Springer Textbooks in Law

Springer Textbooks in Law compiles high-quality educational content aimed at undergraduate and graduate students in all areas of law. All self-contained volumes are authored by accomplished academics and suitable for use in class as well as individual study. Many of them include chapter abstracts, definitions of technical terms, cases and self-assessment exercises, as well as recommended reading sections. This series is an invaluable resource for students and lecturers alike and spans the full range of topics in international and European law, including fundamentals of law and comparative law. Special attention is paid to current and emerging topics such as IT law, intellectual property, human rights as well as dispute resolution, mediation, arbitration – and many more.

Sarah Legner

Digital Competition Law

Competition Law – Digital Markets Act – Platform Regulation

Springer

Sarah Legner
Institute for Business and Tax Law
Kiel University
Kiel, Germany

ISSN 2509-999X ISSN 2510-0009 (electronic)
Springer Textbooks in Law
ISBN 978-3-662-73212-0 ISBN 978-3-662-73213-7 (eBook)
https://doi.org/10.1007/978-3-662-73213-7

Translation from the German language edition: "Digitales Wettbewerbsrecht" by Sarah Legner, © Der/die Herausgeber bzw. der/die Autor(en), exklusiv lizenziert an Springer-Verlag GmbH, DE, ein Teil von Springer Nature 2025. Published by Springer Berlin Heidelberg. All Rights Reserved.

This Springer imprint is published by the registered company Springer-Verlag GmbH, DE, part of Springer Nature.
The registered company address is: Heidelberger Platz 3, 14197 Berlin, Germany

Preface

Digital markets pose special challenges for safeguarding fair and open markets. At a European level, these challenges are addressed through the application of general competition law, as well as the adoption of special rules to address the unique structures of digital markets. In Germany, the legislator decided to add digital-related provisions to its competition law but did not see the need to deviate from the general principles of competition law, that is, did not adopt a distinct regulatory approach.

Against this backdrop, the aim of this textbook is twofold. Firstly, it aims to explain the foundations of European and German competition law, with a special focus on digital markets. The term competition law, as used in the title of the textbook, first refers to the concept commonly employed at the European level. From a German perspective, it primarily encompasses antitrust law. Unfair competition law is excluded. Secondly, the textbook covers the Digital Markets Act and the Platform Regulation. This should not obscure the fact that their objectives differ from those of (general) competition law. However, their genesis and substantive proximity to competition law justify including them under a broad understanding of digital competition law. Both regulations address practices of platform operators that can also be sanctioned by instruments found in general competition law. Taken together, general competition law, the Digital Markets Act, and the Platform Regulation can thus be seen as serving the overarching goal of keeping digital markets open.

The textbook attempts to strike a balance between explaining the fundamentals of competition law, on the one hand, and providing a sector-specific in-depth analysis, on the other. The focus on digital markets is established through the chapters on the Digital Markets Act and the Platform Regulation as regulations specifically designed for digital markets, as well as through an introductory chapter on characteristics of digital markets. Moreover, the discussions of European and German competition law are enriched with many examples related to digitalisation.

The first chapter outlines the relevance of platforms, data, and artificial intelligence for competition in digital markets. It also provides an overview of further regulatory initiatives affecting these phenomena, which often have an indirect impact on the competition debate. One example is the preliminary reference to the ECJ in *Meta (Facebook)* concerning the competence of competition authorities to assess infringements of data protection law. The second chapter presents European competition law. It explains the foundations and basic concepts of the field. The focus lies on the specific challenges for the protection of competition in digital markets. In the context of the cartel prohibition, this includes the use of AI for monitoring and implementing anti-competitive collusion, in abuse control, the particularities of assessing market power and identifying abuses in multi-sided markets, and in merger control, theories of harm based on data and innovation, among other aspects.

Chapters three and four are devoted to sector-specific regulation through the Digital Markets Act and the Platform Regulation. Under the broad conceptual framework adopted here, these regulations also form part of digital competition law. Their genesis and objectives are first explained. For the Digital Markets Act, the gatekeepers as addressees of the regulation are examined, along with an overview of behavioural obligations and the remedies regime, including recent developments. With regard to the Platform Regulation, the focus is on transparency obligations and other conduct requirements. As for remedies, the recently enacted German Implementing Act on Digital Services will be taken into account.

The fifth chapter deals with German competition law, following the same approach as the second chapter. In addition to discussing general foundations, it focuses on sector-specific developments. The most recent amendments to the German Act against Restraints of Competition (ARC) have codified particular rules addressing competition in digital markets. Examples include the criteria for determining market power in sec. 18(2a), (3a), (3b) ARC, the transaction-value threshold in sec. 35(1a) ARC for German merger control, and the abuse prohibition in sec. 19a ARC.

The textbook reflects the state of affairs as of December 2025. I would like to thank Elias Augustin, Miriam Belke, Tabea Jansen, Marie-Luise Lehnert, Emily Törner, and Daniel Verres for their assistance.

Sarah Legner
Kiel, Germany
January 2026

Contents

List of Abbreviations

ACCC	Australian Competition and Consumer Commission
AcP	Archiv für civilistische Praxis
AG	Advocate General
AI	Artificial intelligence
AI Act	Regulation (EU) 2024/1689 of the European Parliament and of the Council of 13 June 2024 laying down harmonised rules on artificial intelligence, OJ [2024] L 2024/1689
ARC	German Law against Restraints of Competition, Gesetz gegen Wettbewerbsbeschränkungen, GWB
BB	Betriebs-Berater
BGB	German Civil Code, Bürgerliches Gesetzbuch
BT-Drs.	Bundestag printed paper; Bundestagsdrucksache
cf.	conferre
ch.	chapter
CMA	Competition and Market Authority
Consumer Rights Directive	Directive 2011/83/EU of the European Parliament and of the Council of 25 October 2011 on consumer rights, OJ [2011] L 304/64
CR	Computer & Recht
Data Act, DA	Regulation (EU) 2023/2854 of the European Parliament and of the Council of 13 December 2023 on harmonised rules for fair access to and use of data, OJ [2023] L 2023/2854
Data Governance Act, DGA	Regulation (EU) 2022/868 of the European Parliament and of the Council of 30 May 2022 on European data governance, OJ [2022] L 152/1
DB	Der Betrieb
DDG	German Implementing Act on Digital Services, Digitale-Dienste-Gesetz
Digital Content Directive	Directive 2019/770/EU of the European Parliament and of the Council of 20 May 2019 on certain aspects of contracts for the supply of digital content and digital services, OJ [2019] L 136/1

Digital Markets Act, DMA	Regulation (EU) 2022/1925 of the European Parliament and of the Council of 14 September 2022 on contestable and fair markets in the digital sector and amending Directives (EU) 2019/1937 and (EU) 2020/1828, OJ [2022] L 265/1
Digital Services Act, DSA	Regulation (EU) 2022/2065 of the European Parliament and of the Council of 19 October 2022 on a single market for digital services and amending Directive 2000/31/EC (Digital Services Act), OJ [2022] 277/1
DOJ	Department of Justice
DSM Directive	Directive (EU) 2019/790 of the European Parliament and of the Council of 17 April 2019 on copyright and related rights in the Digital Single Market, OJ [2019] L 130/92
e.g.	exempli gratia, for example
ECN+ Directive	Directive (EU) 2019/1 of the European Parliament and of the Council of 11 December 2018 on the strengthening of the competition authorities of the Member States with a view to ensuring more effective enforcement of the competition rules and the proper functioning of the internal market, OJ [2019] L 11/3
ed.	edition, publisher
eds.	publishers
EGBGB	Introductory Act to the German Civil Code, Einführungsgesetz zum Bürgerlichen Gesetzbuch
et seq.	et sequentes, and the following
et seqq.	et sequential, and the following
EU	European Union
EuCML	Journal of European Consumer and Market Law
EUMR	Council Regulation (EC) 139/2004 of 20 January 2004 on the control of concentrations between undertakings, OJ [2004] L 24/1
EuR	Zeitschrift Europarecht
EuZW	Europäische Zeitschrift für Wirtschaftsrecht
EYIEL	European Yearbook of International Economic Law
FRAND	Fair Reasonable and Non-discriminatory

FS	Festschrift
GDPR	Regulation (EU) 2016/679 of the European Parliament and of the Council of 27 April 2016 on the protection of natural persons with regard to the processing of personal data and on the free movement of such data, and repealing Directive 95/46/EC, OJ [2016] L 2016/1
GPR	Zeitschrift für das Privatrecht der Europäischen Union
GRUR	Gewerblicher Rechtsschutz und Urheberrecht
GRUR-Prax	Gewerblicher Rechtsschutz und Urheberrecht in der Praxis
GVG	German Judicial System Act, Gerichtsverfassungsgesetz
GWR	Zeitschrift für Gesellschafts- und Wirtschaftsrecht
HHI	Herfindahl-Hirschmann Index
IoT	Internet of Things
JCLE	Journal of Competition Law & Economics
JECLP	Journal of European Competition Law and Practice
JURA	Juristische Ausbildung
JuS	Juristische Schulung
JZ	Juristenzeitung
K&R	Kommunikation & Recht
KritV	Kritische Vierteljahresschrift für Gesetzgebung und Rechtswissenschaft
lit.	littera
LTZ	Legal Tech – Zeitschrift für die digitale Anwendung
MMR	Multimedia und Recht – Zeitschrift für IT-Recht und Recht der Digitalisierung
NJOZ	Neue Juristische Online Zeitschrift
NJW	Neue Juristische Wochenschrift
no.	number
NZKart	Neue Zeitschrift für Kartellrecht
OECD	Organisation for Economic Cooperation and Development
OJ	Official Journal

Omnibus Directive	Directive (EU) 2019/2161 of the European Parliament and of the Council of 27 November 2019 on better enforcement and modernisation of Union consumer protection rules, OJ [2019] L 328/7
p., pp.	page, pages
Platform Regulation; P2B Regulation	Regulation (EU) 2019/1150 of the European Parliament and of the Council of 20 June 2019 on promoting fairness and transparency for business users of online intermediation services, OJ [2019] L 186/57
PND	Personal Navigation Devices
R&D Block Exemption Regulation	Commission Regulation (EU) 2023/1066 of 1 June 2023 on the application of Article 101(3) of the Treaty on the Functioning of the European Union to certain categories of research and development agreements, OJ [2023] L 143/9
R&D	Research and Development
RDi	Recht digital
Representative Actions Directive	Directive (EU) 2020/1828 of the European Parliament and of the Council of 25 November 2020 on representative actions for the protection of the collective interests of consumers, OJ EU 2020 No. L 409/1
Research & Development Block Exemption Regulation, R&D BER	Commission Regulation (EU) 2023/1066 of 1 June 2023 on the application of Article 101 (3) of the Treaty on the Functioning of the European Union to certain categories of research and development agreements, OJ [2023] L 143/9
Sales of Goods Directive	Directive (EU) 2019/771 of the European Parliament and of the Council of 20 May 2019 on certain aspects concerning contracts for the sale of goods, OJ [2019] L 136/28
Specialisation Block Exemption Regulation, Specialisation BER	Commission Regulation (EU) 2023/1067 of 1 June 2023 on the application of Article 101(3) of the European Union to certain categories of specialisation agreements, OJ [2023] 143/20

StGB	German Criminal Code, Strafgesetzbuch
supp.	supplement
TEU	Treaty on European Union
TFEU	Treaty on the Functioning of the European Union
TKG	German Telecommunications Act, Telekommunikationsgesetz
TRIS Directive	Directive (EU) 2015/1535 of the European Parliament and of the Council of 9 September 2015 laying down a procedure for the provision of information in the field of technical regulations and of rules on information society services, OJ [2015] L 241/1
UCP Directive	Directive 2005/29/EC of the European Parliament and of the Council concerning unfair business-to-consumer commercial practices, OJ [2005] 149/22
Unfair Terms Directive	Council Directive 93/13/EEC of 5 April 1993 on unfair terms in consumer contracts, OJ [1995] L 95/29
UWG	German Act against Unfair Competition, Gesetz gegen den unlauteren Wettbewerb
VBER Vertical Block Exemption Regulation	Commission Regulation (EU) 2022/720 of 10 May 2022 on the application of Article 101(3) of the Treaty on the Functioning of the European Union to categories of vertical agreements and concerted practices, OJ [2022] L 134/4
VuR	Verbraucher und Recht
WM	Wertpapier-Mitteilungen
WRP	Wettbewerb in Recht und Praxis
WuW	Wirtschaft und Wettbewerb
ZBJV	Zeitschrift des Bernischen Juristenvereins
ZEuP	Zeitschrift für Europäisches Privatrecht
ZfPW	Zeitschrift für die gesamte Privatrechtswissenschaft
ZHR	Zeitschrift für das gesamte Handelsrecht und Wirtschaftsrecht

ZPO	German Code of Civil Procedure, Zivilprozessordnung
ZRP	Zeitschrift für Rechtspolitik
ZUM	Zeitschrift für Urheber- und Medienrecht
ZVertriebsR	Zeitschrift für Vertriebsrecht
ZWeR	Zeitschrift für Wettbewerbsrecht/Journal for Competition Law

Characteristics of Digital Markets

Contents

S. Legner, *Digital Competition Law*, Springer Textbooks in Law,
https://doi.org/10.1007/978-3-662-73213-7_1

1

1.1 Digital Platforms

1.1.1 Definition and Types of Platforms

Digitalisation has not only led to the development of new products and services but has also given rise to innovative business models. One of the most significant transformations has been the emergence of online platforms, which has fundamentally altered traditional market structures. In digital markets, platforms often act as **intermediaries**,[1] enabling interactions between distinct user groups.[2] Much like other intermediary services, these platforms play a crucial role in shaping what are known as **multi-sided markets**.[3] In such markets, the value created by the platform depends on its ability to attract and coordinate multiple interdependent groups, such as buyers and sellers, users and advertisers, or developers and end-users. For instance, e-commerce platforms like *Amazon* and *eBay* connect individual and commercial sellers with consumers. Search engines and social media platforms, including *Google* and *Facebook*, serve a dual function by offering free content and services to users while monetising access to those users through targeted advertising. Similarly, app distribution platforms such as *Apple's App Store* and *Google Play* link software developers with mobile device users. Ride-sharing and accommodation services like *Uber* and *Airbnb* operate in comparable ways, enabling connections between private service providers—such as drivers or hosts—and end-users through digital interfaces.

While multi-sided markets are a defining feature of the digital economy, they are not exclusive to it. Traditional, non-digital sectors also provide clear examples of multi-sided market structures. One such example is the case of advertising-financed newspapers, which operate simultaneously in two distinct markets: the reader market and the advertising market. On one side, readers consume journalistic content, typically free of charge. On the other side, advertisers pay for access to these readers by purchasing advertising space.[4] The presence of readers increases the newspaper's attractiveness to advertisers, while advertising revenues, in turn, help subsidise or support content production. Another example is the credit card industry, where the platform—in this case, the credit card issuer—serves both cardholders and merchants.[5] Cardholders are provided with convenient payment solutions, while merchants benefit from access to a broader customer base and are charged fees for accepting card payments. The value of the credit card platform increases as more users and merchants participate, again illustrating positive cross-side network effects. In the digital context, multi-sided markets are not just common. They are the norm.[6] In the explanatory memorandum to the ninth amendment

1 Glöckner (2021), sec. 9 mn. 864.
2 German Federal Cartel Office (2016), pp. 8 et seqq.; Fuchs (2024), ARC sec. 18 mn. 70.
3 German Federal Cartel Office (2016), pp. 23 et seqq.; Höppner and Grabenschröer (2015), p. 162.
4 Higher Regional Court of Duesseldorf 22 December 2010 – VI-Kart 4/09, NZG 2011, 543 –*Anzeigengemeinschaft*.
5 Huttenlauch (2025), Article 102 TFEU mn. 57.
6 Körber (2025), EUMR Article 2 mn. 24; Körber (2017), pp. 93 et seq.

of the German Act Against Restraints of Competition (ARC), the legislator explicitly acknowledged the significance of platform-based models. In this context, the term 'platform' is used synonymously with 'multi-sided market.'[7]

Currently, there is **no universally accepted definition** or classification system for platforms. In economic literature, various conceptual frameworks are proposed, and no consensus has emerged on a standardised typology.[8] Similarly, competition law does not operate with a single, unified concept of a platform. Instead, different authorities apply distinct categorizations based on the specific context or regulatory objective. The German Federal Cartel Office proposes a functional classification of platforms based on the type of intermediary service they provide. It distinguishes primarily between **matching platforms** and attention platforms.[9] Matching platforms are those whose core function is to facilitate direct interaction between different user groups.[10] These platforms act as intermediaries that bring together users for the purpose of exchange or engagement. Examples include online job exchanges, dating services, and booking platforms. The Federal Cartel Office further subdivides matching platforms into **transactional and non-transactional** categories.[11] Transactional matching platforms are designed to enable or facilitate economic exchanges between users. Real estate portals and online marketplaces fall into this category, as their users typically aim to conclude commercial transactions—such as the sale of goods or the rental of property. In contrast, non-transactional matching platforms foster interaction without necessarily resulting in an economic transaction. For example, dating platforms enable users to establish personal contact based on compatibility or preferences, but there is no expectation of a formal exchange or payment between the parties involved.

According to the German Federal Cartel Office, **attention platforms** are characterised by their ability to enable one user group to capture the attention of another.[12] In this category, the platform operator functions as an intermediary by creating and managing an environment in which such attention can be effectively directed and monetised. This structure makes the platform operator a valuable contractual partner for advertisers, as it facilitates the targeted placement of advertising content and thereby enhances both its reach and effectiveness. Unlike matching platforms, where the focus is on direct interaction between user groups, attention platforms primarily revolve around the attraction and retention of users' attention as a commodity. The platform gathers and aggregates user activity, preferences, or content consumption patterns, which in turn allows advertisers to target specific audience segments with tailored advertisements. Social networks and online retail platforms are examples of attention platforms.

---

7 Government Justification for the ninth Amendment to the ARC, BT-Drs. 18/10207, p. 47: '*Since a definition will only emerge over time, platforms are used below, as in the economic literature, partly synonymously with the term multi-sided markets.*' [quote translated by author].

8 Pars pro toto Armstrong (2006), pp. 668 et seqq.; Caillaud and Jullien (2003), pp. 309 et seqq.; King (2013), pp. 247 et seqq.

9 German Federal Cartel Office (2016), pp. 23 et seq.

10 German Federal Cartel Office (2016), p. 24.

11 German Federal Cartel Office (2016), p. 23.

12 German Federal Cartel Office (2016), pp. 24 et seqq.

In its revised Notice on Market Definition issued in 2024, the **Commission** also recognises the need to differentiate between various forms of interaction facilitated by platforms. It draws a distinction between transaction platforms and matching platforms,[13] although it adopts a narrower interpretation of the latter compared to the German Federal Cartel Office. According to the Commission, matching platforms are limited to those that enable non-economic interactions between user groups. In this conceptual framework, platforms that facilitate personal or social connections—such as dating services or social networking sites—are classified as matching platforms, while those that support economic transactions are categorised separately as transaction platforms. Thus, for the Commission, these are two alternative types of platforms. By contrast, the German Federal Cartel Office follows a broader classification. It regards transaction platforms as a subtype of matching platforms, since both involve the facilitation of direct interaction between different user groups. From this perspective, the distinction lies not in the nature of the interaction—economic or non-economic—but rather in the outcome of the platform-mediated connection.

Further proposals for categorising platforms have been put forward in **academic literature**. Some scholars suggest that platforms enabling one user group to attract the attention of another—such as advertising-based models—should be considered non-transaction platforms, irrespective of whether a transaction eventually occurs.[14] However, the German Federal Cartel Office has explicitly rejected this approach.[15]

> When applying platform categories in the context of competition law (e.g. defining markets, evaluating market power), it is important to ensure that the term is clearly defined. In European competition law, different understandings of terms prevail than those used by the German Federal Cartel Office for German competition law.

1.1.2 Network Effects

Indirect network effects pose crucial risks for free competition on digital markets. They are a distinctive feature of online platforms and can give rise to **monopolisation tendencies**. Indirect network effects refer to the interactions between different user groups on a platform, illustrating that one user group can benefit from the presence of others (Fig. 1.1).[16]

▶ Example

The benefits for advertisers of placing adverts on a social network or in an online shop increase with the number of end users or customers active on the platform. ◀

13 Commission, Notice on market definition OJ C/2024/1645, mn. 95.
14 Filistrucchi, Geradin, van Damme and Affeldt (2014), pp. 293, 301 et seqq.
15 German Federal Cartel Office (2016), pp. 22 et seq.
16 German Federal Cartel Office (2016), p. 50; Podszun (2025), ARC sec. 18 mn. 151.

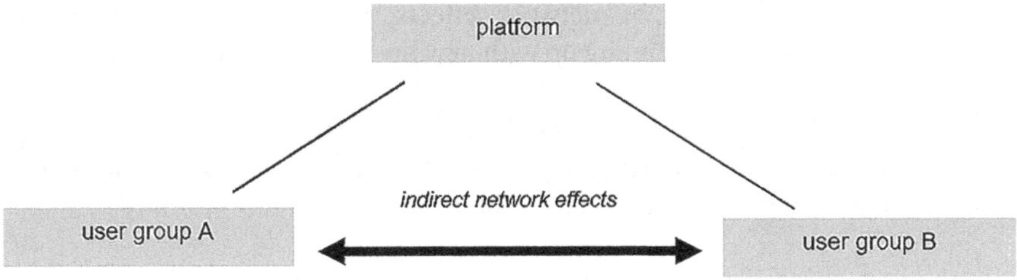

Fig. 1.1 Indirect network effects

In the context of an attention platform,[17] these are defined as **positive** indirect network effects. It is evident that indirect network effects can also be observed on platforms designed for matching,[18] such as auction platforms and dating portals.[19] In the case of **negative** indirect network, however, it is advantageous for one user group if the number of users in another group is as low as possible.[20] Advertisers on search services is one example of this issue. If search customers are shown a large number of adverts, they will find this annoying, potentially leading to a decrease in overall user satisfaction and perceived utility of the platform.[21]

Positive indirect network effects can help platforms to quickly gain market power. In the digital market, there is often a short period of intense competition.[22] The platform operator that successfully navigates this phase is likely to secure a dominant market position, akin to a monopoly. This has the effect of weakening competition in the market. The market will 'tip' in favour of the platform that has gained market power (**tipping**).

However, it should be noted that indirect network effects do not necessarily result in market power. A case-by-case analysis is required. Should negative indirect network effects arise, the presence of a user group on the platform will not assist the operator in building up another user group. In the event of positive indirect network effects, it is essential to examine whether they are **reciprocal or one-sided**.[23] Reciprocal network effects occur, for example, on matching platforms such as booking portals. In this case, the risk of tipping may be more significant than with attention platforms. As demonstrated by the example of the social network, these platforms are characterised by one-sided positive indirect network effects or even one-sided negative indirect network effects.[24]

Innovation-driven competitive pressure also plays a key role in the competitive environment on digital markets. It should be noted that dominant platform opera-

---

17 For the German Federal Cartel Office's understanding of this term, see ▶ 1.1.1.
18 For the German Federal Cartel Office's understanding of this term, see ▶ 1.1.1.
19 Podszun and Schwalbe (2017), pp. 98, 100.
20 German Federal Cartel Office, Decision of 23 November 2017 – B6-35/17, mn. 70 – *CTS EVENTIM/Medusa Music/Four Artists*.
21 Haucap and Wenzel (2011), p. 6.
22 Podszun and Schwalbe (2017), pp. 98, 100.
23 Tamke (2018), pp. 503, 505.
24 Tamke (2018), pp. 503, 505.

1

tors in the market, driven by network effects, are vulnerable to disruption. Competitors achieve this by coming up with new business ideas that are innovative.[25]

▶ Example

In the German social networking sector, *StudiVZ* and *SchülerVZ*, which were once dominant, have now been superseded by *Facebook*. ◀

In the past, these dynamics have repeatedly prompted market-leading platforms to acquire start-ups with a small market share but innovative business ideas at an early stage in order to eliminate innovation-driven competitive pressure.

▶ Example

In 2014, *Facebook* acquired the mobile messaging service *WhatsApp*. The merger did not fulfil the turnover thresholds of European merger control. The Commission was only able to undertake a review of the merger subsequent to a submission by the parties involved, as stipulated in Article 4(5) EUMR, and ultimately cleared it.[26] ◀

Furthermore, **direct network effects** can arise in platform markets. They have an impact on users from the same group and occur when the value of a platform to a user increases alongside the number of other users from that group (◘ Fig. 1.2.)[27]

▶ Example

For users of a social network, the value of the platform increases with the number of friends and acquaintances active on the platform with whom they can share texts, photos or videos. ◀

Direct network effects do not exclusively occur on platforms. They also occur in networks, for example in railway networks or telecommunications networks.[28] In

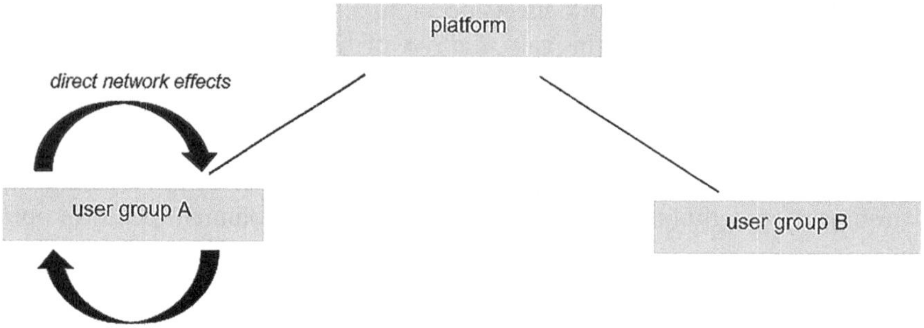

◘ **Fig. 1.2** Direct network effects

25 Körber (2015), pp. 415, 418 et seq.
26 Commission, Decision of 3 October 2014 – COMP/M.7217 – *WhatsApp/Facebook*.
27 Körber (2025), EUMR Article 2 mn. 24b.
28 Glöckner (2021), sec. 9 mn. 861.

the context of competitive analysis, direct network effects are just as important as indirect network effects. This is because they influence the market power of platforms. Direct network effects have been shown to engender 'self-reinforcing tendencies' and have been identified as a contributing factor to market tilting, specifically in cases where they manifest as positive direct network effects.[29]

The competitive impact of direct network effects is intensified if users do not tend to ***multi-homing***, i.e. generally only use one intermediary service of the same type.[30] Single-homing can be observed in the context of social networks, for instance. The dissemination of content across various networks is not without its challenges, as the transferability of content from one platform to another is often limited. This has the effect of creating **lock-in effects**, which make it likely that users will decide to use one platform exclusively, rather than using several social networks at the same time.

> In sec. 18(3a) no. 1 ARC, German competition law lists direct and indirect networks as criteria that must be taken into account when determining a dominant market position, particularly in multi-sided markets and networks.

1.1.3 Price Structures

The indirect network effects described above are often reflected in the pricing structure of the platforms.[31] There are groups of users who typically **do not pay** for the platform's intermediation services.

▶ Examples

In the domain of social networking, private users are not charged a fee when they register. A search service can be used by search customers free of charge. ◀

The rationale behind such an asymmetrical pricing structure becomes apparent when the other user groups of the intermediary service offered by the platform are taken into consideration. As demonstrated by the aforementioned examples, the presence of one-sided indirect networks is evident. The attractiveness of the platform to advertisers is directly proportional to the number of end users active on the platform. It is therefore a profitable strategy for platform operators to offer them their intermediary service free of charge.[32]

However, end users frequently provide data. This is a decisive competitive factor for platform operators.[33] In the context of competition law, this represents a

29 German Federal Cartel Office, Decision of 6 February 2019, B6-22/16, mn. 424 – *Facebook*.
30 Weber and Volz (2015), pp. 356, 358.
31 Höppner and Grabenschröer (2015), pp. 162, 163.
32 Höppner and Grabenschröer (2015), pp. 162, 162.
33 For the role of data for competition in digital markets, see ▶ 1.2.

significant shift in the **traditional understanding of the market** as a place where goods are exchanged.[34] Furthermore, it is imperative for the assessment of **market power** that individual market segments should not be viewed in isolation, but rather, existing interdependencies must be taken into account, irrespective of the market's specific boundaries.

German competition law stipulates in sec. 18(2a) ARC: The assumption of a market is not precluded by the fact that a service is provided free of charge.

Unilateral pricing on platforms is not only a challenge under competition law. In the context of European consumer law, it was also necessary for the legislator to clarify whether free-of-charge contracts fall under the protective provisions that require a 'consumer contract'. According to Article 3(1a) Consumer Rights Directive,[35] it is sufficient for the consumer to 'provide or undertake to provide personal data to the trader' in order to benefit from consumer protection mechanisms—particularly the trader's information obligations and the consumer's right of withdrawal.

1.1.4 Outlook on Other Regulatory Approaches

In addition to the competitive risks associated with market power of large platform operators, there are also risks of disinformation and hate speech, as well as risks to the democratic decision-making process. The EU legislator has addressed these risks by enacting the Digital Services Act.[36]

Furthermore, contract law acknowledges that platform operators often have the authority to unilaterally dictate contractual terms that may be disadvantageous to users. The Platform Regulation[37] establishes a general framework for the terms and conditions of contracts between platform operators and commercial users.[38] The DSM Directive[39] establishes obligations that online content-sharing service providers must adhere to with regard to copyright-protected content uploaded by users.

34 Legner (2023a), pp. 175, 178.

35 Directive 2011/83/EU of the European Parliament and of the Council of 25 October 2011 on consumer rights, OJ [2011] L 304/64.

36 Regulation (EU) 2022/2065 of the European Parliament and of the Council of 19 October 2022 on a single market for digital services and amending Directive 2000/31/EC (Digital Services Act), OJ [2022] L 277/1.

37 Regulation (EU) 2019/1150 of the European Parliament and of the Council of 20 June 2019 on promoting fairness and transparency for business users of online intermediation services, OJ [2019] 186/57. For further details, see ▶ 4.1.1.

38 Consumer contracts are already covered by the Unfair Terms Directive.

39 Directive (EU) 2019/790 of the European Parliament and of the Council of 17 April 2019 on copyright and related rights in the Digital Single Market, OJ [2019] L 130/92.

1.2 Data

1.2.1 Categories of Data

Digital business models are frequently dependent on the collection and processing of substantial amounts of data. It is important to note that there are different types of data. In the field of data protection, a distinction is typically drawn between personal and non-personal data. Personal data can include, for instance, information regarding the location of internet users and their personal preferences.[40] Data is considered to have lost its personal reference only when it has been irreversibly anonymised. This means that it cannot be assigned to a natural person.[41]

Despite the fact that the processing of personal data is in principle dependent on consent in accordance with the GDPR and a fundamental consumer awareness of privacy, users on digital markets often willingly and extensively provide such data (*privacy paradox*).[42]

It is evident that this is applicable to registrations with various platforms, including online marketplaces and social networks. Conversely, undertakings collect information regarding the behaviour of users during their utilisation of the platform service.[43] This facilitates the determination of consumer preferences with regard to the products offered and usage times.

Purely commercial data does not contain any personal reference information. Such information may be protected as trade secrets or by copyright (especially databases).[44] Data can also be **generated** in various ways. Machine-generated data is defined as information created by hardware or software when a machine or device is in operation.[45]

1.2.2 Data and Market Power

From a competition law perspective, gaining a significant advantage in accessing and utilising data can be a factor contributing to **market power**.[46] An undertaking can already gain market power by accessing large quantities of data (*big data*).[47] Of greater importance, however, are the **possibilities for utilising it**.[48] The use of AI has enabled the structuring and processing of large volumes of data in a variety of ways. Notably, the processing speed has been significantly improved. Businesses

40 French Competition Authority and German Federal Cartel Office (2016), p. 5.
41 Klabunde and Horváth (2024), GDPR Article 4 mn. 20.
42 German Federal Cartel Office (2017), pp. 3 et seq.
43 French Competition Authority and German Federal Cartel Office (2016), pp. 6 et seq.
44 Stepanova and Veeck (2024), sec. 4 mn. 6.
45 German Federal Cartel Office (2017), pp. 2 et seq.
46 Körber (2016), 303, 304 et seq.
47 Glöckner (2021), sec. 9 mn. 867.
48 Weber (2014), pp. 169, 173.

can also use their data strategically to enhance products and services, customising them to user needs and securing a competitive advantage.[49]

This is not an issue that is limited to digital markets. However, **competition for quality** and innovation is often particularly important in digital markets. Price competition for intermediary services is not a factor if these services are offered free of charge to end users.[50] Instead, payment is made by the provision of data to the platform operator.

The multi-sided nature of digital markets makes it clear that this approach by platform operators to collect user data is a profitable strategy. By offering services free of charge, a platform can successfully unite a large number of users in a short period of time. Should **indirect network effects**[51] be present, the product will become more attractive to other user groups.

> Numerous behavioural obligations of the Digital Markets Act are linked to data-related strategies of gatekeepers. These obligations include the prohibition of data combination practices and the restriction of the use of commercial users'data in competition with them. The underlying logic of this position is that powerful platform operators, in their capacity as gateways to end users, should refrain from imposing barriers to market entry through the implementation of specific data utilisation strategies. In this regard, the DMA does not require proof of anti-competitive conduct.

In contrast to physical objects, data is defined by its **non-rivalrous** nature. Should an undertaking have access to certain user-generated data, this does not prevent competitors from collecting and using the same data. Therefore, a competitive advantage is primarily derived from the superior access to data that one competitor possesses in comparison to another.[52] For instance, if a competitor has exclusive access to certain data, this can have the effect of foreclosing the market. Conversely, if end users engage in **multi-homing**, that is, using multiple online trading platforms concurrently, it diminishes the competitive advantage that a platform operator gains from the data collected.[53] In some cases, a competitor may possess a 'data advantage' that other businesses are unable to match in a timely fashion.[54]

> According to sec. 18(3a) no. 4 ARC, German competition law considers access to competition-relevant data as a key factor in assessing market dominance, particularly in multi-sided markets and networks.

Data availability can also have a pro-competitive effect if it increases market transparency. Price comparison services, for instance, provide consumers with a

49 Weber (2014), pp. 169, 171.
50 Körber (2016), pp. 303, 305.
51 For further details on indirect network effects, see ▸ 1.1.2.
52 Fuchs (2024), ARC sec. 18 mn. 148a.
53 German Federal Cartel Office (2017), p. 5.
54 German Federal Cartel Office (2017), p. 7.

comprehensive overview of the market offers. This has the potential to initiate price or quality competition.[55]

1.2.3 Data and Restrictions to Competition

It is important to note that data are not only relevant when it comes to assessing market power. Their relevance to competition also gives rise to new forms of competition restriction. The creation of **data pools** may result in the exchange of sensitive information between competitors, which could constitute a violation of the ban on cartels.[56] In the context of merger control, it may be necessary to determine whether undertakings will have access to a larger volume of data as a result of a merger. This can sometimes have the effect of foreclosing the market. In the event of mergers between non-competing undertakings, it is also necessary to consider whether the merged entity could hinder competitors' access to data.[57]

Moreover, the question of whether prohibitions on abuse might result in obligations for an undertaking with market power to grant **access to data** is being discussed.[58] Data can be classified as an 'essential facility' according to the Bronner criteria. German competition law explicitly clarifies this in sec. 19(2) no. 4 ARC. However, it is imperative to maintain a cautious approach when asserting claims regarding data access. It is important to note that undertakings which possess market power are at liberty to enhance their competitive position with competitive instruments.[59]

1.2.4 Outlook on Other Regulatory Approaches

Data is the subject of further regulatory acts. The General Data Protection Regulation (**GDPR**)[60] is a regulation that aims to give individuals more control over their personal data. Despite the fact that data protection law is intended to protect informational self-determination, interdependencies with competition law have become apparent. In the context of data protection law, there are two key questions that competition authorities must address: firstly, whether they are per-

55 French Competition Authority and German Federal Cartel Office (2016), p. 14.
56 For further details on data-related restrictions of competition under Article 101 TFEU, see ► 2.2.2.2.3.
57 On the assessment of vertical and conglomerate mergers under EU merger control, see ► 2.4.4.4.
58 Schweitzer, Haucap, Kerber and Welker (2018), p. 133.
59 For further details on the essential facilities doctrine, see ► 2.3.2.1.7 (EU competition law), ► 5.3.1.5.1 (German competition law).
60 Regulation (EU) 2016/679 of the European Parliament and of the Council of 27 April 2016 on the protection of natural persons with regard to the processing of personal data and on the free movement of such data, OJ [2016] L 119/1.

mitted to investigate breaches of data protection law, and secondly, whether a breach of the GDPR may be considered an abuse of market power.[61]

The Data Governance Act (**DGA**)[62] is designed to optimise the use of data.[63] This also includes the role of data as a market power factor: providers of data intermediation service are intended to facilitate access to data for small businesses alongside large platform operators. The Data Act (**DA**)[64] was passed at the end of 2023. The regulations cover a range of issues, including data exchange and access. Among other things, users of hybrid products will have access to the data generated through their usage.[65]

1.3 Artificial Intelligence

1.3.1 Definition of AI

Technological progress has led to an increasing use of artificial intelligence (AI) in business. AI applications have a variety of uses, extending beyond the scope of an undertaking's internal work procedures.[66] AI systems are also being used by businesses as part of their marketing strategy. On the one hand, this concerns the services offered.[67] Examples include hybrid products of the Internet of Things. Intelligent robot vacuum cleaners and refrigerators are designed to fulfil their functions in conjunction with the digital components integrated into their design or as a result of their connection to the internet. From a competitive perspective, this leads to a greater variety of products. New offerings have the potential to intensify competition and drive innovation. On the other hand, businesses use AI systems to set their competitive parameters, e.g. the quantity offered or the price charged.[68] The capacity of AI systems to process vast quantities of data in a short amount of time is enabling businesses to achieve a competitive advantage.

There is **no universally accepted definition** of artificial intelligence.[69] The term is frequently linked to machine learning processes.[70] AI is trained on the basis of large amounts of data and learns to solve specific problems. This is achieved by

---

61 German Federal Cartel Office, Decision of 6 February 2019 – B6-22/16 – *Facebook*; Higher Regional Court of Duesseldorf 26 August 2019 VI-Kart 1/19 (V), MMR 2019, 742 – *Facebook*; German Federal Supreme Court 23 June 2020 – KVR 69/19, GRUR 2020, 1318, 1326 – *Facebook*; ECJ 4 July 2023 – C-252/21, ECLI:EU:C:2023:537 – *Meta (Facebook)*.

62 Regulation (EU) 2022/868 of the European Parliament and of the Council of 30 May 2022 on European data governance, OJ [2022] L 152/1.

63 Hennemann and Steinrötter (2022), p. 1481; Honer and Schöbel (2024), pp. 648, 650.

64 Regulation (EU) 2023/2854 of the European Parliament and of the Council of 13 December 2023 on harmonised rules for fair access to and use of data, OJ [2023] L 2023/2854.

65 Hennemann and Steinrötter (2022), pp. 1481, 1484.

66 One example of the internal use of AI is *smart factories*, in which companies aim to optimise production processes with the help of AI.

67 Ballestrem, Bär, Gausling, Hack and von Oelffen (2020), p. 2.

68 Legner (2025), pp. 183, 183–190.

69 Niederée and Nejdl (2020), sec. 2 mn. 1.

70 Lauscher and Legner (2022), pp. 367, 369 et seq.

utilising a substantial number of examples to identify the properties of an object that influence its perception.[71] In the context of machine learning, there are three main methods: supervised learning, unsupervised learning and reinforcement learning.[72]

Article 3 no. 1 AI Act[73] provides a broad definition of the term:[74] an AI system is defined as 'a machine-based system designed to operate with varying degrees of autonomy, capable of adaptation once operational, and deriving outputs such as predictions, content, recommendations or decisions from the inputs received for explicit or implicit goals that can influence physical or virtual environments.' Recital 12 AI Act clarifies that 'simpler conventional software systems and programming approaches' are not included. Systems 'based exclusively on rules defined by natural persons for the automatic execution of operations' are not covered by the AI Act. Therefore, the definition includes a core element of the autonomy of an AI system. However, the precise degree of autonomy required in this respect remains unclear. The core element of the definition is therefore autonomy. However, the exact degree of autonomy required in this respect remains unclear.[75]

► Examples

The AI definition of the AI Act includes chatbots, lie detectors and systems for recognising emotions in the workplace. In the context of competition law, other systems have become relevant, e.g. market surveillance software. These do not fall under the regulation's definition of AI due to their lack of ability to act autonomously. ◄

AI systems are frequently categorised according to the **degree of autonomy** they possess. The terms weak and strong AI are commonly used.[76] While weak AI is limited to solving predefined tasks, the development of strong AI aims to create systems that can define tasks independently.[77] The AI systems that have become relevant for competition law—for example, web crawlers and price monitoring software—are predominantly categorised as weak AI according to this understanding. In some cases, a similar distinction is made between semi-automated, automated and autonomous AI systems.[78] In this respect, there are also differences in the scope of action and task areas. However, it is possible that a uniform differentiation or conceptualisation may be in place.[79]

---

71 Lauscher and Legner (2022), pp. 367, 369.
72 Glauner (2024), sec. 1 mn. 3.
73 Regulation (EU) 2024/1689 of the European Parliament and of the Council of 13 June 2024 laying down harmonised rules on artificial intelligence, OJ [2024] L 2024/1689.
74 Criticism of this definition is expressed by Chibanguza and Steege (2024), pp. 1769, 1170; Ebers (2024), p. 1.
75 Chibanguza and Steege (2024), pp. 1769, 1170.
76 Nida-Rümelin (2022), sec. 1 E. mn. 1; Steege (2022), pp. 926, 927.
77 Weak vs. strong AI – a definition < https://ki.thws.de/thematik/starke-vs-schwache-ki-eine-definition/ > (accessed 1 September 2025).
78 Specht and Herold (2018), pp. 40, 41 et seq.
79 Steege (2022), pp. 926, 927.

1

The AI Act provides a categorisation of AI systems based on **risks to fundamental rights**.[80] It differentiates between AI systems with minimal risk (e.g. web crawlers), AI systems with low risk (e.g. chatbots), high-risk AI systems (e.g. AI systems in the field of law enforcement) and prohibited AI systems with unacceptable risks (e.g. AI systems for 'social scoring').

1.3.2 AI and Market Structures

AI systems are strategically employed by undertakings to align their competitive conduct. This includes the use of competitive parameters, i.e. decisions on pricing or quantities offered.

▶ Examples

Web crawlers facilitate the automated search of extensive databases and the monitoring of competitor pricing within the market. Price algorithms enable companies to respond swiftly to competitor pricing strategies and adjust their own prices accordingly. ◀

In its sector inquiry into e-commerce, the Commission reported that approximately two-thirds of retailers who monitored their competitors' pricing on the internet '*used software programmes to adjust their own prices on the basis of competitors' observed prices*.'[81] The Commission has reported that more than 30% of retailers are now using algorithms to automatically adjust their prices in line with market developments.[82]

The application of AI systems can influence market structures. **Market transparency** can be increased if AI systems process large amounts of data in the shortest possible time, thereby providing a reliable overview of competitor market conduct.[83] Algorithms can also **react more quickly** to market observations, making price adjustments in a matter of seconds, which is faster than human players. Unfortunately, it is not possible to provide a generalised answer regarding the impact of this situation on competition. Should a company's price adjustments result in a rapid reaction from competitors, there is a possibility that competition may intensify.[84] However, increased market transparency may weaken competition by enabling undertakings to coordinate via the market (**tacit collusion**).[85] Consequently, the price level rises even in the absence of a prohibited cartel agreement. AI systems are also used to **implement** anti-competitive agreements.[86] Their

80 Frank and Heine (2023), pp. 1281, 1282; Müller-Peltzer and Tanczik (2023), pp. 452, 454.
81 Commission, Final report on the sector enquiry into e-commerce, COM(2017) 229 final, mn. 13.
82 Commission, Final report on the E-commerce Sector Inquiry, COM(2017) 229 final, mn. 603 et seq.
83 Künstner (2019), pp. 36, 37.
84 König (2020), sec. 17 mn. 73.
85 For further details on the principles of tacit collusion, see ▶ 2.2.1.3.
86 Commission, Final report on the sector enquiry into e-commerce, COM(2017) 229 final, 2017, mn. 13.

use can enhance cartel discipline, thereby amplifying the economic harm caused by illegal agreements.

▶ Example

Supplier L has agreed with its dealers that they may not sell to end customers at prices below an agreed minimum price. To ensure compliance with this agreement by all dealers, Supplier L employs price monitoring algorithms that constantly monitor the dealers' prices and report any deviations to Supplier L immediately. ◀

Furthermore, the role of **blockchain** and **smart contracts** in the context of competition law is a subject that is currently being discussed.[87] The term 'smart contract' is used to describe the computerised, automated processing of contracts, representing a further development of well-known goods and cash machines.[88] The insurance industry is an example of an area where blockchain technology has been adopted. Some insurance undertakings have temporarily used blockchain to process flight delay insurance policies.[89] Blockchain technology, also known as distributed ledger technology, gained prominence primarily through the cryptocurrency Bitcoin. Its primary association is with the property of being tamper-proof.[90] Data is stored in a decentralised manner on the computers involved in the network.[91] This renders a centralised location redundant. The term 'blockchain' originates from the way in which transactions are stored in interconnected blocks.[92]

The expansion of blockchain technology has led to the emergence of a wide range of applications for smart contracts.[93] In Germany, the German Federal Supreme Court recently ruled on a case involving the remote disablement of the battery charging option for leased electric vehicles after the termination of the contract.[94] This ruling marks a significant milestone as the first court decision concerning a smart contract. The German Federal Court of Justice concentrated on sec. 307 German Civil Code, which deals with the control of general terms and conditions. The clause in question was considered to be null and void, since it unilaterally favoured the lessors' contractual position.[95] From a competition law perspective, the blockchain's **consensus requirement**, among other things, can present

87 OECD, Blockchain Technology and Competition Policy, 2018 <https://one.oecd.org/document/DAF/COMP/WD(2018)47/en/pdf > (accessed 1 September 2025); Louven and Saive (2018), p. 348; Kumkar (2025), TFEU Article 101 mn. 132.
88 Legner (2023b), pp. 213, 213 et seq.
89 <https://www.de-hub.de/blog/post/eine-hassliebe-blockchain-und-die-versicherungsbranche/> (1 September 2025).
90 Mik (2018), pp. 853, 857.
91 Kaulartz (2016), pp. 474, 476.
92 Möllenkamp (2024), Part 13.6. mn. 4.
93 Hohn-Hein and Bart (2018), pp. 1089, 1090; as, *one of the most important technologies of the future*.
94 German Federal Supreme Court 26 October 2022 – XII ZR 89/21, SVR 2023, 58. See also Higher Regional Court of Duesseldorf 7 October 2021 – 20 U 116/20, MMR 2022, 403; Regional Court of Duesseldorf 11 December 2019 – 12 O 63/19, BeckRS, 51046.
95 German Federal Supreme Court 26 October 2022 – XII ZR 89/21, SVR 2023, 58, 59 et seq.

certain challenges: in order to integrate new information into the blockchain, the majority of participants must agree. It is necessary to ascertain whether this can be considered as prohibited conduct under the European and German ban on cartels.[96] Furthermore, the implementation of anti-competitive agreements could be enhanced through the use of smart contracts.[97]

1.3.3 AI and Price Setting

The use of AI is linked to the importance of data as a competitive factor in digital markets. Platform operators collect extensive user **data**. AI applications facilitate their processing and utilisation. This allows platform operators to create user profiles that they can use, among other things, to provide customised offers. **Personalised prices** are one such example of individualised offers. From an economic perspective, a distinction is made between three forms of price discrimination.[98] In the case of first-degree price discrimination, suppliers set the price that corresponds to the consumer's personal **willingness to pay**. This has not yet been feasible due to a lack of knowledge on the part of providers and individual willingness to pay. However, it seems that this may be possible in the long term, as increasing data availability suggests that an approximation to this may be achievable.[99] In second-degree price discrimination, providers differentiate on the basis of the willingness to pay of different customer groups.[100] One such strategy is offering volume discounts. Second-degree price discrimination allows consumers to decide for themselves which customer groups they want to belong to. For instance, the volume discount only applies to consumers who purchase a significant number of products.

In third-degree price discrimination, providers also differentiate the divergent willingness to pay on the basis of different customer groups. However, consumers cannot self-assign to a group; this is instead determined by the provider.[101] For instance, in the event of a discount for senior citizens at the theatre, it is not the responsibility of the customer to determine whether they wish to receive the discount. Instead, the provider has decided that only consumers who have reached a certain age will receive the discount. From a business perspective, price personalisation is a strategy that can be used to capture a greater share of consumer surplus and thus maximise profits.

First-degree price discrimination: suppliers take into account the individual willingness to pay of each consumer. For instance: negotiations regarding individual prices.

96 Louven and Saive (2018), p. 348.
97 Hoffer and Mirtchev (2019), pp. 239, 242.
98 Hofmann (2016), pp. 1074, 1082; Locher (2018), pp. 292, 296–297.
99 Wagner and Eidenmüller (2019), pp. 220, 225.
100 Legner (2021), pp. 34, 36.
101 Legner (2021), pp. 34, 36.

❗ Second-degree price discrimination: suppliers categorise consumers into groups based on different levels of willingness to pay. Consumers have the option of assigning themselves to the groups. For instance: volume discounts.

❗ Third-degree price discrimination: suppliers divide consumers into groups based on different willingness to pay. The allocation to the group is made by the provider. For instance: discounts for students.

Personalised pricing is not a modern phenomenon, nor is it unique to digital markets. It is worth noting that even in medieval markets, there were instances where lords of the manor would pay more for the same goods.[102] In stationary supermarkets, quantity discounts are also granted. It is a well-established practice for museums to offer reduced admission fees to students. Nonetheless, the phenomenon has attracted particular attention in digital markets. Firstly, algorithm-based data processing means that it is difficult for consumers to understand how the personalised price was calculated (**black box** character of AI).[103] Secondly, consumers have **minimal ability to avoid the personalisation strategies** employed by providers, or to do so with any significant effort.[104] Research indicates that consumers often perceive personalised offers as unfair.[105] From an overall economic perspective, the result is less clear. In principle, the concept of price personalisation facilitates the provision of offers to a broader market segment by adjusting prices accordingly, for instance, for low-income consumers.[106] However, it is not yet clear whether this corresponds to the approach of providers on digital markets.

The use of AI systems also facilitates **price dynamization**. Prices are adjusted in a timely manner to reflect the prevailing market conditions, such as increased demand on specific days of the week or the imminent expiration of an offer.[107] Algorithms facilitate the process of setting dynamic prices for undertakings by enabling swift analysis of relevant data and prompt pricing decisions.[108]

▶ Examples

It is an established phenomenon that the cost of train and flight tickets tends to increase in proportion to the imminent travel date. This is also the case in instances where a limited number of tickets remain available for a given trip.[109] ◀

102 Golland (2020), pp.186, 187.
103 Golland (2020), pp. 186, 187.
104 Golland (2020), pp. 186, 187.
105 ConPolicy, Was Verbraucherinnen und Verbraucher in NRW über individualisierte Preise im Online-Handel denken, final report of a survey commissioned by the Ministry for Climate Protection, Environment, Agriculture, Nature Conservation and Consumer Protection of the State of North Rhine-Westphalia of 21 January 2016, 8 et seq.; Tillmann and Vogt (2018), p. 4.
106 Tillmann and Vogt (2018), pp. 447, 448 et seq.
107 Hofmann (2016), pp. 1074, 1077; Micklitz and Namysłowska (2019), UWG sec. 5 mn. 130.
108 Künstner and Franz (2017), pp. 688, 689.
109 Künstner (2019), pp. 36, 37.

1.3.4 AI and Competition Law Enforcement

The commercial use of AI gives rise to **questions of attribution**. Competition law prohibitions address undertakings.[110] Algorithms themselves do not fall under the concept of undertaking. In this regard, it is essential to clearly define the due diligence obligations, including monitoring and intervention responsibilities, to ensure the accurate application of price-setting and competition law provisions to the undertaking using the algorithm.[111] Similar questions arise in other areas of law. These include the doctrine of legal transactions[112] (conclusion of contracts by AI) as well as contractual and tort law (damage caused by AI).[113]

1.3.5 Outlook on Other Regulatory Approaches

The regulation of AI systems is **an intra- and interdisciplinary** topic in law. In addition to competition law, personalised and dynamic prices are discussed in the context of **unfair competition law**.[114] In principle, retailers are permitted to set their own prices. However, information obligations might follow from Article 8 UCP Directive,[115] which prohibits aggressive commercial practices, or from the general clause of Article 5(1) UCP Directive.

In the context of **consumer protection law**, the Omnibus Directive[116] represents a significant development in the realm of consumer rights enforcement and modernisation. The directive, which came into effect in 2019, stipulates in Article 6(1) (ea) Consumer Rights Directive that consumers must be informed if the price has been personalised on the basis of automated decision-making in the case of distance and off-premises contracts. The German legislator has implemented this requirement in sec. 312d(1) German Civil Code in conjunction with Article 246a sec. 1(1) no. 6 Introductory Act to the German Civil Code (*Einführungsgesetz zum Bürgerlichen Gesetzbuch, EGBGB*). This does not, however, imply a prohibition on price personalisation.

Algorithmic price discrimination has the potential to contravene **anti-discrimination law** if it is found to differentiate between protected characteristics,

110 On the concept of undertaking, see ► 2.1.4.1 (EU competition law), ► 5.1.4.1 (German competition law)

111 Lübke (2021), pp. 723, 751 et seq.

112 Keßler (2017), pp. 589, 592; Kumkar (2020), pp. 801 et seq.; Specht and Herold (2018), pp. 40 et seq.

113 Günther (2014), pp. 45 et seqq.; Hanisch (2014), pp. 27 et seqq.; Schirmer (2016), pp. 660, 664 et seqq.

114 Hofmann (2016), pp. 1074 et seq.

115 Directive 2005/29/EC of the European Parliament and of the Council concerning unfair business-to-consumer commercial practices, OJ [2005] 149/22.

116 Directive (EU) 2019/2161 of the European Parliament and of the Council of 27 November 2019 as regards the better enforcement and modernisation of Union consumer protection rules, OJ [2019] L 328/7.

for example with regard to gender (**gender pricing**).[117] However, such price discrimination can only be considered illegal if price differences are not based on differences in production costs or are justified for other reasons. For instance, it should be noted that retailers frequently produce both male and female product versions, for example in the clothing or drugstore sectors. These versions often, but not always, differ exclusively in terms of colour or design.

The AI Act was implemented in 2024.[118] The regulation adopts a horizontal approach. Its primary focus is on high-risk AI systems. According to Article 6 AI Act, these are AI systems that are used in areas that are particularly sensitive to fundamental rights. Examples include the use of AI in remote biometric identification (Article 6(1) in conjunction with Annex III no. 1 AI Act) or in the context of recruitment (Article 6(1) in conjunction with Annex III no. 4 AI Act). The chosen regulatory approach is based on product safety law. Comprehensive requirements for high-risk AI systems are set out in Article 8 et seqq. The AI Act stipulates that providers of high-risk AI systems must fulfil the Act's provisions before placing these systems on the market. In the context of competition law, pricing AI systems do not typically fall under the category of high-risk AI systems. In terms of restrictions, their use is not subject to any. For AI systems with minimal fundamental rights risk, Article 95 AI Act merely stipulates that codes of conduct must be created by providers and deployers. The **proposal for an AI liability directive**,[119] with the Commission had released in 2022, was withdrawn in February 2025.

References

Armstrong M (2006) Competition in two-sided markets. RAND J Econ 37(3):668–691

Ballestrem J, Bär U, Gausling T, Hack S, von Oelffen S (2020) Künstliche Intelligenz - Rechtsgrundlagen und Strategien in der Praxis. Springer Gabler, Wiesbaden

Caillaud B, Jullien B (2003) Chicken & egg: competition among intermediation service providers. RAND J Econ 34(2):309–328

Chibanguza K, Steege H (2024) Die KI-Verordnung – Überblick über den neuen Rechtsrahmen. NJW 2024:1769–1775

Ebers M (2024) Die KI-Verordnung ante portas: Ein neuer Rechtsrahmen für Legal Tech? LTZ 2024:1–2

Filistrucchi L, Geradin D, van Damme E, Affeldt P (2014) Market definition in two-sided markets: theory and practice. J Compet Law Econ 10(2):293–339

Frank J, Heine M (2023) KI-Einsatz im Betrieb unter der KI-Verordnung. NZA 2023:1281–1284

French Competition Authority, German Federal Cartel Office (2016) Competition Law and Data. Bonn, Paris

Fuchs A (2024) ARC sec. 18. In: Immenga U, Mestmäcker E (eds) Kommentar zum Wettbewerbsrecht, 7th edn. C.H. Beck, Munich

117 Legner (2021), pp. 34 et seqq.

118 Regulation (EU) 2024/1689 of the European Parliament and of the Council of 13 June 2024 laying down harmonised rules on artificial intelligence, OJ [2024] L 2024/1689.

119 Commission, Proposal for a Directive of the European Parliament and of the Council on adapting non-contractual civil liability rules to artificial intelligence (AI Liability Directive), COM(2022) 496 final.

German Federal Cartel Office (2017) Big Data und Wettbewerb. Publication series "Wettbewerb und Verbraucherschutz in der digitalen Wirtschaft", Bonn

German Federal Cartel Office (2016) Market power of platforms and networks. Bonn

Glauner P (2024) § 1 Technische Grundlagen von generativen KI-Modellen. In: Ebers M, Quarch B (eds) Rechtshandbuch ChatGPT - KI-basierte Sprachmodelle in der Praxis. Nomos, Baden-Baden, pp. 21–42

Glöckner J (2021) Kartellrecht – Recht gegen Wettbewerbsbeschränkungen, 3rd edn. Kohlhammer, Stuttgart

Golland A (2020) Datenschutzrechtliche Fragen personalisierter Preise – Herausforderungen von Algorithmen im Schnittbereich von Ethik, Ökonomie und Datenschutz. CR 36(3):186–194

Günther J (2014) Roboter und rechtliche Verantwortung - Eine Untersuchung der Benutzer- und Herstellerhaftung. Herbert Utz Verlag, Munich

Hanisch J (2014) Zivilrechtliche Haftungskonzepte für Robotik. In: Hilgendorf E (ed) Robotik im Kontext von Recht und Moral. Nomos, Baden-Baden, pp. 27–61

Haucap J, Wenzel T (2011) Wettbewerb im Internet: Was ist online anders als offline?. DICE Ordnungspolitische Perspektiven No. 16. Available via https://www.econstor.eu/handle/10419/48625. Accessed 23 Sept 2025

Hennemann M, Steinrötter B (2022) Data Act – Fundament des neuen EU-Datenwirtschaftsrechts? NJW 2022:1481–1486

Hofmann F (2016) Der maßgeschneiderte Preis - Dynamische und individuelle Preise aus lauterkeitsrechtlicher Sicht. WRP 62(9):1074–1081

Hoffer R, Mirtchev K (2019) Erfordert die Blockchain ein neues Kartellrecht? – Die Anwendung von Art. 101 und 102 AEUV sowie der Zusammenschlusskontrolle im Kontext der Blockchain-Technologie. NZKart 2019:239–247

Hohn-Hein N, Bart G (2018) Immaterialgüterrechte in der Welt von Blockchain und Smart Contract. GRUR 2018:1089–1096

Höppner T, Grabenschröer J (2015) Marktabgrenzung bei mehrseitigen Märkten am Beispiel der Internetsuche. NZKart 2015:162–168

Honer M, Schöbel P (2024) Das Gesetz über Künstliche Intelligenz im System der europäischen Digitalregulierung – Ein Überblick. JuS 2024:648–653

Huttenlauch A (2025) Art. 102 TFEU. In: Kersting C, Meyer-Lindemann H, Podszun R (eds) Kommentar zum Deutschen und Europäischen Kartellrecht, 5th edn. C.H. Beck, Munich

Kaulartz M (2016) Die blockchain-technologie. CR 32(7):474–480

Keßler O (2017) Intelligente Roboter – neue Technologien im Einsatz. Voraussetzungen und Rechtsfolgen des Handelns informationstechnischer Systeme. MMR 2017:589–594

King S (2013) Two-sided markets. Aust Econ Rev 46(2):247–258

Klabunde A, Horváth A (2024) GDPR Article 4. In: Ehemann E, Selmayr M (eds) DS-GVO Kommentar, 3rd edn. C.H. Beck, Munich

König C (2020) Sec. 17 KI und Wettbewerbsrecht. In: Ebers M, Heinze C, Krügel T, Steinrötter B (eds) Rechtshandbuch Künstliche Intelligenz und Robotik. C.H. Beck, Munich, pp. 542–572

Körber T (2025) EUMR Article 2. In: Immenga U, Mestmäcker E (eds) Kommentar zum Wettbewerbsrecht, 7th edn. C.H. Beck, Munich

Körber T (2017) Konzeptionelle Erfassung digitaler Plattformen und adäquate Regulierungsstrategien. ZUM 2017:93–101

Körber T (2016) "Ist Wissen Marktmacht?" Überlegungen zum Verhältnis von Datenschutz, "Datenmacht" und Kartellrecht – Teil 1. NZKart 2016:303–310

Körber T (2015) The commission's "next big thing"? NZKart 2015:415–423

Kumkar L (2025) Art. 101 TFEU. In: Gersdorf H, Paal B (eds) Beck'scher Online-Kommentar Informations- und Medienrecht, 49th edn. C.H. Beck, Munich

Künstner K (2019) Preissetzung durch Algorithmen als Herausforderung des Kartellrechts - Verhaltenskoordinierung über Algorithmen und Systeme Künstlicher Intelligenz. GRUR 2019:36–42

Künstner K, Franz B (2017) Preisalgorithmen und Dynamic Pricing: Eine neue Kategorie kartellrechtswidriger Abstimmungen? K&R 2017:688–693

Kumkar L (2020) Rechtsgeschäfte unter Beteiligung automatisierter und autonomer Systeme. K&R 2020:801–807
Lauscher A, Legner S (2022) Künstliche Intelligenz und Diskriminierung. ZfDR 2022:367–390
Legner S (2025) Wettbewerb mit KI. KIR 2025:183–190
Legner S (2023a) Die Marktabgrenzung im Kartellrecht. JURA 2023:175–181
Legner S (2023b) Smart Contracts und Finanzdienstleistungen. VuR 2023:213–218
Legner S (2021) Durchsetzungsdefizite bei Gleichbehandlungsgeboten am Beispiel des Gender Pricing. KritV 104(1):34–60
Locher L (2018) Verschiedene Preise für gleiche Produkte? Personalisierte Preise und Scoring aus ökonomischer Sicht. ZWeR 2018:292–316
Louven S, Saive D (2018) Antitrust by Design – Das Verbot wettbewerbsbeschränkender Abstimmungen und der Konsensmechanismus der Blockchain. NZKart 2018:348–354
Lübke J (2021) Preisabstimmung durch Algorithmen. ZHR 185(2021):723–769
Micklitz H, Namysłowska M (2019) UWG Sec. 5. In: Spindler G, Schuster F (eds) Recht der elektronischen Medien, 4th edn. C.H. Beck, Munich
Mik E (2018) Electronic platforms: openness, transparency & privacy issues. Eur Rev Priv Law 26(6):853–870
Möllenkamp S (2024) Part 13.6. In: Hoeren T, Sieber U, Holznagel B (eds) Handbuch Multimedia-Recht, 62th supp. C.H. Beck, Munich
Müller-Peltzer P, Tanczik V (2023) Künstliche Intelligenz und Daten. RDi 2023:452–458
Nida-Rümelin J (2022) § 1 E. Überblick über die Verwendung der Begriffe starke & schwache Künstliche Intelligenz. In: Chibanguza K, Kuß C, Steege H (eds) Rechtshandbuch Künstliche Intelligenz - Recht und Praxis automatisierter und autonomer Systeme I Generative KI. Nomos, Baden-Baden, pp. 75–90
Niederée C, Nejdl W (2020) Sec. 2 Technische Grundlagen der KI. In: Ebers M, Heinze C, Krügel T, Steinrötter B (eds) Rechtshandbuch Künstliche Intelligenz und Robotik. C.H. Beck, Munich, pp. 38–74
Podszun R (2025) ARC sec. 18. In: Kersting C, Meyer-Lindemann H, Podszun R (eds) Kommentar zum Deutschen und Europäischen Kartellrecht, 5th edn. C.H. Beck, Munich
Podszun R, Schwalbe U (2017) Digitale Plattformen und GWB-Novelle: Überzeugende Regeln für die Internetökonomie? NZKart 2017:98–106
Schirmer J (2016) Rechtsfähige Roboter? JZ 71(13):660–666
Schweitzer H, Haucap J, Kerber W, Welker R (2018) Modernisierung der Missbrauchsaufsicht für marktmächtige Unternehmen. Available via https://www.bmwk.de/Redaktion/DE/Publikationen/Wirtschaft/modernisierung-der-missbrauchsaufsicht-fuer-marktmaechtige-unternehmen.pdf?__blob=publicationFile&v=12. Accessed 25 Sept 2025
Specht L, Herold S (2018) Roboter als Vertragspartner? – Gedanken zu Vertragsabschlüssen unter Einbeziehung automatisiert und autonom agierender Systeme. MMR 2018:40–44
Steege H (2022) Definition von künstlicher Intelligenz in Art. 3 Nr. 1 KI-VO-E. MMR 2022:926–930
Stepanova O, Veeck B (2024) § 4 Datenschutz. In: Ebers M, Quarch B (eds) Rechtshandbuch ChatGPT - KI-basierte Sprachmodelle in der Praxis. Nomos, Baden-Baden, pp. 112–136
Tamke M (2018) Marktmacht in digitalen Märkten nach der 9. GWB-Novelle. NZKart 2018:503–508
Tillmann T, Vogt V (2018) Personalisierte Preise – Diskriminierung 2.0?. Available via ABIDA dossier. https://www.abida.de/sites/default/files/22_Dossier_Personalisierte%20Preise_Online.pdf. Accessed 25 Sept 2025
Wagner G, Eidenmüller H (2019) In der Falle der Algorithmen? Abschöpfen von Konsumentenrente, Ausnutzen von Verhaltensanomalien und Manipulation von Präferenzen: Die Regulierung der dunklen Seite personalisierter Transaktionen. ZfPW 2019:220–246
Weber R (2014) Information at the crossroads of competition and data protection law. ZWeR 2014:169–183
Weber R, Volz S (2015) Kartellrechtlicher Handlungsbedarf im Lichte potenzieller Meinungsmacht von Suchmaschinen. WuW 2015:356–368

European Competition Law

Contents

S. Legner, *Digital Competition Law*, Springer Textbooks in Law,
https://doi.org/10.1007/978-3-662-73213-7_2

2.1 Introduction

2.1.1 Overview

European competition law is primarily governed by the Treaty on the Functioning of the European Union (TFEU) and the European Merger Control Regulation (EUMR). It is structured into three main areas (◘ Fig. 2.1).

Article 101 TFEU establishes the **ban of cartels**. Under Article 101(1) TFEU, agreements and concerted practices between undertakings that may prevent, restrict, or distort competition within the internal market are prohibited. These restrictions can take the form of horizontal agreements—collusive arrangements between competitors—or vertical agreements between businesses operating at different levels of the supply chain. Classic examples of prohibited horizontal restrictions include so-called 'hardcore cartels,' where competitors directly fix prices or allocate markets or customers among themselves. Vertical agreements may also fall under the prohibition, such as those involving resale price maintenance or other restrictions on a distributor's freedom to set prices. However, not all restrictive agreements are unlawful. Article 101(3) TFEU provides an exemption for agreements that generate sufficient pro-competitive benefits to outweigh their anti-competitive effects. This may include improvements in production or distribution, or the promotion of technical or economic progress, provided that consumers receive a fair share of the resulting benefits. Such exemptions are more common for vertical restraints, as recognised by Article 2(1) Vertical Block Exemption.

Article 101 TFEU

1. The following shall be prohibited as incompatible with the internal market: all agreements between undertakings, decisions by associations of undertakings and concerted practices which may affect trade between Member States and which have as their object or effect the prevention, restriction or distortion of competition within the internal market, and in particular those which:
   (a) directly or indirectly fix purchase or selling prices or any other trading conditions;
   (b) limit or control production, markets, technical development, or investment;
   (c) share markets or sources of supply;

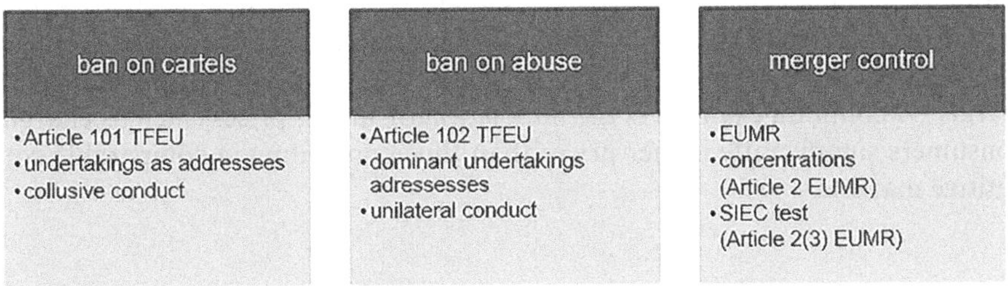

◘ **Fig. 2.1** The pillars of EU competition law

2

(d) apply dissimilar conditions to equivalent transactions with other trading parties, thereby placing them at a competitive disadvantage;

(e) make the conclusion of contracts subject to acceptance by the other parties of supplementary obligations which, by their nature or according to commercial usage, have no connection with the subject of such contracts.

2. Any agreements or decisions prohibited pursuant to this Article shall be automatically void.
3. The provisions of paragraph 1 may, however, be declared inapplicable in the case of:

- any agreement or category of agreements between undertakings,
- any decision or category of decisions by associations of undertakings,
- any concerted practice or category of concerted practices,

which contributes to improving the production or distribution of goods or to promoting technical or economic progress, while allowing consumers a fair share of the resulting benefit, and which does not:

(b) impose on the undertakings concerned restrictions which are not indispensable to the attainment of these objectives;

(c) afford such undertakings the possibility of eliminating competition in respect of a substantial part of the products in question.

Article 102 TFEU prohibits undertakings that hold a dominant position in a given market from abusing that position (**ban on abuse**). The provision targets unilateral conduct—that is, behaviour by a single undertaking acting independently of competitors—which has the effect of distorting or restricting competition. An undertaking is considered dominant when it enjoys a position of economic strength that allows it to act to a significant extent independently of its competitors and customers. While dominance itself is not prohibited, the abuse of such a position is. The rationale behind this prohibition is twofold: to protect the competitive process and to safeguard the interests of other market participants, including consumers. Abuse may take different forms, most notably exclusionary and exploitative conduct. Exclusionary abuse occurs when a dominant undertaking uses its position to hinder or eliminate competitors from the market. This can include practices such as unjustified refusals to supply, predatory pricing, tying and bundling, or entering into exclusivity agreements. Exploitative abuse involves conduct that directly harms the other side of the market. A common example is the imposition of unfair prices, such as charging consumers significantly higher prices than those prevailing in comparable competitive markets.

Article 102 TFEU
Any abuse by one or more undertakings of a dominant position within the internal market or in a substantial part of it shall be prohibited as incompatible with the internal market in so far as it may affect trade between Member States.

Such abuse may, in particular, consist in:

(a) directly or indirectly imposing unfair purchase or selling prices or other unfair trading conditions;
(b) limiting production, markets or technical development to the prejudice of consumers;
(c) applying dissimilar conditions to equivalent transactions with other trading parties, thereby placing them at a competitive disadvantage;
(d) making the conclusion of contracts subject to acceptance by the other parties of supplementary obligations which, by their nature or according to commercial usage, have no connection with the subject of such contracts.

European **merger control** is governed by the European Union Merger Regulation (**EUMR**), which regulates the merger of undertakings that meet the criteria set out in Article 3 EUMR. Specifically, mergers are subject to scrutiny if they have a Community dimension, meaning the undertakings involved exceed certain turnover thresholds specified in Article 1 EUMR. The scope of merger control extends beyond traditional mergers to include the acquisition of control over another undertaking. Merger control operates as a preventive system: the undertakings may only proceed with the merger once it has been cleared by the Commission. The merger may not be implemented unless the Commission gives its approval following a review. The substantive test applied by the Commission in assessing mergers is the SIEC test, established in Article 2(3) EUMR. Under this test, the Commission must prohibit a merger if it leads to a significant impediment to effective competition in the internal market or a substantial part of it. In any event, such an impediment occurs if the merging undertaking would, as a result of the merger, acquire a dominant market position. This might be the case if, for example, the undertakings involved in the merger would have a combined market share that is exceptionally high—such as 80%—and if there are significant barriers to market entry, such as control over essential technical knowledge or resources, which would prevent potential competitors from entering the market.

2.1.2 Historical Context of European Competition Law

European regulations concerning the protection of competition were first established in the **ECSC Treaty**[1] of **1952**. The **EEC Treaty**,[2] which came into force in **1957**, also included provisions for the protection of competition, notably a ban on

1 Treaty establishing the European Coal and Steel Community.
2 Treaty establishing the European Economic Community.

cartels (Article 86) and a ban on abuse of a dominant position (Article 90). However, unlike the ECSC Treaty, which remained in effect until 2002, the EEC Treaty did not include provisions for merger control. In **1999**, the EEC Treaty was replaced by the Treaty of Amsterdam, which amended and consolidated the **EC Treaty**. Under the revised framework, the competition rules were further developed and are now enshrined in Article 81, 82. The current provisions of Article 101 and Article 102 TFEU have been in effect since the **Treaty of Lisbon** in **2009**.

The European Union Merger Regulation (**EUMR**), in its current version, has been in force since **2004**. The original version of the regulation, which was adopted in 1989, introduced the market dominance test as the substantive basis for assessing mergers.[3] The SIEC test replaced the market dominance test in 2004. Before the introduction of the EUMR in 1989, mergers were occasionally assessed under the framework of abuse of a dominant position, which treated anti-competitive mergers as a form of market structure abuse.[4] The possibility of reviewing non-notifiable mergers ex post, based on the prohibition of abuse under Article 102 TFEU, has gained practical significance once again, most notably in the *Towercast* case.[5] This approach is particularly important for the protection of competition in digital markets, where mergers can have a considerable impact on innovation and competitive dynamics—even when they fall below the notification thresholds set out in Article 1 EUMR. One prominent example of such a situation is the acquisition of *WhatsApp* by *Facebook* in 2014. This merger was not subject to notification to the Commission, as the turnover thresholds established by the EUMR were not met.[6] However, the transaction had the potential to significantly affect competition, particularly due to the dynamic, innovation-driven nature of competition in digital markets, which can sometimes make traditional turnover-based thresholds less reflective of actual market power and competitive effects.

The core provisions of European competition law—Articles 101, 102 TFEU, as well as the EUMR—**have not been amended in response to digitalisation**. Where the European legislator has addressed the specific challenges posed by digital markets, it has primarily done so through secondary legislation. In particular, the revised **Vertical Block Exemption Regulation (VBER)**,[7] which has been in force since 2022, takes into account multi-sided business models and new types of restrictions of competition in the digital context. Among the novel issues addressed are narrow and broad price parity clauses, which restrict the terms under which sellers may offer better prices on other platforms or their own sales channels. The revised VBER also clarifies the role of platforms within distribution structures. Specifically,

---

3 Council Regulation (EEC) No 4064/89 of 21 December 1989 on the control of concentrations between undertakings, OJ [1989] L 395/1.

4 ECJ 21 February 1973 – C-6/72, ECLI:EU:C:1973:22 – *Continental Can*.

5 ECJ 16 March 2023 – C-449/21, ECLI:EU:C:2023:207 – *Towercast*.

6 Commission, Decision of 3 October 2014 – COMP/M.7217 – *WhatsApp/Facebook*.

7 Regulation (EU) 2022/720 of 10 May 2022 on the application of Article 101 (3) of the Treaty on the Functioning of the European Union to categories of vertical agreements and concerted practices, OJ [2022] L 134/4.

it states that the operator of an online intermediary service qualifies as a supplier within the meaning of the regulation. Consequently, agreements with undertakings that offer goods and services on the platform qualify as vertical agreements.[8] In addition to the VBER, the horizontal block exemption regulations—namely, the Research and Development (R&D) Block Exemption Regulation[9] and the Specialisation Block Exemption Regulation[10]—were revised in 2023 to reflect contemporary economic conditions, including those shaped by digitalisation and innovation-driven collaboration.

The development of European digital competition law has been shaped primarily by the decision-making practice of the Commission and the **case law** of the European courts. Over the past two decades, the courts have turned to a '**more economic approach**'. This methodological shift marks a departure from per se rules toward a more flexible, effects-based analysis, where the competitive impact of a given practice is assessed on a case-by-case basis. Another element of the more economic approach is the increasing emphasis on consumer welfare as objective of competition law.[11] Although the European courts have framed this development cautiously—as a mere 'concretisation' or clarification of the existing general clauses in the competition rules—it reflects a significant shift. In practice, these interpretations have resulted in what can be described as genuine transformations in how core concepts of competition law are understood and applied, particularly in the context of complex and dynamic digital markets.

► Example

Fidelity rebates—rebates granted by a dominant undertaking to incentivise customers to purchase exclusively or predominantly from it—were regarded as abusive per se under European competition law. The ECJ, in earlier case law, considered such practices inherently capable of restricting competition, particularly by excluding smaller rivals[12] However, this formalistic approach was fundamentally re-evaluated in the landmark judgment of 2017 in *Intel*. In this ruling, the ECJ departed from the per se categorisation and emphasised the need for a case-by-case assessment based on economic effects. The Court held that where a dominant undertaking submits economic evidence suggesting that its rebates were not capable of foreclosing equally efficient competitors, the Commission must conduct an impact-based analysis.[13] ◄

---

8 For further details, see ► 2.2.5.2.1.
9 Commission Regulation (EU) 2023/1066 of 1 June 2023 on the application of Article 101 (3) of the Treaty on the Functioning of the European Union to certain categories of research and development agreements, OJ [2023] L 143/9.
10 Commission Regulation (EU) 2023/1067 of 1 June 2023 on the application of Article 101 (3) of the Treaty on the Functioning of the European Union to certain categories of specialisation agreements, OJ [2023] L 143/20.
11 For further details on the objectives of European competition law, see ► 2.1.3.
12 ECJ 13 February 1979 – C-85/79, ECLI:EU:C:1979:36, para. 90 – *Hoffmann-La Roche*.
13 ECJ 6 September 2017 – C-413/14 P, ECLI:EU:C:2017:632, para. 139 – *Intel/Commission*.

Although not limited to digital markets, this development has had a significant impact on the enforcement of competition law in digital contexts. The shift toward effects-based analyses has also contributed to **longer proceedings**. As a result, the enforcement of competition rules often lags behind the rapid pace of innovation and market evolution in the digital sector. This raises concerns about the timely and effective protection of competition in fast-moving technology markets. One example is the *Google Shopping* case: the Commission found that Google had abused its dominant position in general internet search by systematically favouring its own comparison shopping service in search results while demoting rival services.[14] The Commission opened a formal investigation in 2010, and the final decision was not issued until 2017—7 years later.

Finally, the Commission regularly updates **its communications and guidelines** to reflect new developments in its decision-making practice and to enhance legal certainty for undertakings. In 2022, the Commission revised its **Vertical Guidelines**, which outline the principles governing the assessment of vertical agreements under Article 101 TFEU.[15] The revision took into account changes in commercial practices and aimed to address challenges posed by the increasing importance of online platforms, dual distribution, and other features of the digital economy. In 2023, the **Horizontal Guidelines**, which relate to agreements between actual or potential competitors, were also amended.[16] In this update, the Commission not only responded to recent developments in the digital sector, such as data sharing and digital innovation collaborations, but also placed particular emphasis on providing legal clarity for the assessment of sustainability agreements.

▶ Example

In the updated chapter on the exchange of information, the Commission clarifies that such exchanges may occur not only through direct communication between competitors but also indirectly, including via third parties. This may involve intermediaries such as '*service providers, digital platforms, online tools, or algorithms*'.[17] ◀

In 2023, the Commission has announced its intention to publish guidelines on Article 102 TFEU by 2025. As a preparatory measure, the Commission published amendments to its 2008 enforcement priorities[18] at the end of 2023.[19] Among other things, the updated communication includes important clarifications regarding the as-efficient competitor test, which plays a central role in the effects-based assess-

14 Commission, Decision of 27 June 2017 – AT.39740 – *Google Search (Shopping)*.

15 Commission, Guidelines on Vertical Restraints [2022] OJ C 248/1.

16 Commission, Guidelines on the applicability of Article 101 of the Treaty on the Functioning of the European Union to horizontal co-operation agreements [2023] OJ C 259/1.

17 Commission, Horizontal Guidelines [2023] OJ C 259/1, para. 408.

18 Commission, Amendment to the Commission Notice – Clarifications on the Commission's priorities in the application of Article 82 of the EC Treaty to exclusionary conduct by dominant undertakings [2023] OJ C 116/1.

19 Commission, Clarifications on the Commission's priorities in the application of Article 82 of the EC Treaty to exclusionary conduct by dominant undertakings [2009] OJ C 45/7.

ment of exclusionary abuses. In 2024, The Commission published draft guidelines.[20] In particular, the Commission outlines procedural requirements for presenting evidence of specific instances of exclusionary abuse. This aims to enhance the practical enforceability of Article 102 TFEU.[21] Additionally, the Commission intends to revise the Regulation 1/2003 on the implementation of Articles 101, 102 TFEU. Therefore, it started a consultation process in July 2025.[22] In the area of merger control, the Commission introduced a new Implementing Regulation[23] in early 2023. This regulation aims to simplify and streamline the notification process for merger transactions, particularly by expanding the scope of the simplified procedure. In May 2025, the Commission began a consultation process for the revision of both the Horizontal Merger Guidelines and the Non-Horizontal Merger Guidelines.[24]

2.1.3 Objectives

2.1.3.1 Competitive Process

European competition law primarily protects competition as an institution and treats it as a value in itself.[25] It establishes a **level playing field** that allows undertakings to compete on equal terms for commercial relationships with third parties. To ensure free markets, European competition law safeguards the freedom of action of undertakings.[26] However, this protection does not extend to guaranteeing the survival of all competitors. It is a normal feature of competition that less efficient firms lose customers while stronger ones expand their market share. The founders of the European Economic Community and the early developers of German competition law[27] based their work on **ordoliberal principles**. However, the theoretical foundation for competition in the drafting of the EEC Treaty remained far less detailed than the discussions that shaped the development of German competition law.[28]

---

20 Draft Guidelines on the application of Article 102 of the Treaty on the Functioning of the European Union to abusive exclusionary conduct by dominant undertakings <https://competition-policy.ec.europa.eu/public-consultations/2024-article-102-guidelines_en> (accessed 28 August 2025).

21 Wagner-von Papp (2024), pp. 445 et seq.

22 <https://ec.europa.eu/commission/presscorner/detail/en/ip_25_1795> (accessed 5 September 2025).

23 Commission Implementing Regulation (EU) 2023/914 of 20 April 2023 implementing Council Regulation (EC) No 139/2004 on the control of concentrations between undertakings [2023] OJ EU L 119/22.

24 <https://ec.europa.eu/commission/presscorner/detail/en/ip_25_1141> (accessed 5 September 2025).

25 ECJ 4 June 2009 – C-8/08, ECLI:EU:C:2009:343, para. 38 – *T-Mobile Netherlands*: '*Article 81 EC, like the other competition rules of the Treaty, is designed to protect not only the immediate interests of individual competitors or consumers but also to protect the structure of the market and thus competition as such.*'

26 Möschel (1988), pp. 707, 712.

27 For the historical context of German competition law, see ► 5.1.2.

28 Kling and Thomas (2016), sec. 2 mn. 36.

The protection of competition as an institution is based on a **structural understanding** of how markets function. Market share and the degree of market concentration serve as key indicators for assessing whether effective competition exists. However, a high level of market concentration does not automatically imply a decline in competition. As recognised by competition law, the competitive process functions as a 'discovery procedure' that can produce unpredictable outcomes.[29] In digital markets, structural concerns arise particularly in relation to high market concentration driven by indirect network effects. From a structural perspective, this concentration is often viewed critically. The nature of competition in these markets tends to shift from competition within the market to **competition for the market**. Even so, the specific dynamics of multi-sided platform markets mean that competition still takes place, although through different mechanisms and channels.

2.1.3.2 Consumer Welfare

For about 20 years, European competition law has increasingly followed what is called the **more economic approach**.[30] This shift is linked to two main developments. The first relates to the goals of competition law both the Commission and the European courts now recognise consumer welfare as a goal alongside the protection of competition as such.[31] In conducting an effects-based analysis, a benchmark is needed to assess whether an undertaking's conduct should be regarded as anti-competitive. The consumer welfare standard serves this role, providing a reference point for evaluating outcomes under European competition law. Originally derived from economic theory, consumer welfare can be assessed from both static and dynamic perspectives. In static terms, it is measured through **consumer surplus**, which represents the difference between the actual price paid by a consumer and the maximum price they would have been willing to pay (the reservation price). From a dynamic perspective, consumer welfare increases through broader **product variety** and improved **quality**. These factors that can justify higher prices if they reflect added value for consumers.

This focus on outcomes marks a shift to an **effects-based approach**. That leads to the second major development: how competition law is applied in practice. The Commission and courts are paying closer attention to the real effects of business behaviour on the market. They analyse whether certain agreements, business practices, or mergers actually harm consumers, for example by raising prices or reducing quality. In most traditional markets, the main focus is on how an undertaking's actions affect prices and output. To do this, the Commission uses both qualitative and quantitative tools. One example of a quantitative tool is the UPP (Upward Pricing Pressure) test, which helps assess whether a merger is likely to lead to higher prices.[32] Digital markets, however, often work differently. Many digital services are

---

29 Von Hayek (1994), p. 250.

30 For the more economic approach in the historical context of EU competition law, see ► 2.1.2.

31 Commission, Decision of 26 April 2006 – COMP/M.3916, para. 125 – *T-Mobile Austria/tele.ring*; Commission, Decision of 12 March 2009 – COMP/M.5355, para. 21 – *BASF/Ciba*.

32 Commission, Decision of 12 December 2012 – COMP/M.6497, para. 312 et seq. — *Hutchison 3G Austria/Orange Austria*.

offered to consumers for free or at very low cost, so price is not always the best measure of harm or benefit.[33] Instead, the Commission and courts look at how a company's behaviour affects innovation, product variety, and quality. These effects are harder to measure, but they still matter for consumer welfare.[34] Digital platforms typically offer several advantages for consumers. They can make markets more transparent by helping users compare products and prices more easily. Platforms also reduce transaction costs by allowing users to buy directly from sellers.[35] In addition, large platforms often have access to a lot of user data, which they can use to develop better products and services. Many platforms also monitor the quality of products sold on their sites, which can further benefit consumers.[36] However, since platform operators determine which pieces of information consumers are confronted with, they also shape the formation of consumers' preferences.[37] Accordingly, the question of whether the business models of digital platforms merely enhance consumer welfare is more complex than it may initially appear.

The objectives of safeguarding competition and promoting consumer welfare are, in principle, aligned. Competitive markets tend to produce lower prices, enhanced product quality, and increased innovation, thereby advancing consumer welfare. However, tensions between these goals may arise. In these cases, they require a careful balancing of interests within the framework of European competition law. Such balancing is explicitly addressed in the context of the cartel prohibition through the exemption mechanism provided under Article 101(3) TFEU. This provision allows agreements that would otherwise fall within the scope of the Article 101(1) prohibition to be exempted where they generate sufficient pro-competitive efficiencies. These efficiencies must not only offset the restrictive effects on competition but also benefit consumers, be indispensable to achieving the efficiencies, and avoid eliminating competition in a substantial part of the market. Similarly, both abuse of dominance cases under Article 102 TFEU and merger control assessments under the EUMR recognise the possibility of justifying otherwise anti-competitive conduct or concentrations on the basis of efficiency gains. This so-called **efficiency defence** permits undertakings to argue that their conduct or transaction, while potentially restrictive, yields substantial economic efficiencies that enhance consumer welfare and thus should be deemed compatible with European competition rules.

---

33 For more information of asymmetric price structures in digital markets, see ► 1.1.3.

34 Bostoen (2023), p. 90.

35 Bostoen (2023), p. 210.

36 A critical view on this point is taken by GC 12. December 1991 – T-30/89, ECLI:T:1991:70, para. 118 – *Hilti*: '*As the Commission has established, there are laws in the United Kingdom attaching penalties to the sale of dangerous products and to the use of misleading claims as to the characteristics of any product. There are also authorities vested with powers to enforce those laws. In those circumstances it is clearly not the task of an undertaking in a dominant position to take steps on its own initiative to eliminate products which, rightly or wrongly, it regards as dangerous or at least as inferior in quality to its own products.*'

37 Podszun (2023), p. 20220037.

2.1.3.3 European Single Market

2

In addition to promoting consumer welfare and preserving effective competition, European competition law plays a vital role in achieving the broader goal of **European integration**.[38] Specifically, it supports the development and maintenance of a single internal market, as envisaged in Article 3(3) TEU and Article 26 TFEU. These provisions call for the establishment of an area without internal frontiers, within which goods, services, capital, and persons can circulate freely. By prohibiting anti-competitive agreements and abusive practices that restrict trade between Member States, EU competition law supports market integration. In this context, effective competition is not only valued for its impact on consumer welfare but also as a mechanism for realising the Treaty objective of a functioning internal market.[39]

2.1.4 Scope of Application

2.1.4.1 Personal Scope

European competition law applies to **undertakings**. The term undertaking must be interpreted **autonomously** and independently from European and national legal definitions found in other areas such as commercial or company law. The interpretation of undertaking under Articles 101, 102 TFEU is **functional** and economic in nature.[40] According to settled case law, an undertaking encompasses any entity engaged in an **economic activity**, regardless of its legal status or the way in which it is financed. The concept focuses on the performance of economic functions rather than on the legal form or classification under national law. An economic activity is understood as offering goods or services on a given market. The status of an undertaking is therefore attributed not only to corporations such as limited liability companies (in German law: GmbH) and public limited companies (in German law: AG), but also to partnerships (e.g. in German law: GbR, oHG, KG) and even natural persons, provided they are engaged in market-oriented activities. The key criterion is that participation in economic life must not be purely occasional.[41] Even indirect involvement in market activities may suffice to qualify an entity as an undertaking.[42] For example, research and development efforts aimed at improving product quality or enhancing environmental performance (such as emission reductions in production processes) may constitute economic activity if they are linked to the entity's role in the market.

---

38 ECJ 13 July 1966 – C-56/64, ECLI:EU:C:1966:41 – *Consten and Grundig*.

39 On current developments, see Brinker (2019), TFEU Article 101 mn. 11.

40 ECJ 23 April 1991 – C-41/90, ECLI:EU:C:1991:161, para. 21 – *Höfner and Else*; ECJ 16 November 1995 – C-244/94, ECLI:EU:C:1995:392, para. 14 – *FFSA and others*.

41 Wiedemann (2020), sec. 4 mn. 1.

42 Mestmäcker and Schweitzer (2014), sec. 9 mn. 6.

Definition

The concept of an undertaking in European competition law is interpreted autonomously and functionally. It encompasses any entity engaged in economic activity, regardless of its legal status, legal personality, or method of financing. Legal subjectivity is not a prerequisite. An economic activity refers to any offering or purchasing of goods or services on a given market. The legal form—whether natural person, partnership, or corporation—is irrelevant, as is whether the entity is publicly or privately financed.

► **Examples**

freelance professionals (e.g. lawyers, consultants);[43] commercial banks;[44] large digital platforms (e.g. online marketplaces, social media platforms).[45] ◄

In European competition law, the definition of an undertaking extends beyond individual legal entities.[46] The concept is functional and centres on economic activity rather than legal form. As a result, an economic entity need not possess legal capacity to qualify as an undertaking. Where several legally distinct entities operate under a single centre of control—typically within a corporate group—they may collectively be regarded as a single undertaking for the purposes of competition law.[47] This principle applies even though the **group** itself does not possess legal personality. In such cases, the group as a whole constitutes an economic unit alongside its individual members. The decisive factor is the **absence of market independence**. If the subsidiaries or affiliated companies do not independently determine their conduct on the market but instead follow the strategic direction and instructions of a parent company, there is no competition between them. In such circumstances, the entities functionally constitute one undertaking under the single economic entity doctrine. This interpretation is grounded in the so-called independence postulate, which holds that only entities that independently decide their market behaviour are considered separate undertakings.[48] The lack of legal subjectivity of the corporate group does not preclude it from being treated as an undertaking under European competition rules. This functional approach also applies when assessing liability for infringements of competition law.[49] Legal entities that form part of a single economic unit may be held jointly and severally liable for competition law violations committed by the undertaking as a whole.[50] In the *Akzo* case,

43 ECJ 19 February 2001 – C-309/99, ECLI:EU:C:2002:98 – *Wouters*.
44 ECJ 2 April 2020 – C-228/18, ECLI:EU:C:2020:265 – *Budapest Bank Nyrt*.
45 GC 10 November 2021 – T-612/17, ECLI:EU:T:2021:763 – *Google Shopping*.
46 ECJ 8 May 2013 – C-508/11 P, ECLI:EU:C:2013:289, para. 82 – *ENI*; ECJ 28 June 2005 – C-189/02 P, ECLI:EU:C:2005:408, para. 113 – *Dansk Rørindustri et al.*
47 ECJ 14 March 2019 – C-724/17, ECLI:EU:C:2019:204, para. 37 – *Skanska*; ECJ 11 July 2013 – C-440/11 P, ECLI:EU:C:2013:514, para. 36 – *Stichting A. Portielje*.
48 Glöckner (2021), sec. 4 mn. 380.
49 Mestmäcker and Schweitzer (2014), sec. 9 mn. 3–5.
50 Mestmäcker and Schweitzer (2014), sec. 9 mn. 23.

2

the ECJ ruled that the parent undertaking is liable for a breach of competition law by a subsidiary if, '*although having a separate legal personality, that subsidiary does not decide independently upon its own conduct on the market, but carries out, in all material respects, the instructions given to it by the parent company.*'[51]

While the term undertaking is broad and functional, certain actors fall outside its scope due to the nature of their activities or legal status. **Consumers** are not regarded as undertakings within the meaning of European competition law. Their participation in the market is limited to satisfying personal needs, and they do not engage in economic activity.[52] As such, they are not subject to the prohibitions set out in Articles 101, 102 TFEU. Similarly, employees who do not act independently are not considered addressees of the prohibitions under competition law. Their conduct on the market is directed by instructions from their employer, and they do not make autonomous decisions regarding their market behaviour.[53]

Public authorities acting in a sovereign capacity (i.e. exercising public powers) are not considered undertakings under European competition law.[54] However, when the state or a public body engages in economic activity—for instance, by offering goods or services on the market—it is subject to the competition rules just like any private operator. The state may act not only as a supplier but also as a purchaser. Nonetheless, in the *Fenin* judgment, the GC and the ECJ held that public procurement activities aimed at fulfilling purely non-economic objectives (e.g. provision of public healthcare) do not fall within the scope of competition law, even if they involve the purchase of goods or services.[55] This interpretation highlights a significant divergence from the approach taken in German competition law. Under the German competition law, public procurement activities are generally subject to competition law scrutiny, regardless of the purpose they serve.[56]

The scope of Article 101 TFEU explicitly includes not only individual undertakings but also **associations of undertakings**. These are typically organisations composed of at least two undertakings that are formed to promote or coordinate their members' commercial interests.[57] Examples include trade associations, industry groups, and certain types of cooperatives. These associations are subject to the same cartel prohibition as their members, especially where their activities or decisions restrict competition among undertakings.

51 ECJ 11 July 2013 – C-440/11 P, ECLI:EU:C:2013:514, mn. 38 – *Gosselin*; ECJ 10 September 2009 – C-97/08 P, ECLI:EU:C:2009:536, mn. 58 – *Akzo Nobel.*

52 Zimmer (2025), TFEU Article 101(1) mn. 10.

53 ECJ 4 December 2014 – C-413/13, ECLI:EU:C:2014: 2411, para. 42 – *FNV Kunsten Informatie en Media.*

54 Jennert (2004), pp. 37, 40 et seq.

55 ECJ 11 July 2006 – C-205/03 P, ECLI:EU:C:2006:453 – *FENIN*; CFI 4 March 2003 – T-319/99, ECLI:EU:T:2003:50 – *FENIN.*

56 For further details on the concept of undertaking under German competition law, see ► 5.1.4.1.

57 Kumkar (2025), TFEU Article 101 mn. 10.

2.1.4.2 Substantive Scope

The prohibition of cartels and the prohibition of abuse of a dominant position apply exclusively to anti-competitive practices that are capable **of affecting trade between the member states** of the European Union. Where such an effect on intra-European trade is absent, only national competition law is applicable.[58] Importantly, the threshold for triggering the application of EU competition law is relatively low. It is sufficient if the impact on trade is potential or indirect. Furthermore, the agreements or practices in question must be capable of **appreciably** affecting trade between European countries. This requirement of appreciable effect has been clarified by the Commission through its Guidelines on the effect on trade concept.[59] According to the non-appreciable affectation of trade rule (**NAAT-rule**) an agreement is not capable of appreciably affecting trade between member states if the combined market share of the parties involved does not exceed 5% and the combined EU turnover in the case of horizontal restraints of competition or the EU turnover of the supplier in the case of vertical restraints of competition does not exceed EUR 40 million.[60]

The scope of application of EU merger control is determined by whether a proposed concentration possesses a **Community dimension**, as defined by the turnover thresholds set out in **Article 1 EUMR**.[61] Only mergers that meet these thresholds have to be notified to the Commission for merger control.

The **Digital Markets Act (DMA)**[62] operates alongside European competition law and does not exclude its application. In accordance with Article 1(6) DMA, the enforcement of Articles 101, 102 TFEU remains fully applicable. Consequently, even where an undertaking has been designated as a gatekeeper under Article 3 DMA,[63] it continues to be subject to the general prohibitions of competition law and remains accountable for any anti-competitive conduct.

2.1.4.3 Territorial Scope

The territorial applicability of European competition law is determined by the **effects doctrine**.[64] Under this principle, it is sufficient for an anti-competitive practice to have actual or potential effects within the European internal market. Consequently, European competition rules may apply even when all the undertakings involved are established outside the European Union.[65] Historically, European courts referred to the implementation principle, which focused on whether the anti-competitive conduct was implemented within the internal market. While older case

58 ECJ 30 June 1966 – C-56-65, ECLI:EU:C:1966:38 – *Maschinenbau Ulm*; ECJ 13 July 2006 – C-295/04 and others, ECLI:EU:C:2006:67, para. 41 – *Manfredi*.
59 Commission, Guidelines on the effect on trade concept, OJ [2004] C 101/81, para. 3.
60 Commission, Guidelines on the effect on trade concept, para. 52.
61 For further details, see ► 2.4.3.2.
62 The Digital Markets Act is captured by ► Chap. 3.
63 On the notion of gatekeeper, see ► 3.2.
64 Mestmäcker and Schweitzer (2014), sec. 7 mn. 50.
65 Commission, Decision of 13 May 2009 – COMP/37.990, para. 1749 et seqq. – *Intel*.

law emphasized this approach, the European courts have interpreted the concept of implementation broadly. For example, it is deemed sufficient if undertakings located outside the EU supply goods or services into the internal market that are affected by the anti-competitive practice. In practice, this broad interpretation of implementation results in an outcome that largely aligns with the effects doctrine.[66] Therefore, the result is usually the same as when applying the effects principle.

2.2 Prohibition of Cartels: Article 101 TFEU

2.2.1 Prohibited Conduct

2.2.1.1 Agreements

General Principles

The ban on cartels prohibits restrictions on competition that result from collusive conduct. Article 101(1) TFEU clarifies this by listing three types of prohibited conduct. These serve as means of restricting competition. Undertakings can coordinate by concluding an **agreement**, adopting a **decision**, or engaging in a **concerted practice**.

An agreement exists when the parties reach a mutual understanding about **certain market conduct**.[67] In any case, this may be realized through the conclusion of contract that has a binding effect under civil law.[68] However, a legally binding effect is not required. The concept of an agreement also encompasses so-called gentlemen's agreements, which lack the intention to be legally binding.[69] A **de facto agreement** of intent is sufficient; the undertakings do not need to consider themselves legally bound by it. An agreement may also be concluded implicitly. Unilateral conduct, however, does not fall within the scope of the cartel prohibition.[70]

▶ Example

In the *Adalat* case, the ECJ ruled that the failure of distributors to export medicines to Spain and France—after the manufacturer had reduced the quantity supplied for that purpose—did not constitute an agreement between the distributors and the manufacturer. Rather, the supply reduction was a unilateral act by the manufacturer.[71] The fact that the distributors refrained from exporting could not be interpreted as consent. However, if the manufacturer had imposed sanctions for non-compliance, the distributors' adherence might have constituted implied consent. ◀

66 ECJ 9 March 2017 – C-615/15 P, ECLI:EU:C:2017:190, para. 53 et seq. – *ray tubes*.
67 ECJ 13 July 2006 – C-74/04 P, ECLI:EU:C:2006:460, para. 37 – *Volkswagen II*.
68 Zimmer (2025), TFEU Article 101(1) mn. 76. A contract with which undertakings realise a restriction of competition is void under Article 101(2) TFEU.
69 Grave and Nyberg (2025), TFEU Article 101(1) mn. 227.
70 ECJ 6 January 2004 – C-2/01 P and others, ECLI:EU:C:2004:2 – *Bayer v Commission*.
71 ECJ 6 January 2004 – C-2/01 P and others, ECLI:EU:C:2004:2 – *Bayer v Commission*.

This example illustrates that the reason an undertaking consents to an agreement is irrelevant to the concept of an agreement. A de facto agreement is also sufficient if it results from economic pressure.[72]

Unlike a concerted practice,[73] an agreement does not require the agreed-upon conduct to be implemented.[74] The mere formulation of a shared intention already concretizes the planned market conduct. This marks a key distinction from the concept of concerted practice. Since a concerted practice does not require an agreement on specific market behaviour, it may already be established through the exchange of strategic information.

Agreements Using and Through Algorithms

Algorithms can facilitate the **monitoring** of compliance with anti-competitive agreements by enabling undertakings to observe whether other cartel participants are adhering to the agreed-upon terms. This is particularly relevant in cases of vertical restraints on competition—such as resale price maintenance[75]—where suppliers may use pricing algorithms to promptly detect whether retailers are deviating from a fixed or minimum agreed price.[76]

▶ Example

In both the United States[77] and the United Kingdom,[78] competition authorities have reported cases involving online retailers who agreed on fixed pricing levels for posters sold via the online marketplace *Amazon*. To implement this agreement, the competitors purchased and used price-adjustment software. They programmed the software to set poster prices in line with the collusive agreement. Both the *U.S. Department of Justice* and the *U.K. Competition and Markets Authority* classified this as an anti-competitive agreement facilitated through the use of software. ◀

There is ongoing debate about whether algorithms could, in the future, **independently enter into agreements**.[79] If undertakings deploy algorithms that not only monitor the prices of competitors or retailers but also autonomously determine their own pricing strategies, it is conceivable that AI systems could autonomously adjust prices in a manner that mimics collusive behaviour. In such scenarios, it

---

72 Stockenhuber (2025), TFEU Article 101 mn. 93.
73 On the principles of concerted practices, see ▶ 2.2.1.3.
74 Zimmer 2025, TFEU Article 101(1) mn. 75.
75 For further details on vertical core restrictions, see ▶ 2.2.2.3.1.
76 Commission, Horizontal Guidelines, 2023, para. 379; Dohrn and Huck (2018), pp. 173, 174.
77 DOJ, press release of 6 April 2015 <https://www.justice.gov/opa/pr/former-e-commerce-executive-charged-price-fixing-antitrust-divisions-first-online-marketplace> (accessed 1 September 2025).
78 CMA, Decision of 12 August 2016 – Case no. 50223 – Online sales of posters and frames <https://assets.publishing.service.gov.uk/media/57ee7c2740f0b606dc000018/case-50223-final-non-confidential-infringement-decision.pdf> (accessed 1 September 2025).
79 Dohrn and Huck (2018), pp. 173, 174.

would be necessary to attribute the algorithm's actions to the respective undertaking in order to establish a breach of competition law.[80] The design or programming of the algorithm could serve as the basis for this attribution.[81]

Furthermore, **blockchain technology** is being evaluated as a potential tool for monitoring compliance with anti-competitive agreements.[82] A blockchain is a decentralized network in which data records—referred to as 'blocks'—are chronologically linked. It is considered tamper-proof and transparent. When combined with so-called smart contracts—self-executing programs that carry out transactions automatically based on their code[83]—this technology can also be used to trace payments and enforce collusive arrangements.

2.2.1.2 Decisions

In contrast to an agreement, a decision by an association of undertakings results from a collective expression of will.[84] As with agreements, the civil law validity or enforceability of such a decision is irrelevant to its existence under competition law.[85] Unlike agreements, decisions can be adopted by a majority vote, unless the association's internal rules provide otherwise. In such cases, all members who accept or adhere to the majority decision may be considered to have infringed the prohibition on cartels—even if they did not vote in favour of the decision.[86]

2.2.1.3 Concerted Practices

General Principles

Article 101 TFEU prohibits undertakings from coordinating their conduct in advance of an agreement. The concept of a concerted practice serves as a catch-all provision. It becomes relevant where undertakings do not establish a clearly defined common strategy on the market.[87] It captures any conduct that is incompatible with the principles of free competition and includes

> » any direct or indirect contact between such traders, the object or effect of which is to create conditions of competition which do not correspond to the normal conditions of the market in question.[88]

When competitors coordinate their market behaviour, they reduce the risks and uncertainties that typically arise from independent competition. Coordination alleviates the uncertainty regarding future conduct of competitors, which is a central feature of a functioning competitive market.[89]

---

80 For further details, see ► 2.5.2.
81 Dohrn and Huck (2018), pp. 173, 175.
82 OECD (2018), pp. 5 et seqq.; Kumkar (2025), TFEU Article 101 mn. 132; Louven and Saive (2018), p. 348.
83 On the concept of smart contracts Legner (2023a), pp. 213 et seq.
84 Zimmer (2025), TFEU Article 101(1) mn. 87.
85 Mestmäcker and Schweitzer (2014), sec. 10 mn. 27.
86 ECJ 29 October 1980 – C-209/78, ECLI:EU:C:1980:248, para. 91 – *Van Landewyck*.
87 ECJ 4 June 2009 – C-8/08, ECLI:EU:C:2009:343, para. 26 – *T-Mobile Netherlands*.
88 ECJ 28 May 1998 – C-7/95, ECLI:EU:C:1998:256, para. 87 – *Deere*.
89 Pohlmann (2018), pp. 633, 646.

Concerted practices often occur through the **exchange of commercially sensitive information**, particularly regarding future market conduct.[90] For example, if competitors share information on planned price increases or sales volumes, they may adjust their own behaviour accordingly.[91] In oligopolistic markets, coordination can even be achieved through unilateral public announcements. This practice is known as signalling.[92] If a price announcement is sufficiently detailed or made well in advance, competitors may rely on it when setting their own prices. If, as a result, one undertaking raises its prices following another's public pricing announcement, a coordinated practice may be deemed to exist.[93] Importantly, the announcement need not be explicitly addressed to competitors; a public statement can suffice.[94]

Unlike an agreement, a concerted practice generally requires evidence of **actual market conduct** following from the prior coordination.[95] Parallel behaviour in the market may serve as an indication of such coordination.[96] However, recent decisions by the European courts have set a relatively low threshold for establishing the required market conduct.[97] It is not necessary to show that the conduct resulted in a demonstrable restriction of competition; it is sufficient that the purpose of the coordination was to restrict competition.[98]

! The notion of concerted practice functions as a residual category where no provable agreement can be demonstrated. Unlike agreements, however, proof of an implementing act is required to establish an infringement. It must be demonstrated that the coordination influenced the actual market conduct.

Undertakings are still **permitted** to engage in **tacit collusion**.[99] Under certain market conditions, competitors may coordinate their behaviour across the market implicitly, without entering into an agreement or engaging in concerted practices as prohibited under Article 101 TFEU.[100] A typical example is the oligopolistic petrol station market. Due to **high market concentration, price transparency, and homogeneous products**, competitors can closely monitor each other's behaviour and adjust their own strategies accordingly.

In such markets, undertakings independently adapt their conduct to prevailing market conditions.[101] Nevertheless, this independent yet parallel behaviour can

---

90 ECJ 28 May 1998 – C-7/95, ECLI:EU:C:1998:256, para. 85 – *Deere*.
91 ECJ 14 July 1972 – C-48/69, ECLI:EU:C:1972:70, para. 64 – *ICI*.
92 Wagner-von Papp (2023), TFEU Article 101 mn. 353.
93 Zimmer (2025), TFEU Article 101(1) mn. 99.
94 Commission, Decision of 7 July 2016 – AT.39850 – *Container Shipping* (The proceedings were terminated by way of binding commitments offered by the parties).
95 ECJ 4 June 2009 – C-8/08, ECLI:EU:C:2009:343, para. 51 f. – *T-Mobile Netherlands*.
96 GC 12 April 2023 – T-442/08, ECLI:EU:T:2013:188, para. 137 – *CISAC*.
97 ECJ 4 June 2009 – C-8/08, ECLI:EU:C:2009:343, para. 58 – *T-Mobile Netherlands*.
98 ECJ 8 July 1999 – C-199/92 P, ECLI:EU:C:1999:358, para. 164 – *Hüls*.
99 Böni and Palzer (2009), pp. 477, 479.
100 Wagner-von Papp (2023), TFEU Article 101 mn. 358.
101 Ulmer (1972), p. 13.

2

Prison sentence	A stays silent	A confesses
B stays silent	1 year, 1 year	0 years, 10 years
B confesses	10 years, 0 years	5 years, 5 years

Fig. 2.2 Prisoner's dilemma

result in the emergence of a collusive equilibrium, in which prices remain above competitive levels. This occurs because each undertaking recognises that by maintaining parallel conduct, all participants can achieve higher collective profits.[102] While an individual undertaking could, in the short term, increase its profit by undercutting its rivals' prices, the incentive to deviate from the collusive equilibrium is weakened when market structures suggest that competitors are likely to respond swiftly. The faster the anticipated reaction to a price cut, the smaller the short-term profit from deviating, and the more stable the collusive outcome becomes.

The economic foundation of tacit collusion can be illustrated by the **prisoner's dilemma** in game theory (Fig. 2.2).[103] This model shows that players achieve a **higher collective gain** if they cooperate. In the traditional prisoner's dilemma, this means that both suspects remain silent and do not confess to the crime, resulting in shorter prison sentences for both. However, each individual has an incentive to deviate from the cooperative outcome. If only one confesses, that player avoids punishment, while the other receives a significantly longer sentence. Although defection benefits the individual in the short term, it leads to a worse outcome for both players if they act in the same way. In the context of market behaviour, tacit collusion is only durable over time if competitors are able to discipline any deviation from the collusive arrangement.[104] This is where the so-called **tit-for-tat strategy** becomes relevant. It is based on the principle of reciprocity: if one competitor chooses the most profitable strategy for itself at the expense of others—such as lowering prices—its competitors respond by doing the same.

In the prisoner's dilemma, this means that a confession by one player leads to a confession by the other, resulting in a longer sentence for both compared to the cooperative outcome. In a market setting, this dynamic is reflected in the behaviour of undertakings, especially in oligopolistic sectors like the petrol station market. Since fuel prices are highly transparent and often clearly visible from the roadside, competitors are able to monitor each other's prices closely. If one undertaking reduces its price, others are likely to follow quickly. As a result, the short-term ben-

102 Ewald (2020), sec. 7 mn. 88.
103 On the basics of game theory, see Kerber and Schwalbe (2023), Introduction mn. 182 et seq.
104 Legner (2014), pp. 1, 3.

efit of deviating from the tacitly collusive equilibrium is diminished, making stable coordination more likely.

Parallel conduct, by itself, does not constitute a violation of Article 101 TFEU. Within the framework of the prohibition on cartels, what is prohibited is defined by the **form** of the coordination rather than its effects. The key distinction between unlawful coordination and lawful parallel behaviour lies in the **principle of independence**. Undertakings must determine their market conduct independently. As long as parallel behaviour results from such independent decision-making, it remains outside the scope of Article 101.

! Aligning one's behaviour with that of competitors does not amount to prohibited conduct under Article 101 TFEU, provided that the independence requirement is not breached. However, under Article 102 TFEU, which governs abuse of dominance, such market alignment may contribute to the finding of collective dominance.[105]

Collusion Using Algorithms

The use of algorithms can not only facilitate the monitoring of compliance with anti-competitive agreements but can also play an active role in the **implementation of coordinated conduct**.[106] This may occur, for example, when cartel participants jointly use the same pricing algorithm or rely on identical third-party software. In such cases, the algorithm itself becomes a tool for executing the coordination.

▶ Example

In the *Eturas* case,[107] the provider of an online travel booking platform (E) sent a message to participating travel agencies, stating that discounts were to be limited to a maximum of 3%. Technically, the travel agencies could still apply higher discounts. However, the platform provider implemented technical changes to the system, requiring agencies to complete additional steps in order to offer a higher discount.

The ECJ found that this constituted a concerted practice among the travel agencies. According to the Court's reasoning, the agencies were expected to publicly distance themselves from the communication once they became aware of it. As they failed to do so, the ECJ inferred tacit acceptance, and therefore a concerted practice, indirectly facilitated by the platform provider. This arrangement is an example of a hub-and-spoke constellation, where coordination among competitors occurs through a central intermediary. In this case, the online booking platform was used as the mechanism to implement the coordination. By relying on the same third-party software, the agencies were able to align their pricing behaviour. ◀

105 On the concept of collective dominance, see ▶ 2.3.1.3.
106 For further details, see ▶ 2.2.1.1.
107 ECJ 21 January 2016 – C-74/14, ECLI:EU:C:2016:42 – *Eturas*.

2

Collusion Through Algorithms?

Phenomenon of Algorithmic Collusion

It is increasingly predicted that, in the future, algorithms independently deployed by undertakings will autonomously develop reaction links. This would make **tacit collusion** a **more common** phenomenon. In such scenarios, algorithms would no longer function merely as tools for implementing pre-existing agreements. Instead, they would themselves autonomously establish forms of implicit coordination—forms that, in principle, remain lawful under current competition law frameworks.

Learning Goals

Implicit collusion (tacit collusion) must be clearly distinguished from concerted practices. Coordination that occurs via observation of market signals—without communication or contact—does not fall under the scope of prohibited conduct within the meaning of Article 101 TFEU. Nevertheless, it can produce similar anti-competitive effects and be equally harmful to consumer welfare as explicit collusion.

There is ongoing debate regarding the practical relevance of this concern in the near future.[108] Historically, tacit coordination in compliance with competition law has only occurred under very specific market conditions, such as high concentration, transparency, and product homogeneity. However, some scholars argue that algorithms—because of their capacity to process large volumes of data in real time—may make it possible to monitor and react to competitors' behaviour even in less concentrated and less transparent markets.[109]

With this kind of algorithmic price monitoring, the incentive to compete on price may be significantly reduced. As soon as one undertaking lowers its prices, others may immediately follow suit. This tit-for-tat dynamic implies that the undertaking initiating a price cut would not gain a lasting competitive advantage. Instead, it may trigger a price war that erodes profitability for all. As a result, undertakings may gravitate toward a stable, collusive equilibrium with price levels above competitive norms, even without entering into any formal or informal agreement.

At present, there is insufficient evidence to suggest that the use of algorithms will fundamentally alter market dynamics across the board. Further empirical research is required to assess the potential scope and risks of algorithm-driven tacit collusion.[110] In this context, the possible use of blockchain technology is also being explored.[111] Because blockchain records all transactions in a transparent and immutable ledger, it could increase market transparency and facilitate the algorithmic monitoring of competitors, thereby reinforcing the potential for tacit coordination.[112]

---

108 See Künstner (2019), pp. 36, 37; Kumkar (2025), TFEU Article 101 mn. 134; Mundt (2021), pp. 69, 70.

109 Göhsl (2018), pp. 121, 121.

110 Picht and Freund (2018), pp. 403, 406.

111 Hoffer and Mirtchev (2019), pp. 239, 241 et seqq.; Reimers et al. (2020), p. 64.

112 Kumkar (2025), TFEU Article 101 mn. 132.

Legal Assessment

Implicit collusion is, in principle, not covered by the prohibited conduct of the ban on cartels. Undertakings do not violate the principle of independence if they merely coordinate their conduct via the market. Nevertheless, in view of the increased risk of implicit collusion through algorithms describe aboce, some voices are calling for competition intervention. In particular, it has been proposed that implicit collusion should be assessed **based on its effects**, and that it should fall within the scope of the prohibition under Article 101 TFEU if it results in a reduction of consumer welfare.[113] However, Article 101(1) TFEU adopts a form-based approach, focusing on infringements of the principle of independence between undertakings. Under this framework, the actual effects of the conduct are not decisive for establishing a violation. Instead, the effects become relevant only at the level of the exemption assessment under Article 101(3) TFEU.[114] Moreover, expanding the scope of Article 101(1) TFEU to include effect-based assessments of tacit coordination raises concerns. Such an approach risks blurring the line between legitimate, independent market conduct and prohibited collusion. In practice, it may amount to indirect price regulation by competition authorities, potentially capturing behaviour that is legally permissible under current competition law principles.[115]

The form-based approach of the cartel prohibition under Article 101(1) TFEU should therefore be maintained. At the same time, the principle of independence must be further developed to address the specific challenges posed by algorithm-driven coordination.[116] For instance, it may suffice to establish a prohibited concerted practice if the software used has been programmed in a way that systematically supports the emergence of a collusive equilibrium.[117] An illustrative example would be an algorithm that temporarily increases prices to test competitors' responses and immediately lowers them again if no parallel price increase occurs.[118] Such behaviour may serve as a functional equivalent to communication between undertakings, and thus indicate a concerted practice prohibited under Article 101(1) TFEU.

In cases of algorithm-controlled pricing, liability remains with the undertaking, particularly where a breach of **due diligence obligations** can be established.[119] Undertakings are required to monitor and, where necessary, intervene in the operation of pricing algorithms.[120] Under the principle of effectiveness in EU law, undertakings cannot shield themselves from liability by claiming ignorance of the

113 Thomas (2019), pp. 159–203.
114 Lübke (2021), pp. 723, 746.
115 König (2020), sec. 17 mn. 49; OECD (2017), pp. 49 et seq.
116 Autorité de la concurrence and German Federal Cartel Office (2019), p. 53.
117 Wolf (2019), pp. 2, 9; Ylinen (2018), pp. 19, 22.
118 Autorité de la concurrence and German Federal Cartel Office (2019), p. 53: '*algorithmic communication*'.
119 Ballestrem et al. (2020), p. 1331; Müller-Graff (2020), pp. 1145, 1151; Ylinen (2018), pp. 19, 22.
120 Heinemann (2019), p. 15.

algorithm's effects.[121] To improve the detection and prevention of concerted practices involving algorithmic tools, it is proposed that competition authorities be granted enhanced powers, including ex ante market monitoring.[122] This would allow regulators to respond more effectively to the emerging risks of algorithmically sustained oligopolistic structures, and to intervene at an early stage where harmful coordination is likely to arise.

2.2.2 Restrictions of Competition

2.2.2.1 General Principles

The prohibition on cartels under Article 101(1) TFEU prevents undertakings from engaging in conduct that has the object or effect of preventing, restricting, or distorting competition. In practice, no strict distinction is made between these three terms.[123] Rather, they are collectively understood under the broader concept of a restriction of competition. The examples listed in Article 101(1)(a)–(e) TFEU illustrate typical forms of anti-competitive conduct that are commonly encountered in practice.[124] These include price-fixing, output limitations, market sharing, and similar practices. However, the list is not exhaustive. It serves a clarifying function rather than limiting the scope of the provision, which remains open to capturing other forms of coordination that restrict competition.

A restriction of competition is typically characterised by a limitation on the **freedom of action** of the undertakings involved.[125] In some decisions, reference is also made to the restriction of the freedom of third parties.[126] While the prohibition of hardcore restrictions (such as price-fixing or market sharing) can be justified solely on the basis of the principle of independence between undertakings,[127] European competition practice also considers the broader effects on third parties and the internal market when assessing other forms of restrictions (e.g. purchasing cooperations or research and development agreements). In these cases, the analysis may focus on whether the coordination leads to a significant degree of market power, which is considered detrimental to competition. Such market power can reduce competitive pressure not only among the parties to the agreement but also for external market participants, thereby affecting overall market dynamics and consumer welfare.

It is helpful to distinguish between horizontal and vertical restraints of competition when analysing the prohibition of cartels under Article 101 TFEU, as the two categories differ fundamentally in nature.

---

121 Müller-Graff (2020), pp. 1145, 1151.
122 Lorenzoni (2022), pp. 33, 44.
123 Emmerich and Lange (2024), sec. 4 mn. 26; Mestmäcker and Schweitzer (2014), sec. 11 mn. 1.
124 See Lettl (2021), sec. 2 mn. 74–94.
125 ECJ 24 October 1995 – C-70/93, ECLI:EU:C:1995:344, para. 19 – *Bayerische Motorenwerke/ALD*: '*Furthermore, the agreement reduces each dealer's freedom of commercial action [...].*'
126 ECJ 18 July 2006 – C-519/04 P, ECLI:EU:C:2006:492, paras. 42 et seq. – *Meca Medina*.
127 For further information on hardcore restrictions, see ► 2.2.2.2.1 and 2.2.2.3.1.

- **Horizontal restraints of competition** arise between undertakings operating at the same level of the supply chain, typically as competitors. Classic examples include price-fixing agreements, market or territorial allocation, and output restrictions. The exchange of competitively sensitive information (such as future pricing or production plans) or the joint setting of technical standards may also constitute horizontal restraints. Importantly, agreements between potential competitors are likewise assessed under the framework for horizontal restrictions.[128]
- **Vertical restraints of competition** occur between undertakings operating at different levels of the supply chain, such as between manufacturers and distributors or retailers. Examples include resale price maintenance, where a manufacturer imposes fixed or minimum resale prices on its downstream distributors. Another form is the use of broad best price clauses, whereby a platform operator contractually prevents retailers from offering their goods or services on other sales channels, especially competing platforms, on more favourable terms than those offered on the operator's own platform.

Strictly speaking, all restrictions of competition are horizontal in nature, as they ultimately affect the competitive conditions at a particular level of the market. Vertical restraints, by contrast, concern agreements between undertakings operating at different levels of the supply chain—such as manufacturers and retailers—and therefore do not involve a direct competitive relationship between the parties to the agreement. Nevertheless, vertical restraints can have horizontal effects, as they may restrict competition either upstream or downstream in the market.[129]

Not every distribution agreement constitutes a vertical restraint on competition. While all such agreements involve a degree of exclusivity or limited replicability, this alone is not sufficient.[130] For a vertical restraint to fall within the scope of Article 101(1) TFEU, it must contain elements that go beyond the mere exchange of goods or services, e.g. contractual obligations that restrict pricing, territories, or customer groups. The legal assessment of vertical restraints is more **ambivalent** than that of horizontal ones. It must always be examined whether the restraint also leads to efficiencies that justify its application. In some cases, vertical restraints may enhance the quality of distribution or the availability of pre-sale services, and thus contribute to consumer welfare.[131] For instance, resale price maintenance may help to prevent free-riding among distributors.[132] The Commission addresses this in its Vertical Guidelines:[133]

128 Wagner-von Papp (2023), TFEU Article 101 mn. 301.
129 Thomas (2020), pp. 222, 225.
130 Glöckner (2021), sec. 5 mn. 438.
131 Buccirossi (2015), pp. 747, 749.
132 Commission, Vertical Guidelines, 2022, para. 14.
133 Commission, Vertical Guidelines, 2022, para. 14.

2

» For example, where demand-enhancing pre-sales services are provided by one distributor, such as personalised advice in relation to particular goods or services, this may lead to higher sales by competing distributors offering the same goods or services and thus create incentives among distributors to free-ride on costly services provided by others.

In such cases, the potential anti-competitive effects of a vertical restraint may be offset by its efficiency gains, and an exemption under Article 101(3) TFEU may be considered.

Vertical agreements can also address the **problem of double marginalisation**. This phenomenon arises when both the supplier and the retailer apply their own profit margins independently, resulting in cumulatively higher prices for the final consumer. Through coordinated vertical arrangements, undertakings can internalise the effects of their pricing decisions on each other, potentially leading to lower retail prices and improved overall efficiency in the supply chain.

! When assessing whether an agreement constitutes a restriction of competition under Article 101(1) TFEU, it is essential to distinguish between horizontal restraints—asthose between actual or potential competitors—and vertical restraints, which occur between undertakings operating at different levels of the supply chain.

Traditionally, the distinction between horizontal and vertical restraints is based on a linear distribution structure, typically involving two or three tiers: manufacturer, distributor, and retailer. However, this model is increasingly challenged in the digital economy. **Platform operators**—particularly in online markets—often perform intermediary functions that defy conventional categorisation. They may facilitate transactions between independent users while simultaneously influencing the terms and conditions of those transactions. Moreover, the functional roles in online sales are more fluid, with platform operators often performing tasks traditionally associated with both production and distribution.[134] In some cases, platform operators are also vertically integrated, meaning they offer marketplace services to independent retailers while simultaneously competing with them at the downstream level.

▶ Example

The operator of the *Amazon* marketplace provides third-party retailers with access to its digital sales platform. At the same time, Amazon itself sells products on that platform, thereby competing directly with those retailers. ◀

According to **Article 1(1)(d) VBER**, platform operators are to be qualified as suppliers when they provide online intermediation services. As a result, agreements between a platform operator and a trader who offers goods or services via the plat-

134 Thomas (2020), pp. 222, 238.

form are generally classified as vertical agreements under European competition law.[135]

If a vertically integrated platform—one that also sells goods or services in competition with traders on its own platform—enters into agreements with those traders, this does not, in itself, alter the vertical nature of the agreement. However, the applicability of the VBER may still be excluded in such cases, particularly under Article 2(4)–(6). These provisions limit the exemption's scope where the exchange of information between supplier and buyer does not directly relate to the implementation of the vertical agreement, or is not necessary to improve the production or distribution of the contract goods or services. Importantly, the VBER also explicitly covers vertical agreements concerning online intermediation services, provided the relevant conditions are met.[136]

In the following, this textbook illustrates a non-exhaustive list of examples of horizontal and vertical restrictions of competition. While **traditional forms** of restraints of competition will be included, the focus lays on competitive restraints that have emerged in **digital markets**. The illustration will include the Commission's relevant guidance. The Commission has issued two sets of guidelines: the 2023 **Horizontal Guidelines**,[137] which address cooperation and restrictions between competitors; and the 2022 Vertical Guidelines,[138] which clarify the application of Article 101 TFEU and the VBER to agreements between undertakings at different levels of the supply chain. These guidelines reflect the Commission's enforcement practice and provide businesses with practical guidance, particularly in light of new challenges arising from digital markets. In this context, the Commission and the EU courts have also begun to assess new forms of restraints of competition, especially those involving platforms and algorithmic pricing mechanisms, alongside traditional categories such as price-fixing, market sharing, and resale price maintenance.

2.2.2.2 Horizontal Restrictions of Competition

Hardcore Cartels

Horizontal restrictions of competition include **hardcore cartels**, in which undertakings **directly coordinate** on key **competitive parameters**.[139] Typical forms of such coordination include price-fixing, market sharing, or customer allocation. For instance, if several suppliers agree on a uniform price for selling posters on an online marketplace,[140] this constitutes a prohibited hardcore cartel. The use of **AI** can **facilitate the monitoring and enforcement** of such agreements among cartel members, thereby enhancing the stability and persistence of the cartel.

---

135 For further details on the notion of vertical agreement, see ► 2.2.5.2.1.
136 On the VBER, see ► 2.2.5.5.1.
137 Commission, Guidelines on Horizontal Restraints, OJ [2023] C 259/1.
138 Commission, Guidelines on Vertical Restraints, OJ [2022] C 248/1.
139 Wagner-von Papp (2023), TFEU Article 101 mn. 330.
140 For further details on this example, see ►2.2.1.1.

2

Hardcore cartels are considered restrictions of competition by object. This means that their anti-competitive nature is presumed without the need for detailed market analysis. As such, they **do not qualify for exemption** under competition law and are typically subject to substantial fines.

Agreements on Research and Development

Agreements between competitors in the field of research and development (R&D agreements) can, under certain circumstances, restrict competition, including competition in innovation. At the same time, such agreements may also generate pro-competitive benefits. Therefore, it must first be assessed whether a specific R&D agreement falls within the scope of the prohibition under Article 101(1) TFEU.

No infringement of Article 101 TFEU can be presumed where the cooperation between competitors is necessary to bring a new product or technology to market in the first place.[141] Moreover, when the joint activities are somewhat removed from the market, as in the case of basic research, this often indicates that the cooperation is unlikely to restrict competition.[142]

In practice, R&D agreements assume a wide variety of forms and contents. The Commission addresses this in its Horizontal Guidelines:

> They [R&D agreements] include agreements under which one party finances R&D carried out by another party ('paid-for' R&D); agreements covering the joint improvement of existing products and technologies, and agreements concerning the development of products and technologies that would create an entirely new demand. The R&D cooperation may take the form of a cooperation agreement or a joint venture, namely a jointly controlled company. Undertakings may also cooperate in looser forms, such as technical cooperation in working groups.[143]

Competition concerns may arise where R&D agreements serve as a vehicle to disguise cartel arrangements, such as price-fixing or production limitations.[144] In addition, any potential restrictive effects on competition must be assessed where the agreement involves joint production or commercialisation.[145] If such elements are absent, the focus shifts to whether the agreement nevertheless restricts competition in innovation.[146] To the extent that an R&D agreement does restrict competition and thus falls within the scope of Article 101(1) TFEU, it must then be determined whether the agreement qualifies for an exemption under Article 2(1) R&D Block Exemption Regulation.[147]

---

141 ECJ 4 June 2009 – C-8/08, ECLI:EU:C:2009:343, para. 43 – *T-Mobile Netherlands*.
142 Commission, Horizontal Guidelines, 2023, para. 133 et seq.
143 Commission, Horizontal Guidelines, 2023, para. 52.
144 Commission, Horizontal Guidelines, 2023, para. 141.
145 Commission, Horizontal Guidelines, 2023, para. 144.
146 Commission, Horizontal Guidelines, 2023, para. 144.
147 Commission Regulation (EU) 2023/1066 of 1 June 2023 on the application of Article 101 (3) of the Treaty on the Functioning of the European Union to certain categories of research and development agreements, OJ [2023] L 143/9. For further information, see ► 2.2.5.2.2.

▶ Example

In 2021, the Commission imposed fines on several car manufacturers in the *car emissions* case for violating the prohibition on cartels.[148] The undertakings had coordinated their efforts in the development of selective catalytic reduction (SCR) systems for diesel vehicles. Specifically, they agreed to limit the size of AdBlue tanks used in vehicles sold within the European Economic Area. Although this agreement contributed to improving the vehicles' CO_2 balance, the Commission found that it restricted competition in innovation. The concern was that, in the absence of such coordination, each manufacturer might have pursued more advanced solutions in exhaust gas after-treatment. ◀

In recent years, numerous digitalisation-driven collaborations have emerged with the aim of fostering innovation. These include cooperative arrangements in areas such as **Industry 4.0** and the **Internet of Things**.[149] However, not all such initiatives fall neatly within the categories addressed by the Horizontal Guidelines. This has resulted in a degree of legal uncertainty regarding their assessment under EU competition law.

In particular, uncertainty arises both in relation to the prohibition under Article 101(1) TFEU and the potential for exemption under Article 101(3) TFEU. Where such novel forms of cooperation do not fall within the scope of an existing block exemption regulation, an individual assessment for exemption must be carried out.[150]

▶ Example

Undertakings may collaborate to develop new business models based on existing products. However, under the Commission's current interpretation, R&D agreements typically presuppose the development of new or improved products or technologies, not merely novel uses or applications of existing offerings.[151] ◀

In light of this, affected undertakings have increasingly called on the Commission to make greater use of its clarification tools, in particular, the instrument of negative clearance under Article 10 Regulation 1/2003, as well as informal guidance letters.[152] These instruments can help clarify whether a specific form of cooperation is compatible with Article 101 TFEU. This need is especially pressing given the rapid pace of innovation in digital markets. The dynamic nature of these sectors means that competition assessments may quickly become outdated.[153]

148 Commission, Decision of 8 July 2021 – AT.40178, OJ C 458, 16, para. 7 et seq. – *Car emissions*.
149 Schweitzer, Schallbruch and Wambach (2019), p. 59.
150 For details on this assessment, see ▶ 2.2.5.3.
151 Commission, Horizontal Guidelines, 2023, para. 52.
152 Schweitzer, Schallbruch and Wambach (2019), p. 60.
153 Ecker et al. (2021), p. 41.

2

▶ **Example**

When undertakings that are not initially in a competitive relationship cooperate to explore new applications for IoT technologies, their joint research may give rise to a (potential) competitive relationship.[154] In such cases, the cooperation may need to be reassessed under competition law.

According to the Commission, a potential competitive relationship exists where one undertaking '*would undertake the necessary additional investments or other necessary switching costs to enter the relevant market on which the latter is active.*'[155] In digital markets, these conditions can often be rapidly fulfilled, as the development of new digital products may require no more than a novel idea and relatively modest investment. ◀

Exchange of Information

The exchange of information between competitors concerning their market conduct can, under certain conditions, amount to a restriction of competition. In particular, **market information systems** often involve coordinated exchanges based on predefined reporting procedures.[156] From a competition law perspective, it is crucial to assess whether the information exchanged is capable of reducing strategic uncertainty about competitors' future behaviour.[157] This is particularly likely when commercially **sensitive data** is shared, for instance, regarding pricing, planned output, customer allocation, or product characteristics.[158] By contrast, the exchange of non-sensitive information, such as aggregated data on the general state of an industry, non-confidential technical knowledge, or information relating to industry standards, is generally considered unproblematic under competition law.[159] In such cases, the exchange may even enhance market transparency and intensify competition by enabling more informed decision-making.[160]

In addition to the nature of the information exchanged, the **structure of the relevant market** plays a decisive role in the legal assessment.[161] In concentrated markets, where only a few undertakings are active, enhanced transparency can facilitate tacit coordination, as companies may be able to identify individual competitors based on the shared data.[162] While the exchange of sensitive information can also raise concerns in fragmented markets, a higher frequency of exchange is generally required to reach a level of transparency that could distort competition.[163]

---

154 Ecker et al. (2021), p. 41.
155 Commission, Horizontal Guidelines, 2023, para. 16.
156 Zimmer (2025), TFEU Article 101(1) mn. 271.
157 ECJ 19 March 2015 – C-286/13 P, ECLI:EU:C:2015:184, para. 121 – *Dole Food and Dole Fresh Fruit Europe*.
158 Commission, Horizontal Guidelines, 2023, para. 384 et seq.; Lettl (2021), sec. 2 mn. 38.
159 Commission, Horizontal Guidelines, 2023, para. 386.
160 Krauß (2021), ARC sec. 1 mn. 251.
161 Commission, Horizontal Guidelines, 2023, para. 412.
162 Emmerich and Lange (2024), sec. 4 mn. 53.
163 ECJ 2 October 2003 – C-194/99 P, ECLI:EU:C:2003:527, para. 86 – *Thyssen Stahl*.

The 2023 revision of the Horizontal Guidelines explicitly acknowledges, for the first time, that information exchange can occur **through algorithms**.[164] A key example is the *Eturas* case, where competitors engaged in a concerted practice on pricing by jointly using third-party software.[165] The Commission classifies this type of coordination as an indirect exchange of information. The Commission classifies this type of coordination as an indirect exchange of information.[166] Optimisation algorithms can also be suitable for exchanging information. For example, these algorithms make the decision on the price to be charged for the undertaking and use sensitive information from competitors as a basis for the decision.[167]

The principles outlined above also apply to **online platforms**, including both business-to-consumer (B2C) and business-to-business (B2B) marketplaces.[168] While such platforms often enhance efficiency and market access, they may also enable the exchange of confidential information between commercial users.[169] In B2B environments, undertakings might use platforms not only for transactions but also for integrating production processes.[170]

The principles set out above should also apply to the assessment of the exchange of information on **online platforms**. Online marketplaces are used by undertakings to make their sales more effective. There are not only platforms that enable sales to end consumers. Undertakings sell their services to other undertakings on **business-to-business platforms**. At the same time, confidential information may be exchanged between commercial users via the platform. B2B platforms also offer undertakings the opportunity to network production processes. However, not all data sharing restricts competition. Increased transparency and international trade can have pro-competitive effects.[171] In this context, the **cooperative use of data** should be assessed similarly to physical information exchanges.[172] If the shared data includes sensitive insights into competitors' market conduct or strategies, it may constitute a competition law infringement. If not, shared data pools may promote innovation, enable better resource use, and benefit the overall market.[173] The Commission's Horizontal Guidelines highlight cost savings, the development of new products, and improved algorithmic training as potential efficiencies from cooperative data use.[174] The European Data Strategy further supports this perspective, aiming to leverage data sharing to enhance competitiveness across sectors, particularly in areas such as healthcare and sustainability.[175]

---

164 Commission, Horizontal Guidelines, 2023, para. 368.
165 ECJ 21 January 2016 – C-74/14, ECLI:EU:C:2016:42 – *Eturas*.
166 Commission, Horizontal Guidelines, 2023, para. 368.
167 Commission, Horizontal Guidelines, 2023, para. 402.
168 Zimmer (2025), TFEU Article 101(1) mn. 276.
169 Meyer and Müller (2007), pp. 117, 123.
170 Podszun and Bongartz (2020), p. 2882.
171 Meyer and Müller (2007), pp. 117, 124.
172 Lundqvist (2018), pp. 146 et seq.; Commission, Horizontal Guidelines, 2023, para. 379: '*If pricing practices are unlawful when applied offline, it is highly likely that they are also unlawful when applied online.*'
173 Kumkar (2025), Article 101 TFEU mn. 153.
174 Commission, Horizontal Guidelines, 2023, para. 373.
175 <https://commission.europa.eu/strategy-and-policy/priorities-2019-2024/europe-fit-digital-age/european-data-strategy_de > (accessed 1 September 2025) As part of this strategy, the Commission has proposed the Data Governance Act and the Data Act, see ► 1.2.4.

2

To mitigate competition concerns, undertakings should ensure that only final, aggregated data is accessible to others, reducing the risk of identifying individual market actors.[176] Such transparency can also help smaller competitors gain insights into market conditions.[177] Additionally, appointing an independent trustee to manage data pools can safeguard confidentiality.[178] In **decentralised systems** such as blockchain, data exchange may occur without a central authority, offering further structural safeguards.[179] To promote legal certainty and innovation, the Commission is encouraged to use tools such as negative clearance decisions under Article 10 Regulation 1/2003 and informal guidance letters.[180]

Standardisation Agreements

Competitors often collaborate on the development of standards to define technical or qualitative requirements for products and services.[181] In recent years, European digital regulation has placed increasing emphasis on supplementary forms of self-regulation, such as codes of conduct and technical standards, as instruments to operationalise regulatory obligations. These mechanisms allow state authorities and regulated entities to jointly and consensually specify duties of care. A clear example of this approach is the Digital Services Act. Under Articles 45–47 DSA, stakeholders are encouraged to develop codes of conduct aimed at mitigating systemic risks in the digital environment, including disinformation and hate speech. Additionally, Article 44 DSA highlights the importance of technical standards to facilitate the implementation of the behavioural obligations imposed on designated service providers. A similar reliance on standardisation is found in the AI Act,[182] particularly in the regulation of high-risk AI systems. The AI Act encourages the creation of technical standards to clarify and operationalise due diligence requirements. Notably, Article 40 AI Act establishes that compliance with harmonised standards creates a presumption of conformity with the applicable legal obligations.

When assessing the compatibility of standardisation agreements with Article 101 TFEU, it is essential to determine whether such agreements restrict competition between undertakings. According to the Horizontal Guidelines, standardisation agreements generally have a pro-competitive effect.[183]

These agreements can enhance market integration within the European internal market by facilitating cross-border trade and improving product interoperability. They also contribute to product quality, consumer safety, and technological development.[184] Importantly, standards are typically voluntary, meaning that undertak-

176 Commission, Horizontal Guidelines, 2023, para. 408.
177 Commission, Horizontal Guidelines, 2023, para. 391.
178 Commission, Horizontal Guidelines, 2023, para. 408.
179 Louven and Saive (2018), pp. 348, 350.
180 Schweitzer, Schallbruch and Wambach (2019), p. 59.
181 Commission, Horizontal Guidelines, 2023, para. 465.
182 On further details on the AI Act, see ▶ 1.3.5.
183 Commission, Horizontal Guidelines, 2023, para. 465, 501.
184 Commission, Horizontal Guidelines, 2023, para. 465.

ings are not legally required to comply with them. Instead, each company retains the freedom to adopt or disregard the standard.[185] The Commission also places particular emphasis on the openness of the standard-setting process.[186] A key consideration is whether all interested undertakings had the opportunity to participate in the development of the standard. Transparent and inclusive standard-setting processes help prevent anti-competitive outcomes and ensure that no individual company is unfairly disadvantaged or excluded.

However, standardisation agreements may infringe Article 101(1) TFEU if they restrict innovation competition.[187] This concern arises in particular when standards are given a de facto mandatory character, thereby limiting the freedom of action of participating undertakings. The ECJ has recognised a restriction of competition in cases where competitors agree to produce only products that comply with specific standards, effectively excluding alternative solutions or innovations.[188] In such situations, the agreement may reduce the scope for technological diversity and market entry. Nevertheless, even where a restriction is established, such agreements may still benefit from an exemption under Article 101(3) TFEU if they generate efficiency gains.[189] These can include improvements in product compatibility, reduced transaction costs, or enhanced consumer trust—provided the benefits are passed on to consumers, the restrictions are indispensable, and competition is not eliminated in a substantial part of the market.

Purchase and Sales Agreements

Cooperation between competitors—whether related to the sale of products or joint purchasing arrangements—can restrict competition. The Horizontal Guidelines highlight that the content of such agreements can vary significantly:

» At one end of the spectrum, joint selling agreements may lead to a joint determination of all commercial aspects related to the sale of the product, including price. At the other end, there are more limited agreements that only address one specific commercialisation function, such as distribution, after-sales service, or advertising.[190]

» Joint purchasing arrangements exist in a variety of economic sectors. They may provide for the members to make joint purchases, or they may be limited to the joint negotiation of purchase prices, components of the purchase price or other terms and conditions with a supplier, leaving the actual purchase transactions to be concluded by each party individually, based on the jointly negotiated prices and/or terms and condition.[191]

185 Commission, Horizontal Guidelines, 2023, para. 490.
186 Commission, Horizontal Guidelines, 2023, para. 451.
187 Commission, Horizontal Guidelines, 2023, para. 468.
188 ECJ 13 December 2012 – C-226/11, ECLI:EU:C:2012:795, para. 36 – *Expedia*.
189 Commission, Horizontal Guidelines, 2023, para. 501 et seq.
190 Commission, Horizontal Guidelines, 2023, para. 317.
191 Commission, Horizontal Guidelines, 2023, para. 274.

Purchasing and sales agreements may raise concerns under competition law if they involve price or quantity fixing.[192] Similarly, the exchange of sensitive information between competitors can restrict competition.[193] In the context of buying syndicates, mandatory purchasing obligations may constitute a restriction of competition.[194] The same holds true for sales pools that require compulsory supply.

Where an agreement is not explicitly intended to restrict competition, its assessment must consider the specific market conditions, including the market power of the parties involved. According to the Commission, purchasing or sales agreements become questionable when the parties have a combined market share exceeding 15%.[195] In the case of purchasing agreements, it is important to evaluate market shares at both the upstream procurement level and the downstream sales level.

2.2.2.3 Vertical Restrictions of Competition

Pricing Restrictions

A hardcore vertical restriction is **resale price maintenance** (RPM), where retailers agree to charge a specific price to end customers at the request of the manufacturer.[196] **Fixed and minimum resale prices** are considered prohibited hardcore restrictions under Article 4(a) VBER. They are not eligible for exemption.

European competition law takes a more lenient stance toward **maximum resale price maintenance**, where agreements prevent retailers from exceeding a specified price. Such arrangements may fall outside the scope of the VBER‘s prohibition, provided they do not, in practice, result in fixed or minimum pricing due to pressure.

Non-binding price recommendations generally do not constitute resale price maintenance. However, if a retailer is effectively compelled to adhere to a recommended price, especially through indirect pressure or monitoring, this may amount to a de facto price restriction. In this context, the use of algorithms can facilitate manufacturer oversight and increase the likelihood of unlawful pressure on retailers.[197]

▶ Example

Supplier A issues a recommended retail price of EUR 2.50 per unit for resale to end customers. However, Retailer B chooses not to follow this recommendation and instead sells the product at EUR 1.99. Supplier A becomes aware of this deviation by using a web crawler to monitor retail prices online. In response, A contacts B and instructs him to raise the retail price to the recommended EUR 2.50. When B does not comply, A threatens to withhold future deliveries. ◀

192 Commission, Horizontal Guidelines, 2023, para. 277, 322.
193 Commission, Horizontal Guidelines, 2023, para. 281, 325.
194 Säcker and Mohr (2011), pp. 793, 795.
195 Commission, Horizontal Guidelines, 2023, para. 291, 339.
196 Eilmansberger and Kruis (2018), TFEU Article 101 mn. 183; Zimmer (2025), TFEU Article 101(1) mn. 298.
197 Commission, Sector Inquiry into Electronic Commerce, SWB(2017), 154 final, para. 13; Dohrn and Huck (2018), 173, 175.

The mere use of **price monitoring software** does not, in itself, constitute a violation of the cartel prohibition.[198] However, where a supplier responds to observed price deviations (such as by threatening to suspend deliveries) the originally non-binding price recommendation may become a de facto fixed price.[199] In such cases, the arrangement is no longer exempt but qualifies as a hardcore restriction under EU competition law, and is therefore prohibited.

Additional forms of pressure can also transform a recommendation into a binding commitment. For instance, if the recommended price is printed directly on the product packaging, or if the supplier explicitly threatens to terminate the contract unless the retailer complies with the suggested prices, this may likewise amount to an unlawful restriction of competition.[200]

Prohibitions on Internet Sales

A manufacturer's prohibition on internet sales by its distributors constitutes a vertical restraint of competition.[201] According to **Article 4(e) VBER**, any measure that prevents the effective use of the internet for selling the contract goods or services, either by the buyer or its customers, is considered a hardcore restriction. In a 2018 decision, the Commission further clarified that an outright internet sales ban is not the only form of such a restriction.[202]A requirement that makes online sales subject to prior authorisation, where the manufacturer retains broad discretion in granting or denying that authorisation, may be deemed equivalent to a ban, and is therefore also prohibited under EU competition law.

▶ Example

As part of a selective distribution system, the cosmetics manufacturer Pierre Fabre (PF) required that its products be sold exclusively through physical points of sale, and only in the presence of a qualified pharmacist. PF argued that these restrictions were necessary to preserve the prestigious image of its brand.

The ECJ disagreed. It held that the internet sales ban amounted to a vertical restriction of competition under Article 101(1) TFEU. The Court explicitly stated: '*The aim of maintaining a prestigious image is not a legitimate aim for restricting competition and cannot therefore justify a finding that a contractual clause pursuing such an aim does not fall within Article 101(1) TFEU.*'[203] ◀

Decisions of the ECJ make clear that product-specific justifications are generally not sufficient to support a ban on internet sales. Such a restriction is only permissible if it is explicitly required by statutory regulation. By contrast, other

---

198 Commission, Vertical Guidelines, 2022, para. 191.

199 Example of the use of price monitoring software in the case of resale price maintenance: Commission, Decision of 24 July 2018 – AT.40182, para. 136, 155 – *Pioneer*.

200 Commission, Vertical Guidelines, 2022, para. 188.

201 ECJ 13 October 2011 – C-439/09, ECLI:EU:C:2011:649, para. 47 – *Pierre Fabre Dermo-Cosmétique*; von Hülsen (2012), pp. 299, 302; Peeperkorn and Heimann (2014), pp. 1175, 1176.

202 Commission, Decision of 17 December 2018 – COMP/AT.40428, para. 62 et seqq. – *Guess*.

203 ECJ 13 October 2011 – C-439/09, ECLI:EU:C:2011:649, para. 46 – *Pierre Fabre Dermo-Cosmétique*.

forms of online sales restrictions, such as platform bans,[204] and limitations on online advertising that do not amount to a complete ban on an entire advertising channel may still benefit from the exemption under Article 4(e) VBER.

2

Platform Bans

A platform ban arises when a manufacturer and its retailers agree that products or services may not be sold via third-party online marketplaces, such as *Amazon* or *eBay*. Early cases involving such restrictions were addressed by the German Federal Cartel Office and national courts.[205] In its 2017 *Coty* judgment, the ECJ held that platform bans within **selective distribution systems** for luxury goods can be compatible with Article 101(1) TFEU[206] The Court considered such a restriction a legitimate, objective, and qualitative criterion that can serve to enhance quality-based competition. Consistent with this ruling, the Commission stated in its 2022 Vertical Guidelines that such a restriction may be proportionate where:

> a supplier of luxury goods prohibits its authorised dealers from using online marketplaces as long as this does not indirectly prevent an authorised dealer from effectively using the internet to sell the goods in certain territories or to certain customers.[207]

According to the Commission, platform bans do not inherently restrict access to certain territories or customer groups, particularly where retailers remain free to operate their own online shops. In such cases, the Commission sees no automatic conflict with Article 101 TFEU.[208] However, the legal treatment of non-luxury branded goods remains unsettled. The German Federal Cartel Office has taken a cautious position. It argues that the ECJ's findings in Coty (which concern luxury goods) should **not** be automatically extended **to all branded products.**[209] In its view, brand protection can be achieved through platform-specific quality requirements, making a general ban on platform sales unnecessary.[210] In contrast, the Higher Regional Court of Hamburg has adopted a more permissive stance. In a 2018 decision, it held that platform bans may also be compatible with competition law for non-luxury goods, provided they are part of a selective distribution system and do not restrict effective internet use by authorised distributors.[211] In its 2018 decision, the court argued that

---

204 On the assessment of platform bans under Article 101(1) TFEU, see ► 2.2.2.3.3.

205 German Federal Cartel Office, Decision of 24 October 2013 – B7–1/13–35 – *Sennheiser – Amazon Marketplace*; Higher Regional Court of Schleswig 5 June 2014–16 U (Kart) 154/13, NZKart 2014, 364 – *Digitalkameras*, Higher Regional Court of Frankfurt (on the Main) 22 December 2015–11 U 84/14 (Kart), NZKart 2016, 84 – *Funktionsrucksäcke*; Higher Regional Court of Berlin 19 September 2013–2 U 8/09 Kart, NZKart 2014, 72 – *Schulranzen*.

206 ECJ 6 December 2017 – C-230/16, ECLI:EU:C:2017:941, para. 58 – *Coty Germany*.

207 Commission, Vertical Guidelines, 2022, para. 150.

208 Commission, Vertical Guidelines, 2022, para. 150.

209 German Federal Cartel Office, Wettbewerbsbeschränkungen im Internetvertrieb nach Coty und Asics – wie geht es weiter?, 2018, p. 5.

210 German Federal Cartel Office, Wettbewerbsbeschränkungen im Internetvertrieb nach Coty und Asics – wie geht es weiter?, 2018, p. 5; Kumkar (2018), pp. 119, 138.

211 Higher Regional Court of Hamburg 22 March 2018–3 U 250/16, NZKart 2018, 590, 592 et seq. – *Aloe-Vera-Produkte*.

» it may be proportionate for a supplier of luxury goods to prohibit its authorised distributors from using online marketplaces, as long as this does not indirectly prevent the effective use of the internet by the authorised distributor to sell the goods to particular territories or customers.[212]

This approach has been endorsed by the Union legislator in the amended Vertical Block Exemption Regulation of 2022. According to **recital 15 VBER**, when assessing whether a restriction qualifies as a hardcore restriction under **Article 4(e) VBER**:

» the content and context of the restriction may be taken into account, but it should not depend on the market-specific circumstances or the individual characteristics of the undertakings concerned.

Dual Pricing

A dual pricing system refers to a manufacturer's practice of requiring retailers to charge different prices for the same product, depending on whether it is sold online or in a physical store.[213] Such a system can be compatible with Article 101 TFEU if it serves to **incentivise investment**, particularly in physical retail infrastructure.[214] For example, a manufacturer may wish to **promote brick-and-mortar sales** by allowing retailers to purchase products at a lower price when they are resold via physical outlets. This encourages retailers to maintain a local presence and invest in offline customer service.

Under the previous Vertical Guidelines, dual pricing was generally considered incompatible with European competition law.[215] It was classified as a restriction of passive sales via the internet and, as such, not exemptable under the Vertical Block Exemption Regulation.[216] Although the Commission recognised the interest in supporting offline retail, it permitted such support only in the form of fixed financial subsidies, rather than price differentiation. This restrictive approach was increasingly criticised for being inflexible and outdated, given the evolving role of online commerce.[217]

With the revision of the VBER in 2022, dual pricing is no longer automatically considered a hardcore restriction. Although this change is not explicitly stated in the regulation itself, the Commission clarified its position in the 2022 Vertical Guidelines. The updated guidance reflects the reality that online sales no longer require special protection, as they are now a mature and widely accepted distribution channel. The lawfulness of dual pricing now depends on whether the price

212 Higher Regional Court of Hamburg 22 March 2018–3 U 250/16, NZKart 2018, 590 – *Aloe-Vera-Produkte* [quote translated by author].

213 Commission, Vertical Guidelines, 2022, para. 209; Schuhmacher and Holzweber (2025), TFEU Article 101 mn. 893.

214 Commission, Vertical Guidelines, 2022, para. 209.

215 Commission, Guidelines on Vertical Restraints, OJ [2010] C 130/1, para. 52.

216 Emde (2019), pp. 69, 85.

217 Klauß and Seeliger (2010), pp. 233, 236.

2

difference between online and offline sales is reasonable. The compatibility of dual pricing with the cartel prohibition depends on whether the price differences between online and offline sales are **reasonable.**[218] The Commission **does not require a complex cost analysis** to justify these differences; rather, the assessment focuses on whether the pricing structure reflects legitimate commercial considerations, such as differing levels of investment or service.

Restrictions on the Use of Price Comparison Services and Search Engines

Price comparison services do not enable retailers to sell directly to consumers. Rather, they serve as a complement to online sales and help consumers locate, compare, and access offers made by retailers on the internet.[219] A general prohibition on the use of such services or on search engines as part of a selective distribution system is considered a hardcore restriction under **Article 4(e) VBER.**[220] According to the Commission, such restrictions are anti-competitive because:

> » [s]uch restrictions have the object of preventing the effective use of the internet by the buyer to sell the contract goods or services to particular territories or customers, as they limit the buyer's ability to target customers beyond its physical trading area, inform them about its offers and attract them to its online store or other sales channels.[221]

As the number of online offers continues to grow, it is increasingly important that consumers can obtain a clear and reliable market overview. From the retailer's perspective, using price comparison services and search engines enhances online visibility and helps attract potential customers.[222] A general ban on such services is considered a hardcore restriction under Article 4(e) VBER. However, a limited prohibition, targeting only specific price comparison tools, may be compatible with Article 101 TFEU, provided that alternative services remain available.[223] In such cases, the restriction does not eliminate the retailer's ability to advertise online or reach consumers effectively, and thus may fall outside the scope of a hardcore restriction.

Geoblocking Practices

Blocking offers on the internet for specific regions, for example, preventing consumers in certain countries from purchasing products, constitutes a hardcore restriction under Article 4(b)–(e) VBER.[224] Such measures result in the partitioning of markets and are typically intended to prevent parallel imports.[225]

---

218 Commission, Vertical Guidelines, 2022, para. 209.
219 Kumkar (2025), TFEU Article 101 mn. 145.
220 Commission, Vertical Guidelines, 2022, para. 206; Commission, Decision of 17 December 2018, AT.40428 – *Guess*, para. 118: '*The objective of the online search advertising restriction was to reduce competitive pressure by authorised retailers on Guess' own online retail activities and to keep down its own advertising costs.*'
221 Commission, Vertical Guidelines, 2022, mn. 206.
222 Kumkar (2025), TFEU Article 101 mn. 146.
223 Commission, Vertical Guidelines, 2022, para. 206.
224 Kumkar (2025), TFEU Article 101 mn. 150.
225 GC 27 September 2023 – T-172/21, ECLI:EU:T:2023:587 – *Valve Geoblocking*.

Moreover, these restrictions can impede customers' effective use of the internet as a distribution channel, which is prohibited under Article 4(e) VBER. By limiting cross-border sales, manufacturers undermine the open and integrated nature of the internal market and restrict consumer choice.[226]

► **Example**

According to the GC, an online gaming platform and several game publishers restricted the activation codes for games sold on the platform to function only within specific countries. The Court held that this practice constituted geo-blocking and found that it distorted competition by fragmenting the internal market.[227] ◄

Unlike Article 101 TFEU, which primarily targets anti-competitive agreements and concerted practices, the Geoblocking Regulation[228] also addresses unilateral conduct by traders, thereby offering a broader legal framework to prevent geo-blocking within the internal market. Pursuant to Article 3(1) Geo blocking Regulation, providers are prohibited from blocking or restricting customers' access to their online interfaces based on nationality, place of residence, or place of establishment. Furthermore, Article 4(1) Geo blocking Regulation prohibits applying different general terms and conditions to customers for these same reasons. This regulation complements Article 101 TFEU by extending the prohibition to unilateral practices, which were not previously covered under competition law.[229]

Exclusivity Obligations

Exclusivity agreements represent another type of vertical restraint on competition. A common example is an **exclusive purchasing obligation**, where retailers commit to buying exclusively from a single supplier. Such agreements are not inherently anti-competitive; in fact, they may have pro-competitive effects, for instance by helping to maintain product quality and service standards. The ECJ has emphasized that the **overall economic context** of an exclusive purchasing obligation must be examined to determine whether it restricts competition.[230] Particular attention should be given to the existence of parallel contractual networks, where exclusive purchasing obligations are imposed across multiple distributors. Such a situation may lead to market foreclosure (often referred to as **bundling theory**).[231] Key factors in this assessment include the extent of market coverage achieved by the net-

---

226 Kumkar (2025), TFEU Article 101 mn. 150a.

227 GC 27 September 2023 – T-172/21, ECLI:EU:T:2023:587 – *Valve Geoblocking*.

228 Regulation (EU) 2018/302 of the European Parliament and of the Council of 28 February 2018 on addressing unjustified geo-blocking and other forms of discrimination based on customers' nationality, place of residence or place of establishment within the internal market, OJ [2018] LI 60/1.

229 Bernhard (2019), pp. 472, 472.

230 ECJ 28 February 1991 – C-234/89, ECLI:EU:C:1991:91, para. 19 et seq. – *Delimitis/Henninger Bräu*.

231 Schuhmacher and Holzweber (2025), TFEU Article 101 mn. 1001.

work of exclusive contracts, the duration of these contracts, and the market shares held by the suppliers and retailers involved.

2 The Vertical Block Exemption Regulation addresses exclusive purchasing obligations in **Article 5(1)(a)**. In conjunction with Articles 1, 3 VBER, the regulation sets clear thresholds for exemption. An agreement does not benefit from the exemption if the combined market share of the parties exceeds 30% on the relevant market (Article 3 VBER), the obligation covers more than 80% of the buyer's total procurement of the relevant goods or services (Article 1(f) VBER), and the agreement has a duration of more than 5 years (Article 5(1)(a) VBER).

For the assessment of whether an exclusive arrangement **appreciably**[232] restricts competition, the de minimis Notice[233] applies the bundling theory. Under this approach, if there is a cumulative foreclosure effect (such as where multiple exclusive agreements restrict access to a substantial portion of the market) the appreciability threshold is lowered to 5% market share. By contrast, isolated vertical agreements are typically regarded as appreciable only above a 15% market share.[234]

In the context of **exclusive distribution agreements**, the supplier agrees to sell only to a single distributor within a specific territory. While such arrangements can contribute to efficient market organisation, they may raise concerns about market foreclosure, particularly when they are coupled with measures that prevent parallel imports.[235] However, exclusive distribution agreements can be justified under the concept of market development,[236] particularly when they serve to facilitate market entry. According to the ECJ, '*the agreement proves to be necessary precisely for the penetration of a undertaking into an area in which it was not previously active.*'[237]

Parity Obligations

Parity obligations have gained relevance in digital markets, particularly through mechanisms like best-price clauses.[238] Under such clauses, a platform operator requires retailers to offer the best terms available when selling through the platform, compared to other sales channels.[239] When assessing the impact of these clauses on competition, it's important to distinguish between narrow and broad price parity clauses:

- Narrow price parity clauses prevent retailers from offering more favorable conditions on their own sales channels, such as their own website.[240]

---

232 On the concept of appreciability, see ► 2.2.2.5.

233 Commission, Notice on agreements of minor importance which do not appreciably restrict competition within the meaning of Article 101(1) of the Treaty on the Functioning of the European Union, OJ [2019] C 291/1.

234 For further details, see ► 2.2.2.5.

235 Seeliger (2020), sec. 11 mn. 298.

236 Stockenhuber (2025), TFEU Article 101 mn. 153.

237 ECJ 30 June 1966 – C-56/65, ECLI:EU:C:1966:38, ECR 1966, 284, 304 – *Société Technique Minière/Maschinenbau Ulm.*

238 Schuhmacher and Holzweber (2025), TFEU Article 101 mn. 902.

239 Kirchhoff (2020), sec. 11 mn. 279 f.

240 Alfter and Hunold (2016), pp. 525, 527.

- Broad price parity clauses restrict retailers from offering better terms on third-party platforms as well.[241]

This distinction, initially made by national competition authorities and courts,[242] is now enshrined in the Vertical Block Exemption Regulation. Since 2022, **Article 5(1)(d) VBER** includes broad price parity clauses and declares them non-exempt. Broad price parity clauses can lead to **market foreclosure in intermediary services.**[243] Consumers are less likely to explore other platforms if retailers cannot offer more competitive deals elsewhere. This increases the barriers to entry for potential competitors. Simultaneously, competition among retailers is restricted.[244] While retailers are still free to set the prices on their platform, the broad best-price clause **limits their freedom**. Retailers are effectively compelled to factor in the platform's commission when setting prices on other sales channels.[245]

Narrow price parity clauses, while still **exemptable**, also restrict competition. They are subject to the requirements of Articles 1, 3 VBER. However, their market foreclosure effects are less pronounced compared to broad price parity clauses, as traders can still offer better prices on competing platforms. Under Article 6(1) 1st sentence VBER, the Commission can withdraw the exemption if a narrow price parity clause results in effects that are incompatible with Article 101(3) TFEU. Specifically, this is the case if the market for online intermediation services is highly concentrated and competition between platform operators is significantly restricted due to the cumulative effect of similar agreements across multiple networks, as outlined in **Article 6(1) 2nd sentence VBER**.

2.2.2.4 Object or Effect of Preventing, Restricting or Distorting Competition

The prohibited conduct described above must either have the object or effect of restricting competition. Whether a restriction is considered 'by object' does not depend on the intentions of the parties involved in the agreement. Instead, it must be assessed **objectively**.[246] A restriction by object is **inherently harmful** to competition.[247] This occurs when the negative effects are so likely that there is no need to

---

241 German Federal Supreme Court 18 May 2021 – KVR 54/20, NZKart 2021, 499, 499 – *Booking.com*.

242 German Federal Supreme Court 18 May 2021 – KVR 54/20, NZKart 2021, 499 – *Booking.com* Higher Regional Court of Duesseldorf 4 June 2019 - VI-Kart 2/16 (V), NZKart 2019, 379 – *Enge Bestpreisklausel II*; German Federal Cartel Office 22 December 2015 – B9–121/13 – *Booking.com* decision of 9 January 2015 – VI-Kart 1/14 (V), NZKart 2015, 148 – *HRS*; German Federal Cartel Office 20 December 2013 – B9-66/10 – *HRS*.

243 German Federal Supreme Court 18 May 2021 – KVR 54/20, NZKart 2021, 499, 500 – *Booking.com*.

244 Mörsdorf and Schäfer (2019), pp. 659, 660.

245 German Federal Supreme Court 18 May 2021 – KVR 54/20, NZKart 2021, 499, 500 – *Booking.com*.

246 ECJ 19 March 2015 – C-286/13 P ECLI:EU:C:2015:184, para. 114 – *Dole Food and Dole Fresh Fruit Europe*; Kumkar (2025), Article 101 TFEU mn. 49.

247 ECJ 2 April 2020 – C-228/18, ECLI:EU:C:2020:265, para. 76 – *Budapest Bank et al.*

assess their market impact.[248] If a restriction is deemed to be by object, it automatically falls under the cartel prohibition, regardless of its actual effects.[249] Restrictions by object are always considered appreciable.[250]

2

▶ **Examples**

Examples of horizontal hardcore cartels (such as price fixing or territorial allocation) and vertical hardcore restraints, such as resale price maintenance, are considered restrictions of competition by object.[251] ◀

If a restriction is not deemed to be by object, it will only fall under the cartel prohibition if its anti-competitive effect can be demonstrated. In such cases, all relevant circumstances must be considered, particularly the market conditions.[252] To assess the effect, the affected markets may need to be defined, and the market shares of the undertakings involved in the cartel must be determined.[253] Additionally, the actual market outcomes must be compared to those that would occur in the absence of the agreement.[254]

2.2.2.5 Appreciability

Article 101(1) TFEU only covers restrictions of competition that are **appreciable**.[255] In its **De Minimis Notice**,[256] the Commission clarifies that horizontal restrictions are not considered appreciable if the combined market share of the parties does not exceed 10% in any of the affected markets.[257] For vertical agreements, a restriction of competition is not appreciable if no undertaking involved has a market share above 15% in any of the affected market levels.[258] These market share thresholds are based on **presumptions**. However, restrictions of competition by object represent an important exception: they are always considered appreciable, even below the mentioned market share thresholds.[259]

---

248 ECJ 11 September 2014 – C-67/13 P, ECLI:EU:C:2014:2204, para. 57 – *CB*; Zimmer (2025), TFEU Article 101(1) mn. 145.
249 Zimmer (2025), TFEU Article 101(1) mn. 142.
250 On the concept of appreciability, see ▶ 2.2.2.5.
251 ECJ 25 October 1977 – C-26/76, ECLI:EU:C:1977:167, para. 21 et seq. – *Metro*.
252 ECJ 28 February 2013 – C-1/12, ECLI:EU:C:2013:127, para. 70 – *Ordem dos Técnicos Oficiais de Contas*.
253 Säcker and Zorn (2023), TFEU Article 101 mn. 295. For further details on market definition, see ▶ 2.3.1.1.
254 ECJ 17 October 1994 – T-34/92, ECLI:EU:T:1994:258, para. 49 – *Fiatagri and New Holland Ford*.
255 ECJ 30 June 1966 – C-56/65, ECLI:EU:C:1966:38, p. 304 – *Société Technique Minière/Maschinenbau Ulm*.
256 Commission, Notice on agreements of minor importance which do not appreciably restrict competition under Article 101(1) of the Treaty on the Functioning of the European Union (De Minimis Notice), OJ [2019] C 291/1.
257 Commission, De Minimis Notice, 2019, para. 8 a).
258 Commission, De Minimis Notice, 2019, para. 8 b).
259 ECJ 13 December 2012 – C-226/11, ECLI:EU:C:2012:795, para. 16 – *Expedia*.

In the case of vertical restraints, the bundling theory is also applied to determine appreciability.[260] If a restraint is implemented through a large number of similar agreements, these are considered collectively. As a result, a vertical agreement can reach the appreciability threshold with a market share as low as 5% if at least 30% of the market is covered by the bundle of similar agreements.

2.2.3 Effect on Trade Between Member States

European competition law aims to create a single internal market. Therefore, restrictions of competition that only affect the territory of a single Member State do not violate Article 101 TFEU. Instead, it is required that the restriction is likely to **affect trade between Member States**. The criteria for interstate effects are relatively low.[261] The Commission has clarified these in its guidelines on the concept of the effect on interstate trade, notably through the **NAAT rule**.[262] According to these guidelines, the ability to affect interstate trade is denied if the cartel participants have a combined market share of no more than 5%, and, for horizontal agreements, if the combined turnover of the undertakings, or for vertical agreements, the turnover of the suppliers related to the cartelized goods, does not exceed EUR 40 million.[263]

2.2.4 Unwritten Exceptions

2.2.4.1 Public Interest Defence

The prohibition of cartels has a broad scope. The goal of protecting free competition can, at times, conflict with other objectives of the European Union. To address such conflicts, the ECJ has recognised unwritten exceptions to the cartel ban in certain situations. One category of exceptions relates to the pursuit of other **public interests**. In the *Albany* judgment, the ECJ established that the prohibition on cartels does not apply to **collective agreements between employers and employees**.[264] These agreements promote social policy and uphold the autonomy of collective bargaining, as guaranteed by Articles 153, 155 TFEU.[265] As a result, agreements that may restrict competition within the framework of collective bargaining fall outside the scope of Article 101(1) TFEU.

In the *Meca Medina* case, the ECJ recognised an exception to the prohibition of cartels in favour of **sporting rules**.[266] It held that rules which are '*purely sporting in*

260 Commission, De Minimis Notice, 2019, para. 10.
261 Zimmer (2025), TFEU Article 101(1) mn. 195; Kumkar (2025), TFEU Article 101 mn. 54.
262 NAAT stands for 'no appreciable affectation of trade', cf. Guidelines on the concept of effect on trade between Member States in Articles 81 and 82 of the Treaty, OJ [2004] C 101/81 para. 3.
263 Commission, Guidelines on the effect on trade concept in Articles 81 and 82 of the Treaty, OJ [2004] C 101/81 para. 52.
264 ECJ 21 June 1999 – C-67/96, ECLI:EU:C:1999:430 – *Albany*.
265 Schuhmacher and Holzweber (2025), TFEU Article 101 mn. 27.
266 ECJ 18 July 2006 – C-519/04 P, ECLI:EU:C:2006:492 – *Meca Medina*.

nature'[267]—such as anti-doping regulations—fall outside the scope of Article 101(1) TFEU. These rules do not pursue economic objectives but serve the internal goals of sport, such as preserving its non-profit character and ensuring fair competition among athletes.[268] Another unwritten exception was recognised in the *Wouters* case.[269] The ECJ examined a regulation issued by the Netherlands Bar that prohibited multi-disciplinary partnerships between lawyers and accountants. Although the measure restricted competition, the ECJ found that it did not fall under Article 101(1) TFEU. The regulation aimed to safeguard the proper functioning of the legal profession, particularly the independence of legal advice and the avoidance of conflicts of interest.[270] In doing so, the ECJ gave precedence to the effective **administration of justice** over strict competition rules.

In the *API* case, the Court of Justice of the European Union considered **road traffic safety**.[271] The case concerned decisions made by a committee composed primarily of industry representatives, which determined minimum operating costs in the road freight transport sector. Due to Italian legal requirements, these decisions also indirectly influenced pricing for freight transport services. The ECJ found that the decisions taken within this committee were compatible with Article 101(1) TFEU. One interpretation of the ruling is that the ECJ accepted a restriction of competition in favour of the public interest, specifically, road safety.[272] Others, however, view the decision as more closely aligned with the reasoning in *Wouters*. On this view, the ECJ acknowledged the legitimacy of a state's delegation of regulatory powers to a professional body, and did not treat the resulting decisions as typical agreements between undertakings under Article 101(1) TFEU.[273]

In two decision of December 2023, the ECJ found that unwritten exceptions are not available for competitive restrictions by object.[274] In both the *European Superleague Company* case and the *International Skating Union* case, it declared that the case law mentioned above '*does not apply either in situations involving conduct which, far from merely having the inherent 'effect' of restricting competition, at least potentially, by limiting the freedom of action of certain undertakings, reveals a degree of harm in relation to that competition that justifies a finding that it has as its very 'object' the prevention, restriction or distortion of competition.*'[275]

A current debate concerns whether the promotion of sustainability goals can justify restricting the application of Article 101(1) TFEU.[276] Critics argue against

---

267 ECJ 18 July 2006 – C-519/04 P, ECLI:EU:C:2006:492, para. 27 – *Meca Medina*.

268 ECJ 18 July 2006 – C-519/04 P, ECLI:EU:C:2006:492, para. 31 – *Meca Medina*.

269 ECJ 19 February 2002 – C-309/99, ECLI:EU:C:2002:98 – *Wouters*.

270 ECJ 19 February 2002 – C-309/99, ECLI:EU:C:2002:98, para. 100 – Wouters.

271 ECJ 4 September 2014 – C-184/13 and others, ECLI:EU:C:2014:2147 – *API*.

272 Kokott and Dittert (2014), pp. 15, 18.

273 Schweitzer (2014), pp. 21, 36.

274 ECJ 21 December 2023 – C-333/21, ECLI:EU:C:2023:1011 – *European Superleague Company*, ECJ, 21 December 2023 – C-124/21 P, ECLI:EU:C:2023:1012 – *International Skating Union*.

275 ECJ 21 December 2023 – C-333/21, ECLI:EU:C:2023:1011, para. 186 – *European Superleague Company*; ECJ 21 December 2023 – C-124/21 P, ECLI:EU:C:2023:1012, para. 113 – *International Skating Union*.

276 Cf. Haucap et al. (2023), pp. 68–92; Inderst and Thomas (2022) < https://www.econstor.eu/handle/10419/253671 > (1 September 2025); Nowag (2019), p. 8.

such an unwritten exception, noting that sustainability (when defined broadly in line with the UN Sustainable Development Goals[277]) could potentially justify a wide range of restrictions and undermine the principle of free competition. Moreover, competition and sustainability are not inherently in conflict. In fact, competitive pressure often incentivises companies to innovate and invest in sustainable practices over the long term.[278] For this reason, it is more persuasive to consider sustainability objectives only within the framework of the exemption provided by Article 101(3) TFEU. This is also the approach adopted by the Commission in its 2023 Horizontal Guidelines, which emphasise that sustainability considerations must be assessed under the exemption criteria, rather than serving as a basis for excluding agreements from the scope of Article 101(1) TFEU.[279]

2.2.4.2 Doctrine of Ancillary Restrictions

European case law also excludes agreements restricting competition from the scope of Article 101(1) TFEU if they are a necessary component of a more comprehensive agreement with a **main purpose that is neutral in terms of competition law**.[280] One example is non-compete clauses in subcontractor or undertaking sale agreements. The prerequisite is that the ancillary agreement is **objectively necessary** and **proportionate** in view of the main purpose pursued.[281] A non-competition clause in a undertaking sale agreement may therefore only extend to such a period of time as is necessary for the purchaser to maintain and retain the customer base.[282] In its new Horizontal Guidelines, the Commission states that it must be impossible for the undertakings to carry out the cooperation without the ancillary agreement.[283] The fact that the co-operation would be '*difficult to implement or less* profitable'[284] is not sufficient to exclude the restriction of competition from Article 101(1) TFEU.

In 2019, the Higher Regional Court of Duesseldorf ruled that **narrow price parity clauses** of a hotel booking portal do not fall under Article 101 TFEU as necessary ancillary agreements.[285] The court justified this by stating that

» '*it would permanently disrupt the balanced exchange of services and the balance between the portal service of the parties involved and the remuneration obligation of the hotel bound by the contract if the hotels were able to prevent the claim for remu-*

277 2030 Agenda for Sustainable Development < https://unric.org/de/17ziele/ > (1 September 2025).
278 Legner (2023c), pp. 233 et seqq.
279 Commission, Horizontal Guidelines, 2023, paras. 556 et seq.
280 CFI 18 September 2001 – T-112/99, ECLI:EU:T:2001:215, para. 115 – *M6 and others*; Grave and Nyberg (2025), TFEU Article 101(1) mn. 315.
281 CFI 18 September 2001 – T-112/99, ECLI:EU:T:2001:215, para. 104 – *M6 and others.*
282 Cf. ECJ 11 July 1985 – C-42/48, ECLI:EU:C:1985:327, para. 28 – *Remia.*
283 Commission, Horizontal Guidelines, 2023, para. 34.
284 Commission, Horizontal Guidelines, 2023, para. 34.
285 Higher Regional Court of Duesseldorf 4 June 2019 – VI-Kart 2/16 (V), NZKart 2019, 379 – *Enge Bestpreisklausel II.*

neration from arising by diverting hotel customers who have chosen their hotel using the booking portal to the hotel's own booking options before making a booking by offering a lower room price or better contractual conditions'.[286]

2

Neither the German Federal Supreme Court[287] nor the European legislator in the Vertical Block Exemption Regulation has agreed with this. Merely jeopardising the platform operator's business model by submitting better offers on the undertaking's own websites cannot be sufficient to classify a narrow price parity clause as a necessary ancillary agreement.[288] The German Federal Supreme Court adds that

» *'the suitability or even necessity of a contractual provision to ensure a fair and balanced exchange of services in the bilateral relationship between the contracting parties is not sufficient to exempt an ancillary agreement from the prohibition of Art. 101 I TFEU.'*[289]

The purpose of competition law is not to ensure contractual parity. Rather, the free-rider problem addressed by the Higher Regional Court of Duesseldorf can be taken into account in the context of the exemption requirements under Article 101(3) TFEU. In this context, a comprehensive assessment must be made of the consumer benefits associated with the possibility of more favourable sales via the hotel providers' own websites. The Vertical Block Exemption Regulation now also mentions narrow price parity clauses in Article 6(1) VBER as restrictions of competition that can be exempted on the merits. However, the exemption advantage can be withdrawn by the Commission in individual cases.

2.2.4.3 Concept of Market Development

Restrictions of competition that allow the undertakings involved to access new markets are exempt from the ban on cartels because of their pro-competitive effects.[290] This principle applies to **joint ventures**, such as when multiple construction companies submit a joint bid for a project because no single company could manage the order volume on its own.[291] The market development doctrine can also justify **exclusive distribution agreements**, for instance if absolute territorial protection is required for distributors to establish a presence in a new market.[292] In the context of digital innovations, research and development agreements are exempt if the participating undertakings would be unable to make the necessary

286 Higher Regional Court of Duesseldorf 4 June 2019 – VI-Kart 2/16 (V), NZKart 2019, 379, 381 – *Enge Bestpreisklausel II* [quote translated by author].
287 German Federal Supreme Court 18 May 2021 – KVR 54/20, NZKart 2021, 499 – *Booking.com*.
288 Schuhmacher and Holzweber (2025), TFEU Article 101 mn. 906.
289 German Federal Supreme Court 18 May 2021 – KVR 54/20, NZKart 2021, 499, 501 – *Booking.com* [quote tanslated by author].
290 Stockenhuber (2025), TFEU Article 101 mn. 153.
291 Wagner-von Papp (2023), TFEU Article 101 mn. 306.
292 ECJ 30 June 1966 – C-56/65, ECLI:EU:C:1966:38, p. 304 – *Société Technique Minière/Maschinenbau Ulm*.

investments or lack the technical capabilities to carry out the required research independently.[293]

2.2.4.4 Agency Agreements

Agreements between a commercial agent and their principal may fall outside the scope of Article 101(1) TFEU. A commercial agent is defined by their role in representing the principal's interests in the market.[294] As described by the Commission, such an agent *'no longer acts as an independent economic operator.'*[295] In the *Voestalpine* decision, the GC referred to the commercial agent *'de facto as an auxiliary organ'*[296] of the principal. This characterisation reflects the conditions under which agency agreements fall outside the scope of Article 101(1) TFEU. A commercial agent is a sales intermediary who *'bears **no significant financial or commercial risks**.'*[297] Thus, agreements with an independent distributor who bears their own economic risk, are not excluded from Article 101(1) TFEU. Crucially, how an agent is classified under national law, such as in sec. 84 et seq. German Commercial Code (*HGBHandelsgesetzbuch, HGB*), is not relevant for the purposes of European competition law. Instead, the key criterion is the agent's actual function and the extent of commercial risk assumed within the contractual relationship.

In the context of the digital economy, the Higher Regional Court of Duesseldorf held that price parity clauses agreed between a **hotel booking platform** and hotel operators using the platform did not fall within the scope of the cartel prohibition. The court reasoned that the platform should be regarded as a commercial agent.[298] According to the judgment, the platform's role was limited to *'preparing room bookings ready for conclusion on behalf of the contracting hotel undertakings via the hotel portal.'*[299] Moreover, the court emphasized that the platform exercised *'no influence over the booking conditions.'*[300] The German Federal Supreme Court rightly took a different view.[301] In its reasoning, it highlighted the objective of the agreed price parity clause, which was to address a *'free-rider problem to a not inconsiderable extent'*[302] by controlling one of the most significant competitive parameters. This, the Court found, clearly indicates that the platform does not operate on the market without assuming economic risk. This disqualified the platform from being considered a commercial agent.

---

293 Commission, Horizontal Guidelines, 2023, para. 138.
294 Commission, Vertical Guidelines, 2022, para. 29.
295 Commission, Vertical Guidelines, 2022, para. 30.
296 GC 15 July 2015 – T-418/10, ECLI:EU:T:2015:516, para. 158 – *voestalpine and voestalpine Wire Rod Austria.*
297 Commission, Vertical Guidelines, 2022, para. 30 [emphasis addes by author].
298 Higher Regional Court of Duesseldorf 4 December 2017 – VI-U (Kart) 5/17, NZKart 2018, 54, 55 – *Expedia [quote translated by author].*
299 Higher Regional Court of Duesseldorf 4 December 2017 – VI-U (Kart) 5/17, NZKart 2018, 54, 55 – *Expedia [quote translated by author].*
300 Higher Regional Court of Duesseldorf 4 December 2017 – VI-U (Kart) 5/17, NZKart 2018, 54, 55 – *Expedia [quote translated by author].*
301 German Federal Supreme Court 18 May 2021 – KVR 54/20, NZKart 2021, 499, 502 – *Booking.com.*
302 German Federal Supreme Court 18 May 2021 – KVR 54/20, NZKart 2021, 499, 502 – *Booking.com.*

2

In its 2022 Vertical Guidelines, the Commission also underscores that '*agreements entered into by undertakings active in the online platform economy [...] do not meet the conditions to be categorised as agency agreements.*'[303] The Commission justifies this position on several grounds.[304] First, platform operators typically enter into contracts with a large number of undertakings, making it implausible to view the platform as a dependent extension of any single contracting party. Second, the intermediation role of such platforms, often accompanied by significant market power, enables them to exert considerable influence over the terms under which commercial users offer their goods or services. Third, and importantly, platform operators frequently make substantial investments in the operation of their intermediary services. As a result, they take on economic risks that are incompatible with the role of a commercial agent.

2.2.4.5 Group Privilege

Agreements between entities that form part of the **same economic unit**, and are thus considered a single undertaking within the meaning of Article 101 TFEU, are not subject to the prohibition on cartels.[305] This is because, within such relationships, there is **no independent decision-making autonomy** that could be restricted by an agreement. Instead, the entities operate as a single market participant.[306] For an economic unit to be established, the parent company must exercise actual influence over the subsidiary; mere potential to exert control is insufficient.[307] In assessing the existence of such an economic unit, case law primarily considers the size of the shareholding.[308] Additional factors, such as personal interdependencies, may also be relevant. Where the parent company owns 100% or nearly 100% of the subsidiary, case law presumes the existence of an economic unit.[309] Although the subsidiary may attempt to rebut this presumption, doing so has proven to be virtually impossible in practice.

Learning Goals

In certain areas of competition law, the principle of economic unity is explicitly codified and must be applied with priority over general case law. Within the scope of the VBER, Article 1(2)(2), defines the concept of affiliated undertakings. In the context of European merger control, Article 5(4)–(5) EUMR are particularly relevant. Article 5(4) EUMR governs the calculation of turnover, while Article 5(5) EUMR sets out the rules for the pro rata attribution of shares in joint ventures, both relying on the concept of economic unity. Beyond these procedural and definitional contexts, the existence of an economic unit also has significant implications for liability

303 Commission, Vertical Guidelines, 2022, para. 46.
304 Commission, Vertical Guidelines, 2022, para. 46.
305 For further information on the definition of an undertaking, see ▶ 2.1.4.1.
306 ECJ 24 October 1975 – C-73/95 P, ECLI:EU:C:1996:405 – *Viho*; ECJ 11 April 1989 – C-66/86, ECLI:EU:C:1989:140– *Ahmed Saeed Flugreisen et al.*
307 ECJ 10 September 2009 – C-97/08 P, ECLI:EU:C:2009:536, para. 60– *Akzo Nobel et al.*
308 Stockenhuber (2025), TFEU Article 101 mn. 167.
309 ECJ 29 March 2011 – C-201/09 P, ECLI:EU:C:2011:190, para. 97 – *ArcelorMittal Luxembourg*.

under both competition fines and civil damages. Where a parent company and its subsidiary form a single economic entity, they are jointly and severally liable for infringements of competition law.

2.2.5 Exemption Requirements

2.2.5.1 General Principles

Where an agreement infringes Article 101(1) TFEU, the undertakings involved may nonetheless benefit from an **exemption under Article 101(3) TFEU**. If the exemption criteria are met, the agreement is considered compatible with EU competition law and does not constitute a breach of Article 101 TFEU. Unlike the form-based approach taken under Article 101(1) TFEU, Article 101(3) TFEU introduces an assessment based on the **effects** of the agreement. In essence, a restriction may be exempted where its pro-competitive effects outweigh its negative impact on competition. The exemption criteria reflect the dual purpose of EU competition law: not only to preserve the competitive process, but also to promote **consumer welfare**.[310]

Article 101(3) TFEU sets out four cumulative conditions that must all be satisfied for an exemption to apply:

- The agreement must contribute to improving the production or distribution of goods, or to promoting technical or economic progress;
- Consumers must receive a fair share of the resulting benefits;
- The agreement must not impose restrictions that are not indispensable to achieving these objectives; and
- The agreement must not afford the undertakings the possibility of eliminating competition in respect of a substantial part of the relevant market.[311]

The exemption conditions under Article 101(3) TFEU apply **ipso jure**, without the need for a formal declaration by the Commission. This is confirmed by Article 1(2) Regulation 1/2003.[312] As a result, undertakings must determine on their own whether their agreement meets the exemption criteria. According to Article 2 Regulation 1/2003, the burden of proof rests with the undertakings concerned. Because Article 101(3) TFEU uses broad and flexible language, its application often involves legal uncertainty. To address this, the Commission has issued several **block exemption regulations** (BERs), which define the conditions under which specific types of agreements qualify for exemption. These regulations offer undertakings clearer guidance and greater legal certainty.

---

310 On consumer welfare as objective of EU competition law, see ► 2.1.3.2.
311 For further details on the Article 101(3) TFEU criteria, see ► 2.2.5.3.
312 Previously, the exemption was structured as a prohibition subject to authorisation, meaning that it was the Commission that had to issue the exemption decisions.

2

Where a Block Exemption Regulation applies, its requirements must be assessed first. If the agreement does not meet the criteria for exemption under the relevant BER, it is then necessary to examine whether an individual exemption under Article 101(3) TFEU may still apply. However, such individual exemptions are rare, as the BERs are intended to specify and operationalise the general exemption conditions laid down in Article 101(3) TFEU.

Learning Goals

In addition to Block Exemption Regulations, there are also sector-specific derogations from the cartel prohibition. One prominent example is the agricultural sector, which falls under the special regime established by Article 42 TFEU. In this context, competition rules are set out in sector-specific legislation, such as the Common Market Organisation Regulation.[313] As a result, Article 101 TFEU does not apply at all in these cases. Neither the definition of restrictive practices nor the exemption conditions are relevant.

A number of block exemption regulations are outlined below. The fundamental distinction between horizontal and vertical restraints[314] explains why the Vertical Block Exemption Regulation (VBER)[315] provides a broad exemption for vertical agreements. Under Article 2(1) VBER, all vertical restraints are exempt from the prohibition in Article 101(1) TFEU, provided the conditions are met. In contrast, there is no equally comprehensive exemption for horizontal restraints. Instead, the nature and content of the agreement must be examined to determine whether it falls within the scope of a specific regulation targeting certain types of horizontal cooperation. These include the Research and Development Block Exemption Regulation (R&D BER)[316] and the Specialisation Block Exemption Regulation (Specialisation BER).[317] Where no regulation applies, it becomes necessary to assess whether an individual exemption under Article 101(3) TFEU may be granted.

---

313 Regulation (EU) No 1308/2013 of the European Parliament and of the Council of 17 December 2013 establishing a common organisation of the markets in agricultural products, OJ [2013] L 347/671.

314 For further details on this distinction, see ► 2.2.2.1.

315 Commission Regulation (EU) 2022/720 of 10 May 2022 on the application of Article 101(3) of the Treaty on the Functioning of the European Union to categories of vertical agreements and concerted practices, OJ [2022] 134/4.

316 Commission Regulation (EU) 2023/1066 of 1 June 2023 on the application of Article 101(3) of the Treaty on the Functioning of the European Union to certain categories of research and development agreements, OJ [2023] L 143/9.

317 Commission Regulation (EU) 2023/1067 of 1 June 2023 on the application of Article 101 (3) of the Treaty on the Functioning of the European Union to certain categories of specialisation agreements, OJ EU 2023 No L 143/20.

2.2.5.2 Block Exemptions

Vertical Block Exemption Regulation

Overview

According to Article 2(1) VBER, **vertical agreements** are, in principle, exempt from the prohibition under Article 101(1) TFEU. However, this exemption applies only if the agreement falls within the scope of the VBER. To qualify, the parties involved must satisfy the dual market share thresholds set out in Article 3 VBER. Additionally, the agreement must not include any hardcore restrictions as defined in Article 4 VBER, nor any other excluded restrictions listed in Article 5 VBER. If a hardcore restriction is present, the entire agreement is excluded from the exemption under Article 2(1) VBER. In contrast, if the agreement contains a non-exempted restriction under Article 5 VBER, only that specific provision is excluded, while the remainder of the agreement may still benefit from the exemption.

! Article 2(1) VBER provides that, in principle, all vertical agreements are exempted from the prohibition under Article 101(1) TFEU.

The broad scope for exempting vertical restraints of competition makes it clear that they are essentially different from horizontal ones. It is evident that, in principle, they are less detrimental to competition, as their implementation merely restricts the competitive freedom of action of one party and may result in the generation of efficiencies. A prominent illustration of this phenomenon is the issue of double marginalisation, where a dual mark-up, consequently leading to an elevated sales price, can arise within the distribution chain if manufacturers and retailers establish their prices without considering each other's actions. This results in a disadvantage for consumers.[318] This can be circumvented through the implementation of vertical agreements.

However, vertical restraints of competition can also have detrimental foreclosure effects. The market power of the undertakings involved in the agreement is the key factor in this regard. The Vertical Block Exemption Regulation addresses this by linking its exemption provision in Article 2(1) VBER to the market share threshold in Article 3 VBER. Furthermore, vertical agreements can facilitate the establishment of horizontal agreements between suppliers and buyers.

The Vertical Block Exemption Regulation was comprehensively revised in 2022, with **numerous special provisions for the digital economy** included.

- On the one hand, this pertains to the development of new business models. The intermediary services of platform operators do not align neatly with the classic two- or three-tier distribution structure that the 2010 Vertical Block Exemption Regulation relied on. It is ultimately not possible to clearly assign the role of supplier or buyer to a platform operator. Instead, the tasks that a platform operator performs are situated at the interface between production and distribution.[319] In addition, some platform operators take on a hybrid role. They not

---

318 Commission, Vertical Guidelines, 2022, para. 201.
319 Thomas (2020), pp. 222, 238.

only offer intermediary services, but also compete with their customers at a downstream market level.

- On the other hand, **novel forms of vertical restrictions on competition** have emerged in the digital sector. The compatibility of these restrictions with the prohibition on cartels has been a subject of considerable debate. These include internet distribution bans, platform bans and price parity clauses.[320] The Vertical Block Exemption Regulation explicitly addresses some of these new forms, thereby creating legal certainty.

Scope of Application

Vertical Agreements

Even if the European ban on cartels treats horizontal and vertical restraints of competition in the same way, the two are essentially different. This is shown by the broad exemption of vertical agreements in Article 2(1) VBER. The definition of the term 'vertical agreement' as set out in the regulation is relevant for determining the scope of the exemption. According to Article 1(1)(a) VBER, this includes an agreement between two or more undertakings. For the purposes of the agreement, these undertakings are each **active at a different level of the production or distribution chain**. The agreement concerns the conditions under which the undertakings concerned may purchase, sell or resell goods or services. The VBER generally refers to these entities as 'suppliers' and 'buyers'.

▶ Examples

Agreements between manufacturers and distributors or between wholesalers and retailers are of a vertical nature. ◀

Article 1(1)(d) VBER addresses the complex issue of integrating a platform operator into the distribution structure. According to this provision, an 'undertaking that provides online intermediation services' qualifies as supplier. Consequently, agreements between a platform operator and the undertakings active on the platform are considered vertical agreements.

The Article 2(4), (6) VBER provides for an exception for **hybrid platforms**. Such platforms compete at the downstream market level with the undertakings to which they offer their intermediary services at the upstream market level.

▶ Example

Amazon offers retailers access to its marketplace. Conversely, it competes with these retailers, as it itself acts as a supplier of goods on its own marketplace. ◀

In accordance with Article 2(6) VBER, vertical agreements concerning the provision of online intermediary services are excluded from the VBER's scope of

320 For further details on these vertical restrictions of competition, see ▶ 2.2.2.3.

application if the provider of such services is active as a competitor on the downstream market. While the agreements remain classified as vertical, they are excluded from the exemption outlined in Article 2(1) VBER. The background to this is that there is a risk of horizontal collusion in such constellations, which the VBER does not wish to privilege.

As outlined in Article 2(4),(5) VBER, an additional exception is in place for the exchange of information. The Vertical Block Exemption Regulation does not apply if the transaction does not directly concern the implementation of the vertical agreement, or is not necessary to improve the production or distribution of the contract goods or services. Accordingly, the Vertical Block Exemption Regulation does not cover, for example, the exchange of technical information on contract goods or logistical information on distribution.[321] In the dual distribution scenario, however, it is unlikely that the Vertical Block Exemption Regulation will apply if the parties exchange information on future prices or individual consumers.[322]

Market Share Thresholds

Article 3(1) VBER links the exemption sequence of the regulation to a double market share threshold. The market share of both the supplier and the buyer must not exceed 30%. This takes into account, albeit in a very generalised way, that the competitive effects of vertical agreements depend on the market power of the undertakings involved.

Article 8 VBER stipulates the method for determining market shares. However, when it comes to platform operators, it is challenging to accurately define the markets and determine the market shares. Platforms typically form multi-sided markets.[323] Thus, it must be evaluated whether each user group, that is to say, one market side, should be considered as an independent market, or whether it is preferable for summarise several user groups when defining the market. When assessing the *Microsoft/LinkedIn* merger, the Commission assumed a single market for online recruitment services comprising both job seekers and recruiters.[324] However, a different approach was taken in the *Mastercard* case. With regard to payment card systems, the Commission assumed two separate markets for issuing and acquiring.[325]

Furthermore, platform operators occasionally provide a service to a user group, typically private end users, without requesting financial compensation.[326] Examples include the provision of social networks by *Instagram* or *Facebook*. In this regard, a market share calculation based on turnover is not appropriate. However, the fundamental premise of a market is not negated by the absence of monetary consideration.[327]

---

321 Commission, Vertical Guidelines, 2022, para. 99.
322 Commission, Vertical Guidelines, 2022, para. 100.
323 For details on market delineation in the digital sphere, see ► 2.3.1.1.4.
324 Commission, Decision of 6 December 2016 – M.8124 – *Microsoft/LinkedIn*.
325 Commission, Decision of 19 December 2017 – AT.34579 – *Mastercard*.
326 For details on asymmetric price structures in digital markets, see ► 1.1.3.
327 Commission, Decision of 7 October 2011 – COMP/M.6281 – *Microsoft/Skype*.

2

Hardcore Restrictions

Article 4 VBER enumerates six hardcore restrictions to which the exemption set out in Article 2 VBER does not apply. If they also fail to fulfil the requirements of Article 101(3) TFEU (individual exemption),[328] they are in violation of Article 101 TFEU. In this case, the entire vertical agreement is in breach of competition law and void pursuant to Article 101(2) TFEU.

Article 4(a) VBER deals with **resale price maintenance**.[329] According to this provision, fixed and minimum price maintenance are excluded from the exemption. In contrast, maximum price maintenance and non-binding price recommendations are exempted, unless they actually have the same effect as fixed or minimum selling prices as a result of the exercise of pressure or the granting of incentives.

Article 4(b) VBER covers **territorial and customer restrictions** in **exclusive distribution systems**.

> **Definition**
>
> According to Article 1(1)(h) VBER, an exclusive distribution system means a distribution system where the supplier allocates a territory or group of customers exclusively to itself or to a maximum of five buyers and restricts all its other buyers from actively selling into the exclusive territory or to the exclusive customer group.

Article 4(b) VBER lists five exceptions in (i)–(v), some of which are pertain directly to the nature of an exclusive distribution system. The following are excluded and thus covered by Article 2(1) VBER:

- The restriction of active sales by the exclusive distributor and its direct customers, into a **territory** or to a **customer group** reserved to the supplier or allocated by the supplier exclusively to a maximum of five other exclusive distributors;
- The restriction of active or passive sales by the exclusive distributor and its customers **to unauthorised distributors** located in a territory where the supplier operates a selective distribution system for the contract goods or services;
- The restriction of the exclusive distributor's **place of establishment**;
- The restriction of active or passive sales to end users by an exclusive distributor operating at the **wholesale level of trade**;
- The restriction of the exclusive distributor's ability to actively or passively sell components, supplied for the purposes of incorporation, **to customers who would use them to manufacture the same type of goods** as those produced by the supplier.

According to Article 4(c) VBER, **territorial and customer restrictions** in **selective distribution systems** are considered hardcore restrictions. This also applies to

328 For the criteria laid down in Article 101(3) TFEU, see 2.2.5.3.

329 On the evaluation of resale price maintenance under Article 101(1) TFEU, see ► 2.2.2.3.1.

restrictions on **cross-supplies** and sales to end users by members of the selective distribution system operating at the retail level of trade.

Definition

Pursuant to Article 1(1)(g) VBER, a selective distribution system means a distribution system where the supplier undertakes to sell the contract goods or services, either directly or indirectly, only to distributors selected on the basis of specified criteria and where these distributors undertake not to sell such goods or services to unauthorised distributors within the territory reserved by the supplier to operate that system.

Exceptions are provided for territorial and customer restrictions in Article 4(c)(i)(1)–(5) VBER. These provisions are modelled on those of Article 4(b) VBER.

Article 4(d) VBER covers **territorial and customer restrictions** in **free distribution systems**. The exceptions correspond to those set out in Article 4(b)–(c) VBER.

Article 4(e) VBER concerns the prevention of the effective **use of the internet to sell the contract goods or services.**[330] It is not solely the direct prohibition of internet sales that is encompassed. Other obligations that indirectly impede traders from selling goods to specific customers or in particular territories via the internet are similarly not exempt.[331] This includes, for example, an agreement that a retailer must obtain the manufacturer's authorisation before concluding an online transaction or a prohibition on the retailer setting up its own online shops.[332] A dual pricing system is only subject to Article 4(e) VBER if the price difference between goods sold offline and online is disproportionate and bears no relation to the investment involved in using the distribution channels.[333]

Article 4(e) VBER also refers to '**other restrictions of online sales**' and '**restrictions of online advertising**' that are not intended to prevent the use of an entire online advertising channel. Such restrictions remain exempt. Therefore, producers can still set qualitative requirements for the online sales channels used by retailers. For example, banning online marketplaces does not qualify as a hardcore restriction.[334] It is also permissible to impose requirements on retailers regarding the presentation of goods in their online shops.

Article 4 lit. (f) VBER covers restrictions on the **sale of spare parts**.

Excluded Restrictions

Article 5 VBER lists further restrictions that do not fall under the exemption of Article 2(1) VBER. Unless they exceptionally fulfil the requirements of Article 101 (3) TFEU,[335] they are in violation of the ban on cartels. In such a scenario, the

330 On the evaluation of prohibitions on internet sales under Article 101(1) TFEU, see ► 2.2.2.3.2.
331 Commission, Vertical Guidelines, 2022, para. 206.
332 Commission, Vertical Guidelines, 2022, para. 206.
333 Commission, Vertical Guidelines, 2022, para. 209.
334 Commission, Vertical Guidelines, 2022, para. 207.
335 For the requirements of Article 101 (3) TFEU, see ► 2.2.5.3.

agreement that restricts competition is considered invalid; however, the remaining agreement remains in effect.

2

Article 5(1)(a) VBER addresses any direct or indirect non-compete obligation[336] of a duration of **at least 5 years**.[337] According to Article 1(1)(f) VBER, the term encompasses any direct or indirect obligation causing the buyer not to manufacture, purchase, sell or resell goods or services which compete with the contract goods or services, or any direct or indirect obligation on the buyer to purchase from the supplier or from another undertaking designated by the supplier more than 80% of the buyer's total purchases of the contract goods or services and their substitutes on the relevant market.

Article 5(1)(b) VBER stipulates that **obligations causing the buyer, after termination of the agreement, not to manufacture, purchase, sell or resell goods or services** are not exemptable. A narrow exception, applicable in the event of the fulfilment of four cumulative conditions, is set out in Article 5(3) VBER. One of the stipulated conditions is that the non-compete obligation is limited to a period of 1 year after termination of the agreement.

❗ Post-contractual non-compete obligations may already be exempt from Article 101(1) TFEU if they are a necessary ancillary agreement for the fulfilment of a contractual purpose that is neutral in terms of competition law.[338] If this is the case, exemption is not required. The Vertical Block Exemption Regulation does not need to be examined in this case.

Article 5(1)(c) VBER excludes from the exemption obligations which induce the members of a selective distribution system not to sell the brands of certain competing suppliers. This is intended to promote intra-brand competition.[339]

Article 5(1)(d) VBER addresses **wide price parity clauses**.[340] These are agreements between a platform operator and the businesses using the platform, under which the latter are prohibited from offering, selling, or reselling their goods or services on competing online intermediary platforms under more favourable conditions. Such wide parity clauses are not exempt under the VBER. In contrast, Article 5 VBER does not apply to narrow price parity clauses, which relate only to the supplier's own website. These remain exemptable under the VBER. Furthermore, under Article 6 VBER, the Commission retains the authority to withdraw the exemption in individual cases where justified.

❗ Both narrow and wide price parity clauses fall under the scope of Article 101(1) TFEU, as they restrict competition between platform operators and commercial users of the platform. These clauses are considered vertical restraints of competition. According to a well-founded view, the commercial agent exception does not

---

336 For further details on exclusivity obligations, see ► 2.2.2.3.7.
337 An exception is made in Article 5(2) VBER for goods sold by the customer on premises and land owned by the supplier.
338 For further information on the doctrine of ancillary restrictions, see ► 2.2.4.2.
339 Commission, Vertical Guidelines, 2022, para. 252.
340 For the differentiation between narrow and wide price parity clauses, see ► 2.2.2.3.8.

apply to narrow price parity clauses. Within the scope of the VBER, narrow best-price clauses are generally exempt under Article 2(1). In contrast, wide price parity clauses are not exemptable, as explicitly excluded under Article 5(1)(d) VBER.

Research & Development Block Exemption Regulation

Overview

The Research and Development Block Exemption Regulation (R&D BER) sets out the conditions under which **research and development agreements** are exempt from the prohibition in Article 101(1) TFEU. Pursuant to Article 2(1) R&D BER, certain R&D agreements are exempt from the ban on cartels, provided that the agreement falls within the scope of the Regulation. In contrast to the Vertical Block Exemption Regulation (VBER), the R&D BER is also applicable, in principle, to **horizontal agreements**, i.e., between actual or potential competitors. However, the exemption requirements under the R&D BER are stricter than those under the VBER. This is particularly evident in the market share thresholds set out in Article 6 R&D BER, which determine the applicability of the exemption. Furthermore, the exemption is **time-limited**, applying only for the duration of the research and development activities, as also stipulated in Article 6 R&D BER.

! The assessment of R&D agreements under Article 101(1) TFEU is inherently complex. Where an R&D agreement does not restrict competition, the question of exemption under Article 101(3)TFEU does not arise, as the agreement falls outside the scope of the cartel prohibition altogether.[341]

The broad exemption framework for R&D agreements reflects the understanding that cooperation between undertakings to develop new, or improve existing, products and processes can lead to significant efficiencies. These efficiencies may enhance innovation and deliver benefits to consumers, thereby fostering effective competition.[342]

The R&D BER was **revised in 2023**. While the Regulation continues to distinguish between horizontal and vertical R&D agreements, the conditions for exempting horizontal R&D agreements have become more flexible. Notably, the revised Regulation now explicitly covers agreements concluded during the early phases of joint research and development, as recognized in Recital 16 R&D BER. In addition, under Article 4 R&D BER, access to pre-existing know-how is now only required as a condition for exemption where the parties have opted not to engage in joint exploitation of the results.

Scope of Application

Research and Development Agreements

The term 'research and development agreement' is defined in Article 1(1)(1) R&D BER. It encompasses agreements relating to the **joint research and development**

341 For the assessment of R&D agreements under Article 101(1) TFEU, see ► 2.2.2.2.2.
342 Commission, Horizontal Guidelines, 2023, para. 37.

(whether contractual or collaborative) of contract products and contract technologies. The definition also includes the subsequent joint exploitation (utilisation) of the results of such research and development activities.

No reference is made in the R&D BER to joint research and development aimed at **new business models or business concepts** based on existing products or technologies.[343] This creates a degree of legal uncertainty, particularly for R&D agreements within the digital economy, where innovation often focuses on the use and recombination of existing technologies rather than the creation of entirely new ones. In such cases, only an individual exemption under Article 101(3) TFEU may be available.

Market Share Thresholds

Article 6 R&D BER sets out market share thresholds that vary depending on whether the undertakings involved in the R&D agreement are competitors or not: If the parties **are competitors**, Article 6(1)(a) R&D BER stipulates that the combined market share of the parties to the agreement on the relevant product and technology markets may **not exceed 25%** if the agreement concerns the joint research and development of contract products or technology. In the case of contract research and development, the joint market share of the financing party and all other parties to the agreement must be taken into account in accordance with Article 6(1)(b) R&D BER. The term 'competitor' is defined in Article 1 no. 15 R&D BER. A potential competitor is an undertaking that can realistically be expected to become active on the market within a maximum of 3 years without the research and development agreement.

Article 6(2) R&D BER **does not specify any market share thresholds** for **vertical R&D agreements**. The legislator assumes that such agreements do not restrict innovation competition in principle.[344]

In principle, the exemption **only** applies for **the duration of the research and development activity**. If the research results are jointly **exploited**, the exemption is extended by a **further 7 years**, see Article 6(3) R&D BER. A further extension for an indefinite period is possible pursuant to Article 6(4) R&D BER; the market share threshold of 25% applies again in the case of horizontal agreements.

Requirements from Article 3–5 R&D BER

Articles 3–5 R&D BER set out additional conditions for the application of the exemption under Article 101(3) TFEU. According to Article 3 R&D BER, the parties must ensure **unrestricted access to the final results** of the research and development activities for the purposes of further R&D and their utilisation. Article 4 R&D BER applies to R&D agreements that **do not involve joint exploitation of the results**. In such cases, the exemption is granted only if each party is given access to the other parties' existing know-how, provided that such know-how is indispensable for the exploitation of the results. Conversely, Article 5 R&D BER addresses

343 Ecker et al. (2021), p. 42.
344 Cf. recital 21 R&D BER.

agreements that do include **joint exploitation**. Here, the exemption is conditional upon the joint exploitation being limited to results that are indispensable for the production of the contract products or the application of the contract technologies, and which are either protected by intellectual property rights or constitute know-how.

Hardcore Restrictions

According to Article 8(a) R&D BER, hardcore restrictions, which render an agreement ineligible for exemption, include clauses that limit the parties' freedom to engage in independent research or to collaborate with third parties in fields outside the scope of the R&D agreement. Once the joint research has been completed, a prohibition on further research qualifies as a hardcore restriction only if it extends to the field to which the research and development agreement relates or to a connected field. In addition, Article 8 R&D BER identifies several hardcore restrictions relating to the utilisation of research results: Article 8(b) R&D BER addresses the limitation of output or sales. Under Article 8(c) R&D BER, the fixing of prices for the sale of contract products is not permitted. Pursuant to Article 8(d) R&D BER, restrictions on territories or customer groups for the sale or licensing of the contract products or technologies are likewise inadmissible.

Excluded Restrictions

Article 9 R&D BER lists further restrictions that cannot benefit from exemption under Article 101(3) TFEU. According to Article 9(1)(a) R&D BER, **non-challenge clauses** are not exemptable. These are clauses requiring a party not to challenge the validity of intellectual property rights—such as patents or copyrights—held by other parties, particularly those that were significant for the R&D process or protect its results after the R&D activities have concluded. The rationale behind this rule is that former participants in an R&D collaboration often possess insider knowledge that may allow them to identify wrongfully granted IP rights.[345] They should therefore not be contractually prevented from contesting such rights. Furthermore, Article 9(1)(b) R&D BER prohibits clauses that **prevent parties from granting licences to third parties** for the production of contract products or the application of contract technologies. An exception is made only where the agreement provides for exploitation by one or more parties within the internal market, and such exploitation is carried out in relation to third parties.

Specialisation Block Exemption Regulation

Overview

The Specialisation Block Exemption Regulation (Specialisation BER) lays down the conditions under which specialisation agreements may be exempted from the prohibition in Article 101(1) TFEU. According to Article 2(1) Specialisation BER, such agreements are in principle exempted, provided they meet the Regulation's

345 Commission, Horizontal Guidelines, 2023, para. 175.

2

requirements. Specialisation agreements are typically concluded **between competitors** and involve either the allocation of the production of one or more specific products to a single party, or the joint production of a specific product by the parties. These agreements hold rationalisation potential, as the consolidation of production between competitors may lead to significant quantitative and qualitative efficiencies.[346] By combining their skills, resources, and assets, parties can improve productivity, reduce duplication, and enhance product quality or innovation capacity.[347]

Article 3(1) Specialisation BER sets a **market share threshold of 20%**. The combined market share of the parties on the relevant market must not exceed this threshold for the exemption under the Regulation to apply. However, the exemption does not extend to hardcore restrictions listed in Article 5 Specialisation BER. These include clauses that severely restrict competition and are therefore automatically excluded from exemption, even if the other conditions are met.

The Specialisation BER was **revised in 2023**, introducing more flexible rules compared to its 2010 predecessor. One key change is the expanded scope of unilateral specialisation agreements. While the 2010 version only covered agreements between two parties, the revised Regulation now explicitly includes agreements 'between two or more parties', thereby broadening its applicability.

Scope of Application

The Specialisation BER applies to horizontal agreements which restrict competition. Article 1(1) Specialisation BER identifies three categories of specialisation agreements:

- Unilateral specialisation agreements, where one party agrees to cease production of a particular product and instead undertakes to purchase it from another party, who will produce it exclusively.
- Reciprocal specialisation agreements, where each party agrees to specialise in the production of certain products, while refraining from producing the products assigned to the other party.
- Joint production agreements, in which the parties agree to produce certain products jointly, either through a jointly controlled company or by other forms of collaboration.

To benefit from the exemption under Article 2(1) Specialisation BER, the agreement must satisfy the market share threshold set out in Article 3(1). Specifically, the combined market share of the parties on the relevant market **must not exceed 20%**. In cases where the specialisation products are intermediate products, Article 3(2) Specialisation BER applies a double market share threshold: the 20% threshold must be met both on the market for the intermediate product and on the downstream market where the intermediate product is used.

---

346 Kling and Thomas (2016), sec. 5 mn. 433.

347 Commission, Horizontal Guidelines, 2023, para. 37.

Hardcore Restrictions

Pursuant to Article 5 Specialisation BER, the exemption does not apply to obligations that involve price-fixing for the sale of specialisation products, limiting output or sales, or allocating markets or customers.

2.2.5.3 Article 101(3) TFEU Criteria

If no BER applies to the restriction of competition under examination, or if a BER does apply but its conditions are not fulfilled, an individual exemption under Article 101(3) TFEU must be assessed. This requires an evaluation of whether the four cumulative conditions for exemption are satisfied.

Improvement in the Production or Distribution of Goods or in Technical or Economic Progress

The first requirement for an individual exemption is that the agreement restricting competition must generate efficiencies. The term efficiency is defined in Article 101(3) TFEU as the improvement of the production or distribution of goods and the promotion of technical or economic progress. Improvements in production are achieved when cartelists successfully **reduce production costs** by leveraging existing production capacities more efficiently[348] or developing more cost-effective production processes.[349] With technical and economic progress, Article 101(3) TFEU refers to **dynamic efficiencies**. This includes the accelerated development of new products or improvements in the quality of existing services.[350] R&D agreements can play a key role in generating these efficiencies.

With regard to restrictions on competition agreed between platform operators and retailers, such as price parity clauses or exclusivity agreements, potential efficiencies may include **increased market transparency** and **reduced transaction costs**.[351] When assessing restrictions on the use of online marketplaces, it is important to consider whether such measures serve legitimate objectives, such as preventing the sale of counterfeit goods, ensuring a consistent level of customer service, or protecting the brand's image.[352]

The extent to which non-economic benefits may be considered under Article 101(3) TFEU remains controversial. In past decisions, the Commission and the courts have addressed factors such as job security[353] and environmental protection.[354] However, in its 2023 Horizontal Guidelines, the Commission adopts a strict stance, requiring that benefits must translate into measurable economic efficiencies to qualify for exemption. In particular, the chapter on the newly intro-

---

348 Commission, Decision of 21 December 1994 – IV/34.252, para. 25 – *Philips-Osram*.

349 Commission, Decision of 18 May 1994 – IV/33.640, para. 67 – *Exxon/Shell*.

350 Commission, Guidelines on Article 81(3) EC, 2004, para. 70.

351 German Federal Supreme Court 18 May 2021 – KVR 54/20, NZKart 2021, 499, 501 – *Booking.com*

352 Commission, Vertical Guidelines, 2022, para. 334.

353 ECJ 25 October 1977 – C-26/76, ECLI:EU:C:1977:100, para. 75 – *Metro*.

354 Commission, Decision of 24 January 1999 – IV.F.1/36.718, paras. 55 et seqq. – *CECED*.

2

duced category of sustainability agreements states that environmental benefits from a cartel are only relevant if consumers in the affected markets value them, meaning the benefits must matter to consumers individually.[355] In the context of the digital economy, this issue has not, as far as can be observed, played a significant role.

Fair Share for Consumers

The mere generation of efficiencies is not sufficient to justify an exemption. Rather, consumers must receive a fair share of the resulting benefits. This requirement reflects consumer welfare as an objective of European competition law.[356]

Consumers are 'users of the products covered by the agreement, including producers that use the products as an input, wholesalers, retailers and final consumers.'[357]

❗ The concept of the consumer in competition law is not identical to that in other areas of law, particularly in European private law. While there, the term 'consumer' is understood to refer to a natural person who does not act for commercial or professional purposes. In Article 101(3) TFEU, 'consumer' is defined as the **opposite side of the market** and thus includes persons other than the end consumer as defined under European private law.

Consumer participation in quantitative efficiencies can be achieved, for example, by passing on the cost savings that the cartel members realise in production through reduced sales prices.[358] In terms of qualitative efficiencies, participation gives consumers the opportunity to purchase and utilise products of a higher standard.[359]

The share received by consumers is considered 'fair' if the positive effects at least offset the negative, competition-restricting consequences of the competitive restriction.[360] Therefore, it is not necessary for the advantages to outweigh the disadvantages. In the case of qualitative efficiency gains, depending on the extent of the quality improvement of a product, an appropriate contribution can also be affirmed if the cartelists demand a higher price.[361] The key issue is to quantify the efficiencies.

Indispensability of the Restrictions

Furthermore, the restriction of competition must be indispensable for achieving the claimed efficiency gains. This requirement reflects the **principle of proportionality**.[362] It must be assessed not only whether the efficiencies could have been achieved

---

355 Commission, Horizontal Guidelines, 2023, paras. 582 et seq.
356 On further details on the consumer welfare standard as objective auf EU Competition law, see ► 2.1.3.2.
357 Commission, Guidelines on Article 81(3) EC, 2004, para. 84.
358 Commission, Guidelines on Article 81 (3) EC Treaty, 2004, para. 95.
359 Commission, Guidelines on Article 81 (3) EC Treaty, 2004, para. 102.
360 Schuhmacher and Holzweber (2025), Article 101 TFEU mn. 327.
361 Commission, Guidelines on Article 81 (3) EC Treaty, 2004, para. 102.
362 Kling and Thomas (2016), sec. 5 mn. 290.

in the absence of any restriction, but also whether less restrictive means could have produced the same result.[363] In particular, where the restriction qualifies as a hardcore restriction under a Block Exemption Regulation, there is a strong presumption that it is not indispensable for realising the stated efficiencies.[364]

▶ Example

In relation to the restrictive agreement involving narrow price parity clauses, the platform operator argued that operating its hotel booking platform created significant transparency gains, reduced accommodation prices, and lowered transaction costs for consumers.[365] However, the German Federal Supreme Court comes to the conclusion that the agreement of a narrow price parity clause is not essential for this. There are no indications that without the narrow price parity clause, there would be a competitively relevant deterioration in the range of services in the provision of the search, comparison and booking functions for end consumers or in the increase in reach for the hotels connected to the platform.[366] The free-rider problem put forward by the platform operator, according to which hotel providers would switch to advertising via the platform but conclude the actual contract via their own website, is '*only of marginal importance*' in the opinion of the German Federal Supreme Court.[367] This is because '*according to the results of the consumer survey conducted on its behalf, 99% of consumers who find accommodation for the first time on* ▶ booking.com *would also book it there.*'[368] ◀

No Elimination of Competition

An exemption is precluded if the restriction eliminates competition in a substantial part of the relevant market. This condition aims to protect the competitive process itself. In the long term, both static and dynamic efficiencies depend on effective competition, which provides incentives and direction for innovation and efficiency improvements.[369] As the Commission has emphasised, '*the ultimate aim […] is to protect the competitive process.*'[370] Moreover, if a competitor is excluded from significant parts of the market, it becomes unlikely that consumers will benefit appropriately. In such cases, the absence of sufficient competitive pressure typically reduces the incentive for cartel members to pass on efficiency gains, such as production savings, in the form of lower prices. Market share plays a central role in this assessment. The Commission generally considers an exemption to be ruled out

---

363 Commission, Guidelines on Article 81(3) EC Treaty, 2004, para. 76.
364 ECJ 7 December 2013 – C-68/12, ECLI:EU:C:2013:72, para. 35 – *Slovenská sporiteľňa.*
365 German Federal Supreme Court 18 May 2021 – KVR 54/20, NZKart 2021, 499, 504 – ▶ *Booking.com*
366 German Federal Supreme Court 18 May 2021 – KVR 54/20, NZKart 2021, 499, 504 – ▶ *Booking.com*
367 German Federal Supreme Court 18 May 2021 – KVR 54/20, NZKart 2021, 499, 505 – ▶ *Booking.com* [quote translated by author].
368 German Federal Supreme Court 18 May 2021 – KVR 54/20, NZKart 2021, 499, 505 – ▶ *Booking.com* [quote translated by author].
369 ECJ 25 October 1977 – C-26/76, ECLI:EU:C:1977:167, mn. 20 – *Metro.*
370 Commission, Guidelines on Article 81 (3) EC Treaty, 2004, para. 105.

when the parties to the agreement hold a combined market share of 50% or more.[371] Conversely, if their cumulative market share is below 30%, an exemption may be considered possible.[372]

2

Checklist: Assessing Collusive Conduct Under Article 101 TFEU

1. **Agreement, concerted practice, or decision**

an agreement between undertakings, a decision by an association of undertakings or a concerted practice.

2. **Restriction of competition**
   a) **Horizontal or vertical dimension**: Horizontal agreements occur between actual or potential competitors. Vertical agreements occur between undertakings at different levels of the supply chain (e.g. manufacturer and distributor).
   b) **By object or by effect**: The conduct must have the object or effect of preventing, restricting, or distorting competition within the internal market.
   c) **De minimis doctrine**: The restriction must be appreciable; minor restraints with negligible market impact do not fall under Article 101(1) TFEU.

3. **No exclusion from the scope of Article 101(1) TFEU**

The conduct must not fall outside the **scope of Article 101(1)** due to public interests, lack of competitive significance or pro-competitive effects (e.g., group privilege, public interest defence, doctrine of ancillary restraints)

4. **Effect on trade between Member States**

The agreement must be capable of **affecting trade between Member States**, i.e., have a cross-border dimension within the EU.

5. **No applicable exemption**
   a) **Block exemption regulations**

   Determine whether the agreement benefits from a **block exemption** (e.g. Vertical Agreements BER, R&D BER, Specialisation BER).

   b) **Individual exemption under Article 101(3) TFEU**

   All four cumulative conditions must be satisfied:

- The agreement contributes to **improving production or distribution**, or promotes **technical or economic progress**;
- Consumers receive a **fair share** of the resulting benefits;
- The restrictions are **indispensable to achieving those efficiencies**;
- The agreement does not **eliminate competition** in respect of a substantial part of the relevant market.

371 Commission, Decision of 22 December 1976 – IV/24.510, OJ [1977] L 16/8, 12 – *Gerofabriek*.
372 Ellger (2025), Article 101(3) TFEU mn. 305.

2.3 Prohibition of Abuse: Article 102 TFEU

2.3.1 Market Dominance

2.3.1.1 Market Definition

Product Market

The prohibition set out in Article 102 TFEU targets the abuse of a dominant position by undertakings. It does not apply to all undertakings, but only to those that hold a significant degree of market power. The provision aims to prevent dominant undertakings from exploiting their position in ways that harm competition or consumers.

The assessment of an undertaking's market power is conducted in relation to a **specific market**. Before examining the criteria for determining a dominant position,[373] it is essential to outline the principles of **market definition** in competition law. Market definition serves as a tool to identify the competitive constraints that limit an undertaking's commercial freedom.[374] It delineates the boundaries within which competition takes place by identifying the relevant competitors and substitutable products or services.

According to established case law, a market comprises the geographic area in which undertakings offer or demand products or services that are interchangeable or substitutable from the consumer's perspective.[375] Accordingly, markets must be defined along three dimensions:

- Product market (what is being offered),
- Geographical market (where it is being offered), and
- Temporal market (when relevant, for seasonal or time-limited markets).

The relevant product market is determined by examining **demand-side substitutability**.[376] It comprises 'the range of products that customers of the undertaking(s) involved regard as effective and immediate substitutes.'[377] This assessment must be carried out from the perspective of the demand side of the market, typically the customers in supply markets, by determining which products they consider interchangeable. To identify these substitutes, the analysis must take into account customer preferences regarding product characteristics, price, functionality, intended use, as well as any barriers to switching and associated switching costs.[378] The Commission formulates the central question in this context as follows:

373 For further details on these criteria, see ► 2.3.1.2.
374 Mestmäcker and Schweitzer (2014), sec. 17 mn. 17.
375 Legner (2023d), 175, 175.
376 GC 9 September 2009 – T-301/04, ECLI:EU:T:2009:317, para. 48 – *Clearstream*.
377 Commission, Notice on the relevant market, 2024, para. 26.
378 Commission, Notice on the relevant market, 2024, para. 26.

> *'To what extent and to what readily available substitute products (if any) the customers of the undertaking(s) involved would switch in response to a deterioration in the conditions of supply of the products of the undertaking(s) involved relative to other products?'*[379]

2

An illustrative example is the ECJ's decision in United Brands, where the Court defined the relevant product market for fresh fruit.[380] Despite the availability of other fruits such as apples, oranges, grapes, peaches, and strawberries, the Court found that bananas formed a separate product market due to their specific characteristics, such as constant availability, ease of handling, and appeal across consumer groups. '*The banana has certain characteristics, appearance, taste, softness, seedlessness, easyhandling, a constant level of production which enable it to satisfy the constant needs of an important section of the population consisting of the very young, the old and the sick.*'[381]

European case law also applies the **SSNIP test** as a quantitative method for market definition.[382] SSNIP stands for *Small but Significant Non-transitory Increase in Price.* The term already provides a useful description of the process involved in applying the SSNIP test: When carrying out the test, the first step is to assume the narrowest conceivable market in which the undertaking is hypothetically a monopolist.[383] In the event of the undertaking raising its prices slightly, but not temporarily by 5–10%, the conduct of customers is then observed. If a significant number of consumers switch to an alternative product, causing the price to increase to a level that does not generate profit for the hypothetical monopolist, the SSNIP test indicates that the substitute product also falls within the relevant market segment. The SSNIP test is repeated iteratively until a hypothetical price increase becomes profitable for a hypothetical monopolist. At that point, the boundaries of the relevant product market can be defined. The test relies on the concept of **cross-price elasticity**, which measures the degree to which the demand for one product responds to changes in the price of another. It captures the extent to which products are substitutable from the consumer's perspective based on their price interdependence.[384]

The concept of demand substitutability is complemented by the concept of **supply-side flexibility**. Under this approach, the relevant product market may also include products or services that suppliers could begin to offer without incurring significant additional costs or delays.[385] For example, if a paper manufacturer can quickly and cost-effectively switch from producing standard writing paper to high-quality paper, both types of paper may be considered part of the same relevant product market. This is because potential entry or expansion by existing producers can exert competitive pressure comparable to that of current suppliers.

379 Commission, Notice on the relevant market, 2024, para. 27.
380 ECJ 14 February 1978 – C-27/76, ECLI:EU:C:1978:22, para. 28 et seq. – *United Brands.*
381 ECJ 14 February 1978 – C-27/76, ECLI:EU:C:1978:22, para. 31 – *United Brands.*
382 Commission, Decision of 20 January 2008, COMP/M.4734, para. 95 – *Ineos/Kerling.*
383 Commission, Draft Revised Notice on the Relevant Market, 2024, paras. 29, 59 et seq.
384 Fuchs and Heinemann (2025), Article 102 TFEU mn. 61.
385 ECJ 21 February 1973 – C-6/72, ECLI:EU:C:1973:22, para. 33 – *Continental Can*; Commission 24 March 2004 – COMP/C-3/37.792, para. 334 et seq. – *Microsoft*; *Frenz*, NZKart 2013, 285, 286.

▶ Examples

In the context of the digital economy, the Commission recognises two types of **social network**: those with a private focus, such as *Facebook* and *Instagram*, and those with a professional focus, such as *LinkedIn* and *Xing*.[386] The Commission also recognises that, from a consumer's perspective, these services are not interchangeable: private social networks are used to exchange information with friends and acquaintances, while professional social networks are used to establish professional contacts, promote professional advancement, and search for career options.[387]

When defining the market for **communication applications for smartphones**, including *WhatsApp* and *Facebook Messenger*, the Commission considered how interchangeable the applications were with electronic communication services, such as voice calls, SMS, MMS and emails.[388] Although both types of service fulfil the same communication purposes, communication applications offer consumers additional functions: For example, users can see when their contacts were last online and when they last used the application.[389] There are also differences in pricing: messenger services such as *WhatsApp* are generally free of charge and are not priced based on the number of messages sent. This could be different for SMS and MMS. Messages sent to other countries, in particular, are often charged for separately despite flat-rate offers from telecommunications providers.[390] ◀

Current

The Commission has updated its approach to market definition to reflect recent developments in competition law and digital markets. The original 'Notice on the Definition of the Relevant Market for the Purposes of Community Competition Law' was published in 1997.[391] A revision process began in 2021, followed by the publication of a draft revised Notice in November 2022 and the final version in February 2024.[392] For the first time, the Commission provides guidance on the market definition for multi-sided platforms, addressing the specific challenges posed by platform-based business models.

Geographical Market

Article 9(7) EUMR provides a legal point of reference for the criteria to be taken into account when defining the geographical market.[393] According to this, the geographic market is

386 Commission, Decision of 6 December 2016, M.8124, para. 116 – *Microsoft/Linkedin*.
387 Commission, Decision of 6 December 2016, M.8124, para. 106 et seqq. – *Microsoft/Linkedin*.
388 As a result, the Commission left the market definition open, cf. Decision of 3 October 2014, COMP/M.7217, para. 33 – *Facebook/Whatsapp*.
389 Commission, Decision of 3 October 2014 – COMP/M.7217, para. 30 – *Facebook/Whatsapp*.
390 Commission, Decision of 3 October 2014 – COMP/M.7217, para. 31 – *Facebook/Whatsapp*.
391 Commission, Notice on the definition of the relevant market for the purposes of Community competition law, OJ [1997] C 372/5.
392 Commission, Notice on the definition of the relevant market for the purposes of Union competition law, OJ [2024] C/2024/1645.
393 Von der Groeben, Schwarze and Hirsbrunner (2015), Article 9 EUMR mn. 40.

> » an area in which the undertakings concerned are involved in the supply and demand of products or services, in which the conditions of competition are sufficiently homogeneous and which can be distinguished from neighbouring areas because, in particular, conditions of competition are appreciably different in those areas.

2

Case law is also based on a geographic area with '***sufficiently** homogeneous*'[394] competitive conditions. As the geographic market definition has the same objective as the product market definition, namely to identify the competitive forces acting on a given undertaking, **demand substitutability** must also be taken into account. The SSNIP test can also be applied in this context. The reference is to the geographic area: In the event of a hypothetical monopolist increasing its prices slightly but permanently, would customers then purchase the same products in a different geographic area? In the event of a positive response, the alternative geographic area is also considered to be part of the relevant market.

The relevant geographic market may be definded at various levels—local, regional, national, European or global. In instances where similar services are offered on a global scale by platform operators, a global market may be postulated. A relevant example of this phenomenon is the Commission's decision regarding the merger between *Facebook/WhatsApp*. In this decision, the Commission stated that the market for communication applications for smartphones must be defined '*EEA-wide, if not worldwide.*'[395] The Commission reached a similar conclusion regarding the market for social networking services. It observed that most social networks are available globally and that the services provided across countries or regions are broadly comparable. In particular, there were no significant differences in terms of pricing, functionality, or compatibility with operating systems that would justify a narrower geographic market definition.[396]

❗ In contrast to the Commission's view, the German Federal Cartel Office, in its *Facebook* decision, defined the relevant market for social networks as national, arguing that user preferences and competitive conditions in Germany differed sufficiently from those in other countries to warrant a national market definition.[397]

In the Commission's decision on *Google Android*, a global market for the licensing of operating systems for smart mobile devices was defined, with the exception of China. Additionally, a global market for Android app stores was delineated, also with the exception of China.[398] However, a divergent decision has been made in relation to the market for online advertisements: In view of the linguistic challenges, there is ample evidence to indicate that the markets should be delineated on a national basis.[399]

---

394 ECJ 14 February 1978 – C-27/76, ECLI:EU:C:1978:22, para. 11 – *United Brands*; GC 7 May 2009 – T-151/05, ECLI:EU:T:2009:144, para. 52 – *NVV and others*.

395 Commission, Decision of 3 October 2014, COMP/M.7217, para. 44 – *Facebook/Whatsapp*.

396 Commission, Decision of 3 October 2014 – COMP/M.7217, para. 65 – *Facebook/Whatsapp*.

397 German Federal Cartel Office, Decision of 6 February 2019, B6-22/16, para. 344 – *Facebook*.

398 Commission, Decision of 18 July 2018 – AT.40099, paras. 217 et seqq. – *Google Android*.

399 Commission, Decision of 3 October 2014 – COMP/M.7217, para. 83 – *Facebook/Whatsapp*; Commission, Decision of 18 February 2010 – COMP/M.5727, paras. 91 et seqq. – *Microsoft/Yahoo! Search Business*.

Temporal Market

The temporal market definition concerns the period in which a market exists in its product and geographic scope. It is not always necessary to define this period precisely in order to apply the prohibition of abuse.[400] Nevertheless, should market conditions undergo change in the foreseeable future, it may become necessary to ascertain the competitive forces at a certain point in time. A classic example of this phenomenon would be the sale of tickets to sporting events, such as the Olympic Games.[401] However, competitive conditions in the digital economy can also evolve rapidly if disruptive innovations create new markets or shift competitive forces.

Specifics of Digital Markets

Non-monetary Services

In digital markets, it is common for certain services to be offered to end users free of charge, that is, without requiring a direct monetary payment in exchange for access or use.

► **Examples**

Social networks that only require registration to access do not require consumers to pay money; transaction platforms (e.g. hotel booking platforms or online marketplaces) are accessible free of charge. However, there are also other business models: in the case of dating platforms or music streaming services, end users regularly have to pay to access the platform. ◄

When services are provided free of charge, particular challenges arise in defining relevant markets under competition law. A key question is whether such non-monetary service relationships can constitute a 'market' in the legal sense. Traditionally, a market is defined as a setting where goods or services are **exchanged**, where supply meets demand.[402]

However, excluding free offerings to end consumers from the definition of a relevant market is unconvincing. The provision of services at no monetary cost represents only one side of the multi-sided business models employed by platform operators. A broader perspective, one that considers all user groups involved, reveals why it can be **profit-maximizing** for platforms to offer services to end users free of charge.[403] The presence of a large and active user base enhances the attractiveness of the platform to other paying customer groups. A clear example is advertisers on social media platforms: the more end users a platform reaches, the more valuable it becomes to advertisers seeking targeted advertising opportunities. This leads advertisers to pay higher prices to access the platform's audience. These dynamics illustrate the concept of **positive indirect network effects**, where increased participation by one user group (e.g., end users) increases the value of the platform

400 Podszun (2025), sec. 18 GWB mn. 103.
401 Legner (2023d), pp. 175, 178.
402 Legner (2023d), pp. 175, 178.
403 Legner (2023d), pp. 175, 178.

for another group (e.g. advertisers).[404] Therefore, it is justified and economically sound to treat unpaid service relationships with end users as part of the relevant product market under competition law.

2 The German legislator has explicitly clarified this for German competition law in **sec. 18(2a) ARC**.[405] At EU level, the Commission takes the same view in its amended notice on market definition:

> » Zero monetary prices may be an integral part of multi-sided platforms' business strategy. The fact that a product is supplied at a zero monetary price does not imply that there is no relevant market for that product.[406]

▶ Examples

In its assessment of the *Facebook/WhatsApp* merger, the Commission correctly concluded that messenger services form part of the market for smartphone communication applications, even though they are offered free of charge.[407] This tendency was evident as early as 2010 in the Commission's *Microsoft/Yahoo*! decision[408] with regard to search engines, and was later confirmed in the *Google Shopping* decision.[409] ◀

Learning Goals

Other areas of law have also reacted to the free provision of services to end consumers. For digital contract law, **Article 3(1a) Consumer Rights Directive**[410] stipulates that the provisions for consumer contracts also apply if the consumer does not pay the undertaking a monetary price, but instead provides or undertakes to provide personal data.

When a user group receives a service free of charge, this has significant **implications for market definition**. Most notably, it precludes the application of the SSNIP test, which is traditionally used to assess substitutability based on pricing.[411] In such cases, market definition must instead rely on **non-price parameters**. This approach was evident in the Commission's *Google Shopping* decision, where it defined a market for general search services. These services are typically offered to end users at no monetary cost. In the absence of pricing data, the Commission focused on qualitative factors, particularly the intended use of the services.[412] To

---

404 On the concept of network effects, see ▶ 1.1.2.
405 For further details on sec. 18(2a) ARC, see ▶ 5.3.1.2.
406 Commission, Notice on market definition, 2024, para. 97.
407 Commission, Decision of 3 October 2014 – COMP/M.7217, paras. 20–34 – *Facebook/WhatsApp*.
408 Commission, Decision of 18 February 2010 – COMP/M.5727, para. 85 et seq. – *Microsoft/Yahoo*!
409 Commission, Decision of 27 June 2017 – AT.39740, para. 152 – *Google Search (Shopping)*: '*The fact that a product or service is provided free of charge does not prevent the offering of such a service from constituting an economic activity for the purposes of the competition rules of the Treaty.*'
410 Directive 2011/83/EU of the European Parliament and of the Council of 25 October 2011 on consumer rights, OJ [2011] L 304/64.
411 Commission, Notice on the relevant market, 2024, paras. 96–98.
412 Commission, Decision of 27 June 2017 – AT.39740, para. 163 et seqq. – *Google Search (Shopping)*.

distinguish general search services from other online offerings, such as *Wikipedia* or *IMDb*, the Commission emphasized the functional differences: general search services redirect users to external websites that contain the information sought, whereas content sites directly provide users with specific information (e.g. about a product or topic).[413] Moreover, content platforms are not suitable for broad, general-purpose searches, further underscoring their lack of substitutability with general search engines.[414]

In distinguishing between general and specialised search services, the Commission observed that specialised search services (e.g. *Shopzilla, LeGuide*, or *Idealo*) are limited to providing targeted information or shopping opportunities within a specific content category (e.g. clothing or consumer electronics).[415] In contrast, general search services are designed to retrieve information from the entire internet and to serve a much broader purpose.[416] Beyond this functional distinction, the Commission also considered differences in data sources: while general search engines index the full breadth of publicly available web content, specialised search services often rely on curated or sector-specific sources. The Commission's market definition further took into account the services' differing monetisation strategies. Unlike general search engines, which are primarily financed through advertising, specialised search services generate revenue through multiple channels, including the paid inclusion of products, service fees, and commissions. These differing business models and use cases supported the conclusion that general and specialised search services belong to distinct product markets.[417]

As a modification of the traditional SSNIP test, the Commission has proposed the **SSNDQ test** (*Small but Significant Non-transitory Decrease in Quality*) to assess substitution relationships in markets where services are provided free of charge. Under this approach, consumer behaviour is analysed in response to a hypothetical, minor but lasting deterioration in the quality of the free service.[418] The objective is to determine whether users would switch to alternative services, thereby helping to define the relevant product market. However, the SSNDQ test introduces considerable interpretive challenges. Unlike price increases, which can be measured objectively and applied uniformly, declines in quality are inherently more difficult to quantify and assess.[419] Quality is often multi-dimensional—encompassing aspects such as speed, accuracy, user interface, data protection, or ad intrusiveness—and determining the threshold of a 'significant' deterioration is inherently subjective. As a result, the application of the SSNDQ test leaves substantial room for discretion and judgment, potentially affecting the consistency and reliability of market definitions in practice.

---

413 Commission, Decision of 27 June 2017 – AT.39740, para. 164 – *Google Search (Shopping)*.
414 Commission, Decision of 27 June 2017 – AT.39740, para. 165 – *Google Search (Shopping)*.
415 Commission, Decision of 27 June 2017 – AT.39740, para. 167 – *Google Search (Shopping)*.
416 Commission, Decision of 27 June 2017 – AT.39740, para. 168 – *Google Search (Shopping)*.
417 Commission, Decision of 27 June 2017 – AT.39740, para. 168 – *Google Search (Shopping)*.
418 Commission, Notice on the relevant market, 2024, para. 98.
419 Bostoen (2023), p. 71.

2

▶ **Example**

In its decision on the *Google Android* case, the Commission defined the markets for Android app stores and app stores for other mobile operating systems based on the expected behaviour of OEMs and app developers in the event of a minor but significant deterioration in the quality of the Android app store (e.g. regarding search functions, presentation of results or update functions).[420] ◀

Multi-Sided Markets

The next step involves determining the boundaries of multi-sided markets. A key question is whether the various **user groups** interacting through a platform should be treated as part of a single relevant product market, or whether each side of the platform constitutes a distinct market of its own. The Commission approaches this issue by assessing whether the services offered by the platform operator to the different user groups are **substitutable**.[421] The decisive criterion is the degree of interchangeability from the user's perspective, which depends not only on the **characteristics of the services provided** but also on **behavioural factors**.[422] An important behavioural consideration is whether users tend to multi-home, that is, use several competing platforms simultaneously, or whether they typically concentrate their activities on a single platform. Patterns of single-homing versus multi-homing can significantly influence competitive dynamics and the appropriate definition of the relevant market.

▶ **Examples**

In some cases, separate markets must be defined for different user groups on a platform. For instance, the provision of social networking services to end users and the offering of advertising opportunities to businesses on the same platform are considered distinct markets. These services cater to different user groups and serve fundamentally different purposes. From the users' perspective, they are not substitutable: while end users engage with social networks to share content and communicate with others, advertisers use the platform as a tool to reach potential customers and drive sales. Similarly, in the context of payment systems, the Commission has identified two separate relevant product markets: one for issuing (i.e. providing payment instruments to end users) and one for acquiring (i.e. enabling merchants to accept those instruments).[423] These activities, though functionally connected, target different user groups and are not interchangeable from the perspective of either side. In contrast, in its analysis of online recruitment services, the Commission defined a single multi-sided market that includes both jobseekers and recruiters.[424] ◀

---

420 Commission, Decision of 18 July 2018 – AT.400999, para. 286 – *Google Android.*
421 Commission, Notice on the relevant market, 2024, para. 95.
422 Commission, Notice on the relevant market, 2024, para. 95.
423 Commission, Decision of 19 December 2007 – AT.34579 – *Mastercard.*
424 Commission, Decision of 6 December 2016 – M.8124 – *Microsoft/LinkedIn.*

The Commission also considers the **type of platform** to be a relevant factor in market definition. In its Notice on Market Definition, the Commission distinguishes between **transaction platforms** and **matching platforms**.[425] This classification influences whether user groups on a platform are included within a single multi-sided market or treated as participants in separate relevant product markets.

According to both the Commission and academic literature, transaction platforms (such as payment systems or online marketplaces, where users on different sides of the platform interact directly to conclude a transaction) generally justify a single market definition encompassing both user groups. The close interdependence between the sides makes it appropriate to treat them as part of one integrated market. In contrast, for non-transaction platforms (or matching platforms) where no direct transaction between user groups occurs (such as social media or search engines) the literature often supports defining separate relevant product markets for each user group.[426] This is because the services provided to each group are typically not substitutable and may serve entirely distinct economic functions.

Learning Goals

It is important to note that platform categories are not uniformly defined across jurisdictions. For example, the German Federal Cartel Office interprets the terms differently from the Commission (see ▶ 1.1.1).

2.3.1.2 Single Dominance

Concept of Market Dominance

European competition law does not provide a formal definition of market dominance. However, the concept has been clarified through case law, which has established a consolidated interpretation. According to this jurisprudence, a dominant position refers to:

> » economic strength enjoyed by an undertaking which enables it to prevent effective competition being maintained on the relevant market by affording it the power to behave to an appreciable extent independently of its competitors, its customers and ultimately of the consumers.[427]

! Two core elements characterise market dominance. First, the undertaking must be in a position to prevent effective competition in the relevant market. Second, it must possess the capacity to act independently from its competitors and the opposite side of the market.

The presence of these elements is determined by reference to a number of individual criteria. What is required is an overall assessment that demonstrates a certain degree of market power. A monopoly is not necessary. Even a significantly

425 Commission, Notice on the relevant market, 2024, para. 95.
426 Filistrucchi et al. (2014), pp. 293, 301 et seqq.
427 ECJ 13 February 1979 – C-85/76, ECLI:EU:C:1979:36, para. 38 – *Hoffmann-La Roche*.

lower market share may indicate a dominant position if further structural or behavioural factors are present that provide the undertaking with an independent scope of conduct.

2

The existence of market dominance, in itself, **is not prohibited** under Article 102 TFEU. On the contrary, European competition law recognises that an undertaking may attain such a position through superior performance. What Article 102 TFEU prohibits is the abuse of the position, in particular when the undertaking exploits the degree of autonomy associated with its dominance. The concept of market dominance is therefore a purely objective one.[428]

Criteria

Market Share

By far the most important criterion for determining market dominance is **market share**. The The ECJ assumes that market dominance may exist where an undertaking holds a market share significantly above 40%.[429] For market shares between 25% and 40%, further criteria are required to indicate independent room for condcut.[430] In contrast, a dominant position is unlikely with a market share of less than 25%.[431] In addition to absolute market share, relative market share—that is, the **gap between the undertaking's market share and that of its closest competitor**—is also a relevant factor.[432] For example, if an undertaking holds a 40% market share but competes with another undertaking of comparable size, market dominance may be excluded.

Undertakings involved in abuse cases in digital markets have frequently held very high market shares. In its *Google Shopping* decision,[433] for instance, the Commission found that *Google* held a market share exceeding 90% in the search engine market. Regarding the Android mobile operating system, the Commission assumed a market share of nearly 85% in 2014.[434] Similarly, in 2004, it found that *Microsoft* held a market share of over 90% in the market for PC operating systems.[435]

Nevertheless, it should be borne in mind that the significance of market share may be reduced in digital markets characterised by rapid and **dynamic innovation**.[436] In such environments, even competitors with relatively small market shares can exert substantial competitive pressure, limiting the extent to which a dominant undertaking can act independently. A notable example is the Commission's market dominance assessment in the *Microsoft/Skype* merger case.[437] There, the Commission argued

---

428 Jung (2025), Article 102 TFEU mn. 62.
429 ECJ 13 February 1979 – C-85/76, ECLI:EU:C:1979:36, para. 50 et seq. – *Hofmann-La Roche*.
430 Fuchs and Heinemann (2025), Article 102 TFEU mn. 128.
431 Huttenlauch (2025), Article 102 TFEU mn. 155.
432 CFI 25 March 1999 – T-102/96, ECLI:EU:T:1999:65, mn. 201 – *Gencor*.
433 Commission, Decision of 27 June 2017 – AT.39740 – *Google Search (Shopping)*.
434 Körber (2014), pp. 378, 380.
435 Commission, Decision of 24 March 2004 – COMP/C-3/37.792 – *Microsoft*.
436 Körber (2014), pp. 378, 380 et seqq.
437 GC 11 December 2013 – T-79/12, ECLI:EU:T:2013:635, para. 65 – *Cisco Systems and Messagenet*.

that a market share of 90% does not necessarily render a market unassailable. This conclusion was reached in the context of the video telephony market.

Other Criteria

Furthermore, the level of **barriers to market entry** must be taken into account when assessing market dominance.[438] Such barriers refer to the effort and resources an undertaking must invest in order to enter the market as a viable competitor. These may include substantial investments in production facilities, access to key infrastructure, or specialised technical expertise. The extent of entry barriers is closely linked to the degree of competitive pressure exerted by **potential competition**. Even undertakings that are not yet active in the market can exert a disciplinary influence on a dominant firm if market conditions suggest that new entry is likely in the near future.

In digital markets, barriers to entry may arise from the need for significant investment in research and development, or from access to data, algorithms, or network effects. However, it should also be noted that operating certain digital platforms may require relatively low investment, particularly where services are offered free of charge to end users.[439] In such cases, it is often relatively easy to attract advertising customers, which may reduce entry barriers and increase competitive pressure.

Demand elasticity is another important factor in the assessment of market dominance. If consumers are able and willing to switch to a competitor's product in response to even minor price increases, this limits an undertaking's room for manoeuvre. In such cases, buyer power can act as countervailing power to mitigate market power on the supply side. This dynamic is evident in the food sector, where large retailers, due to their significant purchasing power, are sometimes even able to dictate the conditions under which manufacturers sell their products.[440]

An undertaking's **financial strength** can also increase its scope for independent conduct, particularly when innovation and research and development are key competitive parameters in the market.[441] Additional structural factors, such as ownership links with other undertakings[442] or vertical integration along the supply chain,[443] may likewise contribute to or reinforce market dominance.

Specific Criteria in Digital Markets

In multi-sided digital markets, additional factors play a critical role in the assessment of market dominance. Among the most important are **direct and indirect network effects**.[444]

---

438 Fuchs and Heinemann (2025), Article 102 TFEU mn. 135.

439 German Federal Cartel Office, Decision of 22 October 2015 – B6-57/15, para. 186 – *online dating platform*.

440 German Federal Cartel Office, Sector enquiry into food retail, 2014; *Legner*, Schadenstheorien bei Nachfragemacht, 2019, pp. 20 et seqq.

441 Jung (2025), Article 102 TFEU mn. 101.

442 ECJ 9 November 1983 – C322/81, ECLI:EU:C:1983:313, para. 55 – *Michelin*.

443 ECJ 14 February 1978 – C-27/76, ECLI:EU:C:1978:22, para. 69/71 – *United Brands*.

444 For further details on the concept of network effects, see ► 1.1.2.

2

Learning Goals

- **Direct network effects** occur among users within the same group.[445] The value of a platform increases for each user as the number of other users from that group grows. A common example is social media platforms, sharing texts, photos, or videos becomes more meaningful as more users are available to view and interact with the content.
- **Indirect network effects** arise from interactions between different user groups. For example, the attractiveness of a social network to advertisers increases with the number of active private users. This is an instance of a positive indirect network effect. However, negative indirect effects are also possible, for instance, if a growing number of advertisers diminishes the user experience for private users.[446]

Where direct network effects are strong, users are likely to gravitate toward platforms that already have a large user base. This can significantly raise barriers to entry. New entrants, such as a rival social network, may struggle to gain market traction, as users prefer platforms that already offer access to a broad and active community.

An important factor in this context is whether users are willing to use multiple services simultaneously, a behaviour known as **multi-homing**. If consumers generally do not engage in multi-homing, this tends to strengthen the market power of the incumbent platform operator. The willingness to multi-home often depends on the switching costs involved.[447] For example, users of social networks cannot easily transfer their contacts and data from one platform to another, creating significant **lock-in effects**.[448]

Access to competition-relevant data can also confer substantial market power. By analysing user data, undertakings can tailor their offerings to better meet consumer preferences. Unlike physical goods, data is essentially non-rivalrous, meaning that its use by one firm does not diminish its availability to others. Therefore, it is particularly the advantage in access to data that can translate into market power. Firms with superior data access are better positioned to understand consumer behaviour and to provide customised services or to innovate accordingly.[449] Economies of scope may arise when an undertaking operates multiple platform services and integrates data across them.

Finally, **innovation-driven competitive pressure** in digital markets can affect the relevance of market share thresholds in the dominance assessment.[450] Historical developments in digital markets demonstrate that disruptive innovations can repeatedly emerge, reshaping competitive dynamics and displacing firms that previously held significant market power.

---

445 Körber (2025a), Article 2 EUMR mn. 24b.

446 German Federal Cartel Office 23 November 2017 – B6-35/17, para. 70 – *CTS EVENTIM/Medusa Music/Four Artists*.

447 Article 7 DMA, which aims to promote *multi-homing* for messenger services. For further details, see ► 3.3.3.

448 Podszun and Schwalbe (2017), pp. 98, 100.

449 Tamke (2018), pp. 503, 507.

450 Tamke (2018), pp. 503, 507.

2.3.1.3 Collective Dominance

A market may also be dominated by two or more undertakings. In such cases, these undertakings are considered to hold collective dominance. Although Article 102 TFEU does not expressly define this concept, it has been developed through case law, most notably on the basis of the so-called **Airtours criteria**.[451]

The assessment of **external stability** focuses primarily on the undertakings' combined market share. In this context, the criteria used for assessing individual dominance, such as market shares, barriers to entry, and countervailing buyer power, are relevant. To determine the absence of internal competition, it must be examined whether the market is sufficiently transparent and whether there are deterrence mechanisms to sustain coordination. Market **transparency** allows undertakings to monitor the pricing behaviour of their rivals.[452] This is particularly likely in markets where homogeneous products are sold and pricing is easily observable. A well-known example is the petrol station market, where prices are displayed publicly and in real time. In such settings, undertakings may align their conduct based on market signals, a phenomenon often referred to as tacit coordination. This form of coordination does not require any direct contact between undertakings and thus does not constitute a violation of Article 101 TFEU, but may nonetheless amount to an abuse under Article 102 TFEU if collective dominance is established.

Maintaining a collusive equilibrium requires effective coordination and discipline among firms. Each undertaking inherently faces a temptation to deviate from this equilibrium by slightly undercutting the collusive price to capture a larger market share and boost individual profits. However, such deviations can be **deterred** if undertaking adopt mechanisms to 'punish' non-compliance, thereby reinforcing the stability of the collusion. One common enforcement mechanism is the **tit-for-tat strategy**: when a firm lowers its price to break the agreement, competitors respond by also reducing their prices. This retaliation diminishes the profitability of deviation, making it less attractive for any single undertaking to disrupt the collusive arrangement.

Learning Goals

A collective dominant position, in itself, is not prohibited under competition law. Article 102 TFEU only addresses the abuse of such a position, not its mere existence. Similarly, implicit collusion does not automatically fall within the scope of Article 101 TFEU. For conduct to qualify as a concerted practice under Article 101 TFEU, there must be some form of coordination or understanding between undertakings. Mere parallel behaviour resulting from market transparency or interdependence does not meet this threshold.[453]

To date, collective dominance **has played a limited role in platform markets**. The multi-sided nature of these markets complicates coordination, as any form of

---

451 GC 6 June 2002 – T-342/99, ECLI:EU:T:2002:146 – *Airtours*.
452 Legner (2014), pp. 1, 3.
453 For the difference on concerted practices and tacit collusion, see ► 2.2.1.3.

implicit collusion would need to occur simultaneously across multiple market sides. Nonetheless, the growing use of algorithms may enhance market transparency, particularly on the downstream side, thereby increasing the likelihood and stability of collusive equilibria. In light of these developments, there is an ongoing debate within the context of cartel prohibition as to whether certain forms of tacit collusion should also be subject to legal sanction in the future, particularly when they result in reduced consumer welfare.[454]

2.3.2 Abuse

2.3.2.1 Exclusionary Abuses

General Principles

A dominant undertaking is prohibited from **unfairly impeding** its competitors. This restriction stems from the recognition that competition in the market is already weakened due to the dominant undertaking's significant scope for unilateral conduct.[455] While a dominant undertaking is permitted to pursue profit maximisation and benefit from efficiencies, not every adverse effect on competitors arising from its conduct constitutes an abuse of dominance. Classifying all such effects as abusive would, in effect, prohibit dominance itself—an outcome that is incompatible with Article 102 TFEU.

However, a dominant undertaking must not use its market power to impair genuine competition through '*methods different from those which condition normal competition in products or services.*'[456] In this context, the dominant firm is subject to a '*special responsibility*'[457] to preserve the competitive structure of the market. The concept of abuse under Article 102 TFEU is interpreted objectively, meaning that a finding of abuse does not require proof of intent to exclude competitors. In legal practice, the broad and undefined notion of abuse has been clarified through the development of distinct categories.

> **!** A useful starting point for the case-by-case assessment of abusive conduct is the general principle that both the interests of the parties involved and the protective purpose of Article 102 TFEU must be taken into account. The central aim of Article 102 TFEU is to safeguard the freedom of competition, rather than to protect individual competitors as such.[458]

In principle, the greater the market power of a dominant undertaking, the more constrained it is in terms of permissible conduct. There is a direct relationship between the degree of dominance and the allowed scope of conduct. For example,

454 For further details on this discussion, see ▶ 2.2.1.3.
455 ECJ 6 September 2017 – C-413/14 P, ECLI:EU:C:2017:632, para. 134 – *Intel.*
456 ECJ 13 February 1979–85/76, ECLI:EU:C:1979:36, para. 91 – *Hoffmann-La Roche.*
457 ECJ 6 September 2017 – C-413/14 P, ECLI:EU:C:2017:632, para. 135 – *Intel.*
458 Fuchs and Heinemann (2025), Article 102 TFEU mn. 255.

an undertaking with a market share just above the dominance threshold (e.g. 40%) will generally have more leeway than a quasi-monopolist, whose near-total control of the market significantly limits acceptable forms of competitive behaviour.

In recent years, European case law has increasingly embraced an **effects-based approach** to the enforcement of Article 102 TFEU. This approach requires the Commission to demonstrate the anticompetitive effects of the conduct in question, moving away from a previously dominant form-based approach, which focused more on the formal characteristics of the conduct itself. The courts now demand a more rigorous economic assessment, requiring evidence of how the behaviour in question restricts competition or harms consumer welfare.

► Example

A clear illustration of the shift from a form-based to an effects-based approach in the application of Article 102 TFEU is found in the evolving treatment of loyalty rebates. Under earlier case law, such as *Hoffmann-La Roche*, loyalty rebates granted by a dominant undertaking, i.e. discounts conditioned on customers purchasing all or a large proportion of their needs exclusively from the dominant firm, were considered abusive *per se*.[459] This meant that the conduct was deemed unlawful irrespective of its actual effects on the market or competitors.

However, this formalistic approach was significantly revised by the ECJ in its 2017 ruling in the *Intel* case.[460] The Court held that, where a dominant undertaking submits evidence that its rebate scheme was not capable of restricting competition, the Commission is required to conduct a detailed analysis of the scheme's actual or potential exclusionary effects. In particular, the Court emphasised the need to assess the potential for foreclosure or crowding out of equally efficient competitors.[461] ◄

The **as-efficient competitor test** has gained increasing significance in assessing whether the conduct of a dominant undertaking has exclusionary effects under Article 102 TFEU.[462] The central question is whether the conduct is capable of excluding a competitor that is as efficient as the dominant undertaking itself.[463] The underlying rationale is that EU competition law is intended to protect the competitive process, not individual competitors per se. Accordingly, it does not shield less efficient firms from market exit; such outcomes are considered a natural consequence of effective competition.[464] The test serves as a benchmark to distinguish between legitimate competition on the merits and unlawful exclusionary practices. If a rival that operates as efficiently as the dominant undertaking cannot compete effectively under the conditions imposed by the dominant firm's conduct (e.g. pricing practices or rebate schemes), this may indicate an abuse of dominance.

459 ECJ 13 February 1979 – C-85/76, ECLI:EU:C:1979:36, para. 89 – *Hoffmann-La Roche*.
460 ECJ 6 September 2017 – C-413/14 P, ECLI:EU:C:2017:632 – *Intel*. *See* Legner (2023b), pp. 26, 31.
461 ECJ 6 September 2017 – C-413/14 P, ECLI:EU:C:2017:632, para. 140 – *Intel*.
462 Rohner (2023), pp. 67 et seq.
463 ECJ 27 March 2012 – C-209/10, ECLI:EU:C:2012:172, para. 21 – *Post Danmark*.
464 Barthelmeß (2014), pp. 492, 493.

2

However, the evidentiary threshold for applying the as-efficient competitor test is high. The Commission must present robust economic analysis demonstrating the likely foreclosure effects on efficient rivals. In recent years, several Commission decisions imposing fines under Article 102 TFEU[465] have been annulled or overturned by the EU courts due to insufficient or flawed impact assessments.[466] This trend reflects the judiciary's growing insistence on rigorous, effects-based reasoning in abuse of dominance cases.

European case law recognise a possibility for dominant undertakings to justify potentially abusive conduct under Article 102 TFEU through an **efficiency defence**.[467] This defence is not expressly provided for in the Treaty but has been acknowledged by the courts. The requirements of the efficiency defence are similar to those set out in Article 101(3) TFEU.[468] To succeed, the dominant undertaking must demonstrate that any anti-competitive foreclosure effects are **at least counterbalanced by efficiency gains**. These efficiencies must be passed on to consumers, and the conduct in question must be indispensable to achieving them, i.e. there must be no less restrictive alternative. In addition, the conduct must not eliminate all effective competition.[469]

The requirements for invoking this defence are stringent, and the burden of proof lies entirely with the dominant undertakings. It must provide detailed and substantiated evidence demonstrating the necessity, proportionality, and consumer benefits of the conduct. Given the high evidentiary bar, the efficiency defence has played a limited role in practice so far. Whether it will become a meaningful component of abuse of dominance proceedings remains an open question.[470]

❗ The assessment of abusive conduct under Article 102 TFEU follows a two-stage approach. First, the conduct must be examined to determine whether it constitutes an abuse, with particular attention to its actual or potential effects on competition. If the conduct is found to be abusive, the second stage involves assessing whether the undertaking can justify its behaviour, typically by demonstrating efficiency gains that outweigh the anti-competitive effects. This justification must meet strict criteria, and the burden of proof lies with the dominant undertaking.

To provide greater legal certainty for undertakings, the Commission published in 2008 its Guidance on the Commission's **enforcement priorities** in applying

---

465 For further details on the enforcement, see ► 2.5.

466 ECJ 6 September 2017 – C-413/14 P, ECLI:EU:C:2017:632 – *Intel*; GC 15 June 2022 – T-235/18, ECLI:EU:T:2022:358 – *Qualcomm*; GC 14 September 2022 – T-604/18, ECLI:EU:T:2022:541 – *Google Android*.

467 ECJ 15 March 2007 – C-95/04 P, ECLI:EU:C:2007:166, para. 69 – *British Airways*; ECJ 17 February 2011 – C-52/09, ECLI:EU:C:2011:83, para. 76 – *TeliaSonera*; ECJ 27 March 2012 – C-209/10, ECLI:EU:C:2012:172, para. 40 f. – *Post Danmark*.

468 For further details on the criteria under Article 101(3) TFEU, see ► 2.2.5.

469 ECJ 15 March 2007 – C-95/04 P, ECLI:EU:C:2007:166, para. 86 – *British Airways*.

470 Brand (2025), Article 102 TFEU mn. 159; Fuchs and Heinemann (2025), Article 102 TFEU mn. 214: '*Overall, the impression arises that the addition of an 'efficiency defence'to the objective justification of potentially abusive conduct in the context of the abuse offence is more rhetorical than substantive*' [quote translated by author].

Article 82 EC (now Article 102 TFEU) concerning exclusionary conduct by dominant undertakings.[471] For the first time, the Commission now plans to adopt **guidelines on Article 102 TFEU**.[472] Already at the end of 2023, it issued an **amendment to the 2008 enforcement priorities**,[473] and in 2024, it presented a draft of the 'Guidelines on the application of Article 102 of the Treaty on the Functioning of the European Union to abusive exclusionary conduct by dominant undertakings'.[474] The draft indicates a partial departure from the previously dominant more economic approach. The final content of the guidelines remains to be seen.

The following section examines selected categories of exclusionary abuse based on European case law, with a particular focus on examples from digital markets. In recent years, several high-profile abuse proceedings have been initiated against dominant digital undertakings. This trend is unsurprising, given that digital markets often exhibit structural features—such as strong network effects, high barriers to entry, and data-driven lock-in effects[475]—that tend to entrench market power. As a result, the prohibition of abuse under Article 102 TFEU has gained particular practical relevance in the digital economy. However, the types of abusive conduct discussed below are not unique to digital markets. Many of the case groups were originally developed in more traditional sectors and continue to be of broad relevance across different industries. The aim is therefore to illustrate both the continuity and the specific challenges of applying established abuse categories in the evolving context of digital markets.[476]

Exclusive Agreements

In addition to the prohibition of anti-competitive agreements under Article 101 TFEU, Article 102 TFEU also imposes legal limits on **exclusive purchasing agreements**. When a dominant undertaking enters into such agreements with its customers, they often result in significant market foreclosure due to the undertaking's typically high market share. Even relatively short contract durations can be problematic: case law has held that exclusive agreements with terms as short as 2 years may constitute abusive foreclosure.[477] More recent decisions by the Commission have required dominant undertakings to refrain from concluding exclusive con-

---

471 Communication from the Commission, Guidance on the Commission's enforcement priorities in applying Article 82 of the EC Treaty to abusive exclusionary conduct by dominant undertakings, OJ [2009] C 45/7.

472 https://germany.representation.ec.europa.eu/news/kartellrecht-kommission-kundigt-leitlinien-zu-behinderungsmissbrauch-und-andert-erlauterungen-zu-2023-03-27_de (accessed 24 June 2024). *See* Higer (2023), p. 385.

473 Amendment to the Commission Notice – Clarifications on the Commission's priorities in the application of Article 82 of the EC Treaty to exclusionary conduct by dominant undertakings, OJ [2023] C 116/1.

474 < https://competition-policy.ec.europa.eu/public-consultations/2024-article-102-guidelines_en > (accessed 5 September 2025).

475 For further details on these criteria, see ► 2.3.1.2.

476 One exception may be the case of self-preferencing, a case group that is currently primarily associated with digital markets.

477 ECJ 13 February 1979 – C-85/76, ECLI:EU:C:1979:36, para. 89 – *Hoffmann-La Roche*

2

tracts exceeding 5 years, reflecting a stricter enforcement stance. These restrictions aim to ensure that competing undertakings retain effective access to the market.[478]

In the digital economy, the *Google Search (AdSense)* case[479] serves as a prominent example of alleged abusive exclusive dealing. According to the Commission, *Google* made its online advertising intermediation platform, *AdSense for Search*, available to website operators (referred to as 'publishers'), enabling them to display search-based advertisements and connect with advertisers. However, the Commission found that *Google* had imposed contractual restrictions on these publishers that limited the ability of competing search advertising providers to place ads on the same websites. These exclusivity clauses, in the Commission's view, unduly restricted market access for rivals and thereby constituted an abuse of dominance under Article 102 TFEU.[480] However, in September 2024, the GC annulled the Commission's decision, citing insufficient reasoning in the assessment of competitive effects.[481]

In its 2018 decision in the *Google Android* case, the Commission found that *Google* had engaged in exclusionary conduct by linking revenue-sharing agreements with mobile device manufacturers to exclusivity conditions.[482] Specifically, manufacturers would only receive a portion of *Google's* advertising revenue if they refrained from pre-installing competing general search services. The Commission considered this to have a foreclosure effect on rival search providers and thus to constitute an abuse of dominance under Article 102 TFEU. However, in 2022, the GC annulled this part of the decision.[483] The Court ruled that the Commission had failed to consider all relevant factual and economic circumstances in its assessment of the alleged foreclosure effects, and thus had not met the evidentiary standard required under the effects-based approach.

A similar outcome occurred in the *Qualcomm* case,[484] where the Commission had imposed a fine on *Qualcomm* for making incentive payments to *Apple*, allegedly inducing *Apple* to purchase LTE chipsets exclusively from *Qualcomm*. The Commission considered these payments to be de facto exclusivity arrangements with anti-competitive effects. However, the GC annulled the decision, again citing deficiencies in the Commission's impact analysis.[485]

These cases reflect the growing influence of the more economic approach in abuse of dominance law cases.[486] Under this approach, exclusivity arrangements are not condemned per se but must be assessed based on their actual or likely effects on competition.

---

478 Commission, Decision of 11 October 2007 – COMP/B-1/37966, para. 27 – *Distrigaz*.
479 Commission, Decision of 20 March 2019 – AT.40411 – *Google Search (Adsense)* (annulled by GC 18 September 2024 – T-334/19 P, ECLI:EU:T:2024:634 – *Google AdSense for Search*).
480 Commission, Decision of 20 March 2019 – AT.40411, para. 329 et seq. – *Google Search (Adsense)*.
481 GC 18 September 2024 – T-334/19 P, ECLI:EU:T:2024:634 – *Google AdSense for Search*.
482 Commission, Decision of 18 July 2018 – AT.40099, paras. 1188 et seq. – *Google Android*.
483 GC 14 September 2022 – T-604/18, ECLI:EU:T:2022:541, paras. 698 et seq. – *Google Android*.
484 Commission, Decision of 24 January 2018 – AT.40220 – *Qualcomm*.
485 GC 15 June 2022 – T-235/18, ECLI:EU:T:2022:358 – *Qualcomm*.
486 On further details on the more economic approach, see ► 2.1.2.

Refusal to Supply

A refusal to supply by a dominant undertaking may, under certain conditions, constitute unjustified discrimination within the meaning of **Article 102 2nd sentence (c) TFEU**. This provision prohibits a dominant undertaking from applying dissimilar conditions to equivalent transactions with other trading parties, thereby placing them at a competitive disadvantage.

As a general principle, even a dominant undertaking retains the freedom to choose its contractual partners. However, in exceptional circumstances, Article 102 TFEU may impose a duty to supply or to continue a commercial relationship.[487] The key consideration in assessing the abusiveness of a refusal to supply is whether the affected trading partners have viable alternative sources of supply. The greater their dependency on the dominant undertaking, the more likely it is that a refusal will be deemed abusive. The assessment therefore requires a **comprehensive balancing of interests**, taking into account the dominant undertaking's freedom of contract, the competitive structure of the market, and the potential exclusionary effects of the refusal. A particularly significant subset of refusal-to-supply cases is captured under the essential facilities doctrine. This doctrine applies where the dominant undertaking controls an infrastructure or input that is indispensable for effective competition in a downstream market and where denying access would eliminate that competition.

Online platforms often possess significant market power. Even if they do not qualify as essential facilities, each case must be assessed individually to determine whether a refusal to initiate or continue business relations constitutes an abuse of dominance under Article 102 TFEU. This is particularly relevant in the context of search engines or social networks, which in some cases hold market shares exceeding 90%.[488] Such high levels of concentration can result in substantial dependency for commercial users, including advertisers and retailers.[489] Where a platform delists or blocks access to these users, it can severely impair their ability to reach end consumers. In such cases, the impact on market access and competition must be carefully examined, and the platform's conduct may be subject to stricter scrutiny under the abuse of dominance framework.

▶ Example

In its 2004 decision in the *Microsoft* case,[490] the Commission (upheld in principle by the GC in 2007[491]), found that Microsoft had abused its dominant position in the market for PC operating systems by refusing to disclose interoperability information to competing suppliers of workgroup server operating systems. The Commission held that access to this information was indispensable for rivals to develop interoperable products and compete effectively. Microsoft's refusal was found to hinder innovation and limit consumer choice. ◀

---

487 Paal (2025), Article 102 TFEU mn. 41.
488 See Paal (2025), Article 102 TFEU mn. 42b.
489 Bostoen (2023), p. 161.
490 Commission, Decision of 24 March2004 – COMP/C-3/37.792 – *Microsoft*.
491 GC 17 September 2007 – T-201/04, ECLI:EU:T:2007:289 – *Microsoft*.

Self-Preferencing

2

In the ***Google Shopping*** case, the ECJ found that the dominant search engine operator had abused its market dominance by favouring itself.[492] According to the court's findings, *Google* had placed its own price comparison service *Google Search* at a higher position in the search results in order to encourage search engine users to use it. In contrast, the search engine ranked competing price comparison services in less prominent positions, which meant that users rarely visited these websites. Practices of self-preferencing can be realised by market dominators who offer an intermediary service (here: search engine) at an upstream market level and at the same time compete with commercial users (here: offer of a price comparison service) at a downstream market level. According to the GC, the abuse consists in the fact that

> 'Google was relying on its dominant position on the market for general search services in order to favour its own comparison shopping service on the market for specialised comparison shopping search services by promoting the positioning and display of that comparison shopping service and of its results on its general results pages, as compared to competing comparison shopping services, whose results, given their inherent characteristics, were prone to being demoted on those pages by adjustment algorithms.'[493]

The ECJ affirmed this point of view.[494] Self-preferencing does not fall into one of the previously recognised categories of abuse of market power. In particular, the ECJ did not consider the *Google Shopping* case to fall under the essential facilities doctrine.[495] Rather, there are certain parallels to discrimination, among other things. This is because self-preferential treatment consists of treating one's own services or products better than comparable offers from competitors.[496] However, it is doubtful whether the standard example of Article 102 2nd sentence (c) TFEU can be applied. According to this provision, the market dominator must apply different conditions for equivalent services to trading partners. In the case of self-preferencing, however, it is a matter of different conditions compared to its own range of services.[497] According to the GC, self-preferencing is an '***independent form of leveraging abuse***.'[498] A dominant undertaking is not per se prohibited from extending its market power to other markets by means of leverage. Specific circumstances must be present so that the conduct can no longer be assessed as an expression of competition on the merits. The GC affirmed such specific circumstances

---

492 ECJ 10 September 2024 – C-48/22 P, ECLI:EU:C:2024:726 – *Google Shopping* (see also the decisions of the previous instances: GC 10 November 2021 – T-612/17, ECLI:EU:T:2021:763 – *Google Shopping*; Commission, Decision of 27 June 2017 – AT.39740 – *Google Search (Shopping)*.).
493 GC 10 November 2021 – T-612/17, ECLI:EU:T:2021:763, para. 167 – *Google Shopping*.
494 ECJ 10 September 2024 – C-48/22 P, ECLI:EU:C:2024:726, paras. 157 et seqq. – *Google Shopping*.
495 ECJ 10 September 2024 – C-48/22 P, ECLI:EU:C:2024:726, paras. 118 – *Google Shopping*.
496 Bostoen (2023), p. 97.
497 Akmann (2017), pp. 302, 330 et seq.
498 GC 10 November 2021 – T-612/17, ECLI:EU:T:2021:763, para. 240 – *Google Shopping*.

and emphasised that '*the rationale and value of a general search engine lie in its capacity to be open to results from external (third-party) sources and to display these multiple and diverse sources on its general results page*'.[499] The reasoning suggests that the courts evaluate the self-preferencing practice conducted by Google as abusive conduct specifically designed for general search services. This calls for caution when drawing conclusions for the assessment of self-preferential practices with regard to other intermediary services.[500]

European competition authorities are increasingly scrutinizing self-preferential practices in digital markets. In the *Amazon Buy Box* case, the Commission examined the criteria used to allocate the so-called Buy Box, a prominent feature that allows consumers to easily purchase products with a single click.[501] Winning the Buy Box significantly enhances a retailer's visibility and sales potential. The investigation concluded with commitments from *Amazon*, in which the company pledged, among other things, to ensure equal treatment of all sellers when determining *Buy Box* allocation.

In September 2025, the Commission fined *Google* for self-preferential treatment of its own online display advertising technology service *AdX*.[502] In the Commission's view, *Google's* self-preferencing serves to give its own service a competitive advantage and to squeeze out competing services. *AdX* is an online display advertising technology service where content providers and advertisers negotiate the purchase of display advertising.

Article 6(5) DMA explicitly prohibits gatekeepers from engaging in self-preferencing in rankings, requiring instead that ranking be carried out on transparent, fair, and non-discriminatory terms. Unlike dominant undertakings under Article 102 TFEU, gatekeepers under the DMA are not permitted to justify discriminatory conduct based on efficiencies or other defences.[503]

By contrast, **Article 7 Platform Regulation** addresses self-preferencing more narrowly. It imposes transparency obligations on providers of online intermediation services and online search engines but does not prohibit self-preferencing itself. As a result, such conduct remains permissible under that regulation, provided it is disclosed appropriately.[504]

Rebates

In the analysis of potentially abusive rebate schemes under Article 102 TFEU, it is essential to distinguish between various types of rebates. **Quantity rebates** and **functional rebates** are generally permissible.[505] These forms of rebates reflect genuine efficiency gains achieved by the dominant undertaking, which are then passed

499 GC 10 November 2021 – T-612/17, ECLI:EU:T:2021:763, para. 178 – *Google Shopping*.
500 Achleitner (2022), pp. 253, 260.
501 Commission, Decision of 20 December 2022 – AT.40703 – *Amazon Buy Box*.
502 Commission, Decision of 5 September 2025 – AT.40670 – *Google - Adtech and Data-related practices*.
503 For further details on Article 6(5) DMA, see ► 3.3.2.4.
504 For further details on Article 7 Platform Regulation, see ► 4.3.4.
505 Kling and Thomas (2016), sec. 6 mn. 168 et seq.

on to customers. Because these discounts are tied to cost savings, they are typically unobjectionable from a competition law perspective.

2

By contrast, **loyalty rebates** (also referred to as fidelity rebates) are granted on the condition that a customer sources all or a significant portion of its requirements exclusively or predominantly from the dominant undertaking. The intention behind such rebates is to 'reward' customer loyalty and secure continued patronage. Since the ECJ's landmark judgment in ***Hoffmann-La Roche***, loyalty rebates have been regarded as inherently anti-competitive and thus abusive per se.[506] They were presumed to restrict competition by their very nature. However, the ECJ revised this strict approach in its 2017 ruling in ***Intel***. In that case, the Court held that the classification of loyalty rebates as abusive requires an effects-based analysis.[507] Specifically, it must be assessed whether the rebate scheme is capable of excluding a competitor that is as efficient as the dominant undertaking. This evaluation necessitates a case-by-case assessment of the actual or potential market effects of the rebate. Relevant factors to consider include the conditions under which the rebate is granted;[508] the duration of the rebate scheme; and the magnitude of the rebate offered.[509]

Similarly, **target rebates**, which are contingent upon the customer reaching pre-agreed sales or volume thresholds, must also be assessed in light of their competitive effects.[510] Although structurally different from loyalty rebates, target rebates may raise comparable concerns. As with loyalty rebates, determining whether they are abusive requires a comprehensive examination of all relevant circumstances in the specific case.[511] In particular, it is necessary to examine whether a competitor that is just as efficient as the market dominator is forced out of the market by the rebate practice.

Tying and Bundling

Abusive tying is addressed under **Article 102 2nd sentence (d) TFEU**. According to this provision, a dominant undertaking may not make the sale of one product conditional upon the purchase of another product or service that is neither connected to the main product by necessity nor justified by commercial usage.

▶ Example

A dominant undertaking offers a software licence only on the condition that the customer also purchases specific hardware from it. In this scenario, the hardware is the tied product, while the software licence constitutes the tying product. ◀

506 ECJ 13 February 1979–85/79, ECLI:EU:C:1979:36, para. 89 – *Hoffmann-La Roche*.
507 ECJ 6 September 2017 – C-413/14 P, ECLI:EU:C:2017:632, para. 138 et seqq. – *Intel*.
508 ECJ 6 September 2017 – C-413/14 P, ECLI:EU:C:2017:632, para. 136 – *Intel*.
509 ECJ 6 September 2017 – C-413/14 P, ECLI:EU:C:2017:632, para. 138 et seqq. – *Intel*.
510 Griem (2022), pp. 119, 120.
511 GC 17 June 2014 – T-286/09, ECLI:EU:T:2014:547 – *Intel*.

The first step in assessing the legality of such a practice is to identify the tying and tied products and determine whether they are **separate products**.[512] This requires showing that there is independent demand for each product. Typically, the **tying product** belongs to the market in which the undertaking holds a dominant position. In contrast, bundling refers to practices where consumers can only purchase two or more products as a package.[513]

The rationale behind the prohibition of abusive tying and bundling is to prevent a dominant firm from **leveraging its market power** in one market to gain a competitive advantage (or even dominance) in another, thereby distorting competition. Such practices can lead to market foreclosure, as competing suppliers of the tied product may be excluded from the market.[514]

In the *Microsoft* case, the Commission found that the undertakings had abused its dominant position by tying its *Windows* operating system with its media player.[515] The GC upheld the Commission's decision and emphasised that *Windows Media Player* benefits from '*the ubiquity of that operating system on client PCs, which cannot be counterbalanced by the other methods of distributing media players*'[516] In the *Google Android* case, the Commission criticised the undertaking not only for an exclusivity obligation[517] but also for bundling its mobile apps and services. According to the Commission's findings, the dominant firm required mobile device manufacturers to pre-install its general search app and web browser as a condition for obtaining a licence to use its app store.[518]

Tying practices may be **objectively justified**, particularly where technical necessity can be demonstrated. However, in the *Microsoft* decision, the GC rejected such justification, finding no technical necessity for the integration of the media player with the operating system.[519] Similarly, in the *Google Android* case, the Court found that the company had not demonstrated that it could recoup the costs of developing and maintaining its services through the tying arrangement.[520]

Current

In June 2024, the Commission initiated formal proceedings against *Microsoft* to investigate potential anticompetitive tying practices involving its *Teams* platform, according to an official press release.[521]

---

512 Glöckner (2021), sec. 6, mn. 623.

513 Steinvorth (2020), § 20, mn. 150.

514 ECJ 14 November 1996 – C-333/94 P, ECLI:EU:C:1996:436, para. 27 et seqq. – *Tetra Pak II*; Mestmäcker and Schweitzer (2014), sec. 18, mn. 32.

515 Commission, Decision of 24 March 2004 – COMP/C-3/37.792 – *Microsoft.*

516 ECJ 17 September 2007 – T-201/04, ECLI:EU:T:2007:289, para. 1036 – *Microsoft.*

517 For further details on this part of the case, see ► 2.3.2.1.2.

518 GC 14 September 2022 – T-604/18, ECLI:EU:T:2022:541, para. 274 et seqq. – *Google Android*; Commission 18 July 2018 – AT.40099, para. 714 et seqq. – *Google Android.*

519 GC 17 September 2007 – T-201/04, ECLI:EU:T:2007:289, para. 1098 – *Microsoft.*

520 GC 14 September 2022 – T-604/18, ECLI:EU:T:2022:541, para. 614 – *Google Android.*

521 Commission AT.4073 – *Microsoft Teams II* (proceedings initiated on 25 June 2024), ► https://ec.europa.eu/commission/presscorner/detail/de/ip_24_3446 (5 September 2025).

2

Essential Facilities Doctrine

A dominant undertaking may abuse its market position by denying competitors access to essential facilities. This concept is known as the essential facilities doctrine. The term 'facility' is interpreted broadly and may encompass not only physical infrastructure but also products, services, intellectual property, or information.[522] A facility is considered essential only if it constitutes a non-replicable resource that is indispensable for access to a related upstream or downstream market.[523] The threshold for asserting an access claim is intentionally high, as the doctrine significantly limits the dominant undertaking's rights of ownership and freedom of contract.[524] Moreover, an undertaking is, as a rule, not required to facilitate the business activities of its competitors.[525] Consequently, the ECJ recognizes such intervention only under '*exceptional circumstances*'[526] where a refusal to grant access amounts to an abuse of dominance.

Historically, the Commission has applied the essential facilities doctrine to compel access to key infrastructure, such as ports, requiring operators to accommodate competing ferry services.[527] The doctrine has also gained significant relevance in sectors like energy, telecommunications, and transport, where control over critical infrastructure can effectively limit market access.[528]

The case law of the ECJ has clarified the requirements of the essential facilities doctrine through the **Bronner criteria**. These criteria establish a high threshold for demonstrating that a facility is essential.[529] A key requirement is that the facility must be non-duplicable and that all competitors rely on it to access a specific market.[530] Furthermore, access must be **indispensable** for the competitor's ability to operate in that market. To assess this, it must be examined whether it is economically viable for the competitor to enter the market by alternative means.[531] This analysis is based on the perspective of a competitor with sales volumes comparable to those of the dominant undertaking, not a smaller or less efficient rival.

In the context of digital markets, the question arises whether **search engines** can be classified as essential facilities. Applying the Bronner criteria, a dominant search engine operator could, in theory, be found to abuse its position if it unjustifiably excludes competitors from its index or penalizes rival services in search result rankings.[532] However, there are strong arguments against applying the essential facilities doctrine to search engines. Under *Bronner*, only facilities that constitute the only viable means of accessing a market fall within the doctrine's scope. Despite *Google*'s

---

522 Deselaers (2025), Article 102 TFEU, mn. 466.
523 Hoffmann (2025), sec. 28, mn. 105.
524 Eilmannsberger and Bien (2023), Article 102 TFEU, mn. 341.
525 Körber (2012), pp. 761, 765 et seq.
526 ECJ 6 April 1995 – C-241/91 P and others, ECLI:EU:C:1995:98, para. 50 – *RTE and ITP*.
527 Commission, Decision of 21 December 1993, IV/34.689 – *Sea Containers v. Stena Sealink*; Commission v. 21 December 1993–94/119/EC – *Port of Rodby*.
528 Commission, Decision of 3 December 2009 – COMP/39.316, para. 37–40 – *Gaz de France*.
529 ECJ 26 November 1998 – C-7/97, ECLI:EU:C:1998:569 – *Bronner*.
530 ECJ 26 November 1998 – C-7/97, ECLI:EU:C:1998:569, para. 40 – *Bronner*.
531 ECJ 26 November 1998 – C-7/97, ECLI:EU:C:1998:569, para. 46 – *Bronner*.
532 Paal (2025), Article 102 TFEU, mn. 67.

high market share, the Commission has found that alternative search engines remain accessible to users without significant switching costs.[533] Moreover, search engines do not qualify as non-replicable resources.[534] A market participant seeking entry can, in principle, develop and operate its own search engine, even if doing so entails considerable effort and investment. For these reasons, it is persuasive to reject the classification of search engines as essential facilities and to conclude that the doctrine does not apply in this context.

Learning Goals

In presenting search results, a dominant operator may face legal restrictions under Article 102 TFEU, particularly concerning the prohibition of abusive self-preferencing.[535] If the search engine is designated as a gatekeeper, it must additionally adhere to the conduct obligation set out in Article 6(5) DMA.[536]

With regard to the competitive significance of data in digital markets, the question arises whether claims for **access to data** can be derived from Article 102 TFEU under the essential facilities doctrine. While data may qualify as a facility within this framework, satisfying the access requirements established in *Bronner* poses considerable challenges.[537] Data is non-rivalrous in nature and often accessible through multiple alternative means.[538] Moreover, data protection law establishes that, in principle, it is the data subject who determines who may access their personal data.[539]

In German competition law, the legislator explicitly included the term data as a potential essential facility in sec. 19(2) no. 4 ARC, introduced through the tenth amendment.[540] This provision allows for data access claims under strict conditions. However, this inclusion does not entail any substantive deviation from the legal position under Article 102 TFEU. German abuse of dominance law similarly does not establish a general right of access to data.

In a preliminary ruling of February 2025, the ECJ held that a refusal to grant access may constitute an abuse even where such access is not indispensable for the requesting undertaking to operate on the downstream market.[541] An exclusionary abuse may be present if access is capable of making the '*app more attractive to consumers, where that platform has not been developed by the undertaking in a dominant position solely for the needs of its own business*.'[542] The reference by the Italian

533 Körber (2012), pp. 761, 766.
534 Kersting and Dworschak (2013), pp. 46, 48.
535 On the assessment of self-preferencing practices under Article 102 TFEU, see ▶ 2.3.2.1.4.
536 For further details on Article 6(5) DMA, see ▶ 3.3.2.4.
537 Haucap et al. (2018), p. 133.
538 Haucap et al. (2018), p. 133.
539 Haucap et al. (2018), p. 133.
540 For further details on sec. 19(2) no. 4 ARC, see ▶ 5.3.1.5.
541 ECJ 25 Feburary 2025 – C-233/23, ECLI:EU:C:2025:110 – *Alphabet and Google.*
542 ECJ 25 Feburary 2025 – C-233/23, ECLI:EU:C:2025:110, principle 1 – *Alphabet and Google.*

Council of State concerned *Google*'s refusal to enable interoperability between an app developed by *ENEL*, an energy company, for locating charging stations for electric vehicles and its *Android Auto* operating system. While the app can also be used independently of the operating system, the Court noted that, where the operating system is designed to integrate third-party applications, it must be examined whether *Google*'s refusal restricts competition in the relevant market.

2

2.3.2.2 Exploitative Abuses

General Principles

In addition to exclusionary abuse, exploitative abuse constitutes the second main form of abuse under competition law. It arises when a dominant undertaking imposes **unfair purchase or selling prices** or other **unfair trading conditions**, as set out in **Article 102 2nd sentence (a) TFEU**. The prohibition of exploitative abuse is primarily aimed at protecting the other side of the market, namely, consumer welfare. In practice, however, exploitative abuse has played a comparatively minor role in European competition law. This is largely due to the high threshold for establishing that prices are excessively high.[543] As competition is understood as dynamic process, strict price regulation is generally considered incompatible with the principles of competition law. Accordingly, even dominant undertakings are, in principle, free to set their prices autonomously.

To assess whether prices deviate from a competitive benchmark, the European courts primarily rely on the **comparative market method**.[544] This approach involves using the price level in a market comparable to the one dominated as a reference point to determine whether the dominant undertaking is charging abusively high prices.[545] In European competition law practice, the **geographic comparative market** method is particularly prominent.[546] Courts often select a comparator market located in another part of the European Union. The decisive criterion in choosing a suitable comparator market is its similarity to the dominated market. Such comparability exists when the same product is offered and similar market structures, such as demand patterns, distribution systems, or regulatory environments, are present.

The **temporal comparative market** method relies on the price level that previously prevailed in the relevant market, serving as a benchmark to detect excessive pricing over time. In contrast, the **product comparative market** method uses a different market where other, potentially substitute, products or services are sold. However, this method inherently suffers from a low degree of comparability with the dominated market, due to differences in product characteristics, demand con-

543 Huttenlauch (2025), Article 102 TFEU, mn. 210.

544 ECJ 29 February 1968 – C-24/67, ECLI:EU:C:1968:11, p. 113 – *Parke, Davis & Co. v Probel and Others*; ECJ 16 December 1999 – T-198/98, ECLI:EU:T:1999:341, para. 51 et seq. – *Micro Leader Business*.

545 For comparative market methods in the context of the calculation of damages under sec. 33a ARC, see Legner (2012), pp. 218, 220.

546 ECJ 8 June 1971 – C-78/70, ECLI:EU:C:1971:59, para. 19 – *Deutsche Grammophon/Metro SB*; ECJ 27 February 2014 – C-351/12, ECLI:EU:C:2014:110, para. 87 – *OSA*.

ditions, and cost structures. As a result, case law treats the product comparison market method only as a supplementary tool, rather than a primary basis for assessing exploitative pricing.[547]

An exploitative abuse cannot be established merely because a dominant undertaking charges prices higher than those on a comparable market. Rather, the prices must be '*significantly excessive.*'[548] Whether this threshold is met depends on a case-by-case assessment. Key factors include the degree of comparability between the relevant and the reference market, as well as the extent of the dominant undertaking's market power. Importantly, a 'safety margin' must be applied to the comparative prices to prevent the premature imposition of de facto price regulation. This margin serves as a buffer to ensure that only clearly excessive pricing is deemed abusive under Article 102 TFEU.

In addition, courts have occasionally relied on the **concept of profit margin capping** to approximate a price level consistent with competition.[549] In essence, this approach involves examining the dominant undertaking's profitability to assess whether its profits are 'unreasonably' high. However, such a method is problematic and should be rejected. It rests on the flawed assumption that the economic value of a service can be determined in the abstract. In reality, value is not fixed; it is continuously shaped by the dynamic interplay of supply and demand. Accordingly, there is no objectively 'reasonable' level of profit that can serve as a universal benchmark.[550]

! Whether prices are exceptionally abusively excessive must be assessed using the **comparable market method**. The benchmark for determining a price level consistent with competition is the price prevailing in a market that is comparable to the one dominated. However, not every deviation from this benchmark constitutes an abuse. To avoid premature or overly rigid price control, an additional **safety margin** must be applied. Only when the price significantly exceeds the competitive analogue exploitative pricing can be affirmed.

In addition to Article 102 2nd sentence (a) TFEU, which addresses abusive pricing practices, certain other forms of price-related abuse are referenced in the additional illustrative examples provided in Article 102 2nd sentence TFEU. For instance, Article 102(2)(b) TFEU covers the limitation of production, markets, or technical development to the prejudice of consumers, which may also relate to abusive pricing under certain circumstances. However, the practical relevance of these regulatory examples is limited. In EU legal practice, competition authorities and courts typically assess abusive conduct independently of its classification under a specific example listed in Article 102 2nd sentence TFEU. Moreover, the

547 ECJ 11 November 1986 – C-226/84, ECL:EU:C:1986:421, para. 28 – *British Leyland.*
548 ECJ 13 November 1975 – C-26/75, ECLI:EU:C:1975:150, para. 15/16 – *General Motors Continental.*
549 ECJ 14 February 1978 – C-27/76, ECLI:EU:C:1978:22, para. 248/257 – *United Brands.*
550 Fuchs and Heinemann (2025), Article 102 TFEU para. 229.

listed examples are not exhaustive; they serve merely as illustrative categories.[551] Numerous forms of abusive conduct are not explicitly mentioned in the provision but are nonetheless covered by the general prohibition in Article 102 1st sentence TFEU.

Some of the distinctive features of digital markets will be examined in the following sections. In the context of excessive pricing, particular attention must be paid to the characteristics of multi-sided markets and the dynamic nature of digital business models. In e-commerce, prices are often **individualised** to reflect variations in consumers' willingness to pay and are **dynamically** adjusted in response to real-time demand conditions. In addition, platform operators sometimes provide services to consumers without requiring monetary payment. Typical examples include messenger services and social networks. In such cases, exploitative abuse in the form of excessive pricing is not applicable. Instead, the focus shifts to whether the **terms and conditions** imposed by the platform operator are **unfair**. This form of exploitative abuse targets the contractual terms themselves, particularly the platform's general terms and conditions. For instance, access to a social network often requires users to consent to extensive data processing practices. In this context, the concept of abuse of conditions has gained traction, especially where these terms violate non-competition legal norms, most notably data protection law.[552] As a result, the issue has become increasingly relevant in the application of competition law to standardised contract terms, particularly in the digital economy.[553]

Excessive Pricing

The application of the **comparative market concept** to determine abusive pricing can be particularly **problematic** in the context of multi-sided digital platform markets. These markets are highly dynamic and characterized by rapid technological evolution, which significantly diminishes the long-term informative value of historical price comparisons.[554]

One major issue arises from the inherent tendency of digital markets to 'tilt', that is, to evolve from competitive environments into ones dominated by a single or a few powerful platforms. Prices charged by a platform when it first enters the market may no longer serve as a reliable benchmark once the platform has achieved market dominance. Comparing past and present prices without accounting for changes in market structure may therefore lead to misleading conclusions about the presence of abusive conduct. Moreover, digital platform services are frequently subject to technological innovation and continual improvement.[555] In many cases,

---

551 ECJ 14 October 2010 – C-280/08 P, ECLI:EU:C:2010:212, para.173 – *Deutsche Telekom*.

552 ECJ 4 July 2023 – C-252/21, ECLI:EU:C:2023:537 – *Meta (Facebook)*; German Federal Supreme Court 23 June 2020 – KVR 69/19, NZKart 2020, 473 – *Facebook*; Higher Regional Court of Duesseldorf 26 August 2019 – VI-Kart 1/19 (V), NZKart 2019, 495 – *Facebook*.

553 ECJ 4 July 2023 – C-252/21, ECLI:EU:C:2023:537 – *Meta (Facebook)*; Commission, Decision of 4 March 2024 – AT.40437 – *Apple App Store Practices (music streaming)*.

554 Richter and Zorn (2023), pp. 521, 530.

555 Richter and Zorn (2023), pp. 521, 530.

higher prices for newer products or services reflect quality enhancements or expanded functionalities, rather than an exercise of market power. Such price increases are not inherently objectionable under competition law, as they may be justified by increased value to users. The geographic dimension also presents challenges. In digital platform markets, where leading operators often function on a global scale, identifying an appropriate geographic comparator becomes difficult. The global reach of dominant platforms may mean that no equivalent comparator exists in another region. This further complicates any assessment based on traditional comparative market analysis.[556]

Comparable product markets are often the most readily available basis for assessing pricing behaviour.[557] However, their usefulness is inherently limited in digital platform cases, as the services offered are rarely identical. This undermines the degree of comparability with the market under investigation from the outset. For example, in competition proceedings in the United States, the commission charged by the *Apple App Store* for in-app payments was evaluated against the fees levied by other platform operators, such as *PayPal* and the *Epic Games Store*.[558] While these platforms provide comparable services in a broad sense, they differ significantly in terms of functionality, user base, ecosystem integration, and underlying business models. These differences complicate efforts to draw meaningful conclusions from such comparisons.

Personalised Pricing

Price personalisation involves charging different prices to different customers for the same service, based on variations in their willingness to pay. This practice can take several forms, commonly referred to as degrees of price discrimination.

Learning Goals

First-degree price discrimination (also known as perfect price discrimination) occurs when the supplier tailors prices to the individual willingness to pay of each consumer. This approach requires detailed knowledge of the consumer's valuation and is often implemented through individual price negotiations.

Second-degree price discrimination involves offering a menu of pricing options, allowing consumers to self-select into categories based on their preferences or purchasing behaviour. An example is volume discounts, where consumers who buy larger quantities benefit from lower unit prices.

Third-degree price discrimination occurs when the provider segments the market into distinct groups based on observable characteristics, such as age, occupation,

556 Richter and Zorn (2023), pp. 521, 530.

557 Richter and Zorn (2023), pp. 521, 530.

558 Pars pro toto *Cameron v. Apple Inc*, 4:19-cv-03074, (N. D. Cal.), Complaint 4 June 2019, para. 74 et seqq.; *In re Google Play Developer Antitrust Litigation*, 3:20-cv-05792, (N. D. Cal.); Match Group, LLC v. Google LLC, 3:22-cv-02746, (N.D. Cal.); State of Utah v. Google LLC, 3:21-cv-05227, (N.D. Cal.), Complaint filed 7 July 2021, para. 191.

or location, and sets different prices for each group. Examples include student discounts or reduced fares for seniors.[559]

2

The personalisation of prices by a dominant undertaking does not, in itself, constitute an abusive exploitation under Article 102 TFEU.[560] The practice of tailoring prices to individual customers' willingness to pay is, in principle, lawful. Price personalisation is commonly employed by companies with limited market power, including in offline (analogue) markets.

While the use of algorithms has facilitated the broader adoption of personalised pricing and enhanced the precision with which willingness to pay is estimated, this technological development does not, as such, alter the legal assessment under competition law. Nevertheless, if consumers find it more difficult to recognise personalised pricing strategies in online environments, this may give rise to a need for regulatory intervention. From a de lege ferenda perspective, information obligations should be considered to safeguard consumers' autonomy in decision-making.

The European Union has already taken steps in this direction with the Omnibus Directive, which introduced new transparency obligations into consumer protection law, cf. Article 6(1)(ea) Consumer Rights Directive and Article 7(4)(f) Unfair Commercial Practices Directive. These have been implemented in Germany through, inter alia, sec. 312d(1) German Civil Code (*Bürgerliches Gesetzbuch, BGB*), Article 246a sec. 1(1) first sentence no. 6 German Introductory Act to the Civil Code (*Einführungsgesetz zum BGB, EGBGB),* and sec. 5a, 5b(4) German Act Against Unfair Competition (*Gesetz gegen den unlauteren Wettbewerb, UWG*).

As for the competition law assessment, the impact of personalised pricing on consumer welfare must be carefully evaluated. The effects are ambivalent. On one hand, some argue that personalised pricing can increase access for financially weaker consumers by offering them lower prices than a uniform pricing model would allow.[561] On the other hand, critics contend that such consumers are often disadvantaged in practice, as undertakings tend to offer price advantages less frequently to them.[562]

Dynamic Pricing

In principle, the use of dynamic pricing[563] **does not amount to an abuse of a dominant position through exploitative practices.**[564] The rapid adjustment of prices in response to changes in demand is generally permissible, even for dominant undertakings. An abuse of exploitation may only be found where prices are excessively high, not merely because they are frequently adjusted. If prices are set excessively high within a dynamic pricing model, the general principles governing exploitative pricing apply. The assessment of whether prices are 'too high' involves a compari-

559 For further details on price discrimination, see ► 1.3.3.
560 Körber (2016), 303, 308; Paal (2019), pp. 43, 49.
561 Tietjen and Flöter (2017), pp. 546, 546.
562 Hofmann (2016), pp. 1074, 1076.
563 For further details on the role of AI in dynamic pricing strategies, see ► 1.3.3.
564 Paal (2019), pp. 43, 48.

son with price levels in comparable geographic markets. In this regard, the application of competition law does not differ fundamentally in cases involving dynamic pricing. There are no special considerations that would alter the standard analysis of exploitative conduct solely because prices are adjusted dynamically.[565]

Unfair Trading Conditions

Exploitation of the opposite side of the market by a dominant undertaking is not limited to the imposition of excessively high prices. Other terms and conditions imposed by the dominant firm may also constitute exploitative conduct. This is reflected in Article 102 2nd sentence (a) TFEU, which explicitly refers not only to pricing but also to 'other unfair trading conditions.'[566] Accordingly, an exploitative abuse can be found where a dominant undertaking imposes unreasonable or unjustified conditions on its trading partners. However, it must be emphasised that Article 102 TFEU is not intended to function as a general mechanism for reviewing the substantive fairness of contractual terms. The mere existence of a unilateral contractual arrangement that disadvantages one party is not, in itself, sufficient to establish an abuse of dominance. Rather, such an assessment requires a connection to the protective objectives of competition law—namely, the preservation of market structure, the prevention of distortion of competition, and the safeguarding of consumer welfare.

In its *Apple App Store Practices (music streaming)* case of March 2024, the Commission imposed a fine of EUR 1.8 billion on *Apple* for abusing its dominant position in the market for the distribution of music streaming apps via its App Store.[567] The Commission's assessment centred on an abuse of conditions, rather than pricing. Specifically, Apple was found to have restricted music streaming app developers from informing users about alternative subscription options available outside the App Store ecosystem.[568] According to the Commission, these contractual restrictions were neither necessary nor proportionate to the legitimate economic interests of the dominant undertaking. As a result, users were effectively denied access to potentially cheaper music subscription offers, leading to higher overall costs.[569]

In November 2024, the Commission concluded that *Meta* had also unfair trading conditions on its *Facebook Marketplace*.[570] According to the Commission, Meta's terms of use allowed the dominant undertaking to exploit data from companies competing with *Meta* on its marketplace in order to improve its own ser-

565 Paal (2019), pp. 43, 48.
566 ECJ 27 March 1974 – C-127/73, ECLI:EU:C:1974:25, para. 6/8 – *BRT/SABAM*.
567 Commission, Decision of 4 March 2024 – AT.40437 – *Apple App Store Practices (music streaming)*.
568 Commission, Decision of 4 March 2024 – AT.40437 – *Apple App Store Practices (music streaming)*.
569 Commission, Decision of 4 March 2024 – AT.40437 – *Apple App Store Practices (music streaming)*.
570 Commission, Decision of 14.11.2024 – AT.40684 – *Facebook Marketplace*.

2

vices. Meta mainly relied on ad-related data, which, in the Commission's view, provided the undertaking with 'substantial benefits.'[571]

In its *Meta (Facebook)* decision of July 2023, ECJ addressed the complex relationship between competition law and data protection law.[572] The ruling followed a request for a preliminary ruling by the Higher Regional Court of Duesseldorf, which sought clarification on the extent to which national competition authorities may invoke **violations of the GDPR when assessing an abuse of dominance under sec. 19 ARC**. The referring court asked whether it is compatible with data protection law for a competition authority, when acting within its mandate to monitor abuses of market power, to determine that certain contractual terms and conditions breach the GDPR, and to issue a remedial order on that basis. In essence, the key question was whether a national competition authority is permitted to classify the conduct of a dominant undertaking as exploitative because the relevant contractual terms violate data protection provisions under the GDPR.

The ECJ confirmed that a competition authority may rely on a breach of data protection law as a basis for establishing an abuse of conditions under Article 102 TFEU. In doing so, the Court highlighted the distinct objectives pursued by competition law and data protection law. While competition authorities act to preserve effective market structures and prevent the abuse of dominance, data protection authorities are primarily concerned with safeguarding the fundamental rights and freedoms of individuals in the context of personal data processing, as well as ensuring the free movement of data within the EU.[573] Importantly, the ECJ clarified that when a competition authority finds a violation of the GDPR, it does not overstep into the role of a data protection authority. Rather, it assesses the breach exclusively **to safeguard the competitive process**. The competition authority is thus entitled to determine that certain terms and conditions are exploitative because they infringe data protection norms, insofar as this finding is relevant to identifying an abuse of dominance. Although the request for a preliminary ruling by the Higher Regional Court of Düsseldorf arose in the context of proceedings under German abuse law (sec. 19 ARC),[574] the ECJ's reasoning is expected to have broader significance. Given the substantive alignment between sec. 19 ARC and Article 102 TFEU, the Court's interpretation will likely inform the application of the European prohibition of abuse as well. The judgment thus contributes to the evolving understanding of how data protection considerations may factor into the assessment of exploitative conduct under EU competition law.

2.3.2.3 Effect on Trade Between Member States

The prohibition of abuse under Article 102 TFEU presupposes that the abusive conduct is capable of **affecting trade between Member States**. This requirement distinguishes the scope of Article 102 TFEU from the corresponding national

571 Commission, Decision of 14 November 2024 – AT.40684, paras. 1197 et seqq. – *Facebook Marketplace*.

572 ECJ 4 July 2023 – C-252/21, ECLI:EU:C:2023:537 – *Meta (Facebook)*.

573 ECJ 4 July 2023 – C-252/21, ECLI:EU:C:2023:537, para. 49 – *Meta (Facebook)*.

574 For further details on the German *Facebook* case, see ► 5.3.1.5.3.

competition laws, which apply regardless of any cross-border effect.[575] As with Article 101 TFEU,[576] the threshold for establishing an effect on inter-state trade under Article 102 TFEU is not particularly high. According to the Commission, it is sufficient that it is

» 'possible to foresee with a sufficient degree of probability on the basis of a set of objective factors of law or fact that the agreement or practice may have an influence, direct or indirect, actual or potential, on the pattern of trade between Member States.'[577]

As a general rule, this condition is met if the abusive conduct occurs in more than one Member State. However, the requirement may also be satisfied where the conduct is confined to a part of a single Member State, provided it impedes access to that market by competitors from other Member States.[578]

Checklist: assessing unilateral conduct under Article 102 TFEU

1. Market dominance
   a) Market definition
   - aa) Product market
   - bb) Geographical market
   - cc) Temporal market

   b) Single dominance or collective dominance

2. Abuse

Exclusionary or exploitative abuse

3. Effect on trade between Member States

2.4 Merger Control: EUMR

2.4.1 Introduction

European merger control is governed by the **European Merger Control Regulation** (EUMR).[579] It requires parties to mergers with a Community dimension to notify

575 Fuchs and Heinemann (2025), Article 102 TFEU mn. 24.

576 On this perquisite in the context of the ban on cartels, see ► 2.2.3.

577 Commission, Guidelines on the effect on trade concept in Articles 81 and 82 of the Treaty, OJ [2004] C 101/81, para. 23.

578 Commission, Guidelines on the effect on trade concept in Articles 81 and 82 of the Treaty, OJ [2004] 101/81, para. 97.

579 Council Regulation (EC) No 139/2004 of 20 January 2004 on the control of concentrations between undertakings, OJ 2004 L 24/1.

2

the Commission prior to implementation. According to Article 7(1) EUMR, the merger may not be implemented before it has been authorised by the Commission. Unlike Article 102 TFEU, which targets the abuse of existing market power, the Commission's power to prohibit a concentration under the EUMR is grounded in the **creation or strengthening of market power**. Pursuant to Article 2(3) EUMR, a concentration is prohibited if it is likely to significantly impede effective competition (**SIEC**). The SIEC test is generally satisfied where the merger would result in the creation or strengthening of a dominant position. Thus, merger control under the EUMR is inherently forward-looking, involving a **predictive assessment** of future market developments and competitive dynamics.

Under Article 21(3) EUMR, when the EUMR is applicable, it pre-empts national merger control regimes. This is referred to as '**one-stop-shop principle**'. As a result, the Commission has exclusive jurisdiction over concentrations with a Community dimension. National competition authorities may only intervene where the turnover thresholds under Article 1 EUMR are not met, or where the transaction does not qualify as a concentration under Article 3 EUMR.

The original version of the EUMR was adopted in 1989[580] and has since undergone one comprehensive revision, which took place in 2004. Before the EUMR entered into force, the European Courts occasionally conducted ex post assessments of mergers under Article 102 TFEU.[581] In this context, the concept of an 'abuse of market structure' was developed:

> » *'Abuse may [...] occur if an undertaking in a dominant position strengthens such position in such a way that the degree of dominance reached substantially fetters competition, i.e. that only undertakings remain in the market whose behaviour depends on the dominant one'.*[582]

This legal approach has gained renewed relevance following ECJ's ruling in the *Towercast* case.[583] In that judgment, the Court held that mergers falling outside the scope of both the EUMR and national merger control regimes may nevertheless be subject to scrutiny under Article 102 TFEU.

System of European merger control: The Commission carries out European merger control review in two stages. First, the Commission assesses whether the proposed merger falls under the definition of a **concentration in Article 3 EUMR** and if it meets the **turnover thresholds in Article 1 EUMR**. This is followed by a substantive analysis. The Commission assesses whether the merger will lead to a significant

580 Council Regulation (EEC) No 4064/89 of 21 December 1989 on the control of concentrations between undertakings, OJ EC 1989 No L 395/13.
581 ECJ 21 February 1973 – C-6/72, ECLI:EU:C:1973:22 – *Continental Can.*
582 ECJ 21 February 1973 – C-6/72, ECLI:EU:C:1973:22, para. 26 – *Continental Can.*
583 ECJ 25 March 2023 – C-449/21, ECLI:EU:C:2023:207 – *Towercast.*

impediment to effective competition (**SIEC**), cf. **Article 2(3) EUMR**. If the merger would harm competition, the Commission will prohibit its implementation.

2.4.2 Definition of a Concentration: Article 3 EUMR

2.4.2.1 Merger

The term 'concentration' in Article 3 EUMR refers to a **lasting change in the control structure** of undertakings.[584] Article 3 EUMR distinguishes between two main forms of concentrations: **mergers** (Article 3(1)(a) EUMR) and **acquisitions of control** (Article 3(1)(b) EUMR).

The concept of a 'merger' under Article 3(1)(a) EUMR should be interpreted more narrowly than the broader notion implied by the term 'merger control' commonly used in European competition law. A merger, in the strict sense of Article 3(1)(a) EUMR, occurs when two or more previously independent undertakings or parts thereof combine into a single economic unit. This may take the form of a legal merger. However, Article 3(1)(a) EUMR also encompasses cases where undertakings establish a **common economic management**.[585] In such scenarios, the undertakings retain their legal independence but relinquish their economic autonomy.[586] An example from German corporate law is the 'Gleichordnungskonzern', where companies remain legally independent but are managed under a unified economic structure.

2.4.2.2 Acquisition of Control

While a merger typically involves a relationship of parity between the participating undertakings, an acquisition of control is characterised by a relationship of **dominance and subordination**.[587] In such cases, one undertaking acquires the ability to exercise **decisive influence** over the activities of another.[588] Control refers to the capacity to influence key entrepreneurial, strategic, and personnel decisions within the target undertaking.[589] This influence may be established through rights, agreements,[590] or other means. Most commonly, control arises through the acquisition

584 Commission, Jurisdictional Notice under Council Regulation (EC) No 139/2004 on the control of concentrations between undertakings, OJ 2008 C 95/1, para. 7.
585 Commission, Jurisdictional Notice under Council Regulation (EC) No 139/2004 on the control of concentrations between undertakings, OJ 2008 C 95/1, para. 10.
586 Commission 20 May 1998 – IV/M.1016 – *Price Waterhouse/Coopers & Lybrand.*
587 Whish and Bailey (2024), p. 937.
588 Commission, Jurisdictional Notice under Council Regulation (EC) No 139/2004 on the control of concentrations between undertakings, OJ 2008 C 95/1, para. 16.
589 Riesenkampff and Steinbarth (2025), Article 3 EUMR, mn. 17; Glöckner (2021), sec. 7 mn. 718.
590 Commission 16 December 2015 – M.7839 – *Outokumpu/Hernandez Edelstahl*, paras. 11–14.

2

of shares or assets,[591] but it can also result from personnel links or inter-company agreements that enable one undertaking to steer the business decisions of another.[592]

Control can be acquired either individually or jointly. **Sole control** exists when one undertaking alone gains the ability to exercise decisive influence over another (the target undertaking). In contrast, joint control arises when two or more undertakings share this decisive influence. A common example of **joint control** is when two companies each acquire a 50% stake in a third company.[593]In such a case, they must reach agreement on key decisions, since neither can act unilaterally. However, joint control is also possible with unequal shareholdings, as long as one or more shareholders have veto rights over important strategic decisions, such as business planning, budgeting, or appointing senior management.[594] These veto rights give them real influence, even if they hold less than 50%.

Under Article 3(1)(b) EUMR, joint control only qualifies as a concentration if it involves the creation of a **full-function joint venture**, see **Article 3(4) EUMR**. This means that the joint venture must operate like an independent business and perform all core economic functions on a lasting basis.[595] This differs from German merger control, where the creation of partial-function joint ventures can also trigger merger review if the other legal requirements for a concentration are met.[596]

In the competition for the development of AI, digital corporations have recently engaged in repeatedly recruiting highly qualified personnel away from competitors ('direct hiring').[597] If the undertaking from which they are recruited is no longer able to remain in the market thereafter, it becomes apparent that such conduct may exert a considerable influence on competitive structures. For this reason, it is being considered whether the strategy of direct hiring should be understood as a concentration in the form of an acquisition of control.[598] In cases where the 'transfer' of employees does not rest upon an agreement between the two companies concerned, the legal situation remains unclear. In this respect, there would be no transferring undertaking, although the notion of an acquisition of control generally presupposes the existence of such an undertaking.

---

591 Commission 18 February 2020 – M.5727 – *Microsoft/Yahoo! Search Business*.

592 Körber (2025b), EUMR Art. 3 mn. 57.

593 Commission, Jurisdictional Notice under Council Regulation (EC) No 139/2004 on the control of concentrations between undertakings, OJ [2008] C 95/1, para. 64.

594 Commission, Jurisdictional Notice under Council Regulation (EC) No 139/2004 on the control of concentrations between undertakings, OJ [2008] C 95/1, para. 65.

595 Whish and Bailey (2024), p. 940.

596 On joint ventures in the German merger control framework, see ► 5.4.2.1.

597 < https://www.wsj.com/tech/ai/meta-ai-recruiting-mark-zuckerberg-5c231f75 > (accessed 12 September 2025).

598 Bien and Becker (2024), pp. 81–88.

2.4.3 Community Dimension: Article 1 EUMR

2.4.3.1 Turnover Thresholds

A merger or acquisition is only subject to notification under the EU Merger Regulation (EUMR) if it has a Community dimension as defined in Article 1(1) EUMR. Whether this threshold is met depends on the turnover (i.e. revenue) of the undertakings involved, based on the criteria set out in Article 1(2), (3) EUMR.

According to **Article 1(2) EUMR**, a concentration has a Community dimension if the following two conditions are met:

- The **combined worldwide turnover** of all the undertakings concerned exceeds **EUR 5 billion**, and
- The **EU-wide turnover of at least two** of the undertakings exceeds **EUR 250 million each**.

However, there is an important exception: if each of the undertakings concerned generates more than two-thirds of its EU turnover within one and the same Member State, the case is considered to be of primarily national significance and does not fall under the EUMR. Instead, national competition authorities will review it.[599]

Even if the thresholds in Article 1(2) are not met, a concentration may still have a Community dimension if it satisfies all four criteria in **Article 1(3) EUMR**:

- The **combined worldwide turnover** of all undertakings concerned exceeds **EUR 2.5 billion**.
- In at least **three Member States**, the **combined** national turnover of all undertakings concerned exceeds **EUR 100 million in each**.
- In each of those three Member States, the turnover **of at least two undertakings** is more than **EUR 25 million**.
- The **EU-wide turnover** of at least **two undertakings** concerned exceeds **EUR 100 million each**.

This provision serves as a catch-all rule, ensuring that mergers with significant cross-border effects are still reviewed at the EU level. The two-thirds exception mentioned above also applies here: if all undertakings involved are mainly active in the same Member State, the case may still be handled nationally.

❗ A proposed concentration has a Community dimension if it meets either the turnover thresholds of Article 1(2) EUMR or those of Article 1(3) EUMR.

The rules for calculating turnover are set out in Article 5 EUMR. According to Article 5(4) TFEU, the turnover of affiliated undertakings, such as subsidiaries or

599 Commission, Decision of 15 November 2005 – M.3986 – *Gas Natural/Endesa*.

2

parent companies, must be consolidated. That means that their figures are added together for the purpose of assessing whether the relevant thresholds are met. Importantly, the regulation looks at the total turnover of the undertakings concerned. This means that turnover is not limited to the specific products or markets affected by the merger, but rather includes the undertaking's overall business activities.[600]

Which undertakings are regarded as '**undertakings concerned**' depends on the type of concentration involved. In the case of a merger under Article 3(1)(a) EUMR, the undertakings participating in the merger are those to be considered. For an acquisition of control under Article 3(1)(b) EUMR, the undertakings concerned are generally the acquiring undertaking (or undertakings) and the target undertaking.[601] The turnover of the seller (transferor) is normally not included in the calculation, unless the transferor retains joint control of the target following the transaction.[602]

2.4.3.2 Turnover in the Digital Sector

In recent years, several mergers in digital markets have fallen outside the scope of the EUMR because they did not meet the turnover thresholds set out in Article 1(2) or Article 1(3) EUMR. As a result, they could not be reviewed by the Commission, even though they were strategically important for the future of competition in the digital sector. A prominent example is the acquisition of *WhatsApp* by *Facebook* in 2014.[603] At the time, *WhatsApp*'s turnover was too low to trigger the jurisdictional thresholds under Article 1 EUMR. Nevertheless, *Facebook* was willing to pay approximately USD 19 billion, highlighting the strategic value of the transaction despite the low revenue figures. This illustrates a recurring challenge in digital markets: when young undertakings or start-ups are acquired, their current turnover is often insufficient to bring the concentration under European merger control.[604] However, such undertakings may still have significant competitive potential, particularly if they can grow user numbers rapidly and emerge as future rivals to established players. In some cases, so-called 'killer acquisitions' occur, where dominant firms acquire emerging competitors not to integrate or promote them, but to neutralise a potential future threat to their market position. In digital markets, there is often no clear correlation between turnover and competitive significance, as many digital services initially prioritise user growth and market reach over revenue generation.[605] This disconnect poses a challenge to traditional turnover-based jurisdictional thresholds.

---

600 GC 14 July 2006 – T-417/05, ECLI:EU:T:2006:219 – *Endesa*.

601 Commission, Jurisdictional Notice under Council Regulation (EC) No 139/2004 on the control of concentrations between undertakings, OJ [2008] C 95/1, para. 129.

602 Commission, Jurisdictional Notice under Council Regulation (EC) No 139/2004 on the control of concentrations between undertakings, OJ [2008] C 95/1, para. 139.

603 Commission, Decision of 3 October 2014 – M.7217 – *Facebook/WhatsApp*.

604 Cf. Argentesi et al. (2019), pp. 2 et seq.

605 Crémer et al. (2019), p. 111.

To address the enforcement gaps that arise when mergers in digital markets fall below the jurisdictional thresholds of Article 1 EUMR, Member State competition authorities have the option to refer such transactions to the Commission. This possibility is provided by **Article 22 EUMR**, which allows one or more Member States to request that the Commission examines a merger that does not meet the EUMR thresholds, but nonetheless affects trade between Member States and threatens to significantly affect competition within the territory of the referring state(s).[606] A recent and important clarification came from the ECJ in the *Illumina/Grail* case. The Court held that a Member State authority may not initiate a referral under Article 22 EUMR if the transaction does not fall within the scope of its own national merger control regime.[607] An initiative to transfer jurisdiction can also come from the undertakings involved. According to **Article 4(5) EUMR**, the merging parties may request that the Commission examine the merger if it is notifiable in at least three Member States.[608] In such cases, all the relevant Member States must agree to the referral. This 'one-stop-shop' approach can simplify the process and ensure consistent review at the EU level.

Another potential mechanism for addressing problematic mergers that escape prior scrutiny is **ex post intervention under Article 102 TFEU**, which prohibits the abuse of a dominant market position.[609] However, this approach is legally complex and carries significant uncertainty for the undertakings involved[610] A key limitation is that intervention under Article 102 TFEU requires the existence of dominance after the merger has occurred; it cannot be based on predictive assessments. This differs from the forward-looking analysis required under Article 2(3) EUMR, which allows the Commission to prohibit a merger based on its likely future effects on competition. Moreover, ex post measures such as unbundling (forcing a company to undo a completed merger) are considered highly intrusive and are rarely used in practice. For this reason, preventive merger control mechanisms remain the preferred tool for safeguarding competition in rapidly evolving markets, particularly the digital economy.

The Digital Markets Act (DMA) introduces additional transparency obligations for gatekeepers in relation to mergers and acquisitions. **Article 14 DMA** requires gatekeepers to inform the Commission of any planned concentrations involving other digital services providers, even if these do not meet the thresholds set out in the EUMR. However, this provision does not establish a separate merger control regime. The obligation under Article 14 DMA is limited to providing information. It does not give the Commission the power to approve or prohibit the transaction based on this notification alone. Instead, the aim is to enhance regulatory oversight and enable closer monitoring of acquisitions, especially those involving emerging

606 For further details on referral possibility, see ▶ 2.4.5.4.

607 ECJ 3 September 2024 – C-611/22 P, C-625/22 P, ECLI:EU:C:2024:677 – *Illumina*. The opposite view supported by GC 13 July 2022 – T-227/21, ECLI:EU:T:2022:447 – *Illumina*.

608 On example is the *WhatsApp/Facebook* merger, cf. Commission, Decision of 3 October 2014 – M.7217 – *WhatsApp/Facebook*.

609 For further details, see ▶ 2.4.1.

610 Schweitzer, Schallbruch and Wambach (2019), p. 68.

competitors or innovative start-ups that may not trigger the usual turnover thresholds under the EUMR.[611]

2

From a *de lege ferenda* perspective, it has been proposed that the **turnover thresholds in Article 1 EUMR be lowered.**[612] The goal is to capture mergers that are of competitive significance, especially in digital markets, which often escape review under the current regime. This includes transactions involving start-ups or innovative digital platforms that may not yet generate high revenues but could develop into important competitors. However, this proposal is controversial. One of the main arguments against lowering the thresholds is that it would result in a significant increase in the number of mergers requiring notification, including many in traditional sectors where there is no obvious risk to competition. This would place an additional burden on competition authorities and undertakings without offering clear enforcement benefits. Moreover, lower turnover thresholds are not necessarily well suited to identify the kinds of transactions that are particularly relevant in digital markets.[613] In these markets, the competitive potential of an undertakings does not always correlate with its current turnover. Factors such as user growth, access to data, and network effects may be more important indicators of future market power.

For this reason, it has also been considered whether the Community-wide significance of a **concentration** should not be based solely on turnover figures, but also include a **value-based threshold**, referring to the purchase price or consideration paid in the transaction.[614] Some national legal systems have already introduced such rules. In German merger control, for example, sec. 35(1a) ARC provides an additional notification requirement based on the value of the consideration, which must exceed EUR 400 million, even if the standard turnover thresholds are not met.[615] Austria has also introduced a value-based notification threshold in sec. 9(4) Austrian Cartel Act.

At the European level, however, such a reform of the EUMR is not currently expected. In the context of a 2016 evaluation, the Commission did raise the question of whether purely turnover-based thresholds might unduly limit the scope of merger control[616] Nonetheless, the Competition Commissioner at the time expressed caution, noting the practical challenges involved in applying a value-based threshold. These include difficulties in valuation, legal uncertainty, and increased administrative complexity.[617]

---

611 For further details on Article 14 DMA, see ► 3.3.3.

612 Apel and Polley (2021), pp. 273, 306; Levy et al. (2020), pp. 51, 57.

613 Apel and Polley (2021), pp. 273, 306.

614 Argentesi et al. (2019), p. 45; Motta and Peitz (2020), p. 34.

615 For further details on sec. 35 (1a) ARC, see ► 5.4.2.2.

616 Commission, Evaluation of procedural and jurisdictional aspects of EU merger control, 2016, pp. 2, 5, ► https://ec.europa.eu/smart-regulation/roadmaps/docs/2017_comp_003_evaluation.pdf (9 July 2024).

617 *Vestager*, The future of EU merger control, Speech – International Bar Association 24th Annual Competition Conference, 11 September 2020, pp. 3 et seq.: '*One solution could be a new threshold that's based on the value of the merger, not the sales of the companies. But it's not easy to set a threshold like that at the right level. If it's too high, it doesn't really help – you still end up missing a lot of the cases that matter. On the other hand, if you set it low enough to make sure that you see all those mergers, you risk making companies file a lot of cases that simply aren't relevant. So right now, changing the EUMR, to add a new threshold like this, doesn't seem like the most proportionate solution.*'

2.4.4 Substantive Analysis: Article 2 EUMR

2.4.4.1 General Principles

In assessing the substantive legality of a concentration, the Commission must determine whether the merger should be prohibited or cleared, possibly subject to conditions or commitments. The legal standard for this review is the **SIEC test** as laid down in Article 2(3) EUMR. Under this provision, a merger must be prohibited if it is likely to result in a significant impediment to effective competition within the internal market or a substantial part of it. Article 2(3) TFEU further specifies that such an impediment is deemed to exist in particular where the merger would lead to the **creation or strengthening of a dominant position**. This reflects the traditional **market dominance test**, which remains the core example of a situation in which a concentration may harm competition.[618]

Historically, the Commission primarily applied the market dominance test in its substantive merger review. Where dominance could not be established, the Commission occasionally addressed gap cases. These are cases in which mergers did not result in dominance but were nonetheless expected to significantly impede competition. In such cases, the analysis often remained anchored in structural indicators, such as market shares and concentration levels. Today, however, the Commission increasingly adopts a direct application of the SIEC test. This shift reflects a more effects-based approach in line with the more economic approach already discussed in the context of abuse of dominance under Article 102 TFEU.[619] Within this framework, the concept of individual dominance is now typically assessed under the category of unilateral effects, while collective dominance is analysed in terms of coordinated effects. Despite this alignment, there remain conceptual differences between the traditional market dominance test and the broader SIEC standard. While the former primarily relies on market structure indicators, the SIEC test focuses more on the anticipated competitive effects of the transaction, particularly in terms of consumer welfare. The following sections will follow the structure of Article 2(3) EUMR, beginning with an explanation of market dominance as the standard case referred to in the provision.

To better understand and analyse the competitive effects of a concentration, it is useful to distinguish between three main **types of mergers**:[620]

- Horizontal mergers
- Vertical mergers
- Conglomerate mergers

---

618 Prior to the amendment of the EUMR in 2004, the market dominance test instead of the SIEC test was the standard of review for European merger control.

619 Commission, Decision of 26 April 2006 – COMP/M.3916, paras. 125 et seq. – *T-Mobile Austria/Tele.ring*; Commission, Decision of 13 July 2005 – COMP/M.3653, paras. 326 et seq. – *Siemens/VA Tech*.

620 For further details on these merger types, see ► 2.4.4.4.

A horizontal merger involves undertakings that are active on the same product and geographic market and thus compete directly with each other.[621] The Commission also classifies mergers between potential competitors as horizontal.[622] A vertical merger involves undertakings that operate at different stages of the supply chain, such as a supplier and its customer. These undertakings are not competitors but are connected through a commercial relationship.[623] A conglomerate merger brings together companies that are neither competitors nor part of the same supply chain. These mergers often involve product extensions, such as firms offering similar products in different geographic areas, or complementary products, like hardware and software that function together.[624] One merger may affect competition in more than one way.[625] A single transaction could raise horizontal concerns in one market while also having vertical or conglomerate implications in another.

2.4.4.2 Market Dominance Test

The Commission must prohibit a merger if it would lead to the creation or strengthening of a dominant position. The **concept of market dominance** in this context largely corresponds to the definition used in the context of the prohibition of abuse under Article 102 TFEU.[626] As established under Article 102 TFEU, a dominant position exists where an undertaking can act to a significant extent independently of its competitors and customers. The key question in merger control is whether the merged entity would, after the transaction, possess such a position of independent market power that it could set prices, limit output, or reduce innovation without being effectively constrained by competitive pressure.[627]

! In merger control, the creation or strengthening of market dominance is, in itself, sufficient to justify a prohibition of the transaction. This reflects a form of structural control, which aims to prevent anti-competitive market structures before they arise. In contrast, Article 102 TFEU does not prohibit the mere existence or creation of a dominant position, for example, through internal growth. Dominance as such is not unlawful. What is prohibited is the abuse of that dominant position. This is a form of conduct-based control, which intervenes only when a dominant firm uses its market power in a way that harms competition or consumers.

The criteria for determining market dominance in merger control are, in principle, the same as those applied under the prohibition of abuse in Article 102 TFEU.[628] The first step in the assessment is to **define the relevant market**, which involves examining the market from a product, geographic, and (where relevant) temporal perspective. Once the relevant market has been identified, the analysis focuses on whether the merging undertakings would, after the transaction, gain an

---

621 Körber (2025a), Art. 2 EUMR mn. 401.
622 Commission, Guidelines on Horizontal Mergers, 2004, para. 5.
623 Commission, Guidelines on Horizontal Mergers, 2004, para. 4.
624 Körber (2025a), Article 2 EUMR mn. 580.
625 Riesenkampff and Steinbarth (2025), Article 2 EUMR mn. 118.
626 On the concepts of single dominance and collective dominance, see ► Sects. 2.3.1.2 and 2.3.1.3.
627 GC 21 September 2005 – T-87/05, ECLI:EU:T:2005:333, para. 48 – *EDP*.
628 On the criteria for assessing market dominance, see ► 2.3.1.2.

independent scope of conduct, that is, the ability to act to a considerable extent independently of competitors, customers, or consumers. This is assessed on the basis of both **market structure** and **firm-specific factors**. These include market shares (typically the most important indicator), barriers to entry, access to key inputs or customers, financial resources and vertical integration as well as past market behaviour.

Unlike the prohibition of abuse under Article 102 TFEU, which assesses the conduct of an already dominant undertaking, Article 2(3) EUMR requires a forward-looking, **prognostic assessment**. The Commission must determine whether the proposed merger is likely to result in a significant impediment to effective competition, including through the creation or strengthening of a dominant position. This assessment must not only predict whether the merged entity will gain an independent scope of conduct, but also whether this position is likely to be sustained over time rather than being merely temporary.[629] The anticipated competitive effects must therefore be **durable**. This requirement is particularly important in digital markets, where innovation-driven competition often plays a dominant role. In such environments, dominant positions may prove less stable due to the potential for rapid market disruption, sometimes described as **contestable monopolies**.[630] The Commission addressed this issue in its *Microsoft/Skype* merger decision. It found that traditional indicators, such as market shares, had only limited relevance in the context of consumer communications services.[631] The Commission noted the dynamic nature of the sector, where market shares can shift quickly and innovative entrants may succeed in gaining market position within a short period of time.[632]

Current

In light of the particular dynamics of digital markets, there is growing debate about whether the forecasting standard applied under Article 2(3) EUMR remains fit for purpose. Critics argue that the traditional evidentiary thresholds may be too rigid to effectively address the risks posed by mergers involving fast-moving, innovation-driven firms.[633] Some suggest lowering the standard of proof, making it easier for competition authorities to intervene in cases where the risk of harm is plausible, even if not certain.[634] Others advocate for the introduction of presumption-based rules, which would shift the burden of presentation and proof. For example, if a merger involves a dominant company acquiring a current or potential competitor, it could be presumed to significantly impede effective competition unless the parties can demonstrate otherwise.[635]

---

629 Commission, Decision of 12 November 1992 – IV/M.222, para. 91 – *Mannesmann/Hoesch*.
630 Körber (2012), pp. 761, 765.
631 Commission, Decision of 7 October 2011 – COMP/M.6281, para. 78 – *Microsoft/Skype*.
632 Commission, Decision of 7 October 2011 – COMP/M.6281, para. 123 – *Microsoft/Skype*.
633 Furman et al. (2019), mn. 3.85–87.
634 Stigler Committee (2019), p. 98.
635 Stigler Committee (2019), p. 98.

The market dominance rule in Article 2(3) EUMR is not limited to cases of single dominance. It also extends to situations of collective dominance, consistent with the interpretation of Article 102 TFEU. Although the text of Article 2(3) EUMR does not explicitly refer to collective dominance, the case law of the EU courts has established that such cases fall within the provision's scope.[636] Accordingly, a merger must also be prohibited if it is expected to lead to the creation or strengthening of a position of collective market dominance.

The concept of collective dominance corresponds to that under Article 102 TFEU.[637] It requires, first, that the undertakings concerned no longer compete effectively with one another due to some degree of coordinated conduct on the market. Second, the undertakings must be able to behave collectively to a significant extent independently of external competitive pressure, particularly from other competitors and customers. In such cases, even though no single undertaking holds a dominant position, the joint market behaviour of several firms can still produce similar anti-competitive effects. As a result, EU merger control must also address the risks posed by collective dominance to ensure the continued effectiveness of market competition.

Learning Goals

European case law has clarified the conditions for establishing collective market dominance through the Airtours criteria, developed in the *Airtours/First Choice* case.[638] According to these criteria, collective dominance requires a market structure that allows for sufficient transparency, enables firms to monitor and maintain coordination (discipline), and provides collective competitive independence from external competitors or customers.

The emergence of collective market dominance through a merger presupposes that the relevant market was already highly concentrated prior to the transaction. In other words, only a few competitors must be active in the market. Such oligopolistic market structures make it possible for undertakings to reach a common understanding on market conduct. This phenomenon is known as tacit collusion. For a finding of collective dominance, it is not enough to consider the combined market share of the undertakings involved. It is also essential to examine the transparency of the market and the degree of market homogeneity. These factors determine whether undertakings can coordinate their market conduct and sustain it over time without external interference or defection from within the group.

---

636 ECJ 31 March 1998 – C-68/94, ECLI:EU:C:1998:148, paras. 152 et seqq. – *Kali + Salz*; ECJ 6 June 2002 – T-342/99, ECLI:EU:T:2002:146, paras. 58 et seqq. – *Airtours*.

637 For further details on the Airtours criteria, see ▶ 2.3.1.3.

638 GC 6 June 2002 – T-342/99, ECLI:EU:T:2002:146, para. 58 et seqq. – *Airtours*.

2.4.4.3 SIEC Test

Unilateral Effects

When applying the SIEC criterion under Article 2(3) EUMR, the Commission distinguishes between unilateral and coordinated effects.[639] **Unilateral effects** occur when a merger removes important competitive pressure, thereby increasing the market power of the merged entity. As a result, the merged undertaking gains greater freedom of action, allowing it to **behave independently** of its competitors and customers. This form of market power arises not from collusion, but from the ability of the merged undertaking to act without being constrained by other market players. The creation or strengthening of **single dominance** is the clearest example of a unilateral effect. It reflects a situation where the transaction leads to a single undertaking gaining a dominant position that significantly impairs effective competition.

Learning Goals

In the past, the Commission typically applied the market dominance test first and resorted to the SIEC test only in gap cases, where dominance did not arise but a merger was still likely to significantly impair competition. Today, the Commission often applies the SIEC test directly. This reflects a broader focus on competitive effects rather than structural outcome.

EU case law has clarified that what are known as gap cases fall within the scope of Article 2(3) EUMR.[640] In these cases, the merged entity gains unilateral room for manoeuvre, although it does not become dominant in the structural sense. Recital 25 EUMR explicitly addresses these gap scenarios. Its wording indicates that the term 'significant impediment to effective competition' extends beyond dominance and includes 'the anti-competitive effects of a concentration resulting from the non-coordinated behaviour of undertakings which would not have a dominant position on the market concerned'.

Unilateral effects that go beyond single dominance are most often relevant in **oligopolistic markets**, where only a small number of competitors operate and each holds a high market share.[641] In such markets, the Commission examines whether the merger would eliminate competitive constraints previously applied by the merging parties to each other, or whether it would result in a reduced competitive pressure on remaining competitors.[642] The same criteria used to evaluate market dominance can also be used to assess gap cases.

However, the conditions described in recital 25 EUMR, namely elimination of competitive constraints and reduction of pressure on competitors, are not cumulative requirements. The ECJ made clear that it is sufficient for the Commission to

639 Commission, Guidelines on Horizontal Mergers, 2004, para. 22.
640 Commission, Guidelines on Horizontal Mergers, 2004, para. 25.
641 Commission, Guidelines on Horizontal Mergers, 2004, para. 25.
642 Commission, Guidelines on Horizontal Mergers, 2004, para. 25.

2

demonstrate that the merger eliminates an important competitive constraint between the merging parties.[643] Moreover, the criteria listed in recital 25 EUMR are not exhaustive.[644] In fact, any transaction likely to cause a significant impediment of effective competition, such as the emergence of unilateral scope for price increases, may qualify as a **gap case** under Article 2(3) EUMR.[645]

Below are selected cases where a significant impediment to effective competition has been recognised even in the absence of individual market dominance. The Hutchison/Telefónica UK merger confirmed that an overriding probability of an impediment is sufficient to justify intervention.[646] A significant impediment may arise in the case of **close competitors**, where the products of merging undertakings are highly interchangeable. Even if one undertaking does not gain a dominant position because, for example, another competitor holds a larger market share the merged entity may command unilateral scope to raise prices due to the elimination of competitive pressures between the merging parties.[647] In such circumstances, the UPP test (Upward Pricing Pressure) provides a useful quantitative tool to estimate the potential price impact resulting from the merger.[648]

In homogeneous markets, unilateral effects beyond individual market dominance may occur when a merger enables competitors to raise prices by **reducing capacity**, particularly if they are the only undertakings with excess capacity.[649] In the T-*Mobile Austria/tele.ring* case, the Commission recognised a gap case and approved the merger only subject to conditions.[650] Although the combined entity did not become dominant in terms of market share, the merger removed an important competitive force, namely *tele.ring*, a small but potent **maverick**, thereby granting the merged entity unilateral scope for higher pricing.

Coordinated Effects

Coordinated effects occur when undertakings in an oligopolistic market adopt unilateral conduct through coordination.[651] The most established form of coordinated effects is **collective dominance**, but scholarship raises the possibility that coordinated effects may emerge even when collective dominance is not established.[652]

2.4.4.4 Merger Types

Horizontal Merger

In order to concretise the competitive effects of a merger project, a distinction must be made between the types of mergers described above (cf. ► 2.4.4.1).

643 ECJ 13 July 2023 – C-376/20 P, ECLI:C:EU: 2023:561, para. 114 – *Hutchison/Telefónica UK*.
644 ECJ 13 July 2023 – C-376/20 P, ECLI:C:EU: 2023:561, para. 114 – *Hutchison/Telefónica UK*.
645 ECJ 13 July 2023 – C-376/20 P, ECLI:C:EU: 2023:561, para. 112 – *Hutchison/Telefónica UK*.
646 ECJ 13 July 2023 – C-376/20 P, ECLI:C:EU: 2023:561, para. 88 – *Hutchison/Telefónica UK*. The ECJ contradicts the GC' decision (28 May 2020 – T-399/16, ECLI:EU:T:2020), which had required a high degree of probability.
647 Riesenkampff and Steinbarth (2025), Article 2 EUMR mn. 163.
648 For the further method of the GUPPI (*gross upward pricing pressure index*) see Commission 12 December 2012 – COMP/M.6497, para. 314 – *Hutchison 3G Austria/Orange Austria*.
649 Glöckner (2021), sec. 7 mn. 737.
650 Commission, Decision of 26 April 2006, COMP/M.3916 – *T-Mobile Austria/Tele.ring*.
651 Commission, Guidelines on Horizontal Mergers, 2004, mn. 39.
652 Kling and Thomas (2016), sec. 8 mn. 248.

Horizontal mergers result in an increase in **market share concentration**. The **Herfindahl-Hirschman Index (HHI)** is commonly used to assess changes in market concentration following such mergers.[653] It is calculated by summing the squares of the market shares of all undertakings in the relevant market.[654]

▶ **Example**

Before the merger, firm A holds 30%, B 20%, C 20%, and firms D, E, and F each hold 10%. The pre-merger HHI is therefore: $30^2 + 20^2 + 20^2 + 10^2 + 10^2 + 10^2 = 2000$. If competitors If competitors A and B merge (combined market share = 50%), the post-merger HHI becomes: $50^2 + 20^2 + 10^{(2)} + 10^2 + 10^2 = 3200$. ◀

In addition to considering the absolute level of the HHI, the Commission evaluates the delta, i.e., the difference between the post-merger and pre-merger HHI. In this example, the delta is 3200–2000 = 1200, significantly above the threshold of 150. According to the Commission's Horizontal Merger Guidelines, such an increase may indicate potential competition concerns,[655] in this case, regarding the merger between A and B. However, HHI values alone do not justify a presumption that the merger should be prohibited. Instead, a qualitative assessment of market structure and other relevant factors is necessary to determine whether the merger would lead to the creation or strengthening of a dominant market position.

In addition to the criteria already discussed in relation to Article 102 TFEU, the effects on **innovation competition** can become particularly significant in the context of merger control. This is especially relevant in **digital markets**, where disruptive innovations have previously displaced firms with established market power. An example is the Commission's approval of the *Facebook/WhatsApp* merger,[656] which was later criticized. Although *WhatsApp* was not a strong competitor at the time, it was already exerting considerable competitive pressure as an innovative start-up. Critics argued that the merger eliminated this pressure, ultimately to the detriment of innovation competition. This reflects a broader strategy employed by dominant firms: acquiring emerging competitors with high growth potential at an early stage.[657] Such acquisitions are often facilitated by the acquirers' substantial financial resources. Innovation-related concerns have also played a role in merger control decisions in other sectors, such as pharmaceuticals[658] and crop protection products.[659] However, not every acquisition of an innovative start-up should be viewed as anti-competitive. In some cases, the acquired firm may benefit from the acquiring platform's resources and financial strength, which can help scale and further develop its innovative business model.[660]

---

653 GC 22 June 2022 – T-584/19, ECLI:EU:T:2022:386, para. 375 et seqq. – *thyssenkrupp*.
654 Commission, Guidelines on Horizontal Mergers, 2004, para. 16.
655 Commission, Guidelines on Horizontal Mergers, 2004, para. 20.
656 Commission, Decision of 3 October 2014, Case M.7217 – *Facebook/WhatsApp*.
657 Haucap et al. (2018), pp. 122 et seq.
658 Commission, Decision of 4 August 2015 – M.7559, paras. 58 et seqq. – *Pfizer/Hospira*.
659 Commission, Decision of 27 March 2017 – M.7932, paras. 1975 et seq. – *Dow/DuPont*.
660 Bostoen (2023) p. 238; Crémer et al. (2019), p. 110.

2

The Commission has also examined **data-related theories of harm** in horizontal mergers within the digital sector. A key consideration is whether the merging parties gain independent scope for strategic conduct through the combination of their data sets.[661] Superior access to data may enable the merged entity to raise barriers to entry. This can affect both potential new entrants and existing competitors. For new entrants, increased data concentration may hinder their ability to compete effectively. For incumbents, the merger may worsen their competitive position by limiting access to comparable data resources or weakening their ability to innovate.[662] Moreover, depending on the diversity and quality of the combined data sets, the merged entity may also be better positioned to extract further insights through advanced analytics, thereby reinforcing its competitive advantage.[663]

▶ Examples

In the *Meta/Kustomer* case, which the Commission cleared subject to conditions, it examined, among other issues, the extent to which *Meta* could access Kustomer's data post-merger. The Commission assessed whether this access would give Meta a competitive advantage in its role as a provider of online advertising services. It ultimately concluded that such an advantage would indeed arise.[664]

In contrast, in the *Facebook/WhatsApp* case, the Commission investigated the potential exclusionary effects of *Facebook* gaining access to *WhatsApp* user data.[665] However, it rejected this theory of harm, noting the high barriers to accessing such data. For instance, changes to *WhatsApp*'s terms of service would have been required.[666] Moreover, the Commission found no clear evidence that access to *WhatsApp's* data would significantly strengthen *Facebook*'s position in the online advertising markets.[667] ◀

Vertical Merger

In contrast to horizontal mergers, vertical mergers do not lead to an addition of market shares. However, they can still result in the creation or strengthening of a dominant position through **market foreclosure effects**.[668] This can occur, for example, when the merged entity is able to restrict access to essential inputs, thereby making it more difficult for competitors to enter or remain in the market.[669] According to Guidelines on the Assessment of Non-Horizontal Mergers, the Commission first assesses whether the merged entity has the **ability** to foreclose the

661 Holzweber (2016), pp. 104, 108.
662 Holzweber (2016), pp. 104, 108.
663 Holzweber (2016), pp. 104, 109.
664 Commission, Decision of 27 January 2022 – M.10262, paras. 533 et seqq. – *Meta/Kustomer*.
665 Commission, Decision of 3 October 2014 – M.7217, paras. 180 et seq. – *Facebook/WhatsApp*.
666 Commission, Decision of 3 October 2014 – M.7217, para. 185 – *Facebook/WhatsApp*.
667 Commission, Decision of 3 October 2014 – M.7217, paras. 187 et seqq. – *Facebook/WhatsApp*.
668 Commission, Guidelines on non-horizontal mergers, 2008, para. 18.
669 Wilson (2025), sec. 29 mn. 114.

market. It then considers whether the entity also has the **incentive** to do so from an economic perspective.[670]

The **combination of personal** data in the context of vertical mergers can also lead to exclusionary effects.[671] This is particularly relevant when the merged entity gains a significant advantage over its competitors through superior access to data.[672] However, such foreclosure concerns are less likely to arise if similar data can be collected by other market participants.[673] In its clearance decision in the *Google/DoubleClick* case, the Commission found that data on internet usage behaviour could also be obtained by competing firms. As a result, it concluded that *DoubleClick* did not offer a unique service.[674] The Commission noted that 'other companies active in online advertising have the ability to collect large amounts of more or less similar information that is potentially useful for advertisement targeting.'[675]

The role of access to **non-personal data** in shaping competitive dynamics is also increasingly being discussed, particularly in relation to its importance in specific markets.[676]

▶ Example

In the *TomTom/Tele Atlas* case, the Commission examined whether non-personal data. in this instance, digital map databases, constituted a critical input that could be subject to foreclosure.[677] These databases are essential for the functioning of portable navigation devices. The Commission assessed whether the merged entity would be in a position to foreclose competing PND manufacturers and software developers, for example by raising prices, providing lower-quality maps, or delaying updates.[678] While it found that the merged entity had the ability to engage in such foreclosure, it concluded that it lacked sufficient economic incentives to do so.[679] ◀

Innovation competition can also serve as a relevant criterion when assessing unilateral effects in vertical mergers.

▶ Example

In the *Intel/McAfee* case, the Commission examined whether the merger could reduce innovation by impairing the interoperability of third-party products.[680] The concern was that the vertical integration resulting from the merger might give Intel the ability and incentive to restrict access to essential technical information required for software development. According to the Commission's findings, *Intel* could have limited competitors' access to such information post-merger, thereby preventing them from ensuring their

---

670 Commission, Guidelines on non-horizontal mergers, 2008, paras. 33 et seqq, 40 et seqq.
671 Wilson (2025), sec. 29 mn. 115.
672 Holzweber (2016), pp. 104, 109.
673 Commission, Decision of 9 January 2014 – COMP/M.7023, para. 626 – *Publicis/Omnicom*.
674 Commission, Decision of 11 March 2008 – COMP/M.4731, para. 268 – *Google/DoubleClick*.
675 Commission, Decision of 11 March 2008 – COMP/M.4731, para. 269 – *Google/DoubleClick*.
676 Holzweber (2016), pp. 104, 108.
677 Commission, Decision of 14 May 2008 – COMP/M.4854 – *TomTom/Tele Atlas*.
678 Commission, Decision of 14 May 2008 – COMP/M.4854, para. 193 – *TomTom/Tele Atlas*.
679 Commission, Decision of 14 May 2008 – COMP/M.4854, paras. 210, 230 – *TomTom/Tele Atlas*.
680 Commission, Decision of 26 January 2011 – COMP/M.5984 – *Intel/McAfee*.

security software was fully compatible with Intel's processors and chipsets. This advantage would have remained exclusive to *McAfee*. ◄

Conglomerate Merger

The effects of conglomerate mergers can vary significantly. In principle, the Commission considers them to be less problematic than horizontal mergers.[681] However, certain effects must still be carefully assessed, as they may lead to the creation or strengthening of a dominant position by the merged entity. Among these are **tying and bundling practices**, which can have a foreclosure effect that disadvantages competitors.[682] In such cases, the merged entity seeks to leverage its market power from one market affected by the merger into another. This is commonly referred to as **leveraging**. The strategy can apply to both complementary and substitutable products.[683] The Commission has already examined such leveraging effects in the context of digital markets, where the risks of foreclosure through bundling and data-driven advantages are particularly pronounced.

► Example

In the *Microsoft/LinkedIn* case, the Commission assessed whether the merger would enable the combined entity to leverage *Microsoft*'s strong position in sales intelligence solutions software into other software markets.[684] The Commission rejected this anticipated leveraging effect because *LinkedIn*'s position in the sales intelligence market was not sufficiently strong, and the market itself was highly differentiated.[685] In contrast, the Commission did confirm another leveraging effect: it found that *Microsoft* could use its market power in the PC operating systems market to strengthen its position in the professional social networking market.[686] ◄

It should be noted that not every tying or bundling strategy results in the merger being prohibited. Instead, it must be assessed whether the merged entity already holds market power in at least one of the markets affected by the practice.[687] Additionally, there must be an economic incentive to engage in tying or bundling. Thus, the strategy should be expected to increase the profits of the undertakings concerned.[688]

---

681 Commission, Guidelines on non-horizontal mergers, 2008, para. 92.
682 Commission, Guidelines on non-horizontal mergers, 2008, paras. 96, 97.
683 Kling and Thomas (2016), sec. 8 mn. 282.
684 Commission, Decision of 6 December 2016 – COMP/M.8124, paras. 218 et seq. – *Microsoft/LinkedIn*.
685 Commission, Decision of 6 December 2016 – COMP/M.8124, paras. 222 et seq. – *Microsoft/LinkedIn*.
686 Commission, Decision of 6 December 2016 – COMP/M.8124, paras. 295 et seq. – *Microsoft/LinkedIn*.
687 Commission, Guidelines on non-horizontal mergers, 2008, para. 99.
688 Commission, Guidelines on non-horizontal mergers, 2008, para. 105 et seq.

Other consequences of conglomerate mergers include **portfolio effects**. This occurs when the merged entity strengthens its market power by expanding its range of products. A broad product portfolio alone is generally not enough to create such an advantage.[689] However, it can become significant if competitors offer a smaller selection[690] and customers are incentivized to buy all products from the same supplier.[691] In some cases, the merged entity may even be able to 'force' customers to purchase the entire portfolio, particularly when it includes products on which customers are dependent.[692]

Spill-over effects arise when the merged entity benefits from leveraging existing expertise or established post-merger infrastructure across different markets.[693]

► Example

In its assessment of the *Boeing/McDonnell Douglas* merger, the Commission noted that the merged entity would gain improved access to research funding[694] This advantage was expected to benefit *Boeing*, which was already dominant in the civil aviation sector prior to the merger. ◄

Another potential theory of harm in conglomerate mergers is the **strengthening of financial resources.**[695]A financially stronger merged entity may be able to cross-subsidize its products or offer discounts, which can deter new competitors from entering the market.[696]

2.4.4.5 Efficiency Defence

The anti-competitive effects of a merger may be justified by efficiency gains.[697] Whether and which efficiency gains can be expected is examined as part of the **efficiency defence**. In this context, the undertakings involved bear the burden of presenting and proving these gains.[698]

A legal basis for the efficiency defence is found in recital 29 EUMR:

» In order to determine the impact of a concentration on competition in the common market, it is appropriate to take account of any substantiated and likely efficiencies put forward by the undertakings concerned.

---

689 Commission, Decision of 18 October 2001 – COMP/M.2608, para. 34 – *INA/FAG*.
690 Commission, Decision of 15 October 1997 – COMP/M.938, paras. 100 et seq. – *Guinness/Grand Metropolitan*.
691 Commission, Decision of 15 July 2005 – COMP/M.3732, para. 131 – *Procter & Gamble/Gillette*.
692 Commission, Decision of 17 July 2009 – COMP/M.5547, paras. 99 et seqq. – *Koninklijke Philips Electronics/Saeco International Groups*.
693 Körber (2025a), Article 2 EUMR mn. 606.
694 Commission, Decision of 30 July 1997 – IV/M.877, paras. 83 et seqq. – *Boeing/McDonnell Douglas*.
695 ECJ 14 December 2005 – T-210/01, ECLI:EU:T:2005:456, paras. 201 et seqq. – *General Electric*.
696 Körber (2025a), EUMR Article 2 mn. 605.
697 Zimmer (2004), 250, 262 et seq; Thomas (2017), 13(2), 346, 366 et seqq. A different view is taken by Körber (2025a), Article 2 EUMR mn. 359.
698 GC 6 July 2010 – T-342/07, ECLI:EU:T:2010:480, para. 403 – *Rynair*.

2

Furthermore, Article 2(1)(2)(b) EUMR requires that 'the interests of intermediate and final consumers and the development of technical and economic progress, insofar as this serves the consumer and does not hinder competition' be taken into account when assessing a merger.

The Commission outlines the requirements for the efficiency defence in its guidelines.[699] First and foremost, efficiency gains must **benefit consumers**.[700] These benefits may, for example, arise if the merged entity reduces sales prices due to savings in production costs.[701] It must be likely that such cost savings will actually be passed on to consumers, which largely depends on the merged entity's market power.[702] If the entity holds a monopoly-like position, competitive pressure may be insufficient to compel price reductions. In the context of vertical mergers, incentives to lower prices may also stem from avoiding double marginalisation. This refers to a situation where both supplier and retailer add mark-ups to costs, resulting in higher prices for consumers.[703] By integrating vertically, the merged entity can eliminate one layer of mark-up, potentially reducing final prices. Additionally, dynamic efficiencies can be considered. These occur when consumers benefit from new or improved products brought about by the merger.[704] The prerequisite that efficiencies benefit consumers aligns with the overarching objective of protecting consumer welfare.[705] Similarly, the conditions for exemption under Article 101(3) TFEU[706] and the possibility of justification under Article 102 TFEU[707] also require that efficiencies provide advantages to consumers. The Commission places greater weight on efficiencies that materialize promptly[708] and insists that these benefits accrue to consumers in the same markets where the merger raises competition concerns.[709] In digital markets, price-related benefits may be less prominent, as many services are offered to consumers free of charge. Instead, positive effects for consumers often arise through increased innovation, improved product quality, or greater variety. However, this shift in focus towards dynamic efficiencies presents challenges, particularly in quantifying these benefits.

Secondly, the efficiencies must be **merger-specific**.[710] This means the efficiencies must result directly from the merger and could not be achieved through other

---

699 Commission, Guidelines on Horizontal Mergers, 2004, para. 76 et seqq.; Commission, Guidelines on Nonhorizontal Mergers, 2008, para. 53.

700 Commission, Guidelines on Horizontal Mergers, 2004, para. 79 et seq.

701 Commission, Guidelines on Horizontal Mergers, 2004, para. 80.

702 Commission, Guidelines on Horizontal Mergers, 2004, para. 84.

703 Ewald (2020), sec. 7 mn. 64.

704 Commission, Guidelines on Horizontal Mergers, 2004, para. 81.

705 For further details on the consumer welfare standard as objective of EU competition law, see ► 2.1.3.2.

706 On the criteria under Article 101(3) TFEU, see ► 2.2.5.

707 ECJ 27 March 2012 – C-209/10, ECLI:EU:C:2012:172, para. 40 – *Post Danmark*; ECJ 17 February 2011 – C-52/09, ECLI:EU:C:2011:83, paras. 75 et seqq. – *TeliaSonera Sverige*.

708 Commission, Guidelines on Horizontal Mergers, 2004, para. 79.

709 Commission, Guidelines on Horizontal Mergers, 2004, para. 79.

710 Commission, Guidelines on Horizontal Mergers, 2004, para. 85.

means, such as entering into a licensing agreement. Thirdly, the efficiencies must be **verifiable**.[711] Verifiability poses a high hurdle in merger control practice, as the burden of proof lies with the merging parties. They must demonstrate not only whether efficiencies will materialize but also to what extent. The Commission requires concrete quantitative evidence in this regard.[712] For example, in Form CO, undertakings are asked to specify efficiency gains in numerical terms and explain how these figures are calculated.[713]

Finally, the efficiencies must be sufficient to strengthen the merged entity's ability and incentive to enhance competition for the benefit of consumers, thereby **offsetting the merger's potential adverse effects on competition**.[714] For example, in the *UPS/TNT Express* case, the Commission acknowledged the quality improvements claimed by the merging parties as an efficiency gain. However, these were ultimately deemed insufficient to outweigh the expected harm to competition across all affected markets.[715]

The requirements for meeting the prerequisites of an efficiency defence are stringent. In practice, many merging parties present efficiency claims, but the Commission often finds these insufficient to justify the expected restrictions on competition.[716]

2.4.5 Merger Control Procedure

2.4.5.1 Notification

Merger projects that meet the criteria for formal merger control under Article 3, 1 EUMR must be **notified** to the Commission in accordance with Article 4 EUMR. For this purpose, undertakings are required to submit the **Form CO**.[717] The obligation to notify arises once the agreement has been concluded, a public takeover bid has been announced, or a controlling interest has been acquired (see Article 4(1) EUMR). Before the formal notification is submitted, it is common for the parties to engage in an informal pre-notification phase with the Commission to clarify procedural and substantive issues.[718]

---

711 Commission, Guidelines on Horizontal Mergers, 2004, para. 86.

712 Commission, Guidelines on Horizontal Mergers, 2004, para. 86.

713 Commission Regulation (EC) No 802/2004 of 7 April 2004 implementing Council Regulation (EC) No 139/2004 on the control of concentrations between undertakings, OJ [2004] L 133/1, 20, para. 9.3, i)-iv).

714 Commission, Guidelines on Horizontal Mergers, 2004, para. 77.

715 Commission, Decision of 30 January 2013 – COMP/M.6570 – *UPS/TNT Express*.

716 Cf. e.g. Commission, Decision of 6 October 2004 – COMP/M.3099 – *Areva/Urenco/ETC JV*; Commission, Decicion of 26 April 2006 – COMP/M.3916 – *T-Mobile Austria/Telering*; Commission 22 June 2009 – COMP/M.5335 – *Lufthansa/SN Airholdings*; Commission, Decision of 4 September 2012 – COMP/M.6314 – *Telefónica UK/Vodafone UK/Everything Everywhere/JV*; Commission, Decision of 28 May 2014 – COMP/M.6992 – *Hutchison 3G UK/Telefonica Ireland*; Commission, Decision of 2 July 2014 – COMP/M.7002 – *M&G/Alliance Medical*.

717 Commission Regulation (EC) No 802/2004 of 7 April 2004 implementing Council Regulation (EC) No 139/2004 on the control of concentrations between undertakings, OJ [2004] 133/1.

718 Kling and Thomas (2016), sec. 8 mn. 368.

The obligation to notify a transaction is closely linked to the prohibition on implementation set out in **Article 7 EUMR**. Under this provision, a concentration may not be implemented either before it has been notified or before it has been approved by a Commission decision. The concept of **implementation** is interpreted broadly, even partial implementation of the transaction may constitute a breach of Article 7 EUMR.[719] A violation of this prohibition, commonly referred to as gun jumping, can result in significant fines. The Commission has recently exercised its enforcement powers in this regard on multiple occasions.[720]

2.4.5.2 Phase I Investigations

Once a merger project is notified, the Commission enters the preliminary examination phase pursuant to **Article 6 EUMR**. During this phase, the Commission must issue a decision within **25 working days**. In exceptional cases, this period may be extended to 35 working days, for example, if the Commission gains jurisdiction following a referral by a Member State[721] or if the notifying parties propose commitments, cf. Article 10(1) EUMR.

During the preliminary examination phase, the Commission assesses whether the notified transaction constitutes a concentration within the meaning of the EUMR. If this is not the case, it issues a decision under Article 6(1)(a) EUMR, thereby terminating the procedure. Alternatively, if the Commission concludes that the concentration does not raise serious competition concerns, it clears the transaction pursuant to Article 6(1)(b) EUMR. **Clearance** at this stage may also be granted subject to conditions and obligations, where necessary to address potential competition concerns.

However, if the Commission concludes that the notified concentration raises serious doubts as to its compatibility with the internal market, it initiates a Phase II investigation (**main examination procedure**) pursuant to Article 6(1)(c) EUMR. If the Commission fails to issue a decision within the time limits set out in Article 10(1) EUMR, the transaction is deemed to be cleared under the principle of **fictitious authorisation**, cf. Article 10(6) EUMR. There is also the possibility of a **simplified procedure**, in which the Commission clears the transaction by way of a short-form decision.[722] This procedure is used for cases that are straightforward and unlikely to raise competition concerns. In 2023, over 80% of notified concentrations were approved under this simplified process.[723]

---

719 On the concept of warehousing, see GC 18 May 2022 – T-609/19, ECLI:EU:T:2022:299, paras. 53 et seqq. – *Canon*.

720 Commission, Decision of 6 September 2022 – COMP/M.10188 – *Illumina/Grail*; Commission, Decision of 27 June 2019 – COMP/M.8179 – *Canon/Toshiba Medical Systems Corporation*.

721 On the possibilities of referral, see ► 2.4.5.4.

722 Commission Notice on the simplified treatment of certain concentrations under Council Regulation (EC) No 139/2004 on the control of concentrations between undertakings, OJ [2023] C 160/1.

723 < https://competition-policy.ec.europa.eu/mergers/statistics_en > (accessed 5 September 2025).

2.4.5.3 Phase II Investigations

If the notified concentration meets the relevant criteria and the Commission, in its preliminary examination, identifies serious competition concerns, it will initiate an in-depth investigation under **Article 8 EUMR** (Phase II). The standard time limit for this main examination procedure is **90 working days**, as set out in Article 10(3) EUMR. This period may be extended to 105 working days if the merging parties submit proposed commitments. Should the Commission fail to reach a decision within this timeframe, the authorisation fiction of Article 10(6) EUMR applies. If, during the main investigation, the Commission's initial doubts about the merger's compatibility with the internal market under Article 2(3) EUMR are confirmed, it will issue a Statement of Objections. In line with Article 18 EUMR, the parties must then be given the opportunity to respond.

The Commission may conclude the procedure by clearing the concentration if it finds that the competition concerns are not substantiated. This clearance may be unconditional or **subject to commitments and conditions** imposed under Article 8(2) EUMR. However, if the Commission determines that the merger would significantly impede effective competition, it is required **to prohibit** the transaction pursuant to Article 8(3) EUMR.

2.4.5.4 Referrals of Concentrations

In principle, the Commission's competence to review a concentration is determined by the criteria set out in Articles 1, 3 EUMR.[724] However, for transactions that do not meet the turnover thresholds of Article 1 EUMR, several referral mechanisms exist.

One such mechanism allows **the parties**, prior to notification, to request that the Commission examines the transaction under **Article 4(5) EUMR**, even if the concentration lacks a Community dimension. This referral is available when the proposed transaction falls within the scope of national merger control rules in **at least three Member States**. If none of the Member States concerned objects to the referral, the case is deemed to have a Community dimension by virtue of Article 4(5) EUMR, and the Commission gains jurisdiction. This procedure enables undertakings to avoid the burden of multiple parallel national filings. A notable example is the *Facebook/WhatsApp* merger, where the parties made use of the Article 4(5) EURM referral mechanism. Although the transaction did not meet the EU turnover thresholds, it was accepted by the Commission and ultimately cleared during the preliminary review phase pursuant to Article 6(1)(b) EUMR.[725] Conversely, if the turnover thresholds of Article 1 EUMR are met, undertakings can request that the transaction is not examined by the Commission but by a Member State, see Article 4(4) EUMR. The prerequisite is that 'the concentration may significantly

---

724 On the definition of a concentration, see ► 2.4.2; for the prerequisites of a community dimension of a merger, see ► 2.4.3.

725 Commission, Decision of 3 October 2014, COMP/M.7212 – *Facebook/WhatsApp*.

impede competition in a market within a Member State which has all the characteristics of a distinct market.'

2

In addition, following notification, national competition authorities may request a referral of the case to the Commission under **Article 22 EUMR**. This mechanism allows for referral even when the transaction does not meet the EUMR turnover thresholds, provided that it affects trade between Member States and threatens to significantly affect competition within the territory of the referring Member State(s). In its *Illumina/Grail* ruling of 2022, the EC confirmed that a Member State may request a referral under Article 22 EUMR even if it lacks jurisdiction to review the concentration under its own national law.[726] However, in 2024, the ECJ reversed its position, holding that such a referral must be based on the referring authority's own jurisdiction to assess the transaction. This interpretation significantly narrows the scope of Article 22 EUMR referrals, limiting Member States' ability to request Commission intervention in such cases.[727]

Despite this restriction, Article 22 EUMR remains a valuable tool for addressing so-called killer acquisitions. This term refers to a strategy often employed by large digital or pharmaceutical firms to eliminate nascent competitors before they become a significant threat. Even where the Article 1 EUMR thresholds are not met, Article 22 EUMR referrals can provide a legal basis for the Commission to assess and potentially prohibit such mergers. Nonetheless, the inherent difficulty in forecasting future competitive harm continues to pose challenges for effective enforcement.

Gatekeepers also have specific obligations under DMA. According to **Article 14 DMA**, gatekeepers must inform the Commission of any intended concentration involving digital services, regardless of whether the transaction meets the thresholds of the EUMR.[728] This obligation ensures that the Commission is made aware of potentially significant transactions at an early stage.

The information provided under Article 14 DMA can serve as a basis for the Commission to scrutinise such transactions through a referral under Article 22 EUMR, even if the concentration does not meet the jurisdictional thresholds set out in Article 1 EUMR. In this way, the Article 22 referral mechanism allows for a more comprehensive and flexible review of merger activity in the digital economy.

> ❗ The referral mechanism under Article 22 EUMR plays a crucial role in enabling the Commission to assess mergers that fall below the thresholds of Article 1 EUMR. However, the ECJ, in contrast to the GC's interpretation in the *Illumina/Grail* case, held that a referral request by a national competition authority requires that the authority have jurisdiction to review the concentration under its own national law. This interpretation limits the scope of Article 22 EUMR referrals, curbing the Commission's ability to rely on broad, jurisdiction-neutral referrals.

726 GC 13 July 2022 – T-227/21, ECLI:EU:T:2022:447 – *Illumina*.
727 ECJ 3 September 2024 – C-611/22 P, C-625/22 P, ECLI:EU:C:2024:677 – *Illumina*.
728 See ► 4.3.3.

2.4.5.5 Judicial Review

Under Article 21(2) EUMR, parties to a merger control decision have the right to seek judicial review. In particular, an **action for annulment under Article 263 TFEU** is generally admissible. Such actions fall under the jurisdiction of the GC, and must be brought within 2 months of the contested decision.

A wide range of Commission decisions may be challenged, including prohibition decisions, divestment or unbundling orders issued for breach of the standstill obligation, and clearance decisions that are subject to burdensome conditions or obligations.[729] In addition, under Article 263(4) TFEU, third parties not directly involved in the Commission proceedings may also bring an action, provided they are directly and individually affected by the decision. This may include competitors, customers, or suppliers of the merging parties.[730] Judgments of the GC may be appealed to the ECJ on points of law, pursuant to Article 256(1) TFEU.

Checklist: Assessing a Concentration Under the EUMR

1. Formal Merger Control
   a) Definition of a merger under Article 3 EUMR (acquisition of assets, acquisition of control).
   b) Turnover thresholds under Article 1 EUMR (worldwide and domestic sales thresholds).

2. Substantive analysis—Option 1: Market Dominance Focus
   a) Market dominance test: Would the merger create or strengthen a dominant position under Article 2(3) EUMR?
   b) If no individual dominance is found: gap cases directly under the SIEC criterion
   c) Efficiency defence

3. Substantive analysis—Option 2: SIEC / Unilateral and Coordinated Effects
   a) Unilateral effects: single market dominance; if not, gap cases
   b) Coordinated effects: collective dominance; if not, gap cases
   c) Efficiency defence (as above).

729 Glöckner (2021), sec. 7 mn. 768.
730 Glöckner (2021), sec. 7 mn. 767.

2.5 Enforcement

2.5.1 Public Enforcement

Besides the national competition authorities, the Commission is responsible for the administrative enforcement of European competition law, as established in Article 4 Regulation 1/2003.[731] Pursuant to Article 7(1) Regulation 1/2003, the Commission may issue **cease-and-desist orders** requiring an undertaking to bring an infringement of competition rules to an end.

Furthermore, under Article 7(2) Regulation 1/2003, the Commission is empowered to impose **remedies** necessary to effectively terminate the infringement. These remedies may be either **structural** or **behavioural** in nature. Structural remedies typically involve changes to the organisation or assets of the undertaking, for example, an obligation to grant competitors or customers access to a specific technology or infrastructure.[732] Behavioural (or conduct) remedies, by contrast, may require modifications to certain practices, such as changes to general terms and conditions or pricing policies.[733] In selecting appropriate remedies, the Commission must observe the **principle of proportionality**. Accordingly, structural remedies may only be imposed where no equally effective behavioural remedy is available to address the competition concerns.

The Commission's power to impose remedies under Article 7 Regulation 1/2003, even in response to a single infringement of competition law, stands in contrast to the framework of DMA. Under Article 18(1) DMA, the Commission may impose remedies on gatekeepers only where there is evidence of a **systematic non-compliance** with the obligations set out in Article 5, 6, or 7 DMA. According to Article 18(3) DMA, a systematic infringement is presumed where the gatekeeper has committed at least three violations within an 8-year period.[734] Only in such cases may the Commission impose non-financial remedies, including structural measures such as divestitures or functional separation, provided these are necessary and proportionate to ensure effective compliance.

Under **Article 9 Regulation 1/2003**, the Commission has the power to make commitments offered by undertakings legally binding. Where a company is under investigation for a potential infringement of EU competition law, it may voluntarily propose commitments that it considers appropriate to address the Commission's concerns. The Commission then assesses whether the proposed commitments are sufficient to eliminate the identified competition issues. If it finds them adequate, the Commission may adopt a commitment decision, rendering the measures binding on the undertaking. At the same time, the Commission closes its

731 Council Regulation (EC) No 1/2003 of 16 December 2002 on the implementation of the rules on competition laid down in Articles 81 and 82 of the Treaty, OJ [2003] L 1/1.
732 Ritter and Wirtz (2025), Regulation 1/2003 Article 7 mn. 48.
733 Anweiler (2025), Regulation 1/2003 Article 7 mn. 46.
734 For further details on Article 18(3) DMA, see ► 3.4.1.

investigation without reaching a formal finding of infringement, stating that there is no longer a need to pursue further action regarding the conduct in question.[735]

▶ Example

In cases involving abuse of dominance in the digital sector, dominant undertakings have frequently offered commitments to resolve proceedings initiated under Article 102 TFEU. A notable case is the Commission's investigation into *Amazon*'s e-book distribution agreements in 2015. The Commission expressed concerns that Amazon had included parity clauses in its contracts with e-book publishers.[736] These clauses required publishers to ensure that Amazon always received terms at least as favourable as those offered to its competitors, including in terms of pricing and selection. The Commission took the preliminary view that such clauses could restrict competition and constituted an abuse of dominance under Article 102 TFEU.

In response, *Amazon* offered commitments not to enforce existing parity clauses and to refrain from including such clauses in future agreements with e-book suppliers.[737] The Commission assessed these commitments and, concluding that they addressed the competition concerns, adopted a commitment decision under Article 9 Regulation 1/2003, making the commitments legally binding.[738] As a result, the proceedings were formally closed without a finding of infringement. ◀

2.5.2 Especially: Fines

In cases of infringement of the prohibition on cartels or the prohibition on abuse of dominance, the Commission may impose fines under **Article 23(2) Regulation 1/2003**. The level of fines has increased significantly in recent years, reflecting the severe consequences that violations of EU competition law can have for undertakings.

▶ Examples

In March 2024, the Commission imposed a EUR 1.4 billion fine on *Apple* for infringing Article 102 TFEU.[739] The case concerned the distribution conditions imposed on music streaming providers in the App Store, which the Commission considered abusive. In the *Google Shopping* decision, the Commission fined *Google* EUR 2.4 billion for engaging in self-preferencing practices, favouring its own comparison shopping service in search results at the expense of rivals.[740] ◀

735 Ritter and Wirtz (2025), Regulation 1/2003 Article 9 mn. 29.
736 For a detailed assessment of these clauses under EU competition law, see ▶ 2.2.2.3.
737 Commission, Decision of 4 May 2017 – AT.40153, para. 17 – *e-book distribution agreements*.
738 Commission, Decision of 4 May 2017 – AT.40153, para. 1 – *e-book distribution agreements*.
739 Commission, Decision of 4 March 2024 – AT.40437 – *Apple App Store Practices (music streaming)*.
740 Commission, Decision of 27 June 2017 – AT.39740 – *Google Search (Shopping)*.

2

A fine may only be imposed if the infringement is committed **culpably**. Intent exists where the undertaking knew that its conduct infringed competition law.[741] However, actual awareness is not required; it is sufficient that the undertaking should have recognised the illegality.[742] A mistake of law, i.e. an incorrect understanding of the legal prohibition, does not generally exempt an undertaking from liability. Negligence arises when the undertaking could have recognised that its conduct was unlawful, had it exercised reasonable care.[743]

Importantly, the use of AI, for instance, in automated price-setting systems, does not relieve undertakings of responsibility. Undertakings have a duty of care when deploying AI tools, and cannot 'hide' behind algorithmic systems to escape liability.[744] The use of AI does not shield undertakings from culpability for infringements of Article 101 TFEU, particularly in the context of collusive practices.

The fine imposed under Article 23(2) Regulation 1/2003 may amount to up to **10% of the total worldwide turnover of the undertaking** in the preceding business year. This ceiling functions as a **cap**, not as a formula for calculating fines.[745] The actual calculation is guided by the Commission's Guidelines on fines, but the 10% limit defines the legal maximum. The term 'undertaking' in Article 23 Regulation 1/2003 is interpreted by the ECJ as referring not merely to a single legal entity, but to the broader **economic unit** engaged in the infringing conduct.[746] This means that, although the fine is formally addressed to a particular legal person, all entities forming part of the same economic unit at the time of the infringement are considered jointly and severally liable.[747]

This principle has been most notably applied to the liability of parent companies for competition law infringements committed by their wholly-owned or nearly wholly-owned subsidiaries. The decisive factor is whether the subsidiary exercises market autonomy. Where the parent company holds 100% or nearly 100% of the subsidiary's shares, it is presumed that the parent exerts decisive influence, thereby forming a single economic unit with the subsidiary[748] If the shareholding is below this threshold, additional evidence, referred to as 'plus factors', must be considered to determine whether the parent exercised decisive influence. Conversely, liability can also extend downward, such that a subsidiary may be held liable for the conduct of its parent company.[749] In addition, sister companies within the same corporate group may be held jointly liable where they form part of the same economic unit.[750]

---

741 ECJ 8 November 1983 – C-96/82 and others, ECLI:EU:C:1983:310, p. 3429 – *IAZ and others.*

742 GC 6 April 1995 – T-143/89, ECLI:EU:T:1995:64, para. 41 – *Ferriere Nord.*

743 ECJ 14 February 1978 – C-27/76, ECLI:EU:C:1978:22, para. 299/301 – *United Brands.*

744 For further details on the functions of algorithms for establishing collusion, see ► 2.2.1.3.3.

745 ECJ 8 December 2011 – C-389/10, ECLI:EU:C:2011:816, para. 99 – *KME Germany et al.*

746 For further details on the concept of undertaking under EU competition law, see ► 2.1.4.1.

747 ECJ 10 April 2014 – C-231/11 P and others, ECLI:EU:C:2014:256 – *Commission v Siemens Austria and others.*

748 ECJ 14 July 1972 – C-48/69, ECLI:EU:C:1972:70, para. 132/135 – *ICI.*

749 ECJ 6 October 2021 – C-882/19, ECLI:EU:C:2021:800 – *Sumal.*

750 ECJ 6 October 2021 – C-882/19, ECLI:EU:C:2021:800 – *Sumal.*

When calculating a fine under Article 23(2) Regulation 1/2003, the Commission follows a structured methodology outlined in its Guidelines on fines. The process begins with the determination of a basic amount, which is assessed in light of several factors, including the nature and gravity of the infringement, its actual or potential impact on the internal market, the duration of the conduct, and its geographic scope.[751] Once the basic amount has been established, it may be adjusted to reflect aggravating or mitigating circumstances. Aggravating factors include a long duration of the infringement, intentional conduct by the undertaking, or attempts to obstruct the Commission's investigation, such as destroying evidence or failing to comply with information requests.[752] By contrast, mitigating circumstances may lead to a reduction in the fine. These include the undertaking's willingness to cooperate with the Commission, prompt termination of the unlawful behaviour, or limited involvement in the infringement.

In the context of cartel investigations, the Commission's Leniency Notice provides specific conditions under which undertakings may benefit from a reduction or complete waiver of the fine.[753] Full immunity may be granted to the first undertaking that supplies decisive evidence of the infringement. Additionally, the Commission uses settlement procedures to reward cooperation and procedural efficiency.[754] Undertakings that acknowledge their participation in the infringement and agree to a simplified procedure may receive a further reduction in the fine, typically up to ten percent.

2.5.3 Private Enforcement

Contracts that infringe the prohibition of cartels under Article 101(1) TFEU are deemed automatically void pursuant to Article 101(2) TFEU. This nullity applies to the entire agreement or the offending provisions, depending on whether the remainder of the contract can stand independently in legal and economic terms. In contrast, the invalidity of contractual provisions that contravene the prohibition of abuse under Article 102 TFEU is not explicitly regulated at the EU level. However, in German competition law, such invalidity arises by applying sec. 134 German Civil Code in conjunction with Article 102 TFEU.[755] According to sec. 134 German Civil Code, legal acts that violate a statutory prohibition are null and void unless the law provides otherwisc. Thus, contractual clauses that result from or contribute

751 Commission, Guidelines on the method of setting fines imposed pursuant to Article 23(2)(a) of Regulation No 1/2003 OJ [2006] C 201/2, paras. 12 et seqq.
752 Nowak (2025), Regulation 1/2003 Article 23 mn. 33.
753 Commission, Notice on the non-imposition or reduction of fines in cartel cases, OJ [2016] C 298/17.
754 Regulation (EC) No 622/2008 of 30 June 2008 as regards the conduct of settlement proceedings in cartel cases, OJ [2008] L 171/3.
755 Huttenlauch (2025), TFEU Art. 102 Rn. 358.

2

to an abuse of market dominance may be rendered void under national civil law due to their incompatibility with EU competition rules.

European competition law does not, in itself, provide a direct civil law basis for damages claims. However, in its landmark judgments in *Courage v. Crehan*[756] and *Manfredi,*[757] the ECJ affirmed that individuals and undertakings have the right to claim compensation for harm suffered as a result of conduct infringing European competition law, in particular Articles 101, 102 TFEU. The legal basis for such claims must be found in the **national legal systems** of the Member States.[758] Nonetheless, the exercise of this right is subject to two key principles of European law. First, the **principle of equivalence** requires that the procedural rules governing the enforcement of EU competition law rights must not be less favourable than those applicable to similar domestic actions. Second, the **principle of effectiveness** ensures that national rules do not render the exercise of EU rights practically impossible or excessively difficult.

In 2014, the EU legislator adopted the Cartel Damages Directive[759] to facilitate the effective enforcement of actions for damages in the Member States. The Directive aims to harmonise key aspects of private enforcement across the EU, ensuring that individuals and businesses harmed by competition law infringements, particularly cartel conduct, can obtain full compensation. The concept of undertaking employed in the Cartel Damages Directive reflects the interpretation established under Article 101 TFEU and Regulation 1/2003.[760] It refers to the economic unit, regardless of its legal form or capacity.[761] Consequently, all entities forming part of the economic unit at the time of the infringement may be held jointly and severally liable for the resulting harm. Since directives are not directly applicable in Member States, pursuant to Article 288(3) TFEU, their provisions require national transposition. In Germany, the legislator implemented the Cartel Damages Directive through sec. 33 et seq. ARC. The specific provisions governing the transposition are discussed in detail in the chapter on German competition law.[762]

2.6 Proceedings

2.6.1 Administrative Proceedings

The Commission may initiate administrative proceedings on its own initiative if it suspects an infringement of Article 101 or Article 102 TFEU. The decision to initi-

756 ECJ 20 September 2001 – C-453/99, ECLI:EU:C:2001:465, para. 19 et seqq. – *Courage/Crehan.*

757 ECJ 13 July 2006 – C-295/04 and others, ECLI:EU:C:2006:461, para. 58 et seqq. – *Manfredi.*

758 For details on the German provisions that enable the private enforcement of EU competition law, see ► 5.5.3.

759 Directive 2014/104/EU of the European Parliament and of the Council of 26 November 2014 on certain rules governing actions for damages under national law for infringements of the competition law provisions of the Member States and of the European Union, OJ [2014] L 349/1.

760 On the concept of undertaking, see ► 2.1.4.1.

761 ECJ 14 March 2019 – C-724/17, ECLI:EU:C:2019:204, para. 47 et seqq. – *Skanska.*

762 For further details on sec. 33 et seq. ARC, see ► 5.5.3.

ate proceedings lies within the Commission's discretion, reflecting the **principle of opportunity**.[763] Alternatively, proceedings may be triggered by a formal complaint submitted by a third party. However, the submission of a complaint does not entitle the complainant to compel the Commission to take action.[764] Once the Commission formally initiates proceedings, the competence of national competition authorities to pursue enforcement in relation to the same conduct under Article 101 or Article 102 TFEU ceases. This is laid down in Article 11(6) Regulation 1/2003 and ensures a clear allocation of responsibilities and avoiding duplication of enforcement efforts.

Before adopting any investigative measures, the Commission must have an **initial indication** or suspicion of a possible infringement.[765] Under Article 18 Regulation 1/2003, it is empowered to request all necessary information from undertakings or associations of undertakings. Pursuant to Article 19 Regulation 1/2003, the Commission may also conduct interviews with individuals or representatives of undertakings to clarify facts or gather additional evidence.

In accordance with Articles 20, 21 Regulation 1/2003, the Commission is further authorised to carry out inspections, including unannounced visits, both at the business premises of undertakings and, in certain cases, at other premises, such as private homes, if there is a reasonable suspicion that evidence is being kept there. These investigatory powers are essential for uncovering competition law infringements, particularly where evidence may not be voluntarily disclosed. Undertakings are under a legal obligation to cooperate with the Commission during investigations. This duty of cooperation applies especially to requests for information and on-site inspections, and non-compliance may result in the imposition of fines under Article 23 Regulation 1/2003.[766]

In addition to the adoption of cease-and-desist orders under Article 7 Regulation 1/2003 and the binding effect of commitments pursuant to Article 9, the Commission may also impose **interim measures under Article 8 Regulation 1/2003**. This instrument allows the Commission to intervene swiftly in order to prevent serious harm to the competitive process during the course of an ongoing investigation. However, the threshold for the adoption of interim measures at the European level is high. Such measures may only be imposed where there is a prima facie finding of an infringement and a risk of serious and irreparable damage to competition. The potential harm must also be reasonably foreseeable based on the circumstances of the case. In comparison, the German legislator has opted for a more flexible approach. Under sec. 32a ARC, the standard for issuing interim measures is less stringent. While a risk of serious harm remains a requirement, the

763 Ritter and Wirtz (2025), Article 7 Regulation 1/2003 mn. 10.
764 Dieckmann (2020), sec. 41 mn. 8.
765 Dieckmann (2020), sec. 42 mn. 4.
766 Dieckmann (2020), sec. 42 mn. 8.

2

procedural barriers are lower, thereby facilitating the use of interim relief by the German competition authority. This divergence reflects a more proactive stance in German law toward the preservation of effective competition pending the outcome of a full investigation.[767]

In light of the growing importance of digital markets and the increasing complexity of uncovering competition law infringements involving AI, there is ongoing debate about whether the investigative powers of competition authorities should be expanded.[768] One proposal under discussion is the introduction of algorithmic control mechanisms, allowing authorities to directly assess the functioning and effects of AI-driven systems used by undertakings.[769] Another idea is to shift from a purely reactive enforcement model to a more proactive, ex ante monitoring of digital markets.[770] In this context, it is being considered whether the Commission should systematically observe market developments and evaluate how the deployment of AI technologies may affect market structures, potentially giving rise to anti-competitive outcomes. At present, the Commission already possesses a tool for broader market scrutiny in the form of sector inquiries, as provided for under Article 17 Regulation 1/2003. This provision enables the Commission to investigate entire sectors of the economy where price rigidity, lack of transparency, or other structural indicators suggest that competition may be restricted or distorted, even in the absence of a specific infringement. Furthermore, there are increasing calls to use AI in the service of enforcement, enabling authorities to identify patterns of collusion or abuse more efficiently.[771] For instance, it has been reported that the Swiss Competition Authority has employed algorithms to detect restrictive agreements among construction companies.[772]

2.6.2 Fine Proceedings

In administrative fine proceedings under European competition law, the formal initiation of the procedure is typically preceded by a **preliminary investigation** phase.[773] During this phase, the Commission seeks to establish the relevant facts and, where necessary, exercises its investigative powers under Regulation 1/2003. Once the Commission has gathered sufficient evidence, it issues a Statement of Objections, in which it sets out the legal and factual basis on which it intends to

767 See ► 3.6.1.

768 Künstner (2019), pp. 36, 42.

769 OECD, Algorithms and Collusion: Competition Policy in the Digital Age (2017), 2; http://www.oecd.org/daf/competition/Algorithms-and-colllusion-competition-policy-in-the-digital-age.pdf (9 June 2024).

770 Künstner (2019), pp. 36, 42.

771 Künstner (2019), pp. 36, 42; Lorenzoni (2022), 15(26), 33, 40 et seqq.

772 Competition Commission, case report on the analysis of bids in construction tenders, ► https://www.weko.admin.ch/weko/de/home/aktuell/medieninformationen/nsb-news.msg-id-64011.html (9.6.2024).

773 Feddersen (2009), Article 23 regulation 1/2003 mn. 2.

impose a fine.[774] The undertakings concerned are then given the opportunity to respond to the allegations, both in writing and, if requested, at an oral hearing.[775] This ensures respect for the rights of defence. Following this procedural stage, the Commission may adopt a decision imposing a fine in what is, at the European level, a simple administrative procedure.[776] This stands in contrast to German competition law, where the imposition of fines follows a procedure that must comply with the formal requirements of administrative offence law ('Ordnungswidrigkeitenrecht'), which includes higher procedural safeguards and judicial involvement.[777]

A Commission decision imposing a fine may be challenged by bringing an action for annulment under **Article 263(4) TFEU**. Jurisdiction lies with the **GC**. Pursuant to Article 31 Regulation 1/2003, the GC has unlimited jurisdiction to review the Commission's decision, including the power to annul, reduce, or increase the fine imposed. An appeal against the GC's judgment may be brought before the ECJ. However, the ECJ's review is limited to points of law. That means it does not reassess the factual findings of the GC.

2.6.3 Civil Proceedings

Civil proceedings for competition law damages are conducted exclusively before national civil courts. The procedural rules governing such actions are determined by national law. In Germany, the relevant provisions are set out in sec. 33 et seqq. ARC, which are explained in detail in the chapter on German competition law.[778] However, European case law plays a significant role in shaping the interpretation and application of these national provisions. In particular, national courts may refer questions of EU law to the ECJ for a **preliminary ruling**, in accordance with **Article 267 TFEU**, where the interpretation of the Cartel Damages Directive is at issue.

In key decisions such as *Skanska*[779] and *Sumal*,[780] the ECJ clarified that the definition of 'undertaking' under the Directive must be understood in line with the established European competition law concept, namely, as an economic unit, irrespective of legal form. This interpretation is binding on national courts and must inform the application of national transposition measures, in accordance with the principle of directive-conforming interpretation. As a result, the uniform application of EU competition law is safeguarded across Member States, even in the context of decentralized civil enforcement.

774 Feddersen (2009), Article 23 regulation 1/2003 mn. 26.
775 GC15 March 2000 – T-25/95, ECLI:EU:T:2000:77, para. 653 – *Cimenteries CBR*.
776 Meyer (2025), Article 101 TFEU mn. 205.
777 For further details on German fine proceedings, see ► 5.6.2.
778 For further details civil proceedings under civil proceedings, see ► 5.6.3.
779 ECJ 14 March 2019 – C-724/17, ECLI:EU:C:2019:204 – *Skanska*.
780 ECJ 6 October 2021 – C-882/19, ECLI:EU:C:2021:298 – *Sumal*.

2.7 Review Questions

1. What are multi-sided markets? Give examples.

Multi-sided markets are markets in which a single provider offers services to two or more distinct user groups, known as market sides or counterparties, and where interdependencies exist between these groups (▸ 1.1.1). The value of the platform to one group typically increases with the participation of the other group(s), a phenomenon referred to as indirect network effects.

In the digital economy, multi-sided markets are particularly prevalent. For example, platform operators, such as those running social media networks, provide services to private end users (who access content or social interactions) and to advertisers (who seek to reach those users through targeted advertising). The more users the platform attracts, the more valuable it becomes to advertisers, and vice versa. Multi-sided market structures also exist in traditional sectors. A common example is newspapers and magazines, which serve readers on one side by providing content, and advertisers on the other by offering advertising space. Again, the appeal to advertisers depends on the size and demographics of the readership.

2. What is meant by network effects? Give examples from the digital economy.

Network effects refer to the interdependencies within and between different user groups on a multi-sided platform market (▸ 1.1.2). They describe how the value of a product or service increases or decreases for users depending on the number of other users engaging with the same platform. There are two main types of network effects:

Direct network effects occur within a single user group. For instance, on social media platforms, the benefit to an individual user increases as more other private users join and interact. The platform becomes more attractive as the user base grows, due to enhanced opportunities for communication and engagement. Indirect network effects occur between different user groups on the platform. These can be positive, when an increase in one group benefits the other. For example, on online trading platforms such as Amazon or eBay, the value for retailers increases as the number of end users (i.e. potential buyers) grows. A larger consumer base leads to more visibility and sales opportunities. These can also be negative, when growth in one group harms the other, such as when increased advertiser activity on a platform leads to a degraded user experience for consumers due to excessive or intrusive ads.

3. In which ways can algorithms contribute to or facilitate unlawful collusive conduct?

In the context of the ban on cartels, algorithms can take on several roles that influence how collusive behaviour is implemented, maintained, or even potentially initiated (► 2.2.1.1; ► 2.2.1.3).

Firstly, algorithms may be used to monitor compliance with cartel agreements. By continuously tracking prices, outputs, or market behaviours, algorithms allow undertakings to detect deviations from collusive arrangements quickly. This enhances cartel discipline, as participants are deterred from undercutting or cheating on the agreement due to the risk of immediate detection. As a result, when such cartels are uncovered, the fines imposed by competition authorities may be higher due to the increased stability and duration of the infringement.

Secondly, the use of identical or coordinated algorithms facilitate the implementation of anticompetitive agreements. When all cartel participants rely on the same pricing software or algorithmic system, alignment in behaviour can be achieved more easily, sometimes even without direct communication.

Lastly, there is an ongoing academic and policy debate about whether algorithms could autonomously achieve collusion, without any explicit human agreement. This scenario refers to so-called 'tacit algorithmic collusion', where algorithms, through learning and market interaction, may reach a stable collusive outcome on their own. However, such cases remain hypothetical; to date, there is no known instance of fully autonomous algorithmic collusion being observed or sanctioned in practice.

4. What issue is addressed by the term 'algorithmic oligopolisation'?

The term 'algorithmic oligopolisation' refers to the concern that the use of algorithms may alter market dynamics in such a way that undertakings are able to coordinate their market behaviour without entering into explicit agreements. This phenomenon is known as tacit collusion (cf. ► 2.2.1.3.3). Traditionally, tacit coordination is considered feasible only in exceptional cases, particularly where market conditions are favourable: namely, where the market is highly concentrated, products are homogeneous, and a high degree of transparency allows firms to observe and react to one another's behaviour. Under such circumstances, undertakings may raise prices above the competitive level simply by anticipating and mirroring their rivals' conduct, without infringing Article 101 TFEU. The use of pricing or monitoring algorithms could enhance this risk. Algorithms can significantly increase the speed of reaction and improve market transparency, which may facilitate coordination. However, there is no conclusive evidence to date that algorithmic tools can enable or sustain tacit collusion in markets that lack the typical structural conditions for coordination.

5. A manufacturer prohibits its dealers from using the internet as a distribution channel within a selective distribution system. Is this agreement compatible with the European ban on cartels? Variation: What would be the legal assessment if the manufacturer, while generally allowing both online and offline sales, offers dealers lower resale prices for sales in physical stores?

The agreement in which the manufacturer prohibits dealers from using the internet as a sales channel violates Article 101 TFEU. It constitutes a vertical restriction of competition that limits the dealers' freedom to determine how and where they sell the goods (► 2.2.2.3.2). Such a restriction is classified as a hardcore restriction under Article 4(e) VBER. Accordingly, the agreement cannot benefit from a block exemption, regardless of the market shares of the undertakings involved. From the classification as hardcore restriction also follows that the agreement is presumed to be unlawful and, in principle, cannot be exempted under Article 101(3) TFEU, unless truly exceptional circumstances can be shown.

In the variation, where the manufacturer does not prohibit online sales but offers lower resale prices for offline sales (a dual pricing system), the legal assessment differs. This arrangement does not automatically constitute a restriction of competition. It reflects the recognition that the internet is now a well-established sales channel and does not require special protection compared to traditional brick-and-mortar outlets. Whether such dual pricing is compatible with Article 101 TFEU depends on whether the price differences are justified and proportionate, e.g. to reflect legitimate differences in the costs incurred for each sales channel. The Commission does not require detailed cost accounting, but the price advantage for offline sales must remain reasonable and not result in an indirect restriction of online sales (**cf.** ► 2.2.2.3.4).

6. How are price parity clauses assessed under Article 101 TFEU? Please name the relevant provisions in the VBER.

Price parity clauses(also referred to as best-price clauses or most-favoured-nation clauses) arise when a platform operator requires commercial users not to offer their goods or services at better conditions elsewhere. A distinction is made between narrow price parity clauses, where the restriction applies only to the provider's own website; and broad price parity clauses, where it applies to third-party platforms as well.

Both forms of price parity clauses are classified as vertical restraints under Article 101(1) TFEU because they limit the pricing freedom of commercial users and can foreclose alternative sales or distribution channels, especially in platform markets (**cf.** ► 2.2.2.3.8). Narrow parity clauses generally fall outside the scope of the VBER (i.e. they are not automatically exempted), but they are not classified as hardcore or excluded restrictions. Their legality must therefore be assessed individually under Article 101(3) TFEU. Broad parity clauses, by contrast, are expressly designated as 'excluded restrictions' under Article 5(1)(d) VBER. This means that they are not covered by the block exemption, regardless of the market shares of the parties. As such, they require an individual assessment and are less likely to be justified under Article 101(3) TFEU, especially if they lead to market foreclosure or reduce inter-platform competition.

7. Can a vertical agreement between a platform operator and commercial users be exempt from Article 101 TFEU under the commercial agent privilege?

The commercial agent privilege excludes certain agreements from the scope of Article 101 TFEU. Specifically, it applies where the agent is not acting as an independent economic operator, but is instead integrated into the principal's business organisation and bears no significant commercial or financial risk in relation to the contracts concluded on the principal's behalf (► 2.2.4.4). However, this exemption generally does not apply to platform operators. Platforms typically act as independent intermediaries that broker transactions between commercial users and end customers. They bear their own economic risks, operate on behalf of multiple undertakings, and frequently set or influence commercial terms, such as pricing rules or access conditions. The fact that platform operators serve many commercial users and exercise a significant degree of control makes it inappropriate to consider them as mere auxiliary agents within the meaning of the commercial agent doctrine. As such, agreements between platform operators and commercial users will usually fall within the scope of Article 101 TFEU, and must be assessed accordingly under the rules on vertical restraints.

8. How are platform operators integrated into the VBER?

Platform operators do not conform to the traditional two- or three-tier distribution model (manufacturer–wholesaler–retailer) on which the VBER is largely based. Instead, they typically operate at the interface between production and distribution, facilitating transactions between commercial users and end customers, often without owning the products or services themselves. To address this structural divergence, Article 1(1)(d) VBER explicitly provides that undertakings offering online intermediation services are to be treated as suppliers with respect to the undertakings that use their services. This legal clarification ensures that agreements between a platform operator and the commercial users who offer goods or services via the platform are treated as vertical agreements for the purposes of Article 101 TFEU (► 2.2.5.2.1.2). This classification is important because it means that platform agreements can benefit from the safe harbour offered by the VBER, provided all the other conditions (such as market share thresholds and absence of hardcore restrictions) are met. However, platform operators that also compete with their users (so-called hybrid platforms) may be excluded from the benefit of the block exemption under Article 2(6) VBER.

9. Platform operators occasionally offer services to end users free of charge. What consequences does this have for the market definition under competition law?

2

At first glance, offering services free of charge raises the question of whether a market exists at all, as markets are typically defined by the exchange of goods or services for consideration. However, this narrow view does not reflect the reality of multi-sided platform markets, where services may be provided to one user group (e.g. private end users) at no monetary cost while being financed through transactions with another user group (e.g. advertisers or business users). In such cases, positive indirect network effects play a crucial role: platforms often offer free access to consumers in order to attract scale on one side of the market, which in turn increases the platform's value on the other side. As a result, the provision of a service free of charge does not preclude the existence of a relevant market. This understanding is reflected in European competition law. The Commission's Notice on Market Definition recognises that non-monetary exchanges, particularly in digital markets, can form the basis of a relevant market (**cf.** ► 2.3.1.1.4).

10. What criteria should be taken into account when defining product markets in the digital sector?

In the digital sector, market definition is particularly complex due to the prevalence of multi-sided platform markets. These platforms typically provide services to several distinct user groups. When defining the product market, a key question is whether the services to these different user groups belong to a single integrated market or constitute separate relevant markets. The Commission, in its Notice on Market Definition, provides guidance tailored to digital markets. It considers substitutability as one main criterion. The decisive factor is whether the services provided to different user groups are substitutable from the users' perspective. If they are not, this may justify defining separate markets for each user group. The Commission also takes into account the platform type: It distinguishes between transactional platforms (e.g. online marketplaces) and Matching or advertising platforms (e.g. social media). Moreover, the Commission considers network effects: Their existence and nature are relevant in assessing how user groups relate to one another and how demand on one side of the platform influences the other (**cf.** ► 2.3.1.1.4.2).

11. Should the essential facilities doctrine be applied to dominant search engine operators?

One argument against applying the essential facilities doctrine to search engines is that a resource should only be considered 'essential' if there is no realistic alternative for market access. Although certain search engines (such as *Google Search*) hold very high market shares, alternative providers do exist and can be accessed by users without substantial switching costs. This suggests that access to a dominant search engine is not strictly indispensable. Moreover, search engines are not inherently non-replicable infrastructures. In principle, a market participant seeking to enter the market could develop its own search engine, even if doing so may require significant investment and time. Therefore, the criteria for classifying a search engine as an essential facility may not be met (**cf.** ► 2.3.2.1.7).

12. What does the ECJ understand by an abusive self-preferencing practice under Article 102 TFEU?

The ECJ defines self-preferencing as conduct by a dominant undertaking that operates an intermediation service at the upstream market level while simultaneously competing with commercial users at the downstream level, and uses its market position to unfairly favour its own offerings, for example, through preferential ranking. In doing so, the undertaking leverages its upstream market power to strengthen its position in adjacent or downstream markets. This practice has been scrutinised by the Commission and the EU courts in the *Google Shopping* case (ECJ 10 September 2024 – C-48/22 P, ECLI:EU:C:2024:726; GC 10 November 2021 – T-612/17, ECLI:EU:T:2021:763; Commission, Decision of 27 June 2017 – AT.39740) (► 2.3.2.1.4).

13. Can dynamic or personalised pricing constitute exploitative abuse under Article 102 TFEU?

Neither personalised nor dynamic pricing constitutes an exploitative abuse under Article 102 TFEU per se. Making use of individual customers' willingness to pay is, in principle, permissible and must remain so even for dominant undertakings. Similarly, dominant firms are allowed to respond swiftly to changing demand by adjusting prices. However, exploitative abuse may arise where a dominant undertaking sets prices that are excessively high (**cf.** ► 2.3.2.2.3; ► 2.3.2.2.4).

14. What are the challenges associated with applying the turnover thresholds in Article 1 EUMR to mergers in the digital sector?

In the digital sector, so-called 'buy-out strategies' have increasingly been observed in recent years. These involve the early acquisition of innovative and potentially competitive start-ups by large digital firms, with the aim of preventing future competition that might threaten their market dominance. Such transactions are commonly referred to as 'killer acquisitions'. From a merger control perspective, the challenge is that these acquisitions often fall below the turnover thresholds set out in Article 1 EUMR and therefore escape notification requirements (**cf. 2.4.1.2.2**). One mechanism that enables the Commission to still review such transactions is a referral by Member State authorities under Article 22 EUMR, or, alternatively, a request by the undertakings concerned pursuant to Article 4(5) EUMR.

15. What data-related harm theories are discussed under the SIEC test?

In both horizontal and vertical mergers, superior access to data can lead to foreclosure effects that harm competitors, for example, by enabling product improvements through data analysis. However, a foreclosure effect requires that competitors lack comparable opportunities to collect data. Additionally, there must be sufficient incentives to pursue foreclosure strategies (**cf. 2.4.3.3.1; 2.4.3.3.2**).

2.8 Landmark ECJ Decisions

- ECJ 25 Feburary 2025 – C-233/23, ECLI:EU:C:2025:110 – *Alphabet and Google*
- ECJ 10 September 2024 – C-48/22 P, ECLI:EU:C:2024:726 – *Google Shopping*
- ECJ 3 September 2024 – C-611/22 P, C-625/22 P, ECLI:EU:C:2024:677 – *Illumina*
- ECJ 13 July 2023 – C-376/20 P, ECLI:C:EU: 2023:561 – *Hutchison/Telefónica UK*
- ECJ 4 July 2023 – C-252/21, ECLI:EU:C:2023:537 – *Meta (Facebook)*
- ECJ 25 March 2023 – C-449/21, ECLI:EU:C:2023:207 – *Towercast*
- ECJ 22 March 2022 – C-151/20, ECLI:EU:C:2022:203 – *Nordzucker*
- ECJ 22 March 2022 – C-117/20, ECLI:EU:C:2022:202 – *pbost*
- ECJ 6 October 2021 – C-882/19, ECLI:EU:C:2021:800 – *Sumal*
- ECJ 25 February 2021 – C-857/19, ECLI:EU:C:2021:139 – *Slovak Telekom*
- ECJ 14 March 2019 – C-724/17, ECLI:EU:C:2019:204 – *Skanska*
- ECJ 6 December 2017 – C-230/16, ECLI:EU:C:2017:941 – *Coty Germany*
- ECJ 6 September 2017 – C-413/14 P, ECLI:EU:C:2017:632 – *Intel*
- ECJ 21 January 2016 – C-74/14, ECLI:EU:C:2016:42 – *Eturas*
- ECJ 19 March 2015 – C-286/13 P, ECLI:EU:C:2015:184 – *Dole Food and Dole Fresh Fruit Europe*
- ECJ 4 September 2014 – C-184/13, ECLI:EU:C:2014:2147 – *API*
- ECJ 7 December 2013 – C-68/12, ECLI:EU:C:2013:72 – *Slovenská sporiteľňa*
- ECJ 13 December 2012 – C-226/11, ECLI:EU:C:2012:795 – *Expedia*
- ECJ 27 March 2012 – C-209/10, ECLI:EU:C:2012:172 – *Post Danmark*
- ECJ 13 October 2011 – C-439/09, ECLI:EU:C:2011:649 – *Pierre Fabre Dermo-Cosmétique*
- ECJ 17 February 2011 – C-52/09, ECLI:EU:C:2011:83 – *TeliaSonera*
- ECJ 14 October 2010 – C-280/08 P, ECLI:EU:C:2010:212 – *Deutsche Telekom*
- ECJ 4 June 2009 – C-8/08, ECLI:EU:C:2009:343 – *T-Mobile Netherlands*
- ECJ 17 September 2007 – T-201/04, ECLI:EU:T:2007:289 – *Microsoft*
- ECJ 18 July 2006 – C-519/04 P, ECLI:EU:C:2006:492 – *Meca Medina*
- ECJ 13 July 2006 – C-295/04, ECLI:EU:C:2006:461 – *Manfredi*
- ECJ 19 February 2002 – C-309/99, ECLI:EU:C:2002:98 – *Wouters*
- ECJ 20 September 2001 – C-453/99, ECLI:EU:C:2001:465 – *Courage/Crehan*
- ECJ 28 February 1991 – C-234/89, ECLI:EU:C:1991:91 – *Delimitis/Henninger Bräu*

- ECJ 26 November 1998 – C-7/97, ECLI:EU:C:1998:569 – *Bronner*
- ECJ 25 October 1977 – C-26/76, ECLI:EU:C:1977:100 – *Metro*

References

Achleitner R (2022) Selbstbegünstigung als Konzept des Marktmissbrauchs unter Art. 102 AEUV. Das Grundsatzurteil des EuG zu Google Shopping als Initialzündung für einen Wandel in der Digitalwirtschaft? – Anmerkung zum Urteil des EuG v. 10.11.2021, Case T-612/17 (Google and Alphabet v Commission [Google Shopping]). EuR 2022:253–270

Akmann P (2017) The theory of abuse in Google search: a positive and normative assessment under EU Competition Law. J Law Technol 2017:302–376

Alfter M, Hunold M (2016) Weit, eng oder gar nicht? Unterschiedliche Entscheidungen zu den Bestpreisklauseln von Hotelportalen. WuW 2016:525–531

Anweiler J (2025) Regulation 1/2003 Article 7. In: Kersting C, Meyer-Lindemann HJ, Podszun R (eds) Kartellrecht, 5th edn. C.H. Beck, Munich

Apel K, Polley R (2021) "Gap cases" in der formellen Fusionskontrolle der FKVO? ZWeR 2021:273–316

Argentesi E, Buccirossi P, Calvano E, Duso T, Marrazzo A, Nava S (2019) Ex-post assessment of merger control decisions in digital markets. Lear, Rome

Autorité de la concurrence and German Federal Cartel Office (2019) Algorithms and competition

Ballestrem J, Bär U, Gausling T, Hack S, Oelffen S (2020) Künstliche Intelligenz - Rechtsgrundlagen und Strategien in der Praxis. SpringerGabler, Wiesbaden

Barthelmeß S (2014) Die Intel-Entscheidung des Europäischen Gerichts: Per se Missbräuchlichkeit von Ausschließlichkeitsrabatten unter Art. 102 AEUV und eingeschränkte Bedeutung des "as-efficient-competitor"-Tests. NZKart 2014:492–496

Bernhard J (2019) Die Geoblocking-Verordnung in der Praxis. NJW:472–476

Bien F (2023) TFEU Article 102. In: Säcker F (ed) Münchener Kommentar zum Wettbewerbsrecht, 4th edn. C.H. Beck, Munich

Bien F, Becker B (2024) Das Anwerben von Mitarbeitern im Lichte der deutschen und europäischen Fusionskontrolle – Teil 1. WuW 2024:81–88

Böni F, Palzer C (2009) Kollektive Marktbeherrschung - Sinnbild für "Des Kaisers neue Kleider"? WuW 2009:477–488

Bostoen F (2023) Abuse of platform power – leveraging conduct in digital markets under EU Competition Law and beyond. Concurrences, Paris

Brand O (2025) TFEU Article 102. In: Jaeger W, Kokott J, Pohlmann P, Schroeder D, Seeliger D (eds) Frankfurter Kommentar zum Kartellrecht, 111th supp. Dr. Otto Schmidt, Cologne

Brinker I (2019) TFEU Article 101. In: Becker U, Hatje A, Schoo J, Schwarze J (eds) EU-Kommentar, 4th edn. Helbing Lichtenhahn Verlag, Basel

Buccirossi P (2015) Vertical restraints on e-commerce and selective distribution. J Compet Law Econ 11(3):747–773

Crémer J, de Montjoye Y, Schweitzer H (2019) Competition policy for the digital era. Publications Office for the European Union, Brussels

Dieckmann H (2020) Sec. 41, 42. In: Wiedemann G (ed) Handbuch des Kartellrechts, 4th edn. C.H. Beck, Munich

Dohrn D, Huck L (2018) Der Algorithmus als "Kartellgehilfe"? – Kartellrechtliche Compliance im Zeitalter der Digitalisierung. DB 2018:173–179

Ecker B, Geerenstein D, Gronemeyer A, Janka S, Jansen G, Kiparski G, Lau N, Polley R, Scheibe A, Suchsland U, Wegner A (2021) Industrie 4.0 - Kartellrechtliche Betrachtungen, 2nd edn. BMWi, Berlin

Eilmansberger T, Kruis T (2018) TFEU Article 101. In: Streinz R (ed) Beck'sche Kommentare EUV/AEUV, 3rd edn. C.H. Beck, Munich

Ellger R (2025) TFEU Article 101 (3). In: Immenga U, Mestmäcker E (eds) Kommentar zum Wettbewerbsrecht, 7th edn. C.H. Beck, Munich
Emde R (2019) Qualitativ-selektive Vertriebssysteme und Internetvertrieb – mehr als ein Jahr nach "Coty". ZVertriebsR 2019:69–86
Emmerich V, Lange K (2024) Kartellrecht, 16th edn. C.H. Beck, Munich
Ewald C (2020) Sec. 7. In: Wiedemann G (ed) Handbuch des Kartellrechts, 4th edn. C.H. Beck, Munich
Feddersen C (2009) Article 23 Regualation 1/2003. In: Grabitz E, Hilf M, Nettesheim M (eds) Das Recht der Europäischen Union, 40th supp. C.H. Beck, Munich
Filistrucchi L, Geradin D, van Damme E, Affeldt P (2014) Market definition in two-sided markets: theory and practice. J Compet Law Econ 10(2):293–339
Fuchs A, Heinemann A (2025) TFEU Article 102. In: Immenga U, Mestmäcker E (eds) Kommentar zum Wettbewerbsrecht, 7th edn. C.H. Beck, Munich
Furman J, Coyle D, Fletcher A, McAuley D, Marsden P (2019) Unlocking Digital Competition, Report of the Digital Competition Expert Panel. London. Available via: https://assets.publishing.service.gov.uk/media/5c88150ee5274a230219c35f/unlocking_digital_competition_furman_review_web.pdf. Accessed 10 July 2024
Glöckner J (2021) Kartellrecht – Recht gegen Wettbewerbsbeschränkungen, 3rd edn. Kohlhammer, Stuttgart
Göhsl F (2018) Algorithmic Pricing and Article 101 TFEU. WuW 2021:121–126
Grave C, Nyberg J (2025) TFEU Article 101(1). In: Kersting C, Meyer-Lindemann H, Podszun R (eds) Kommentar zum Deutschen und Europäischen Kartellrecht, 5th edn. C.H. Beck, Munich
Griem F (2022) Wettbewerbliche Wirkungen von Kopplungsrabatten. NZKart 2022:119–126
Haucap J, Kerber W, Schweitzer H, Welker R (2018) Modernisierung der Missbrauchsaufsicht für marktmächtige Unternehmen. Nomos, Baden-Baden
Haucap J, Podszun R, Rüdiger H, Kreuter-Kirchhof C, Rohner T, Rösner A, Offergeld P, May A (2023) Wettbewerb und Nachhaltigkeit in Deutschland und der EU. BMWK, Duesseldorf
Heinemann A (2019) Algorithmen als Anlass für einen neuen Absprachebegriff? Working paper, Zurich
Higer D (2023) Die jüngste Initiative der Kommission zu Art. 102 AEUV: Abkehr von einer bloßen Prioritätenmitteilung hin zu Leitlinien. NZKart 2023:385–392
Hirsbrunner S (2015) EUMR Article 9. In: von der Groeben H, Schwarze J, Hatje A, Terhechte J (eds) Europäisches Unionsrecht, 7th edn. Nomos, Baden-Baden
Hoffer R, Mirtchev K (2019) Erfordert die Blockchain ein neues Kartellrecht? – Die Anwendung von Art. 101 und 102 AEUV sowie der Zusammenschlusskontrolle im Kontext der Blockchain-Technologie. NZKart 2019:239–247
Hoffmann J (2025) In: Dauses MA, Ludwigs M (eds) Handbuch des EU-Wirtschaftsrechts, 64th supp. C.H. Beck, Munich, p H.I. sec. 3
Hofmann F (2016) Der maßgeschneiderte Preis. WRP 2016:1074–1081
Holzweber S (2016) Daten als Machtfaktor in der Fusionskontrolle. NZKart 2016:104–112
Hülsen P (2012) Ausgewählte praktische Probleme des selektiven Vertriebs aus kartellrechtlicher Sicht. ZVertriebsR 2012:299–232
Huttenlauch A (2025) TFEU Article 102. In: Kersting C, Meyer-Lindemann H, Podszun R (eds) Kommentar zum Deutschen und Europäischen Kartellrecht, 5th edn. C.H. Beck, Munich
Inderst R, Thomas S (2022) Legal Design in Sustainable Antitrust. ZBW - Leibniz Information Centre for Economics, Kiel/Hamburg
Jennert C (2004) Wirtschaftliche Tätigkeit als Voraussetzung für die Anwendbarkeit des europäischen Wettbewerbsrechts. WuW 2004:37–46
Jung C (2025) TFEU Article 102. In: Grabitz E, Hilf M, Nettesheim M (eds) Das Recht der Europäischen Union, 85th supp. C.H. Beck, Munich
Kerber W, Schwalbe U (2023) Introduction. In: Säcker F (ed) Münchener Kommentar zum Wettbewerbsrecht, 4th edn. C.H. Beck, Munich
Kersting C, Dworschak S (2013) Leistungsschutzrecht für Presseverlage: Müsste Google wirklich zahlen? – eine kartellrechtliche Analyse. NZKart 2013:46–53

Kirchhoff W (2020) Sec. 11. In: Wiedemann G (ed) Handbuch des Kartellrechts, 4th edn. C.H. Beck, Munich
Klauß I, Seeliger D (2010) Auswirkungen der neuen Vertikal-GVO und Vertikal-Leitlinien auf den Internetvertrieb. GWR 2010:233–236
Kling M, Thomas S (2016) Kartellrecht, 2nd edn. Verlag Franz Vahlen, Munich
Kokott J, Dittert D (2014) Die Pflicht zur Berücksichtigung außerwettbewerblicher Belange im Rahmen von Art. 101 AEUV und ihre praktische Umsetzung. In: Monopolies Commission (ed) Politischer Einfluss auf Wettbewerbsentscheidungen – Wissenschaftliches Symposium anlässlich des 40-jährigen Bestehens der Monopolkommission. Baden-Baden, Nomos, pp. 15–16
König C (2020) In: Ebers M, Heinze C, Krügel T, Steinrötter B (eds) Künstliche Intelligenz und Robotik, 1st edn. C.H. Beck, Munich, Sec. 17
Körber T (2012) Google im Fokus des Kartellrechts. WRP 2012:761–772
Körber T (2014) Machtmissbrauch durch Android? – Zum Wettbewerb auf den Märkten für mobile Betriebssysteme und Anwendungen. NZKart 2014:378–386
Körber T (2016) "Ist Wissen Marktmacht?" Überlegungen zum Verhältnis von Datenschutz, "Datenmacht" und Kartellrecht – Teil 1. NZKart 2016:303–310
Körber T (2025a) EUMR Article 2. In: Immenga U, Mestmäcker E (eds) Kommentar zum Wettbewerbsrecht, 7th edn. C.H. Beck, Munich
Körber T (2025b) FKVO Article 3. In: Immenga U, Mestmäcker E (eds) Kommentar zum Wettbewerbsrecht, 7th edn. C.H. Beck, Munich
Krauß K (2021) ARC sec. 1. In: Bunte H (ed) Kartellrecht – Kommentar, 14th edn. Luchterhand, Munich
Kumkar L (2018) Zur Zulässigkeit pauschaler Plattformverbote im Internetvertrieb von Luxuswaren - Die Entscheidung des Europäischen Gerichtshofs in der Rechtssache Coty Germany. ZWeR 2018:119–140
Kumkar L (2025) TFEU Article 101. In: Gersdorf H, Paal B (eds) BeckOK Informations- und Medienrecht, 49th edn. C.H. Beck, Munich
Künstner K (2019) Preissetzung durch Algorithmen als Herausforderung des Kartellrechts - Verhaltenskoordinierung über Algorithmen und Systeme Künstlicher Intelligenz. GRUR 2019:36–42
Legner S (2012) Schadensberechnung bei Hardcore-Kartellen. KSzW 2012:218–224
Legner S (2014) Die Preisbildung im Oligopol und mögliche Gegenmaßnahmen (Sektoruntersuchung Kraftstoffe). Freilaw 2014:1–8
Legner S (2023a) Smart Contracts und Finanzdienstleistungen. VuR 2023:213–218
Legner S (2023b) Entscheidungen zum europäischen Kartellrecht im Jahr 2022. GPR 2023:26–36
Legner S (2023c) Climate change and competition - how can European Competition Law pro-mote sustainability? EYIEL 2023:233–260
Legner S (2023d) Marktabgrenzung im Kartellrecht. JURA 2023:175–181
Lettl T (2021) Kartellrecht, 5th edn. C.H. Beck, Munich
Levy N, Mostyn H, Buzata B (2020) Reforming EU merger control to capture 'killer acquisitions'. Compet Law J 2020:51–67
Lorenzoni I (2022) Why do competition authorities need artificial intelligence? Yearb Antitrust Regul Stud 15(26):33–55
Louven S, Saive D (2018) Antitrust by Design – Das Verbot wettbewerbsbeschränkender Abstimmungen und der Konsensmechanismus der Blockchain. NZKart 2018:348–354
Lübke J (2021) Preisabstimmung durch Algorithmen. ZHR 185(2021):723–769
Lundqvist B (2018) Competition and data pools. EuCML 2018:146–154
Mestmäcker E, Schweitzer H (2014) Europäisches Wettbewerbsrecht, 3rd edn. C.H. Beck, Munich
Meyer F (2025) TFEU Article 101. In: Jaeger W, Kokott J, Pohlmann P, Schroeder D, Kulka M (eds) Frankfurter Kommentar zum Kartellrecht, 111th edn. Dr. Otto Schmidt, Cologne
Meyer L, Müller U (2007) Die Zukunft des Geheimwettbewerbs in einer vernetzten Welt. WuW 2007:117–119
Mörsdorf O, Schäfer L (2019) Kartellrechtliche Bewertung von Plattformparitätsklauseln – zugleich Anmerkung zum Urteil des OLG Düsseldorf in Sachen Booking. NZKart 2019:659–666

2

Möschel W (1988) Wettbewerbspolitik aus ordoliberaler Sicht. In: von Gamm O, Raisch P, Tiedemann T, Festschrift für Gerd Pfeiffer zum 60. Geburtstag am 23. September 1988, Heymann, Köln, pp 707–723

Motta M, Peitz M (2020) Big tech mergers. Discussion Paper Series CRC TR 224, London

Müller-Graff P (2020) Algorithmen im Kartellrecht. In: Benicke C, Huber S (eds) National, International, Transnational: Harmonischer Dreiklang im Recht, Festschrift für Herbert Kronke zum 70. Geburtstag am 24. Juli 2020. Gieseking Verlag, Bielefeld, pp 1145–1154

Mundt A (2021) Algorithmen und Wettbewerb in einer digitalen Welt. NVertriebsR:69–71

Nowag J (2019) Competition law's sustainability gap? Tools for an examination and a brief overview. LundLawCompWP 3/2019:149–165

Nowak C (2025) Article 23 reg. 1/2003. In: Kersting C, Meyer-Lindemann H, Podszun R (eds) Kommentar zum Deutschen und Europäischen Kartellrecht, 5th edn. Beck, Munich

OECD (2017) Algorithms and Collusion, Competition policy in the digital age. Available via: https://www.oecd.org/content/dam/oecd/en/publications/reports/2017/05/algorithms-and-collusion-competition-policy-in-the-digital-age_02371a73/258dcb14-en.pdf. Accessed 1 Sept 2025

OECD (2018) Blockchain Technology and Competition Policy. Available via: https://one.oecd.org/document/DAF/COMP/WD(2018)47/en/pdf. Accessed 1 Sept 2025

Paal B (2019) Missbrauchstatbestand und Algorithmic Pricing – Dynamische und individualisierte Preise im virtuellen Wettbewerb. GRUR 2019:43–53

Paal B (2025) TFEU Article 102. In: Gersdorf H, Paal BP (eds) BeckOK Informations- und Medienrecht, 49th edn. C.H. Beck, Munich

Peeperkorn L, Heimann M (2014) Keine Neuigkeiten für Drittplattformverbote – Die Bedeutung des "Pierre Fabre"-Urteils des EuGH für den Onlinevertrieb. GRUR 2014:1175–1178

Picht P, Freund B (2018) Competition (law) in the era of algorithms. Eur Compet Law Rev 39(9):403–410

Podszun R (2023) From competition law to plaform regulation – regulatory choices for the digital markets act. Economics 17(1):1–13

Podszun R (2025) In: Kersting C, Meyer-Lindemann HJ, Podszun R (eds) Kommentar zum Deutschen und Europäischen Kartellrecht, 5th edn. C.H. Beck, Munich, p Sec. 18 GWB

Podszun R, Bongartz P (2020) B2B-Marktplätze und IoT-Plattformen in der kartellbehördlichen Praxis. BB:2882–2891

Podszun R, Schwalbe U (2017) Digitale Plattformen und GWB-Novelle: Überzeugende Regeln für die Internetökonomie? NZKart 2017:98–106

Pohlmann P (2018) Algorithmen als Kartellverstöße. In: Kokott J, Pohlmann P, Polley R (eds) Europäisches, deutsches und internationales Kartellrecht – Festschrift für Dirk Schroeder. Dr. Otto Schmidt, Cologne, pp 633–656

Riesenkampff A, Steinbarth S (2025) EUMR Article 3. In: Kersting C, Meyer-Lindemann H, Podszun R (eds) Kommentar zum Deutschen und Europäischen Kartellrecht, 5th edn. C.H. Beck, Munich

Riesenkampff A, Steinbarth S (2025) EUMR Article 2. In: Kersting C, Meyer-Lindemann H, Podszun R (eds) Kommentar zum Deutschen und Europäischen Kartellrecht, 5th edn. C.H. Beck, Munich

Reimers T, Brack S, Modest C (2020) Blockchain-Kooperationen im Bereich Supply Chain - Kartellrechtliche Rahmenbedingungen. WuW 2020:64–70

Richter A, Zorn A (2023) Die Wiederentdeckung des Ausbeutungsmissbrauchs im europäischen Recht - eine Analyse missbräuchlichen Preissetzungsverhaltens am Beispiel des Pharmasektors und digitaler Plattformen. NZKart 2023:521–531

Ritter K, Wirtz M (2025) Regulation 1/2003 Article 7. In: Immenga U, Mestmäcker E (eds) Kommentar zum Wettbewerbsrecht, 7th edn. C.H. Beck, Munich

Rohner T (2023) Art. 102 AEUV und die Rolle der Ökonomie – Eine Weiterentwicklung des more economic approach. Nomos, Baden-Baden

Säcker F, Mohr J (2011) Die Beurteilung von Einkaufskooperationen gemäß Art. 101 Abs. 1 und Abs. 3 AEUV. WRP 2011:793–808

Säcker F, Zorn A (2023) TFEU Article 101. In: Säcker F, Bien F, Meier-Beck P, Montag F (eds) Münchener Kommentar zum Wettbewerbsrecht, 4th edn. C.H. Beck, Munich

Schuhmacher F, Holzweber S (2025) TFEU Article 101. In: Grabitz E, Hilf M, Nettesheim M (eds) Das Recht der Europäischen Union, 85th supp. C.H. Beck, Munich

Schweitzer H (2014) Die Bedeutung nicht-wettbewerblicher Aspekte für die Auslegung von Article 101 TFEU im Lichte der Querschnittsklauseln. In: Monopolkommission (ed) Politischer Einfluss auf Wettbewerbsentscheidungen -Wissenschaftliches Symposium anlässlich des 40-jährigen Bestehens der Monopolkommission. Nomos, Baden-Baden, pp 11–38

Schweitzer H, Schallbruch M, Wambach A (2019) Ein neuer Wettbewerbsrahmen für die Digitalwirtschaft – Bericht der Kommission Wettbewerbsrecht 4.0, Berlin

Seeliger D (2020) Sec. 11. In: Wiedemann G (ed) Handbuch des Kartellrechts, 4th edn. C.H. Beck, Munich

Steinvorth T (2020) Sec. 20. In: Wiedemann G (ed) Handbuch des Kartellrechts, 4th edn. C.H. Beck, Munich

Stigler Committee (2019) Digital platforms - final report. Chicago. Available via: https://www.chicagobooth.edu/research/stigler/events/antitrust-competition-conference. Accessed 10 July 2014

Stockenhuber P (2025) TFEU Article 101. In: Grabitz E, Meinhard H, Nettesheim M (eds) Das Recht der Europäischen Union, 85th supp. C.H. Beck, Munich

Tamke M (2018) Marktmacht in digitalen Märkten nach der 9. GWB-Novelle. NZKart 2018:503–508

Thomas S (2017) The known unknown: in search for a legal structure of the significance criterion of the SIEC test. J Compet Law Econ 13(2):346–387

Thomas S (2019) Harmful signals: cartel prohibition and oligopoly theory in the age of machine learning. J Compet Law Econ 15(2–3):159–203

Thomas S (2020) Die digitale Ökonomie zwischen vertikaler und horizontaler Wettbewerbsbeschränkung. ZHR 184(2020):222–248

Tietjen D, Flöter B (2017) Dynamische und personalisierte Preise: Welche lauterkeitsrechtlichen Schranken gelten für Unternehmen? GRUR-Prax 2017:546–548

Ulmer P (1972) Abgestimmte Verhaltensweisen im Kartellrecht. C.F. Müller, Karlsruhe

Von Hayek F (1994) Freiburger Studien – Gesammelte Aufsätze, 2nd end. Mohr Siebeck, Tübingen

Wagner-von Papp F (2023) Article 101. In: Säcker F (ed) Münchener Kommentar zum Wettbewerbsrecht, 4th edn. C.H. Beck, Munich

Wagner-von Papp F (2024) Leitlinienentwurf zu Behinderungsmissbräuchen. WuW 2024:445–446

Whish R, Bailey D (2024) Competition law, 11th edn. Oxford University Press, Oxford

Wiedemann G (2020) Sec. 4. In: Wiedemann G (ed) Handbuch des Kartellrechts, 4th edn. C.H. Beck, Munich

Wilson T (2025) H.I. sec. 4. In: Dauses M, Ludwigs M (eds) Handbuch des EU-Wirtschaftsrechts, 64th supp. C.H. Beck, Munich

Wolf M (2019) Algorithmengestützte Preissetzung im Online-Einzelhandel als abgestimmte Verhaltensweise – Ein Beitrag zur Bewältigung des "Predictable Agent" über Art. 101 Abs. 1 AEUV. NZKart 2019:2–10

Ylinen J (2018) Digital Pricing und Kartellrecht. NZKart 2018:19–22

Zimmer D (2004) Significant Impediment to Effective Competition – Das neue Untersagungskriterium der EU-Fusionskontrollverordnung. ZWeR 2004:250–267

Zimmer D (2025) In: Immenga U, Mestmäcker E (eds) TFEU Article 101(1), 6th edn. C.H. Beck, Munich

Digital Markets Act

Contents

S. Legner, *Digital Competition Law*, Springer Textbooks in Law,
https://doi.org/10.1007/978-3-662-73213-7_3

3.1 Introduction

3.1.1 Overview

3

The Digital Markets Act (hereinafter: DMA)[1] is a European regulation[2] aimed at ensuring contestability and fairness in digital markets. It serves objectives distinct from those of general EU competition law, which primarily seeks to protect competition itself and promote consumer welfare. Importantly, within its scope of application, the DMA does not replace competition law. Instead, both legal frameworks **apply concurrently**, as clarified in Article 1(6) DMA.

▶ **Examples**

If a gatekeeper favours its own price comparison service over those of competitors in the ranking of search results (e.g. *Google Search*), it may breach the prohibition on self-preferencing under Article 6(5) DMA. If the gatekeeper also holds a dominant market position, this conduct could simultaneously constitute an abuse of dominance under Article 102 TFEU, by unfairly disadvantaging rivals.[3]

If a gatekeeper makes access to its social networking service (e.g. *Facebook*) conditional upon users consenting to the merging of personal data from multiple sources, this may infringe Article 5(2) DMA, which prohibits certain forms of data combination. If the company also holds a dominant position, such behaviour may further violate Article 102 TFEU as an abuse of unfair trading conditions.[4] ◀

As a result of the simultaneous applicability of the DMA and competition law, it is possible that a gatekeeper's conduct may breach the DMA while still complying with Article 102 TFEU. This divergence in legal outcomes stems from the **distinct objectives** pursued by each legal framework.

▶ **Example**

Gatekeeper T, which holds a 25% market share, operates an online intermediary platform for hotel services. T only permits business users (e.g. hotels) to list their offerings on the platform if they agree not to provide better accommodation conditions (e.g. lower prices or better terms) on their own websites.[5] In this scenario, T is in breach of the DMA but

1 Regulation (EU) 2022/1925 of the European Parliament and of the Council of 14 September 2022 on contestable and fair markets in the digital sector, OJ EU 2022 No. L 265/1.

2 The DMA is an EU regulation within the meaning of Article 288 TFEU. Unlike directives, regulations do not require transposition into national law in order to have effect. Rather, they are directly applicable and binding in all their parts in every Member State.

3 ECJ 10 September 2024 – C-48/22 P, ECLI:EU:C:2024:726 – *Google Shopping*.

4 For a competition law assessment of this practice, see ECJ 4 July 2023 – C- 252/21, ECLI:EU:C:2023:537 – *Meta (Facebook)*; German Federal Supreme Court 23 June 2020 – KVR 69/19, NZKart 2020, 473 – *Facebook*; German Federal Cartel Office, Decision of 6 February 2019 – B6-22/16 – *Facebook*.

5 Christodoulou and Holzwarth (2022), pp. 540, 543.

its conduct does not violate competition law. Specifically, T violates Article 5(3) DMA, which prohibits gatekeepers from preventing business users from offering different conditions through their own direct online sales channels compared to those offered through the gatekeeper's platform. At first glance, one might also consider a potential violation of Article 101 TFEU, which prohibits anti-competitive agreements, particularly vertical restraints. However, in this case, the restriction is exempt under Article 2(1) VBER because the market share thresholds set out in Article 3 VBER are met.

Furthermore, the restriction imposed by T qualifies as a narrow price parity clause, i.e., it only applies to the prices displayed on the business user's own website and not across all distribution channels. Under Article 6 VBER, such clauses are generally exempt from the prohibition under Article 101 TFEU. In contrast, broad price parity clauses, which restrict pricing across all online channels, are not exemptible under Article 5(1)(d) VBER. ◄

The DMA sets out two detailed catalogues of conduct obligations in Articles 5, 6 DMA, specifically tailored to address harmful practices associated with digital business models. In addition, Article 7 DMA establishes interoperability obligations for certain messenger services. However, these obligations do not apply to all companies. The DMA's provisions are binding only on gatekeepers. Gatekeepers are large digital firms that, due to their significant size and entrenched market position, wield substantial influence over competition dynamics and end users. The DMA focuses on specific core platform services, as defined in Article 2(2) DMA, which include social networks (e.g. *Facebook, Instagram, X*), online search engines (e.g. *Google Search, Bing, Yahoo*), web browsers (e.g. *Google Chrome, Mozilla Firefox, Apple Safari*) and messenger services (e.g. *WhatsApp, Signal, Threema*), among others.

Importantly, an undertaking that meets the substantive criteria for gatekeeper status (primarily turnover thresholds and user base figures) is not automatically subject to the DMA. Before the obligations apply, the Commission must formally designate the undertaking as a gatekeeper through a regulatory procedure.

➤ So far, the Commission has carried out two rounds of designations and designated several undertakings as gatekeepers under the DMA. In September 2023, the following companies were designated as gatekeepers: *Alphabet, Apple, Meta, Microsoft, Amazon,* and *ByteDance*. The core platform services affected include social networks (*TikTok* (*ByteDance*), *Facebook* and *Instagram* (*Meta*), *LinkedIn* (*Microsoft*)), intermediation services (*Google Maps, Amazon Marketplace*), video-sharing platforms (e.g. *YouTube*), search engines (e.g. *Google Search*), and operating systems (*Android* (*Alphabet*), *iOS* (*Apple*), *Windows* (*Microsoft*). In May 2024, ► Booking.com was added to the list of gatekeepers. *TikTok Ads* (*ByteDance*) and *X Ads* (*X*) were not designated. In addition, the Commission concluded that the social network *X* does not meet the criteria to qualify as a gatekeeper. In April 2025, the Commission decided that *Facebook Marketplace*—contrary to its initial assessment in 2023—no longer qualifies as a gatekeeper. The Commission referred in particular to the decline in the number of business users reached in 2024.

3

The prohibitions in Articles 5, 6 DMA are **precisely formulated** provisions. Unlike the general clauses found in competition law, they are tailored to address specific types of conduct. They enable faster and more effective enforcement of the DMA. Some of these prohibitions are **derived from past or ongoing competition law proceedings**, and as such, they may anticipate the legal assessment that would otherwise be conducted under traditional competition law rules.[6] For instance, Article 5(2) DMA prohibits certain forms of data aggregation unless effective consent is obtained in accordance with data protection law. Under competition law, however, it remains unresolve to what extent a violation of data protection rules can amount to an abuse of conditions under Article 102 TFEU. Some obligations under the DMA, such as the restriction on narrow price parity clauses in Article 5(3) DMA, go beyond what is currently prohibited under competition law. Importantly, gatekeepers **cannot justify their conduct by referencing efficiency gains.**[7] Moreover, a breach of the DMA's obligations does not depend on actual harm to competition. This strict, per se approach is designed to facilitate swift and consistent enforcement of the DMA's rules.

The Commission is responsible for enforcing the behavioural obligations set out in the DMA. It has the authority to impose **fines** for culpable infringements of these obligations. In cases of systematic non-compliance the Commission may, following a market investigation, impose remedial measures. These can include structural remedies, such as unbundling, which may be applied as a measure of last resort.

▶ Example

Undertaking T, with an annual turnover of EUR 10 billion, has been designated by the Commission as a gatekeeper under the DMA. T operates an online intermediation service for hotel bookings through its platform. T imposes contractual restrictions on hotel undertakings using its platform, prohibiting them from offering better conditions on competing platforms or their own websites. This constitutes a violation of the prohibition on most-favoured-nation clauses set out in Article 5(3) DMA.

The Commission, acting under Article 29 DMA, adopts a formal decision finding that T has breached its obligations under the DMA. In accordance with Article 30 DMA, the Commission is also empowered to impose a fine of up to 10% of T's total annual turnover, which in this case may amount to up to EUR 1 billion. ◀

The DMA is silent on **private enforcement**, particularly with regard to claims for injunctive relief and damages. However, it is now widely accepted that the principle of effectiveness under EU law requires that such private enforcement must be possible.[8] In response, the German legislator, through the 11th amendment to the

6 Bostoen (2023), p. 263 et seqq.
7 Van den Boom (2022), pp. 57, 64.
8 Herbers et al. (2023), pp. 185, 187 et seq.

ARC, has established a legal basis for the private enforcement of the DMA. Under the amended provisions, claims for injunctive relief and removal pursuant to sec. 33 ARC, as well as claims for damages under sec. 33a ARC, can now be asserted in the event of violations of Articles 5, 6 or 7 DMA.

3.1.2 Legislative Process

The DMA is intended to **close gaps** in competition law in digital markets. In recent years, it has become apparent that competition law proceedings regularly take too long to keep pace with the fast-moving conditions of the digital economy. In particular, the Commission has conducted a number of proceedings against large digital undertakings for abuse of a dominant market position. However, it regularly takes many years or even decades for these proceedings to be finalised. For example, the Commission took almost seven years to reach its decision in the *Google Shopping* case.[9]

One reason for the **prolonged enforcement of competition law** is the undefined legal concepts of the prohibitions. Broad general clauses, such as the concept of 'abuse' in Article 102 TFEU or 'significant impediment to effective competition' in Article 2 EUMR, offer flexibility and can also be applied to new digital business models. At the same time, however, they are accompanied by legal uncertainty. The legal concepts are regularly only concretised through European case law. In addition, there are guidelines that summarise the prevailing understanding of the European courts and the Commission. In the last two decades, the courts have tightened the requirements for proving the detrimental effects of abusive conduct on competition.[10] In-depth economic analyses of the impact of abusive behaviour are required.[11] At the same time, the undertakings concerned have the option of justification in the form of an *efficiency defence*.[12] These peculiarities of the application of competition law in digital markets mean that law enforcement 'lags behind' the fast-moving market conditions.

Against this background, the DMA offers a kind of counter-draft to Article 102 TFEU. Its prohibitions are comparatively detailed and are intended to leave little room for interpretation. In contrast to competition law, 'justifications on economic grounds' (recital 23 DMA) are not to be considered. The prohibitions of the DMA apply regardless of the effects of the gatekeepers' conduct in individual cases.

9 Commission, Decision of 27 June 2017 – AT.39740 – *Google Search (Shopping)*.

10 Podszun (2023b), p. 20220037.

11 For further details on the more economic approach in the context of Article 102 TFEU, see ► 2.3.2.1.1.

12 For the concept of efficiency defence in competition law, see ► 2.4.4.5.

▶ **Example**

Pursuant to sec. 19a(2) 1st sentence no. 1(a) ARC, the German Federal Cartel Office may prohibit an undertaking with paramount cross-market significance for competition from favouring its own offers over those of competitors when arranging access to procurement and sales markets. The prerequisite is that the self-preferential treatment causes competitive harm. Pursuant to sec. 19a(2) 2nd sentence ARC, the undertaking concerned can provide justification. Article 6(5) DMA also prohibits self-preferencing. However, the gatekeeper is denied the possibility of justification. Furthermore, the Commission does not have to examine specific effects on competition. Rather, the gatekeeper is prohibited per se from favouring the services and products it offers itself in the ranking. ◀

The downside of the specified obligations is that they offer **little flexibility**. At the same time, the requirements can become outdated relatively quickly if digital business models change. The DMA takes this risk into account by providing mechanisms for updating its provisions: On the one hand, Article 12 DMA gives the Commission far-reaching powers to adopt delegated acts in accordance with Article 291 TFEU in order to supplement the obligations. Unlike regulations, delegated acts do not have to go through the ordinary legislative procedure and can therefore tend to be adopted more quickly. Secondly, the market investigation in Article 19 DMA provides for a specific procedure in which the Commission determines the need to update the DMA. It remains to be seen to what extent this approach will prove to be practicable.

3.1.3 Objectives

3.1.3.1 Relationship to (General) Competition Law

The DMA is designed to safeguard contestability and fairness in digital markets. It is, therefore, not part of competition law, as explicitly stated in Article 1(6) DMA. Instead, the DMA constitutes a form of sector-specific regulatory law tailored to the unique dynamics of core platform services.[13] This classification is also evident from the legal basis of the regulation: the DMA is founded on Article 114 TFEU, which empowers the EU to adopt measures aimed at the approximation of national laws for the purpose of ensuring the functioning of the internal market.[14] In contrast, the European legislator did not rely on Article 103 TFEU, the legal basis typically used for enacting secondary legislation in the field of competition law, including measures to enforce the prohibitions set out in Articles 101, 102 TFEU.

13 Recital 11 DMA states: '*This Regulation pursues an objective that is complementary to, but different from that of protecting undistorted competition on any given market, as defined in competition-law terms, which is to ensure that markets where gatekeepers are present are and remain contestable and fair [...]*'.

14 Larouche and de Streel (2021), pp. 542, 545.

The DMA and competition law apply in parallel, as they pursue distinct objectives. The DMA is designed to ensure contestability and fairness in digital markets through ex ante regulation. In contrast, competition law seeks to protect the freedom of competition and promote consumer welfare, primarily through ex post enforcement (and merger control).

Learning Goals

While the DMA does not affect the application of national or EU competition law, as explicitly stated in Article 1(6) DMA, it does have a blocking effect under **Article 1(5) DMA**. This provision precludes Member States from imposing additional obligations on designated gatekeepers aimed at ensuring contestable and fair digital markets. The goal is to establish a uniform regulatory framework across the EU, avoiding fragmentation and legal uncertainty. In this respect, the DMA enjoys **priority of application**.

Learning Goals

Against this background, the compatibility of sec. 19a ARC with the blocking effect of Article 1(5) DMA has been subject to legal debate. Sec. 19a ARC, introduced in 2021, targets large digital players that exhibit paramount cross-market significance for competition,[15] These are practically the same group of companies that may be designated as gatekeepers under the DMA. Moreover, overlaps in prohibited conduct exist. For example, sec. 19a(2) 1st sentence no. 5 ARC empowers the German Federal Cartel Office to prohibit such undertakings from refusing data portability, where this may restrict competition. Similarly, Article 6(9) DMA obliges gatekeepers to enable effective, free-of-charge data portability for end users.

Learning Goals

Nevertheless, it is persuasive to conclude that sec. 19a ARC is not in principle precluded by the blocking effect of Article 1(5) DMA.[16] The provision remains applicable alongside the DMA, due to key differences in legal basis and enforcement approach: Sec. 19a ARC is grounded in competition law and linked to the concept of abuse. It requires a demonstration of competitive harm and provides for justification by the undertaking concerned.[17] In contrast, the DMA imposes ex ante obligations on gatekeepers without requiring proof of harm or allowing for efficiency defences. This reflects a divergence in objectives: Sec. 19a ARC aims to **protect freedom of competition**, while the DMA seeks to ensure contestability and fairness, as outlined in Article 1(6) DMA.

---

15 On the concept of paramount significance for competition across markets, see ► 5.3.2.2.

16 Bongartz (2022), pp. 72, 74; Herbers et al. (2023), pp. 185, 187; Jovanovic and Greiner (2021), pp. 678, 679; Käseberg and Gappa (2023), DMA Article 1 mn. 28; Zimmer and Göhsl (2021), pp. 29, 59. A different view is taken by Paal and Kumkar (2021), pp. 809, 815.

17 Jovanovic and Greiner (2021), pp. 678, 679.

Learning Goals

However, once an undertaking is designated as a gatekeeper by the Commission, the DMA takes precedence over national rules that duplicate or add to its obligations. In such cases, the blocking effect under Article 1(5) DMA applies. As a result, sec. 19a ARC remains relevant in three main scenarios: when an undertaking has not (yet) been designated as a gatekeeper; when the conduct at issue does not relate to core platform services as defined by the DMA; or when the conduct falls outside the scope of the DMA's regulatory provisions.[18]

Learning Goals

This interpretation was confirmed by the German Federal Supreme Court in April 2024, in its *Amazon* decision, where the Court upheld the parallel applicability of sec. 19a ARC and the DMA, while recognising the DMA's priority in areas explicitly regulated by European law.[19] The decision clarifies that the court interprets the concept as one aimed at addressing cross-market concentration tendencies. In doing so, the court makes clear that sec. 19a ARC is intended to enable intervention before further entrenchment of economic power occurs in the digital sector.

3.1.3.2 Contestability

The primary objective of the DMA is to ensure **contestability** in digital markets, that is, to keep markets open. The aim is to ensure that competition has a real opportunity to enter and challenge established players. This objective is closely aligned with the traditional competition law goal of protecting the freedom of competition, although it differs in a crucial respect: no proof of actual competitive harm is required for a finding that contestability has been impaired.[20]

In this context, the theory of contestable markets is instructive. It emphasises that even **potential competition**, the credible threat of market entry, can exert a disciplining effect on dominant undertakings. Competitive pressure may arise not only from existing rivals but also from the realistic possibility that other undertakings could enter the market in the near future.[21] Maintaining contestability is particularly challenging in digital markets, which are prone to 'tipping' due to their structural characteristics.[22] These include direct and indirect network effects, economies of scale, and high fixed costs coupled with low marginal costs, all of which can lead to the entrenchment of dominant positions. To address these risks, the behavioural obligations imposed on gatekeepers under Articles 5, 6 DMA are designed to lower entry barriers and prevent the foreclosure of potential rivals. This is further clarified in Article 12(5)(a)(i) DMA, which provides that a gatekeeper's practice may impair contestability if it creates or reinforces barriers that make **market entry** more difficult.

---

18 Käseberg and Gappa (2023), DMA Article 1 mn. 29.

19 German Federal Supreme Court 24 April 2024 – KVB 56/22, NZKart 2024, 500, 503 et seqq. – *Amazon*.

20 Burchardi (2022), pp. 610, 615.

21 Schweitzer (2021), pp. 503, 511.

22 For further details on the multi-sided nature of digital markets, see ► 1.1.

▶ Example

A gatekeeper is required to allow business users to conclude contracts with end users outside the gatekeeper's platform, even where the initial contact between the two was established via the gatekeeper's platform service. Pursuant to Article 5(4) DMA, the gatekeeper must also permit business users to advertise such external offers on its platform. For instance, a business user may promote its app on the gatekeeper's app store, while providing end users the option to download the app directly from the business user's own website—bypassing the gatekeeper's distribution channel.[23] This provision is designed to foster multi-homing, i.e. the simultaneous use of multiple platforms or services by end users or business users. By reducing dependence on a single gatekeeper platform, the DMA aims to enhance contestability in digital markets, particularly in the area of online intermediation services. ◀

Access to critical inputs, especially data, can be decisive for market entry and effective competition.[24] Recognising this, the DMA imposes data access obligations on gatekeepers to reduce barriers to entry and level the playing field. Under Article 6(11) DMA, gatekeepers that provide search engine services must grant competing providers access to query, click, and view data, subject to FRAND (fair, reasonable, and non-discriminatory) terms. This is intended to ensure that rivals can improve their own services through comparable data-driven insights. In addition, Article 6(10) DMA requires gatekeepers to provide business users with access to data generated in the context of their use of a core platform service. This includes, for example, transactional data or customer interactions relevant to the business user's commercial activity on the platform. The DMA also introduces data portability obligations. According to Article 6(9) DMA, end users must be able to freely and effectively transfer their data—for instance, from one social network to another. This not only empowers users but also facilitates switching between services, thereby enhancing contestability in digital markets.[25]

The DMA also seeks to promote **competition within platform ecosystems themselves**, not only across markets. Many platform operators are vertically integrated, meaning they not only provide intermediation services but also compete directly with business users on downstream markets. This hybrid role can create significant competitive advantages, particularly when the gatekeeper has access to commercially sensitive data generated by users of its platform. To address this risk, Article 6(2) DMA prohibits gatekeepers from using non-public data obtained through the provision of their core platform services to gain an unfair advantage in downstream markets. This includes, for example, data relating to the activities, transactions, or performance of business users. The aim is to prevent predatory practices and ensure that third-party business users can compete on the platform on equal terms. A similar concern was the subject of the *Amazon Marketplace* competition

---

23 Podszun et al. (2022), pp. 3249, 3251. On the evaluation of this conduct in the context of Article 102 TFEU, see Commission, Decision of 4 March 2024 – AT.40437 – *Apple App Store Practices (music streaming)*.

24 For details on the role of data in competition in digital markets, see ▶ 1.2.

25 Podszun et al. (2022), pp. 3249, 3252.

law investigation by the Commission.[26] The case focused on whether *Amazon*, in its dual role as platform operator and retailer, used data from third-party sellers active on its marketplace to undercut or exclude them, thereby distorting competition.[27] In addition, Article 6(5) DMA prohibits self-preferencing by gatekeepers—for instance, favouring their own products or services in ranking, display, or access conditions. This rule is also designed to strengthen competition within the platform environment by ensuring a neutral and non-discriminatory treatment of business users.

3

Finally, the obligations imposed by the DMA are also intended to prevent gatekeepers from **leveraging their considerable economic power into adjacent markets**.[28] According to Article 5(7) DMA, gatekeepers are prohibited from making access to one of their core platform services conditional upon the use of other services they offer—such as their identification service, web browser, or payment system. This is designed to prevent the bundling of services in a way that restricts user choice, locks in users, or distorts competition in related markets.[29]

3.1.3.3 Fairness

Furthermore, the DMA aims to promote fairness in digital markets.[30] This principle is elaborated in Article 12(5)(b) DMA, which states that an **imbalance between the rights and obligations** of business users is considered unfair if it results in a **disproportionate advantage** for the gatekeeper. However, the DMA does not provide a precise standard or criteria to determine when such an imbalance exists or when an advantage becomes disproportionate.[31] Recital 33 DMA offers some guidance, emphasizing that business users and alternative providers 'should have the ability to adequately capture the benefits resulting from their innovative or other efforts. This suggests that fairness entails a reasonable and equitable distribution of rights and obligations that reflects the contributions and investments of business users within the platform ecosystem.

> The principle of fairness also plays a prominent role in other pieces of European legislation governing the digital sector. In particular, the Platform Regulation addresses the structural power imbalance between business users and platform operators.[32] Recital 2 Platform Regulation highlights that 'the growing intermediation of transactions through online intermediation services, fuelled by strong data-driven indirect network effects, leads to an *increased dependence of such business users*, particularly micro, small and medium-sized enterprises (SMEs), on

---

26 Commission, Decision of 20 December 2022 – AT.40462 – *Amazon Marketplace*.

27 The proceedings were terminated by means of commitments.

28 Schweitzer (2021), pp. 503, 512.

29 On a corresponding competition law procedure, see Commission, Decision of 4 March 2024 – AT.40437 – *Apple App Store Practices (music streaming)*.

30 On the relationship between contestability and fairness, see e.g. van den Boom (2022), pp. 57, 62.

31 Van den Boom (2022), pp. 57, 63.

32 On the objectives of the Platform Regulation, see ▶ 4.1.3.

those services in order for them to reach consumers'.[33] The AI Act[34] also envisages the development of fair AI systems, cf. e.g. recital 27 AI Act.[35] In order to achieve this, training data sets must be relevant, sufficiently representative, and to the best extent possible, free of errors and complete in view of the intended purpose' (Article 10(3) AI Act), among other things. In addition, the AI Act strives for transparency. Article 13(1) AI Act states that High-risk AI systems 'shall be designed and developed in such a way as to ensure that their operation is sufficiently transparent to enable deployers to interpret a system's output and use it appropriately.'

The DMA introduces a form of content control over contractual relationships between gatekeepers and **business users**. This is evident in several obligations. For example, Article 6(5) DMA requires gatekeepers to ensure that their ranking practices are based on transparent, *fair*, and non-discriminatory criteria. Moreover, Article 6(11) DMA obliges gatekeepers to provide third-party online search engine providers, upon request, with access to ranking, query, click, and view data on *fair*, reasonable, and non-discriminatory (FRAND) terms.

The concept of fairness under the DMA also extends to **end users**, although its application in this context is somewhat more limited. The Commission's ability to update the list of obligations is activated, under Article 12(5)(b) DMA, specifically by practices that threaten fairness in relation to business users. Nonetheless, recital 2 DMA makes clear that end users are also encompassed within the DMA's fairness objective. Several obligations can be interpreted as furthering this aim. For instance, Article 5(2) DMA safeguards the decision-making autonomy of end users by conditioning the legality of data combination practices on the effective consent of the end user, in accordance with data protection law. In addition, Article 5(6) DMA prohibits gatekeepers from preventing either business users or end users from reporting unlawful conduct to competent authorities.

3.1.4 Scope of Application

3.1.4.1 Personal and Territorial Scope

According to Article 1(2) DMA, the regulation applies to all core platform services offered or provided by gatekeepers to business users or end users within the European Union, regardless of the gatekeeper's place of establishment.[36] In line with the **marketplace principle**, the focus lies on the location of the users rather than that of the gatekeeper.[37] This broad territorial scope serves a dual purpose: to

33 Emphasis added.
34 Regulation (EU) 2024/1689 of the European Parliament and of the Council of 13 June 2024 laying down harmonised rules on artificial intelligence, OJ [2024] L 2024/1689.
35 For further insights on algorithmic fairness, see e.g. Kattnig et al. (2024), p. 106053; Westerstrand (2025), p. 107864.
36 Käseberg and Gappa (2023) DMA Article 1 mn. 9.
37 Kumkar (2024) DMA Article 1 mn. 23.

protect users located in the EU and to ensure the proper functioning and fairness of digital markets within the Union.[38] The DMA's territorial scope is therefore aligned with the **effects doctrine**, which also underpins the application of European competition law. Under this principle, the decisive factor is whether the conduct in question has substantial effects within the EU market.[39] For business users, the applicability of the DMA requires that they are established in the EU, meaning they must operate through a **fixed establishment** within the Union.[40] In contrast, for end users, mere presence within the EU is sufficient. They must **be located** in the territory of the Union at the time the service is offered.

3

3.1.4.2 Temporal Scope

The DMA entered into force on 1 November 2022 and became fully applicable on **2 May 2023**. In accordance with Article 3(3) DMA, undertakings providing core platform services that meet the relevant thresholds were required to notify the Commission by 3 July 2023. Following such notification, the Commission has 45 working days under Article 3(4) DMA to assess the submissions and formally designate the undertakings as gatekeepers. Once designated, gatekeepers are subject to the DMA's behavioural obligations within six months, as stipulated in Article 3(10) DMA. Consequently, for those undertakings designated in early September 2023, the compliance deadline fell on 8 March 2024. From that date onward, designated gatekeepers are required to adhere to the full set of obligations and prohibitions laid out in the DMA.

3.2 Gatekeepers

3.2.1 Undertaking

The obligations set out in the DMA apply to gatekeepers, a category of undertakings that provide core platform services and hold significant economic power. The term undertaking is defined in **Article 2(27) DMA** as any entity engaged in an **economic activity**, irrespective of its legal form or the manner in which it is financed. This definition aligns with the established interpretation in European competition law.[41] As a result, the scope of the DMA is not limited to individual legal entities; a **group of undertakings** may also qualify as a gatekeeper, provided it meets the criteria set out in the regulation.[42]

38 Heinze and Kettler (2025) § 11 mn. 65.
39 Käseberg and Gappa (2023) DMA Article 1 mn. 9. On the effects doctrine under European competition law, see ► 2.1.4.3.
40 Heinze and Kettler (2025) § 12 mn. 67. On the understanding of this term under Article 49 TFEU, see e.g. Forsthoff (2025) TFEU Article 49 mn. 16.
41 On this term under competition law, see ► 2.1.4.1.
42 Lettl (2023), pp. 953, 954.

3.2.2 Core Platform Services

According to Article 3(1)(b) DMA, only undertakings that provide at least one core platform service can be designated as gatekeepers. The DMA does not define this term. Instead, it provides a closed list of ten specific services in Article 2(2) DMA, which are deemed to constitute core platform services. These include:
- Online intermediation services (e.g. online marketplaces such as *eBay, Zalando*, or *Amazon Marketplace*; platforms like ► Booking.com)
- Online search engines (e.g. *Google, Bing, Yahoo*)
- Online social networking services (e.g. *Instagram, LinkedIn*)
- Video-sharing platform services (e.g. *YouTube, Vimeo*)
- Number-independent interpersonal communication services (e.g. *WhatsApp, Signal, Threema*)
- Operating systems (e.g. *Windows, macOS, Android, iOS*)
- Web browsers (e.g. *Chrome, Safari, Firefox*)
- Virtual assistants (e.g. *Alexa, Siri*)
- Cloud computing services (e.g. *Apple iCloud, Google Drive, Microsoft One-Drive*)
- Online advertising services (e.g. *Google Ads, Amazon Ads*)

The term core platform service is intended to be *technology-neutral*. That means that the type of device through which the service is accessed or provided is irrelevant.[43]

While the Commission may initiate a market investigation under Article 19 DMA to assess whether additional services should be regulated, it cannot unilaterally amend the list of core platform services. Unlike other provisions of the DMA, Article 2(2) DMA is not subject to amendment through a delegated act under Article 12 DMA. Any expansion of the list must follow the legislative procedure outlined in Article 294 TFEU. The Commission may therefore only propose legislative amendments to Article 2(2) DMA, which must then be adopted by the European Parliament and the Council.

3.2.3 Requirements of the Gatekeeper Status

3.2.3.1 General Requirements

The gatekeeper status of an undertaking offering core platform services depends on the fulfilment of two conditions. First, the undertaking must satisfy the substantive criteria set out in Article 3(1) DMA. Second, it must be formally designated as a gatekeeper by the Commission in accordance with the same provision (see ► 3.2.4). **Article 3(1) DMA** lays down **three cumulative substantive requirements**. Firstly, the undertaking must have a significant impact on the internal mar-

43 Bongartz and Kirk (2023) DMA Article 2 mn. 7.

3

ket. Secondly, it must provide a core platform service that functions as an important gateway for business users to reach end users. Thirdly, it must enjoy a durable and entrenched position in its operations, or it must be foreseeable that it will acquire such a position in the near future.

When these conditions are met, the undertaking is considered to wield substantial economic influence. However, it is important to note that gatekeeper status does not require a finding of market dominance within the meaning of Article 102 TFEU. Unlike traditional competition law assessments, the DMA **does not require a definition of the relevant market**.[44] Gatekeeper status and dominance are distinct legal concepts and must be assessed independently. The presence of one does not imply the other. For instance, gatekeeper designation does not primarily hinge on market share but rather on the undertaking's ability to control access to key user groups, thereby acting as a bottleneck between business users and end users.[45]

3.2.3.2 Presumptions under Article 3(2) DMA

Article 3(2) DMA establishes a system of **rebuttable presumptions** for each of the three substantive criteria set out in Article 3(1) DMA. These presumptions are designed to streamline the Commission's assessment of whether an undertaking qualifies as a gatekeeper. This approach aligns with the ex ante regulatory framework of the DMA, which aims to ensure timely identification of undertakings subject to the obligations in Articles 5, 6, 7 DMA. The presumptions operate as follows:

- **Significant impact on the internal market** is presumed under Article 3(2)(a) DMA if the undertaking has achieved an EU **annual turnover of at least EUR 7.5 billion** in each of the last three financial years, or recorded an average market capitalisation or equivalent fair market value of at least EUR 75 billion in the last financial year, and provided the same core platform service in at least three Member States.
- The status of a core platform service as an **important gateway** for business users to reach end users is presumed under Article 3(2)(b) DMA if, in the preceding financial year the service had at **least 45 million monthly active end users** established or residing in the EU, and at least **10,000 yearly active business users** established in the EU.
- A **entrenched and durable position**, or the foreseeable attainment thereof, is presumed under Article 3(2)(c) DMA if the undertaking has satisfied both the turnover/valuation and user thresholds set out above for each of **the past three financial years**.

To ensure consistency and transparency, Article 3(6) DMA empowers the Commission to adopt delegated acts specifying the methodologies undertakings must use to determine whether they meet the relevant thresholds. This enables a uniform application of the presumptions across different market participants.

---

44 Kumkar (2022), pp. 347, 349.
45 Kumkar et al. (2024) Preamble DMA mn. 23.

Overview: Presumption of gatekeeper status (Article 3(2) DMA)

Criterion	Presumption Threshold	Reference Period
1. Significant impact on the internal market	- Annual EU turnover ≥ EUR 7.5 billion **or**- Average market capitalisation ≥ EUR 75 billion **and** provision of the same core platform service in ≥ 3 Member States	Last **three financial years** (turnover)Last **financial year** (capitalisation)
2. Core platform service as an important gateway	- ≥ 45 million **monthly active end users** residing or established in the EU **and**- ≥ 10,000 **yearly active business users** established in the EU	**Previous financial year**
3. Entrenched and durable position	- Thresholds for **turnover or capitalisation** (see point 1) **and**- Thresholds for **user numbers** (see point 2)	**Each of the last three financial years**

3.2.3.3 Gatekeeper Status without Presumptions: Assessment under Article 3(8) DMA

- An undertaking may still be designated as a gatekeeper even if it does not meet one or more of the rebuttable presumptions set out in Article 3(2) DMA.[46] In such cases, the Commission conducts an individualised assessment based on a catalogue of **qualitative criteria** listed in **Article 3(8) DMA**. The following factors must be considered in the assessment:
- **Size of the undertaking** (a): This includes turnover, market capitalisation, overall business activities, and market position. These elements indicate whether an undertaking possesses the capacity to transfer its economic power across markets, potentially contributing to market tipping.[47]
- **Number of business and end users** (b): The analysis must examine whether the undertaking's user base falls just below or far below the thresholds set in Article 3(2) DMA. A growing user base increases the platform's relevance as a gateway between business users and end users.
- **Network effects and data advantages** (c): These are central to digital platform economics. Strong direct and indirect network effects can accelerate the accumulation of market power.[48] Additionally, superior access to user data allows undertakings to improve targeting and product optimisation, reinforcing their competitive advantage.
- **Economies of scale and scope** (d): Platforms that benefit from cost reductions due to increased output (scale) or from operating across multiple services (scope) can consolidate their market position and deter competition more effectively.

---

46 In these instances, the Commission must carry out a market investigation for gatekeeper designation, see ► 3.5.1.2.

47 Legner (2025) § 13 mn. 16.

48 On the concept of network effects, see ► 1.1.

3

- **User and business lock-in** (e): The degree of user loyalty—and the switching costs associated with moving to alternative providers—can entrench an undertaking's market position. The assessment also considers whether users typically multi-home, i.e. use several platforms in parallel, or rely on a single provider.[49]
- **Conglomerate structure and vertical integration** (f): A vertically integrated or conglomerate group may gain additional advantages, such as the ability to cross-subsidise services or combine data sets across different platforms. This integration can reinforce market dominance across layers of the digital value chain.
- **Other relevant structural characteristics** (g): This catch-all provision allows the Commission to take into account any other features of the undertaking's business model or service structure that may be relevant to gatekeeper status. This ensures flexibility in the assessment and accommodates evolving market practices.

3.2.4 Designation

3.2.4.1 Designation Procedure

The DMA provides for two distinct procedures by which the Commission can designate an undertaking as a gatekeeper. The first is a simplified and expedited **notification procedure**, applicable when the undertaking fulfils the presumption criteria set out in Article 3(2) DMA. In this case, the undertaking is under a legal obligation to notify the Commission within two months of meeting the thresholds, pursuant to Article 3(3) DMA. Once the Commission has received the notification, it has **45 days** to adopt a designation decision in accordance with Article 3(4) DMA.

Where an undertaking either does not meet the thresholds under Article 3(2) DMA or claims to rebut the presumption, the designation process follows a more complex route via a **market investigation** in accordance with Article 17 DMA. The possibilities for rebutting the presumption are **very limited**.[50] According to Article 23 DMA, rebuttal is only permitted in exceptional circumstances. Efficiency arguments or purely economic considerations are excluded from the rebuttal process, as they are not relevant to the assessment of gatekeeper status.[51] The burden of proof lies with the undertaking seeking to rebut the presumption.[52] If the Commission finds the rebuttal unconvincing, it rejects the arguments in accordance with Article 3(5)(1) DMA, and issues a designation decision within 45 days of receipt of the rebuttal.

49 Legner (2025) § 13 mn. 19.
50 A critical view is taken by Haus and Weusthof (2021), pp. 318, 321; Körber (2021), pp. 379, 384.
51 Käseberg and Gappa (2023) DMA Article 3 mn. 19.
52 Lettl (2023), pp. 953, 959.

However, if the undertaking succeeds in rebutting the presumption, the Commission may initiate a full market investigation under Article 17 DMA, as foreseen in Article 3(5)(3) DMA. This procedure is more detailed and investigative in nature than the notification process. Where the market investigation is initiated following a rebuttal of the presumption, it should be completed within **five months**. In contrast, if the undertaking does not meet the thresholds in Article 3(2) DMA at all and is being assessed independently, the Commission is expected to conclude the market investigation within **twelve months**.

In both cases, the Commission assesses whether the undertaking meets the gatekeeper criteria based on the comprehensive list of indicators set out in Article 3(8) DMA. For this purpose, it is granted **investigative powers**. These include the ability to issue formal requests for information under Article 21 DMA, conduct interviews under Article 22 DMA, and carry out inspections under Article 23 DMA. These inspections closely resemble the dawn raids familiar from Article 20 Regulation 1/2003.

3.2.4.2 Designation Decision

The outcome of the procedure is formalised in a Commission **decision**, which identifies the undertaking as a gatekeeper and specifies the particular core platform services for which gatekeeper status is established. Following the decision, the undertaking must comply with the relevant conduct obligations under Articles 5, 6, 7 DMA no later than **six months after designation**. If a gatekeeper fails to comply with these obligations, the Commission may adopt a non-compliance decision in accordance with Article 29 DMA. In the event of a culpable infringement, it may impose fines of up to ten percent of the gatekeeper's total annual turnover, pursuant to Article 30 DMA.[53]

To ensure that the designation remains appropriate over time, the Commission is required by Article 4(2) DMA to review **every three years** whether the undertaking continues to satisfy the gatekeeper conditions under Article 3(1) DMA. In addition, the undertaking itself may request such a review at any time, as provided by Article 4(1) DMA. If it is found that the conditions are no longer fulfilled, the Commission is obliged to revoke the designation.

Checklist: Assessing a gatekeeper position

1. Entity qualifies as an **undertaking** pursuant to Article 2(27) DMA
2. Entity provides at least one **core platform service** pursuant to Article 2(2) DMA
3. **Requirements under Article 3(1) DMA** are fulfilled, either through the presumptions in Article 3(2) DMA or based on the criteria in Article 3(8) DMA.
4. Entity has been formally **designated** as a gatekeeper by the Commission pursuant to Article 3(3)–(8) DMA.

53 For further details, see ► 3.5.2.

3.3 Obligations

3.3.1 Obligations under Article 5 DMA

3

Article 5 DMA sets out a series of specific prohibitions which, according to the European legislator, leave comparatively little room for interpretation. As stated in recital 31 DMA, these obligations are intended to be 'clear and unambiguous' and enable undertakings to comply without the need for further clarification.[54] Unlike sec. 19a ARC,[55] the obligations under Article 5 DMA do not require activation by an official decision; they apply directly upon designation as a gatekeeper. However, practical application of the provision will ultimately determine whether this legislative approach is effective. A closer reading of the list of prohibitions reveals that, despite their formal clarity, some provisions allow for considerable interpretative leeway. Moreover, significant questions remain regarding the technical implementation of certain obligations, which may challenge the assumption of straightforward compliance.

▶ Example

Article 5(2) DMA requires that end users be given a genuine choice regarding their consent to the combination of data by ensuring the availability of an equivalent alternative service. It remains to be seen how the Commission will define the requirements for such an equivalent service to be offered by the gatekeeper to users who refuse to give their consent. ◀

3.3.1.1 Prohibition on Data Combination Practices: Article 5(2) DMA

Article 5(2) DMA imposes a prohibition on certain data combination practices by gatekeepers. Such practices are only permissible if two cumulative conditions are met. First, the gatekeeper must obtain the **effective consent** of the end user, in accordance with the requirements set out under the GDPR. Second, end users must have been given a **specific choice** as to whether to grant such consent. Recital 37 DMA further clarifies that where end users choose not to consent, the gatekeeper is obliged to provide them with a functionally equivalent, non-personalised alternative to the service offered to users who do consent. This ensures that refusal of consent does not result in a degraded user experience or constitute a form of indirect coercion. The prohibited data combination practices include several distinct forms of cross-service data usage:

- The processing of personal data from end users who interact with third-party services that rely on the gatekeeper's core platform services, particularly for the purpose of delivering online advertising services (a).

---

54 For a critical view on this point, see Bostoen (2023), p. 263 et seqq.; Simone and Laudando (2025), p. 3.

55 On this provision, see ▶ 5.3.2.

- The combining of personal data from the relevant core platform service with personal data from other core platform services, other services offered by the gatekeeper, or from third-party services (b).
- The cross-use of personal data obtained through one core platform service in the gatekeeper's other services, and vice versa (c).
- The sign in of end users to other services provided by the gatekeeper in order to enable the combining of their personal data (d).

Similar issues were targeted by the German Federal Cartel Office's proceedings in the *Facebook* case, which centred on the competitive risks arising from extensive data pooling practices.[56] The Office found an abuse of business terms pursuant to sec. 19(1) ARC, holding that access to the social network was conditional upon end users' consent to the merging of their personal data from various *Facebook* services and third-party websites.[57] The proceedings are currently pending before the Higher Regional Court of Duesseldorf, where one of the key legal questions concerns whether infringements of data protection law can constitute a form of competitive harm. In contrast, under Article 5(2) DMA, this issue does not arise. The provision contains an explicit reference to the GDPR and does not require the demonstration of harm to competition. The prohibition stands independently of any assessment of market effects. Substantively, the prohibition under Article 5(2) DMA serves a dual purpose. On the one hand, it seeks to promote the contestability of digital markets by lowering barriers to entry, particularly by limiting the gatekeeper's ability to entrench its position through data consolidation. On the other hand, it enhances user autonomy, ensuring that individuals retain control over how their personal data is used across services. This autonomy is a central component of the fairness objective underpinning the DMA.[58]

Article 5(2) DMA is one of the first obligations under the DMA that the Commission decided to enforce. In April 2025, the Commission imposed a fine of EUR 200 million on *Meta* for breaching Article 5(2) DMA.[59] In its decision, the Commission held that, until March 2024, the social networks *Facebook* and *Instagram* could only be used free of charge if users agreed to the gatekeeper's practice of processing and combining personal data for the purpose of delivering personalised advertising. Users who refused to consent were instead required to pay a monthly fee. According to the Commission, this 'consent-or-pay' model did not provide consumers with a '*less personalised but equivalent alternative*' to the services concerned.[60] Consequently, the gatekeeper failed to provide users with the specific choice required under Article 5(2) DMA.[61]

---

56 German Federal Cartel Office, Decision of 6 February 2019 – B6-22/16 – *Facebook*.

57 For further details on this case, see ► 5.3.1.5.3.

58 Bueren and Weck (2022) DMA Article 5 mn. 8 speak of '*protection of privacy*' [quote translated by author]. On the fairness objective, see ► 3.1.3.3.

59 Commission, Decision of 23 April 2025 – DMA.100055 – *Meta – Article 5(2)*.

60 Commission, Decision of 23 April 2025 – DMA.100055 – *Meta – Article 5(2)*, para. 88.

61 Commission, Decision of 23 April 2025 – DMA.100055 – Meta – Article 5(2), paras. 87 et seqq.

3.3.1.2 Prohibition of Most-Favoured-Nation Clauses: Article 5(3) DMA

3

Article 5(3) DMA prohibits gatekeepers from preventing business users from offering the same products or services to end users through third-party online intermediary services or their own direct online distribution channels at different prices or under different conditions than those offered through the gatekeeper's platform. This provision effectively bans gatekeepers from imposing most-favoured-nation clauses, including both narrow and broad price parity clauses. Such clauses are prohibited due to their market foreclosure effects: when end users consistently find the best offers on the gatekeeper's platform, it becomes increasingly difficult for competing platform providers to attract business users and establish a foothold in the market.

Learning Goals

Broad price parity clauses prevent business users from offering better terms on any other sales channels, while narrow price parity clauses restrict better offers only on specific channels, often limited to the commercial user's own website.[62]

The prohibition also extends to measures having an equivalent effect, such as demanding higher commission fees from business users who provide better conditions through other sales channels. Article 5(3) DMA imposes stricter rules **than the existing competition law framework**. While broad price parity clauses imposed by a dominant undertaking are already prohibited under Article 102 TFEU, as well as the cartel prohibition under Article 101 TFEU,[63] narrow price parity clauses currently benefit from an exemption under Article 2(1) VBER, provided that none of the parties to the agreement holds a market share exceeding 30%.[64] In contrast, broad best-price clauses are explicitly non-exemptable under Article 5(1)(d) VBER.

3.3.1.3 Prohibition of Anti-Steering: Article 5(4) DMA

Pursuant to Article 5(4) DMA, gatekeepers are prohibited from restricting business users from 'redirecting' end users to alternative distribution channels. This provision ensures that business users can inform their customers about offers available outside the gatekeeper's platform, thereby promoting competition and user choice.

▶ Example

An audiobook provider that distributes its app via a gatekeeper's platform must be allowed to inform users (within the app or through other means) that more favourable prices or offers are available on its own website.[65] ◀

Importantly, this prohibition on obstructing advertising and redirection applies specifically to end users who have already entered into a business relationship with the commercial user (so-called acquired end users). This distinction reflects the

---

62 For further details, see ▶ 2.2.2.3.8.
63 See ▶ 2.2.2.3.8.
64 On the assessment of price parity clauses under the VBER, see ▶ 2.2.5.2.2.4.
65 Heinz (2023) DMA Article 5 mn. 62.

DMA's goal of opening up closed platform ecosystems and encouraging multi-homing, where users engage with multiple services or platforms simultaneously (see recital 40 DMA).

The prohibition of anti-steering is one of the few obligations the Commission has already enforced. In April 2025, the Commission imposed a fine of EUR 500 million on *Apple* for violating Article 5(4) DMA.[66] According to the Commission, *Apple* restricted app developers' freedom to provide users with information on prices.[67] Moreover, in many cases, *Apple* only permitted so-called 'link-outs' to redirect customers to other sales channels, while at the same time restricting this practice in several ways.[68]

A similar rule exists under German competition law: sec. 19(2) 1st sentence no. 2(b) ARC includes a parallel provision applicable to undertakings with paramount cross-market significance for competition.[69]

3.3.1.4 Obligation to Enable Access to Externally Acquired Content: Article 5(5) DMA

Under Article 5(5) DMA, gatekeepers are required to ensure that end users can access and use content, subscriptions, functionalities, or other elements through the software applications of business users, via the gatekeeper's core platform services. This obligation applies regardless of whether the content was obtained through the gatekeeper's platform or from an external source.

► Example

A gatekeeper operating an app store[70] must allow users of music streaming applications on its end devices to access music subscriptions purchased outside the app or app store ecosystem.[71] ◄

The scope of content covered by this obligation includes, but is not limited to, music, podcasts, videos, and digital newspapers.[72] Importantly, a violation of Article 5(5) DMA does not only arise from explicit access restrictions included in the gatekeeper's terms of service. It also encompasses indirect or unilateral practices that hinder access, such as excessively lengthy authorisation processes, technical barriers, or compatibility issues intentionally imposed by the gatekeeper.[73] The overarching aim of this obligation is to facilitate multi-homing in the acquisition

---

66 Commission, Decision of 23 April 2025 – DMA.100109 – *Apple - Online Intermediation Services - app stores - AppStore - Art. 5(4).*
67 Commission, Decision of 23 April 2025 – DMA.100109, paras. 59 et seqq. – *Apple - Online Intermediation Services - app stores - AppStore - Art. 5(4).*
68 Commission, Decision of 23 April 2025 – DMA.100109, paras. 90 et seqq. – *Apple - Online Intermediation Services - app stores - AppStore - Art. 5(4).*
69 On this provision, see ► 3.3.2.3.
70 An app store is qualified as intermediary service pursuant to Article 2 no. 5 DMA.
71 König (2025) § 12 mn. 35.
72 Heinz (2023) DMA Article 5 mn. 100.
73 Heinz (2023) DMA Article 5 mn. 109.

and use of digital content, which lowers market entry barriers and fosters a more competitive and open digital ecosystem.

3.3.1.5 Prohibition against Hindering Legal Complaints: Article 5(6) DMA

3

Under Article 5(6) DMA, gatekeepers are prohibited from preventing business users or end users from reporting violations of the DMA to a competent authority. This provision safeguards users' ability to inform authorities of breaches by gatekeepers, particularly those that undermine contestability and fairness in the digital sector. The prohibition primarily targets violations of the DMA's obligations but also extends to infringements of related legal frameworks, including general contract law, competition law, unfair competition law, data protection law, and consumer protection law.[74] The aim is to ensure that enforcement authorities remain functional and that legal violations are effectively investigated and prosecuted. A breach of Article 5(6) DMA occurs, for example, if a gatekeeper blocks a commercial user's account on its online marketplace after the user reports a suspected violation—such as improper use of business data by the gatekeeper—to the Commission.[75]

3.3.1.6 Prohibition of Tying other Services: Article 5(7) DMA

Under Article 5(7) DMA, gatekeepers are prohibited from conditioning the use of their core platform services on the simultaneous use of specific other services they provide—such as identification services, web browser engines, or payment systems.

▶ Example

A gatekeeper operating an app store cannot require app developers to use its proprietary payment system for in-app purchases as a condition for distributing their apps.[76] ◀

This anti-tying provision is designed to keep digital markets open and competitive. It prevents gatekeepers from leveraging their dominance in one area to gain or entrench power in adjacent markets.

3.3.1.7 Prohibition of Tying Core Platform Services: Article 5(8) DMA

Under Article 5(8) DMA, gatekeepers are prohibited from tying one core platform service to another. Specifically, they may not require users to **subscribe** to or register with additional **core platform services** in order to access or use another of the gatekeeper's core services.

▶ Example

A gatekeeper operating an online marketplace may not condition its use on customers also subscribing to the gatekeeper's cloud service.[77] ◀

---

74 Podszun (2023a) DMA Article 5 mn. 126.
75 Podszun et al. (2022), pp. 3249, 3251.
76 Heinz (2023) DMA Article 5 mn. 136.
77 Podszun et al. (2022), pp. 3249, 3251.

This prohibition aims to lower barriers to market entry and reduce the competitive advantages gatekeepers may gain through excessive data accumulation across services. The provision builds on concerns previously addressed by the Commission under Article 102 TFEU. In the *Google Android* case, the Commission found that the dominant firm had unlawfully tied access to its app store to the pre-installation of its search engine and web browser by device manufacturers.[78] A similar, yet broader, provision can be found in sec. 19a(2) 1st sentence no. 3(b) ARC. Unlike Article 5(8) DMA, it is not limited to registration requirements or core platform services and applies to companies with paramount cross-market significance for competition.

3.3.1.8 Advertising Transparency Obligations: Article 5(9), (10) DMA

Article 5(9) DMA and Article 5(10) DMA impose obligations on gatekeepers to ensure transparency in online advertising, both for advertisers and publishers. Under Article 5(9) DMA, gatekeepers must provide **advertisers**—upon request and free of charge—daily information about each advertisement. This includes pricing details, fees charged, performance metrics, and the amount paid to the publisher. Similarly, Article 5(10) DMA requires that gatekeepers provide **publishers**—again on request and free of charge—with daily information regarding the remuneration received, the price paid by the advertiser, and the key metrics used to calculate both.

The purpose of these transparency requirements is to illuminate the conditions that the gatekeeper establishes for adverts. By enhancing **visibility into pricing and performance data**, the DMA aims to empower advertisers and publishers to make informed choices and switch to alternative platforms if they find the gatekeeper's conditions unsatisfactory.

3.3.2 Obligations under Article 6 DMA

The prohibitions listed in Article 6 DMA are in principle as specific as the obligations set out in Article 5 DMA. However, the legislator has separated these two sets of duties. This distinction reflects the recognition that the obligations under Article 6 DMA often require a higher degree of specification. Their implementation can be technically complex and may involve balancing competing interests. To address this, Article 8 DMA introduces the mechanism of a **regulatory dialogue**. This process is initiated at the discretion of the Commission, typically upon request by a gatekeeper. Importantly, it is not contingent upon a specific infringement. Rather, it functions as a tool of ex ante regulation. It aims at collaboratively shaping effective compliance measures.[79]

78 Commission, Decision of 18 July 2018 – AT.40099 - *Google Android*.
79 König (2025) sec. 12 mn. 11.

3.3.2.1 Prohibition on the Use of Non-Public Commercial User Data: Article 6(2) DMA

Article 6(2) DMA prohibits gatekeepers from using non-public data obtained from business users through the provision of core platform services in order to compete with those users. This provision specifically targets **vertically integrated gatekeepers**, that is, those who act as intermediaries for business users (e.g. via marketplaces, app stores, or ad services) while simultaneously offering competing products or services in downstream markets.[80] The provision seeks to prevent gatekeepers from exploiting their dual role and the resulting conflicts of interest, particularly in cases where the gatekeeper could gain a competitive advantage not based on superior performance but on privileged access to sensitive commercial data.

3

> **▶ Example**
>
> A prominent illustration of the scenario addressed by Article 6(2) DMA is the *Amazon Marketplace*. On this platform, *Amazon* not only acts as an intermediary by enabling third-party business users to offer goods and services to end users, but also operates as a direct competitor by selling its own products through the same interface.[81] In its role as platform operator, Amazon obtains access to a broad range of non-public data relating to the activities of business users. This includes data provided by sellers when listing products (such as pricing and inventory levels), as well as behavioural data generated through user interaction with those listings, such as click-through rates, purchase conversions, and customer reviews.[82] ◀

The prohibition under Article 6(2) DMA applies specifically to the use of non-public data '**in competition**' with business users. It is still unclear how narrowly the Commission will interpret the required competitive relationship. One possible approach is to apply the established principles of market definition from competition law[83] to assess both actual and potential competition between the gatekeeper and business users.[84] Importantly, the restriction is not absolute: the gatekeeper remains permitted to use commercial user data when providing non-competing services.

3.3.2.2 Uninstallation and Default Setting Flexibility: Article 6(3) DMA

Under Article 6(3) DMA, gatekeepers are required to ensure that end users can uninstall pre-installed software applications and change default settings on their devices or platforms. These actions must be possible 'in a simple manner,' which means the process must be user-friendly and accessible. The rationale behind this obligation is to prevent the gatekeeper's market power from being leveraged into adjacent markets by steering users toward its own services through pre-installation or default configurations. The provision takes into account behavioural tendencies

80 Serafimova (2024) Article 6 DMA mn. 7.
81 Seip and Berberich (2021), pp. 44, 46.
82 Wolf-Posch (2023) DMA Article 6 mn. 6.
83 For the principles of market delineation in competition law, see ▶ 2.3.1.1.
84 Wolf-Posch (2023) DMA Article 6 mn. 9 et seq.

of end users, namely, their inertia or preference for maintaining the default state rather than taking the effort to seek and activate alternatives.[85] This obligation draws on principles established under Article 102 TFEU. For example, the GC held that *Microsoft* had abused its dominant position by pre-installing *Windows Media Player* on its *Windows* operating system, thereby disadvantaging competing media software.[86] The prohibition also addresses default settings for virtual assistants, an area in which the Commission has found that users tend to stick with pre-selected services for extended periods.[87]

3.3.2.3 Authorisation to Install Apps: Article 6(4) DMA

Article 6(4) DMA requires gatekeepers to allow the installation and use of third-party software applications on their operating systems. Gatekeepers must also enable the operation of alternative app stores on their platforms. This obligation includes supporting **sideloading**, that is, permitting users to download and install applications from sources outside the gatekeeper's own app store.[88]

► Example

If a gatekeeper operates a mobile operating system, it is not permitted to block the download or installation of third-party app stores. Article 6(4) DMA is designed to facilitate the installation of alternative app stores.[89] ◄

However, to address legitimate concerns related to **system security**, such as the risk of malware or fraudulent apps, Article 6(4)(2) DMA allows gatekeepers to implement necessary protective measures.[90] If a gatekeeper can demonstrate that specific restrictions are essential to safeguard the integrity of its operating system, it may lawfully limit the use of certain third-party applications.

3.3.2.4 Prohibition of Self-preferencing: Article 6(5) DMA

Article 6(5) DMA prohibits gatekeepers from engaging in self-preferencing. Specifically, when ranking services, gatekeepers must not favour their own offerings over comparable services provided by third parties. Instead, rankings must be based on transparent, fair, and non-discriminatory criteria.

This prohibition is modelled on the *Google Shopping* case, where the ECJ found that the dominant search engine operator had abused its position by prioritising its own price comparison service in search results over competing third-party services.[91] Recital 51 DMA further clarifies that the prohibition of self-preferencing

85 Herbers (2023) DMA Article 5 mn. 25.
86 EC 17 September 2007 – T-201/02, ECLI:EU:T:2007:289 – *Microsoft*.
87 Commission, Final report – sector inquiry into consumer Internet of Things, 2022, SWD(2022) 10 final, paras. 457 et seq.
88 Herbers (2023) DMA Article 6 mn. 53.
89 Podszun et al. (2022), pp. 3249, 3252.
90 Herbers (2023) DMA Article 6 mn. 77.
91 ECJ 10 September 2024 – C 48/22 P, ECLI:EU:C:2024:726 – *Google Shopping*.

applies not only to search rankings but also to other contexts, such as the display of apps in app stores or the ranking of news content on social networks. Notably, the rule applies to services that are merely 'similar,' meaning a direct competitive relationship is not required.[92] It is sufficient that the gatekeeper's and third-party services fall within the same general category.[93] However, the scope of Article 6(5) DMA is narrower than that of sec. 19a(2) 1st sentence no. 1 ARC, which extends beyond ranking to prohibit other forms of self-preferencing.[94]

3

3.3.2.5 Prohibition of Restrictions on Switching Options: Article 6(6) DMA

Under Article 6(6) DMA, gatekeepers are required to ensure that end users can freely switch between apps and services accessed via the gatekeeper's core platform services. For instance, on an operating system, users must be able to choose their preferred web browser independently. The gatekeeper may not limit this choice to browsers offered by providers with whom it maintains contractual relationships.[95] Importantly, the provision prohibits not only outright bans on switching, but also any measures that restrict or hinder the switching process. This includes, for example, making it more difficult for users to access alternative apps or limiting their functionality.[96] Recital 53 DMA highlights that this obligation serves to enhance product diversity and protect users' freedom of choice. A corresponding rule is found in sec. 19a(2) 1st sentence no. 2 ARC, which similarly prohibits gatekeepers from restricting switching behaviour.

3.3.2.6 Interoperability Obligation: Article 6(7) DMA

Article 6(7) DMA imposes an interoperability obligation on gatekeepers that provide an operating system or virtual assistant, while also offering services or hardware accessed through those core platform services. These gatekeepers must ensure that third-party providers are able to interoperate with the same functionalities that the gatekeeper uses for its own services.

▶ Example

A voice assistant must be capable of interacting not only with the gatekeeper's own apps, but also with apps developed by third parties.[97] ◀

This obligation aims to prevent vertically integrated gatekeepers from leveraging their dual role to gain unfair advantages unrelated to performance, such as by denying third parties access to essential system functions. Such practices can lead to lock-in effects and distort competition in downstream markets.[98]

---

92 Heinz (2023) DMA Article 6 mn. 91.
93 Heinz (2023) DMA Article 6 mn. 91.
94 For more information on this provision, see ▶ 5.3.2.3.
95 Podszun et al. (2022), pp. 3249, 3252.
96 Herbers (2023) DMA Article 6 mn. 126.
97 Podszun et al. (2022), pp. 3249, 3252.
98 Herbers (2023) DMA Article 6 mn. 137.

Current
In March 2025, the Commission issued two decisions under Article 8 DMA (regulatory dialogue) specifying the interoperability requirements for *Apple*'s iPhones, iPads and devices from other providers.[99]

3.3.2.7 Data Access for Advertisers and Publishers: Article 6(8) DMA

Under Article 6(8) DMA, gatekeepers are required to provide advertisers and publishers—upon request and free of charge—with access to the performance measurement tools and relevant data necessary to conduct an independent evaluation of their advertising inventory. Similar to the right to information set out in Article 5(9), 5(10) DMA,[100] this provision is designed to enhance transparency in the gatekeeper's advertising services. By enabling advertisers and publishers to independently assess performance, the regulation facilitates more effective comparisons between different advertising services. Recital 58 DMA notes that this increased transparency is expected to strengthen market dynamics by encouraging advertisers and publishers to consider alternative platform operators, thereby promoting competition.

3.3.2.8 Data Portability: Article 6(9) DMA

Pursuant to Article 6(9) DMA, gatekeepers must ensure that end users can, upon request and free of charge, effectively port the data they have provided or that has been generated through their use of the core platform service.

▶ **Example**
If a user switches from one sales platform to another, they are entitled to transfer data related to their past purchases to the new platform.[101] ◀

The data portability obligation is designed to reduce switching costs and enable multi-homing, thereby lowering entry barriers for competing platforms. In addition to promoting competition, the provision also aims to ensure greater fairness in the relationship between gatekeepers and end users.[102]

3.3.2.9 Data Access for Business Users and Search Engine Operators: Article 6(10), (11) DMA

Article 6(10) DMA grants business users a right to free, effective, high-quality, and continuous real-time access to the data they have provided or that has been generated through their use of the gatekeeper's core platform services. This right facili-

99 Commission, Decision of 19 March 2025 – DMA.100204 – *SP – Apple – Article 6(7) – process*; Commission, Decision of 19 March 2025 – DMA.100203 – *Apple – Operating systems – iOS – Article 6(7) – SP – Features for Connected Physical Devices.*
100 For further details on these provisions, see ▶ 3.3.1.8.
101 Wolf-Posch (2023) DMA Article 6 mn. 178.
102 Wolf-Posch (2023) DMA Article 6 mn. 179.

3

tates switching to alternative platform providers and enables business users to analyse data in order to optimise their own offerings. By levelling the informational playing field, the provision helps reduce the gatekeeper's data-driven competitive advantage. This data access right complements Article 6(2) DMA, which prohibits gatekeepers from using commercially sensitive user data in competition with their business users.[103] Together, these provisions aim to ensure a fairer and more transparent commercial environment.

Article 6(11) DMA introduces a distinct data access right for online search engine operators. Gatekeepers operating a search engine must, upon request, grant access to data on rankings, queries, clicks, and views relating to both paid and unpaid search results generated by end users. Access must be provided on fair, reasonable, and non-discriminatory (FRAND) terms. This right applies not only to rival search engine operators, but also to those not in direct competition with the gatekeeper. The underlying rationale, as reflected in recital 61 DMA, is that search engine markets are characterised by strong network effects: the more search queries processed, the more refined the algorithm becomes, and the higher the quality of the search results.[104] As a result, newer or smaller search engines face significant barriers to market entry due to limited data and reduced result relevance. By granting access to key performance data, Article 6(11) DMA aims to enable alternative search engine providers to improve their services and better compete in a highly concentrated market.

3.3.2.10 Obligation to Provide Access to App Stores, Online Search Engines, and Online Social Networks: Article 6(12) DMA

Article 6(12) DMA imposes an obligation on gatekeepers to grant business users access to core platform services, specifically, app stores, online search engines, and social networking services, under FRAND conditions. The rationale behind this obligation is the that these particular core platform services are especially prone to imbalances in bargaining power. Without regulation, gatekeepers could impose terms that unduly disadvantage business users.[105] By requiring access on FRAND terms, the DMA aims to ensure a level playing field and prevent contractual conditions that may be exploitative or discriminatory. Article 6(12) DMA introduces a substantive review of the access conditions imposed by gatekeepers, effectively subjecting them to a form of content control to safeguard fairness and market contestability.

3.3.2.11 Obligation to Provide Appropriate Conditions for Terminating Core Platform Services: Article 6(13) DMA

To safeguard users' freedom of choice, Article 6(13) DMA requires that the conditions for terminating the provision of a core platform service must not be disproportionate. According to recital 63 DMA, the cancellation process must not be

---

103 For further details on Article 6(2) DMA, see ► 3.3.2.1.
104 Wolf-Posch (2023) DMA Article 6 mn. 256.
105 Schwab (2023) DMA Article 6 mn. 284.

more complex than the process for subscribing to the service. Cancellation conditions are deemed disproportionate, for example, if the gatekeeper imposes unnecessary procedural barriers or demands additional fees to terminate the contract. This provision aims to prevent lock-in effects and ensure that users can easily exercise their right to discontinue the use of a service without facing undue burdens.

3.3.3 Further Obligations

Further obligations are set out in **Article 7 DMA**, specifically concerning interpersonal communication services such as messenger platforms. Under this provision, a gatekeeper operating such a service must provide an interoperability interface to enable interaction with third-party communication services.[106] The aim, according to the EU legislator, is to ensure that over time, users of different messenger services can communicate seamlessly with one another—for example, enabling a message to be sent from *WhatsApp* to *Signal* and vice versa. This obligation supports user choice, reduces lock-in effects, and fosters greater competition in the digital communications market.

Article 14 DMA introduces a notification obligation for gatekeepers with regard to mergers. While the DMA does not establish a separate merger control regime, the prohibition or approval of mergers continues to fall under the scope of the EUMR.[107] However, gatekeepers are required to inform the Commission of any intended concentration within the meaning of Article 3 EUMR,[108] if the undertakings involved provide core platform services, operate in the broader digital sector, or facilitate data collection. This obligation applies regardless of whether the transaction meets the turnover thresholds under Article 1 EUMR[109] or triggers review under any national merger control rules. This early notification requirement aims to enhance transparency and allow the Commission to monitor market dynamics and potential accumulations of digital power—even in cases that might otherwise escape formal merger review under existing thresholds.

The notification obligation under Article 14 DMA is related to Article 22 EUMR.[110] Under Article 22 EUMR, a Member State may refer a transaction to the Commission for review—even if the transaction does not meet the jurisdictional thresholds of either EU or national merger control regimes.[111] This provision enables scrutiny of mergers that could otherwise escape regulatory oversight. Article 14 DMA plays a supportive role by ensuring that the Commission and national competition authorities receive timely information about planned transactions involving gatekeepers. Specifically, it targets mergers where the undertakings involved operate in the digital sector, offer core platform services, or enable

106 Podszun et al. (2022), pp. 3249, 3252.
107 For further details on European merger control, see ► 2.4.
108 For the definition of concentration, see ► 2.4.2.
109 For the community dimension of merger, see ► 2.4.3.
110 Maher (2024), pp. 273, 278.
111 On this point, see ► 2.4.5.4.

significant data collection. Even if such mergers fall below conventional turnover thresholds, they may still raise substantive competition concerns. In this context, the Article 14 DMA obligation helps the Commission detect and assess potentially anti-competitive acquisitions (such as killer acquisitions) and contributes to the identification of core platform services that may become relevant in future notification decisions or market investigations under the DMA or European competition law.

3.4 Enforcement

3.4.1 Public Enforcement

As a rule, the enforcement of EU regulations lies with the Member States. This reflects the principle of subsidiarity. However, in exceptional cases, direct enforcement may be assigned to the Commission, provided that the regulation expressly grants such competence. This is the case with the DMA, which entrusts exclusive enforcement powers to the Commission. Pursuant to **Article 29 DMA**, the Commission may issue a **non-compliance decision** if a gatekeeper fails to comply with an obligation set out in Articles 5, 6 or 7 DMA. This decision must be adopted following the advisory procedure under Article 50(2) DMA, which requires the Commission to obtain an opinion from the Advisory Committee on Digital Markets. In its decision, the Commission must also set a reasonable deadline within which the gatekeeper must bring the infringement to an end.

The Commission may impose structural or behavioural remedies under Article 18(1) 3rd sentence DMA, but only where a gatekeeper has systematically infringed its obligations under Articles 5, 6 or 7 DMA and has thereby maintained, strengthened, or expanded its position in relation to its core platform services.[112] This represents a departure from the competition law regime under Article 7 Regulation 1/2003, which does not require a systematic pattern of abuse as a precondition for imposing remedies.[113]

Under Article 18(3) DMA, a systematic infringement is presumed if the Commission has issued at least **three non-compliance decisions** against the gatekeeper within an **eight-year period**. However, the text of Article 18 DMA does not clearly specify whether the infringement must be the cause of the gatekeeper maintaining, strengthening, or expanding its position. However, a systematic non-compliance poses a serious threat to the DMA's objectives of contestability and fairness only where it results in maintaining, strengthening or extending a gatekeeper position.[114]

112 On this point, see ► 2.5.1.
113 Bueren and Weck (2022) DMA Article 5 mn. 18.
114 Legner (2025) § 13 mn. 41.

❗ Unlike Article 7 Regulation 1/2003, which allows for remedies following any established infringement of competition law, Article 18 DMA permits the imposition of remedial measures only in cases of systematic non-compliance by a gatekeeper with the obligations set out in Articles 5, 6, 7 DMA.

Conduct remedies under Article 18 DMA may require a gatekeeper either to refrain from certain practices or to take specific positive actions. In appropriate cases, the Commission may also impose a temporary ban on mergers involving the gatekeeper. In contrast, structural remedies may involve more far-reaching measures, such as an order to divest parts of the undertaking. These remedies aim to address the root causes of economic power consolidation resulting from systematic non-compliance. When selecting and imposing remedies, the Commission is bound by the principle of proportionality.[115]

The imposition of remedies under the DMA requires a special procedure. The Commission must assess the existence of systematic non-compliance as part of a **market investigation pursuant to Article 18 DMA.**[116] Only if such a pattern of repeated infringement is established structural or far-reaching conduct remedies can be imposed. In contrast, where a gatekeeper commits a single or isolated infringement, the Commission is limited to issuing a cease-and-desist order. This procedural distinction reflects the DMA's graduated enforcement approach and mirrors certain competition law proceedings under Article 102 TFEU, which served as models for the conduct obligations in Articles 5, 6 DMA.[117]

In cases of systematic non-compliance, a gatekeeper may offer **commitments** pursuant to **Article 25 DMA**. It is within the Commission's discretion to assess whether the proposed commitments are suitable to effectively address and remedy the infringement. This mechanism provides a flexible enforcement tool aimed at restoring compliance without necessarily resorting to the imposition of structural remedies. By contrast, in the case of simple infringements, the DMA does not permit the use of commitments. The Commission is limited to issuing a non-compliance decision under Article 29 DMA. This strict approach is intended to ensure the swift cessation of unlawful conduct and reinforces the DMA's ex ante regulatory character.[118]

3.4.2 Especially: Fines

If a gatekeeper culpably violates its conduct obligations under the DMA, the Commission may impose a fine pursuant to **Article 30(1)(a) DMA**. The fine may amount to up to 10% of the gatekeeper's total worldwide turnover in the preceding

115 Legner (2025) § 13 mn. 89.
116 For details on market investigations, see ► 3.5.1.2.
117 See e.g. Commission, Decision of 27 June 2017 – AT.39740 – *Google Search (Shopping)*; Commission, Decision of 18 July 2018 – AT. 40099 – *Google Android*; Commission, Decision of 20 March 2019 – AT.40411 – *Google Search (AdSense)* (annulled by the GC 18 September 2024 – T-334/19 P, ECLI:EU:T:2024:634 – *Google AdSense for Search*).
118 Legner (2025) § 13 mn. 92.

3

financial year. This mirrors the fine level set out in Article 23(2) Regulation 1/2003 for competition law infringements.[119] In cases of repeated infringement, the fine may be even higher: if the gatekeeper commits a second offence within eight years, which is identical or similar and concerns the same core platform service, the fine may be increased to up to 20% of its total worldwide turnover under **Article 30(2) DMA**. Furthermore, a fine of up to 10% may also be imposed if the gatekeeper fails to comply with remedies adopted in a systematic non-compliance procedure under Article 18(1) DMA, or if it breaches commitments that have been made binding pursuant to Article 25 DMA, cf. Article 30(1) DMA.

In the case of culpable **formal violations**, such as a breach of the information obligation under Article 14 DMA regarding mergers,[120] or the failure to provide timely information during the notification procedure under Article 3 DMA,[121] the Commission may impose a fine of up to 1% of the gatekeeper's annual worldwide turnover, pursuant to Article 30(3)(a) DMA.

When determining the amount of the fine, the Commission must take into account the nature, gravity, and duration of the infringement, as well as any recurrence, in accordance with Article 30(4) DMA. For formal violations, the procedural impact—such as delays in enforcement or review—must also be considered. Repeat offences will typically result in higher fines, while a reduction may be granted if the violation was committed negligently rather than intentionally.

Pursuant to Article 30(4) DMA, the severity, duration, and any repetition of the infringement must be considered when **determining the amount of a fine**. In cases of formal violations, the Commission must also take into account any procedural delays resulting from the offence. Repeat infringements are treated as aggravating factors and typically lead to higher fines.[122] Conversely, if the offence was committed negligently rather than intentionally, a reduction in the fine is appropriate in favour of the gatekeeper.

3.4.3 Private Enforcement

3.4.3.1 Regulatory Framework for Private Enforcement

Initially, it was disputed whether the obligations imposed by the DMA could also be enforced before national courts under civil law.[123] The DMA itself is largely silent on this matter. However, several provisions suggest that the European legislator envisages the possibility of private enforcement. Notably, Article 39 DMA regulates the cooperation between national courts and the Commission. Such cooperation presupposes that national courts may, in fact, be called upon to interpret and apply provisions of the DMA.[124] Moreover, recital 42 DMA explicitly

119 For details on Article 23(2) Regulation 1/2003, see ► 2.5.2.
120 For details on Article 14 DMA, see ► 4.3.3.
121 On the designation procedure under Article 3 DMA, see ► 3.2.4.1.
122 Milde (2025) § 14 mn. 51.
123 Körber (2021), p. 436; Zimmer and Göhsl (2021), pp. 29, 52.
124 Becker (2023), pp. 403, 406.

affirms the right of business users and end users to raise concerns about unfair practices by gatekeepers, including before national courts. This indicates a clear intent to allow for judicial redress at the national level. In addition, the general principles of Union law, particularly the **principle of effectiveness**, require that directly applicable Union law, such as the DMA, must be capable of enforcement through private legal actions. Limiting enforcement solely to public authorities would not guarantee the full effectiveness of the DMA's provisions.[125] Therefore, private enforcement mechanisms must be available to complement public enforcement, ensuring that the objectives of the DMA can be fully realized in practice.[126]

3.4.3.2 Implementation in German Competition Law

3.4.3.2.1 Overview

With the 11th Amendment to the ARC in 2023, the German legislature established a framework for private enforcement of the DMA. This was primarily achieved through the expansion of sec. 33 et seq. ARC.[127] In doing so, Germany must comply with the principle of equivalence, as set out in Article 4(3) TEU. This requires that rights under the DMA must be enforceable to the same extent as comparable rights under national law.[128] Since 2023, the right to injunctive relief and removal under **sec. 33(1) ARC** has explicitly applied to violations of Articles 5, 6, 7 DMA. Additionally, **sec. 33a(1) ARC** allows for the recovery of damages in cases of culpable breaches of DMA obligations.

The inclusion of the obligations under Articles 6 DMA within the scope of sec. 33 and 33a ARC demonstrates that their specification through regulatory dialogue with the Commission under Article 8 DMA does not preclude their self-executing nature. In other words, the obligations under Article 6 DMA remain sufficiently clear and binding to serve as a basis for private enforcement.[129] German implementation thereby meets the conditions established by the ECJ for the private enforcement of Union law, namely that the relevant provisions must be 'clear, precise, and unconditional'.[130]

Sec. 33b ARC extends the binding effect of Commission decisions to gatekeeper designations under Article 3 DMA, as well as to findings of infringements of the obligations laid down in Article 5, 6, 7 DMA. While a Commission finding of a breach is not a prerequisite for initiating private enforcement (i.e., stand-alone actions remain permissible), the formal designation of an undertaking as a gatekeeper by the Commission is a necessary precondition.[131] An undertaking becomes subject to the obligations of the DMA only upon such designation. Decisions

125 ECJ 20 September 2001 – C-453/99, ECLI:EU:C:2001:465, para. 23 et seqq. – *Courage and Crehan*; ECJ 13 July 2006 – C-295/04 and others, ECLI:EU:C:2006:461, para. 58 et seqq. – *Manfredi*.
126 Becker (2023), pp. 403, 406.
127 For further details on the German implementing provisions, see ► 3.4.3.2.
128 ECJ 14 March 2019 – C-724/17, ECLI:EU:C:2019:204 – *Skanska*.
129 Schweitzer (2021), pp. 503, 541.
130 AG Geelhoed, Opinion of 13 December 2001 – C-253/00, ECLI:EU:C:2001:697, para. 37 – *Muñoz and Superior Fruiticola*.
131 Richter and Gömann (2023), pp. 208, 209.

adopting commitments under Article 25 DMA or under Article 18(6) DMA, however, are not binding under sec. 33b ARC.[132] Nevertheless, following the reasoning of the *Gasorba* judgment,[133] such decisions may serve as indications or prima facie evidence when assessing a possible DMA infringement in civil proceedings.[134] Notably, specifications of conduct obligations under Article 6 DMA, developed through the regulatory dialogue with the Commission, do not fall within the scope of the binding effect under sec. 33b ARC. These specifications, while relevant, are not themselves legally binding on national courts for the purposes of private enforcement.

3

Further procedural facilitation is provided by sec. 33g ARC, which has been extended to cover DMA violations by means of a reference to sec. 33a ARC. This provision enables claimants to demand the surrender of evidence and the provision of information, enhancing the enforceability of private claims under the DMA. The statute of limitations applicable to DMA-related claims is governed by sec. 33h(1)–(5) ARC. In principle, the limitation period for claims under sec. 33(1) and sec. 33a(1) ARC is five years. This aligns with the standard limitation periods for competition law claims under German law and ensures consistency in the enforcement of Union competition rules at the national level.

3.4.3.2.2 Standing to Bring Claims

Any affected party may assert claims for injunctive relief and damages under sec. 33(1) ARC. Sec. 33(3) ARC further clarifies that such claims are available to any person who has been **affected by the infringement**, either as a competitor or another market participant. Whether a party is considered affected by a breach of the DMA depends on the specific nature of the conduct obligation in question. Some obligations, such as the prohibition on the use of non-public data under Article 6(2) DMA or the ban on hindering advertising services under Article 5(4) DMA, primarily affect business users, including business users operating on the gatekeeper's platform. For certain provisions, the group of entitled parties is even more narrowly defined. For example, the data access rights under Article 5(9), (10) DMA are granted specifically to advertisers and publishers, meaning only these parties are eligible to bring related claims. By contrast, other obligations under the DMA are designed to protect end users as well. For instance, the prohibition against restricting access to legal remedies (Article 5(6) DMA) and the requirement to allow the uninstallation of pre-installed apps (Article 6(3) DMA) also confer rights directly upon end users. The scope of standing, therefore, varies significantly depending on the purpose and addressee of the individual DMA provision at issue.

During 2025, the first court decisions in Germany applying the DMA's provisions were issued. In August 2025, the Regional Court of Mainz ruled that *Google* violated Article 5(8) DMA[135] by preferencing its own mail service, *Gmail*.[136] The

132 Richter and Gömann (2023), pp. 208, 211.
133 ECJ 23 November 2017 – C-547/16, ECLI:EU:C:2017:891, para. 29 – *Gasorba*.
134 Richter and Gömann (2023), pp. 208, 211.
135 For further details on this obligation, see ▶ 3.3.1.7.
136 Regional Court of Mainz 12 August 2025 – 12 HK O 32/24, NZKart 2025, 561.

claimant, a provider of competing email services, argued that using other email services (such as *gmx.de* or *web.de*) on Android mobile phones was more complicated and less user-friendly compared to *Google*'s own service. The decision is not yet final, as *Google* has filed an appeal.

3.4.3.2.3 Damage

In actions for damages under the DMA, the claimant bears the burden of demonstrating and proving the harm suffered. The types of damage resulting from violations of the DMA can vary widely and are highly dependent on the specific nature of the infringement in question.

Sec. 33a(2) ARC provides a **rebuttable presumption of harm** for breaches of the prohibition on cartels. However, this presumption **does not apply** to infringements of the DMA's conduct obligations. From a legal policy perspective, this exclusion is controversial. Practical experience with the private enforcement of competition law has shown that proving damages, particularly in follow-on actions, often presents significant challenges. Similar evidentiary difficulties are likely to arise in the context of DMA enforcement. That said, it must be acknowledged that the DMA's conduct obligations are more closely aligned with the abuse of dominance provisions under sec. 19 et seq. ARC and Article 102 TFEU, which also fall outside the scope of the presumption in sec. 33a(2) ARC. Furthermore, the obligations under the DMA are highly heterogeneous in nature: they target a broad array of platform behaviours and are intended to protect various categories of users, including business users, advertisers, and end users.

Despite this diversity, the legislator recognises that violations of these obligations typically have a substantial negative effect on the contestability and fairness of digital markets.[137] In light of this, the introduction of a statutory presumption of harm, at least for certain categories of DMA infringements, should be seriously considered to facilitate effective private enforcement. In accordance with sec. 287 German code of civil procedure, courts may estimate the amount of damages once liability has been established. This provision plays a crucial role in easing the evidentiary burden on claimants, particularly in complex digital market contexts where quantifying harm with precision may be difficult.

3.4.3.2.4 Relationship to Competition Law Enforcement

Affected parties are also entitled to seek injunctive relief, removal, and damages under sec. 33, 33a ARC for infringements of competition law.[138] Given that the same conduct may constitute both a violation of the DMA's obligations and an infringement of competition law prohibitions (such as those under sec. 19a ARC or Article 102 TFEU) the question arises as to how parallel enforcement proceedings under both legal regimes should interact.

---

137 Richter and Gömann (2023), pp. 208, 212.

138 For further details on private enforcement of competition law infringements, see ► 2.5.3, ► 3.5.3.

3

Numerous questions regarding this issue are still open. One key issue concerns the extent to which disclosure obligations and evidence obtained in competition law proceedings can be used in parallel DMA-related actions. For example, it remains to be clarified whether claimants can rely on findings or evidence from competition law investigations in follow-on DMA proceedings, or whether such use would be restricted by procedural or substantive rules. In light of the differing regulatory approaches and objectives pursued by competition law and the DMA, a clear procedural separation of enforcement mechanisms may be desirable. Whereas general competition law is grounded in the prohibition of market power abuse and anti-competitive agreements, the DMA establishes a system of ex ante regulation designed to promote contestability and fairness in digital markets. While complementary, the two regimes serve distinct purposes and apply different legal standards. As the body of case law and enforcement practice develops, greater clarity will be needed to define the points of interaction between DMA enforcement and enforcement of competition law provisions.

3.4.3.3 Collective Redress and Representative Actions

The obligations under the DMA are also open to collective enforcement mechanisms. The DMA has been explicitly integrated into the Directive (EU) 2020/1828 on representative actions for the protection of the collective interests of consumers.[139] Specifically, the DMA was added to Annex I no. 67 Representative Action Directive by Article 52 DMA. Moreover, **Article 42 DMA** expressly confirms that the Representative Action Directive applies to representative actions brought against violations of Articles 5, 6, 7 DMA that affect the collective interests of consumers. With that, the European legislator acknowledges that a single violation of the DMA's obligations could potentially impact a significant number of consumers. Representative actions can enhance the deterrent effect of the obligations, thereby promoting fairness and contestability in digital markets.

The German legislature has classified the DMA as a consumer protection law within the meaning of **sec. 2(2) no. 56 German Injunctive Relief Act** (Unterlassungsklagengesetz, UKlaG). As a result, the entities authorised under sec. 3 German Injunctive Relief Act may bring actions for removal and injunctive relief pursuant to sec. 2(1) German Injunctive Relief Act. In addition, entities recognised under sec. 2 German Consumer Redress Act (Verbraucherrechtedurchsetzungsgesetz, VDuG) are entitled to bring redress actions and model declaratory actions under sec. 1(1) German Consumer Redress Act. This facilitates the collective enforcement of DMA rights, particularly in cases where systemic infringements affect large numbers of consumers.

In May 2025, the Higher Regional Court of Cologne ruled on an application for interim relief filed by a German consumer association concerning *Meta*'s plans

139 Directive (EU) 2020/1828 of the European Parliament and of the Council of 25 November 2020 on representative actions for the protection of the collective interests of consumers, OJ [2020] L 409/1.

to train its AI system.[140] Among other things, the consumer association argued that Meta's conduct violated Article 5(2)(b) DMA.[141] The court, however, held that *Meta*'s intended use of personalised user data from its social networks *Facebook* and *Instagram* for AI training purposes did not violate the DMA, since there was no 'combining' of data within the meaning of Article 5(2)(b) DMA.[142] According to the court, training data typically does not allow the identification of individuals. The notion of 'combining' under the DMA, by contrast, presupposes the deliberate aggregation of different data relating to the same person.[143] The decision was rightly criticised. Although the court used several methods of interpretation to analyse the provision, it failed to establish its link to the DMA's overarching goal of promoting contestability and fairness.[144]

3.5 Proceedings

3.5.1 Administrative Proceedings

3.5.1.1 Investigation Procedures

A non-compliance decision under Article 29 DMA requires that the Commission first conduct a formal investigation. This procedure is **initiated by a decision** pursuant to Article 20 DMA, which marks the official opening of proceedings. According to Article 29(2) DMA, the Commission must issue its decision within **12 months** of initiating the proceedings. Before concluding the investigation, the Commission is required to submit a preliminary assessment to the gatekeeper concerned, in accordance with Article 29(3) DMA. This ensures procedural fairness and allows the gatekeeper to respond to the Commission's findings before a final decision is made.

The Commission possesses extensive investigative powers throughout the process, including the ability to conduct inspections, request information, and interview employees. Notably, many of these powers may be exercised prior to the formal initiation of proceedings. However, even in the pre-investigative phase, the Commission must have an **initial suspicion** of non-compliance.[145] Such suspicion may arise through the Commission's own market monitoring activities or through notifications from third parties under Article 27 DMA, including business users, competitors, consumers, or other stakeholders.

In the context of its investigations under the DMA, the Commission is endowed with extensive investigatory powers. Article 21 DMA authorises the Commission to request **information** from undertakings in two forms: through a simple request

140 Higher Regional Court of Cologne 23 May 2025 – 15 UKl 2/25, NZKart 2025, 393 – *Facebook KI-Training*.
141 On this provision, see ► 3.3.1.1.
142 Higher Regional Court of Cologne 23 May 2025 – 15 UKl 2/25, NZKart 2025, 393, 393 et seq. – *Facebook KI-Training*.
143 Higher Regional Court of Cologne 23 May 2025 – 15 UKl 2/25, NZKart 2025, 393, 394 – *Facebook KI-Training*.
144 On further points of criticism, see Hornkohl and Ribera Martínez (2025).
145 Milde (2025) § 14 mn. 7.

3

under Article 21(1) DMA, or a formal information order under Article 21(3) DMA. Notably, and in contrast to Article 18 Regulation 1/2003, the DMA explicitly allows these requests to extend to 'data, algorithms, and information on tests. This reflects the digital-specific focus of the regulation. In addition to written requests, the Commission may also conduct **interviews** and record the statements of individuals, in accordance with Article 22 DMA. However, such interviews require the consent of the person concerned.

Further, Article 23 DMA empowers the Commission to carry out **on-site inspections**. Undertakings are legally obliged to tolerate such inspections. The Commission may enter business premises, examine and copy business records, and request explanations from employees regarding documents or facts relevant to the investigation. These powers closely mirror those available under Article 20 Regulation 1/2003, which governs competition law investigations, but are tailored to the enforcement needs of the DMA.

Pursuant to **Article 24 DMA**, the Commission is empowered to adopt **interim measures** in urgent cases where there is a risk of serious and irreparable harm to business users or end users of gatekeepers. The threshold for such measures is set high.[146] In addition to urgency, a preliminary assessment must indicate a likely violation of the obligations set out in Articles 5, 6, 7 DMA. To ensure the exceptional character of interim measures, the Commission cannot impose them unilaterally; it must consult the Advisory Committee on Digital Markets (cf. Articles 24 3rd sentence, 50(2) DMA).

Decisions on non-compliance under Article 29 DMA can be challenged before the GC by way of an action for annulment pursuant to **Article 263(4) TFEU**. However, such actions do not have suspensive effect, meaning the decision remains effective while the case is pending. Similarly, although decisions initiating proceedings under Article 20 DMA may in principle be contestable, challenges are unlikely to succeed in practice given the procedural nature of these acts and their compliance with legal standards.

3.5.1.2 Market Investigations

The DMA introduces a special procedure for **market investigations** aimed at conducting thorough inquiries into digital market structures and identifying systematic infringements. These investigations are resource-intensive and bear similarities to **sector inquiries** under **Article 17 Regulation 1/2003** and **sec. 32e ARC**. However, sector inquiries differ fundamentally in their purpose: they focus solely on analysing sector-specific competitive conditions, whereas DMA market investigations are geared towards assessing gatekeeper status and compliance.

The Commission may initiate market investigations for **three reasons**. Firstly, under **Article 17 DMA**, a market investigation is required in two specific scenarios related to **gatekeeper designation**.[147] First, it is necessary when the Commission

146 Milde (2025) § 14 mn. 84.

147 On further details of the designation procedure, see ▶ 3.2.4.1.

intends to designate an undertaking as a gatekeeper, but the entity does not meet one or more of the thresholds set out in Article 3(2) DMA for the presumption of gatekeeper status. Second, a market investigation is mandated if the undertaking meets these thresholds but submits credible and substantiated arguments to rebut the presumption. In both cases, the criteria enumerated in **Article 3(8) DMA** serve as the guiding framework for assessing the gatekeeper position.[148]

Secondly, pursuant to **Article 18 DMA**, the Commission may initiate a market investigation to identify **systematic infringements** of obligations imposed on gatekeepers. If such infringements are confirmed following the investigation, the Commission is empowered to impose appropriate measures to address the violations.[149]

Thirdly, the DMA is designed to adapt to the rapid evolution of the digital sector and includes mechanisms for timely regulatory updates.[150] In this regard, **Article 19 DMA** provides for market investigations aimed at assessing whether **updates** are necessary to the regulation itself. Specifically, through these investigations, the Commission evaluates whether additional services should be added to the list of core platform services under Article 2(2) DMA, or whether there are emerging practices that undermine contestability and fairness but are not yet prohibited by the current provisions of Articles 5, 6, 7 DMA.

Market investigations are initiated by a **formal decision** in accordance with Article 16 DMA. Although the wording of Article 16 DMA does not explicitly require an initial suspicion for launching an investigation, it is generally expected that there are specific indications pointing to the existence of the relevant grounds for the market investigation. During the investigation, the Commission has access to its investigative powers as set out in Articles 21 et seq. DMA.

The maximum duration of market investigations varies depending on the underlying reason for the inquiry. For market investigations related to gatekeeper designation, the Commission must complete the process within **five months** if the investigation is triggered by the rebuttal of the presumption established under Article 3(2) DMA, as provided in Article 17(3) DMA. In contrast, where an undertaking does not meet the presumption thresholds, the Commission aims to complete the investigation within **twelve months**, pursuant to Article 17(1) DMA. This twelve-month timeframe also applies to market investigations initiated due to suspected systematic infringements of conduct obligations under Article 18(1) DMA. The longest investigation periods are reserved for market inquiries addressing new services or emerging practices. Under Article 19(3) DMA, the Commission may take up to **eighteen months** to conduct the investigation and prepare proposals for amendments to the DMA, reflecting the need for a thorough and careful assessment in such cases.

---

148 See ► 3.2.3.3 for the criteria under Article 3(8) DMA.

149 For more details on the public enforcement of the DMA, see ► 3.4.1.

150 Larouche and de Streel (2021), pp. 542, 557.

3.5.1.3 Investigation by National Competition Authorities

Pursuant to **Article 38(7) DMA**, national competition authorities are empowered to initiate administrative proceedings **to investigate breaches** of the obligations under Articles 5, 6, 7 DMA. For example, the German legislator has implemented this provision in sec. 32g(1) ARC. In this context, the national authorities have access to their regular investigative powers. It is assumed that such proceedings may run in parallel with investigations into violations of sec. 19a ARC.

3

However, if the investigations establish that a DMA infringement has occurred, the authority to issue a cease-and-desist order remains exclusively with the Commission, as stipulated in Article 29 DMA. Consequently, the national competition authority concludes its investigation by submitting a **report to the Commission**, cf. Article 38(7)(2) DMA.[151]

Even if a national competition authority can make legal violations of the DMA the subject of its investigation, it has no authority to halt or sanction such violations.

Article 38 DMA sets out additional provisions governing the cooperation between national competition authorities and the Commission. These provisions apply in particular to proceedings based on competition law provisions that are initiated against gatekeepers. Given that the same or closely related conduct by digital undertakings may fall under both competition law and the DMA, national authorities are required to inform the Commission of the **initiation of such proceedings**, in accordance with **Article 38(2), (3) DMA**. This obligation to notify does not limit the investigative or enforcement powers of national authorities. The same applies to decisions by national competition authorities to impose fines; such decisions remain within its competence, even when they relate to conduct that may also fall within the scope of the DMA.

National competition authorities may initiate competition law proceedings even after an undertaking has been designated as a gatekeeper. In such cases, they are required to notify the Commission in accordance with Article 38(2), (3) DMA.

3.5.2 Fine Proceedings

In order to impose a fine on a gatekeeper under **Article 30 DMA**, the Commission must first initiate formal proceedings by adopting a decision pursuant to Article 20(1) DMA. Where the fine concerns an infringement of the obligations under Articles 5, 6 or 7 DMA, a prior decision of non-compliance under Article 29 DMA is also required. The fine may be imposed in a separate decision or directly in connection with the non-compliance decision.

151 Van den Boom (2022), pp. 57, 67.

The administrative act imposing the fine may be challenged before the GC by way of an **action for annulment** pursuant to Article 263(4) TFEU. An appeal against the GC's judgment may be brought before the ECJ. Under Article 45 DMA, the ECJ has the authority to conduct a full review of the Commission's discretionary decisions, including those related to the imposition and calculation of fines.

Both competition law and the DMA provide for fines as enforcement measures. This raises the question of when the principle of **ne bis in idem**, as enshrined in Article 50 CFR, is infringed—particularly if the Commission initiates both DMA proceedings and proceedings under **Article 102 TFEU** in relation to the same underlying conduct. This issue is especially relevant in cases where conduct obligations under the DMA are inspired by previous competition law decisions, meaning the same behaviour may violate both the DMA's goals of ensuring fairness and contestability and the competition law objective of protecting market freedom.

In principle, a violation of the ne bis in idem principle requires a **threefold identity**: First, the earlier decision must be final. Second, it must concern the same facts. Third, it must affect the same protected legal interest.[152] However, in recent rulings, *Nordzucker*[153] and *bpost*,[154] ECJ appears to interpret the third requirement (identity of the protected legal interest) more narrowly, thereby limiting the scope of ne bis in idem. The ECJ clarified that the identity of the legal interest is relevant only at the justification stage of an interference with Article 50 CFR, rather than as part of the factual identity test. Based on this evolving case law, it can be argued that DMA enforcement and competition law enforcement pursue distinct regulatory objectives.[155] Consequently, the same conduct may, in principle, be sanctioned under both regimes without necessarily breaching Article 50 CFR. To address potential concerns about disproportionate sanctions, the Commission seeks to mitigate this overlap at the penalty stage. Pursuant to recital 86 DMA, the Commission will take into account fines already imposed on the gatekeeper for the same conduct when determining the amount of any DMA-related penalty.

Regarding German competition law, the principle of ne bis in idem also becomes relevant when the German Federal Cartel Office conducts proceedings against a gatekeeper under sec. 19a ARC in parallel with proceedings by the Commission under the DMA. Given that both sec. 19a ARC and Articles 5, 6 DMA apply to the same category of undertakings and may address substantially identical conduct, the imposition of double sanctions should be avoided. In such cases, care must be taken to ensure compliance with Article 50 CFR, and parallel enforcement should not result in duplicate penalties for the same factual and legal infringement.[156]

152 ECJ 25 February 2021 – C-857/19, ECLI:EU:C:2021:139 – *Slovak Telekom*.
153 ECJ 22 March 2022 – C-151/20, ECLI:EU:C:2022:203 – *Nordzucker*.
154 ECJ 22 March 2022 – C-117/20, ECLI:EU:C:2022:202 – *pbost*.
155 Huerkamp and Nuys (2023) DMA Article 30 mn. 21; Käseberg and Gappa (2023) DMA Article 1 mn. 33.
156 Huerkamp and Nuys (2023) DMA Article 30 mn. 24.

3

3.5.3 Civil Proceedings

In Germany, pursuant to **sec. 87 1st sentence ARC**, the regional courts have exclusive jurisdiction at first instance for civil actions brought under secs. 33, 33a ARC arising from violations of Articles 5, 6, 7 DMA, regardless of the value in dispute. Local jurisdiction is determined according to the general rules of secs. 12 et seq. German Code of Civil Procedure. In addition to the general forum of the defendant's domicile (cf. **secs. 12, 17 German Code of Civil Procedure**), special jurisdictions may apply. If a contractual relationship exists between the plaintiff and the gatekeeper, jurisdiction may also lie with the court at the place of performance under **sec. 29a German Code of Civil Procedure**. Moreover, the special jurisdiction for torts under **sec. 32 German Code of Civil Procedure** is applicable, as many DMA-related claims may involve unauthorised acts. The place of performance in such cases is any location where a material element of the infringement under the DMA occurs.[157]

Appeals are governed by the general rules of the German Code of Civil Procedure. Under the conditions of sec. 511(2) German Code of Civil Procedure, an appeal against a first-instance judgment may be brought before the Higher Regional Court. If the requirements of sec. 543 German Code of Civil Procedure are fulfilled—namely, if the matter is of fundamental significance or requires a decision by the highest court to ensure uniform jurisprudence—an appeal may be lodged with the German Federal Court of Justice pursuant to sec. 542 German Code of Civil Procedure.

3.6 Review Questions

1. What are the objectives of the DMA?

The DMA aims to promote contestability and fairness in the digital sector, as outlined in Article 1(2) DMA. These overarching goals are further specified in Article 12(5) DMA.

Contestability refers to the ability of new and existing companies to compete effectively in digital markets. Its objective is to lower entry barriers and foster competition, both among platform operators and within the platforms themselves. Contestability is undermined when gatekeepers create or strengthen obstacles that prevent other businesses from entering or expanding in the market. It is also impaired when rival platform operators are denied access to essential inputs that gatekeepers control.

Fairness is an outcome-oriented principle. It seeks to address and prevent imbalances in the relationship between gatekeepers and their business users, particularly where such imbalances result in disproportionate rights or obligations. Additionally,

157 Schmidt (2024) ARC sec. 87 mn. 39.

certain conduct obligations under the DMA (e.g. Articles 5(2), 6(3) DMA) are specifically designed to safeguard end users' freedom of choice (for further details, see ► 3.1.3.2 and 3.1.3.3).

2. What is the relationship between the DMA and (general) competition law?

According to Article 1(6) DMA, the Digital Markets Act does not affect the application of existing competition law. This means that competition law rules apply in addition to the conduct obligations set out in the DMA.

In particular, this parallel application includes provisions such as sec. 19a ARC. While both the DMA and sec. 19a ARC may target similar types of behaviour by the same undertakings, sec. 19a ARC is grounded in the abuse of dominance concept under competition law. As such, it allows for potential justifications based on efficiency considerations, which are not typically available under the DMA's strict obligations. Sec. 19a ARC primarily aims to protect the freedom of competition. However, once a company has been designated as a gatekeeper by the Commission under the DMA, the DMA takes precedence. In this case, sec. 19a ARC may no longer apply to behaviours covered by the DMA, due to the DMA's blocking effect.

That said, sec. 19a ARC remains relevant in three situations: when a company has not yet been designated as a gatekeeper; when the conduct does not relate to core platform services; or when the practices in question are not explicitly addressed by the DMA (► 3.1.3.1).

3. How is the territorial scope of the DMA determined?

The territorial scope of the DMA is defined in Article 1(2) DMA. The DMA applies to all core platform services that a gatekeeper provides or offers to business users or end users located within the European Union. This means that the location of the gatekeeper is irrelevant. What matters is whether the services are targeted at or have an impact on users in the EU. This approach aligns with the 'effects doctrine' found in European competition law, which extends legal obligations to conduct that has a substantial effect within the EU. For business users, the DMA applies if they are established in the EU. For end users, residence in the EU is sufficient (► 3.1.4.1).

4. How is it determined whether an undertaking is subject to the obligations under Articles 5, 6, 7 DMA?

An undertaking is subject to the obligations under Articles 5, 6, 7 DMA if it has been designated as a gatekeeper by the Commission. This designation requires that the undertaking fulfils the criteria set out in Article 3(1) DMA and has formally been identified as a gatekeeper through one of the procedures provided by the regulation. The DMA establishes two different pathways for designation. The first is the notification procedure, which applies when an undertaking exceeds the quantitative thresholds related to turnover and user numbers as specified in Article 3(2) DMA. In this case, the undertaking is presumed to be a gatekeeper and must notify the Commission accordingly.

3

The second pathway involves a market investigation under Article 17 DMA. This procedure is triggered either when the undertaking, despite meeting the thresholds, successfully rebuts the presumption of gatekeeper status, or when the undertaking does not meet the thresholds but may still hold a significant position in the market that justifies its designation. In such cases, the Commission assesses the undertaking's position based on a range of qualitative factors, including market structure, market conduct, and characteristics specific to the undertaking, as outlined in Article 3(8) DMA (► 3.2.4).

5. How do the DMA's obligations differ from the ban on abuse under Article 102 TFEU?

While the DMA contains precisely defined prohibitions, Article 102 TFEU relies on broad and generally formulated legal concepts. A key distinction lies in the evidentiary requirements. Under Article 102 TFEU, establishing an infringement requires proof of anti-competitive effects. In contrast, the DMA imposes obligations on gatekeepers without requiring a demonstration of actual or potential harm to competition. Moreover, unlike Article 102 TFEU, the DMA does not allow for justification based on efficiency gains. Undertakings cannot defend non-compliance by arguing that their conduct leads to improved efficiency or consumer benefits (► 3.1.1).

6. What is the difference between the obligations under Articles 5, 6 DMA?

In contrast to the obligations under Article 5 DMA, the obligations under Article 6 DMA are open to specification. To facilitate their effective implementation, Article 8 DMA provides for a regulatory dialogue between the Commission and the gatekeeper. This dialogue allows the parties to clarify how specific obligations should be fulfilled in practice. It may be initiated at the Commission's discretion, either on its own initiative or at the request of the gatekeeper. Importantly, this dialogue is not linked to a particular legal violation but functions as a tool of ex ante regulation to define proportionate and workable compliance solutions. Nevertheless, the obligations under both Article 5 and Article 6 remain directly applicable and enforceable (► 3.3.2).

7. Why do Article 5(7), (8) DMA contain prohibitions on tying?

Article 5(7) DMA prohibits gatekeepers from making access to one of their core platform services conditional on the use of another specific service they offer, such as identification services, web browser engines, or payment systems. This rule addresses scenarios where users are effectively forced to accept bundled services, limiting their freedom of choice and restricting competitors' access to users. Article 5(8) DMA further prohibits gatekeepers from combining or linking their core platform services in ways that could entrench their market position. This includes practices that artificially integrate different services, making it more difficult for rivals to compete on individual service components. These prohibitions serve multiple objectives. First, they aim to lower barriers to market entry for competing service providers. Second, they seek to curb the data advantages gatekeepers gain through cross-service user tracking. Finally, they are designed to prevent the leveraging of market power from one service to another, thereby limiting gatekeepers' ability to dominate adjacent markets. (► 3.3.1.6, ► 3.3.1.7).

8. Why does Article 6(2) DMA prohibit gatekeepers from using data collected from business users when competing with them?

This prohibition addresses the conflict of interest inherent in the gatekeeper's hybrid role: on the one hand, the gatekeeper provides a platform or infrastructure for business users; on the other, it may act as a direct competitor to those same users on the platform. By virtue of their position, gatekeepers have access to a vast amount of commercially sensitive data that third-party businesses do not. If gatekeepers were allowed to exploit this data in competition, they could distort market dynamics and entrench their dominance. The objective of Article 6(2) DMA is therefore to ensure a level playing field and to foster fair competition on the platform. By limiting the gatekeeper's ability to use upstream data in its own downstream operations, the DMA aims to encourage market openness, business innovation, and greater competitive pressure (► 3.3.2.1).

9. What is the purpose of the obligation to provide information on mergers under Article 14 DMA?

Article 14 DMA imposes an obligation on gatekeepers to inform the Commission about any planned mergers or acquisitions, even if the transaction does not meet the notification thresholds under the EUMR. This requirement applies in cases where the merging or target undertaking provides core platform services, offers other digital services, or enables the collection of user data.

The purpose of this provision is to enhance the Commission's ability to monitor and assess acquisitions in the digital sector, particularly those that could escape traditional merger control due to their limited turnover. By increasing transparency around gatekeepers' acquisition strategies, Article 14 DMA allows the Commission to detect potentially problematic transactions at an early stage. This is especially relevant for 'killer acquisitions' that target emerging competitors before they can become a serious competitive threat. Moreover, the obligation supports greater use of the referral mechanism under Article 22 EUMR, which allows national competition authorities to refer cases to the Commission, even when national thresholds are not met. In addition, the information provided under this obligation contributes to the Commission's broader understanding of developments in core platform services and may inform decisions in future market investigations or the designation of new gatekeepers (► 3.3.3).

10. On what occasions can the Commission initiate market investigations under the DMA?

The DMA provides the Commission with the authority to initiate market investigations on three specific occasions, each serving a distinct regulatory purpose. First, under Article 17 DMA, the Commission may conduct a market investigation to designate a company as a gatekeeper. This is necessary in cases where the undertaking does not meet the quantitative thresholds set out in Article 3(2) DMA, or where it has successfully rebutted the presumption of gatekeeper status. In such instances, a market investigation enables the Commission to assess whether the undertaking nonetheless holds a position of entrenched and durable economic power with significant impact on the internal market. Second, Article 18 DMA allows the Commission to open a market investigation if there is a suspicion that a gatekeeper is systematically non-compliant with its obligations under the DMA. If this suspicion is confirmed, the Commission may impose proportionate behavioural or structural remedies to address the root causes of the non-compliance and prevent its recurrence. Third, pursuant to Article 19 DMA, the Commission can initiate a market investigation to assess whether there is a need to update or expand the list of core platform services (as defined in Article 2(2) DMA) or to revise the catalogue of obligations laid down in Articles 5, 6, 7 DMA (► 3.5.1.2).

11. What are the legal consequences of a breach of the DMA's obligations?

According to Article 30(1)(a) DMA, the Commission may impose fines where it finds that a gatekeeper has failed to comply with the DMA's obligations. These fines can reach up to 10% of the gatekeeper's total worldwide turnover in the preceding financial year. The DMA also foresees stricter penalties in cases of repeated infringements. Under Article 30(2) DMA, if a gatekeeper commits a similar or identical infringement concerning the same core platform service within a period of eight years, the Commission may impose a fine of up to 20% of the gatekeeper's annual global turnover (► 3.5.2).

12. What additional powers does the Commission have in the event of systematic breaches of the DMA's obligations?

If, in the course of a market investigation under Article 18 DMA, the Commission determines that a gatekeeper has systematically infringed its obligations under the DMA, and that such conduct has contributed to the maintenance, strengthening, or extension of its gatekeeper position, the Commission is empowered to adopt remedial measures of both a behavioural and structural nature. Behavioural remedies may include specific obligations aimed at ensuring future compliance, such as changes to business practices or enhanced transparency requirements. Structural remedies can include far-reaching measures such as the divestiture of parts of the undertaking. However, the Commission must adhere to the principle of proportionality when deciding on the appropriate remedy (► 3.4.1).

13. Can the obligations of the DMA be enforced under private law?

The DMA does not explicitly address the issue of private enforcement. However, the principle of effectiveness under EU law supports the possibility that individuals and businesses affected by violations of the DMA may invoke its provisions before national courts. This principle requires that rights granted by EU law must be effectively protected by Member States, including through judicial remedies. Further support for private enforcement can be found in national legislative developments. Notably, the German legislature has acknowledged the enforceability of DMA obligations through private law. In the context of the 11th amendment to the ARC, it introduced provisions that provide a legal basis for claims for injunctive relief, removal, and damages in cases of DMA violations, cf. secs. 33(1), 33a(1) ARC (► 3.4.3).

14. What role does national competition authorities play in enforcing the DMA's obligations?

National competition authorities do not have direct enforcement powers under the DMA. The authority to enforce the DMA lies exclusively with the Commission. However, the national authorities do play a supportive role. Pursuant to Article 38(7) DMA, they may conduct administrative investigations into possible breaches of the obligations laid down in Articles 5, 6, 7 DMA. Once their investigation is complete, it must submit a report to the Commission. It is then for the Commission to decide whether to initiate formal enforcement proceedings (► 3.5.1.3).

15. Can the same conduct be fined both under competition law and the DMA?

Dual sanctions are possible as long as they comply with the ne bis in idem principle, which prohibits a person or undertaking from being penalised twice for the same offence. In its *bpost* judgment, the ECJ clarified that a double fine is permissible where the two legal regimes pursue different objectives. In this case, competition law and regulatory law (such as the DMA) serve distinct purposes: the former focuses on protecting competition in the market, while the latter seeks to impose specific ex ante obligations on designated gatekeepers. Nevertheless, when imposing fines for overlapping conduct, authorities must ensure close coordination. They are required to take into account any previous penalties imposed for the same or similar behaviour to avoid disproportionate punishment. This means that, while a double fine is not categorically excluded, its application must be carefully assessed to ensure fairness and proportionality in line with EU fundamental rights (► 3.5.2).

References

Becker C (2023) Privatrechtliche Durchsetzung des Digital Markets Act. ZEuP 2023:403–434

Bongartz P (2022) § 19a GWB – a keeper? – Die bleibende Bedeutung der Vorschrift im Abgleich mit dem DMA-Entwurf –. WuW 2022:72–82

Bongartz P, Kirk A (2023) Article 2 DMA. In: Podszun R (ed) Commentary Digital Markets Act. Nomos, Baden-Baden

Bostoen F (2023) Understanding the Digital Markets Act. Antitrust Bull 68(2):263–306

Bueren E/Weck T (2022) Article 5 DMA. In: Säcker F, Meier-Beck P, Bien F, Montag F (eds) Münchener Kommmentar zum Wettwerbsrecht. 4th edn. C.H.Beck, Munich

Burchardi S (2022) Die Selbstbegünstigung von Plattformunternehmen im Fokus des Kartell- und Regulierungsrechts. NZKart 2022:610–616

Christodoulou K, Holzwarth J (2022) Die neue Vertikal-GVO: Das moderne Vertriebskartellrecht 3.0. Neue Zeitschrift für Kartellrecht 2022:540–547

Forsthoff U (2025) Article 49 TFEU. In: Grabitz E, Hilf M, Nettesheim M (eds) Das Recht der Europäischen Union: EUV/AEUV, 85th edn. C.H.Beck, Munich

Haus F, Weusthof AL (2021) The Digital Markets Act - a gatekeeper's nightmare? WuW 2021:318–325

Heinz S (2023) Article 5(3),(4),(5),(7),(8), Article 6(5) DMA. In: Podszun R (ed) Commentary Digital Markets Act, 2023. Nomos, Baden-Baden

Heinze C, Kettler T (2025) § 11 scope of application and relationship to other instruments. In: Steinrötter B, Heinze C, Denga M (eds) EU Platform Regulation – a handbook, 1st edn. Nomos/Beck/Hart Publishing, Baden-Baden/Munich/Oxford

Herbers B (2023) Article 6(3), (4), (6), (7), Article 7, Article 14 DMA. In: Podszun R (ed) Commentary Digital Markets Act, 2023. Nomos, Baden-Baden

Herbers B, Savary F, Gräf S (2023) (K)ein Monopol der Kommission bei der Torwächter-Regulierung – Welche Rolle spielt der Digital Markets Act im deutschen Recht? GRUR-Prax 2023:185–188

Hornkohl L, Ribera Martínez A (2025) The Higher Regional Court Cologne Barks Up The Wrong (Data) Tree: The Court's Interpretation of Article 5(2)(b) DMA in the Meta AI Case, Kluwer Competition Law Blog. https://legalblogs.wolterskluwer.com/competition-blog/the-higher-regional-court-cologne-barks-up-the-wrong-data-tree-the-courts-interpretation-of-article-52b-dma-in-the-meta-ai-case/. Accessed 25 Sep 2025

Huerkamp F, Nuys M (2023) Articles 16–19, 30–36 DMA. In: Podszun R (ed) Commentary Digital Markets Act, 2023. Nomos, Baden-Baden

Jovanovic D, Greiner J (2021) DMA: Überblick über den geplanten EU-Regulierungsrahmen für digitale Gatekeeper – Paradigmenwechsel im Umgang mit digitalen Plattformen? MMR 2021:678–682

Käseberg T, Gappa S (2023) Article 1 DMA. In: Podszun R (ed) Commentary Digital Markets Act, 2023. Nomos, Baden-Baden

Kattnig M, Angerschmid A, Reichel T, Kern R (2024) Assessing trustworthy AI: technical and legal perspectives of fairness in AI. Computer Law & Security Review 55:106053

König C (2025) § 23 Obligations for gatekeepers. In: Steinrötter B, Heinze C, Denga M (eds) EU Platform Regulation – a handbook, 1st edn. Nomos/Beck/Hart Publishing, Baden-Baden/Munich/Oxford

Körber T (2021) Lessons from the Hare and the Tortoise: legally imposed self-regulation, proportionality and the right to defence under the DMA – Part 1. NZKart 2021:379–384

Kumkar L (2022) Der Digital Markets Act nach dem Trilog-Verfahren – Neue Impulse für den Wettbewerb auf digitalen Märkten. RDi 2022:347–354

Kumkar L (2024) Article 1 DMA. In: Jaeger W, Kokott J, Pohlmann P, Schroeder D, Seeliger D (eds) Frankfurter Kommentar zum Kartellrecht, 108th supp. Dr. Otto Schmidt, Cologne

Kumkar L, Nehl H, Serafimova M (2024) Preamble Digital Markets Act. In: Jaeger W, Kokott J, Pohlmann P, Schroeder D, Seeliger D (eds) Frankfurter Kommentar zum Kartellrecht, 108th supp. Dr. Otto Schmidt, Cologne

Larouche P, de Streel A (2021) The European Digital Markets Act: a revolution grounded on traditions. JECLP 12(7):542–560

Legner S (2025) § 13 Market investigation. In: Steinrötter B, Heinze C, Denga M (eds) EU Platform Regulation – a handbook, 1st edn. Nomos/Beck/Hart Publishing, Baden-Baden/Munich/Oxford

Lettl T (2023) Die Normadressaten des Gesetzes über digitale Märkte (Digital Markets Act). WM 2023:953–1004

Maher I (2024) Regulatory design in the EU Digital Markets Act: no solo run for the European Commission. J Antitrust Enforce 12(2):273–279

Milde S (2025) § 14 Powers of and cooperation with authorities/enforcement. In: Steinrötter B, Heinze C, Denga M (eds) EU Platform Regulation – a handbook, 1st edn. Nomos/Beck/Hart Publishing, Baden-Baden/Munich/Oxford

Paal B, Kumkar L (2021) Wettbewerbsschutz in der Digitalwirtschaft – Die wichtigsten Neuerungen der 10. GWB-Novelle im Überblick. NJW 2021:809–815

Podszun R (2023a) DMA Article 5(6) DMA. In: Podszun R (ed) Commentary Digital Markets Act, 1st edn. Nomos, Baden-Baden

Podszun R (2023b) From competition law to platform regulation – regulatory choices for the Digital Markets Act. Economics 17(1):20220037

Podszun R, Bongartz P, Kirk A (2022) Digital Markets Act – Neue Regeln für Fairness in der Plattformökonomie. NJW 2022:3249–3254

Richter AC, Gömann M (2023) Private Enforcement des DMA – Ein Ausblick am Beispiel Amazons. NZKart 2023:208–213

Schmidt K (2024) § 87 GWB. In: Immenga/Mestmäcker (founders) Commentary Wettbewerbsrecht, 7th edn. C.H.Beck, Munich

Schwab A (2023) Article 6(12) DMA. In: Podszun R (ed) Commentary Digital Markets Act, 1st edn. Nomos, Baden-Baden

Schweitzer H (2021) The art to make gatekeeper positions contestable and the challenge to know what is fair: a discussion of the Digital Markets Act Proposal. ZEuP 2021:503–544

Seip F, Berberich M (2021) Der Entwurf des Digital Markets Act. GRUR Prax 2021:44–47

Serafimova M (2024) Article 6 DMA. In: Jaeger W, Kokott J, Pohlmann P, Schroeder D, Seeliger D (eds) Frankfurter Kommentar zum Kartellrecht, 108th supp. Dr. Otto Schmidt, Cologne

Simone C, Laudando A (2025) Principles and obligations of the Digital Markets Act in regulating the economic power of gatekeepers: Positive, negative or trade-off effects? Electronic Markets 35:42

van den Boom J (2022) What does the Digital Markets Act harmonize? – exploring interactions between the DMA and national competition laws. Eur Compet J 19(1):57–85

Westerstrand S (2025) Fairness in AI systems development: EU AI Act compliance and beyond. Inf Softw Technol 187:107864

Wolf-Posch A (2023) Article 5(9)(10), Article 6(2),(8)–(10). In: Podszun R (ed) Commentary Digital Markets Act. Nomos, Baden-Baden

Zimmer D, Göhsl JF (2021) Vom New Competition Tool zum Digital Markets Act: Die geplante EU-Regulierung für digitale Gatekeeper. ZWeR 2021:29–61

Platform Regulation

Contents

S. Legner, *Digital Competition Law*, Springer Textbooks in Law,
https://doi.org/10.1007/978-3-662-73213-7_4

4.1 Introduction

4.1.1 Overview

The Platform Regulation[1] is a European regulation with the aim of promoting **fairness and transparency in favour of business users** when using online intermediary services and search engines. Indirectly, it also aims to **protect consumers**.

The regulation establishes **transparency obligations** for providers of online intermediation services and search engines. These obligations apply, on the one hand, to the terms and conditions governing **the use of their services**. According to Articles 3 and 4 Platform Regulation, providers must clearly communicate the grounds for suspension, termination, and other relevant conditions affecting business users.

On the other hand, the regulation also requires transparency regarding specific aspects of platform design and conduct. Providers must disclose the key parameters used to determine **rankings**, as set out in Article 5 Platform Regulation. They are also required to inform business users of any **self-preferencing practices**, in accordance with **Article 7 Platform Regulation**, and the use of **most-favoured-nation clauses**, as provided in **Article 10 Platform Regulation**. Unlike European competition law and the DMA, the Platform Regulation does not impose bans on such practices. Instead, its focus is limited to transparency: service providers must inform business users about these practices but are not prohibited from engaging in them. Finally, Articles 11–13 Platform Regulation introduce procedural safeguards for business users. Providers must establish internal complaint-handling systems and offer access to mediation in the event of disputes, helping to ensure that conflicts are addressed in a fair and timely manner.

▶ Example

Service provider D sells goods to consumers through its own platform. In response to search queries by consumers, the goods offered by D are displayed at the top of the search results, thus appearing before competing offers from other business users. According to Article 7(1) Platform Regulation, D is required to explain this differentiated treatment to business users, outlining the most important economic, commercial, and legal considerations that justify the preferential ranking.

Although self-preferencing is permitted under the Platform Regulation, it is not without limits. A prohibition on self-preferencing could arise from other legal frameworks, including Article 102 TFEU or Article 6(5) DMA. However, these provisions are limited to certain types of undertakings. To be subject to these regulations, D would need to either be dominant in the market (under Article 102 TFEU), or qualify as a gatekeeper (under Article 6(5) DMA). ◀

1 Regulation (EU) 2019/1150 of the European Parliament and of the Council of 20 June 2019 on promoting fairness and transparency for business users of online intermediation services, OJ EU [2019] L 186/57.

The Platform Regulation operates alongside existing antitrust law and the DMA, as clarified in Article 1(4), (5) Platform Regulation.[2] It does not present a standalone or exhaustive set of rules but rather complements the existing regulatory frameworks.[3] The DMA, in recital 12, explicitly affirms that it does not preclude the application of the Platform Regulation; instead, both regulations are intended to operate in parallel. In Germany, the enforcement of the Platform Regulation's requirements was initially pursued solely under private law, relying on injunctive relief and claims for damages. Under sec. 8a German Act Against Unfair Competition (*Gesetz gegen den unlauteren Wettbewerb, UWG*),[4] collective actions are also possible. However, starting in May 2024, the German Federal Network Agency (Bundesnetzagentur) gained the authority to enforce the transparency obligations set out in the Platform Regulation through cease-and-desist orders, as per sec. 22(1) and sec. 30 German Implementing Act on Digital Services (*Digitale-Dienste-Gesetz, DDG*).[5] The Agency can also impose fines under sec. 33(3) German Implementing Act on Digital Services for violations of various ordinance requirements.

4.1.2 Legislative Process

The Platform Regulation, which came into force in 2020, was the first piece of legislation to be adopted as part of the Commission's broader digital strategy[6] that began in 2015. It specifically targets competitive risks in digital markets, marking an early response within European law to the dependency of business users on large platform operators, a trend that has since been addressed in various other legislative areas.[7] Unlike traditional regulatory frameworks, the Platform Regulation does not fit neatly into any specific area of law, nor does it present a closed or exhaustive regulatory approach. As a result, it serves as a foundational piece in a wider legal landscape.[8] In 2022, the European legislator responded to the growing challenges of digital markets by enacting additional legislative instruments: the DMA and the DSA.

The Platform Regulation itself is a highly detailed piece of legislation. For instance, Article 3(2) Platform Regulation sets out specific requirements, including strict deadlines, for service providers to amend their general terms and conditions. However, in contrast to the DMA and the DSA, the Platform Regulation provides greater flexibility to member states regarding the legal consequences of non-compliance. While the newer regulations primarily rely on administrative law and the imposition of fines, the Platform Regulation leaves the decision on whether to establish public enforcement mechanisms up to individual member states.

2 Arncken (2025) sec. 16 mn. 4.
3 Arncken (2025) sec. 16 mn. 4.
4 Federal Law Gazette Part I 2003, p. 1414.
5 Federal Law Gazette Part I 2024 no. 149.
6 Commission, A Digital Single Market Strategy for Europe, COM(2015) 192 final.
7 Hoffer and Lehr (2019), pp. 10, 19.
8 Busch (2024), pp. 210 et seqq.

4.1.3 Objectives

4.1.3.1 Relation to (General) Competition Law

As outlined in Article 1(1) Platform Regulation, the Regulation imposes obligations on providers of online intermediary services and search engines to promote fairness and transparency in favour of business users. While the Regulation directly targets business-user interests, it indirectly protects consumers as well, since it only applies to intermediary services that facilitate sales to consumers, as clarified in recital 3 Platform Regulation. Importantly, the Platform Regulation is not a part of (general) competition law; instead, it serves as sector-specific regulation with distinct objectives. This is further supported by the competence established in Article 114 TFEU, which provides the legal basis for the adoption of the Platform Regulation, distinguishing it from broader competition law.

4.1.3.2 Fairness and Transparency

Although the goals of the Platform Regulation are sector-specific and distinct from those of competition law, the legislative considerations for its adoption stem from the same structural challenges that undermine competition in digital markets. The core objective of fairness in the Platform Regulation arises from the recognition that online intermediary services and search engines have increasingly become critical 'bottlenecks' through which business users must pass to reach consumers.[9] This dependency creates a power imbalance, where business users rely heavily on platform operators for their business success. The terms and conditions that platform operators unilaterally set for their services act as a primary tool for exercising this power. In this context, platform operators are sometimes referred to as 'private legislators',[10] highlighting their ability to shape the terms under which business users operate, often without meaningful input from those users.

The Platform Regulation introduces, for the first time at the European level, a control mechanism for general terms and conditions in favour of business users. Prior to this, the 1993 Unfair Terms Directive[11] applied only to general terms and conditions used in consumer contracts. Some national legal frameworks, such as sec. 310(1), 307 German Civil Code (*Bürgerliches Gesetzbuch, BGB*), extend this control to cover terms and conditions in business-to-business contracts. However, this broader protection stems from national lawmakers' decisions to include undertakings within the scope of such protections. From a European perspective, the Platform Regulation marks the first time that a regulation specifically addresses the control of general terms and conditions for business users.

---

9 Ernst (2020), p. 735.
10 Schweitzer (2019), p. 1.
11 Council Directive 93/13/EEC of 5 April 1993 on unfair terms in consumer contracts, OJ [1995] L 95/29.

Learning Goals

The power imbalance resulting from the unilateral determination of terms of use by platform operators extends beyond the scope of the Platform Regulation and intersects with various areas of law, including contract law and unfair competition law. In the context of reviewing general terms and conditions, the key question often revolves around whether the terms cause a significant imbalance in the parties' rights and obligations, cf. Article 3 Unfair Terms Directive, sec. 307(1) German Civil Code. Here, both under EU and German law, fundamental rights come into play. Even when fundamental rights are not directly applicable to the contractual relationship between private individuals, they must still be considered due to their indirect horizontal effects. This balancing of interests has been particularly relevant in cases involving hate speech and content moderation. For instance, in a recent ruling, the German Federal Supreme Court acknowledged that service providers have the authority to set stricter terms of use than those prescribed by law.[12] However, the Court emphasized that any conflicting fundamental rights must be carefully balanced through the principle of practical concordance.

Learning Goals

Since 2022, **Article 14 DSA** has introduced a further provision for the monitoring of terms and conditions by providers of intermediary services. In line with the Platform Regulation, Article 14(1) DSA does not impose restrictions on the content of permissible clauses within the terms and conditions. However, Article 14(4) DSA goes a step further, requiring that service providers apply and enforce the restrictions outlined in their terms and conditions in a manner that is 'diligent, objective and proportionate.' This provision also emphasizes that service providers must take into account the rights and legitimate interests of all parties involved, as well as the fundamental rights of users. The application of these requirements has sparked debate as to whether they establish a content review mechanism for terms and conditions. Different interpretations have emerged regarding the extent to which these obligations compel a direct review of the substance of the clauses, and how they may impact the ability of platforms to enforce rules in a fair and transparent manner.[13]

The Platform Regulation seeks to address practices that stem from the superior negotiating power of service providers, as outlined in Articles 5 et seq. Platform Regulation.[14] The legislator recognizes the potential for abuse in these practices, which can disproportionately disadvantage business users. This concern is reinforced by the frameworks of both competition law and the DMA, which impose

---

12 German Federal Supreme Court 29 September 2021 – III ZR 179/20, III ZR 192/20, GRUR 2021, 1433, 1439 – *Hassrede*.

13 This view is supported by Raue (2025) DSA Article 14 mn. 74 et seqq.; Legner (2024b), pp. 99, 105; Wischmeyer and Meißner (2023), pp. 2673, 2674. A critical view is taken by Berberich (2025) sec. 5 mn. 35.

14 Kumkar (2022), pp. 530, 537.

limits on certain practices that contribute to this imbalance. Among these practices are the design of rankings and the use of price parity clauses. In competition law, these practices are often addressed under Article 102 TFEU.[15] Relevant provisions in the DMA that tackle these issues include Article 5(3) DMA and Article 6(5) DMA.[16]

Additionally, the Platform Regulation aims to mitigate this power imbalance through the introduction of mandatory dispute resolution mechanisms, set out in Articles 11–13 Platform Regulation. These provisions are designed to offer a framework for resolving conflicts and ensuring a fairer relationship between platform operators and business users.[17]

The transparency introduced by the Platform Regulation aims to empower business users by enabling them to more reliably assess their competitive position and business opportunities on digital platforms. However, the regulatory approach of the Platform Regulation faces criticism for a key limitation: while it provides valuable information about the potentially disadvantageous position of business users, it does not directly enhance their negotiating power. Merely knowing that their position on a platform may be suboptimal does not necessarily enable business users to leverage better terms or switch to more favourable platforms. This raises doubts about whether the mere disclosure of contractual imbalances will result in meaningful changes, such as switching to other platforms or reorganizing sales channels. In many cases, business users might still find themselves locked into disadvantageous agreements due to network effects, high switching costs, or lack of alternative platforms.

The DMA, passed about two years after the Platform Regulation, is therefore rightly regarded as a 'follow-up'[18] or an 'extension'[19] of the earlier regulation. While the Platform Regulation lays the groundwork for transparency, the DMA builds on this foundation by introducing stricter obligations for gatekeepers.[20] The DMA aims to regulate platform conduct more comprehensively, offering more robust protections for business users by setting out specific do's and don'ts for large platform operators.[21]

While the Platform Regulation and DMA diverge in their specific objectives, there is no inherent conflict between their aims. The pursuit of fairness and transparency in favour of business users ultimately supports the promotion of competition in digital markets. This aligns with the contestability goal of the DMA, which seeks to ensure that markets remain open and competitive. Recital 8 Platform Regulation underscores that the conduct obligations outlined within the Regulation

15 For the evaluation of price party clauses under Article 101 TFEU, see ► 2.2.2.3.8; for further details on self-preferencing within the abuse framework of Article 102 TFEU, see ► 2.3.2.1.4.
16 For further details on these provisions, see ► 3.3.1.2 and 3.3.2.4.
17 Busch (2020), pp. 133, 134.
18 Bostoen (2023), p. 219.
19 Arncken (2025) sec. 16 mn. 5.
20 Bania (2023), p. 116.
21 On potential incoherences between the DMA and the Platform Regulation, see Bania (2023), pp. 116, 117.

are designed to 'recognise and safeguard the important innovation potential of the wider online platform economy and allow for healthy competition.' This reflects a broad recognition that a transparent and fair environment can lead to greater market dynamics, benefiting both business users and consumers.

However, when it comes to the concept of fairness, the DMA and the Platform Regulation have different interpretations. The DMA uses fairness to strike a balance between the rights and obligations of business users and gatekeepers (cf. Article 12(5)(b) DMA).[22] The fairness goal in the DMA is closely tied to achieving a more equitable market outcome, for example, ensuring that business users can compete on a level playing field. In contrast, the Platform Regulation defines fairness more narrowly, primarily focusing on providing transparent information to business users regarding their competitive position on a platform. This approach targets reducing information asymmetries between business users and platform operators, with the aim of promoting transparency and informed decision-making. Therefore, while the DMA focuses on market outcomes, the Platform Regulation seeks to enhance fairness by addressing information imbalances between platforms and business users.[23]

4.1.3.3 Consumer Protection

The obligations set forth in the Platform Regulation primarily address the bilateral relationship between service providers and business users. However, the Regulation also has an indirect protective effect for consumers. Platforms, particularly those that establish multi-sided markets, serve various user groups, not just business users.[24] In these markets, business users typically represent only one side of the platform. Other user groups, such as consumers, constitute additional sides of the market. On platforms like online marketplaces, social networks, or online search engines, consumers regularly interact with the platform. They use it to explore business offers and may even enter into direct transactions with business users. In this context, the Platform Regulation assumes a **three-party relationship**, where service providers connect business users and consumers, each with distinct roles and interests. While the Regulation focuses on ensuring fairness and transparency for business users, the consumer protection element is inherently woven into the design of the platform's service offering and the interactions between the platform, business users, and consumers (◘ Figs. 4.1 and 4.2).

Article 2 no. 4 Platform Regulation defines a consumer as 'any natural person who is acting for purposes which are outside this person's trade, business, craft or profession.'

This definition aligns with the prevailing understanding of the term in European private law (cf. eg. Article 2 no. 6 Digital Content Directive,[25] Article 2 no. 2 Sale of

---

22 For the fairness objective of the DMA, see ► 3.1.3.3.

23 Bueren and Weck (2022) DMA Article 5 mn. 30.

24 On the functioning of digital platforms, see ► 1.1.1.

25 Directive 2019/770/EU of the European Parliament and of the Council of 20 May 2019 on certain aspects of contracts for the supply of digital content and digital services, OJ [2019] L 136/1.

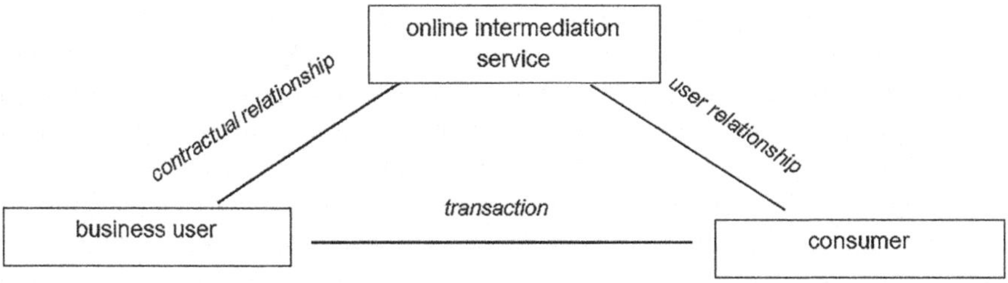

Fig. 4.1 The three-party relationship of online intermediation services

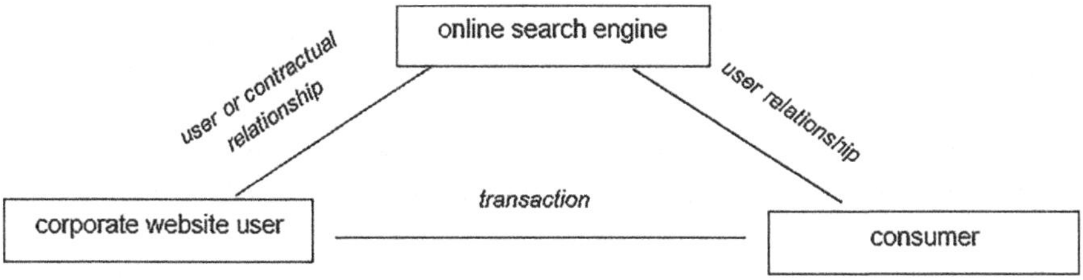

Fig. 4.2 The three-party relationship of online search engines

Goods Directive,[26] Article 2 no. 1 Consumer Rights Directive[27]). In the context of competition law, this definition underscores a critical distinction: the consumer protection objectives pursued by the Platform Regulation are conceptually different from the consumer welfare typically addressed by European antitrust law. While competition law primarily focuses on maintaining competitive market conditions to benefit consumers indirectly, the Platform Regulation directly aims to safeguard consumer interests through specific protections in the digital platform economy.

The consumer protection pursued by the Platform Regulation differs fundamentally from the competition law objective of maximizing consumer welfare.

Recital 3 Platform Regulation clarifies how fairness and transparency towards business users can indirectly foster consumer protection. A transparent online environment enhances **consumer confidence in the digital economy**, ensuring that consumers are better informed when making choices. This aligns with the broader regulatory goals of various consumer protection directives (such as the Consumer Rights Directive, Sale of Goods Directive, and Digital Services Directive) all of which aim to empower consumers and strengthen their freedom of choice in the marketplace. In this context, the Platform Regulation emphasizes the need for consumers to be sufficiently informed about available offers, reflecting the model of the

26 Directive (EU) 2019/771 of the European Parliament and of the Council of 20 May 2019 on certain aspects concerning contracts for the sale of goods, OJ [2019] L136/28.

27 Directive 2011/83/EU of the European Parliament and of the Council of 25 October 2011 on consumer rights, OJ [2011] L 304/64.

informed consumer. This ensures that consumers can make well-informed decisions and are not subject to manipulation or limited choices.[28] Recital 4 DMA further highlights this connection, particularly for the business model of online search engines. It states: 'The ranking of websites by providers of online search engines, including of those websites through which corporate website users offer their goods and services to consumers, has an important impact on consumer choice and the commercial success of those corporate website users.' This reflects how the ranking systems used by search engines shape the information consumers see, influencing their decisions and ultimately their purchasing behaviour.

Learning Goals

The Platform Regulation shares important parallels with other digital regulation acts in terms of consumer protection. Notably, both the DSA and the Omnibus Directive of 2019[29] also aim to safeguard consumer interests in the digital economy. The Omnibus Directive, in particular, introduced new information obligations for platforms regarding ranking parameters, price personalization, and the legal distribution of responsibilities between business users and platform operators.[30] These provisions ensure that consumers are better informed about the dynamics that influence their online choices, particularly concerning how platforms organize and present content. The Platform Regulation can ultimately be seen as a hybrid framework that combines elements of contract law, unfair competition law, and competition law.[31]

4.1.4 Scope of Application

4.1.4.1 Geographical Scope

The geographical scope of the Platform Regulation is determined by the modified marketplace principle outlined in Article 1(2).[32] The Regulation applies regardless of the location of the service providers. The key factor for its applicability is whether the business users receiving the intermediary services are located in the EU—either through their place of residence or establishment. However, the concept of establishment should not be interpreted too broadly. The requirements for business users should be applied as strictly as the residence requirements.[33]

28 Legner (2024a), pp. 649, 654.

29 Directive (EU) 2019/2161 of the European Parliament and of the Council of 27 November 2019 on better enforcement and modernisation of Union consumer protection rules, OJ [2019] L 328/7. The Omnibus Directive contains amendments to the UCP Directive and the Consumer Rights Directive.

30 For further details on the Omnibus Directive, see ► 1.3.4.

31 Arncken (2025) sec. 16 mn. 3; Alexander (2020), pp. 945, 946.

32 Arncken (2025) sec. 16 mn. 46.

33 Arncken (2025) sec. 16 mn. 50.

Additionally, the consumers to whom the business users offer their services must also be located within the EU. This ensures that the Platform Regulation's protections are applied not only to business users within the EU but also to consumers interacting with these businesses.

4.1.4.2 Temporal Scope

The Platform Regulation came into force on 31 July 2019 and has been applicable since 12 July 2020. As a regulation, it applies directly in all Member States without the need for national transposition. The German provisions related to public enforcement under the German Implementing Act on Digital Services came into effect on 14 May 2024.

4.2 Addressees

4.2.1 Online Intermediation Services

The Platform Regulation applies to providers of online intermediary services. According to **Article 2(2) Platform Regulation**, a service qualifies as an online intermediary service if it meets the following three criteria:

- It is an information society service as defined in Article 1(1)(b) TRIS Directive.[34]
- It enables business users to offer goods or services to consumers.
- The provision of the service to business users is based on a contractual relationship between the service provider and the business users.

▶ Examples

Online marketplaces (e.g. *Amazon, eBay*), app stores (e.g. *Google Play*), social networks (e.g. *Facebook, Instagram*), travel portals (e.g. ▶ Booking.com) ◀

Information society services, as defined in Article 1(1)(b) TRIS Directive, are services that meet the following criteria: they are generally provided for remuneration, at a distance, by electronic means, and at the individual request of a recipient. The second condition for qualifying as an online intermediary service pertains to the intermediary activity. It is essential that the service provider acts as an intermediary between two market sides, in this case, between business users and consumers. This means that the platform facilitates the brokering of transactions, even if a transaction does not ultimately occur. The location of the transaction,

34 Directive (EU) 2015/1535 of the European Parliament and of the Council of 9 September 2015 laying down a procedure for the provision of information in the field of technical regulations and of rules on information society services, OJ [2015] L 241/1.

should it occur, is irrelevant to the definition.[35] Notably, business-to-business platforms are excluded from the scope of the Platform Regulation. Messenger services are also not covered by the Regulation. While transactions may be concluded through these services, they do not enable the intermediary role required by the Regulation.[36]

The third requirement pertains to the internal relationship between the service provider and business users. Specifically, a contractual relationship is necessary for the service provider to offer the intermediary service. This requirement distinguishes it from the business model of online search engines, which do not establish a contractual relationship with the operators of the websites they index (as discussed below). This contractual relationship is pivotal as it ties the service provider to specific transparency obligations regarding general terms and conditions (Articles 3 et seq. Platform Regulation).

Unlike general competition law or the DMA, which often require a dominant or powerful market position to trigger specific obligations, the Platform Regulation applies to all service providers, regardless of their market position.

4.2.2 Online Search Engines

Certain obligations set out in the Platform Regulation also apply to online search engines. According to **Article 2(5) Platform Regulation**, an online search engine is defined as a digital service that allows users to input queries in order to perform searches on any topic across all websites, returning results that help users access information related to their search.

▶ Examples

Google, *Bing* and *Firefox* ◀

The term 'search engine' must be interpreted broadly: it refers to services that index and search across the open web. This distinguishes them from more limited search functions that operate only within specific websites or content sources.[37] While most obligations under the Platform Regulation apply specifically to online intermediary services, search engines are nonetheless subject to certain transparency requirements. Notably, these include obligations related to the transparency of ranking systems (Article 5(2) Platform Regulation) and the prohibition of self-preferencing practices (Article 7(2) Platform Regulation).

35 Alexander (2020), pp. 945, 947.
36 Ernst (2020), p. 735.
37 Arncken (2025) sec. 16 mn. 38.

4.3 Obligations

4.3.1 Transparency Obligations: Article 3 Platform Regulation

Article 3(1) Platform Regulation establishes **transparency obligations** regarding the general terms and conditions that form part of the contractual relationship between providers of online intermediary services and their business users. These obligations include:
- the use of clear and comprehensible language in the general terms and conditions;
- ensuring that the general terms and conditions are easily accessible prior to the conclusion of the contract;
- providing information on the reasons upon which the service provider may decide to suspend or terminate the provision of its services.

Article 3(2) Platform Regulation addresses the procedure for amending the general terms and conditions. Service providers are permitted to make changes to their terms only after the expiration of a 'reasonable and proportionate' notice period. The Regulation sets out detailed requirements for this process, including conditions under which the notice period may be waived (cf. Article 3(4) Platform Regulation) and a minimum notice period of 15 days (cf. Article 3(2) Platform Regulation).

4.3.2 Restriction, Suspension, and Termination: Article 4 Platform Regulation

Article 4 of the Platform Regulation addresses situations in which a provider of an online intermediary service intends to restrict, suspend, or terminate the provision of its service to a specific business user. According to Article 4(1), (2) Platform Regulation, the service provider is required to justify such a decision. This justification must be communicated to the affected business user no later than at the time the measure is implemented.

Additionally, the business user concerned must have access to an internal complaints handling system to challenge the decision. Article 4 Platform Regulation functions as a lex specialis to Article 17 DSA, which generally obliges service providers to provide reasons for imposing restrictions on any user (not only business users).[38]

4.3.3 Ranking: Article 5 Platform Regulation

Article 5 Platform Regulation imposes transparency obligations on both providers of online intermediary services and online search engines with regard to the rank-

38 Raue (2025) DSA Article 17 mn. 5.

ing of search results or offers displayed on their platforms.[39] Both types of service providers must clearly set out the main parameters used to determine ranking, including the main parameters determining ranking and the reasons for the relative importance of those main parameters.

4 Article 5(2) Platform Regulation specifically addresses online search engines, recognizing that they often operate without a contractual relationship with the websites they index. As a result, the ranking parameters cannot be disclosed through general terms and conditions. Instead, search engine operators are required to provide a publicly accessible and easily understandable explanation of their ranking criteria.

► Example

A service provider might rank listed offers based on a combination of factors such as the date the offer was placed, the product characteristics, and consumer reviews submitted on the platform. In this case, the provider must explain not only which factors are used but also why they are weighted in a particular way. ◄

The position of offers or websites in platform rankings significantly influences how they are perceived by consumers.[40] Insights from behavioural economics demonstrate that consumers pay far more attention to results displayed on the first page of an online search engine than to those appearing on subsequent pages. The same principle applies to the order of listings on online marketplaces. In light of this, Article 5 Platform Regulation requires service providers to inform users about the parameters used to determine ranking. This transparency allows business users to better understand and evaluate their competitive prospects for reaching consumers through the platform.

Article 5 Platform Regulation is limited to transparency obligations. It does not impose any requirements regarding the substance or fairness of the ranking itself. Providers of online intermediary services and online search engines retain full discretion to determine the ranking parameters they apply. In particular, hybrid service providers remain free to give preferential treatment to their own offers.[41] Furthermore, pursuant to Article 5(3) Platform Regulation, ranking may lawfully take into account factors such as payments made by users or the use of additional services offered by the platform provider.

► Example

If business users pay an additional commission to the operator of an online marketplace, their offers may be displayed in a more prominent position within the ranking. ◄

---

39 Nolteernsting (2025), pp. 11 et seqq.

40 Schneider and Kremer (2020), pp. 1128, 1133.

41 For details on Article 7 Platform Regulation, see ► 4.3.4.

Learning Goals

The Union legislator has introduced similar information obligations in consumer protection law. Article 7a(4)(a) UCP Directive[42] and Article 6a(1)(a) Consumer Rights Directive require that consumers be informed if payments or other commercial considerations affect the ranking of search results on online marketplaces.

4.3.4 Self-Preferencing: Article 7 Platform Regulation

The transparency obligations set out in Article 7 Platform Regulation specifically target hybrid platforms, that is, providers of online intermediation services or online search engines that not only facilitate transactions or searches, but also offer their own products or services in direct competition with business users on the same platform. Such dual roles create a heightened risk of self-preferencing, where the platform operator may give preferential treatment to its own offerings, for example, by ranking them more prominently than those of competing business users. A common case is online marketplaces where the platform operator itself sells products to consumers. Similarly, search engines operated by companies offering their own services may display those services more favourably in the results. While the Platform Regulation does not prohibit self-preferencing, Article 7 Platform Regulation imposes transparency requirements. Service providers must clearly **disclose** any differentiated treatment of their own goods, services, or websites in comparison to those of business users. This enables business users to better understand potential biases in how their offers are ranked and presented, and allows for more informed commercial decision-making.

Learning Goals

Article 6(5) DMA[43] and **sec. 19a(2) 1st sentence no. 1(a) ARC**[44] also address self-preferential practices. There are two differences to Article 7 Platform Regulation: Firstly, competittion law and the Digital Markets Act prohibit self-preferencing under specific conditions. Secondly, the prohibitions only address selected platform operators, namely gatekeepers (Article 6(5) DMA) resp. undertakings with paramount cross-market significance for competition (sec. 19a(2) sentence 1 no. 1(a) ARC). Additionally, in the *Google Shopping* case,[45] the ECJ prohibited the self-preferential conduct of a dominant search engine operator under **Article 102 TFEU.**[46]

42 Directive 2005/29/EC of the European Parliament and of the Council concerning unfair business-to-consumer commercial practices, OJ [2005] 149/22.
43 For further details on this provision, see ► 3.3.2.4.
44 For further details on this provision, see ► 5.3.2.3.
45 ECJ 10 September 2024 – C-48/22 P, ECLI:EU:C:2024:726 – *Google Shopping*.
46 For further information on this case, see ► 2.3.2.1.4.

4.3.5 Data Access: Article 9 Platform Regulation

Through the provision of intermediary services, platform providers regularly gain access to data belonging to both business users and consumers. Under Article 9(1), (2) Platform Regulation, service providers are required to inform business users whether, and to what extent, they have access to such data. Access to this data is highly significant for the economic success of the platform operator.[47] At the same time, it is crucial that the competitive position of business users is not adversely affected. For example, access to data on consumer purchasing behaviour can provide business users with important competitive advantages, as highlighted in recital 33 Platform Regulation. Accordingly, service providers must clearly communicate the options available to business users regarding access to this data. Recital 35 Platform Regulation further emphasizes that such transparency measures 'contribute to increased data sharing and enhance, as a key source of innovation and growth, the aims to create a common European data space.' Article 9 Platform Regulation focuses solely on transparency obligations regarding data access. It does not regulate the conditions under which service providers may collect or process data. These matters are governed by **data protection law**. If a service provider grants access to personal data, the requirements of the GDPR must be observed.[48] In the absence of other legal bases, such access generally requires the data subject's explicit consent.

Importantly, the Platform Regulation does not grant business users a legal right to access platform-collected data. However, under German competition law, sec. 20(1a) 2nd sentence ARC provides a legal basis for a potential claim to data access in cases of exclusionary abuse by relatively powerful platform operators.[49]

Additional obligations exist under the DMA. Article 5(9), (10) DMA imposes specific data access rights for advertisers and publishers, enhancing transparency and fairness in digital advertising markets. In contrast to the Platform Regulation, the DMA also restricts how gatekeepers may use collected data. Article 5(2) DMA[50] prohibits the combination of personal data across services without proper user consent. Article 6(2) DMA[51] prohibits hybrid gatekeepers from using data obtained from business users to compete against them on the platform. These rules aim to strengthen the competitive position of business users and enhance contestability.

4.3.6 Differentiated Treatment: Article 10 Platform Regulation

If a service provider includes **price parity clauses** in its contractual arrangements with business users, it is required under Article 10 Platform Regulation to disclose the reasons for doing so. This explanation must be made easily and publicly acces-

47 Wiedemann (2024) ch. 1.3 mn. 174. On the significance of data for competition in digital markets, see ► 1.1.2.

48 On the relationship between the Platform Regulation and the GDPR, see Schneider and Kremer (2020), pp. 1128, 1135.

49 For further information on sec. 20(1a) 2nd sentence ARC, see ► 5.3.3.2.

50 For further details on Article 5(2) DMA, see ► 3.3.1.1.

51 For further details on Article 6(2) DMA, see ► 3.3.2.1.

sible. Price parity clauses restrict the pricing autonomy of business users. They typically oblige the business user not to offer better prices or conditions either on their own website (narrow price parity clauses) or on other platforms (broad price parity clauses) than those offered via the service provider's platform. Article 10 Platform Regulation ensures that such restrictions are made transparent to business users so they can take them into account when deciding whether to enter into a contractual relationship with the platform provider.

However, the Platform Regulation's transparency obligations exist alongside more substantive legal limitations established under competition law and the DMA. Both narrow and broad price parity clauses may infringe **Article 101 TFEU**.[52] In particular, broad price parity clauses are not eligible for exemption under **Article 5(1)(d) VBER**, whereas narrow price parity clauses may benefit from the exemption under Article 2(1) VBER. For designated gatekeepers under the DMA, **Article 5(3) DMA** imposes a blanket ban on the use of any form of price parity clause, regardless of whether it is narrow or broad.[53] Notably, gatekeepers are not permitted to justify such clauses on the basis of efficiency gains. Article 10(2) Platform Regulation clarifies that the information obligation it imposes does not affect the applicability of stricter substantive rules under competition law or the DMA. Therefore, the transparency requirements of Article 10 Platform Regulation only have practical relevance in those instances where the use of a price parity clause is not already prohibited under those regimes.

4.3.7 Complaint-Handling and Mediation: Articles 11–13 Platform Regulation

Articles 11–13 Platform Regulation are designed to strengthen dispute resolution in favour of business users. To this end, providers of online intermediation services are required to establish an internal complaints-handling system that allows business users to submit complaints relating to the service. If internal resolution proves unsuccessful, the dispute must be referred to mediation, provided both parties agree. These mechanisms aim to enhance the legal protection available to business users and contribute to mitigate the imbalance in negotiating power between platform operators and business users.

4.4 Enforcement

4.4.1 Public Enforcement

The Platform Regulation delegates the organisation and implementation of enforcement mechanisms to the Member States. Recital 46 Platform Regulation

52 For the evaluation of price parity clauses under Article 101 TFEU, see ► 2.2.2.3.8.
53 For further details on Article 5(3) DMA, see ► 3.3.1.2.

explicitly clarifies that Member States are **not obliged 'to provide for ex officio enforcement** or to impose fines'.

Until early 2024, Germany enforced the Platform Regulation exclusively through private claims. However, with the entry into force of the German Implementing Act on Digital Services in May 2024, the German legislator introduced public enforcement, including the possibility of imposing fines and corrective measures for violations of the Platform Regulation. Under **sec. 22(1) German Implementing Act on Digital Services**, the **German Federal Network Agency** (*Bundesnetzagentur, BNetzA*) is designated as the competent supervisory authority. In particular, Pursuant to sec. 30 German Implementing Act on Digital Services in conjunction with sec. 202 German Telecommunications Act (*Telekommunikationsgesetz, TKG*), the Federal Network Agency is empowered to request remedial actions and ensure compliance.[54] However, unlike in competition law, the Federal Network Agency does not have the authority to make voluntary commitments legally binding.[55] By contrast, Article 25 DMA allows the Commission to make commitments binding once a systematic infringement has been established.[56] In the Netherlands, it is the Authority for Consumers and Markets (*Autoriteit Consument & Markt, ACM*) that may impose fines for violations of the Platform Regulation.[57] In France, the order no. 2021-1734 (Arrêté du 22 décembre 2021) allows the imposition of fines. Other Member States, however, still rely solely on private enforcement.

4.4.2 Especially: Fines

In Germany, the culpable violation of several key obligations under the Platform Regulation may result in administrative fines pursuant to sec. 33(3) German Implementing Act on Digital Services. The fine regime covers breaches of provisions in Articles 3, 4, 5, 7, 11, and 12 Platform Regulation. Specifically, the following obligations are sanctionable:

- Obligation of providers of online intermediation services to ensure that the identity of the business user providing the goods or services on the online intermediation services is clearly visible, cf. Article 3(5) Platform Regulation (sec. 33(3) no. 1 German Implementing Act on Digital Services)
- Obligation to justify the restriction, suspension, or termination of service to a business user, cf. Article 4(1), (2), (5) Platform Regulation (sec. 33(3) no. 2 German Implementing Act on Digital Services)
- Obligation to provide an internal complaints-handling procedure in cases of service restriction, suspension, or termination, cf. Article 4(3) 1st sentence Plat-

54 Wischmeyer and Meißner (2024) DDG sec. 30 mn. 22.

55 Wischmeyer and Meißner (2024) DDG sec. 30 mn. 23.

56 For further details on the public enforcement of the DMA, see ► 3.4.1.

57 < https://www.acm.nl/en/publications/acm-now-authorized-enforce-european-platform-business-regulation> (accessed 4 September 2025).

form Regulation (sec. 33(3) no. 3 German Implementing Act on Digital Services)

- Obligation of online search engine providers to offer the possibility for the corporate website user to inspect the contents of a third party notification that led to changes in ranking, cf. Article 5(4) Platform Regulation (sec. 33(3) no. 3 German Implementing Act on Digital Services)
- Obligation to reinstate the business user without delay following a revocation of the restrictive measure, cf. Article 4(3) 2nd sentence Platform Regulation (sec. 33(3) no. 4 German Implementing Act on Digital Services)
- Obligation to provide a statement of reasons on a durable medium upon termination of service, unless a notice period applies, cf. Article 4(4)(2) Platform Regulation (sec. 33(3) no. 5 German Implementing Act on Digital Services)
- Obligation of online search engines to present the main ranking parameters, their weighting, and information on effects of remuneration on rankings, keep this information up to date, and reflect changes accordingly, cf. Article 5(2),(3),(5) Platform Regulation (sec. 33(3) no. 6, 7 German Implementing Act on Digital Services)
- Obligation of online search engine providers to explain any differentiated treatment of their own services, cf. Article 7(2), (3) Platform Regulation (sec. 33(3) no. 8 German Implementing Act on Digital Services)
- Obligation of online intermediation service providers to establish an internal complaints management system and inform business users accordingly, cf. Article 11(1), (2), (4) Platform Regulation (sec. 33(3) nos. 9–14 German Implementing Act on Digital Services)
- Obligation to provide information on the functioning and effectiveness of mediation either before or during the process, cf. Article 12(6) Platform Regulation (sec. 33(3) no. 15 German Implementing Act on Digital Services)

According to sec. 33(6) German Implementing Act on Digital Services the maximum fine for violations of the obligations listed in sec. 33(3) nos. 1, 3, 4, 9, 10, and 11 German Implementing Act on Digital Services is up to EUR 300,000. For breaches of the remaining provisions, specifically sec. 33(3) nos. 2, 5–8, 12–14, and 15 German Implementing Act on Digital Services, the maximum fine is up to EUR 100,000.

! The fine provisions in sec. 33(3) German Implementing Act on Digital Services are highly differentiated. Not all violations of transparency obligations under the Platform Regulation are subject to administrative fines for culpable breaches. In particular, providers of online intermediation services are not subject to fines for non-compliance with transparency obligations related to ranking parameters (Article 5(1) Platform Regulation), self-preferential practices (Article 7(1) Platform Regulation), and price parity clauses (Article 10 Platform Regulation). By contrast, providers of online search engines can be fined under sec. 33(3) nos. 6, 7, 8 German Implementing Act on Digital Services if they fail to meet their transparency obligations concerning the main parameters used for ranking and their relative weighting, the updating of this information, and the disclosure of any differentiated treatment (e.g. self-preferencing practices).

4.4.3 Private Enforcement

4.4.3.1 Consequence of Invalidity

4

Provisions that fail to meet the transparency requirements set out in Article 3(1) Platform Regulation are deemed **void ex tunc** pursuant to Article 3(3). According to recital 20 Platform Regulation, the remaining contractual provisions **remain valid**, provided they are severable from the non-compliant clauses. This principle aligns with sec. 306(1) German Civil Code. Any resulting contractual gap must be addressed through supplementary interpretation of the agreement.[58]

4.4.3.2 Individual Legal Action

The Platform Regulation leaves the determination of further legal consequences to the Member States.[59] Under Article 15(1) Platform Regulation, Member States are required to ensure the 'adequate and effective enforcement' of its provisions. However, the Regulation does not establish individual rights of action. Article 14(9) Platform Regulation merely clarifies that claims arising under legal provisions outside the scope of the Platform Regulation remain unaffected.

Under German law, in the event of a breach of transparency obligations, **contractual claims for damages** under **secs. 280(1), 241(2) German Civil Code** must first be examined.[60] Such a claim requires that the breach of a secondary contractual obligation, specifically, the failure to comply with a duty arising under the Platform Regulation, also results in actual damage. With regard to the independent enforceability of individual obligations, it is necessary to distinguish whether these constitute autonomous ancillary duties within the contractual relationship.[61]

In addition, breaches of the Platform Regulation may give rise to claims under unfair competition law. The obligations imposed by the Regulation qualify as rules of market conduct;[62] hence, their violation constitutes an infringement under sec. 3a German Act Against Unfair Competition.[63] This triggers the legal consequences provided for in unfair competition law. Primarily, this includes a right to injunctive relief under **sec. 8(1) German Act Against Unfair Competition**, which may be asserted by any competitor pursuant to sec. 8(3) No. 1 German Act Against Unfair Competition. Furthermore, a claim for damages by competitors is available under sec. 9(1) German Act Against Unfair Competition.

Pursuant to sec. 2(1) no. 4 German Act Against Unfair Competition, the term 'competitor' requires the existence of a specific competitive relationship. Such a relationship will typically be found between a commercial user and an online intermediary service provider, or between a business operating a website and an online

58 Alexander (2024) Platform regulation Article 3 mn. 46.
59 Schneider and Kremer (2020), pp. 1128, 1132.
60 Köhler (2025) Platform regulation Article 14 mn. 49 et seq.
61 Tribess (2025) sec. 18 mn. 94.
62 Dreher and Kulka (2023) mn. 526.
63 Höppner and Wick (2022) Platform regulation Article 14 mn. 3.

search engine provider.[64] For a competitive relationship to exist, it is sufficient that the commercial conduct of one undertaking is specifically capable of adversely affecting the position of another with respect to its supply or demand activities.[65] In this context, the term competitor is to be interpreted more broadly than in competition law and does not depend on a strict market definition. The obligations imposed by the Platform Regulation underscore the extent to which platform operators can influence the supply-side activities of business users, whether through ranking algorithms, self-preferencing practices, or other forms of preferential treatment. As such, the potential for a competitive relationship in the sense of sec. 2(1) no. 4 German Act Against Unfair Competition is regularly fulfilled.

4.4.3.3 Collective Action

In addition to individual legal remedies, **Article 14 Platform Regulation** requires Member States to ensure the availability of collective redress mechanisms. To implement this obligation, the German legislator introduced sec. 8a Act Against Unfair Competition. Under this provision, **associations, organizations, and public bodies** that meet the criteria set out in Article 14(3), (4) Platform Regulation are entitled to pursue claims for injunctive relief and removal in accordance with sec. 8(1) and sec. 3a German Act Against Unfair Competition. The introduction of representative actions at the EU level is intended to address the limitations of individual legal actions. Business users, often dependent on platform intermediation services, may be reluctant to initiate proceedings on their own due to concerns over commercial repercussions or legal costs.[66]

Germany has not yet designated any qualified entities authorized to bring collective actions under the Platform Regulation. In contrast, Austria has already designated several bodies, including the Federal Competition Authority (*Bundeswettbewerbsbehörde, BWB*) and the Austrian Federal Economic Chamber (*Wirtschaftskammer Österreich, WKÖ*).[67] Since May 2024, the German Federal Network Agency has been granted authority under sec. 22(2) German Implementing Act on Digital Services to designate eligible associations, organizations, and public bodies for this purpose.

4.5 Proceedings

4.5.1 Administrative Proceedings

In Germany, under sec. 22(1) German Implementing Act on Digital Services, the German Federal Network Agency is the competent authority and may initiate

64 Tribess (2025) sec. 18 mn. 17 et seq.
65 Keller (2021) UWG sec. 2 mn. 133.
66 Höppner and Wick (2022) Platform regulation Article 14 mn. 1.
67 https://www.bwb.gv.at/weitere-kompetenzen/p2b-plattform-verordnung (accessed 4 September 2025).

administrative proceedings ex officio.[68] To investigate potential violations of the Platform Regulation, sec. 30 German Implementing Act on Digital Services confers a range of investigative powers upon the Agency. Specifically, the Federal Network Agency may request information pursuant to sec. 30 German Implementing Act on Digital Services in conjunction with sec. 203(1) 1st sentence,(2) 1st sentence,(6) 1st, 3rd–6th sentence German Telecommunications Act. Additionally, it is authorized to gather evidence by hearing witnesses, conducting inspections, and commissioning expert reports, in accordance with sec. 30 German Implementing Act on Digital Services in conjunction with sec. 205 German Telecommunications Act.

The Agency is also empowered to enter and search business premises under sec. 30 German Telecommunications Act in conjunction with sec. 204(1) no. 3, (2), (3) German Telecommunications Act. Furthermore, it may seize objects pursuant to sec. 30 German Telecommunications Act in conjunction with sec. 206 German Telecommunications Act. The formal legality of administrative acts issued by the Germany Federal Network Agency is governed by sec. 32(3) German Implementing Act on Digital Services, which requires the inclusion of a statement of reasons and information on available legal remedies. In the event of an objection or an action for annulment, sec. 31(2) 1st sentence German Implementing Act on Digital Services provides that such legal challenges do not have suspensive effect.

4.5.2 Fine Proceedings

In Germany, the authority responsible for imposing fines under the Platform Regulation is the Federal Network Agency, as stipulated in **sec. 33(8) no. 2 German Implementing Act on Digital Services**. As a general rule, the procedural framework is governed by the provisions of the German Code of Administrative Offences (*Ordnungswidrigkeitengesetz, OWiG*) and the German Criminal Code (*Strafgesetzbuch, StGB*).[69] Accordingly, proceedings are typically initiated based on the principle of discretion. Pursuant to sec. 67 German Administrative Offences Act, the individual concerned has the right to contest the fine by filing an objection (*Einspruch*).

4.5.3 Civil Proceedings

There are no special procedural rules governing civil actions arising from breaches of obligations under the Platform Regulation. In Germany, as a rule, the general provisions of the German Code of Civil Procedure (*Zivilprozessordnung, ZPO*) apply. Subject-matter jurisdiction is primarily determined by the amount in dispute, pursuant to secs. 23, 71 German Judicial System Act (*Gerichtsverfassungsgesetz,*

68 Wischmeyer and Meißner (2024) DDG sec. 30 mn. 13.
69 Papathanasiou (2024) DDG sec. 33 mn. 65.

GVG). In addition to the general place of jurisdiction under secs. 12, 17 German Code of Civil Procedure, typically the registered office of the defendant legal entity, special jurisdiction may apply under sec. 32 German Code of Civil Procedure in cases involving tortious claims.

Where claims are brought under unfair competition law, particularly under sec. 8(1) German Act Against Unfair Competition, sec.14 German Act Against Unfair Competition is relevant. Under sec. 14(1) German Act Against Unfair Competition, exclusive subject matter jurisdiction lies with the regional courts. Furthermore, sec. 14(2) Act Against Unfair Competition provides for special venues, including a so-called 'flying venue' (*fliegender Gerichtsstand*), allowing plaintiffs to bring actions in the district where the infringement occurred.

The provisions on dispute resolution in Articles 11 et seq. Platform Regulation do not impose any mandatory preconditions for admissibility. In particular, a business user is not required to exhaust mediation procedures before initiating legal action.[70]

The available legal remedies include an appeal (*Berufung*) under secs. 511 et seq. German Code of Civil Procedure and, where applicable, an appeal on points of law (*Revision*) under secs. 542 et seq. German Code of Civil Procedure.

4.6 Review Questions

1. What are the objectives of the Platform Regulation?

The objective of the Platform Regulation is to promote fairness and transparency for business users who rely on online intermediation services and online search engines. To achieve this, the Regulation imposes transparency obligations on providers of such services. These include requirements related to ranking criteria, terms and conditions, and access to data, all intended to enable business users to better evaluate and improve their competitive position on the platform. In addition to supporting fair business practices, the Regulation also serves an indirect consumer protection function. While it does not directly regulate consumer rights, its scope is limited to intermediary services that facilitate commercial transactions between business users and consumers (▶ 4.1.3).

2. What is the relationship between the Platform Regulation, competition law, and the DMA?

The Platform Regulation operates alongside both European competition law and the DMA. It does not replace or override these legal frameworks but complements them by addressing specific fairness and transparency issues in the platform economy. With respect to competition law, the parallel application is explicitly con-

70 Tribess (2024) Platform regulation Article 11 mn. 43.

firmed in Article 1(4), (5) Platform Regulation. These provisions clarify that the Regulation is without prejudice to the application of European or national competition rules. Similarly, the DMA acknowledges its coexistence with the Platform Regulation. Recital 12 DMA expressly states that the DMA does not preclude the application of the Platform Regulation. Each instrument serves distinct but overlapping goals: while the Platform Regulation focuses on transparency and fair contractual practices for business users of online intermediation services, the DMA targets systemic market imbalances caused by gatekeepers and imposes specific obligations on them (▶ 4.1.1, ▶ 4.1.3.1).

3. How is the geographical scope of application of the Platform Regulation determined?

The geographical scope of the Platform Regulation is defined in Article 1(2) and follows a modified marketplace principle. In contrast to traditional jurisdictional approaches, the location or registered office of the online intermediation service provider is not decisive. What matters is whether the business users to whom the intermediary service is provided have their place of residence or establishment within the European Union. Additionally, the consumers to whom these business users offer their goods or services must also be located in the EU. This approach ensures that the Regulation applies to platform-mediated commercial relationships that are economically anchored within the internal market, even if the platform operator itself is established outside the Union (▶ 4.1.4.1).

4. Who are the addressees of the transparency and other obligations under the Platform Regulation?

The obligations set out in the Platform Regulation are primarily directed at providers of online intermediation services. According to Article 2(2) Platform Regulation, this term refers to information society services that facilitate direct transactions between business users and consumers and provide their services to business users on a contractual basis. Typical examples include online marketplaces and app stores. In addition to intermediation services, certain provisions of the Platform Regulation also apply to online search engines. As defined in Article 2(5) Platform Regulation, these are digital services that allow users to perform searches of all websites on the basis of a specific query related to any subject (▶ 4.2).

5. What does Article 5 Platform Regulation stipulate with regard to rankings?

Article 5 Platform Regulation establishes transparency obligations concerning the main parameters that determine ranking and, where applicable, their relative importance. These obligations apply to both providers of online intermediation services and online search engines. The aim is to ensure that business users and corporate website users are adequately informed about how rankings are determined, allowing them to better understand how their visibility on a platform is shaped and to assess their competitive position (► 4.3.3).

6. Article 7 Platform Regulation establishes transparency obligations with regard to self-preferential practices of hybrid platforms. Which offences under competition law and the DMA complement these obligations?

Self-preferencing practices are addressed both by existing antitrust prohibitions and by the DMA. The ECJ has ruled that self-preferential conduct by a dominant search engine operator violates Article 102 TFEU, which prohibits abuse of a dominant market position. Similarly, sec. 19a(2) 1st sentence no. 1(a) ARC forbids undertakings with paramount cross-market significance for competition from favouring their own offers in terms of presentation. Furthermore, Article 6(5) DMA prohibits designated gatekeepers from preferentially ranking their own services or products above comparable third-party offerings (► 4.3.4).

7. What does Article 10 of the Platform Regulation say about price parity clauses?

Article 10 Platform Regulation imposes transparency obligations concerning price parity clauses but does not prohibit such clauses outright. In practice, these transparency requirements apply primarily to price parity clauses that are not automatically void due to violations of other competition rules, such as Article 101 TFEU or Article 5(3) DMA. In particular, narrow price parity clauses, which restrict business users from offering lower prices on other platforms but do not extend to other sales channels, may comply with competition law if they benefit from an exemption under Article 2(1) VBER (► 4.3.6).

8. Why do Article 11–13 Platform Regulation promote dispute resolution?

The Platform Regulation recognizes the one-sided dependency of business users on platform operators. Business users rely heavily on these platforms as intermediaries to ensure their services gain visibility and attract consumer demand. This dependence creates a significant power imbalance, which can become particularly problematic in the event of disputes. To address this imbalance and facilitate fairer outcomes, Articles 11–13 Platform Regulation encourage the use of out-of-court dispute resolution mechanisms. These consensual processes aim to provide quicker, less adversarial, and more accessible solutions than formal litigation, helping to restore balance between platform operators and business users (► 4.3.7).

9. Under German law, how can a business user take action if a service provider breaches transparency obligations?

Beyond the nullity consequence outlined in Article 3(3) Platform Regulation, the Regulation leaves the organization of legal consequences to national legislators. In

Germany, if a business user suffers damage as a result of such a violation, they may assert a claim for damages under secs. 280(1), 241(2) German Civil Code. Additionally, the business user can seek injunctive relief under sec. 8(1), (3) no. 1 Act Against Unfair Competition. As a competitor under sec. 2(1) no. 4 Act Against Unfair Competition, the business user is also authorized to initiate legal proceedings. A breach of an obligation under the Platform Regulation is considered an unlawful act under sec. 3a Act Against Unfair Competition, providing further legal basis for action (► 4.4.3.2).

10. Under German law, are collective legal remedies available to enforce transparency obligations under the Platform Regulation?

Article 14 Platform Regulation provides for the possibility of representative actions to ensure the effective enforcement of transparency obligations. In Germany, this provision has been implemented through sec. 8a German Act Against Unfair Competition. Under this framework, specific associations, organisations, and public bodies may be entitled to bring collective legal actions on behalf of affected business users. The authority to designate such eligible entities lies with the German Federal Network Agency, as set out in sec. 22(2) German Implementing Act on Digital Services (► 4.4.3.3).

11. Is the Platform Regulation subject to public enforcement in Germany?

Although the Platform Regulation does not require public enforcement by Member States, Germany has opted to establish such a mechanism. In May 2024, enforcement powers were transferred to the Federal Network Agency through secs. 22(1), 30 German Implementing Act on Digital Services. These provisions empower the authority to investigate infringements and impose corrective measures where necessary (► 4.4.1).

12. Does German law impose fines for non-compliance with the Platform Regulation?

Under sec. 33(3) German Implementing Act on Digital Services, the culpable breach of certain—though not all—obligations under the Platform Regulation may be sanctioned with fines. This applies to violations of specific obligations, including those laid down in Articles 3, 4, 5, 7, 11 and 12 Platform Regulation. The amount of the fine depends on the nature of the violation. According to sec. 33(6) German Implementing Act on Digital Services, a fine of up to EUR 300,000 may be imposed for infringements listed under sec. 33(3) nos. 1, 3, 4, 9, 10 and 11 German Implementing Act on Digital Services. For breaches of nos. 2, 5–8, and 12–15, the maximum fine is EUR 100,000 (► 4.4.2).

References

Alexander C (2020) Anwendungsbereich, Regelungstechnik und einzelne Transparenzvorgaben der P2B-Verordnung. WRP 2020:945–954

Alexander C (2024) Article 3 Platform Regulation. In: Köhler H, Bornkamm J, Feddersen J (eds) Kommentar Gesetz gegen den unlauteren Wettbewerb, 42nd edn. Beck, Munich

Arncken D (2025) § 15 scope of application. In: Steinrötter B, Heinze C, Denga M (eds) EU Platform Regulation – a handbook, 1st edn. Nomos/Beck/Hart Publishing, Baden-Baden/Munich/Oxford

Bania K (2023) Fitting the Digital Markets Act in the existing legal framework: the myth of the "without prejudice" clause. Eur Compet J 19:116–149

Berberich M (2025) § 5 Due diligence obligations, content moderation and procedural fairness. In: Steinrötter B, Heinze C, Denga M (eds) EU Platform Regulation – a handbook, 1st edn. Nomos/C.H.Beck/Hart Publishing, Baden-Baden/Munich/Oxford

Bostoen F (2023) Abuse of platform power – leveraging conduct in digital markets under EU competition law and beyond. Concurrences, Paris

Bueren E/Weck T (2022) Article 5 DMA. In: Säcker F, Meier-Beck P, Bien F, Montag F (eds) Münchener Kommmentar zum Wettwerbsrecht. 4th edn. C.H.Beck, Munich

Busch C (2020) The P2B Regulation (EU) 2019/1150: towards a "procedural turn" in EU platform regulation? EuCML 2020:133–134

Busch C (2024) Platform regulation beyond DSA and DMA: which role for the P2B Regulation? J Antitrust Enforce 12(2):201–206

Dreher M, Kulka M (2023) Wettbewerbs- und Kartellrecht – Eine systematische Darstellung des deutschen und europäischen Rechts, 12th edn. C.F. Müller, Heidelberg

Ernst S (2020) Fairness und Transparenz – Die P2B-Verordnung – Regeln zwischen Verkaufsplattformen und Unternehmern. CR 2020:735–739

Hoffer R, Lehr A (2019) Onlineplattformen und Big Data auf dem Prüfstand – Gemeinsame Betrachtung der Fälle Amazon, Google und Facebook. NZKart 2019:10–20

Höppner T, Wick J (2022) In: Busch C (ed) Kommentar Verordnung (EU) 2019/1150 zur Förderung von Fairness und Transparenz für gewerbliche Nutzer von Online-Vermittlungsdiensten (P2B-VO), 1st edn. C.H.Beck, Munich

Keller E (2021) sec. 2 UWG. In: Harte-Bavendamm H, Henning-Bodewig F (eds) Kommentar Gesetz gegen den unlauteren Wettbewerb, 5th edn. C.H.Beck, Munich

Köhler H (2025) Article 14 Platform Regulation. In: Höhler H, Feddersen J (eds) Kommentar Gesetz gegen den unlauteren Wettbewerb, 43rd edn. C.H.Beck, Munich

Kumkar L (2022) Plattform-Recht revisited: Umgang mit den Marktordnungen digitaler Plattformen de lege lata et ferenda. ZEuP 2022:530–564

Legner S (2024a) Informationspflichten des europäischen Verbrauchervertragsrechts im digitalen Zeitalter – Quo Vadis? ZEuP 2024:649–673

Legner S (2024b) Der Digital Services Act – Ein neuer Grundstein der Digitalregulierung. ZUM 2024:99–111

Nolteernsting K (2025) The European regulatory framework of ranking transparency on platform markets – P2B + P2C = P2U. IIC (2025). https://doi.org/10.1007/s40319-025-01625-1

Papathanasiou K (2024) § 33 DDG. In: Heldt A, Legner S (eds) Kommentar Digitale Dienste Gesetz, 1st edn. Nomos, Baden-Baden

Raue B (2025) Art. 14, Art. 17 DSA. In: Raue B, Hofmann F (eds) Digital Services Act Article-by-Article Commentary. Nomos/C.H.Beck/Hart Publishing, Baden-Baden/Munich/Oxford

Schneider N, Kremer S (2020) Ein zweiter, kritischer Blick auf die P2B-Verordnung: Nachhaltige Veränderung des Plattformökosystems? WRP 2020:1128–1136

Schweitzer H (2019) Digitale Plattformen als private Gesetzgeber: Ein Perspektivwechsel für die europäische "Plattform-Regulierung". ZEuP 2019:1–12

Tribess A (2024) Article 11 Platform Regulation. In: Fritzsche J, Münker R, Stollwerk C (eds) Beck'scher Online-Kommentar zum UWG, 24th edn. C.H.Beck, Munich

Tribess A (2025) § 17 Complaint-handling, mediation, enforcement and monitoring. In: Steinrötter B, Heinze C, Denga M (eds) EU Platform Regulation – a handbook, 1st edn. Nomos/C.H.Beck/Hart Publishing, Baden-Baden/Munich/Oxford

Wiedemann F (2024) Kapitel 1.3 Online-Plattformen. In: Heckmann D, Paschke A (eds) juris PraxisKommentar Internetrecht Das Recht der Digitalisierung, 8th edn. Juris, Saarbruecken

Wischmeyer T, Meißner P (2023) Horizontalwirkung der Unionsgrundrechte – Folgen für den Digital Services Act. NJW 2023:2673–2678

Wischmeyer T, Meißner P (2024) § 30 DDG. In: Heldt A, Legner S (eds) Kommentar Digitale Dienste Gesetz, 1st edn. Nomos, Baden-Baden

German Competition Law

Contents

S. Legner, *Digital Competition Law*, Springer Textbooks in Law,
https://doi.org/10.1007/978-3-662-73213-7_5

5.1 Introduction

5.1.1 Overview

German competition law is governed by the Act against Restraints of Competition[1] (hereinafter: ARC). Similar to European competition law, it is structured around three main pillars (◘ Fig. 5.1).

The **prohibition of cartels** under **sec. 1, 2 ARC** closely mirrors Article 101 TFEU, which governs the European ban on cartels. Pursuant to sec. 2(2) ARC, the block exemption regulations adopted by the European legislator also apply to the German provision in sec. 1 ARC. However, unlike Article 101 TFEU, the application of the German ban on cartels does not require an effect on interstate trade, making it applicable to purely domestic cases as well.

The **prohibitions on abuse** are set out in sec. 19, 19a, and 20 ARC. In addition to the European prohibition of abuse of a dominant market position under Article 102 TFEU, which is essentially identical in substance to **sec. 19 ARC**, German competition law includes further prohibitions. Specifically, **sec. 20 ARC** addresses undertakings that do not meet the threshold of market dominance. These undertakings with relative market power are prohibited from engaging in certain unilateral conduct. According to Article 3(2) 2nd sentence Regulation 1/2003 (commonly referred to as the 'German clause'), this is consistent with European law, as it allows member states to adopt and apply on their territory stricter national laws which prohibit or sanction unilateral conduct.

With **sec. 19a ARC**, the German legislator introduced a prohibition targeting **undertakings of paramount significance for competition across markets** as part of the 10th amendment to the ARC in 2021. This new offence primarily aims to

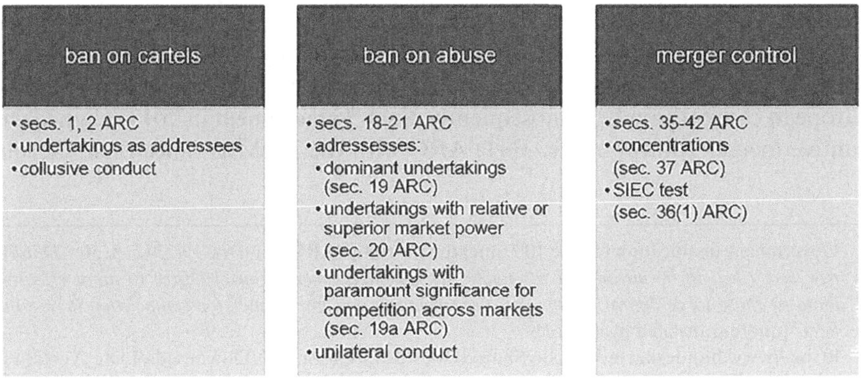

◘ **Fig. 5.1** The pillars of German competition law

1 Federal Law Gazette Part I 2023 no. 405.

address large digital groups.[2] The enforcement mechanism differs from that of sec. 19 and sec. 20 ARC: an undertaking becomes subject to the prohibition only after a determination by the German Federal Cartel Office. By August 2025, the German Federal Cartel Office had already initiated 12 proceedings based on sec. 19a ARC.[3] Furthermore, sec. 21 ARC contains additional specific national prohibitions, including the boycott prohibition and other expressly defined offences.[4]

5

Merger control is governed by **sec. 35–43a ARC**. The turnover-related thresholds in sec. 35 ARC are lower than those under the European regime. With the 9th amendment to the ARC in 2017, the legislator introduced a new, transaction-related merger control threshold in sec. **35(1a) ARC**. Accordingly, in addition to the turnover of the undertakings involved, the value of the consideration for the merger is also relevant for determining the applicability of German merger control. The rationale behind this amendment was the legislative aim to ensure that merger control remains an institution '*that can keep pace with the ever faster economic cycles, especially in light of the advancing digitalisation and networking of the economy and society*.'[5] Due to competitive conditions in digital markets, even a (still) small undertaking can be competitively significant because of its high innovation potential. This relevance, however, is not reflected in turnover figures but rather in the purchase price the acquirer is willing to pay.[6] Since the 8th amendment to the ARC came into force in 2013, the substantive standard for merger control aligns with the SIEC test under Article 2(3) EUMR. Pursuant to sec. 36(1) ARC, the German Federal Cartel Office must prohibit a merger if it leads to a significant impediment to effective competition.[7]

5.1.2 Historical Context of German Competition Law

The ARC, which entered into force on 1 January 1958, has undergone a total of eleven amendments up to early 2024. The **7th amendment** to the ARC, adopted in 2005,[8] significantly harmonised German competition law with the provisions of European competition law. Subsequently, the **8th amendment** in 2013[9] aligned substantive merger control in sec. 36(1) ARC with the EUMR. Since then, German

2 Government justification for the 10th amendment to the ARC, BT-Drs. 19/2342, p. 56: '*Thirdly, a new sec. 19a will be introduced to enable the German Federal Cartel Office to more effectively monitor those large digital groups that are of paramount importance for competition across markets.*' [quote translated by author].

3 https://www.bundeskartellamt.de/SharedDocs/Publikation/DE/Downloads/Liste_Verfahren_Digitalkonzerne.pdf?__blob=publicationFile&v=8 (accessed 6 September 2025).

4 Lettl (2021), sec. 9 mn. 198 et seqq.

5 Government justification for the 9th amendment to the ARC, BT-Drs. 18/10207, p. 70 [quote translated by author].

6 Government justification for the 9th amendment to the ARC, BT-Drs. 18/10207, p. 71.

7 Federal Law Gazette Part I 2013, p. 1738.

8 Federal Law Gazette Part I 2005, p. 1954.

9 Federal Law Gazette Part I 2013, p. 1738.

merger control has also been based on the SIEC test, mirroring Article 2(3) EUMR, which has been in force since 2004. The traditional market dominance test has been retained in German law as a standard example within this framework.

With the **9th Amendment** to the ARC in 2017,[10] the legislator introduced specific provisions addressing digital markets within the frameworks of abuse control and merger regulation. The stated objective was to '*ensure effective merger control and protection against the abuse of market power*' in light of the growing digitalisation of the economy.[11] An important addition was **sec. 18(2a) ARC**, which clarifies that the existence of a market is not precluded merely because a service is offered free of charge. This provision reflects the understanding that, in multi-sided digital markets, certain user groups may access intermediary platform services without paying a monetary fee.[12] Typical examples include social media or online market-places, where private users often create and use accounts at no cost. Given the indirect network effects between end users and commercial users on these plat-forms, such models can still be highly profitable for platform operators.[13] It is therefore unconvincing to dismiss the existence of a market simply due to the absence of a monetary exchange with end users. Sec. 18(2a) ARC explicitly addresses this issue. However, the provision does not define the criteria required to establish the existence of a market in such cases. It is therefore left to legal practice and case law to develop and refine these criteria.

To facilitate the assessment of dominant market positions in digital markets, the catalogue of criteria under **sec. 18(3a) ARC** has been expanded. This provision introduces additional factors relevant to digital competition, including direct and indirect network effects, access to competition-relevant data, and innovation-driven competitive pressure. These are described as 'special factors that character-ise multi-sided markets and networks in particular and distinguish them from traditional markets.'[14] While multi-sided markets and networks are not exclusive to the digital sector, they are particularly prevalent there. The tendency of digital markets to 'tilt', that is, to tip in favour of a single provider, is largely driven by direct network effects among users of the same group, as well as indirect network effects between different user groups. With regard to access to competitively relevant data, the legislator highlights one of the most crucial competitive factors in the digital economy. Here, market power does not necessarily manifest through pricing flexibility; rather, it may arise from (exclusive) control over large volumes of data, which can be just as decisive for competitive dynamics.[15]

The competitive significance of innovation in digital markets stems from struc-tural characteristics that often favour a 'winner-takes-all' dynamic.[16] In such envi-

10 Federal Law Gazette Part I 2017, p. 1416.
11 Government justification for the 9th amendment to the ARC, BT-Drs. 18/10207, p. 1 [quote trans-lated by author].
12 Government justification for the 9th amendment to the ARC, BT-Drs. 18/10207, p. 48.
13 Legner (2023), pp. 175, 178.
14 Government justification for the 9th amendment to the ARC, BT-Drs. 18/10207, p. 48 [quote translated by author].
15 Government justification for the 9th amendment to the ARC, BT-Drs. 18/10207, p. 49.
16 Schweitzer et al. (2018), p. 12.

ronments, firms primarily compete through innovation: a company that successfully introduces a novel product or service can capture the market and establish a dominant position. By contrast, price competition is largely irrelevant in cases where services are provided to end users free of charge. History has shown that even firms with substantial market power can be overtaken by competitors with more innovative business models. As a result, the competitive pressure arising from research and development activities plays a crucial role in shaping the evolution and dynamics of digital markets.[17]

In the context of merger control, sec. 35(1a) ARC introduced an additional threshold based on the consideration paid for a transaction. This amendment was prompted by the *Facebook*/*WhatsApp* merger, which did not fall under either the European or German merger control regimes due to *WhatsApp*'s low turnover.[18] Notably, the acquisition price was USD 19 billion.[19] The economic significance of such transactions lies in the disproportion between the target's low or non-existent turnover and the exceptionally high purchase price.[20] This suggests that acquiring firms recognize the disruptive potential of the target's business model and seek to neutralize innovation-driven competitive threats at an early stage. As a result, such mergers may contribute to further consolidation of market power in digital markets. In addition, the 9th Amendment to the ARC also implemented the EU Cartel Damages Directive, which is reflected in secs. 33a et seq. ARC.[21] These provisions aim to strengthen private enforcement of competition law by facilitating claims for damages.

The **10th Amendment** to the ARC entered into force on 19 January 2021.[22] With this amendment, the German legislator introduced several new provisions specifically tailored to the conditions of the digital economy. One of the central reforms is sec. 19a ARC, which establishes a special abuse control mechanism for undertakings with paramount significance for competition across markets. Although the wording of the provision does not explicitly mention them, it is clear that the legislator primarily intended this provision to target large digital groups.[23] Unlike secs. 19, 20 ARC, the abuse control under sec. 19a ARC is structured as a two-stage process. First, the cartel office must issue a decision formally designating an undertaking as having paramount cross-market significance. In the second stage, it may issue a separate order prohibiting specific forms of unilateral conduct pursuant to sec. 19a(2) ARC. The examples of prohibited conduct listed in sec. 19a(2) ARC

17 Government justification for the 9th amendment to the ARC, BT-Drs. 18/10207, p. 51: '*disruptive […] changes*' [quote translated by author].

18 The Commission examined the merger because it was notifiable in three member states and *Facebook* had requested the Commission's examination. However, the Commission did not see any competition concerns and cleared it.

19 Government justification for the 9th amendment to the ARC, BT-Drs. 18/10207, p. 71.

20 Government justification for the 9th amendment to the ARC, BT-Drs. 18/10207, p. 71.

21 Directive 2014/104/EU of the European Parliament and of the Council of 26 November 2014 on certain rules governing actions for damages under national law for infringements of the competition law provisions of the Member States and of the European Union, OJ [2014] L 349/1.

22 Federal Law Gazette Part I 2021, p. 2.

23 Government justification for the 11th amendment to the ARC, BT-Drs. 19/23492, p. 73.

reflect practices already observed in the digital economy, such as the preferential treatment of a vertically integrated platform's own services (cf. sec. 19a(2) no. 1 ARC) or the restriction of interoperability and data portability (cf. sec. 19a(2) no. 5 ARC).

Additionally, the prohibition of abuse of relative or superior market power has been expanded to include a right to data access under sec. 20(1a) ARC, as well as an anti-tipping provision in sec. 20(3a) ARC. Furthermore, the national legislator has implemented the ECN+ Directive[24] (aimed at strengthening the enforcement powers of national competition authorities) through sec. 50a et seq. ARC.

The **11th Amendment** to the ARC entered into force on 7 November 2023.[25] It introduced a widely discussed **new competition instrument in sec. 32f(3) ARC**, which empowers the German Federal Cartel Office to impose far-reaching remedial measures, including structural remedies such as unbundling, following the conclusion of a sector inquiry. The stated objective is to address competition problems that '*cannot be remedied through merger control and do not derive their restrictive nature from anti-competitive agreements, concerted practices, or the abuse of market power.*'[26] Importantly, the imposition of such measures does not require proof of a violation of competition law. Instead, it is sufficient for the authority to determine, based on the findings of a sector inquiry, that a significant and persistent distortion of competition exists, whether in a single market, at least one nationwide market, several individual markets, or across multiple markets. According to sec. 32f(3) 7th sentence ARC, potential remedies may include: granting third-party access to data; obliging undertakings to establish transparent, non-discriminatory, and open norms and standards; or requiring the organisational separation of undertakings or business units. To justify this 'New Competition Tool,' the legislator specifically pointed to competition challenges in the digital sector. The government's explanatory memorandum refers to European studies advocating for a 'market structure-based competition instrument' as a way to enhance regulatory oversight in digital markets.[27] While the newly introduced sec. 32f ARC reflects this approach, its scope of application is not limited to digital markets.

In addition, **sec. 32g ARC** was amended to grant the German Federal Cartel Office the authority to **investigate potential infringements of the Digital Markets Act (DMA)**[28] that have effects in Germany. However, pursuant to Articles 20 et seq. DMA, enforcement of the regulation lies exclusively with the Commission.

---

24 Directive (EU) 2019/1 of the European Parliament and of the Council of 11 December 2018 on the strengthening of the competition authorities of the Member States with a view to ensuring more effective enforcement of the competition rules and the proper functioning of the internal market, OJ [2019] L 11/3.

25 Federal Law Gazette Part I 2023 no. 294.

26 Government justification for the 11th amendment to the ARC, BT-Drs. 20/6824, p. 27 [quote translated by author].

27 Government justification for the 10th amendment to the ARC, BT-Drs. 20/6824, p. 19.

28 On the DMA, see section 3.

The national authority may conduct preliminary investigations and submit its findings to the Commission, but it is not empowered to enforce the DMA independently.[29]

The German government in office until late 2024 had already begun preparing the 12th amendment to the ARC. Among other things, the previous government intended to address the role of sustainability considerations in the assessment of cartels, consumer protection, ministerial authorisation, and private enforcement. However, following the government's collapse, enactment of the amendment will be delayed. The current government has not yet announced its plans regarding a reform of the ARC.

5.1.3 Objectives

5.1.3.1 Competitive Process

From an intellectual-historical perspective, German competition law is rooted in ordoliberalism. In the 1930s, the Freiburg School, led by *Walter Eucken* and *Franz Böhm*, established the theory of perfect competition as its foundational principle.[30] According to this school of thought, market power poses a threat to free competition. Böhm's well-known dictum encapsulates this perspective. He emphasised that 'competition is the most ingenious instrument of disempowerment in history.'[31]

While this idea continues to shape the foundation of German competition law, it no longer dominates in its pure form. Its influence is evident in several core elements of the ARC: the prohibition of collusion (secs. 1–2 ARC), the stricter behavioural obligations imposed on undertakings with market power (secs. 19–21 ARC), and the merger control provision in sec. 36(1) ARC. Even under the SIEC test, a merger may be prohibited solely on the grounds that it would lead to the creation or strengthening of a dominant market position, even in the absence of concrete anti-competitive effects. The initial drafters of the ARC recognised that perfect competition is an unattainable ideal.[32] Consequently, the ordoliberal framework now exists alongside other theoretical approaches within the ARC's structure. One such alternative is the concept of workable competition, which focuses more on market outcomes than structural market conditions.[33] From this perspective, achieving optimal competitive intensity does not necessarily require a polypolistic market structure. Even today, the structural approach remains a defining element of German competition law. Many key legal standards are still tied to the existence

29 Government justification for the10th amendment to the ARC, BT-Drs. 20/6824, p. 38.
30 Möschel (2014), pp. 42, 44 et seqq.
31 Böhm (1963), pp. 37, 46 [quote translated by author].
32 Rittner (2006), pp. 125, 131.
33 Kantzenbach (1967), pp. 16 et seq.

of market power, with market share continuing to serve as one of the most important indicators in its assessment.

5.1.3.2 Consumer Welfare

German competition law does not articulate the protection of consumer welfare as explicitly as European competition law does. Nonetheless, it is now widely accepted that consumer welfare, in line with EU competition principles, constitutes an **additional objective** of the ARC. This effects perspective is reflected in several provisions. For instance, the exemption criteria under **sec. 2 ARC** mirror the wording of Article 101(3) TFEU, signalling a shared focus on efficiency gains and benefits for consumers. Similarly, the SIEC test, introduced as the standard for merger control under **sec. 36(1) ARC** with the 8th amendment in 2013,[34] further illustrates the shift towards an effects-based analysis. Under this test, a merger must be prohibited if it would significantly impede effective competition. While the market dominance test continues to serve as a prominent example, it is no longer the sole standard. Moreover, the German legislator's intention to harmonise national competition law with European rules was already evident in the 7th amendment to the ARC in 2005,[35] marking a broader trend toward legal convergence with European competition enforcement.

For the concept of consumer welfare, reference can be made to the corresponding principles under European competition law.[36] In static terms, consumer welfare is typically measured by consumer surplus, which is defined as the difference between the reservation price(that is, the consumer's maximum willingness to pay) and the actual price paid for a good or service. In dynamic terms, consumer welfare is enhanced through innovation and progress, which manifest in increased product variety, improved product quality, and technological advancements. These factors contribute to long-term consumer benefits that extend beyond immediate price effects. In the context of digital markets, additional considerations come into play. It is often emphasised that consumers benefit not only from lower transaction costs but also from increased market transparency, facilitated by intermediary services such as search engines or online marketplaces. These platforms enable consumers to access information more efficiently, compare prices, and make more informed purchasing decisions, thereby enhancing overall consumer welfare.

5.1.3.3 Additional Objectives

Beyond consumer welfare and the protection of competition as such, German competition law also pursues further objectives, which are reflected in specific provisions of the ARC. One prominent example is the **protection of small and medium-**

34 Federal Law Gazette Part I 2013, p. 1738.
35 Government justification for the 7th amendment to the ARC, BT-Drs. 15/3640, p. 1.
36 On further details on the consumer welfare standard as objective in EU competition law, see ▶ 2.1.3.2.

sized enterprises (SMEs). Sec. 3 ARC provides for a tailored exemption from the general cartel prohibition, explicitly facilitating cooperation among SMEs.[37] This aims to support their competitive viability by allowing certain agreements that might otherwise be considered anti-competitive, provided they meet defined criteria. Sec. 20 ARC introduces a special prohibition of abuse designed to protect undertakings that are economically dependent on others holding relative or superior market power. Unlike sec. 19 ARC and Article 102 TFEU, this provision does not require the existence of market dominance. It is sufficient that a bilateral imbalance of power exists between the contracting parties.[38] In particular, sec. 20(3) ARC addresses situations where undertakings possess superior market power in comparison to SME competitors. It prohibits specific unfair practices that can hinder smaller rivals, thereby underscoring the law's protective stance toward SMEs.

Since the 9th Amendment to the ARC, the German Federal Cartel Office has held competences in the area of **consumer protection**, as set out in sec. 32e(6) ARC. This provision allows the authority to conduct a sector inquiry if there are reasonable grounds to suspect significant, persistent, or repeated infringements of consumer protection regulations, provided these infringements are of a nature or scale likely to adversely affect the interests of a large number of consumers.[39] While the German Federal Cartel Office is granted extensive investigatory powers under this provision, it does not have the authority to impose remedies in response to any infringements it identifies. Consumer protection must be clearly distinguished from the protection of consumer welfare discussed above. Whereas consumer welfare pertains to market outcomes, particularly in terms of efficiency, prices, and innovation, consumer protection under sec. 32e(6) ARC aligns more closely with the objectives of unfair competition law and European private law. Here, the consumer is regarded as structurally inferior to businesses, especially with regard to information asymmetry and bargaining power, and is thus considered in need of legal safeguards to ensure fair treatment in market transactions.

In German abuse law, considerations beyond pure competition concerns, such as those arising from the **law on general terms and conditions**, may be taken into account. This approach was notably applied in the German Federal Cartel Office's 2019 decision in the Facebook case, where **data protection law** played a central role in the assessment. In that case, the authority incorporated data protection considerations into its balancing of interests to establish an abuse of market power.[40] The ECJ later confirmed that the Federal Cartel Office may consider violations of data

---

37 Grave and Nyberg (2025), sec. 3 ARC mn. 3.

38 Paal (2025), sec. 20 ARC mn. 9.

39 One example is the sector enquiry into messenger and video services, cf. German Federal Cartel Office 15 May 2023 – V-28/20 https://www.bundeskartellamt.de/SharedDocs/Publikation/DE/Sektoruntersuchungen/Sektoruntersuchung_MessengerVideoDienste.html (accessed 9 September 2025).

40 German Federal Cartel Office, Decision of 6 February 2019 – B6-22/16 – *Facebook*.

protection law insofar as they are relevant to assessing an abuse of dominance.[41] However, this should not be misunderstood as an expansion of competition law to pursue non-competition objectives independently. Rather, such considerations are admissible only insofar as they serve the enforcement of competition law in cases of market power abuse.

5.1.4 Scope of Application

5.1.4.1 Personal Scope

German competition law, in line with European competition law,[42] is based on the notion of the **undertaking** as an **economic entity**. This classification is independent of the undertaking's legal form, the duration of its operations, or any intention to generate profit. The decisive criterion is the performance of an economic activity in the market. In the context of German competition law, the term is interpreted **functionally**, with emphasis on the nature of the activity rather than its organisational structure. Although the concept of undertaking also appears in other areas of German law, such as commercial law, company law, and contract law, the prevailing definitions in those fields are not determinative for competition law purposes.

! The concept of an undertaking under German competition law corresponds, in principle, to that applied in European competition law and must likewise be interpreted in a functional manner.

While German competition law recognises slightly different approaches to defining an undertaking, these do not result in substantive deviations from the European concept. German law distinguishes between **absolute and relative undertakings**. Absolute undertakings meet the definition by virtue of their legal form alone, whereas relative undertakings are defined by the nature of the economic activity they perform.[43]

▶ Example

A craftsman is considered an undertaking when engaged in business activities related to his freelance work; however, he is not regarded as such when making purely private purchases. ◀

The state is not considered an undertaking within the meaning of competition law when acting in a sovereign capacity. However, where it operates as an economic actor in the market, the position is different. This is expressly confirmed in **sec. 185(1) ARC**, which provides that competition law also applies to undertakings wholly or partly owned, managed, or operated by the public sector. Under German

---

41 ECJ 4 July 2023 – C-252/21, ECLI:EU:C:2023:537 – *Meta Platforms*.
42 On the concept of undertaking under EU competition law, see ▶ 2.1.4.1.
43 Kling and Thomas (2016), sec. 16 mn. 6–9.

law, this extends to the procurement activities of the state, provided they are conducted under private law.[44] For example, when the state purchases office supplies or equipment for police officers, it is acting as an undertaking on the market. By contrast, European case law excludes procurement activities serving a non-economic purpose, such as those of a social or military nature, from the definition of an undertaking.[45] At this point, the **German concept is therefore broader in scope** than its European counterpart.

5 It remains an open question whether this divergence in case law can be sustained or whether the German concept of an undertaking must ultimately be subordinated to that of European competition law. The primacy of Union law, as enshrined in Article 3 Regulation 1/2003, may speak against retaining the broader German definition.[46] Under this provision, Member States may impose stricter rules than those of European competition law only within the framework of abuse of dominance. However, the concept of an undertaking determines the personal scope of application of all competition law provisions. The German Federal Supreme Court has not yet issued a ruling on this matter. Nevertheless, recent decisions suggest a tendency to maintain the existing German approach.[47]

5.1.4.2 Substantive Scope

With respect to the substantive scope of application, only a few economic sectors remain exempt from the general provisions of competition law. This is reflected in sec. 28–31b ARC. One example concerns the press and publishing sector. Sec. 30 ARC permits vertical price fixing for magazines and books, while the German Book Price Fixing Act (*Buchpreisbindungsgesetz*)[48] makes such price regulation mandatory for books. Sec. 28 ARC further contains a special provision for the agricultural sector.

5.1.4.3 Territorial Scope

The territorial scope of application of German competition law is determined, analogous to European competition law, by the effects doctrine.[49] **Sec. 185(2) ARC** operates as a special conflict-of-laws rule, providing that the provisions apply to all restrictions of competition producing effects in Germany, even if ini-

---

44 German Federal Supreme Court 26 May 1987 – KZR 13/85, NJW 1988, 772, 773 – *Krankentransporte*; German Federal Supreme Court 18 January 2000 – KVR 23/98, NJW-RR 1999, 342, 343 – *Tariftreueerklärung*; Higher Regional Court of Duesseldorf 12 February 1980, NJW 1981, 585, 586 – *Gleichbehandlung aller Anbieter bei öffentlichen Aufträgen*.

45 ECJ 11 July 2006 – C-205/03 P, ECLI:EU:C:2006:453 – *Fenin*; GC 4 March 2003 – T-319/99, ECLI:EU:T:2003:50 – *Fenin*.

46 Klees (2017), sec. 130 ARC mn. 15 et seqq.

47 German Federal Supreme Court 6 November 2013 – KZR 61/11, NZKart 2014, 31, 32 et seq. – *VBL-Gegenwert I*; German Federal Supreme Court 24 January 2017 – KZR 47/14, NZKart 2017, 242 – *VBL-Gegenwert II*.

48 Federal Law Gazette Part I 2002, p. 3448.

49 Wiedemann (2020), sec. 5 mn. 23.

tiated abroad.[50] It is immaterial where the undertakings involved are registered or where their agreements were concluded.[51] Conversely, the mere fact that an undertaking participating in the restriction of competition has its registered office in Germany does not, by itself, trigger the application of German competition law. The decisive criterion is whether the restriction produces effects within German territory.

► **Examples**

An online gaming platform based in the United States agrees with game publishers located in other countries that activation codes for games distributed via the platform will function only in specified territories. For instance, a game purchased in France cannot be activated or used in Germany.

Two undertakings established in France divide the German market between them so that one supplies exclusively to the north of Germany, while the other concentrates its activities on the south. ◄

5.1.5 Relation to European Competition Law

The German **prohibition of cartels** in sec. 1, 2 ARC and the German **prohibition of abuse** in sec. 19 ARC apply **in parallel** with the European prohibition of cartels in Article 101 TFEU and the European prohibition of abuse in Article 102 TFEU. National competition authorities are therefore required to apply both German and European provisions, as stipulated in Article 3(1) Regulation 1/2003, a rule reiterated for clarification in sec. 22(1) ARC.

With regard to the **substantive relationship** between the two regimes, Article 3(2) 1st sentence Regulation 1/2003 and sec. 22(2) ARC provide that no stricter rules than those in European competition law may apply to agreements or concerted practices. An exception (the so-called German clause) is set out in Article 3(2) 2nd sentence Regulation 1/2003 and sec. 22(3) ARC: Member States may adopt or maintain **stricter national provisions** on the abuse of market power. German law makes use of this option through **sec. 20 ARC**, which prohibits abusive conduct by undertakings with relative market power, even if they do not hold a dominant position. Moreover, sec. 19a ARC addresses undertakings of paramount significance for competition across markets, a status that does not necessarily coincide with dominance.[52] This, too, can be regarded as a stricter national provision within the meaning of Article 3(2) 2nd sentence Regulation 1/2003.

50 Rehbinder and von Kalben (2024), sec. 185 ARC mn. 107.
51 Wiedemann (2020), sec. 5 mn. 23.
52 Government justification for the 10th amendment to the ARC, BT-Drs. 19/23492, p. 75: '*The criteria [of sec. 19a(1) 2nd sentence ARC] do not have to be fulfilled cumulatively and their order is not intended to specify a weighting.*' [quote translated by author].

Learning Goals

The relationship between sec. 19a ARC and the obligations under the DMA appears to be marked by potential conflict. Article 1(5) DMA establishes a blocking effect on Member State provisions that seek to impose additional obligations on gatekeepers aimed at ensuring contestable and fair markets. However, sec. 19a ARC is generally regarded as falling within the scope of Article 1(6) DMA. Accordingly, the DMA does not affect the application of existing competition law provisions such as sec. 19a ARC.[53]

The **one-stop-shop principle** applies to merger control under European and German law. Where the scope of European merger control is engaged pursuant to Article 1 EUMR, the German Federal Cartel Office is precluded from examining the merger. This follows directly from Article 21(3)(1) EUMR. If the turnover thresholds set out in Article 1 EUMR are not met, or if the transaction does not qualify as a merger under Article 3 EUMR, the German merger control provisions contained in sec. 35 et seq. ARC may apply instead.[54]

Article 22 EUMR empowers the Commission to review mergers lacking a Community dimension due to unmet turnover thresholds, provided that at least one Member State requests a referral and that the merger affects trade between Member States while significantly threatening competition within the territory of the requesting Member State's territory. Conversely, under **Article 9 EUMR**, the Commission may refer a merger to a Member State's competition authority for examination. Such referral requires that the concentration threatens to affect significantly competition in a market within that Member State, which presents all the characteristics of a distinct market, or that it affects competition in a market within that Member State, which presents all the characteristics of a distinct market and which does not constitute a substantial part of the common market.

5.2 Prohibition of Cartels: Secs. 1, 2 ARC

5.2.1 Introduction

Since the 7th amendment to the ARC in 2005, the wording of the cartel prohibition in **secs. 1, 2 ARC** has been rendered **almost identical to that of the European cartel prohibition** set out in **Article 101 TFEU**. This alignment permits the use of the Commission's guidelines and communications, which elaborate on the requirements of Article 101 TFEU, to inform the interpretation of sec. 1 ARC. There are two principal differences between sec. 1 ARC and Article 101 TFEU. First, an infringement of the German cartel prohibition **does not require an effect on trade between Member States.**[55] Consequently, the German cartel prohibition also cov-

53 Achleitner (2022), pp. 359, 364; Käseberg and Gappa (2023), Article 1 DMA mn. 28.

54 Westermann (2025), Article 21 EUMR mn. 6.

55 For further details on this prerequisite under Article 101(1) TFEU, see ▶ 2.2.3.

ers purely local anti-competitive agreements, such as those affecting only a single region or city.[56] Nonetheless, the existence of an effect on trade between Member States does not preclude the application of sec. 1 ARC. Second, unlike Article 101(1) TFEU, sec. 1 ARC **does not provide illustrative examples** of restrictions of competition. However, this absence does not result in any substantive divergence, as the elements of prohibited conduct and restriction of competition are interpreted in line with European law.

A systematic, though not substantive, difference lies in the fact that the German legislator has placed the conditions for exemption in a provision separate from the prohibition itself, namely sec. 2 ARC. Sec. 2(1) ARC is identical in wording to Article 101(3) TFEU. Sec. 2(2) ARC applies the **European block exemption regulations** to the German cartel prohibition, irrespective of whether the agreement in question is likely to affect trade between Member States. In this respect, too, reference can be made to the chapter on European competition law.[57] Sec. 2(2) ARC constitutes a **dynamic reference**, meaning that subsequent amendments to European block exemption regulations automatically apply under German law.[58] In addition, sec. 3 ARC specifies the exemption requirements for small and medium-sized cartels with the aim of protecting small and medium-sized enterprises (SMEs). This provision seeks to increase legal certainty in their favour and to encourage cooperative arrangements among them.[59]

The following chapter does not address the elements of the prohibition identical to those contained in Article 101 TFEU with the same level of detail as in the context of the European cartel prohibition. Instead, the emphasis will be placed on decisions of the German Federal Cartel Office and the national courts.

5.2.2 Prohibited Conduct

The prohibition of cartels under sec. 1 ARC presupposes collusive conduct. Mirroring the wording of Article 101 TFEU, sec. 1 ARC identifies three forms of prohibited conduct: agreements, concerted practices, and decisions. Substantively, these terms are to be interpreted in the same manner as under European law.[60] Where a restriction of competition affects trade between Member States, Article 3(2) Regulation 1/2003 provides that the application of the European cartel prohibition to such concerted conduct is mandatory.

Any **legal or economic consent** is sufficient to constitute an 'agreement' under sec. 1 ARC; the parties' intention to be legally bound is not required.[61] Where the agreement also qualifies as a contract in the legal sense, it is void pursuant to

56 Kling and Thomas (2016), sec. 19 mn. 2.
57 For further details on the EU block exemption regulations, see ► 2.2.5.2.
58 Glöckner (2021), mn. 433.
59 Ellger (2024), sec. 3 ARC mn. 8.
60 For further details on Article 101(1) TFEU, see ► 2.2.1.
61 Zimmer (2024), sec. 1 ARC mn. 36.

sec. 134 German Civil Code (*Bürgerliches Gesetzbuch, BGB*) in conjunction with sec. 1 ARC.[62] The concept of an agreement does not extend to unilateral measures, such as non-binding price recommendations. However, the German Federal Cartel Office (applies a broad interpretation of the term. In the Contact Lenses case, the German Federal Cartel Office held that the ostensibly non-binding nature of a price recommendation could be called into question if it was 'subsequently and again' reiterated, thereby giving it 'emphasis.'[63] In such circumstances, an agreement is deemed to exist. In its Guidance on the Prohibition of Price Maintenance in the Stationary Food Retail Sector (*Hinweise zum Preisbindungsverbot im Bereich des stationären Lebensmitteleinzelhandels*), the German Federal Cartel Office further emphasised that even subtly expressed threats in the event of non-compliance with a price recommendation can negate its non-binding character.[64] This expansive approach was recently confirmed in the Pfanner decision,[65] in which the German Federal Cartel Office categorised price recommendations as agreements where the manufacturer threatened to block deliveries in the event of deviations and, in some cases, terminated supply relationships entirely as a sanction for price reductions. The German Federal Supreme Court has, to date, left open the question of whether it will endorse this broad interpretation.[66]

In a paper published in 2020, the German Federal Cartel Office examined the interfaces between **algorithms and collusion**, distinguishing **three scenarios** for the use of algorithms.[67] The first scenario, mirroring the approach taken in European competition law,[68] concerns situations in which an **algorithm is used as a supporter** of an anti-competitive practice established in advance.[69] As an example, the German Federal Cartel Office referred to the Poster case from the United Kingdom,[70] in which undertakings employed pricing software to implement a pre-existing agreement between competitors. The second scenario is described as **collusion between competitors supported by algorithms and involving a third party**.[71] Here, the German Federal Cartel Office differentiates between alignment of conduct at the algorithm (code) level and alignment at the level of the input data used (data level).[72] The determination of whether such conduct constitutes a prohibited alignment must be made on a case-by-case basis, taking into account both the

---

62 Wiedemann (2020), sec. 3 mn. 2.

63 German Federal Cartel Office, Decision of 25 September 2009 – B3-123/08, para. 44 – *Kontaktlinsen* [quotes translated by author].

64 German Federal Cartel Office, Hinweise zum Preisbindungsverbot im Bereich des stationären Lebensmitteleinzelhandels, 2017, para. 66.

65 German Federal Cartel Office, Decision of 19 February 2024 – B10-21/12 – *Pfanner*.

66 German Federal Supreme Court 6 November 2012 – KZR 13/12, NZKart 2013, 84 – *UVP for backpacks*.

67 German Federal Cartel Office, Algorithmen und Wettbewerb, 2020, p. 5 et seqq.

68 On the role of algorithms within the EU ban on cartels, see ► 2.2.1.1.

69 German Federal Cartel Office, Algorithmen und Wettbewerb, 2020, p. 6.

70 CMA, Decision of 12 August 2016 – Case no. 50223 – Online sales of posters and frames https://assets.publishing.service.gov.uk/media/57ee7c2740f0b606dc000018/case-50223-final-non-confidential-infringement-decision.pdf (accessed 1 September 2025). For further details on this case, see ► 2.2.1.1.

71 German Federal Cartel Office, Algorithmen und Wettbewerb, 2020, p. 7.

72 German Federal Cartel Office, Algorithmen und Wettbewerb, 2020, p. 7.

information exchanged regarding the algorithm's use and the market power of the undertakings involved.[73]

Learning Goals

There are already initial practical examples of the second application scenario.[74] One is found in the facts underlying the ECJ's decision in *Eturas*.[75]

The third scenario, **collusion brought about by the parallel use of individual algorithms**, is regarded by the German Federal Cartel Office as a hypothetical case.[76] This scenario considers whether algorithms could, in effect, coordinate autonomously, thereby engaging in prohibited collusive conduct that would nonetheless be attributable to the undertakings deploying them. The German Federal Cartel Office rightly emphasises, however, that the use of algorithms for mere market observation must remain permissible as a transparency-enhancing tool.

Learning Goals

For further details, reference can be made to the chapter on the European cartel prohibition,[77] where it is also explained how algorithms might (theoretically) succeed in creating a reaction mechanism through the market, thereby giving rise to implicit collusion, which is in principle permissible.

The **concerted practice** functions as a catch-all offence, covering situations in which coordination between parties has not advanced to the point of an agreement of intent. A concerted practice exists where undertakings '*deliberately allow practical cooperation to take the place of competition associated with risks and thus [contravene] the basic idea of competition law, according to which every entrepreneur must independently determine his market conduct.*'[78]

As in European competition law, the concept of concerted practice under sec. 1 ARC has acquired particular practical relevance in the context of information exchange.[79] The German Federal Supreme Court emphasises that concerted practice constitutes a two-part offence: in addition to the contact between undertakings, there must also be corresponding conduct on the market.[80] However, **tacit collusion** in the market remains permissible where competitors simply observe each other's behaviour without engaging in actual cooperation. The German Federal Cartel Office considers this to be the case, for example, in the petrol station

73 German Federal Cartel Office, Algorithmen und Wettbewerb, 2020, p. 8.
74 For further details on these examples, see ► 2.2.1.3.
75 ECJ 21 January 2016 – C-74/14, ECLI:EU:C2016:42 – *Eturas*.
76 German Federal Cartel Office, Algorithmen und Wettbewerb, 2020, p. 8.
77 See ► 2.2.1.3.
78 German Federal Supreme Court 12 April 2016 – KZR 31/14, NZKart 2016, 371, 372 – *Gemeinschaftsprogramme* [quote translated by author].
79 German Federal Supreme Court 12 April 2016 – KZR 31/14, NZKart 2016, 371, 372 – Gemeinschaftsprogramme; German Federal Supreme Court 13 July 2020 – KRB 99/19, NZKart 2020, 602, 603 – *Bierkartell*; Higher Regional Court of Duesseldorf 12 July 2017 – VI-U Kart 16/13, NZKart 2017, 481 – *Einspeisung von Fernsehprogrammignalen III*.
80 German Federal Supreme Court 13 July 2020 – KRB 99/19, NZKart 2020, 602, 603 – *Bierkartell*.

markets.[81] Owing to the homogeneous and transparent nature of these markets, undertakings can 'communicate' a higher price level even in the absence of collusion or other coordinated action. In such cases, sec. 1 ARC does not apply. Pursuant to sec. 47k ARC, the German Federal Cartel Office has established a Market Transparency Unit (*Markttransparenzstelle*) to mitigate the risk of collusion, with collected price data being made available to consumers in real time.

According to the case law of the German Federal Supreme Court, a decision by an association of undertakings exists if the association '*expresses its serious intention to coordinate the market conduct of its members.*'[82] This interpretation corresponds to the understanding of the term under Article 101 TFEU. The effectiveness of such a resolution under civil or company law is irrelevant for the purposes of sec. 1 ARC.[83]

5.2.3 Restrictions of Competition

5.2.3.1 Principles

As under Article 101 TFEU, a distinction must be drawn between horizontal and vertical restraints of competition when applying the German prohibition of cartels. The two forms of restraint differ in nature. This is reflected, on the one hand, in the simplified exemption requirements applicable to vertical agreements, and on the other, in the historical development of German competition law. Prior to the entry into force of the 7th amendment to the ARC in 2005, German law contained a separate provision for the prohibition of vertical agreements. This was set out in sec. 14 ARC (old version) and covered only vertical price maintenance. Other vertical agreements were subject solely to abuse control under sec. 16 ARC (old version). Sec. 1 ARC (old version) applied exclusively to horizontal agreements.[84] The inclusion of vertical agreements within the scope of today's sec.1 ARC is persuasive, particularly in the context of digital markets. Platform operators whose agreements with commercial users are classified as vertical often possess significant market power, making the restrictive effects of such agreements readily apparent.

In addition to the chapter on Article 101 TFEU, certain categories of horizontal and vertical restraints of competition are set out below. In principle, the principles set out with regard to European competition law[85] apply equally to sec. 1 ARC.

---

81 German Federal Cartel Office, Sektoruntersuchung Kraftstoffmärkte, 2011.

82 German Federal Supreme Court 14 August 2008 – KVR 54/07, NJOZ 2008, 4318, 4318 – *Lottoblock* [quote translated by author].

83 Zimmer (2024), sec. 1 ARC mn. 39.

84 Glöckner (2021), mn. 493-497.

85 For further details on the European principles, see ► 2.2.2.

5.2.3.2 Horizontal Restrictions of Competition

Hardcore Cartels

In parallel with the legal situation under Article 101 TFEU, sec. 1 ARC also covers hardcore cartels. These are agreements in which undertakings directly coordinate a key parameter of competition. Such infringements regularly attract substantial fines.

► Examples

Price agreements, territorial or customer allocations, quota arrangements ◄

Research and Development Agreements

For the assessment of research and development agreements under sec. 1 ARC, reference can be made to the Commission's Horizontal Guidelines.[86] According to these guidelines, the link of the cooperation to a specific product or technology is particularly relevant. If the research and development agreement concerns early innovation effort it is unlikely to restrict competition. The extent to which the agreement includes joint commercialisation or production is also a decisive factor. The history of German competition law shows that research and development collaborations have always been viewed ambivalently: on the one hand, co-operation that serves purely research purposes is generally unlikely to restrict competition; on the other hand, such agreements can nevertheless alter market conditions.[87] Where an R&D co-operation restricts competition, it must be examined whether it qualifies for exemption under sec. 2(2) ARC in conjunction with the R&D Block Exemption Regulation.

In digital markets, research and development co-operation may relate, in particular, to Industry 4.0 technologies, the Internet of Things, or AI-related research topics.[88] Where such collaborations are of a novel type, making their assessment under competition law uncertain for the undertakings involved, they may request a so-called 'chairman's letter' from the German Federal Cartel Office pursuant to sec. 32c(2) ARC. This is an informal communication in which the Office indicates that it will refrain from initiating proceedings. Undertakings, however, have no legal entitlement to receive such a notification; its issuance lies within the discretion of the Federal Cartel Office.[89] By contrast, if the undertakings concerned can demonstrate a 'significant legal and economic interest,' sec. 32c(4) ARC grants them the right to obtain a formal decision as to whether the authority considers there to be grounds for intervention.

---

86 Commission, Horizontal Guidelines, 2023, para. 133 et seqq.
87 Zimmer (2024), sec. 1 ARC mn. 146.
88 For further details, see ► 2.2.2.2.
89 Bach (2024), sec. 32c ARC mn. 36.

Exchange of Information

Cases concerning the exchange of information have to date primarily involved price reporting. In such arrangements, undertakings use a reporting centre to obtain information on the prices charged by their competitors and the terms on which contracts have been concluded.[90] The Federal Court of Justice has held that such reporting procedures, although lacking binding character, can nevertheless restrict competition by reducing its secrecy.[91] This is particularly true where the procedure enables participants to identify which competitor has reported which prices.[92] Even non-identifying price reporting procedures may raise competition law concerns: while they do not directly reveal which undertaking demands the reported conditions, they may still facilitate reactive conduct among undertakings in concentrated markets.[93]

Similar principles apply when information is exchanged through the use of algorithms.[94] Algorithms can serve as an effective means of facilitating such exchanges. In the *Eturas* case decided by the ECJ, this became relevant when competitors used the same algorithm, leading to coordinated outcomes.[95] The German Federal Cartel Office has addressed cases of **cooperative data use** on platforms as a sub-category of information exchange.[96] It has stressed that '*the parties and others must act independently of each other and maintain the necessary safeguards to shield transaction-related information from third parties.*'[97] This aligns with the approach taken in the Commission's Horizontal Guidelines:

> » *Participants in a reciprocal data-sharing arrangement such as a data pool should in principle only have access to their own information and the final, aggregated, information of other participants. Technical and practical measures can ensure that a participant is unable to obtain commercially sensitive information from other participants individually*.'[98]

▶ Example

The German Federal Cartel Office raised no competition concerns regarding the creation of an electronic trading platform for steel products.[99] The platform's purpose was to open up access to digital sales channels to a larger group of smaller suppliers and customers

90 Zimmer (2024), sec. 1 ARC mn. 163.
91 German Federal Supreme Court 29 January 1975 – KRB 4/74, NJW 1975, 1599 – *Aluminium-Halbzeug*.
92 Higher Regional Court of Duesseldorf 26 July 2002 – Kart 37/01 (V), WuW 2002, 1091 – *Transportbeton Sachsen*.
93 German Federal Cartel Office 11 April 2007 – B3-578/06 – *Phonak/GN Store Nord*.
94 For further details on the use of algorithms, see ▶ 2.2.2.2.
95 ECJ 21 January 2016 – C-74/14, ECLI:EU:C:2016:42 – *Eturas*.
96 German Federal Cartel Office, Decision of 25 September 2000, B5-40/00 – *Covisint*; German Federal Cartel Office, Decision of 26 January 2001 – B3-110/00 – *RubberNetwork*.
97 German Federal Cartel Office, Decision of 23 October 2000 – B3-76/00 [quote translated by author].
98 Commission, Horizontal Guidelines, 2023, para. 408.
99 German Federal Cartel Office, Decision of 27 February 2018 – B5-1/18-001 [following quotes translated by author].

and to facilitate the search for suitable contractual partners. The Office examined whether the increased market transparency resulting from the platform's operation could restrict competition. It concluded that the platform was structured so that '*providers cannot access data that would allow conclusions to be drawn about the competitive conduct of their competitors.*' Moreover, it ensured that '*neither specific prices nor availability information is displayed for existing or new customers on the platform outside of the login area.*' ◄

Standardisation Agreements

As explained in relation to the European ban on cartels, standardisation agreements can both intensify competition and enhance market transparency.[100] However, they may also restrict innovation competition. The Commission's Guidelines on Horizontal Agreements apply mutatis mutandis to their assessment under German competition law.[101] Until the 7th amendment to the ARC entered into force, German competition law contained special provisions on standardisation as well as on type and condition cartels. These have now been repealed, and such agreements are assessed under the general prohibition of cartels pursuant to secs. 1, 2 ARC. In practice, the German Federal Cartel Office has repeatedly emphasised that participation in standardisation processes must remain open and non-discriminatory, and that access to essential standard-related technologies should be granted on fair, reasonable and non-discriminatory (FRAND) terms.

Purchase and Sales Agreements

Purchasing pools can restrict **competition on the demand side**, particularly where they involve purchasing commitments.[102] Such commitments need not be based on a formal legal agreement; they may also result from the exertion of economic pressure that effectively causes customers to abandon their individual purchasing activities. By contrast, where cooperation between buyers enables them to enter a market and purchase products in the first place, the arrangement will generally not be considered a restriction of competition.

Learning Goals

In contrast to the case law of the European courts, the German Federal Supreme Court takes the view that the procurement activities of the public sector fall within the competition-law functional concept of an undertaking, even where these activities serve non-economic purposes.[103]

With respect to sales syndicates, the assessment focuses on the effects on competition. A restriction of competition is likely where participating undertakings are obliged to market their products exclusively through a joint organisation. Even in the absence of such an obligation, concerns under sec. 1 ARC may arise if under-

100 Kling and Thomas (2016), sec. 19 mn. 124.
101 For the evaluation of standardisation agreements under Article 101 TFEU, see ► 2.2.2.2.
102 German Federal Supreme Court 12 November 2002 – KZR 11/01, NJW 2003, 1748 – *Ausrüstungsgegenstände für Feuerlöschzüge*.
103 For further details on this issue, see ► 5.1.4.1.

takings voluntarily refrain from selling their products outside the joint structure.[104] This may be the case, for example, where the syndicate imposes most-favoured-nation clauses requiring the participating undertakings to offer it conditions no less favourable than those granted to other buyers.[105]

5.2.3.3 Vertical Restrictions of Competition

Pricing Restrictions

As in European competition law, sec. 1 ARC prohibits both **fixed and minimum resale price maintenance.**[106]

5

▶ **Examples**

'The resale price is EUR 25.00.'; 'The resale price is at least EUR 49.95.' ◀

The legal assessment of **maximum resale price maintenance** is more controversial. While such arrangements allow retailers to reduce prices, potentially benefiting consumers, they may also impair innovation competition by preventing price increases above a set ceiling.[107] Above all, they restrict the retailer's competitive freedom of action. As a general rule, maximum price maintenance constitutes a restriction of competition under sec. 1 ARC. Prior to the 7th amendment to the ARC, it was prohibited under sec. 14 ARC (old version).

▶ **Example**

'The maximum resale price is EUR 15.00.' ◀

Within the scope of the exemption, the VBER applies by virtue of the dynamic reference in sec. 2(2) ARC. Accordingly, maximum resale price maintenance is exempted if it falls within the scope of application of the Block Exemption Regulation pursuant to Article 2(1) VBER.

Non-binding price recommendations remain permissible unless they have the de facto effect of fixed or minimum prices. The German Federal Cartel Office adopts a strict interpretation: the non-binding character of a price recommendation is already called into question if it is 'subsequently and again' raised for discussion and thereby 'emphasised.'[108] Pressure may also arise if the manufacturer advertises the 'recommended' price directly to end customers.[109]

---

104 Zimmer (2024), sec. 1 ARC mn. 131.

105 German Federal Supreme Court 19 June 1975 – KVR 2/74, NJW 1975, 1837 – *Zementverkaufsstelle Niedersachsen*.

106 German Federal Supreme Court 15 March 1973 – KZR 11/72, NJW 1973, 1238 – *Bremsrollen*; Higher Regional Court of Duesseldorf 13 September 2006 – VI-Kart 2/06 (OWi), BeckRS 2006, 12713 – *OTC-Präparate*.

107 Zimmer (2024), ARC sec. 1 mn. 95.

108 German Federal Cartel Office, Decision of 25 September 2009 – B3-123/08 [quotes translated by author].

109 German Federal Supreme Court 8 April 2003 – KZR 3/02, NJW 2003, 2682 – *1 Riegel extra*.

Prohibitions on Internet Sales

The complete exclusion of distribution via the Internet constitutes a violation of the German cartel prohibition.[110] Such exclusion does not amount to a qualitative selection of distribution channels.[111] Under the VBER, the complete ban on internet sales is classified as a hardcore restriction pursuant to Art. Article 4(e) VBER.[112] In its 2009 decision regarding the contact lens case, the German Federal Cartel Office held that a total prohibition of online sales was unlawful.[113] The manufacturer had justified the ban on grounds of health protection, but this argument was rejected.

Platform Bans

The question of whether platform bans, i.e., a manufacturer's prohibition on selling products via online trading platforms, violate sec. 1 ARC has been **assessed inconsistently by German courts**. The Berlin Regional Court held that the exclusion of sales via the *eBay* platform constituted a breach of competition law.[114] The court reasoned that the manufacturer's requirements were '*in any case not based on objective aspects of a qualitative nature*', as they generally excluded sales via the internet platform eBay regardless of compliance with any qualitative standards. In other words, '*the general ban on the sale of goods via eBay*' did not constitute a legitimate qualitative criterion for selecting resellers.[115] This assessment was subsequently confirmed by the Higher Regional Court of Berlin.[116]

▶ **Example**

Simplified facts on the decisions regarding *Schulranzen* according to the Regional Court of Berlin 5 August 2008 – 16 O 287/08: A manufacturer of high-quality school backpacks and satchels had established specific criteria for selecting retailers authorized to distribute its products. Among these criteria, the manufacturer prohibited sales via eBay and comparable online auction platforms, stating that such sales were not permitted '*according to the current state of the design of these formats*.'[117] The manufacturer argued that this restriction was necessary to maintain a high standard of service.[118] Additionally, it claimed that auction platforms had degenerated in public perception into a '*flea market*.'[119] ◀

---

110 Zimmer (2024), ARC sec. 1 mn. 214.
111 Dethof (2012), pp. 503, 514.
112 For further details on Article 4(e) VBER, see ▶ 2.2.5.2.1.
113 German Federal Cartel Office, Decision of 25 September 2009 – B3-123/08 – *Kontaktlinsen*.
114 Regional Court Berlin 5 August 2008 – 16 O 287/08, GRUR-RR 2009, 115 – *eBay-Verbot*.
115 Regional Court Berlin 5 August 2008 – 16 O 287/08, GRUR-RR 2009, 115, 116 – *eBay-Verbot* [quotes translated by author].
116 Higher Regional Court of of Berlin 19 September 2013 – 2 U 8/09 Kart, NZKart 2014, 72 – *Schulranzen*.
117 Regional Court Berlin 5 August 2008 – 16 O 287/08, GRUR-RR 2009, 115, 115 – *eBay-Verbot* [quote translated by author].
118 Higher Regional Court of Berlin 19 September 2013 – 2 U 8/09 Kart, NZKart 2014, 72 juris-mn. 14 (not printed in NZKart reference) – *Schulranzen*.
119 Regional Court Berlin 21 April 2009 – 16 O 729/07 Kart, BB 2009, 1381, 1381 juris-mn. 23 (not reprinted in BB reference) – *eBay-Verbot* [quote translated by author].

In a parallel case concerning the sale of school wreaths and sacks, the Higher Regional Court of Karlsruhe reached a different conclusion.[120] The court held that a platform ban did not violate sec. 1 ARC or Article 101 TFEU. It reasoned that

> » *the requirements for distributing branded products via the Internet, like those for a physical retail shop, pertain to the necessary equipment and setup of the reseller. If a reseller wished to sell online, they had to maintain an Internet presence that met these requirements. According to the court, sales via eBay and comparable auction platforms did not satisfy the prescribed criteria, as these platforms did not meet the standards set by the manufacturer. In this sense, the court treated platform distribution as a suitable qualitative criterion within a selective distribution system. The Mannheim Regional Court reached a similar conclusion, supporting the view that such restrictions could be compatible with competition law'.*[121]

The Higher Regional Court of Karlsruhe considered platform distribution to be a valid **qualitative criterion for a selective distribution system**, a view also supported by the Mannheim Regional Court.[122]

In the context of **luxury perfumes** sold through a selective distribution system, the Higher Regional Court of Frankfurt on the Main held that a prohibition on using third-party sales platforms for online sales does not constitute a hardcore restriction, provided the manufacturer allows the use of search engines or price comparison sites.[123] European case law had previously indicated that platform bans can serve as an appropriate selection criterion, particularly for luxury goods.[124] In 2018, the Higher Regional Court of Hamburg extended this reasoning, assuming that platform bans may also be permissible for products that are not technically high-quality or luxury items.[125] The case in question concerned the sale of food supplements and cosmetics.

The **values set out in the VBER** are relevant for the future evaluation of platform bans under sec. 1 ARC. According to the updated VBER, platform bans may be permissible in the selective distribution of **branded goods**. Recital 15 VBER specifies that, when determining whether a restriction constitutes a hardcore restriction under Article 4(e) VBER, 'the content and context of the restriction, but should not depend on market-specific circumstances or the individual characteristics of the parties'. The 2022 Vertical Guidelines also cite '*high-quality or high-*

---

120 Higher Regional Court of Karlsruhe 25 November 2009 – 6 U 47/08 Kart, GRUR-RR 2010, 109 – *Schulranzen*.

121 Higher Regional Court of Karlsruhe 25 November 2009 – 6 U 47/08 Kart, GRUR-RR 2010, 109, 111 – *Schulranzen* [quote translated by author].

122 Regional Court Mannheim 14 March 2008 – 7 O 263/07 Kart, GRUR-RR 2008, 253 – *Schulranzen*.

123 Higher Regional Court of Frankfurt (on the Main) 12 July 2018 – 11 U 96/14 (Kart), GRUR 2018, 1171 – *Luxusparfüm im Internet II*.

124 ECJ 6 December 2017 – C-230/16, ECLI:EU:C:2017:941 – *Coty Germany*, see 2.2.2.3.3.

125 Higher Regional Court of Hamburg 22 March 2018 – 3 U 250/16, NZKart 2018, 590 – *Aloe Vera-Produkte*.

technology products'[126] as examples of goods for which selective distribution, including the exclusion of certain platforms, may be justified.

Restrictions on the Use of Price Comparison Services and Search Engines

German case a ban on the use of price comparison services to constitute an unauthorised, **non-exempt vertical restriction of competition**.[127] The Higher Regional Court of Duesseldorf held that a general prohibition on such services '*impairs [retailers'] competitive room for manoeuvre*,'[128] affecting not only intra-brand competition but also inter-brand competition. The Federal Court of Justice had already reached the same conclusion in 2017 in the *Asics* case.[129] This approach aligns with the current interpretation under Article 4(e) VBER.[130] At the same time, specific requirements for how goods are presented on a retailer's own website remain permissible.[131] For instance, manufacturers may require the use of photos of a certain minimum quality[132] or demand that retailers provide telephone advice to customers.[133]

Parity Obligations

The German Federal Cartel Office and German case law have repeatedly examined price parity clauses used by hotel booking platforms. In assessing these clauses under competition law, a distinction is made between **narrow and broad price parity clauses**. Narrow price parity clauses prevent providers from offering more favourable prices or better conditions on their own websites, effectively restricting only direct website pricing. In contrast, broad price parity clauses extend this restriction to other alternative distribution channels, including bookings through competing platforms, thereby having a wider impact on market competition.

The German Federal Cartel Office considers both narrow and broad price parity clauses to be **incompatible with sec. 1 ARC** because they restrict the competitive freedom of retailers.[134] Under these clauses, retailers cannot offer better prices either on their own websites or through alternative sales channels, which effectively forecloses competition. This strengthens the platform operator's position in the market for intermediary services, as end users are likely to focus on the platform

---

126 Commission, Vertical Guidelines, 2022, para. 149.
127 Higher Regional Court of Duesseldorf 5 April 2019 – VI-Kart 2/16 (V), NZKart 2019, 503 – *Preisvergleichsportale*.
128 Higher Regional Court of Duesseldorf 5 April 2019 – VI-Kart 2/16 (V), NZKart 2019, 503, 505 – *Preisvergleichsportale* [quote translated by author].
129 German Federal Supreme Court 12 December 2017 – KVZ 41/17, NZKart 2018, 96 – *Asics*.
130 For further details, see ► 2.2.2.3.
131 Regional Court Mannheim 14 March 2008 – 7 O 263/07, GRUR-RR 2008, 253, 256 – *Schulranzen* (on sec. 20 ARC).
132 Zimmer (2024), sec. 1 ARC mn. 214.
133 Dreyer and Lemberg (2012), pp. 2004, 2008.
134 German Federal Cartel Office, Decision of 20 December 2013 – B9-66/10, mn. 153 et seq. – *HRS Bestpreisklausel*; German Federal Cartel Office, Decision of 22 December 2015 – B9-121/13, mn. 159 et seqq. – *Booking.com*.

offering the best terms, leaving little incentive to explore other channels. Narrow price parity clauses mitigate these effects to some extent, as they only prevent more favourable pricing on the retailer's own website.

In 2019, the Higher Regional Court of Duesseldorf held that narrow price parity clauses were a necessary ancillary part of the platform usage agreement between hotel providers and booking platforms, and therefore **excluded them from sec. 1 ARC.**[135] The court reasoned that without such clauses, a free-rider problem would arise: hotels could divert customers acquired via the platform to their own websites.[136] However, the German Federal Supreme Court disagreed, ruling that narrow price parity clauses are not objectively necessary for the business model of a hotel booking platform.[137] Instead, they serve to combat the free-rider problem by restricting the price as the most important competitive parameter to a significant degree.[138] Consequently, the Federal Supreme Court considers both narrow and broad best-price clauses incompatible with sec. 1 ARC and Article 101 TFEU.

Regarding exemptions under sec. 2 ARC, the VBER also plays a key role for the German ban on cartels. Broad price parity clauses are considered non-exemptable under **Article 5(1)(d) VBER**. Narrow price parity clauses, while still constituting a vertical restriction of competition, are generally exempted within the scope of the VBER. However, under Article 6 VBER, the exemption can be withdrawn in individual cases.

Exclusivity Agreements

Exclusivity agreements arise when customers commit to purchasing exclusively or predominantly from a particular supplier, or conversely, when suppliers commit to supplying exclusively or predominantly to a specific customer. Such agreements can potentially foreclose the market and therefore violate sec. 1 ARC. The assessment of whether a violation occurs follows the principles established under Article 101 TFEU,[139] taking particular account of the market coverage of the agreement, its duration, and the market shares of the parties involved. The VBER does not protect agreements that exceed certain thresholds: a total market share of more than 30 % (cf. Article 3 VBER), coverage of more than 80 % of the total procurement of the contract goods or services on the relevant market (cf. Article 1(f) VBER), or a duration exceeding five years (cf. Article 5(1)(a) VBER).

This aligns with German case law principles. In the gas supply contracts case, the German Federal Supreme Court ruled that contracts under which customers

---

135 Higher Regional Court of Duesseldorf 4 June 2019 – VI-Kart 2/16 (V), NZKart 2019, 379 – *Enge Bestpreisklausel II*. In contrast, in 2016, the Higher Regional Court of Duesseldorf ruled otherwise, cf. Higher Regional Court of Duesseldorf 4 May 2016 – VI-Kart 1/16 (V), NZKart 2016, 291 – *Booking.com*.

136 Higher Regional Court of Duesseldorf 4 June 2019 – VI-Kart 2/16 (V), NZKart 2019, 379, 382 – *Enge Bestpreisklausel II*.

137 German Federal Supreme Court 18 May 2021 – KVR 54/20, GRUR 2021, 1213 – *Booking.com*.

138 German Federal Supreme Court 18 May 2021 – KVR 54/20, GRUR 2021, 1213, 1216 – *Booking.com*.

139 On exclusivity agreements in the context of EU competition law, see ► 2.2.2.3.

source around 80–100% of their requirements from a single supplier should not exceed a term of two years.[140] Where the supply volume covers 50–80% of requirements, a contract term of up to four years is generally permissible.[141] The Court reached this conclusion by considering the supplier's market power and the barriers to market entry.[142] Using the bundling theory, it also accounted for the market coverage achieved through the supplier's contracts.

▶ Example

In the *Eventim* case, the German Federal Cartel Office found that the exclusive agreement violated sec. 1 ARC. Under this agreement, the contracting parties committed to sell their tickets exclusively or predominantly through the operator of Germany's largest ticketing platform.[143] The foreclosure effect was significant because *Eventim* held a dominant position in the market. Additionally, the agreement breached sec. 19 ARC.[144] Due to the platform's high market share, the agreement could not benefit from an exemption under Article 2(1) VBER. ◀

5.2.3.4 Object or Effect of Preventing, Restricting or Distorting Competition

A violation of sec. 1 ARC arises when a restriction of competition has either an object or an effect, in line with the principles of Article 101 TFEU.[145] A restriction is considered to have the object of restricting competition if it is inherently harmful to competition by its very nature, without the need for further analysis of its market effects. If it cannot be classified as having the object of restricting competition, it must then be assessed based on its actual or potential effects on the market to determine whether it constitutes a restriction of competition.

5.2.3.5 Appreciability

The German Federal Cartel Office has issued a **De Minimis Notice**[146] to clarify the threshold of appreciability for competition law enforcement. Similar to the Commission's de minimis notice,[147] it explains when the Office will generally refrain

140 German Federal Supreme Court 10 February 2009 – KVR 67/07, NJW-RR 2009, 1635, 1638 – *Gaslieferverträge*.
141 German Federal Supreme Court 10 February 2009 – KVR 67/07, NJW-RR 2009, 1635, 1638 – *Gaslieferverträge*.
142 German Federal Supreme Court 10 February 2009 – KVR 67/07, NJW-RR 2009, 1635, 1638 et seq. – *Gaslieferverträge*.
143 Higher Regional Court of Duesseldorf 3 April 2019 – Kart 2/18 (V), NZKart 2019, 282 – *Ticketvertrieb II*; German Federal Cartel Office, Decision of 4 December 2017 – B6-132/14-2 – *Eventim*.
144 German Federal Cartel Office, Decision of 4 December 2017 – B6-132/14-2, paras. 71 et seqq. – *Eventim*.
145 For further details on these conditions under Article 101(1) TFEU, see ▶ 2.2.2.4.
146 German Federal Cartel Office, Notice no. 18/2007 des Bundeskartellamtes über die Nichtverfolgung von Kooperationsabreden mit geringer wettbewerbsbeschränkender Bedeutung, 2007.
147 Notice on agreements of minor importance which do not appreciably restrict competition within the meaning of Article 101(1) of the Treaty on the Functioning of the European Union, OJ [2019] C 291/1.

from initiating proceedings due to the insignificance of a restriction.[148] For horizontal agreements, the Office typically does not pursue action under sec. 1 ARC or Article 101 TFEU if the market share of the undertakings involved does not exceed **10%** on any of the relevant markets.[149] For vertical agreements, the corresponding threshold is **15%**.[150] Core restrictions, however, are excluded from this de minimis approach. These include agreements that fix prices or price components for third parties, or that restrict production, procurement, or sales.

5.2.4 Unwritten Exceptions

5.2.4.1 Principles

In line with European law, German case law recognises **unwritten exceptions** to the ban on cartels. These are instances, where the literal wording of sec. 1 ARC is fulfilled, but the agreement is not considered contrary to the purpose and meaning of the provision. Because German and European cartel prohibitions operate concurrently, reference can be made to the European framework.[151] Under Article 101 TFEU, European case law has recognised certain non-competitive interests, such as the freedom to conclude collective agreements, the interests of sport, and the legislative powers of bar associations, as grounds for excluding agreements from the prohibition. Additionally, doctrines like the commercial agent privilege, market development doctrine, and group privilege have been developed. German competition law has its own particularities in this regard, but these do not disrupt the overall alignment with European law. The primary differences lie in the terminology used for the restrictions and the justifications cited by German case law.

5.2.4.2 Idea of Immanence

According to the concept of immanence (*Immanenztheorie*), the prohibition of cartels under sec. 1 ARC must undergo teleological reduction when a restriction of competition is necessary to achieve the main purpose of an agreement that is otherwise neutral in terms of competition law.[152] This aligns with the concept of ancillary restraints under Article 101 TFEU.[153] The concept has practical relevance in cases

148 German Federal Cartel Office, Announcement no. 18/2007 des Bundeskartellamtes über die Nichtverfolgung von Kooperationsabreden mit geringer wettbewerbsbeschränkender Bedeutung, 2007, mn. 1.

149 German Federal Cartel Office, Announcement no. 18/2007 des Bundeskartellamtes über die Nichtverfolgung von Kooperationsabreden mit geringer wettbewerbsbeschränkender Bedeutung, 2007, mn. 8.

150 German Federal Cartel Office, Notice no. 18/2007 des Bundeskartellamtes über die Nichtverfolgung von Kooperationsabreden mit geringer wettbewerbsbeschränkender Bedeutung, 2007, mn. 9.

151 See ► 2.2.4.

152 German Federal Supreme Court 3 May 1988 – KZR 17/87, NJW 1988, 273 – *neuform-Artikel*; German Federal Supreme Court 19 October 1993 – KZR 3/92, NJW 1994, 384 – *Ausscheidender Gesellschafter*.

153 On the concept of ancillary restraints, see ► 2.2.4.2.

such as non-competition clauses in **business sale agreements**, which serve to protect the value of the undertaking, including goodwill and existing expertise.[154] Post-contractual non-compete and customer protection clauses are also commonly agreed in **subcontractor agreements**. While such clauses restrict competition, they are exempt from sec. 1 ARC if necessary to prevent the loss of customers from the undertaking.[155] Compatibility with sec. 1 ARC requires that the non-competition obligation is limited to what is necessary in terms of subject matter, territory, and duration. If the clause exceeds what is necessary, a reduction in its scope must be examined.[156]

5.2.4.3 Working Group Privilege

The working group privilege (‘*Arbeitsgemeinschaftsgedanke*’) is based on the principle that competitors who can only participate in the market jointly, such as by submitting a bid for a tendered construction project,[157] do not restrict competition through their cooperation but rather promote it.[158] This closely aligns with the concept of market development recognised under European law.[159] In the digital context, the working group concept can facilitate collaboration, for example, in developing new solutions in Industry 4.0.[160] The German Federal Court of Justice applies the concept when independent action by competitors would be economically or commercially unreasonable,[161] without requiring proof that an undertaking could not operate independently.[162]

5.2.5 Exemption Requirements

5.2.5.1 Principles

The requirements for exemption from the ban on cartels are governed by sec. 2(1) ARC, which mirrors the conditions set out in Article 101(3) TFEU. Under sec. 2(2) ARC, there is a dynamic reference to the European block exemption regulations, meaning these also apply when assessing exemptions under German cartel law. The examination follows the same sequence as in European law: it must first be determined whether a block exemption regulation applies. If it does not apply, or if it

154 German Federal Supreme Court 23 June 2009 – KZR 58/07, NZG 2010, 76 – *Gratiszeitung Hallo*; Higher Regional Court of Duesseldorf 15 August 2007 – VI-U (Kart) 11/07, BeckRS 2008, 3524 – *Anzeigenblatt-GU*; Dreher and Kulka (2023), mn. 1048.

155 Higher Regional Court of Duesseldorf 15 May 2019 – VI-W (Kart) 4/19, NZKart 2019, 386, 388 – *Nachvertragliches Wettbewerbsverbot*.

156 Dreher and Kulka (2023), mn. 1052.

157 German Federal Supreme Court 13 December 1983 – KRB 3/83, BB 1984, 364 – *Bauvorhaben Schramberg*.

158 Müller-Feldhammer (2019), pp. 463, 464.

159 See ► 2.2.4.3.

160 Ecker et al. (2021), p. 44.

161 German Federal Supreme Court 13 December 1983 – KRB 3/83, BB 1984, 364 – *Bauvorhaben Schramberg*; German Federal Supreme Court 5 February 2002 – KZR 3/01, GRUR 2002, 644. 646 – *Jugend- und Frauenennachtfahrten*.

162 Higher Regional Court of Duesseldorf 17 January 2018 – VII-Verg 39/17, NZKart 2018, 153, 154 – *Bidding consortium for dredging work*.

does not grant an exemption in the specific case, the next step is to assess the possibility of an individual exemption under sec. 2(1) ARC. In this process, it is crucial to remember that block exemption regulations are intended to concretise the general requirements for specific categories of restrictions on competition.

5.2.5.2 Block Exemptions

Sec. 2(2) ARC contains a **dynamic reference** to the current version of the block exemption regulations.[163] By doing so, the German legislator has, to some extent, transferred its regulatory authority to the European legislator.[164] This reference means that even in cases where a cartel is not likely to affect interstate trade, an exemption must first be assessed under the European block exemption regulations. The dynamic reference has been criticised on constitutional grounds,[165] particularly with regard to the principle of democracy, which requires that state laws be based on the will of the people.[166] Nevertheless, the reference is considered sufficiently specific, and, importantly, the German legislator retains the ability to revoke it at any time.[167]

5.2.5.3 Sec. 2 ARC Criteria

The requirements for an individual exemption under sec. 2(1) ARC are identical to those of Article 101(3) TFEU and must all be satisfied cumulatively. First, the agreement must result in efficiency gains; second, consumers on the opposite market side must receive an appropriate share of these benefits; third, the restriction of competition must be indispensable for achieving the efficiencies; and fourth, the agreement must not eliminate competition in a substantial part of the relevant markets.

Both static and dynamic **efficiency gains** are relevant, such as cost reductions through economies of scale or scope, or the introduction of new product variants that enhance market variety and consumer welfare. **Appropriate** consumer participation requires that the efficiencies at least offset the negative effects of the restriction, though they do not need to outweigh them. The assessment of whether competition is eliminated depends largely on the cartel's market coverage; if competitive pressure is too weak, consumer participation may already be lacking because the cartel members have little incentive to pass on cost savings to the market.

Checklist: Assessing Collusive Conduct Under Sec. 1, 2 ARC

1. **Agreement, concerted practice, or decision**
   an agreement between undertakings, a decision by an association of undertakings or a concerted practice.

163 Ehricke and Blask (2003), pp. 722, 724; Ellger (2024), sec. 2 ARC mn. 233.
164 If no Block Exemption Regulation applies or no exemption results from it, the possibility of individual exemption pursuant to sec. 2(1) ARC remains.
165 Ehricke and Blask (2003), pp. 722, 725–727; Heyers (2025), sec. 2 ARC mn. 12 et seq.
166 Ehricke and Blask (2003), pp. 722, 725.
167 Ellger (2024), sec. 2 ARC mn. 234; Schneider (2021), sec. 2 ARC mn. 66.

2. **Restriction of competition**
   (a) **Horizontal or vertical dimension**: Horizontal agreements occur between actual or potential competitors. Vertical agreements occur between undertakings at different levels of the supply chain (e.g., manufacturer and distributor).
   (b) **By object or by effect**: The conduct must have the object or effect of preventing, restricting, or distorting competition within the internal market.
   (c) **De minimis doctrine**: The restriction must be appreciable; minor restraints with negligible market impact do not fall under sec. 1 ARC.

3. **No exclusion from the scope of sec. 1 ARC**

The conduct must not fall outside the **scope of sec. 1 ARC** due to public interests, lack of competitive significance or pro-competitive effects (e.g., group privilege, idea of immanence)

4. **No applicable exemption**
   (a) **Block exemption regulations**

Determine whether the agreement benefits from a **block exemption** (e.g. Vertical Agreements BER, R&D BER, Specialisation BER), cf. **sec. 2(2) ARC**

(b) **Individual exemption under sec. 2(1) ARC**

All four cumulative conditions must be satisfied:

- The agreement contributes to **improving production or distribution**, or promotes **technical or economic progress**;
- Consumers receive a **fair share** of the resulting benefits;
- The restrictions are **indispensable to achieving those efficiencies;**
- The agreement does not **eliminate competition** in respect of a substantial part of the relevant market.

5.3 Prohibition of Abuse: Secs. 18-21 ARC

5.3.1 Abuse of Market Dominance: Sec. 19 ARC

5.3.1.1 Introduction

Sec. 19(1) ARC largely corresponds to the prohibition of abuse under **Article 102 TFEU** in European competition law.[168] In contrast to Article 102 TFEU, however, a violation of the German provision does not require any potential to affect interstate trade. The examples set out in sec. 19(2) ARC differ from those in Article 102(2) TFEU, though this divergence is not relevant to the substantive scope of the prohibitions. In German legal practice, these statutory examples have assumed far greater importance than in the application of Article 102 TFEU. When applying the German prohibition of abuse, the Federal Cartel Office and the courts regu-

168 See ► 2.3.

larly distinguish between obstruction or discrimination (no. 1), exploitative abuse (no. 2), discriminatory splitting of conditions (no. 3), cases falling under the essential facilities doctrine (no. 4), and infringements of the prohibition on tapping (no. 5).

Overview of the Standard Examples under Sec. 19(2) ARC:
No. 1: Unfair hindrance of other undertakings or objectively unjustified discrimination.

No. 2: Exploitative abuse by demanding fees or other terms and conditions that deviate from those which would most likely prevail under conditions of effective competition.

No. 3: Discriminatory splitting of conditions by imposing less favourable charges or other terms and conditions than those applied by the dominant undertaking to similar customers in comparable markets.

No. 4: Denial of access to essential facilities that are objectively necessary for participation in an upstream or downstream market.

No. 5: 'Tapping' by requesting another undertaking to grant advantages to the dominant undertaking without an objectively justified reason.

German competition law also contains **prohibitions without counterparts in European competition law**. Sec. 19a ARC targets undertakings with paramount significance for competition across markets.[169] While the DMA[170] addresses similar concerns, it differs in its approach. Furthermore, sec. 20 ARC prohibits certain conduct by undertakings with relative market power even when they fall short of market dominance.[171] Although such rules have no equivalent in European competition law, they are consistent with European law by virtue of Article 3(2) 2nd sentence Regulation 1/2003, which allows member states to impose stricter competition rules on unilateral conduct.

! Unlike European competition law, the German prohibition of abuse is not limited to dominant undertakings. Sec. 20 ARC also applies to undertakings with a strong market position, while sec. 19a ARC targets undertakings with paramount significance for competition across markets.

5.3.1.2 Market Definition

Product Market

The prohibition of abuse under sec. 19 ARC applies only to undertakings with a dominant market position. As with Article 102 TFEU, the first step is to assess whether market dominance exists. This requires defining the relevant market under competition law, taking into account product, geographic, and, where appropriate, temporal dimensions.

---

169 For further details on sec. 19a ARC, see ► 5.3.2.
170 On the DMA, see section 3.
171 For further details on sec. 20 ARC, see ► 5.3.3.

In German competition law, as in European competition law,[172] the relevant product market is mainly defined using the **demand market concept**. This approach focuses on determining which products are interchangeable from the perspective of the demand side, based on their characteristics, intended use, and price (**demand-side substitutability**). The assessment hinges on actual consumer behaviour rather than purely objective or scientific considerations.[173] German case law typically places particular weight on the intended use of the products.[174] Price differences may also be relevant, though they usually play a secondary role. The German Federal Cartel Office, in line with European practice, has at times employed the **SSNIP test**[175] to assess demand substitutability.[176] The German Federal Supreme Court stresses that the test may serve as a helpful tool but cannot be the sole determinant of market definition.[177] The demand market concept is modified concept of **supply-side flexibility**. Products that are not currently offered, but whose production would be possible in the short term and without significant economic effort for the undertakings, are also part of the relevant product market.[178]

▶ Examples

When applying the demand market concept, the German Federal Cartel Office (consistent with European practice[179]) has distinguished between separate but related markets in the digital sector. For example, in the case of social networks, it differentiated between markets for social media services themselves, online advertising markets, and ancillary services such as social plug-ins, central log-ins, and measurement and analysis tools.[180]

Within online advertising, it further drew a line between search-based advertising (where ads are shown in response to specific search queries) and non-search-based advertising (e.g. display ads on websites or in social media feeds).[181] In its sec. 19a ARC decision in the *Alphabet–Google* case, the authority identified a distinct market for general search services, separating it from both content providers and specialised search services.[182] This mirrors the Commission's approach.[183]

---

172 For market definition in the context of EU competition lase, see ▶ 2.3.1.1.

173 German Federal Supreme Court 26 May 1987 – KVR 4/86, GRUR 1987, 928, 929 – *Gekoppelter Kartenverkauf*.

174 German Federal Supreme Court 19 March 1996 – KZR 1/95, WRP 1996, 905, 907 – *Pay-TV-Durchleitung*; German Federal Supreme Court 30 March 2011 – KZR 6/09, WRP 2011, 909, 910 – *MAN contract workshop*.

175 In detail ▶ 2.3.1.1.1.

176 German Federal Cartel Office, Decision of 30 September 2005 – B9-50/05 – *Railion/RBH*.

177 German Federal Supreme Court 4 March 2008 – KVR 21/07, NJW-RR 2008, 996.

178 German Federal Supreme Court 16 January 2007 – KVR 12/06, GRUR 2007, 520, 520 – *National Geographic II*.

179 Commission 3 October 2014 – COMP/M.7217 – *Facebook/Whatsapp*.

180 German Federal Cartel Office, Decision of 6 February 2019, B6-22/16, paras. 167 et seq., 352 et seq., 365 et seq. – *Facebook*.

181 German Federal Cartel Office, Decision of 6 February 2019, B6-22/16, para. 353 – *Facebook*.

182 German Federal Cartel Office, Decision of 30 December 2021 – B7-61/21, paras. 242 et seq. – *Alphabet-Google*.

183 Cf. e.g. Commission, Decision of 27 June 2017 – AT.39740, paras. 154 et seq. – *Google Search (Shopping)*; Commission, Decision of 18 July 2018 – AT.40099, paras. 323 et seq. – *Google Android*.

The reasoning was that specialised search services cater to a predefined and narrow user intent, such as finding the best flight or comparing product prices, whereas general search services must be able to respond to an unlimited range of queries across the entire internet. This requires significantly more complex indexing, crawling, and interpretation capabilities.[184] The German Federal Cartel Office also found that switching between general and specialised search services is limited, because the services differ substantially in their scope, technology, and the user needs they address.[185] ◄

Geographical Market

5

The relevant geographic market under German competition law is determined similarly to the product market, but instead of comparing products, the focus is on geographic areas.[186] The key question is: in which area do sufficiently homogeneous competitive conditions exist, so that firms can reasonably compete under similar conditions? This area may extend beyond Germany's borders if competition conditions are similar across regions. Sec. 18(2) ARC explicitly clarifies that the relevant geographic market can exceed the national scope of the law.[187] The analysis relies purely on economic criteria, such as the ease of cross-border supply, transport costs, regulatory barriers, and consumer behaviour, rather than legal or political boundaries.[188]

► Examples

Even when digital platforms are globally accessible, competition can still be geographically limited. The relevant geographic market is defined by the areas from which competitive pressures actually arise. For example, the German Federal Cartel Office has treated social networks as a national market.[189] While accessible worldwide, users mainly connect with others in Germany,[190] and services are often offered under national domains (e.g. facebook.de).[191] Switching to networks in other countries is constrained by direct network effects, meaning users cannot easily or economically migrate to foreign platforms.[192]

Similarly, online dating portals are considered national markets because users primarily seek contacts within their own country.[193] Search engines can also be national

---

184 German Federal Cartel Office, Decision of 30 December 2021 – B7-61/21, para. 250 – *Alphabet-Google*.

185 German Federal Cartel Office, Decision of 30 December 2021 – B7-61/21, para. 252 – *Alphabet-Google*.

186 German Federal Supreme Court 13 July 2004 – KVR 2/03, GRUR 2004, 1048, 1049 – *Sanacorp/ANZAG*.

187 Podszun (2025), sec. 18 ARC mn. 92.

188 Podszun (2025), sec. 18 ARC mn. 92.

189 German Federal Cartel Office, Decision of 6 February 2019 – B6-22/16 – *Facebook*.

190 German Federal Cartel Office, Decision of 6 February 2019 – B6-22/16, para. 346 – *Facebook*.

191 German Federal Cartel Office, Decision of 6 February 2019 – B6-22/16, para. 348 – *Facebook*.

192 German Federal Cartel Office, Decision of 6 February 2019 – B6-22/16, para. 350 – *Facebook*.

193 German Federal Cartel Office, Decision of 22 October 2015 – B6-57/15, para. 126 – *online dating platform*.

markets due to country-specific search results and national domains,[194] reflecting localized demand and competitive conditions.[195] ◄

Temporal Market

The temporally relevant market refers to the period during which the substitution relationships identified for the product and geographic market actually exist. When products or services are offered on a regular basis, defining a temporal market is generally not crucial for assessing abuse. However, it becomes relevant in situations where the competitive landscape changes quickly, such as the sale of tickets for sporting events like the Olympic Games, where consumers have only a short window to switch providers or access alternatives.[196]

Specifics of Digital Markets

Non-monetary Services

Similar to European competition law,[197] German competition law has debated whether unpaid or free-of-charge services can be considered part of a relevant market. With the 9th amendment to the ARC in 2017, the legislator clarified this issue by incorporating **sec. 18(2a) ARC**, explicitly stating that the existence of a market is not excluded merely because a service is offered free of charge. The German Federal Cartel Office had already treated such services as part of a relevant market in certain decisions,[198] although some older statements had suggested the opposite approach.[199]

! Sec. 18(2a) ARC explicitly provides that the existence of a market is not excluded simply because a service is offered free of charge.

Sec. 18(2a) ARC clarifies that offering a service free of charge *does not prevent* the assumption of a relevant market, but it does not define the **criteria** for when such gratuitous service relationships are considered part of an economic market. German case law has interpreted this in light of the principle that competition law seeks to capture **economic activity**. While monetary payment is the most obvious form of

---

194 German Federal Cartel Office, Decision of 22 October 2015 – B6-57/15, para. 126 – *online dating platform*.

195 German Federal Cartel Office, Decision of 8 September 2015 – B-126/14, para. 152 – *Google/VG Media*.

196 Fuchs (2024), sec. 18 ARC para. 67.

197 For further details, see ► 2.3.1.1.4.

198 German Federal Cartel Office, Decision of 25 June 2015 – B6-39/15 – *Online-Immobilienplattformen*; German Federal Cartel Office 22 October 2015 – B6-57/15 – *Online-Datingplattform*. See also German Federal Cartel Office 6 February 2019 – B6-22/16, para. 246 – *Facebook*: '*The fact that users do not pay a monetary fee for the private use of Facebook.com does not change the fact that the service is used to satisfy a specific need of the user in an economic sense and that the users therefore have the economic function of consumers of the product.*' [quote translated by author].

199 German Federal Cartel Office, Decision of of 3 April 2008 – B7-200/07 – *Kabel Deutschland/Orion*: '*A free service [...] cannot be regarded as a market service, since the latter conceptually presupposes an exchange relationship in return for payment.*' [quote translated by author].

consideration on traditional markets, on multi-sided digital platforms economic value can also arise from the provision of data[200] or user attention. For instance, the ability to deliver targeted advertising to a large user base carries significant economic value. **Positive indirect network effects** further amplify this value: as the number of end users on a platform increases, the benefit for advertisers or other business partners also grows. A parallel example is hotel booking platforms, where a larger user base increases the likelihood of hotel bookings through the platform, generating revenue via commissions.[201] This illustrates why digital platform operators may profitably offer free services to end users. When the free service is integral to the platform's profit-maximizing business model, it must be attributed economic value[202] and can therefore be treated as part of a relevant market under competition law.

▶ Example

To treat the free service relationship between consumers and *Google*'s general search service as a market under competition law, the German Federal Cartel Office highlights that the operation of the search engine is financed by third parties, specifically *Google*'s advertising customers. This financing is connected to the search service through indirect network effects.[203] Additionally, the Office points out that the user data collected from searches has clear economic value. This data allows *Google* to enhance the search functionality for users, making the service more attractive, and to increase the relevance of advertisements, thereby generating higher advertising revenues.[204] ◀

When applying the **demand market concept** to free service relationships, the analysis focuses on the **intended use and functions** of the platform rather than on a monetary price. Because the service is provided at zero cost, the traditional SSNIP test is ineffective. A small percentage increase in a zero price remains zero. Some literature proposes the **SSNDQ test**, which considers how consumers would react to a small but permanent deterioration in the quality[205] of the free service.[206] However, this approach faces practical challenges. It is difficult to measure objectively what constitutes a 'small deterioration' in quality,[207] and reliable data to predict consumer behaviour may be scarce.[208] In fast-moving, innovation-driven markets, any available data can quickly become outdated, further complicating the analysis.

200 Podszun (2025), sec. 18 ARC mn. 35.
201 Podszun (2025), sec. 18 ARC mn. 37.
202 Legner (2023), pp. 175, 179.
203 German Federal Cartel Office, Decision of 8 September 2015 – B6-124/14, para. 132 – *Google/VG Media*.
204 German Federal Cartel Office, Decision of 8 September 2015 – B6-124/14, para. 134 – *Google/VG Media*.
205 For example, the display of more annoying adverts when using social media could be considered.
206 For further details on the SSNDQ test, see ▶ 2.3.1.1.
207 Podszun and Schwalbe (2017), pp. 98, 102.
208 Fuchs (2024), sec. 18 ARC mn. 5.

Multi-Sided Markets

When defining multi-sided markets, the key question is whether the platform's different **user groups** belong to a single relevant product market or should be treated as separate markets. The German Federal Cartel Office applies the **demand market concept** to answer this question. The critical factor is whether the services provided to the different user groups are interchangeable from the perspective of those users.[209] If the services are considered substitutable by the users, the different groups are treated as part of the same market.

For property platforms[210] and online dating portals,[211] the German Federal Cartel Office has concluded that the different user groups belong to a single market. In the case of dating platforms, the Office holds that it is unnecessary to separate the 'market for men' from the 'market for women,'[212] as the platform provides a standardized service: facilitating personal and private contact between the two groups through a matching process.[213] Similarly, for property platforms, the service requested by property sellers and property seekers is uniformly classified as an intermediary service.[214] The existing indirect network effects between user groups do not justify treating them as separate markets.

In other cases, the services provided by a platform operator are not interchangeable. This is particularly clear when one user group receives the service free of charge, as with end users of social media or search services, while another user group pays a fee, such as advertisers.[215] From a demand perspective, these services are not substitutable because they satisfy different needs. Although indirect network effects exist between these groups, they do not justify defining a single market; however, these effects must be considered when analysing the platform operator's dominant position.[216]

The German Federal Cartel Office also considers the type of platform when delineating the market, distinguishing between **matching and attention platforms**.[217] For matching platforms, multiple user groups are generally allocated to a single market, whereas for attention platforms, separate product markets

209 German Federal Cartel Office, Market power of platforms and networks, 2016, p. 31.
210 German Federal Cartel Office, Decision of 25 June 2015 – B6-39/15 – *Online-Immobilienplattformen*.
211 German Federal Cartel Office, Decision of 22 October 2015 – B6-57/15, para. 71 – *Online-Datingplattform*: '*A delineation of markets along the platform pages – namely the user group of women on the one hand and the user group of men on the other – is not to be made.*' [quote translated by author].
212 German Federal Cartel Office, Decision of 22 October 2015 – B6-57/15, para. 75 – *Online-Datingplattform*.
213 German Federal Cartel Office, Decision of 22 October 2015 – B6-57/15, para. 75 – *Online-Datingplattform*.
214 German Federal Cartel Office, Decision of 5 June 2015 – B6-39/15, case report p. 3 – *Online-Immobilienplattformen*; German Federal Cartel Office, Decision of 24 July 2015 – B8-76/15, case report pp. 2 et seq. – *Online-Vergleichsplattformen*; German Federal Cartel Office, Market Power of Platforms and Networks, 2016, p. 31.
215 German Federal Supreme Court 23 June 2020 – KVR 69/19, NZKart 2020, 473 – *Facebook II*.
216 Fuchs (2024), sec. 18 ARC mn. 73b.
217 German Federal Cartel Office, Market Power of Platforms and Networks, 2016, pp. 23 et seq.

are assumed. However, this cannot be understood as a rigid requirement: separate markets may also be recognized for matching platforms if competitive conditions differ between the market sides, for example due to multi-homing by a user group.[218] The overarching objective of market definition is to identify the immediate competitive environment and the competitive forces acting on an undertaking. If competitive conditions differ significantly between two sides of a platform, separate markets must be assumed, regardless of the platform's categorisation.[219]

Learning Goals

5

Platform categorisation is applied inconsistently in competition practice. The types of platforms identified by the Commission in its market definition notice do not align with the categorisation used by the German Federal Cartel Office.[220]

5.3.1.3 Single Dominance

Concept of Single Dominance

In contrast to European competition law, German law expressly defines the concept of market dominance in **sec. 18 ARC**. In substance, this definition does not differ significantly from European law. Under national abuse law, a dominant market position is understood as the unilateral scope for conduct that allows an undertaking to act, to a certain extent, independently of its competitors, customers, or suppliers.[221] This independence does not imply complete freedom from competitive constraints but rather the ability to influence market conditions, prices, or terms of trade without being effectively restrained by other market participants.

Sec. 18(1) ARC distinguishes three categories of market dominance, the first of which, set out in sec. 18(1) no. 1 ARC, concerns **monopolists** that operate entirely without competitors and hold the entire market share. While large digital companies such as *Google* in the market for general search services[222] or *Facebook* in the market for social networks[223] may, according to the authorities' assessments, reach market shares exceeding 90%, this alone does not amount to a monopoly but rather to what is referred to as a quasi-monopoly. Genuine monopolies are more often found in regulated sectors such as telecommunications or rail transport, where legal or structural conditions effectively exclude competition. The exclusive ownership of a patent can also create a monopoly, as it grants the right to prevent any other undertaking from producing or selling the protected invention.[224] The German Federal Supreme

218 German Federal Cartel Office, Market Power of Platforms and Networks, 2016, pp. 69 et seqq.

219 For further details on different types of platforms, see ► 1.1.1.

220 For further details on these categorisations, see ► 1.1.1. and ► 2.3.1.2.

221 German Federal Supreme Court 3 July 1976 – KVR 4/75, GRUR 1977, 169, 172 – *Vitamin-B-12*.

222 Commission, Decision of 27 June 2017 – AT.39740, paras. 273 et seqq. – *Google Search (Shopping)*.

223 German Federal Cartel Office, Decision of 6 February 2019, B6-22/16, para. 389 et seq. – *Facebook*.

224 Wiedemann (2020), sec. 23 mn. 27.

Court has further recognised that most collecting societies hold monopoly positions due to the legal and practical exclusivity of their rights management activities.[225]

Sec. 18(1) no. 2 ARC applies to undertakings that face no significant competition, the **quasi-monopolists**.[226] According to case law, such a position is typically assumed where an undertaking holds a market share of around 90 % or more.[227] This situation is not uncommon in certain digital markets, where strong network effects, high entry barriers, and the accumulation of user data can reinforce such dominance. While market share remains an important indicator, its evidential weight may be reduced if other competitive parameters, such as the pace of innovation, the quality of the products or services, or the potential for disruptive market entry, play a role in shaping the market dynamics. Nevertheless, when an undertaking's market share exceeds 90 %, it is generally difficult to refute the presumption of market dominance.

Sec. 18(1) no. 3 ARC broadens the concept of **market dominance** to include undertakings that hold a dominant position without necessarily having a monopoly or quasi-monopoly. The assessment of such dominance requires a comprehensive evaluation of various factors. In addition to the non-exhaustive list of criteria in sec. 18(3) ARC (such as market share, barriers to market entry, and access to sales and procurement markets) sec. 18(3a) ARC lists additional factors, which are specifically designed for multi-sided markets. These include the presence and strength of network effects, the extent to which users engage in parallel use of competing services (multi-homing), and the degree of innovation-driven competitive pressure.

In practice, the distinctions between the three groups of cases under sec. 18(1) ARC are often not applied strictly. For example, in the *Alphabet-Google* case, the German Federal Cartel Office considered *Google*'s market share of more than 80 % in the market for general search services in Germany, combined with the fact that no competitor either individually or collectively exceeded a 20 % share, to be sufficient to establish market dominance.[228] This approach reflects the fact that, regardless of which case group under sec. 18(1) ARC applies, the legal consequence is the same: the undertaking becomes subject to the prohibition of abuse in sec. 19 ARC. However, the degree of market dominance remains relevant in assessing the expectations placed on the undertaking's competitive conduct This is because the greater an undertaking's market power, the stricter the standards to which its conduct must conform under competition law. An undertaking with overwhelming market strength, such as a quasi-monopolist, is expected to exercise its position with heightened responsibility. Conversely, where market dominance is only just established, the scope of these obligations may be narrower, though the undertaking remains fully subject to the prohibition of abuse.

225 German Federal Supreme Court 30 January 1970 – KZR 3/69, GRUR 1970, 200, 200 – *Tonbandgeräte-Importeur.*

226 Podszun (2025), sec. 18 ARC mn. 106.

227 Higher Regional Court of Frankfurt (on the Main) 3 February 1972 – 6 U 68/71, GRUR 1973, 83, 85 – *Kunststoffkästen*; Higher Regional Court of Berlin 18 February 1969 – Kart V 34/67, WuW 1969, 623 – *Handpreisauszeichner*.

228 German Federal Cartel Office, Decision of 30 December 2021, B7-61/21, para. 264 – *Google Alphabet*.

Criteria

Market Share: Sec. 18(3) no. 1, (4) ARC

In practice, market share remains the primary indicator when assessing market dominance, and this principle also generally applies to digital markets despite their specific structural features. The Higher Regional Court of Duesseldorf confirmed this in its *Ticketvertrieb* decision, noting that market share is the central measure of an undertaking's market success and that this assessment is equally valid for platform markets.[229] Under sec. 18(4) ARC, there is a legal presumption of a dominant market position if an undertaking holds a **market share of at least 40%**. This presumption is, however, rebuttable. The undertaking in question can present evidence
5 demonstrating that it is not dominant despite meeting the threshold. In administrative proceedings, the presumption only plays a role if there is a case of non liquet, meaning the factual situation is unclear.[230] The formal burden of proof in such cases rests with the competition authority. In practice, market share is the most important factor in determining market dominance. Despite their special structures, this also applies in principle to digital markets. In its *Ticketvertrieb* decision, the Higher Regional Court of Duesseldorf stated that '*market share [...] is the key indicator of a undertaking's market success [and this] applies in general, including in relation to platform markets*.'[231]

Other structural or behavioural market factors can diminish the significance of market share as an indicator of dominance. In heterogeneous markets, for example, competitive pressure from close competitors is usually more relevant than that from undertakings offering products with characteristics that differ substantially from those of the market leader.[232] Potential competition or substitution competition may also limit an undertaking's ability to act independently. In digital markets, innovation-driven competitive pressure can come from undertakings that currently have low market shares, which is one reason why killer acquisitions occur, where dominant firms acquire small start-ups early to neutralise the innovative potential they might otherwise bring to the market.

When analysing market dominance, it is important to consider not only the absolute market share but also the **size of the gap between the dominant undertaking and its competitors**.[233] In digital markets, large absolute market shares are often accompanied by considerable market share gaps, which further expand an undertaking's strategic leeway.

---

229 Higher Regional Court of Duesseldorf 5 December 2018 – VI-Kart 3/18 (V), NZKart 2019, 53, 56 – *ticket distribution*.

230 Wiedemann (2020), sec. 23 mn. 41.

231 Higher Regional Court of Duesseldorf 5 December 2018 – VI-Kart 3/18 (V), NZKart 2019, 53, 56 – *Ticketvertrieb* [quote translated by author].

232 In this respect, the demand market concept represents a rough filter. Different competitive proximity ratios can therefore exist within the same market.

233 German Federal Supreme Court 4 March 2008 – KVR 21/07, NJW-RR 2008, 996, 999 – *Soda Club II*; German Federal Supreme Court 16 January 2007 – KVR 12/06, GRUR 2007, 520, 523 – *National Geographic II*beck.

For markets where services are provided free of charge,[234] **calculating** market shares can be challenging. In the *Google/VG Media* case, the German Federal Cartel Office measured *Google*'s market share in the market for general search services by looking at the proportion of search queries in Germany handled by *Google Search*.[235] In proceedings against Facebook, the authority calculated Facebook's market share in the social network market based on the number of daily active users.[236]

Other Criteria: Sec. 18(3) ARC

The **financial strength** of undertakings, as addressed in sec. 18(3) no. 2 ARC, is another factor that can significantly shape the competitive landscape. Superior financial resources can have a deterrent effect on potential competitors, as they may discourage entry or expansion by signalling that the dominant firm can withstand aggressive competition or sustain prolonged investment periods.[237] This is particularly relevant in markets characterised by innovation-driven competitive pressure, where financial strength directly affects an undertaking's capacity to invest in research and development.[238]

With the 10th amendment to the ARC, the legislator introduced **access to competition-relevant data** as an explicit criterion for assessing market dominance in sec. 18(3) no. 3 ARC. This addition reflects the growing recognition that control over valuable data sets can be a decisive source of market power. Sec. 18(3a) no. 3 ARC reiterates the relevance of data access, but in the specific context of multi-sided markets and networks, making it a lex specialis for such cases. While the provision in sec. 18(3a) ARC is tailored to platform-based and network-driven market structures, sec. 18(3) no. 3 ARC clarifies that data access can also be a decisive factor in markets beyond the digital economy. The rationale is that exclusive or superior access to large, high-quality, or unique data sets can strengthen a company's position by improving product quality, enabling targeted advertising, optimising pricing strategies, or raising barriers to entry for competitors.

Superior **access to procurement or sales markets**, as referred to in sec. 18(3) no. 4 ARC, can also provide an undertaking with greater room for manoeuvre. Having its own sales branches or having concluded (permissible) exclusivity agreements with suppliers can strengthen its market position.[239] Interdependencies with other undertakings, pursuant to sec. 18(3) no. 5 ARC, may also enhance access to procurement and sales opportunities.[240]

---

234 For further details on non-monetary services in the context of market definition, see ► 5.3.1.2.4.

235 German Federal Cartel Office, Decision of 8 September 2015, B6-126/14, para. 154 – *Google/VG Media*.

236 German Federal Cartel Office, Decision of 6 February 2019, B6-22/16, paras. 389 et seqq. – *Facebook*.

237 German Federal Supreme Court 25 June 1985 – KVR 3/84, NJW-RR 1986, 525, 526 – *Edelstahlbestecke*; German Federal Supreme Court 21 February 1978 – KVR 4/77, GRUR 1978, 439, 442 – *Kfz-Kupplungen*.

238 Podszun (2025), ARC sec. 18 mn. 125.

239 German Federal Cartel Office, Leitfaden zur Marktbeherrschung, 2012, mn. 51.

240 Fuchs (2024), sec. 18 ARC mn. 130.

Barriers to market entry, as referred to in sec. 18(3) no. 6 ARC, strengthen the market power of competitors already active on the market. Such barriers may arise, for example, from the technical expertise required to operate in the market or from innovation capacities.[241] **Potential competition** is linked to the level of market entry barriers, pursuant to sec. 18(3) no. 7 ARC. Potential competitive pressure comes from undertakings that are not currently active on the market but are likely to enter in the future.[242] The merely theoretical possibility of entering the market does not create any meaningful competitive pressure; rather, imminent market entry must be realistic.[243]

The ability to **switch** its supply or demand to other goods or commercial services, as referred to in sec. 18(3) no. 8 ARC, is relevant for market definition in the form of supply-side switching flexibility, a concept that modifies the demand market concept.[244] However, the extent to which this criterion is relevant for determining market power is debatable. The ability of the **opposite side of the market** to switch to other undertakings, pursuant to sec. 18(3) no. 9 ARC, depends not only on the number of competitors but also on the level of switching costs, which influences customer behaviour.[245] In addition, buyer power can neutralize supply power as countervailing power. This is evident, for example, in the food retail sector, where manufacturers face powerful retailers that, due to their bargaining strength, can sometimes unilaterally impose their desired purchasing conditions. On end-customer markets, by contrast, the market opposition is fragmented, and no countervailing buyer power exists.

Specific Criteria in Digital Markets: Sec. 18(3a) ARC

Since the 9th amendment to the ARC in 2017, additional market structure criteria have been introduced in sec. 18(3a) ARC. These criteria are to be considered when determining market dominance in multi-sided markets and networks. They should be understood as a supplement: the general catalogue of criteria in sec. 18(3) ARC is not replaced by sec. 18(3a) ARC, but rather supplemented and further specified.

Sec. 18(3a) no. 1 ARC initially addresses **direct and indirect network effects**. The concept and mechanisms of network effects have already been explained in the first chapter of this book.[246]

Learning Goals

Direct network effects occur when the value of a service increases for a user group as more participants join the same group. For example, a social network becomes more relevant to private users as the total number of active users grows.

---

241 Fuchs (2024), sec. 18 ARC mn. 132.
242 Podszun (2025), sec. 18 ARC mn. 137.
243 German Federal Supreme Court 15 December 2015 – KZR 92/13, NZKart 2016, 276, 278 – *Pelican/Pelikan*.
244 See ► 2.3.1.1.1.
245 Fuchs (2024), sec. 18 ARC mn. 138.
246 See ► 1.1.

Learning Goals

Indirect network effects arise from interactions between different user groups. For instance, advertisers placing ads on a search engine platform benefit from an expanding base of end users.

Whether network effects strengthen market power or create competitive pressure must be assessed on a case-by-case basis.[247] Network effects can generate self-reinforcing dynamics, enabling a platform to rapidly acquire significant market power and even **'tip' the market** in a short period.[248] This tendency is particularly evident in reciprocal indirect network effects, which occur on matching platforms such as hotel booking portals or dating platforms.[249] In these cases, the value of the platform for one user group increases as the size of the other group grows. One-sided indirect network effects, such as those between end users and advertisers on attention platforms, can also contribute to the concentration of digital markets.[250]

In addition, it must be examined whether circumstances exist that counteract the market power typically associated with network effects. Such factors include, for example, users' tendency to engage in multi-homing, i.e. the parallel use of several platforms, as well as strong differentiation between the intermediary services offered by competing platforms.[251] Moreover, network effects can also enhance the dynamics of digital markets, fostering rapid shifts in market conditions and thereby mitigating the consolidation of entrenched power positions.[252]

▶ Examples

When reviewing the proposed merger between *Verivox* and *ProSiebenSat.1*, the German Federal Cartel Office rejected the forecast of a tipping of the market despite the existence of reciprocal indirect network effects. The authority argued that tipping presupposes a platform holding a clear lead in market position and other decisive competitive factors, which was not the case here.[253]

In the *OCPE II/Elite Medianet* case, the German Federal Cartel Office likewise dismissed the risk of market tipping. It emphasised that '*the market for online dating platforms is characterised by a high degree of platform differentiation designed to satisfy heterogeneous demand, which makes a concentration on just one platform unlikely*.'[254] The authority also highlighted that '*in both user groups, a large proportion of users engage in*

---

247 German Federal Cartel Office, Market Power of Platforms and Networks, 2016, p. 54.

248 German Federal Cartel Office, Decision of 24 July 2015 – B8-76/15, case report, p. 4 – *Online-Vergleichsplattformen*.

249 German Federal Cartel Office, Market Power of Platforms and Networks, 2016, p. 55; German Federal Cartel Office 24 July 2015 – B8-76/15, case report, p. 3 – *Online-Vergleichsplattformen*.

250 Fuchs (2024), sec. 18 ARC mn. 144.

251 German Federal Cartel Office 22 October 2015 – B6-57/15, paras. 147 et seqq. – *OCPE II/Elite Medianet*.

252 German Federal Cartel Office, Decision of 22 October 2015 – B6-57/15, para. 143 – *OCPE II/Elite Medianet*.

253 German Federal Cartel Office, Decision of 24 July 2015 – B8-76/15, case report, p. 4 – *Online-Vergleichsplattformen*.

254 German Federal Cartel Office, Decision of 22 October 2015 – B6-57/15, para. 147 – *OCPE II/Elite Medianet* [quote translated by author].

multi-homing in the narrower sense. The analysis of the data submitted by the notifying parties shows that 72% of respondents use several online dating platforms at the same time.'[255] ◄

5

Sec. 18(3a) no. 2 ARC refers to the **parallel use of services**, commonly known as multi-homing. This describes the tendency of users to rely on multiple platform services simultaneously. Multi-homing mitigates the market power of platform operators and enables the continued existence of smaller providers. Multi-homing is more likely where platform offerings are differentiated and services are available free of charge or at only a low cost. User conduct is also shaped by the costs of switching to alternative services.[256] These switching costs may stem not only from fees but also from disadvantages associated with changing providers.[257] For example, personalisation effects resulting from long-term use can create lock-in and increase switching costs.[258] Legal frameworks may reduce such costs. Under Article 20 GDPR, users have a right to data portability, though this right applies only to personal data. In addition, Article 6(9) DMA grants end users a right to the free and effective portability of data they have generated in connection with a gatekeeper's core platform service.[259] Gatekeepers must also ensure permanent, real-time access to these data.

Sec. 18(3a) no. 3 ARC requires that **economies of scale in connection with network effects** be taken into account when assessing market dominance. This criterion is closely linked to sec. 18(3a) no. 1 ARC, which addresses the existence of network effects, and should therefore be evaluated in conjunction with it.[260] Economies of scale may already be relevant under sec. 18(3) no. 6 ARC, which lists barriers to market entry.[261] Their explicit inclusion in sec. 18(3a) ARC underlines that they represent an additional factor strengthening market power beyond network effects alone. In platform markets, high fixed costs typically arise when establishing the technical and organisational infrastructure of the platform,[262] whereas variable costs per additional user are comparatively low. As the user base grows, significant economies of scale are created, which can reinforce the competitive advantages of established platforms and raise barriers to entry for new competitors.

Sec. 18(3a) no. 4 ARC lists **access to competition-relevant data** as a criterion for assessing market dominance. This reflects the central role of data as a parameter of competition in the digital economy.[263] The provision functions as a lex specialis to sec. 18(3) no. 2 ARC, which addresses the financial strength of undertakings. In practice, access to data is particularly relevant in multi-sided platform markets,

255 German Federal Cartel Office, Decision of 22 October 2015 – B6-57/15, para. 153 – *OCPE II/ Elite Medianet* [quote translated by author].
256 Fuchs (2024), sec. 18 ARC mn. 145.
257 Podszun (2025), sec. 18 ARC mn. 155.
258 Kühling and Gauß (2007), pp. 751, 752.
259 For further details on Article 6(9) DMA, see ► 3.3.2.8.
260 Government justification for the 9th ARC amendment, BT-Drs. 18/10207, p. 51.
261 Paal (2025), sec. 18 ARC mn. 12; Podszun and Schwalbe (2017), pp. 98, 100.
262 Podszun (2025), sec. 18 ARC mn. 156.
263 See ► 1.2.

where user interactions generate large volumes of valuable information. However, data advantages can also create market power in more traditional industries.[264] An undertaking with privileged access to competition-relevant data gains an independent scope of conduct vis-à-vis competitors. Unlike tangible goods, data are non-rivalrous: multiple undertakings could, in principle, use the same data simultaneously. Yet, if access is restricted to a single undertaking, foreclosure effects arise that can exclude rivals from the market. Access to competition-relevant data enables undertakings to innovate, refine, and personalise their products, thereby strengthening their competitive position. The provision covers only competition-relevant data, which in most cases concerns user data.[265]

Sec. 18(3a) no. 5 ARC introduces **innovation-driven competitive pressure** as an additional criterion in the assessment of market dominance. In digital markets, this form of competition is often of particular importance. Even where competition on the market is limited, dynamic rivalry may occur for the market, fuelled by disruptive innovations.[266] As In such cases, the explanatory power of market shares as an indicator of market power diminishes. Disruptive innovations have reshaped market structures in the past, for instance, in the field of social networks. At present, the development of generative AI technologies illustrates how new innovations can fundamentally alter competitive dynamics. Whether innovation-driven pressure should be taken into account in the dominance test depends on the degree of concreteness and immediacy of the innovation threat.[267] It is not sufficient that the dominant position might, in theory, be undermined at some unspecified point in the future. As case law stresses, '*the mere prospect that a dominant market position could disappear at some point*'[268] does not neutralise market power.

Intermediation Power: Sec. 18(3b) ARC

The **intermediation power** under sec. 18(3b) ARC constitutes another criterion specifically tailored to digital markets. In assessing the market power of an undertaking that operates as an intermediary on multi-sided markets, the relevance of its intermediation services for access to procurement and sales markets must be considered. This provision acknowledges the distinctive structures of digital markets. Unlike traditional distribution systems, digital platforms function as intermediaries between different market sides. In this role, they act as gateways to access:[269] they control visibility and reach, for instance by ranking search results, and thus determine the discoverability of commercial users' offers for end users.[270]

264 Fuchs (2024), sec. 18 ARC mn. 148.
265 Fuchs (2024), sec. 18 ARC mn. 148.
266 German Federal Supreme Court 23 June 2020 – KVR 69/19, GRUR 2020, 1318, 1323 – *Facebook.*
267 German Federal Supreme Court 23 June 2020 – KVR 69/19, GRUR 2020, 1318, 1323 – *Facebook.*
268 German Federal Supreme Court 23 June 2020 – KVR 69/19, GRUR 2020, 1318, 1323 – *Facebook* [quote translated by author].
269 Volmar (2020), 170, 170 speaks of '*bottleneck*'.
270 Körber (2020), pp. 290, 292 f.

If competition in the market for the intermediation service is limited, the platform gains market power. The degree to which a platform operator can control market access is not determined solely by its market share; user behaviour also plays a role. In particular, if users tend to rely exclusively on a single platform (single-homing), this reinforces the platform's intermediation power.[271] Additionally, vertical integration, where the platform operator also competes with commercial users on the platform, can further strengthen and complement its intermediation power.[272]

5.3.1.4 Collective Dominance

5

Concept of Collective Dominance

In contrast to Article 102 TFEU, German abuse law provides a definition for the notion of collective market dominance. Under **sec. 18(5) ARC**, two conditions must be satisfied for collective dominance to exist. First, there must be no significant competition between the jointly dominant undertakings, meaning a **lack of internal competition**. Second, the undertakings as a group must possess an independent scope of conduct with respect to their competitors and the other side of the market, indicating a **lack of external competition**.

A lack of internal competition exists when there is close mutual responsiveness between the undertakings. One indication of this is uniform conduct on the market: the undertakings do not compete with each other but instead coordinate their market behaviour in a manner permitted under Article 101 TFEU and sec. 1 ARC. High market concentration facilitates such responsiveness. Consequently, collectively dominant undertakings are typically found in oligopolistically structured markets. Product homogeneity and market transparency further support **tacit collusion**, as they make it easier for undertakings to observe competitors' behaviour and react quickly. Competitors attempting to break the collusive equilibrium (for example, by lowering their prices) can be effectively 'punished' by others responding in kind, following a tit-for-tat strategy.[273] The criteria in sec. 18(5) ARC align with the *Airtours* criteria developed by European case law for assessing collective market dominance.[274]

▶ Example

In the petrol station markets, the German Federal Cartel Office has confirmed the existence of collective market dominance.[275] ◀

Criteria

The same criteria for individual market dominance apply when assessing the absence of external competition. Sec. 18(6) ARC provides two market share-based presumptions: a group of up to three undertakings is presumed collectively domi-

---

271 Volmar (2017), pp. 386, 391.
272 Government justification for the 9th ARC amendment, BT-Drs. 18/10207, p. 70.
273 For further details on tacit collusion, see ▶ 2.3.1.3.
274 On the *Airtours* criteria, see ▶ 2.3.1.3.
275 German Federal Cartel Office, Sektoruntersuchung Kraftstoffmärkte, 2011.

nant if their combined **market share reaches 50%**, and **a group of up to five undertakings if it reaches two-thirds**.

Sec. 18(7) ARC outlines how undertakings can rebut the presumption of market dominance. First, they may show that the competitive conditions between them are likely to give rise to significant competition. It is not sufficient to demonstrate that competition currently exists; the market structure must indicate with reasonable probability that competition will persist in the future.[276] Second, undertakings can rebut the presumption by showing that they do not hold a dominant market position relative to other competitors. This requires challenging the relevance of their market share for their market power, for example, by demonstrating the presence of potential competition or low barriers to market entry.

For digital markets, the German Federal Cartel Office assumes that '*transaction platforms with pronounced indirect network effects, combined with numerous competition parameters, have a rather low probability of collusion*.[277] Regarding matching platforms,[278] the Office reaches a similar conclusion, citing '*relatively pronounced indirect network effects and the existence of numerous competition parameters*,'[279] which make the likelihood of implicit collusion '*rather low*.'[280] Collusion is further complicated by the need for competitors to coordinate across multiple sides of the market.[281]

5.3.1.5 Abuse

Exclusionary Abuses

General Principles

According to **sec. 19(2) no. 1 ARC**, a dominant undertaking is prohibited from unfairly impeding or discriminating against other undertakings without objective justification. The notion of exclusionary conduct is interpreted broadly and covers any **detrimental restriction of another undertaking's competitive freedom**.[282] Actual impairment is not required; it is sufficient that the conduct is capable of impeding competition.[283]

---

276 Podszun (2025), sec. 18 ARC mn. 182.

277 German Federal Cartel Office, Decision of 20 April 2015 – B6-39/15, case report, p. 5 – *Online-Immobilienplattformen*; German Federal Cartel Office, Decision of 24 July 2015 – B8-76/15, case report, p. 5 – *ProSiebenSat.1/Verivox* [quote translated by author].

278 For further details on different types of platforms, see ► 1.1.

279 German Federal Cartel Office, Decision of 22 October 2015 – B6-57/15, para. 200 – *Online-Datingplattform* [quote translated by author].

280 German Federal Cartel Office, Decision of 22 October 2015 – B6-57/15, para. 200 – *Online-Datingplattform*; German Federal Cartel Office 24 July 2015 – B8-76/15, case report p. 5 – *Online-Vergleichsplattform* [quote translated by author].

281 Thomas (2025), sec. 36 ARC mn. 228.

282 German Federal Supreme Court 22 September 1981 – KVR 8/80, GRUR 1982, 60 – *Original-VW-Ersatzteile II*; Higher Regional Court of Duesseldorf 12 December 2001 – U (Kart) 4/01 GRUR 2002, 831, 831 – *Förderung der regionalen Wirtschaft*.

283 Higher Regional Court of Duesseldorf 30 March 2016 – VI-U (Kart) 10/15, NJOZ 2016, 1161, 1173.

Discrimination arises where a dominant undertaking **treats one undertaking differently from other, comparable undertakings**. Unequal treatment falls within the scope of the prohibition only if it concerns undertakings that are sufficiently similar, typically those offering the same type of service at the same market level.[284] Case law further requires that the differential treatment has a detrimental effect on the competitive position of the undertaking concerned.[285] Such unequal treatment constitutes abuse only in the absence of an objective justification.

The inequity of an impediment or the absence of an objective justification for discrimination must be assessed on the basis of a comprehensive **balancing of interests**, taking into account the purpose of competition law, which is to safeguard the freedom of competition.[286] This requires weighing the individual interests of the undertakings concerned against the overarching objective of protecting competitive freedom. The dominant undertaking's market power must also be considered: the greater its scope of action, the stronger its duty to avoid obstructing or discriminating against other undertakings.

At the same time, even dominant undertakings retain a basic right to act autonomously on the market, for instance, to decide whom to supply and under what conditions.[287] In principle, there is no obligation to actively promote the business opportunities of competitors. Beyond the goals of competition law, considerations of public interest[288] and the principles of European competition law may also play a role in the balancing process.[289]

! To determine whether an impediment is unfair or discrimination lacks objective justification, a comprehensive balancing of interests is required, guided by the objective of competition law to safeguard the freedom of competition.

Exclusive Agreements

As already discussed in relation to Article 102 TFEU,[290] a dominant undertaking may unfairly restrict competitors by imposing exclusive purchasing obligations. German practice applies the benchmarks of the VBER, which presumes exclusivity where purchasing obligations exceed 80% of demand and extend beyond five

---

284 Fuchs (2024), sec. 19 ARC mn. 92.

285 German Federal Supreme Court 24 October 2011 – KZR 7/10, GRUR 2012, 84, 87 – *Wholesaler termination*.

286 German Federal Supreme Court 10 December 2019 – KZR 57/19, NZKart 2020, 141, 142 – *Werbeblocker IV*.

287 German Federal Supreme Court 12 November 1991 – KZR 2/90, GRUR 1992, 199, 200 – *Aktionsbeiträge*.

288 German Federal Supreme Court 7 November 2006 – KZR 2/06, GRUR 2017, 616, 617 – *Bevorzugung einer Behindertenwerkstatt*: '*Neither the public sector as the norm addressee of sec. 20 I ARC nor another dominant company is fundamentally prevented from being guided by public welfare interests when selecting several applicants*.' [quote translated by author].

289 German Federal Supreme Court 11 November 2008 – KVR 17/08, GRUR 2009, 424, 435 – *Bau und Hobby*: '*In any case, the assessment of Community law must be included in the consideration pursuant to sec. 20 I ARC*'. [quote translated by author].

290 For further details, see ► 2.3.2.1.

years (see Article 1(f), Article 5(1)(a) VBER). Case law, for instance, has found supply contracts of a dominant gas supplier with terms of up to 20 years to constitute an unfair restriction.[291]

Exclusivity obligations may also infringe the prohibition of cartels.[292] Where such obligations are compatible with Article 101 TFEU and sec. 1 ARC, they do not constitute a violation of sec. 19 ARC.[293] **Price parity clauses** can have effects comparable to exclusivity clauses:[294] they restrict the freedom of commercial platform users to set prices and reduce their incentive to contract with other platform operators.[295]

Refusal to Supply

Exclusionary abuse may arise both from a refusal to enter into business relationships and from the termination of existing supply relationships. In digital markets, this can take the form of blocking accounts that commercial users have opened as sellers on platforms.[296] As a rule, a dominant undertaking remains free to decide with whom it concludes contracts.[297] However, its heightened responsibility to safeguard residual competition in the dominated market may impose additional obligations. For example, the undertaking may be required to observe a reasonable notice period, allowing the customer to prepare for the termination of the business relationship.[298] Within **selective distribution systems**, it is recognised that a dominant manufacturer may apply **qualitative criteria** in choosing its distributors, provided this is done in a non-discriminatory manner.[299] Legitimate criteria include, for instance, the professional qualifications of dealers or the provision of additional services such as repair facilities.

In the case of luxury goods, it may be legitimate for a dominant undertaking to impose a general ban on distribution via online platforms (**platform ban**).[300] Whether such a ban can also be justified for other categories of products has so far been assessed inconsistently in German case law.[301] For example, the Higher Regional Court of Hamburg held that, in the case of food supplements and cosmet-

---

291 Higher Regional Court of Duesseldorf 7 November 2001 – U (Kart) 31/00, WuW 2002, 494 – *Stadtwerke Aachen.*

292 For further details on Article 101(1) TFEU, see ► 2.2.2.3; for further details on sec. 1 ARC, see sec. 5.2.2.3.

293 German Federal Supreme Court 8 April 2014 – KZR 53/12, NZKart 2014, 411, 413 – *VBL-Versicherungspflicht.*

294 Fuchs (2024), sec. 19 ARC mn. 181a.

295 German Federal Cartel Office, Decision of 22 December 2015 – B 9-121/13, para. 313 – *Hotelportalmarkt.*

296 Berghaus and Mekhalfia (2021), pp. 82, 83.

297 German Federal Supreme Court 24 June 2003 – KZR 32/01, GRUR 2003, 893, 895 – *Schülertransporte.*

298 German Federal Supreme Court 10 February 1987 – KZR 6/86, NJW 1987, 3197, 3200 – *Freundschaftswerbung.*

299 German Federal Supreme Court 25 October 1988 – KVR 1/87, GRUR 1989, 220, 222 – *Lüsterbehangsteine*; Bechtold (2003), 3729, 3729 et seqq.

300 Fuchs (2024), sec. 19 ARC mn. 134.

301 For further details on this discussion, see ► 5.2.3.3.3.

ics, the manufacturer's interest in restricting platform distribution outweighed the interests of distributors, such that the resulting hindrance was not considered disproportionate.[302] In light of values reflected in the VBER,[303] it appears persuasive to accept platform bans also for certain other high-quality or high-tech products.

Quantitative selection may also be permissible. It is characterised by the fact that the dominant undertaking admits only a limited number of distributors into its distribution system.[304] Because such a limitation entails a foreclosure effect, stricter requirements for justification apply.[305] In addition, a dominant undertaking may be obliged to ensure **transparency** in the selection of its business partners. Guidance can also be drawn from other legal regimes. Under **Article 3(1)(c) Platform Regulation**, providers of online intermediation services must state in their general terms and conditions the reasons for restricting access to their services by commercial users. These assessments can be taken into account in the competition-law balancing of interests when assessing unfair impediment or lack of objective justification.[306] Some courts, for example, assume that the justification requirement under Article 4(2), (5) Platform Regulation must be considered when evaluating the termination of a business relationship. The Regional Court of Hannover held that, where '*the operator of an online sales platform merely justifies the deactivation of a seller's account by stating that the seller [...] has violated the terms of use [...],*'[307] the seller may assert a claim for reactivation of the account pursuant to sec. 33(1), sec. 19(2) no. 1 ARC. Other courts, however, take the view that a dominant undertaking is obliged to provide reasons even outside the scope of the Platform Regulation when terminating a business relationship.[308]

Learning Goals

The Platform Regulation governs the bilateral relationship between providers of online intermediation services and their commercial users.[309] It primarily imposes transparency obligations. Beyond the duty to provide reasons for restricting or terminating contractual relationships, Articles 5, 7 Platform Regulation require providers to disclose information on the parameters of ranking and on potential self-preferential practices. However, the Platform Regulation does not establish sub-

---

302 Higher Regional Court of Hamburg 22 March 2018 – 3 U 250/16, NZKart 2018, 590, 591 et seq. – *Aloe Vera-Produkte.*

303 For details on the VBER, see ► 2.2.5.2.

304 Kling and Thomas (2016), sec. 20 mn. 119.

305 Fuchs (2024), ARC sec. 19 mn. 136.

306 Regional Court Munich I 12 May 2021, Ref. 37 O 32/21, BeckRS 2021, 10613, para. 75: '*Regulation (EU) 2019/1150, which entered into force on 12 July 2020, does not supersede the antitrust provisions, but stands on its own [...] Its assessments can be indirectly taken into account in the application of antitrust law.*' [quote translated by author]; Kohser and Jahn (2020), pp. 273, 275.

307 Regional Court Hannover 22 July 2021 – 25 O 221/21, GRUR-RS 2021, 24622 [quote translated by author].

308 Regional Court Munich I 12 May 2021 – 37 O 32/21, NZKart 2021, 370, 372 et seq. – *Amazon Kontensperrung II*; German Federal Cartel Office, Decision of 17 July 2019 – B2-88/18, para. 5 – *Amazon Geschäftsbedingungen.*

309 On the addresses of the Platform regulation, see ► 4.2.

stantive prohibitions or restrictions. Its function is therefore limited to enhancing transparency and predictability in platform–business relations, while leaving the assessment of competitive harm and the prohibition of abusive practices to competition law.

Essential Facilities Doctrine

The essential facilities doctrine, exemplified in **sec. 19(2) no. 4 ARC**, constitutes a subcategory of exclusionary conduct. Under this doctrine, a dominant undertaking abuses its market position if it refuses to supply another undertaking, or to grant access to infrastructure facilities, for a reasonable fee. Such supply or access must be objectively necessary for the other undertaking to operate on an upstream or downstream market. Additionally, the refusal of access must pose a threat to eliminate competition on that market.

The 10th amendment to the ARC in 2021 expanded the scope of the essential facilities doctrine. Whereas the offence was previously limited to 'networks and other infrastructure facilities,' it now generally encompasses the supply of certain types of goods or commercial services.[310] The legislator justifies this change by noting that the offence had previously been relevant primarily to physical infrastructure, such as airports, seaports,[311] or sports facilities,[312] and intellectual property rights, but that it also covers 'a denial of access to platforms or interfaces.'[313] Additionally, access to data was explicitly included as a standard example in sec. 19(2) no. 4 ARC. According to the legislator, this amendment is merely declaratory,[314] as the essential facilities doctrine had already occasionally been applied to information in practice.[315]

A claim under sec. 19(2) no. 4 ARC arises only if access is '**objectively necessary**' for the undertaking to operate on the upstream or downstream market. The 10th amendment to the ARC clarified the rationale for access. Previously, the law stated that it was 'not possible for the undertaking to operate as a competitor of the dominant undertaking on the upstream or downstream market without shared use.' The amendment is intended solely to clarify the provision and to facilitate the application of the principles of **substitutability** and **duplicability** from Article 102 TFEU to sec. 19(2) no. 4 ARC.[316]

The key prerequisite is that the undertaking cannot gain access to the market by any other means, not even through its own efforts.[317] Because a claim to access

---

310 Government justification for the 10th ARC amendment, BT-Drs. 19/23492, p. 72.

311 German Federal Supreme Court 14 July 2011 – III ZR 200/10, WM 2012, 371, 375 – *Flughafen Berlin-Tegel.*

312 Higher Regional Court of Koblenz 13 December 2012 – U 73/12 Kart, NZKart 2013, 164 – *Nürburgring*.

313 Government justification for the 10th ARC amendment, BT-Drs. 19/23492, p. 72 [quote translated by author].

314 Government justification for the 10th ARC amendment, BT-Drs. 19/23492, p. 72.

315 Higher Regional Court of Berlin 23 June 2003 – 2 U 20/02 Kart, WRP 2004, 112, 113 et seqq. – *Gera-Rostock*.

316 Fuchs (2024), sec. 19 ARC mn. 328.

317 Kling and Thomas (2016), sec. 20 mn. 209.

significantly restricts the dominant undertaking's freedom of competition and property rights, the requirement of objective necessity is high. It is not sufficient that market entry is merely difficult, for example, because it is economically marginally viable. Rather, it must be absolutely unreasonable from a commercial point of view to set up another infrastructure unit.[318] Objective necessity may therefore be affirmed if the infrastructure cannot be duplicated, for instance due to legal constraints such as construction or environmental regulations.[319]

5

The extension of the essential facilities offence to include **data** does not create a general right of access, given the high threshold for claiming access. A claim under sec. 19(2) no. 4 ARC remains an exception that must be justified. A dominant undertaking is generally not obliged to promote third-party competition. The mere existence of a large data pool does not automatically render it an essential facility.[320] Other undertakings can, in principle, collect their own data from users. Even though data is a critical competitive parameter in digital markets, this does not mean that access to it is objectively necessary for market entry. Empirical evidence from digital markets shows that innovative start-ups have been able to achieve significant market power without having access to the same data as established competitors.[321] Exceptional cases may exist, for example, when exclusive machine data for the Internet of Things is involved.[322] In any case, the provisions of the GDPR must be respected when accessing personal data.[323]

According to a widely accepted view, search engines do not qualify as an essential facility.[324] Even if certain search engine operators hold market shares exceeding 90% in national European markets, it is not objectively necessary for undertakings to be ranked according to 'fair' criteria in order to access customers.[325]

Other Forms of Abusive Conduct

Unfavourable exclusionary strategies can be implemented through **tying and bundling practices**. In such cases, a dominant undertaking offers one service or product in combination with another. While two or more products can be purchased only as a package in cases of bundling, tying practices tying practices only restrict the separate purchase of the tied product, whereas the other one can be purchased individually. Both practices can create a leverage effect if the undertaking holds a very strong market position in the market for the tying product. By tying, the dominant undertaking can 'leverage' its market power into the market for the tied product. A classic example from German practice is the sale of labels tied to the

318 Klumpe (2025), sec. 19 ARC mn. 205 [quote translated by author]. See also Higher Regional Court of Hamburg 19 June 2002 – 5 U 28/02, WuW 2003, 514 – *Online-Ticketshop*.

319 German Federal Supreme Court 11 December 2012 – KVR 7/12, NZKart 2013, 160, 160 et seqq. – *Fährhafen Puttgarden II*.

320 Körber (2020), pp. 290, 292.

321 Körber (2020), pp. 290, 292.

322 Körber (2020), pp. 290, 292.

323 Dreher and Kulka (2023), mn. 1297.

324 For further details on this discussion, see ▶ 2.3.2.1.7.

325 Kersting and Dworschak (2013), pp. 46, 48; Körber (2012), pp. 761, 766.

purchase of a labelling machine.[326] However, tying practices are not inherently unfair. They are not considered abusive if competitors are not significantly harmed. Tying may also be justified for functional or technical reasons, such as when tying equipment and compatible materials ensures proper functionality, and the use of materials from competing manufacturers would compromise the equipment.[327]

In the case of **rebates**, a distinction must be made, as explained in the context of Article 102 TFEU,[328] between quantity and functional rebates, which are generally unproblematic under competition law,[329] and loyalty or target rebates, which may have a predatory effect. German practice has already considered loyalty rebates abusive when their aim is to force competitors out of the market. It remains to be seen how the case-by-case impact analysis required by the ECJ's Intel decision of 2017 under Article 102 TFEU[330] will influence the assessment of loyalty rebates under sec. 19(1) ARC.

In a recent decision, the Higher Regional Court of Düsseldorf held that the **blocking of an undertakings's *Facebook* page** without a prior or immediate subsequent statement of reasons constitutes exclusionary conduct under sec. 19 (1), (2) no. 1 ARC.[331] Such considerations had previously only arisen in the context of reviewing platform terms and conditions under sec. 307 German Civil Code.[332] The novelty of the decision lies in the finding that the absence of reasons for the account suspension may at the same time amount to an abuse of dominance under German competition law. The court emphasised that a balancing of the affected fundamental rights, operating through indirect third-party effect, is required between the dominant platform operator and the undertaking concerned.[333]

Exploitative Abuses

General Principles

The example contained in **sec. 19(2) no. 2 ARC** addresses exploitative abuse. A dominant undertaking is prohibited from imposing prices or other contractual terms that deviate from those which would most likely prevail under conditions of effective competition. This assessment involves a hypothetical analysis of the price

---

326 Higher Regional Court of Berlin 18 February 1969 – Kart V 34/67, WuW 1969, 623 – *Handpreisauszeichner*.

327 Fuchs (2024), sec. 19 ARC mn. 183.

328 For further details, see ► 2.3.2.1.5.

329 A different view is expressed by German Federal Supreme Court 12 July 2013 – KVR 11/12, NZKart 2013, 462, 462 – *laboratory chemicals*: '*An examination of the individual case is always decisive. This may also reveal that the granting of a volume discount constitutes an anti-competitive obstruction of individual companies.*' [quote translated by author].

330 ECJ 6 September 2017 – C-413/14 P, ECLI:EU:C:2017:632 – *Intel*.

331 Higher Regional Court of Düsseldorf 2 April 2025 – VI-U (Kart) 5/24, NZKart 2025, 262, 264 et seq. – *Filmwerkstatt Düsseldorf II*.

332 German Federal Supreme Court 29 Juli 2021 – III ZR 179/20, NJW 2021, 3179 – *Hassredevorwurf*.

333 Higher Regional Court of Düsseldorf 2 April 2025 – VI-U (Kart) 5/24, NZKart 2025, 262, 266 – *Filmwerkstatt Düsseldorf II*.

level and contractual terms that would be expected to emerge under conditions of effective competition. Exploitative abuse differs fundamentally from exclusionary abuse. While exclusionary conduct is aimed at driving competitors from the market, exploitative conduct targets the other side of the market, especially consumer welfare.[334]

In practice, various methods have been developed to estimate the price level that would exist under competitive conditions. Foremost among these is the **comparator market method**, which is explicitly mentioned in sec. 19(2) no. 2 ARC.[335] This method determines the benchmark by examining prices charged on markets that are structurally comparable to the dominated market. Its reliability therefore depends on the extent to which comparable markets can be identified. In the temporal comparative market method, prices from the period before the undertaking achieved market dominance serve as the reference point.[336] A geographic comparator market, by contrast, is a market in which the same products are offered but within a different geographic area, such as another regional market.[337] If foreign markets are used as a reference, it must be ensured that regulatory conditions do not differ in a way that undermines comparability. Comparability is weakest in product comparator markets, where entirely different products are considered. Only markets offering products that are very similar to those in the dominated market should be taken as valid benchmarks.[338]

Regardless of the comparator market chosen, the price level identified there can only serve as an approximation of the hypothetical price that would prevail on the dominated market. This is because prevailing market conditions are rarely identical.[339] For this reason, adjustments must often be made by applying **premiums or discounts**. In some approaches, the comparative market price is treated merely as a 'base,' from which the hypothetical competitive price is derived through further estimations[340] Once this hypothetical price has been established, case law requires a comparison with the price actually charged by the dominant undertaking. Only if the latter **deviates significantly** from the benchmark can exploitative abuse be assumed.[341] The threshold of significance depends on the degree of market dominance the stronger the market power, the lower the tolerance for excessive deviations.[342]

334 For the largely corresponding principles in Article 102 TFEU, see ► 2.3.2.2.

335 Legner (2012), pp. 218, 220 on the comparative market methods in the context of the calculation of damages under sec. 33a ARC.

336 Higher Regional Court of Duesseldorf 14 March 2018 – VI-U (Kart) 7/16, NZKart 2018, 238 – *Mitbenutzung von Kabelkanalanlagen*.

337 German Federal Supreme Court 19 June 2007 – KRB 12/07, WuW 2008, 457 – *Papiergroßhandel*.

338 Higher Regional Court of Duesseldorf 14 March 2018 – VI-U (Kart) 7/16, NZKart 2018, 235, 238 – *Mitbenutzung von Kabelkanalanlagen*.

339 Wiedemann (2020), sec. 23 mn. 202.

340 Klumpe (2025), sec. 19 ARC mn. 161 et seq.

341 German Federal Supreme Court 28 June 2005 – KVR 17/04, NJW 2006, 2333 – *Stadtwerke Mainz*.

342 German Federal Supreme Court 28 June 2005 – KVR 17/04, NJW 2006, 2333 – *Stadtwerke Mainz*.

In addition to the comparator market method, German competition law has at times relied on a **cost-control approach** to establish exploitative abuse.[343] This method involves analysing the cost components underlying price formation and comparing them with the price actually charged. However, such an approach faces similar objections to the concept of profit margin capping known from European abuse law,[344] which has occasionally been applied by the German Federal Cartel Office. Both methods rest on assumptions of what constitutes 'reasonable' costs or profit margins. Yet such benchmarks are inherently problematic, as no fixed values exist. The economic value of a product is continuously shaped by supply and demand and cannot be reduced to a static factor.[345]

The prohibition of exploitative abuse under sec. 19(2) no. 2 ARC has played only a limited role in German practice. This is largely due to the practical difficulties of producing sufficient evidence. The provision also extends beyond excessive pricing to cover exploitation through '**other terms and conditions**'. This type of abuse is referred to as abuse of conditions, or more broadly, exploitative contractual terms. In legal doctrine and practice, this form of abuse is usually treated as a distinct category, separate from price-related exploitation. In recent years, competition authorities and courts have increasingly relied on the general prohibition in sec. 19(1) ARC when addressing abusive conditions. This approach avoids the evidentiary challenges involved in determining what 'other terms and conditions' would most likely have prevailed under hypothetical competitive market conditions.

The abuse of dominance through **discriminatory pricing and terms** under sec. 19(2) no. 3 ARC represents another form of exploitative conduct. Unlike sec. 19(2) no. 2 ARC, where the benchmark is a hypothetical competitive price, the standard of comparison here is the price or terms applied by the dominant undertaking on comparable markets. **sec. 19(2) no. 5 ARC** addresses a specific form of exploitative abuse related to buyer power. The so-called 'tapping prohibition' prevents a dominant buyer from demanding advantages from other undertakings without an objectively justified reason.

Excessive Pricing

In addition to the general principles for determining abusively excessive prices, a notable example from digital markets illustrates the application of exploitative abuse. In November 2015, the German Federal Cartel Office initiated proceedings against two undertakings that held a strong position in the digital supply of audiobooks in Germany.[346] According to the Office, these undertakings attempted to renegotiate licence agreements with audiobook publishers, under which end customers would be able to listen to a specific number of audiobooks for a fixed

343 German Federal Supreme Court 14 December 2021 – KZR 23/18, NZKart 2022, 154, 155 – *Kabelkanalanlagen II*.

344 German Federal Cartel Office, Decision of 14 February 2003 – B11-45/01 – *TEAG*.

345 Fuchs (2024), sec. 19 ARC mn. 232.

346 German Federal Cartel Office, press release of 16 November 2015 'Bundeskartellamt leitet Verfahren gegen Audible/Amazon und Apple ein', https://www.bundeskartellamt.de/SharedDocs/Meldung/DE/Pressemitteilungen/2015/16_11_2015_Audible.html (accessed 8 September 2025).

monthly fee. The publishers contended that the terms demanded by the dominant customers **did not cover their costs**, suggesting the potential application of a margin-squeezing strategy. The German Federal Cartel Office ultimately discontinued the proceedings because the undertakings were willing to amend their terms and conditions starting January 2017.[347] Applying the **comparator market concept** to multi-sided platform markets presents particular challenges. These difficulties arise both from the rapid pace of digital markets and from the frequently observed asymmetric cost structures across the different sides of the platform.[348]

Personalised Pricing and Dynamic Pricing

5

The principles regarding price personalisation and dynamic pricing established under Article 102 TFEU apply mutatis mutandis to German abuse law. A dominant undertaking's practice of personalising prices does not, in itself, constitute exploitative abuse.[349] In principle, the undertaking is permitted to tailor prices to the individual willingness of customers to pay. Similarly, a dominant undertaking is allowed to adjust prices rapidly in response to changes in market demand.[350]

Unfair Trading Conditions

Exploitative practices are not limited to pricing; other contractual terms and conditions can also be structured in a way that constitutes abuse of a dominant market position. **Sec. 19(2) no. 2 ARC** explicitly includes '**other terms and conditions**' as a standard example: if these terms deviate from what would very likely have resulted under conditions of effective competition, they may amount to an abuse of conditions. In practice, the German Federal Cartel Office occasionally relies directly on the general clause in **sec. 19(1) ARC** when assessing such abuses.[351] This approach reflects the fact that sec. 19(2) no. 2 ARC primarily requires application of the comparative market method, and determining the content of non-price terms in a hypothetical competitive scenario is particularly challenging.[352]

To determine whether the terms and conditions imposed by a dominant undertaking are abusive, an **overall assessment** of the bundle of services is generally required.[353] Where reference is made to sec. 19(1) ARC, it must be examined whether the terms unilaterally deviate from the principles of fairness enshrined in dispositive law to the detriment of the business partner.[354] In German competition

---

347 German Federal Cartel Office, press release of 19 January 2017 'Bundeskartellamt stellt Verfahren gegen Audible/Amazon und Apple ein', https://www.bundeskartellamt.de/SharedDocs/Meldung/DE/Pressemitteilungen/2017/19_01_2017_Audible_Amazon.html (accessed 8 September 2025).

348 For further details, see ► 2.3.2.2.

349 Körber (2016), pp. 303, 308.

350 Paal (2019), pp. 43, 48.

351 For example, in the *Facebook proceedings*, see German Federal Cartel Office, Decision of 6 February 2019, B6-22/16 – *Facebook*.

352 Fuchs (2024), sec. 19 ARC mn. 211.

353 German Federal Supreme Court 6 November 1983 – KVR 13/83, GRUR 1985, 318, 319 – *Favorit*.

354 German Federal Supreme Court 6 November 2013 – KZR 61/11, NZKart 2014, 31, 32 – *VBL-Gegenwert I*; Fuchs (2024), sec. 19 ARC mn. 211c.

law practice, general terms and conditions have been the primary focus of abuse-of-conditions claims. Concepts of fairness are derived in this context from content-control provisions under sec. 307 et seq. German Civil Code. However, a mere violation of general terms and conditions law is not sufficient to establish an abuse of market power. Competition law does not aim to transform the contractual self-determination of the parties into heteronomy.[355] Rather, the terms and conditions must result from the market power or significant superiority of power of the dominant undertaking.[356] It must be assessed whether the business partners are materially hindered in their competitive activities by the imposed terms.[357] Moreover, evaluations of fundamental rights may also be incorporated into the balancing of interests.[358]

▶ Example

In the ***Amazon GTC* case**, the German Federal Cartel Office investigated a potential abuse of conditions.[359] According to the Office's findings, *Amazon*'s general terms and conditions were non-transparent and contained extensive limitations of liability in favour of the market-dominating company. In addition, they granted *Amazon* an immediate right of termination without the need to provide reasons. The proceedings were eventually discontinued after Amazon committed to amend its general terms and conditions worldwide.

The Office explained its reasoning for treating the general terms and conditions as a potential abuse of conditions: '*Not every clause in the terms and conditions that was potentially disadvantageous or even severely burdensome for dealers was to be criticized under competition law. Rather, the decisive factor was whether, taken as a whole, the use of the respective terms and conditions significantly jeopardized the retailers' competitive activity on the marketplace or made it impossible for them, in particular because they had no possibility of enforcing the fulfillment of Amazon's main contractual obligations.*'[360] ◀

Although there are some older decisions, the abuse of conditions in digital markets has recently gained renewed attention. One reason for this is that services are often offered free of charge to private users, so there is no price level that could be classified as exploitative. Instead, the focus has shifted to the terms and **conditions governing data processing**.[361]

355 German Federal Supreme Court 7 June 2016 – KZR 6/15, NZKart 2016, 328 – *Pechstein*.

356 German Federal Supreme Court 6 November 2013 – KZR 61/11, NZKart 2014, 31, 34 – *VBL-Gegenwert I*. See also German Federal Supreme Court 24 January 2017 – KZR 47/14, NZKart 2017, 242 – *VBL Gegenwert II*; German Federal Supreme Court 7 June 2016 – KZR 6/15, NZKart 2016, 328 – *Pechstein*.

357 German Federal Cartel Office, Decision of 17 July 2019 – B2-88/18, case report p. 9 – *Amazon AGB*.

358 German Federal Supreme Court 7 June 2016 – KZR 6/15, NZKart 2016, 328, 332 – *Pechstein*.

359 German Federal Cartel Office, Decision of 17 July 2019 – B2-88/18 – *Amazon AGB*.

360 German Federal Cartel Office, Decision of 17 July 2019 – B2-88/18, case report p. 9 – *Amazon AGB* [quote translated by author].

361 Körber (2016), 348, 348 et seqq.

In the high-profile ***Facebook* case**, which has not yet been finally decided by the highest court, the German Federal Cartel Office found an abuse of conditions under sec. 19(1) ARC by the market-dominant social network provider.[362] According to the Office, users were required to accept the provider's terms and conditions in order to access the network. Among other requirements, users had to consent to the collection and consolidation of user data outside the social network. The Offices considered such consent not to be voluntary under the data protection standards of Articles 6, 9 GDPR, as access to the platform was conditional on acceptance of these terms. A central issue in the case is the extent to which an abuse of conditions can be enforced based on non-competition law judgments. The German Federal Cartel Office's decision relied on a **violation of GDPR provisions**, whereas the Higher Regional Court of Duesseldorf, ruling in interim relief proceedings, denied any **competitive harm** resulting from the data protection breach.[363] The court stressed that '*the use of contractual terms and conditions that are impermissible under the legal system does not, by itself, indicate a threat to the protected interests of the Cartel Act (freedom to compete on the merits and openness of market access)*.'[364]

5

The German Federal Supreme Court subsequently ruled in line with the German Federal Cartel Office, taking the opposite view of the Higher Regional Court of Duesseldorf:

> » '*There is no serious doubt that the contested terms of use lead to an anti-competitive market result, because this would not be expected under conditions of functioning competition.*'[365]

By making consent to data aggregation mandatory, the market-dominant provider effectively imposes an extension of services on users without their consent. Under conditions of effective competition, alternative offerings that align with user preferences would be expected to emerge.[366] At the same time, the social network's terms of use created a crowding-out effect to the detriment of competitors, as the personalisation of the intermediary service enhanced the market dominator's offering relative to competing services.[367]

The decisions of both the Higher Regional Court of Duesseldorf and the Federal Court of Justice were rendered in the context of interim relief proceedings. It therefore remains open how the courts will decide in the main proceedings. In 2023, the ECJ ruled on the questions referred by the Higher Regional Court of Duesseldorf regarding the relationship between abuse control and data protection law. It held

---

362 German Federal Cartel Office, Decision of 6 February 2019 – B6-22/16 – *Facebook*.

363 Higher Regional Court of Duesseldorf 26 August 2019 – VI-Kart 1/19 (V), MMR 2019, 742 – *Facebook*.

364 Higher Regional Court of Duesseldorf 26 August 2019 – VI-Kart 1/19 (V), MMR 2019, 742, 745 – *Facebook* [quote translated by author].

365 German Federal Supreme Court 23 June 2020 – KVR 69/19, GRUR 2020, 1318, 1326 – *Facebook* [quote translated by author].

366 German Federal Supreme Court 23 June 2020 – KVR 69/19, GRUR 2020, 1318, 1328 – *Facebook*.

367 German Federal Supreme Court 23 June 2020 – KVR 69/19, GRUR 2020, 1318, 1329 – *Facebook*.

that national competition authorities are not precluded from examining potential infringements of data protection law insofar as this is necessary to assess and clarify anti-competitive conduct.[368] It remains to be seen how the Higher Regional

Another issue raised by the *Facebook* decision concerns the required **causal link** between a dominant market position and unlawful contractual conditions. Two approaches can be distinguished. Under the concept of **conduct causality**, there must be a direct causal connection between the undertaking's market power and the imposition of unlawful terms of use; in other words, the dominant undertaking could only have enforced the terms by virtue of its market power.[369] By contrast, under the concept of **result causality**, it is sufficient that the undertaking's market power results in the unlawful terms and conditions producing an anti-competitive effect.[370]

In the *Facebook* case, the Higher Regional Court of Duesseldorf adopted the stricter approach of conduct causality and denied such a link, reasoning that users would likely have accepted the social network's terms of access even in the absence of a dominant market position.[371] The Federal Cartel Office[372] (and probably also the Federal Court of Justice[373]) relied instead on the broader approach of result causality. With the **10th amendment to the ARC** in 2021, the legislature followed the position of the Federal Court of Justice and **revised the wording of sec. 19(1) ARC** accordingly.[374] Whereas the old version prohibited 'the abuse of a dominant market position,' the new version clarifies that 'an abuse by a dominant undertaking' is prohibited. This legislative change confirms that result causality is sufficient, thereby rejecting the requirement of strict conduct causality.

Checklist: Prohibition of Abuse of Dominance under sec. 19 ARC

1. Dominant market position

To establish dominance, the relevant market must first be defined and the undertaking's position within it assessed.

a) Market definition

- Product market: Which goods or services are considered substitutable by demand or supply?
- Geographical market: In which area do competitive conditions apply homogeneously?

368 ECJ 4 July 2023 – C-252/21, ECLI:EU:C:2023:537 – *Meta (Facebook)*. For further details on this decision, see ► 2.3.2.2.5.

369 Fuchs (2024), sec. 19 ARC mn. 212a.

370 Fuchs (2024), sec. 19 ARC mn. 72.

371 Higher Regional Court of Duesseldorf 26 August 2019 – VI-Kart 1/19 (V), MMR 2019, 742, 746 et seq. – *Facebook*.

372 German Federal Cartel Office, Decision of 6 February 2019, B6-22/16, para. 873 – *Facebook*.

373 German Federal Supreme Court 23 June 2020 – KVR 69/19, GRUR 2020, 1318, 1325 – *Facebook*.

374 Government justification for the 10th ARC amendment, BT-Drs. 19/23492, p. 71: '*The amendment to paragraph 1 is therefore intended to clarify that the abuse of conditions – like the entire offence of sec. 19 ARC – does not require that the abusive conduct was only possible for the company due to its dominant market position.*' [quote translated by author].

- Temporal market (if applicable): Is competition limited to certain periods or subject to seasonal fluctuations?

b) Market dominance (sec. 18 ARC)
- Single dominance: Presumption if an undertaking holds a market share of at least 40 % (sec. 18(4) ARC).
- Collective dominance: Presumption if no more than three undertakings hold a dominant position jointly (sec. 18(6) ARC), or up to five undertakings together account for at least two-thirds of the market (sec. 18(7) ARC).

5

2. Abuse of dominance (sec. 19 ARC)
Once dominance is established, the next step is to assess whether abusive conduct is present.
a) Types of abuse
- Exploitative abuse: The dominant undertaking exploits customers or suppliers, e.g. through excessive prices or unfair conditions.
- Exclusionary abuse: The dominant undertaking obstructs competitors, e.g. through predatory pricing, margin squeezes, or discriminatory practices.

b) Balancing of interests
It must be determined whether the conduct can be justified by legitimate business reasons or efficiencies that outweigh its restrictive effects.
c) Causality
A causal link between the dominant position and the abusive conduct must be established. According to the amended sec. 19(1) ARC, result causality suffices: it is enough that the abuse could only occur due to market power; strict 'conduct causality' is no longer required.

5.3.2 Abuse of a Position of Paramount Significance for Competition Across Markets: Sec. 19a ARC

5.3.2.1 Introduction

The abuse offence contained in sec. 19a ARC was introduced with the 10th amendment to the ARC in response to the competitive challenges posed by digital markets. The provision reflects the German legislator's reaction to increasing market power of large digital platforms and can be understood as a kind of counter-draft to the DMA.[375] Unlike the DMA, sec. 19a ARC is rooted in competition law and is primarily aimed at safeguarding effective competition and protecting consumer welfare.[376] By contrast, the DMA constitutes sector-specific regulatory law. Its

375 For further details on the DMA, see section 3.
376 Schweitzer (2024), sec. 19a ARC mn. 27.

objectives are different: it focuses on ensuring contestability of digital markets and safeguarding fairness in the dealings of large gatekeepers.

Sec. 19a(1) ARC introduces a new addressee category: the prohibition of abuse applies to undertakings of **paramount significance for competition across markets**. Unlike sec. 19 ARC, market dominance is not a prerequisite for this addressee status. The provision is explicitly designed to protect competition even in markets that are not yet dominated.[377] At the same time, mere dominance on a single market is not sufficient to establish paramount cross-market significance. The concept represents a new, autonomous notion of cross-market power, distinct from the dominance criteria under sec. 19 and sec. 20 ARC. The decisive step lies with the **German Federal Cartel Office**: it must first determine by order that an undertaking qualifies as being of paramount significance for competition across markets. Only upon such a finding does the undertaking become subject to the obligations and prohibitions of sec. 19a ARC.

❗ Sec. 19a ARC is not directly applicable. An undertaking only becomes an addressee of this provision once the German Federal Cartel Office has formally determined that it is of paramount significance for competition across markets.

Sec. 19a(2) ARC conclusively sets out specific prohibitions, several of which are derived from abuse practices previously observed in digital markets. In contrast to sec. 19 and sec. 20 ARC, the provision **does not contain a general clause**. This legislative choice aims to enhance legal certainty and accelerate enforcement. Nevertheless, the scope of interpretation remains broad in some instances. To mitigate this, most prohibitions are illustrated through **exhaustive prohibitions**, which provide guidance and clarification.

Like under sec. 19 and sec. 20 ARC, undertakings of paramount significance for competition across markets may invoke **grounds of justification**. However, there is a systematic difference: the conduct-related prohibitions of sec. 19a(2) ARC **do not automatically apply** to every undertaking classified by the Federal Cartel Office as being of paramount importance.[378] Instead, a further administrative decision is required. Only once the Federal Cartel Office issues an order prohibiting specific conduct under the catalogue of sec. 19a(2) ARC, and this order becomes final, does the prohibition take effect.[379]

▶ Example

With regard to data processing conditions, the German Federal Cartel Office examined a potential infringement by *Google* of Sec. 19a(2) 1st sentence no. 4a ARC.[380] This provision prohibits undertakings of paramount cross-market significance for competition from creating or substantially increasing barriers to market entry through the process-

---

377 Glöckner (2021), mn. 681.
378 Dreher and Kulka (2023), mn. 1421.
379 Government justification for the 10th amendment to the ARC, BT-Drs. 19/23492, p. 78.
380 German Federal Cartel Office, Decision of 5 October 2023 – B7-70/21 – *Google Datenverarbeitung*.

ing of competitively relevant data. The Office criticised in particular that '*the creation of a Google account as well as the use of Google's services by non-registered users [...] lacked sufficient granularity of the setting options.*'[381] The proceedings were ultimately concluded by way of commitments. ◄

5.3.2.2 Paramount Significance for Competition Across Markets

Concept

5

Sec. 19a(1) ARC does not define the term paramount significance for competition across markets. It constitutes a new, independent concept of market power. This form of power is neither 'less' nor 'more' than market dominance, but rather an aliud.[382] Its defining characteristic is that it is not confined to a specific market but extends across entire ecosystems.[383] This approach also relieves the German Federal Cartel Office of the need to undertake a detailed market definition when applying sec. 19a ARC.[384]

The legislator has emphasised that only a small number of undertakings will regularly meet this threshold. These are undertakings with resources and a strategic position that allow them to exert considerable influence over the business activities of third parties or to expand into new markets and sectors with relative ease.[385] A consolidated position of power of some duration is required.[386] However, a monopoly position is not necessary. Even in oligopolistic settings, an undertaking may qualify as having paramount cross-market significance.[387]

As of January 2024, the German Federal Cartel Office has designated *Meta (Facebook), Alphabet (Google), Amazon, Microsoft* and *Apple* as undertakings of paramount importance across markets.[388] The designation orders against *Amazon* and *Apple* were upheld by the German Federal Supreme Court.[389] The other designation orders issued by the Federal Cartel Office became final and binding without being challenged.

❗ The concept of outstanding cross-market significance for competition is an independent form of market power (sui generis). It cannot be equated with, or reduced to, the traditional notion of market dominance.

---

381 German Federal Cartel Office, Decision of 5 October 2023 – B7-70/21 – Google *Datenverarbeitung* [quote translated by author].
382 Franck and Peitz (2021), pp. 513, 517.
383 Schweitzer (2024), sec. 19a ARC mn. 92.
384 Schweitzer (2024), sec. 19a ARC mn. 94.
385 Government justification for the 9th amendment to the ARC, BT-Drs. 19/23492, p. 73.
386 Schweitzer (2024), sec. 19a ARC mn. 102.
387 Nothdurft (2021), sec. 19a ARC mn. 31.
388 https://www.bundeskartellamt.de/DE/DigitalWirtschaft/VerfahrenGegenGrosseDigitalkonzerne/verfahrengegengrossedigitalkonzerne_node.html (accessed 8 September 2025).
389 German Federal Supreme Court 23 April 2024 – KVB 56/22, NZKart 2024, 500 – *Amazon*; German Federal Supreme Court 18 March 2025 – KVB 61/23, NZKart 2025, 332 – *Apple*.

Criteria

Sec. 19a(1) 2nd sentence ARC contains a non-exhaustive **catalogue of criteria** that must be taken into account when assessing whether an undertaking is of paramount significance for competition across markets. The first criterion listed is the existence of **market dominance** on one or more markets (sec. 19a(1) 2nd sentence **no. 1** ARC). However, market dominance is neither a necessary nor a sufficient condition for being classified as an addressee of sec. 19a ARC. Rather, it represents only one factor among several in the overall assessment.[390] Market dominance can, nonetheless, increase the risk of market tipping, particularly where positive network effects and economies of scope are present.[391] Although sec. 19a ARC does not require a strict market definition, the practice of the German Federal Cartel Office demonstrates that the authority regularly examines whether dominant positions exist and accords them a certain weight in the overall analysis. Given the digital focus of sec. 19a ARC, the special criteria for multi-sided markets pursuant to **sec. 18(3a), (3b) ARC** are of particular relevance in this context.[392]

▶ **Examples**

In its decision to designate *Meta* as an undertaking of paramount significance for competition across markets, the Office emphasised that Meta '*holds a dominant position with its core service Facebook on the platform and network market for social networks for private users in Germany and is also at least very strong in the area of social media advertising.*'[393]

In its case report on *Amazon*, the Office stated that it was able to '*establish a dominant position of Amazon on the German market for the provision of online marketplace services for commercial traders.*'[394]

With regard to *Google*, the Office found that '*market dominance within the meaning of sec. 19a(1) 2nd sentence no. 1 ARC […] exists in any event on the market for general search services vis-à-vis search users, which is to be defined on a Germany-wide basis. Google has had a very high market share in this market for a long time, which, at consistently over 80%, more than doubles the threshold for the presumption of dominance.*'[395] ◀

In determining whether an undertaking possesses paramount significance for competition across markets, the assessment also takes into account its **financial strength** and access to other resources, cf. sec. 19a(1) 2nd sentence **no. 2** ARC. These factors enable the undertaking to expand its ecosystem and reinforce its cross-market influence.[396] Resources in this context include technical expertise, data pro-

---

390 Nothdurft (2021), sec. 19a ARC mn. 41.
391 German Federal Cartel Office, Decision of 30 December 2021 – B7-61/21, para. 306 – *Alphabet*.
392 For further details on these criteria, see ▶ 5.3.1.3.2.
393 German Federal Cartel Office, Decision of 2 May 2022 – B6-22/21, para. 117 – *Meta* [quote translated by author].
394 German Federal Cartel Office, Decision of 5 July 2022 – B2-55/21, case report p. 3 – *Amazon* [quote translated by author].
395 German Federal Cartel Office, Decision of 30 December 2021 – B7-61/21, para. 62 – *Alphabet* [quote translated by author].
396 Schweitzer (2024), sec. 19a ARC mn. 109.

cessing capacities, and the size of an existing customer base. Financial strength may indicate innovation potential and confer competitive advantages, allowing the undertaking to maintain or expand its market power.[397]

▶ Examples

In its ruling on *Alphabet*, the German Federal Cartel Office noted that '*the absolute level of Google's global group turnover and its growth trajectory, which doubled to USD 182.5 billion within five years, demonstrates the company's exceptional financial strength.*'[398] In its decision regarding *Meta*, the Office observed that Meta holds '*more than approximately 7,500 patents in the USA, acquired through both its own research and development activities and strategic acquisitions,*'[399] and that the company's research efforts are '*distributed across multiple areas of computer science, closely aligned with its social media operations and strategic plans in this domain.*'[400] ◀

5

The **vertical integration** of an undertaking and its simultaneous activity on otherwise interconnected markets can contribute significantly to an undertaking's paramount importance for competition (sec. 19a(1) 2nd sentence **no. 3** ARC). Operating across multiple market levels or interconnected markets allows a company to leverage synergies, expand its influence, and strengthen its cross-ecosystem power.[401] A typical example is a platform with a hybrid role: it not only provides intermediary services to commercial users at an upstream level but also competes with these same users at a downstream level, creating a strategic advantage. The legislator highlights this dynamic, noting that '*undertakings that operate digital platforms and networks can be of central importance for various markets due to the advantages of conglomerate structures and the occupation of key positions relevant to competition.*'[402] It is not required, however, that the undertakings's vertical integration or its other interconnected business segments focus exclusively or predominantly on digital platform activities.[403]

▶ Example

In its decision regarding *Alphabet*, the German Federal Cartel Office emphasized the interconnection of *Google*'s services. It stated: '*Google's activities as a provider of a general search service on the one hand and as a provider of specialised ('vertical') search services on the other are particularly closely linked. Google's specialised search services include, for example, the product and price comparison service Google Shopping. On the*

397 German Federal Cartel Office, Decision of 30 December 2021 – B7-61/21, para. 376 – *Alphabet*.
398 German Federal Cartel Office, Decision of 30 December 2021 – B7-61/21, para. 383 – *Alphabet* [quote translated by author].
399 German Federal Cartel Office, Decision of 2 May 2022 – B6-22/21, para. 632 – *Meta* [quote translated by author].
400 German Federal Cartel Office, Decision of 2 May 2022 – B6-22/21, para. 631 – *Meta* [quote translated by author].
401 Reiter (2024), pp. 101, 104 et seq.
402 Government justification for the 10th amendment to the ARC, BT-Drs. 19/23492, p. 73 [quote translated by author].
403 German Federal Supreme Court 18 March 2025 – KVB 61/23, NZKart 2025, 332, 335 – *Apple*.

one hand, Google can use the interconnectedness of these services to design and optimise its Google Search service. On the other hand, by selecting which and how search results and other content or adverts are displayed via the general search, Google can influence which websites users are likely to click on, or whether they click on any other websites at all. Search engines in general are essential for finding web content.'[404] ◄

As with the determination of market dominance (cf. sec. 18(3) no. 3, (3a) no. 4 ARC), the assessment of paramount cross-market significance for competition also requires examining the extent to which the undertaking has access to competition-relevant data (sec. 19a(1) 2nd sentence **no. 4** ARC). Access to data that is superior to that of competitors enables more precise insights into consumer behaviour and preferences, which can constitute a decisive competitive advantage.[405]

► Example

In its assessment of *Amazon*, the German Federal Cartel Office stated that the undertaking '*has cross-service access to extensive and high-quality data that is unlikely to be available in the same form to competing marketplace operators in particular.*'[406] ◄

The significance of the undertaking's activity for the **access of third parties to procurement and sales markets** must also be considered in the overall assessment (sec. 19a(1) 2nd sentence **no. 5** ARC). This includes the relevant intermediation power when evaluating market dominance (see sec. 18(3b) ARC) or a relatively strong market position (see sec. 20(1) 2nd sentence ARC). Intermediation power arises when an undertaking acts as an intermediary between different market sides and occupies a central role in market access, making commercial users dependent on the platform to sell their products. This power is not solely determined by market share but can also be reinforced by user behaviour. If multi-homing is uncommon, meaning that end users generally do not use multiple platforms in parallel, this further strengthens the undertaking's intermediation power.[407]

► Example

With regard to *Amazon*'s business model, the German Federal Cartel Office highlights the platform's intermediation power, with particular reference to the Prime programme. The Office notes: '*In addition, the broad positioning on the supply side, which (increasingly) covers all consumer needs, and the interlinking of its offers opens up a wide range of opportunities for Amazon to bind the user group of consumers to itself in various ways and to retain them in the ecosystem. In particular, this enables Amazon to encourage consumers*

---

404 German Federal Cartel Office, Decision of 30 December 2021 – B7-61/21, para. 104, 105 – *Alphabet* [quote translated by author].

405 For further details on data access as a criterion in the context of assessing market dominance, see ► 5.3.1.3.

406 German Federal Cartel Office, Decision of 5 July 2022 – B2-55/21, case report, p. 5 – *Amazon*. The German Federal Supreme Court confirmed the finding of *Amazon*'s paramount cross-market significance for competition in 2024, see German Federal Supreme Court 23 April 2024 – KVB 56/22 – *Amazon*.

407 Reiter (2024), pp. 101, 105 et seq.

to increasingly fulfil their consumption needs on the Amazon portal, so that they are no longer accessible to competitors, or only to a limited extent, due to this pull effect. The Prime customer loyalty programme is particularly successful in using the various Prime benefits (first and foremost Prime shipping) to encourage users to consume more in the ecosystem, which is then no longer accessible to other providers with their offers.'[408] ◀

5

Designation Order

Pursuant to sec. 19a(1) 3rd sentence ARC, the German Federal Cartel Office's designation order is limited to a period of **five years**. The order is immediately enforceable. The undertaking concerned may lodge an appeal (*Beschwerde*) against the order under sec. 73(1) ARC; however, such an appeal has **no suspensive effect**.[409] Exclusive jurisdiction for appeals lies with the German Federal Supreme Court, as provided in sec. 73(5) ARC.

5.3.2.3 Abuse

Under sec. 19a(2) 1st sentence no. 1 ARC, the German Federal Cartel Office may prohibit an undertaking of paramount cross-market significance for competition from engaging in **self-preferencing practices**. Unlike the general competition law framework, there is no blanket prohibition of self-preferencing for dominant undertakings. Undertakings with market power may still compete and expand their position through competitive means.[410] However, for undertakings that dominate an entire ecosystem, self-preferencing can be anti-competitive and may contribute to the further entrenchment of digital markets.[411] To justify such practices, undertakings may argue that the preferential treatment is based on legitimate competitive measures.

▶ **Examples**

Self-preferencing can take various forms. Examples include highlighting one's own offers in search or platform rankings, either through better placement or visual emphasis such as colour coding. Another common practice is preventing end users from uninstalling pre-installed applications, thereby restricting their choice. ◀

Learning Goals

The significance of self-preferencing has been illustrated in the *Google Shopping* proceedings initiated by the Commission under Article 102 TFEU, addressing abuse of a dominant market position.[412] At the European level, Article 6(5) DMA prohibits self-preferencing in relation to rankings. The provision targets undertak-

---

408 German Federal Cartel Office, Decision of 5 July 2022 – B2-55/21, case report, p. 4 – *Amazon* [quote translated by author].

409 Grünwald (2025), sec. 19a ARC mn. 161.

410 German Federal Supreme Court 24 October 2011 – KZR 7/10, GRUR 2012, 84, 86 – *Grossisten-kündigung*; German Federal Supreme Court 31 January 2012 – KZR 65/10, NJW 2012, 2110, 2111 – *Vertriebsumstellung*.

411 Paal (2025), sec. 19a ARC mn. 16.

412 Commission 27 June 2017 – AT.39740 – *Google Search (Shopping)*; confirmed by ECJ 10 September 2024 – C-48/22 P, ECLI:EU:C:2024:726 – *Google Shopping*.

ings designated as gatekeepers by the Commission.[413] Sec. 19a(2) 1st sentence no. 1 ARC extends beyond the scope of the DMA. Unlike the DMA's ranking-specific restriction, the German provision addresses self-preferencing in a broader range of contexts, covering any preferential treatment that can reinforce a company's cross-market position.

An undertaking with paramount cross-market significance for competition may be prohibited from implementing measures that **impede** other undertakings in their business activities on **procurement or sales markets** if the undertaking's operations are crucial for access to these markets, as set out in sec. 19a(2) 1st sentence no. 2 ARC. This provision targets actions by which the undertaking seeks to **secure its invulnerability within the ecosystem**. Examples include measures that compel downstream undertakings to exclusively pre-install the programs of the norm addressee. A breach of sec. 19a(2) 1st sentence no. 2 ARC can also occur if the norm addressee obstructs other undertakings from advertising their own offers.

Learning Goals

Some of the abuse scenarios covered by sec. 19a(2) 1st sentence no. 2 ARC are similarly prohibited for gatekeepers under Articles 5, 6 DMA. These include Article 5(3) DMA, which bans most-favoured-nation clauses; Article 5(4) DMA, which restricts limitations on advertising on the gatekeeper's platform; Article 6(3) DMA, which requires that software applications on the gatekeeper's operating system can be uninstalled easily; and Article 6(4) DMA, which obliges the gatekeeper to allow the installation of third-party software applications on its operating system.

Pursuant to sec. 19a(2) 1st sentence no. 3 ARC, an undertaking with paramount cross-market significance for competition may be prohibited from engaging in practices that **impede competitors** in markets where it can rapidly expand its position. Such strategies aimed at quickly acquiring substantial market power are commonly referred to as 'rolling up markets.'[414] Although the statutory wording does not explicitly state this limitation, sec. 19a(2) 1st sentence no. 3 ARC is intended to cover only exclusionary practices that are not based on legitimate competitive means. Examples may include predatory pricing strategies or bundled offers.[415] The addressee of the standard is assumed to have the potential to quickly gain market power if it possesses a significant advantage in accessing customers or data.[416]

Sec. 19a(2) 1st sentence no. 4 ARC addresses **data processing practices** by undertakings of paramount cross-market significance that disadvantage other undertakings. No. 4(a) provides the example of conditioning the use of services on users consenting to the processing of data from other services of the undertaking or from a third-party provider without offering sufficient choice. This reflects the

413 For further details on Article 6(5) DMA, see ► 3.3.2.4.
414 Government justification for the 10th amendment to the ARC, BT-Drs. 19/23492, p. 76.
415 Government justification for the 10th amendment to the ARC, BT-Drs. 19/23492, p. 76.
416 Government justification for the 10th amendment to the ARC, BT-Drs. 19/23492, p. 76.

access conditions to the social network that the German Federal Cartel Office found to constitute an abuse in the *Facebook* case.[417] For gatekeepers, **Article 5(2) DMA** addresses similar situations, but unlike sec. 19a ARC, it explicitly references the **GDPR**. Within the scope of sec. 19a ARC, the principles of the GDPR can still be applied regarding the processing of personal data.[418] Additionally, undertakings may be prohibited from processing data obtained from other undertakings for purposes beyond what is necessary to provide their own services to those undertakings, provided that insufficient choice is available, as set out in sec. 19a(2) 1st sentence no. 4(b) ARC.

5

▶ **Example**

In the *Google Data Processing* proceedings, which concluded in October 2023 with the submission of commitments, the German Federal Cartel Office examined whether *Google*'s data processing terms violated sec. 19a(2) sentence 1 no. 4(a) ARC. The Office noted, among other points: '*First of all, there is a lack of sufficient granularity in the setting options both when setting up a Google account and when using Google's services as a non-registered user. Users do not have the option to reject cross-service data processing or to restrict data processing to the Google end-user service in the context in which the data was generated.*'[419] '*[…] Finally, when setting up a Google account, the required equivalence of consent and rejection is missing. In the context of so-called 'express personalisation,' there is only the option to accept the intended data processing, but no option to reject it.*'[420] ◀

Sec. 19a(2) 1st sentence no. 5 ARC addresses practices that **hinder or prevent product interoperability or data portability**. Product interoperability reduces lock-in effects and facilitates switching between the offerings of different competitors.[421] Similarly, data portability enables users to transfer their data between platforms more easily, thereby enhancing competitive dynamics.[422] The imposition of obligations under sec. 19a(2) sentence 1 no. 5 ARC requires the German Federal Cartel Office to demonstrate that competition would otherwise be harmed.[423] Pursuant to sec. 19a(2) 1st sentence no. 6 ARC, designated undertakings may be prohibited from providing **inadequate or misleading information** to other undertakings. This includes information regarding the quality or handling of services, which could make it difficult for competitors to reliably assess and compare offerings.[424] The legislator primarily had online advertising in mind when drafting this provision. Undertakings with paramount cross-market significance for competition often

---

417 German Federal Cartel Office, Decision of 6 February 2019 – B6-22/16 – *Facebook*.
418 Schweitzer (2024), sec. 19a ARC mn. 195.
419 German Federal Cartel Office, Decision of 5 October 2023 – B7-70/21, para. 51 – *Google Datenverarbeitung*.
420 German Federal Cartel Office, Decision of 5 October 2023 – B7-70/21, para. 54 – *Google Datenverarbeitung*.
421 Paal (2025), sec. 19a ARC mn. 27.
422 Schweitzer (2024), sec. 19a ARC mn. 202.
423 Schweitzer (2024), sec. 19a ARC mn. 208.
424 Government justification for the 10th ARC amendment, BT-Drs. 19/23492, p. 77; Nothdurft (2021), sec. 19a ARC mn. 110.

hold information advantages that, if exploited, can adversely affect competitive conditions.

Learning Goals

There are overlaps with Article 5(9) DMA, which requires gatekeepers to provide each advertiser using their online advertising services with specific information regarding the terms of service. Similarly, Article 6(8) DMA addresses related obligations, stipulating that gatekeepers must, among other requirements, grant advertisers free access to performance measurement tools and the data collected. These provisions align with sec. 19a(2) 1st sentence no. 6 ARC in ensuring that undertakings with significant cross-market influence do not use information asymmetries to the detriment of competition.

Sec. 19a(2) 1st sentence no. 7 ARC prohibits undertakings of paramount cross-market significance from demanding **disproportionate advantages** from other undertakings, constituting a clear prohibition of exploitation. This provision is analogous to the prohibition of 'tapping' under sec. 19(2) no. 5 ARC,[425] and existing case law on that provision can generally inform the interpretation of sec. 19a ARC.

▶ Example

An illustrative example provided by the legislator refers to a norm addressee who demands, in exchange, that press publishers grant free licenses for copyrighted content that are not necessary for the provision of the brokerage service.[426] ◀

Checklist: Prohibition of Abuse of Paramount Cross-Market Significance for Competition pursuant under sec. 19a ARC

1. Undertakings of paramount cross-market significance for competition (sec. 19a(1) ARC)

a) Concept of paramount cross-market significance for competition

The assessment of an undertaking's cross-market significance is based on a combination of criteria, including: market dominance on one or more markets; financial strength and access to resources; vertical integration and activity on interconnected markets; access to competition-relevant data; significance of the undertaking for third-party access to procurement and sales markets

b) Designation by the German Federal Cartel Office

The German Federal Cartel Office issues a designation order to identify undertakings of paramount significance for competition across markets. Such orders are limited to five years and are immediately enforceable, with appeals directed exclusively to the German Federal Supreme Court.

---

425 For further details on sec. 19(2) no. 5 ARC, see ▶ 5.3.1.5.

426 Government justification for the 10th ARC amendment, BT-Drs. 19/25868, p. 118.

2. Abuse (sec. 19a(2) ARC)

The following practices are prohibited for undertakings of paramount cross-market significance:

No. 1: Self-preferencing

No. 2: Disabling or limiting competitors

No. 3: 'Rolling up' or consolidating markets

No. 4: Data processing practices that create barriers to competition

No. 5: Impeding interoperability or data portability

No. 6: Providing insufficient or misleading information

No. 7: Demanding disproportionate advantages from commercial partners

5.3.3 Abuse of Relative or Superior Market Power: Sec. 20 ARC

5.3.3.1 Introduction

Under sec. 20 ARC, German competition law takes a distinctive approach by extending certain prohibitions to undertakings with relative or superior market power, even if they do not meet the threshold of market dominance. Unlike European law, which focuses on dominant undertakings, sec. 20 ARC establishes a stricter rule than Article 102 TFEU. This approach is consistent with European law under Article 3(2) Regulation 1/2003.[427]

Learning Goals

Article 3(2) 1st sentence Regulation 1/2003 prevents national legislators from imposing stricter rules on collusive conduct than those under European competition law. However, for unilateral conduct, Article 3(2) 2nd sentence Regulation 1/2003 allows stricter national regulations.

Sec. 20(1) 1st sentence ARC extends the prohibitions against unjustified discrimination and unfair impediment from sec. 19(2) no. 1 ARC to undertakings with **relative market power**. This framework has already been applied in the context of digital markets to address abuses of relative market power.

► Example

In its assessment of price parity clauses, the German Federal Cartel Office did not resolve whether the *Booking* platform held a dominant market position. Instead, it examined the platform's relative market power under sec. 20(1) ARC and concluded that the platform had abused its market power pursuant to sec. 20(1) in conjunction with sec. 19(2) no. 1 ARC. This finding was made alongside a determination of a violation of sec. 1 ARC and Article 101 TFEU.[428] ◄

427 For further details on the relation to EU competition law, see ► 5.1.5.

428 German Federal Cartel Office, Decision of 22 December 2015 – B9-121/13, mn. 302 – *Booking.com*.

Sec. 20(1) 2nd sentence ARC provides a special extension of the concept of relative market power for undertakings acting as **intermediaries on multi-sided markets**, which includes platform providers.

Sec. 20(1a) 1st sentence **ARC**, introduced by the 10th amendment to the ARC, emphasizes the role of data in determining relative market power. It clarifies that relative market power may also arise from controlling data that other undertakings depend on for their business activities. Sec. 20(1a) 2nd sentence ARC further expands the concept of abuse under sec. 20(1) ARC in conjunction with sec. 19(1), (2) ARC, according to which a **refusal** to grant access to data in return for reasonable remuneration can constitute an unreasonable obstruction.

Sec. 20(3) ARC addresses undertakings with **superior market power**. Unlike relative market power, which focuses on the dependence of customers or suppliers, superior market power is assessed horizontally, i.e., in relation to small and medium-sized competitors. Norm addressees are prohibited from using their market power to directly or indirectly unfairly hinder competitors. Sec. 20(3) 2nd-4th sentences ARC further concretize this prohibition by providing illustrative examples of abusive conduct.

Sec. 20(3a) ARC provides a digital-economy-specific regulatory example. It establishes that an unreasonable impediment occurs if an undertaking with superior market power on a multi-sided market hinders competitors from **independently achieving network effects**, thereby creating a serious risk of restricting competition on the merits to a significant extent. This is designed to prevent the market from 'tilting' in favour of the dominant player. Sec. 20(3a) ARC is commonly referred to as the **anti-tipping rule**,[429] aiming to allow the competition authority to intervene at an early stage before market tipping occurs.[430]

▶ **Example**

A platform operator prohibits its users from multi-homing.[431] ◀

Sec. 20(2) ARC extends the prohibition of tapping, which previously applied to dominant buyers, to buyers with relative market power. This ensures that even buyers who are not dominant cannot demand disproportionate advantages from suppliers. Sec. 20(4) ARC introduces an easing of the burden of proof in favour of small and medium-sized competitors that are impeded, a principle commonly referred to as the 'bear trap doctrine,' making it easier for these undertakings to demonstrate an abuse of relative or superior market power.[432] Sec. 20(5) ARC supplements these rules by addressing trade, professional, and quality mark associations, prohibiting them from refusing admission to an undertaking in a manner that unfairly hinders competition. Collectively, these provisions broaden the scope of competition protection, covering not only dominant undertakings but also those with relative market power and collective gatekeeping by associations.

429 Podszun (2024), sec. 20 ARC mn. 255.
430 Government justification for the 10th ARC amendment, BT-Drs. 19/23492, p. 83.
431 Government justification for the 10th ARC amendment, BT-Drs. 19/23492, p. 83.
432 Markert (2024), sec. 20 ARC mn. 249.

Overview of Sec. 20 ARC (Digital Market-Specific Provisions Are in Bold):
sec. 20(1) 1st sentence ARC: Prohibition of unfair impediment and unjustified discrimination for undertakings with relative market power

sec. 20(1) 2nd sentence ARC: Extension of the concept of relative market power to include dependence on intermediaries

sec. 20(1) 3rd sentence ARC: Presumption of demand-related dependency

sec. 20(1a) ARC: Extension of the concept of relative market power to include data-related dependency

sec. 20(2) ARC: Prohibition of abuse of relative buyer power

sec. 20(3) ARC: Prohibition of unfair hindrance for undertakings with superior market power

sec. 20(3a) ARC: Anti-tipping rule as a regulatory example for the abuse of superior market power

sec. 20(4) ARC: Bear-catching doctrine as a facilitation of evidence in favour of impeded small and medium-sized competitors

sec. 20(5) ARC: Prohibition of unjustified refusal of admission to associations

5

5.3.3.2 Abuse of Relative Market Power

Concept of Relative Market Power

An undertaking has relative market power if other undertakings at the upstream or downstream market level are **dependent** on it. Unlike the assessment of market dominance,[433] the determination of relative market power is not primarily market-wide. Instead, it focuses on bilateral relationships with customers or suppliers.[434] Sec. 20(1) 1st sentence ARC defines dependence as a situation in which other undertakings **do not have sufficient and reasonable alternative options**. Additionally, there must be a clear imbalance in countervailing power between the undertaking and its counterparties. Case law has further specified this concept by identifying **four groups of cases**:

- **Assortment-related dependence**: This exists when a retailer must include a specific branded product in its assortment in order to remain competitive.[435] The branded article must have reached such a level of reputation that consumers expect it to be available.[436] Within this category, two sub-cases can be distinguished. Top position dependence arises when consumers specifically expect the presence of a particular brand. Top-of-the-range dependence, by contrast, does not focus on a single brand; instead, the retailer's competitiveness requires it to carry a certain number of recognised branded products within a product

433 For further details on the concept of market dominance, see ► 5.3.1.3.

434 Glöckner (2021), sec. 6 mn. 666.

435 German Federal Supreme Court 12 December 2017 – KZR 50/15, GRUR 2018, 441, 442 et seq. – *Rimowa*; German Federal Supreme Court 4 November 2003 – KZR 2/02, NJW-RR 2004, 689, 689 et seq. – *Depotkosmetik im Internet*.

436 German Federal Supreme Court 20 November 1975 – KZR 1/75, GRUR 1976, 206 – *Rossignol*.

group.[437] A classic example is the Federal Court of Justice's 1975 decision affirming dependency on the *Rossignol* brand product range.[438]

- **Undertaking-related dependence**: Such a dependency exists when customers are bound to a manufacturer through long-term supply relationships and switching to alternative suppliers would entail significant effort.[439] This is particularly relevant for authorised dealers. Dependence may arise, for example, where customers have invested in specialised machines or tools tailored to the manufacturer's products,[440] or where their customer base has largely been built up through the distribution of the manufacturer's goods.[441]
- **Scarcity-related dependence**: Relative market power can also arise when a sudden shortage leaves customers dependent on a specific supplier. Case law confirmed such dependence during the 1973 oil crisis, where petrol station operators were deemed dependent on oil companies for supply.[442]
- **Demand-related dependence**: Suppliers may become dependent on a particular customer.[443] This can result from product specialisation or from the customer's key market position.[444] Sec. 20(1) 3rd sentence ARC provides a presumption of demand-driven dependence: such dependence is assumed where a customer regularly receives special benefits from a supplier, beyond standard price discounts or service charges, that are not granted to comparable customers.

Since the 10th amendment to the ARC, sec. 20 ARC contains two additional categories of dependency that are specifically tailored to the **digital context**. These are dependency on intermediaries, cf. sec. 20(1) 2nd sentence ARC, and data-related dependency, cf. sec. 20(1a) 1st sentence ARC.

- **Dependence on intermediaries**: Similar to sec. 18(3b) ARC in the context of determining a dominant market position, sec. 20(1) 2nd sentence ARC incorporates the concept of intermediation power into the assessment of relative market power. The underlying idea is that platforms, where commercial users are correspondingly dependent, can assume a key role or even act as a 'bottleneck' for access to other market sides.[445] Commercial users rely on the platform operator to broker their offers. Relative market power of an intermediary is therefore to be assumed under sec. 20(1) 2nd sentence ARC if the users are dependent on its intermediation services in such a way that sufficient and reasonable alternatives are lacking.

---

437 German Federal Supreme Court 9 May 2000 – KZR 28/98, GRUR 2000, 1108 – *Designer-Polstermöbel*.
438 German Federal Supreme Court 20 November 1975 – KZR 1/75, GRUR 1976, 206 – *Rossignol*.
439 German Federal Supreme Court 23 January 2018 – KZR 48/15, NZKart 2018, 191, 193 – *Jaguar-Vertragswerkstatt II*.
440 Stammwitz (2025), sec. 20 ARC mn. 28.
441 Higher Regional Court of Stuttgart 23 March 1979 – 2 W (Kart.) 8/79, WuW 1979, 491 – *Porsche-Vertragshändler*.
442 Higher Regional Court of Berlin 4 July 1974 – Kart 27/74, WuW 1974, 767 – *AGIP II*.
443 Glöckner (2021), sec. 6 mn. 670.
444 Stammwitz (2025), sec. 20 ARC mn. 32.
445 Körber (2020), pp. 290, 292.

▶ **Example**

Case law has affirmed the relative market power of an intermediary where an undertaking generates a large proportion of its turnover through sales via its platform.[446] ◀

- **Data-related dependence**: Pursuant to sec. 20(1a) 1st sentence ARC, dependency arises if an undertaking controls access to data on which other undertakings rely. The decisive prerequisite is that access to the data is necessary for other undertakings to carry out their business activities, for example, to operate on the market effectively or to bring their services to bear in competition.[447] No dependency exists if the undertaking can easily obtain the relevant data elsewhere.[448] It must also be taken into account that data is a non-rivalrous resource, meaning that its use by multiple undertakings in parallel does not diminish its value.

5

▶ **Example**

In June 2023, the German Federal Cartel Office assumed that providers of integrated mobility services were dependent on data in relation to the rail passenger transport forecast data collected by *Deutsche Bahn*.[449] ◀

Abuse

Sec. 20(1) ARC prohibits undertakings with relative market power from abusing their position. The scope of prohibited conduct corresponds in principle to that which is prohibited for dominant undertakings, as follows from the **reference to sec. 19(1),(2) ARC** in sec. 20(1) 1st sentence ARC. Accordingly, undertakings with relative market power are prohibited from unfairly hindering or unjustifiably discriminating against the undertakings dependent on them.

Sec. 20(1a) 2nd sentence ARC adds a digital-economy-specific example of abusive conduct: the **refusal to grant access to data** on which dependent undertakings rely, even if they are willing to pay a **reasonable fee**. Such a refusal may amount to an exclusionary abuse.[450] The key question is whether the refusal is unfair in light of all circumstances. For this assessment, several factors must be considered: whether the dependent undertaking is willing to pay an appropriate fee, the positive effects on competition of granting access to the data, potential negative effects on incentives for the data holder to invest in collecting further data,[451] the importance of the data for the business success of the dependent undertaking, and the burden on the obliged undertaking in providing access.[452]

---

446 Regional Court of Munich I 31 March 2021 – 37 O 32/21, NZKart 2021, 198 – *Amazon-Kontosperrung*.
447 Podszun (2024), sec. 20 ARC mn. 129.
448 Government justification for the 10th ARC amendment, BT-Drs. 19/23492, p. 81.
449 German Federal Cartel Office, Decision of 26 June 2023 – B9-144/19.
450 Podszun (2024), sec. 20 ARC mn. 142.
451 Podszun (2024), sec. 20 ARC mn. 155.
452 Podszun (2024), sec. 20 ARC mn. 159, 161.

Learning Goals

For undertakings that are designated as gatekeepers, additional data access obligations may arise from Article 5(9), (10) DMA.[453] These provisions impose duties on gatekeepers to provide business users and advertisers with access to certain data generated through their use of the gatekeeper's services. Beyond the DMA, Article 9(1) Platform Regulation also requires providers of online intermediation services to explain to their commercial users what data is accessible and on what terms.[454] While this provision does not itself establish an access obligation, it enhances transparency. Such transparency obligations can play a crucial role in practice: they make it easier to determine whether a relatively market-powerful service provider is unlawfully refusing access under sec. 20(1a) 2nd sentence ARC.[455]

5.3.3.3 Abuse of Superior Market Power

Concept of Superior Market Power

Sec. 20(3) ARC extends the prohibition of unfair impediment and unjustified discrimination to undertakings with superior market power. Unlike sec. 20(1) ARC, which focuses on vertical relationships of dependency, the concept of superior market power is based on a **horizontal comparison** with the market position of competitors.[456] The provision applies only in relation to **small or medium-sized undertakings**, which may be dependent. This contrasts with sec. 20(1) ARC, which, since the 10th amendment to the ARC,[457] no longer contains such a restriction. The classification of a competitor as small or medium-sized is primarily determined by turnover. The threshold of less than EUR 10 million laid down in sec. 35(2) 1st sentence ARC can serve as a guide.[458] In addition, a relative size comparison with the turnover of competitors must be undertaken. The decisive factor in establishing superior market power is the existence of a significant power differential in relation to small and medium-sized competitors.[459] Unlike the concept of market dominance, the threshold of dominance itself does not need to be reached. However, the same assessment criteria apply as in the determination of market dominance,[460] albeit with a lower threshold of market power.

Abuse

Sec. 20(3) 1st sentence ARC prohibits undertakings with superior market power from unfairly impeding dependent competitors. Sentence 2 concretises this prohibition by providing three illustrative examples: the sale of food below cost price

453 On these provisions, see ► 3.3.1.8.
454 On this provision, see ► 4.3.5.
455 Podszun (2024), sec. 20 ARC mn. 103.
456 Glöckner (2021), sec. 6 mn. 674.
457 Government justification for the 10th ARC amendment, BT-Drs. 19/23492, p. 79.
458 Lübbert and Schöner (2020), sec. 24 mn. 12.
459 Higher Regional Court of Duesseldorf 19 December 2001 – Kart 21/00 (V), WuW 2002, 151 – *Wal-Mart*; Higher Regional Court of Duesseldorf 13 November 2000, Kart 16/00 (V), WUW 2001, 169 – *Freie Tankstellen*.
460 For further details on the assessment of market dominance, see ► 5.3.1.3.

(no. 1), the sale of other goods below cost price on more than an occasional basis (no. 2), and the imposition of a margin squeeze (no. 3).

The **anti-tipping rule under sec. 20(3a) ARC** establishes a digital-market-specific abuse prohibition. An undertaking is considered to abuse its superior market power on a multi-sided market, as defined in sec. 18(3a) ARC, if it hinders competitors from independently realising network effects, thereby creating a serious risk that competition on the merits will be significantly restricted. The rule is grounded in competition economics, recognizing that digital markets tend to 'tip' toward dominance, often due to indirect network effects – a phenomenon seen as '*one of the greatest threats to competitive functioning in these markets*'.[461] The wording of the provision is broad, potentially causing legal uncertainty in practice,[462] as the absence of standard examples makes the scope of prohibited conduct less predictable. Sec. 20(3a) ARC is also designed as a **preventative provision**, enabling early intervention before market tipping occurs.

5

The prohibition under sec. 20(3a) ARC is not intended to cover situations where an increase in market power results from legitimate competition on the merits.[463] A careful **balancing of interests** is required to determine whether the undertaking with superior market power is simply seeking to retain its customers legitimately or whether its conduct creates a real risk of restricting competition on the merits.[464] For instance, undertakings that already hold significant market power could foster monopolisation tendencies by making it harder for users to multi-home, meaning to use multiple platform services simultaneously.[465] Similarly, cases may arise where platforms retain users by offering particularly attractive or even free services through cross-financing.[466]

Checklist: Prohibition of Abuse of Relative Market Power under Sec. 20 ARC

1. Relatively powerful market position
   (a) Relative market power in a vertical relationship, sec. 20(1), (1a) ARC
   - Assortment-related dependence
   - Undertaking-related dependence
   - Scarcity-related dependence
   - Demand-driven dependence
   - Dependence on intermediaries
   - Data-related dependence

   (b) Relative market power in a horizontal relationship, sec. 20(3) ARC

2. Abuse
   (a) In the case of relative market power in a vertical relationship:

---

461 Polley and Kaup (2020), pp. 113, 115 [quote translated by author].
462 Körber (2020), pp. 290, 293; Polley and Kaup (2020), pp. 113, 115.
463 Paal and Kumkar (2021), pp. 809, 813.
464 Cetintas (2020), pp. 446, 446; Westermann (2022), sec. 20 ARC mn. 133 et seq.
465 Schweitzer, Haucap, Kerber and Welker (2018), p. 63.
466 Podszun (2024), sec. 20 ARC mn. 285.

- Unfair impediment under sec. 20(1), (1a) ARC in conjunction with sec. 19(1), (2) no. 1 ARC
- Passive discrimination under sec. 20(2) ARC in conjunction with sec. 19(2) no. 5 ARC
  (b) In the case of relative market power in a horizontal relationship: Unfair impediment under sec. 20(3), (3a) ARC

5.4 Merger Control: Secs. 35–43a ARC

5.4.1 Introduction

National merger control in Germany is governed by **secs. 35–43a ARC**. The rules differ from European merger control (Articles 1, 3 EUMR) in two key aspects: the turnover thresholds in sec. 35 ARC and the definition of a concentration in sec. 37 ARC. National merger control only applies if the criteria for European merger control are not met. Pursuant to Article 21(3) EUMR, member states may not apply their national law to mergers with a Community dimension, reflecting the **one-stop-shop principle**.[467] Responsibility for national merger control lies exclusively with the German Federal Cartel Office; the state cartel authorities do not have enforcement powers in this area.

Order of Review
Given the primacy of European merger control, a transaction may only be assessed under the national control regime pursuant to sec. 35 et seq. ARC once it has been established that the criteria for the application of Articles 1, 3 EUMR are not satisfied (the one-stop-shop principle).

While the criteria in sec. 35 and sec. 37 ARC differ from those of European merger control, there are significant parallels in the substantive standard of review for mergers. Since the 8th amendment to the ARC came into force in 2013, the German Federal Cartel Office has applied the **SIEC test** under sec. 36(1) ARC when assessing proposed mergers. The previous standard, the market dominance test, remains as a benchmark, similar to its continued use under the 2004 amendment to the ECMR. Consequently, the German legislator has aligned the national merger control regime with European merger control, aiming to promote cross-border convergence and a level playing field.[468] The only notable difference is the balancing clause in sec. 36(1) 2nd sentence no. 1 ARC, which requires clearance of a merger if the parties can demonstrate that the merger will improve competitive

467 Möller (2025), sec. 35 ARC mn. 44.
468 Steinvorth (2020), sec. 20 mn. 3.

conditions and that these improvements outweigh any impediment to competition. While this clause has no direct equivalent in Article 2(3) EUMR, its substance is effectively recognised in European merger control.[469]

In contrast to the EUMR, German national merger control provides for **ministerial approval under sec. 42 ARC**. This provision allows the Federal Minister for Economic Affairs and Energy, upon request, to authorise a merger that has been prohibited by the German Federal Cartel Office.[470] The standard of review for such approval is not based on competition law. Instead, the Minister assesses the merger in light of macroeconomic benefits and overriding public interests. If these considerations outweigh the anticipated impediment to competition, ministerial authorisation may be granted.

As national merger control, like its European counterpart, operates as an **ex ante control regime**, a two-stage review structure is required. In the formal phase of merger control, the definition of a merger (sec. 35 ARC) and the turnover thresholds (sec. 37 ARC) must be examined. If a merger project does not meet these criteria, it is not subject to notification to the German Federal Cartel Office. In its *MetalKustomer* decision, the German Federal Supreme Court recently clarified that the Federal Cartel Office is authorised to establish the parties' notification obligation by way of an order.[471]

5.4.2 Formal Merger Control: Sec. 35, 37 ARC

5.4.2.1 Definition of Merger

Acquisition of Assets

While Article 3 EUMR only recognises mergers (Article 3(1)(a) EUMR) and the acquisition of control (Article 3(1)(b) EUMR),[472] the definition of a merger in sec. 37 ARC is broader. It is divided into four elements. The first element is the acquisition of assets, regulated in **sec. 37(1) no. 1 ARC**. In order to fall within the concept of concentration under sec. 35(1) no. 1 ARC, it is sufficient if a substantial part of the assets is acquired. This requirement is met if the acquired share of assets is either quantitatively significant in relation to the total assets[473] or qualitatively significant in its own right.[474] In any case, the acquired share of assets must enable the acquirer to alter the market position of the acquiring undertaking.[475]

469 Körber (2025), Article 2 EUMR mn. 523.

470 For further details on the ministerial approval, see ► 5.4.3.4.

471 German Federal Supreme Court 17 June 2025 – KVR 77/22, NZKart 2025, 442 – *MetalKustomer*.

472 For further details on Article 3 EUMR, see ► 2.4.2.

473 German Federal Supreme Court 20 November 1975 – KVR 1/75, GRUR 1976, 327, 327 – *Zementmahlanlage I*: '*quantitatively sufficiently high*'.

474 German Federal Supreme Court 20 November 1975 – KVR 1/75, GRUR 1976, 327, 328 – *Zementmahlanlage I.*

475 German Federal Supreme Court 10 October 2006 – KVR 32/05, GRUR 2007, 517, 519 – *National Geographic I.*

▶ Example

Case law has recognised that the acquisition of a substantial part of the assets of a cement plant,[476] as well as the acquisition of a registered trademark, falls within the scope of sec. 37(1) no. 1 ARC. ◀

Acquisition of Control

A merger pursuant to **sec. 37(1) no. 2 ARC** is deemed to occur when one or more undertakings (the parent undertaking or undertakings) acquire control over another undertaking (the subsidiary). This is the most practically relevant form of merger.[477] Control is defined as the ability of one undertaking to exercise a decisive influence over the activities of another.[478]

Sec. 37(1) no. 2(a) ARC lists ownership and usage rights to all or part of an undertaking's assets as standard examples of control. Such usage rights conveying control may, for instance, arise through the conclusion of business transfer agreements.[479] If an undertaking acquires ownership, the merger element of the acquisition of assets under sec. 37(1) no. 1 ARC is usually fulfilled at the same time. Furthermore, sec. 37(1) no. 2(b) ARC refers to rights or contractual arrangements that grant a decisive influence over the composition, deliberations, or resolutions of an undertaking's corporate bodies. In practice, the most significant case of control acquisition is the acquisition of voting shares in an undertaking. This often overlaps with the merger offence of share acquisition under sec. 37(1) no. 3 ARC. However, unlike the acquisition of shares, the determining factor for control is not tied to surpassing certain thresholds but to whether decisive influence can actually be exercised.

If **two or more undertakings** acquire **control** over another undertaking, this constitutes the creation of a joint venture. Where both undertakings hold a 50% stake, they exercise joint control. However, joint control may also arise in cases of unequal shareholdings if the minority shareholder is granted veto rights over key aspects of the joint venture's strategic decisions. Such rights typically cover areas such as the business plan, major investments, management appointments, or the annual budget.[480] These safeguards ensure that even a minority shareholder can exert a decisive influence on the strategic direction of the joint venture.[481] Unlike Article 3(4) EUMR,[482] German merger control does not require the joint venture to be a full-function joint venture, i.e. operating on a lasting basis with all the functions of an autonomous economic entity. Instead, sec. 37(1) no. 2 ARC also extends to **partial-function joint ventures**, thereby applying a broader scope than EU merger control.[483]

476 German Federal Supreme Court 23 October 1979 – KVR 3/78, GRUR 1980, 253 – *Zementmahlanlage II*.
477 Steinvorth (2020), sec. 19 mn. 57.
478 Emmerich and Lange (2024), sec. 32 mn. 6; Steinvorth (2020), sec. 19 mn. 58.
479 Kling and Thomas (2016), sec. 22 mn. 28.
480 Kling and Thomas (2016), sec. 22 mn. 34.
481 Emmerich and Lange (2024), sec. 32 mn. 9.
482 For details on the legal situation under EU merger control, see ▶ 2.4.2.2.
483 Kersting (2025), sec. 37 ARC mn. 49.

The current debate surrounding 'direct hiring', i.e. the poaching of highly skilled employees (e.g. in the AI sector), which may be subject to notification, also affects German merger control.[484] This would be the case if the 'transfer' of employees were part of a broader agreement between two competitors. Cases where no such agreement exists are more difficult to assess. In these instances, there is no selling company from which the acquisition of control actually originates. However, since the effects on market structure can be significant even without such an agreement, a broad interpretation of the merger should be considered.[485]

Acquisition of Shares

The acquisition of shares constitutes a merger pursuant to sec. 37(1) no. 3 ARC if an undertaking acquires capital or voting rights in another undertaking and thereby crosses either the **50% threshold** (lit. a)) or the **25% threshold** (lit. b)). Unlike the acquisition of control under sec. 37(1) no. 2 ARC, the acquisition of shares does not require that the purchaser be able to exert decisive influence over the target undertaking. Control is therefore not a prerequisite. The rationale for this provision lies in the assumption that, from a 25% shareholding onwards, the acquirer is likely to be able to influence the target undertaking's market conduct in practice, even if not formally in control.[486] What matters in this context is solely whether the statutory thresholds are exceeded. If they are, the merger offence is deemed to be fulfilled, irrespective of whether the acquirer actually gains strategic influence.

► Example

If an associated undertaking already holds 20% of the shares and acquires a further 8%, it exceeds the 25% threshold with this acquisition transaction and thus realises an acquisition of shares pursuant to sec. 37(1) no. 3(b) ARC. By contrast, if the undertaking already holds 26% and acquires a further 20%, no new threshold is crossed. Since the 25% threshold has already been exceeded and the 50% threshold is not reached, there is no acquisition of shares under sec. 37(1) no. 3 ARC. ◄

The **fiction of a partial merger of the parents** pursuant to sec. 37(1) no. 3 3rd sentence ARC provides that the creation of a joint venture is not only assessed as a merger between the parents and the joint venture itself, but is also deemed to constitute a merger between the parent undertakings with regard to the markets in which the joint venture is active.[487] The aim of this legal fiction is to allow the German Federal Cartel Office to assess the effects of the transaction on the competitive relationship between the parent companies themselves. The relevance of this fiction already arises at the stage of formal merger control, as all parent under-

484 German Federal Cartel Office, press release of 29 November 2024 'Taking over employees may be subject to merger control in Germany – Bundeskartellamt not competent to review Microsoft/Inflection transaction as Inflection has no substantial operations in Germany' https://www.bundeskartellamt.de/SharedDocs/Meldung/EN/Pressemitteilungen/2024/29_11_2024_Microsoft.html (accessed 12 September 2025).

485 Bien and Becker (2024), pp. 81, 81–88.

486 Government justification for the 5th ARC amendment, BT-Drs. 11/4610, p. 19.

487 Emmerich and Lange (2024), sec. 32 mn. 21.

takings acquiring at least 25% of the shares in the joint venture are considered 'undertakings concerned' within the meaning of sec. 35 ARC. This ensures that potential competitive restraints resulting from the cooperation of the parent undertakings can be reviewed. In this context, it must also be taken into account that the establishment of joint ventures may fall under both merger control rules and the general prohibition of anticompetitive agreements in sec. 1 ARC. This 'two-barriers theory' (*Zwei-Schranken-Theorie*) reflects the parallel applicability of merger control provisions and cartel prohibition rules.[488]

Significant Competitive Influence

As a catch-all provision, sec. 3(1) no. 4 ARC covers cases in which a undertaking acquires significant competitive influence over another undertaking. The focus is on transactions that neither convey control pursuant to sec. 37(1) no. 2 ARC nor reach the thresholds of sec. 37(1) no. 3 ARC.[489] This primarily includes the acquisition of shares that do not reach the threshold of 25%. Only those opportunities to exert influence that are mediated under undertaking law are covered by the catch-all provision.[490] The question of whether the competitive influence is significant must be examined on a case-by-case basis. A mere minority shareholding that remains below the threshold of 25 % is not sufficient in any case. Rather, so-called plus factors are required.[491] These must mean that the influenced undertaking cannot act independently of the influencing undertaking on the market.[492] Examples include information rights that open up the possibility of exerting influence despite a mere minority shareholding.[493]

5.4.2.2 Scope of Application

Pursuant to **sec. 35(1) ARC**, a merger is subject to notification if two cumulative turnover thresholds are met. First, the undertakings involved must have generated total **worldwide turnover** of more than **EUR 500 million** in the last financial year preceding the merger (no. 1). Second, at least one of the undertakings involved must have achieved domestic turnover of more than **EUR 50 million**, while another undertaking involved must have achieved turnover exceeding **EUR 17.5 million**. Only when both conditions are satisfied does the obligation to notify the German Federal Cartel Office arise (no. 2).

If the domestic turnover threshold under sec. 35(1) no. 2 ARC is not reached, a merger may still be subject to notification under **sec. 35(1a) ARC**, provided that all four criteria are cumulatively fulfilled:

---

488 Emmerich and Lange (2024), sec. 32 mn. 23.

489 Riesenkampff and Steinbarth (2025), sec. 37 ARC mn. 28.

490 German Federal Supreme Court 21 December 2004 – KVR 26/03, WRP 2005, 352. 353 et seq. – *Deutsche Post/trans-o-flex*; Paschke (2025) sec. 37 ARC mn. 71.

491 Higher Regional Court of Duesseldorf 6 July 2005 – Kart 26/04 (V), BeckRS 2005, 30359418 – *Bonner Zeitungsdruckerei*; Kling and Thomas (2016), sec. 22 mn. 54.

492 Higher Regional Court of Duesseldorf 23 November 2005 – VI-2 Kart 14/04, AG 2006, 504 – *Mainova/Aschaffenburger Versorgungs GmbH*.

493 German Federal Supreme Court 21 December 2004 – KVR 26/03, WRP 2005, 352, 353 et seq. – *Deutsche Post/trans-o-flex*.

- the worldwide turnover of the undertakings involved exceeds EUR 500 million pursuant to sec. 35(1) no. 1 ARC (no. 1)
- at least one investee has generated domestic turnover of more than EUR 50 million, while neither the acquiree nor any other investee has generated more than EUR 17.5 million each (no. 2)
- the value of the **consideration for the transaction** exceeds EUR 400 million (no. 3)
- the target undertaking carries out **substantial business activities in Germany** (no. 4)

5

The turnover threshold in sec. 35(1a) ARC is a transaction-related threshold, as it does not tie the notification requirement exclusively to turnover levels but instead to the **value of the consideration** under sec. 35(1a) no. 3 ARC. Introduced by the 9th amendment to the ARC in 2017, the provision was designed to close a regulatory gap, particularly in the digital economy. The legislative background was the *Facebook/WhatsApp* merger, which was highly significant from a competition law perspective but nevertheless fell below the turnover thresholds of European merger control.[494] The purpose of the transaction-related threshold is to capture acquisitions where the target undertaking generates little or no turnover, but its competitive relevance is reflected in a high purchase price. This approach recognises that innovation plays a decisive role as a driver of competition in digital markets and that leading undertakings may seek to neutralise potential future competitors at an early stage through strategic acquisitions.[495]

Regarding the fourth condition under sec. 35(1a) ARC, in its *Meta/Kustomer* decision, the German Federal Supreme Court stated that, for the assessment of whether a **substantial national business activity** exists, it is decisive whether the activity in question leads to the proposed merger creating competitive risks for markets located within Germany.[496] In the *Meta/Kustomer* case, it was therefore sufficient that *Kustomer* processed data of German end customers for foreign direct clients. The fact that *Kustomer* did not have direct business customers in Germany to any significant extent did not alter the applicability of merger control.

In its 2022 background paper, the German Federal Cartel Office notes that between 2009 and 2019, more than 400 mergers involving *Alphabet, Amazon, Apple, Meta*, and *Microsoft* were completed. Most of these transactions would not have triggered merger review under the traditional turnover thresholds, as the parties involved did not meet the required revenue levels.[497]

494 The Commission was only able to examine the transaction because the parties to the merger had requested this pursuant to Article 4(5) EUMR, see Commission 3 October 2014 – M.7217 – *Facebook/WhatsApp*.

495 Körber (2017), pp. 93, 98.

496 German Federal Supreme Court 17 June 2025 – KVR 77/22, NZKart 2025, 442, 446 et seqq. – *Meta/Kustomer*.

497 German Federal Cartel Office, Fusionskontrolle im digitalen Zeitalter – Herausforderungen und Entwicklungsperspektiven, 2022, p. 6.

In June 2024, the German Federal Cartel Office conducted its first main examination under sec. 35(1a) ARC, but ultimately cleared the transaction without conditions.[498] The case involved the biotechnology sector, which is highly driven by innovation. Although the turnover thresholds of sec. 35(1) ARC were not met, the parties agreed on a purchase price of approximately EUR 2.8 billion for the acquisition of an 'innovative biotechnology undertaking,' according to the German Federal Cartel Office.[499]

Sec. 38(4a) ARC specifies how the consideration for a merger is to be calculated. It includes all assets and other monetary benefits that the seller receives from the acquirer in connection with the merger, as well as the value of any liabilities assumed by the acquirer. Consequently, the value of the consideration is generally determined by **agreement between the parties**, and there are no objective methods for its calculation.[500] This creates a risk of manipulation, as the parties are largely free to set the purchase price.[501] Moreover, the purchase price is often embedded in a complex contractual structure of rights and obligations, which may be difficult to fully assess.[502] In addition, the final price may not always be known when the contract is concluded or executed, due to price adjustment clauses or contingent rights to determine performance.[503]

For the purpose of turnover-related thresholds, only the turnover of the **undertakings involved** is relevant. Which undertakings are considered 'involved' depends on the type of merger: In the case of an acquisition of assets under sec. 37(1) no. 1 ARC, the undertakings involved are the acquirer and the undertaking whose assets are being acquired.[504] For an acquisition of control under sec. 37(1) no. 2 ARC, the involved undertakings are the acquirer and the target over which control is obtained. If multiple undertakings acquire control jointly, all controlling undertakings and the joint venture itself are considered involved.

In the case of an acquisition of shares pursuant to sec. 37(1) no. 3 ARC, the selling undertaking is not considered involved; instead, the acquirer and the undertaking whose shares are acquired are classified as participating undertakings.[505] The fiction of a partial merger of the parents under sec. 37(1) no. 3 3rd sentence ARC must also be taken into account, meaning that all parent undertakings acquiring at least 25% of the shares in a joint venture are considered participating undertakings. Finally, for mergers involving the acquisition of significant competitive influence under sec. 37(1) no. 4 ARC, the involved undertakings are the acquirer of the influence and the undertaking that comes under that influence.

498 German Federal Cartel Office, press release of 17 June 2024 – *Thermo Fisher Scientific/Olink*, https://www.bundeskartellamt.de/SharedDocs/Meldung/DE/Pressemitteilungen/2024/17_06_2024_Olink_Fischer.html?nn=49408 (accessed 8 September 2025).

499 German Federal Cartel Office, press release of 17 June 2024 – *Thermo Fisher Scientific/Olink*, https://www.bundeskartellamt.de/SharedDocs/Meldung/DE/Pressemitteilungen/2024/17_06_2024_Olink_Fischer.html?nn=49408 (accessed 8 September 2025).

500 Meyer-Lindemann (2025), sec. 35 ARC mn. 47.

501 Baranowski and Glaßl (2017), pp. 199, 206.

502 Meyer-Lindemann (2025), sec. 35 ARC mn. 57.

503 Thomas (2025), sec. 35 ARC mn. 76.

504 Thomas (2025), sec. 37 ARC mn. 56.

When calculating turnover for the purpose of merger control, **special provisions for certain sectors** must be observed. According to sec. 38(2) ARC, only three-quarters of turnover is taken into account in the area of trade in goods. Sec. 38(3) ARC provides specific multipliers for the press and broadcasting sectors: in the case of publishing, producing, and distributing newspapers and magazines, turnover is multiplied by four; in the case of producing, distributing, and organising radio programmes, turnover is multiplied by eight. In addition, sec. 38(4) ARC contains special provisions for calculating turnover in the financial services sector.

5.4.2.3 Obligation to Notify after Sector Enquiry

With the 10th amendment to the ARC, which entered into force in 2021, the legislator introduced an additional notification requirement for mergers in sec. 39a(1) ARC old version. Under this provision, the German Federal Cartel Office could require an undertaking to notify any merger in specific economic sectors if certain conditions were met. In addition to a turnover threshold, these conditions included the market position of the undertakings involved and 'objectively comprehensible indications [...] that future mergers could significantly impede effective competition in Germany in the specified economic sectors.'[506] The obligation applied if the requirements of sec. 39a(2) ARC old version were fulfilled.

With the 11th amendment to the ARC, the legislator linked this instrument more closely to the sector enquiry.[507] Pursuant to **sec. 32f(2) ARC**, the obligation to notify can now be imposed following the conclusion of a sector enquiry. The order must relate to specific economic sectors and is limited to a duration of three years. According to sec. 32f(2) 5th sentence ARC, the order can be extended up to three times for a further three years each. The prerequisite is that there are 'objectively comprehensible indications that **effective competition in Germany [...] could be significantly impeded by future mergers**.' This extension of the notification regime is designed to enable the German Federal Cartel Office to examine mergers that fall below the turnover thresholds of sec. 35 ARC but could nevertheless have a considerable impact on competition.[508]

5.4.3 Substantive Analysis: Sec. 36 ARC

5.4.3.1 Market Dominance Test

Just like European merger control under Article 2(3) EUMR, the substantive review of mergers by the German Federal Cartel Office is based on the SIEC test. According to sec. 36(1) ARC, a merger must be prohibited if it would significantly impede effective competition. The legislator provides the market dominance test as

---

505 Thomas (2025), sec. 37 ARC mn. 223.

506 Legal text translated by author.

507 For further details on the amendments to the ARC, see ► 5.1.2.

508 Government justification for the 11th ARC amendment, BT-Drs. 20/6824, 17, 28; see Franck (2024b), pp. 246, 249.

the **standard example**: a significant impediment to competition is deemed to exist in particular where the merger results in the creation or strengthening of a dominant position on the relevant market.

The concept of market dominance in sec. 36 ARC largely mirrors the understanding of the term under sec. 18, 19 ARC. Accordingly, the definition in **sec. 18(1) ARC** is applicable. Under this provision, it is sufficient if it can be expected that the merged entity will attain a dominant position vis-à-vis its competitors, cf. sec. 18(1) no. 3 ARC. The assessment is carried out on the basis of the non-exhaustive list of criteria in sec. 18(3) ARC, which provide guidance for determining dominance. In addition, the statutory presumption of market dominance in sec. 18(4) ARC, based on a market share of at least 40%, also applies within the framework of merger control.[509] Where mergers affect digital markets, the specific factors codified for multi-sided markets in sec. 18(3a),(3b) ARC must also be taken into account.[510]

▶ Example

In its decision in the *CTS EVENTIM/Medusa Music/Four Artists* case, the German Federal Cartel Office prohibited the merger on the grounds that it would have strengthened *CTS*'s dominant position in the markets for ticketing system services.[511] In its analysis, the authority placed particular emphasis on the role of indirect network effects under sec. 18(3a) no. 1 ARC in multi-sided ticketing system markets. The acquisition of another organiser not only directly affected the competitive position of rival ticketing systems but also intensified the dependence of advance booking offices on the *CTS* system.[512] This increased dependence in turn reinforced the significance of the *CTS* system for organisers.[513] The Federal Cartel Office concluded that these indirect network effects would amplify the foreclosure effects anticipated from the merger, thereby justifying its prohibition. ◀

A **strengthening of market dominance** requires that the merger enhances the undertakings' independent room for manoeuvre, meaning that the overall intensity of competition is reduced. According to sec. 36(1) ARC, the cartel office will also prohibit a merger if it is expected to create or reinforce a **collective dominant position**. This presupposes that there is no significant competition between two or more undertakings with respect to certain goods or services, and that, taken together, they hold at least an overriding market position within the meaning of sec. 18(1) ARC, as clarified in sec. 18(5) ARC. On platform markets, however, the

509 Kahlenberg (2025), sec. 36 ARC mn. 31; critical comment: Thomas (2025), sec. 36 ARC mn. 40.
510 German Federal Cartel Office, Decision of 23 November 2017 – B6-35/17, paras. 154 et seqq. – *CTS EVENTIM/Medusa Music/Four Artists*.
511 German Federal Cartel Office, Decision of 23 November 2017 – B6-35/17, para. 141 – *CTS EVENTIM/Medusa Music/Four Artists*.
512 German Federal Cartel Office, Decision of 23 November 2017 – B6-35/17, para. 282 – *CTS EVENTIM/Medusa Music/Four Artists*.
513 German Federal Cartel Office, Decision of 23 November 2017 – B6-35/17, para. 283 – *CTS EVENTIM/Medusa Music/Four Artists*.

Federal Cartel Office generally considers the risk of tacit collusion to be relatively low.[514]

Past market developments may serve as important indicators of whether the merged entity is likely to attain a dominant position.[515] However, the decision to prohibit or clear a merger ultimately constitutes a **forecasting exercise**.[516] For this, it is generally sufficient that dominance can be predicted '*with some probability*';[517] a high degree of certainty is not required. The relevant time frame for such a prognosis cannot be defined in abstract terms, but in practice, authorities often consider a period of around three to five years post-merger.[518] In the digital economy, however, the rapid pace of change and innovation renders such predictions particularly complex and uncertain.[519]

▶ Example

If a small but highly innovative competitor is acquired, the forecasting exercise becomes complex. It may be difficult to assess how the competitor's business model would have evolved and whether it would have been capable of disrupting the market power of established undertakings. Such uncertainty is especially pronounced in innovation-driven markets, where competitive pressure often arises not from current market shares but from the potential of emerging firms to introduce breakthrough products, technologies, or business models.[520] ◀

Against this background, some scholars and policymakers have argued that the level of probability required for a prohibition under sec. 36 ARC should be lowered.[521] The reasoning is that in dynamic and innovation-driven markets, high certainty is rarely attainable, yet the risks of under-enforcement may be considerable if potentially disruptive competitors are absorbed by dominant players. A more nuanced approach has also been suggested, according to which the extent of the expected impediment to competition should be weighed against the degree of probability required: the greater the potential harm to effective competition, the lower the evidentiary threshold for predicting such harm ought to be.[522] However, this proposal raises concerns about legal certainty.[523] The current wording of sec. 36

514 German Federal Cartel Office, Decision of 20 April 2015 – B6-39/15, case report, p. 5 – *Online-Immobilienplattformen*; German Federal Cartel Office 24 July 2015 – B8-76/15, case report, p. 5 – *ProSiebenSat.1/Verivox*.

515 Kahlenberg (2025), sec. 36 ARC mn. 18.

516 Higher Regional Court of Duesseldorf 26 March 2014 – VI-U (Kart) 43/13, NZKart 2014, 185, 186 – *Phonak III*.

517 German Federal Supreme Court 19 June 2012 – KVR 15/11, NZKart 2013, 36, 37 et seq. – *Haller Tagblatt*.

518 German Federal Supreme Court 19 June 2012 – KVR 15/11, NZKart 2013, 36, 37 – *Haller Tagblatt*; German Federal Cartel Office, Leitfaden zur Marktbeherrschung in der Fusionskontrolle, 2012, mn. 12.

519 German Federal Cartel Office, Fusionskontrolle im digitalen Zeitalter, 2022, p. 9.

520 See Bourreau and de Streel (2020), p. 5.

521 ACCC, Digital Platform Services Inquiry, 2022, p. 106.

522 Furman, Cyle, Fletscher, McAuley and Marsden (2019), mn. 3.88 et seqq.

523 German Federal Cartel Office, Fusionskontrolle im digitalen Zeitalter, 2022, p. 38.

ARC does not require an assessment of the quantitative degree of impediment to competition. Rather, any significant impediment to effective competition is sufficient to justify a prohibition. Introducing a sliding scale between the intensity of harm and the degree of probability could blur the clarity of the legal standard.

Unlike the Commission,[524] the German Federal Cartel Office generally approaches its substantive review by first assessing the creation or strengthening of market dominance as the standard example of a SIEC under sec. 36(1) ARC. Only if such dominance cannot be established does it typically move on to consider the broader SIEC test in its own right.[525] This two-step approach reflects the fact that the market dominance test has a long-standing tradition in German merger control and remains the most familiar analytical framework. Nevertheless, there are exceptions to this tendency. A prominent counter-example is the *Edeka/Tengelmann* case, where the Federal Cartel Office did not limit its assessment to dominance but referred directly to the SIEC criterion.[526] In that case, the authority examined unilateral effects on competition arising from the merger, showing a willingness to apply the SIEC test independently of the dominance concept where the circumstances of the case required it.

5.4.3.2 SIEC Test

When applying the SIEC criterion, German merger control distinguishes between unilateral and coordinated effects. **Unilateral effects** include individual market dominance as the standard example already discussed. **Coordinated effects**, by contrast, cover collective dominance. Beyond these categories, German practice also recognises that further cases of unilateral effects can exist which amount to a significant impediment to effective competition without simultaneously meeting the market dominance rule example, the so-called **gap cases**. This approach was made explicit in the *Cordes & Graefe KG* case, in which the Federal Cartel Office stated:

> Even if the creation or strengthening of an individual dominant position of the parties to the merger cannot be established, unilateral effects may occur as a result of the proposed merger that lead to a significant impediment to effective competition.[527]

---

524 On the Commissions' approach, see ► 5.4.3.

525 Government justification for the 8th amendment to the ARC, BT-Drs. 17/9852, p. 28: '*The creation or strengthening of a dominant market position always constitutes a significant impediment to effective competition (market dominance as a standard example). Prohibitions will probably continue to be based predominantly on this criterion in the future.*' [quote translated by author].

526 German Federal Cartel Office, Decision of 31 March 2015 – B2-96/14 – *Edeka/Tengelmann*. See also German Federal Cartel Office, Decision of 12 March 2012 – B1-30/11 – *Xella/H+H*.

527 German Federal Cartel Office, Decision of 10 March 2014 – B5-134/13 – *Cordes & Graefe KG* [quote translated by author]. For an exemplary assessment of *gap cases* (with a negative result), see German Federal Cartel Office, Decision of 11 June 2015 – B6-22/15, paras. 172 et seqq. – *Funkel/Springer*: '*Furthermore, the transaction is not expected to significantly impede effective competition through non-coordinated effects below the threshold of market dominance [...].*' [quote translated by author].

Although there are relatively few practical examples, it can be assumed—consistent with the interpretation of the SIEC criterion under Article 2(3) EUMR—that gap cases will primarily be identified in oligopolistic market structures.[528] Non-exhaustive categories have already been described in the chapter on European merger control.[529] Among them, particular importance is attached to the merger of close competitors in a heterogeneous market, where the merged entity gains room for price increases without simultaneously becoming dominant.[530] In the case of homogeneous goods, unilateral effects may arise if the merging parties are especially close competitors and have superior possibilities for expanding capacity compared to other players.[531] Finally, for digital markets, a particularly relevant category is the elimination of a still small but highly potent competitor whose mere presence disciplines larger rivals.

5.4.3.3 Merger Types

Horizontal Merger

In order to concretise the competitive effects of a merger, a distinction can be made between three **types of mergers**:
- Horizontal mergers
- Vertical mergers
- Conglomerate mergers

A horizontal merger occurs when the parties are direct competitors on the same relevant market, which means that the merger results in an **addition of market shares**. On platform markets, such a concentration can create a particular risk of tipping if the market share differences between the platforms are significant.[532] Network effects may amplify this risk by increasing the merged entity's scope for independent conduct.[533] For this reason, when assessing market power in the context of horizontal mergers on multi-sided markets, the interdependencies between the different user groups must always be considered.[534]

Whether network effects strengthen the merged entity's position depends to a large extent on user behaviour. If users engage in single-homing, i.e. they are active on only one platform, the risk of monopolisation is higher than in the case of multi-homing, where users typically use several platforms in parallel (cf. sec. 18(3a) no. 2 ARC).[535] The German Federal Cartel Office has also observed that in cases where two platform operators merge in a market in which a strong competitor remains active,

528 Thomas (2025), sec. 36 ARC mn. 247 et seq.

529 On further details on gap cases, see ► 2.4.4.3.

530 On a close competitive relationship, see German Federal Cartel Office, Decision of 14 March 2014 – B3-135/13, paras. 382 et seqq. – *Kliniken Esslingen*.

531 German Federal Cartel Office, Decision of 11 June 2015 – B6-22/15, para. 174 – *Funke/Springer*.

532 German Federal Cartel Office, Decision of 24 July 2015 – B8-76/15, case report p. 4 – *ProSieben-Sat.1/Verivox*.

533 German Federal Cartel Office, Fusionskontrolle im digitalen Zeitalter, 2022, p. 25.

534 For further details, see ► 5.3.1.2.

535 German Federal Cartel Office, Decision of 20 April 2015 – B6-39/15, case report p. 4 – *Online-Immobilienplattformen*.

> » this can mean that the reduction in the number of platforms does not – as is regularly the case in one-sided markets – lead to a lower, but possibly even an increase in competitive intensity, since a lower number of platforms simplifies the internalisation of network effects and thus improves the competitive opportunities of the platforms.[536]

It is also important to note that in digital markets, the mere fact that a merger takes place in an innovation-driven environment does not suffice to affirm that innovation pressure will constrain the merged entity. According to sec. 18(3a) no. 5 ARC and the practice of the Federal Cartel Office, what is required is '*concrete evidence of such a dynamic or disruptive process within the forecast period to be taken as a basis*'.[537] Only if such evidence exists can innovation-related considerations meaningfully influence the competitive assessment.

Vertical Merger

A vertical merger arises when the undertakings involved are active at different levels of the supply chain.[538] The main competitive concern in such constellations is that the merged entity may be able to foreclose rivals by restricting access to essential inputs or sales channels.[539] For a foreclosure scenario to be relevant, two conditions must be met: first, the merged entity must have the ability to engage in foreclosure; second, it must also have an incentive to do so.[540] The incentive element depends on whether such strategies are expected to be profitable overall for the merged entity. The extent to which foreclosure can lead to a strengthening of market power is determined by the merged entity's access to sales and procurement markets (cf. sec. 18(3) no. 3 ARC), and by the possibility for market opponents to evade the foreclosure (cf. sec. 18(3) no. 8 ARC), among other things. For example, if a vertical merger results in the loss of a significant customer, this may restrict the sales opportunities of non-vertically integrated distributors. However, if a sufficient number of other customers are present at the downstream level or in neighbouring markets who can absorb comparable volumes, the risk of foreclosure is reduced.

In digital markets, vertical mergers can have particularly far-reaching consequences. The acquisition of undertakings active on downstream market levels can strengthen the market power of established platform operators.[541] These platforms often hold a gatekeeper position, as commercial users rely on them to reach end customers due to the high concentration of digital markets. Moreover, as high-

536 German Federal Cartel Office, Decision of 20 April 2015 – B6-39/15, case report p. 4 – *Online-Immobilienplattformen* [quote translated by author].
537 German Federal Cartel Office, Decision of 23 November 2017 – B6-35/17, para. 198 – *CTS EVENTIM/Medusa Music/Four Artists* [quote translated by author].
538 German Federal Cartel Office, Leitfaden Marktbeherrschung, 2012, para. 129.
539 German Federal Cartel Office, Leitfaden Marktbeherrschung, 2012, paras. 134 et seqq., 143 et seqq.
540 German Federal Cartel Office, Leitfaden Marktbeherrschung, 2012, paras. 141 et seqq., 147 et seqq.
541 German Federal Cartel Office, Fusionskontrolle im digitalen Zeitalter, 2022, p. 28.

lighted in the context of European merger control, access to superior data can be a decisive factor.[542] If the merged entity gains or expands privileged access to relevant data sets, this may allow it to foreclose competitors by denying them the data necessary to compete effectively.

Conglomerate Merger

5

Conglomerate mergers are characterised by the fact that the undertakings involved neither stand in a direct competitive relationship nor operate at different levels of the supply chain. Despite this, they can still give rise to competitive concerns, particularly through foreclosure effects. A typical mechanism in this respect is tying or bundling, whereby the merged entity combines its products in such a way that it can extend its existing market power into neighbouring or complementary markets.[543] In the digital economy, conglomerate mergers are especially relevant because foreclosure strategies can be implemented in a subtle yet highly effective way.[544]

▶ Example

If undertaking M markets an operating system and pre-installs the Internet browser of target undertaking Z, customers will automatically be provided with this browser when purchasing the operating system. This practice can place competing browsers at a competitive disadvantage, since customers may be less inclined to download or switch to alternatives. ◀

Network effects reinforce such strategies. Where the user bases of the linked products overlap, the attractiveness of the bundled offering grows, thereby amplifying the market power of the merged entity.[545] This has two main implications: first, competitors may be excluded or at least placed at a severe disadvantage; second, the barriers to market entry rise significantly. As a result, the disciplining effect of **potential competition**, which is often particularly important in fast-moving digital markets, is weakened.

5.4.3.4 Efficiency Defence

German case law on the recognition of an **efficiency defence** in merger control is less clearly defined than at the European level. Nonetheless, statements by the German Federal Supreme Court can be interpreted to suggest that efficiencies may be considered as a justification in the context of German merger control.[546] Conceptually, this is persuasive. The replacement of the market dominance test with the SIEC test through the 8th amendment to the ARC in 2013 aimed to align national merger control with European standards. Under the SIEC criterion, the

542 German Federal Cartel Office, Fusionskontrolle im digitalen Zeitalter, 2022, p. 29.
543 German Federal Cartel Office, Leitfaden Marktbeherrschung, 2012, paras. 165 et seqq.
544 German Federal Cartel Office, Fusionskontrolle im digitalen Zeitalter, 2022, p. 30.
545 German Federal Cartel Office, Fusionskontrolle im digitalen Zeitalter, 2022, p. 8.
546 German Federal Supreme Court 23 September 2014 – KVZ 82/13, NZKart 2015, 56, 57 – *Xella*: '*an imminent significant impediment to effective competition [can be inferred from the realisation of*

key consideration is the merger's impact on consumer welfare. Accordingly, both negative effects (such as increased scope for price rises) and positive effects (such as efficiency gains) must be taken into account. In line with the approach in European merger control, it is therefore reasonable to allow undertakings to invoke an efficiency defence under sec. 36(1) ARC.[547]

Regarding the requirements for an efficiency defence, the principles applied in European merger control are also relevant.[548] Efficiencies may be taken into account if they result in tangible **benefits for consumers**. In digital markets, specific advantages can arise when data or functionalities are combined, as this may improve the quality or scope of services offered.[549] Additionally, consumers can benefit from the scale of large platforms through one-stop shopping, which reduces transaction and search costs by allowing users to access multiple services on a single platform rather than engaging with several separate providers.

It must also be established whether the efficiencies are **merger-specific**, meaning that the efficiencies can only be realised through the merger itself.[550] The parties to the merger bear the burden of demonstrating that the efficiencies are indispensable for the merger and that they are **verifiable**. The evidentiary standard is as stringent as under European competition law.[551] In practice, it is often challenging for undertakings to prove efficiencies to the extent that they outweigh the anti-competitive effects of the merger. In particular, the types of efficiencies mentioned above will generally not suffice to justify merger-related restrictions on competition in digital markets when the merger involves large competitors.[552]

5.4.3.5 Ministerial Approval

Sec. 42 ARC establishes the concept of ministerial authorisation. Under this provision, the Federal Minister for Economic Affairs and Energy may approve a merger that has been prohibited by the German Federal Cartel Office if the expected restriction of competition is outweighed by macroeconomic benefits or if the merger is justified by an overriding public interest. This contrasts with European merger control, which does not provide for such a political gateway. While the German Federal Cartel Office assesses merger projects solely based on competition-related criteria using the SIEC test, the ministerial review also takes into account

the rule example] [...] if [...] no circumstances are established from which contrary effects could arise.' [quote translated by author].

547 German Federal Cartel Office, Decision of 17 December 2019 – B4-80/19, paras. 458 et seqq. – *Loomis/Ziemann*; Esser and Höft (2023), pp. 447, 455.

548 German Federal Cartel Office, Decision of 31 March 2015 – B2-96/14, para. 380 – *EDEKA/Tengelmann*; German Federal Cartel Office, Decision of 17 December 2019 – B4-80/19, para. 458 et seqq. – *Loomis/Ziemann*.

549 German Federal Cartel Office, Fusionskontrolle im digitalen Zeitalter, 2022, p. 31.

550 German Federal Cartel Office, Decision of 31 March 2015 – B2-96/14, paras. 382 et seq. – *EDEKA/Tengelmann*.

551 German Federal Cartel Office, Decision of 31 March 2015 – B2-96/14, paras. 380 et seq. – *EDEKA/Tengelmann*; German Federal Cartel Office, Decision of 14 May 2014 – B3-135/13, paras. 285 et seq. – *Klinikum Esslingen/Kreiskliniken Esslingen*.

552 German Federal Cartel Office, Fusionskontrolle im digitalen Zeitalter, 2022, p. 32.

non-competitive, public-interest considerations. Relevant public-interest reasons in past authorisation procedures have included environmental protection,[553] media plurality and press diversity,[554] a secure energy supply,[555] and the international competitiveness of German undertakings.[556] Overall, the practical significance of ministerial authorisation has remained limited. Since its introduction in 1973, only fifteen ministerial authorisation procedures have been completed, alongside 23 applications for approval.[557]

The ministerial authorisation is controversial from a legal policy perspective. Critics have repeatedly called for its abolition, arguing that it threatens both the protection of competition and the independence of the German Federal Cartel Office. Nevertheless, the legislator has retained the instrument to this day. So far, ministerial authorisation has not played a role in digital markets. The main risks to effective competition in the digital environment arise instead from the fact that the competition authority cannot review or prohibit all mergers relevant to competition under its current intervention thresholds. Importantly, ministerial authorisation cannot be used to challenge or overturn a merger that has been cleared by the authority. It only becomes relevant in the opposite constellation, where a merger has been prohibited but its implementation is considered exceptionally desirable for reasons of public interest.

The ministerial authorisation is **controversial from a legal policy perspective**. Critics have repeatedly called for its abolition,[558] arguing that it threatens both the protection of competition and the independence of the German Federal Cartel Office. Nevertheless, the legislator has retained the instrument to this day. So far, ministerial authorisation has not played a role in digital markets. The main risks to effective competition in the digital environment arise instead from the fact that the competition authority cannot review or prohibit all mergers relevant to competition under its current intervention thresholds. Importantly, ministerial authorisation cannot be used to challenge or overturn a merger that has been cleared by the authority. It only becomes relevant in the opposite constellation, where a merger has been prohibited but its implementation is considered exceptionally desirable for reasons of public interest.

---

553 German Federal Ministry for Economic Affairs and Energy, Decision of 5 July 2002 – IB1-220840/129 – *E.ON/Ruhrgas*.

554 Monopolies Commission, Sondergutachten 36: Zusammenschlussvorhaben der Georg von Holtzbrinck GmbH & Co. KG mit der Berliner Verlag GmbH & Co. KG, 2003, para. 41 et seqq.

555 German Federal Ministry for Economic Affairs and Energy, Decision of 1 February 1974 – IB5-810607 – *VEBA/Gelsenberg*.

556 German Federal Ministry for Economic Affairs and Energy, Decision of 16 June 1992 – IB6-220840/105 – *BayWa/WLZ*.

557 Overview of previous applications for ministerial authorisation pursuant to sec. 24(3)/sec. 42 ARC, as of 6 September 2019 https://www.bmwk.de/Redaktion/DE/Downloads/Wettbewerbspolitik/antraege-auf-ministererlaubnis.pdf?__blob=publicationFile&v=1 (6 September 2025).

558 Podszun (2016), pp. 617, 617.

5.4.4 Merger Control Procedure: Sec. 39–43a ARC

5.4.4.1 Notification

If a merger project fulfils the thresholds set out in secs. 35, 37 ARC, the undertakings involved are obliged to notify the German Federal Cartel Office in accordance with **sec. 39 ARC**. The required contents of the notification are listed in sec. 39(3) ARC. In practice, notifications to the German Federal Cartel Office tend to be less extensive than those submitted to the Commission, which is responsible where the European merger control thresholds are met.[559]

The obligation to notify is directly linked to the **prohibition on implementation under sec. 41(1) ARC**: the undertakings involved may only implement a merger once it has been authorised by the German Federal Cartel Office. A breach of this prohibition leads, pursuant to sec. 41(1) 2nd sentence ARC, to the invalidity of the legal transactions concerned. Moreover, undertakings risk fines under sec. 81(2) no. 1 ARC. Where an unlawfully implemented merger also fulfils the conditions for prohibition under sec. 36(1) ARC, the German Federal Cartel Office must order its dissolution pursuant to sec. 41(3) ARC.

5.4.4.2 Phase I Investigations

After notification, the German Federal Cartel Office carries out the phase I review (preliminary examination) under sec. 40(1) 1st sentence ARC. This stage must be completed within **one month**. In this phase, the authority decides either to open the phase II review (main examination) because of competition concerns or to **approve** the project **informally**. If the authority decides to open phase II, it informs the parties with what is commonly called the '**monthly letter**.'[560] In contrast to European merger control,[561] if the authority does not issue a decision within the one-month period, this does not result in automatic ('fictitious') clearance. The deadline is only a cut-off point for the authority to decide whether to proceed to a more detailed review.[562]

5.4.4.3 Phase II Investigations

If the German Federal Cartel Office initiates a phase II review (main examination), it must decide within **four months** whether to authorise or prohibit the project, cf. sec. 40(2) 2nd sentence ARC. If no decision is issued within this deadline, the merger is deemed to have been cleared ('fictitious clearance'). The four-month period starts with the receipt of the complete notification by the German Federal Cartel Office. This differs from European merger control, where the opening of phase II is decisive for the start of the time limit.[563] The deadline may be extended—for example, pursuant to sec. 40(2) 4th sentence no. 1 ARC, if the parties agree to an extension.

559 Kling and Thomas (2016), sec. 22 mn. 174.
560 Riesenkampff and Steinbarth (2025), sec. 40 ARC mn. 5.
561 For the legal situation under EU merger control, see ► 2.4.5.2.
562 Riesenkampff and Steinbarth (2025), sec. 40 ARC mn. 4.
563 For the legal situation under EU merger control, see ► 2.4.5.3.

If the German Federal Cartel Office has to request information under sec. 59 ARC because the parties failed to respond in time or in full for reasons within their control, the expiry of the deadline is suspended. The phase II procedure ends with either the prohibition or the clearance of the project. Clearance may also be granted subject to conditions and obligations, cf. sec. 40(3) ARC. The decision is issued by way of **administrative act**, cf. sec. 40(2) 1st sentence ARC.

5.4.4.4 Judicial Review

5

The parties involved can lodge an appeal against a prohibition decision pursuant to sec. **73 ARC**. This right is also available to third parties under sec. 73(2) ARC. For this, it is sufficient that the third party meets the requirements for being summoned under sec. 54(2) no. 3 ARC.[564] In practice, this may include competitors of the merged entity who are affected by a clearance decision.[565] The appeal must be filed within one month, cf. sec. 74(1) ARC. The time limit begins with the notification of the administrative act. The competent court is the Higher Regional Court of Duesseldorf. Appeals on points of law against its decisions may be lodged with the German Federal Supreme Court in accordance with sec. 77 ARC, provided that leave to appeal has been granted. At this stage, the appellant may only rely on errors of law.

Checklist: Assessing a Concentration Under German Merger Control

1. Formal Merger Control
   (a) Definition of a merger under sec. 37 ARC (acquisition of assets, acquisition of control, acquisition of shares, or significant influence).
   (b) Turnover thresholds under sec. 35 ARC (worldwide and domestic sales thresholds; check sec. 35(1a) for transaction-based thresholds in digital or innovative sectors).

2. Substantive analysis – Option 1: Market Dominance Focus
   (a) Market dominance test: Would the merger create or strengthen a dominant position under sec. 36 ARC?
   (b) If no individual dominance is found: gap cases directly under the SIEC criterion
   (c) Efficiency defence
   (d) Ministerial authorisation under sec. 42 ARC

3. Substantive analysis – Option 2: SIEC / Unilateral and Coordinated effects
   (a) Unilateral effects: single market dominance; if not, gap cases
   (b) Coordinated effects: collective dominance; if not, gap cases
   (c) Efficiency defence
   (d) Ministerial authorisation under sec. 42 ARC

564 Glöckner (2021), sec. 2 mn. 306.
565 Glöckner (2021), sec. 7 mn. 799.

5.5 Enforcement

5.5.1 Public Enforcement

5.5.1.1 Cease-and-Desist Orders and Commitments in the Event of Breach of Competition Law

Pursuant to sec. 32 ARC, the national competition authorities[566] are empowered to issue cease-and-desist orders if an undertaking has violated prohibitions under German or European competition law. These orders constitute an **administrative act** under sec. 35 German Federal Administrative Procedure Act (*Bundesverwaltungsverfahrensgesetz, VwVfG*). The authority is not limited to issuing a simple prohibition. Instead, it can mandate remedial measures under sec. 32(2) ARC. These measures can be either structural or behavioural.

Structural remedies may involve the sale of part of a business or granting access to infrastructure facilities.[567] Such measures affect the corporate structure and are particularly relevant in abuse cases, with most practical examples drawn from Commission practice. Behavioural remedies, by contrast, are aimed at modifying behaviour. Examples include requiring a dominant undertaking to supply certain customers in the future or imposing a price cap.[568] When choosing between remedies, the authority must apply the **principle of proportionality**. For this reason, behavioural orders are usually given priority, as they are generally less intrusive and preferable if equally suitable.

! The issuance of a cease-and-desist order does not require fault on the part of the undertaking with regard to the competition law breach. In contrast, culpability is necessary for imposing fines under sec. 81(1), (2) ARC and for claims for damages under sec. 33a ARC.

In addition, competition authorities can make commitments offered by undertakings binding pursuant to **sec. 32b ARC**. An undertaking may propose measures to remedy a competition law infringement, which can bring the proceedings to a close through mutual agreement with the authority. The authority evaluates whether the proposed commitments are suitable to address the competition concern. If satisfied, it declares the commitments binding and indicates that it will not exercise its powers under sec. 32, 32a ARC. Importantly, such a commitment decision does not constitute a statement on whether the undertaking's conduct actually violated competition law, nor does it guarantee that the conduct will not constitute a violation in the future.[569]

---

566 For the division of responsibilities between the German Federal Cartel Office and the cartel offices of the federal states, see ► 5.6.1.

567 Emmerich (2024), sec. 32 ARC mn. 33.

568 Higher Regional Court of Duesseldorf 3 April 2019 – Kart 2/18, NZKart 2019, 282, 286 – *Ticketvertrieb II*; Emmerich (2024), sec. 32 ARC mn. 36.

569 Bach (2024), sec. 32b ARC mn. 2.

5.5.1.2 Remedial Measures in the Event of Distortion of Competition

Distortion of Competition

With the 11th amendment to the ARC in 2023, the legislator introduced novel measures under **sec. 32f ARC** as part of the administrative consequences. These measures presuppose that a **sector enquiry** has been conducted pursuant to sec. 32e ARC. A sector enquiry is an investigation without the need for specific suspicion, focusing on an entire sector of the economy. Its purpose is to provide a detailed analysis of the competitive situation. There is cause for such an enquiry if, for example, rigid prices or other indications suggest that competition in the sector may be restricted or distorted.[570]

► Example

In 2023, the German Federal Cartel Office completed a sector enquiry into online advertising.[571] Among other aspects, it analysed the central role of online advertising for the business models of multi-sided platforms and examined the prevailing market structures. According to the authority, the search engine *GoogleSearch* (operated by *Alphabet*) plays a particularly significant role in this sector. ◄

The measures to improve competition under sec. 32f ARC **do not presuppose a breach of competition law prohibitions**. This means that the German Federal Cartel Office can intervene in the market structure independently of any infringement. In this respect, the new power to intervene is described as a '*paradigm shift in competition law*.'[572] The legislator justified its introduction with reference to gaps in protection.[573] One such gap concerns **implicit collusion**. As explained in the context of the cartel prohibition,[574] the growing use of algorithms increases the risk that tacit collusion, which in itself does not fall under Article 101 TFEU or sec. 1 ARC, may cease to be an exceptional case. The **speed and adaptability of algorithmic reactions** could even enable implicit collusion in less concentrated and less transparent markets. The legislator also pointed to gaps in the area of abuse control (Article 102 TFEU; secs. 19, 19a, 20 ARC).[575] In its view, high market concentration can be harmful even in the absence of abusive conduct, for instance, if it leads to low or declining incentives for the efficient use of resources or for the development of new or improved products and services.[576]

In addition to the completion of a sector enquiry, intervention under sec. 32f ARC requires the existence of a **significant and continuing malfunctioning of com-**

570 Otto (2025), sec. 32e ARC mn. 1.

571 German Federal Cartel Office, Sektoruntersuchung Online-Werbung – Abschlussbericht https://www.bundeskartellamt.de/SharedDocs/Publikation/DE/Sektoruntersuchungen/Sektoruntersuchung_Online_Werbung_Abschlussbericht.html (6 September 2025).

572 Körber (2023b), p. 5, 5 [quote translated by author].

573 Government justification for the 11th ARC amendment, BT-Drs. 20/6824, p. 15 et seq.

574 For further details, see ► 2.2.1.3.

575 Government justification for the 11th ARC amendment, BT-Drs. 20/6824, p. 16.

576 Government justification for the 11th ARC amendment, BT-Drs. 20/6824, p. 27.

petition. Sec. 32f(5) 1st sentence ARC provides standard examples of when such a disturbance may be assumed. These include:

- Unilateral supply or demand power,
- Restrictions on market entry, market exit, undertakings' capacities, or on switching to another supplier or buyer,
- Uniform or coordinated conduct, and
- Compartmentalisation of input factors or customers through vertical relationships.

Sec. 32f(5) 2nd sentence ARC supplements this by providing a non-exhaustive list of criteria that must be taken into account when assessing whether competition is impaired. Finally, pursuant to sec. 32f(5) 3rd sentence ARC, a distortion is considered ongoing if it has either persisted for at least three years or occurred repeatedly, and if there are no indications that it is highly likely to cease within the next two years.

Remedial Measures

If the German Federal Cartel Office finds a significant and continuing malfunctioning of competition under sec. 32f ARC, it may impose **structural or conduct remedies**. Sec. 32f(3) 7th sentence ARC provides examples of such interventions. The authority may, for instance, prohibit undertakings that significantly contribute to the distortion from granting or restricting access to data, interfaces or networks. It may also prohibit the unilateral disclosure of information or order the organisational separation of business units. In particularly severe cases, especially concerning undertakings with paramount significance for competition across markets under sec. 19a ARC,[577] the authority can even impose **unbundling** as a structural remedy pursuant to sec. 32f(4) ARC. This represents the most far-reaching intervention, as it directly alters the ownership structure of a company.

The German Federal Cartel Office's new 'unbundling instrument' has been the subject of considerable debate.[578] Critics argue that it interferes with entrepreneurial ownership structures and restricts the free play of competition. Constitutional concerns have also been raised.[579] Moreover, doubts remain as to whether the requirement of a 'substantial and continuous disruption of competition' is precise enough to capture the gaps in protection identified by the legislator.[580] As this is a purely national provision, there is also a risk of fragmenting the internal market.[581] By contrast, the Commission does not have comparable powers under Regulation 1/2003[582] or under the DMA.[583]

---

577 For further details on the term undertaking with paramount significance for competition across markets, see ► 5.3.2.2.
578 Körber (2023b), pp. 5, 6 et seq.; Kühling et al. (2023), pp. 250 et seqq.; Rohner (2023), pp. 386, 387.
579 Körber (2023a), pp. 193, 194; Paal and Kieß (2022), pp. 678, 681 et seq.
580 Wagner-von Papp (2023), pp. 301, 302.
581 Kühling and Engelbracht (2024), sec. 32f ARC mn. 50.
582 For further details on the public enforcemenf of EU competition law, see ► 2.5.1.
583 For further details on the public enforcemenf of the DMA, see ► 3.4.1.

5.5.2 Especially: Fines

Pursuant to **sec. 81(1),(2) no. 1, 2(a) ARC**, a culpable infringement of Articles 101, 102 TFEU, or of sec. 1, 19, 20 ARC, as well as the breach of enforceable orders under sec. 19a(2) ARC, constitutes an administrative offence. With the 9th amendment to the ARC in 2017, sec. 81a(1) ARC was introduced to clarify that in German competition law, the liability extends to the entire economic entity. This means that not only the legal entity whose managers committed the offence can be fined, but also 'other legal entities' forming part of the same economic unit at the time of the offence, provided they exercised a decisive influence on the infringing entity.
5 Importantly, these other entities can be held liable even if they neither knew nor should have known about the competition law infringement.[584]

Pursuant to sec. 81c(2) 2nd sentence ARC, the maximum fine is set at 10% of the undertaking's total turnover in the financial year preceding the authority's decision. Unlike Article 23 Regulation 1/2003,[585] however, this does not function as a cap but as a framework for calculating fines.[586] The relevant turnover is that of the entire economic entity (sec. 81c(2), (3), (5) 1st sentence ARC).

In competition fine law, the term undertaking refers to the economic unit. This means that the fine is addressed to the economic entity, and its overall turnover forms the basis for the fine calculation. Nevertheless, a fine can only be imposed on an entity with legal capacity. In practice, this usually means that the parent company of the group is the addressee of the fine.

According to sec. 81d ARC, both the gravity of the infringement and its duration must be taken into account when calculating a fine. The German Federal Cartel Office has set out its approach in the Guidelines for the Assessment of Fines in Cartel Offence Proceedings (*Leitlinien für die Bußgeldbemessung in Kartellordnungswidrigkeitenverfahren*).[587] These new guidelines became necessary after the legislator revised the rules on fines in sec. 81 et seq. ARC in order to implement the ECN+ Directive.[588] The guidelines are binding on the German Federal Cartel Office, but not on the courts. The fine calculation follows a multi-stage process: Firstly, the German Federal Cartel Office determines an initial value based on the undertaking's turnover.[589] Secondly, this amount is adjusted by taking into

584 Glöckner (2021), sec. 2 mn. 227.

585 For further details on Article 23 Regulation 1/2003, see ► 2.5.2.

586 German Federal Supreme Court 26 February 2013, KRB 20/12, NZKart 2013, 195 – *Grauzementkartell.*

587 https://www.bundeskartellamt.de/SharedDocs/Publikation/DE/Leitlinien/Bu%C3%9Fgeldleitlinien_Oktober2021.pdf?__blob=publicationFile&v=4 (6 September 2025).

588 Directive (EU) 2019/1 of the European Parliament and of the Council of 11 December 2018 on the strengthening of the competition authorities of the Member States with a view to ensuring more effective enforcement of the competition rules and the proper functioning of the internal market, OJ [2019] L 11/3.

589 German Federal Cartel Office, Leitlinien für die Bußgeldbemessung in Kartellordnungswidrigkeitenverfahren, 2021, paras. 8 et seqq.

account all relevant circumstances.[590] These include, in particular, the type and duration of the infringement as well as the role the undertaking played in committing the competition offence.

▶ Example

If an undertaking has a turnover of EUR 100 million, the authority may set the initial value at a certain percentage of that figure (e.g. 5%). This results in an initial fine of EUR 5 million. The final amount may then be adjusted upwards if the infringement lasted several years or if the undertaking played a leading role, or downwards if its involvement was minor or if it cooperated with the authority. ◀

If an undertaking cooperates with the competition authorities as a a **leniency witness** and helps uncover a competition infringement, cf. secs. 81h–81n ARC, this will be taken into account as a mitigating factor when calculating the fine. Full **immunity** from fines is possible under sec. 81k ARC if the undertaking submits evidence that enables the authority to obtain a search warrant at the time the leniency application is received. In addition, the general conditions under sec. 81j ARC must be fulfilled. These include serious, continuous and swift cooperation with the authority throughout the proceedings. If the undertaking is not the first to submit such decisive evidence, it can still benefit from a **reduction** of the fine. According to sec. 81l ARC, this requires that the evidence submitted provides significant added value for the authority's investigation. The German Federal Cartel Office has clarified the requirements in its Guidelines on the Leniency Programme (*Leitlinien zum Kronzeugenprogramm*).[591]

In order to close gaps in legal protection, sec. 81a(2) ARC provides that in cases of universal succession and partial universal succession through a split, fines under sec. 81a(1) ARC can also be imposed on the legal successor. This principle is further extended by sec. 81a(3) ARC to undertakings that assume economic succession. In this respect, sec. 81a(2), (3) ARC goes further than the liability of the universal successor under sec. 30(2a) German Code of Administrative Offences (*Gesetz über Ordnungswidrigkeiten; OWiG*). Unlike the legal situation under the German Code of Administrative Offences, pursuant to sec. 81a(2) 3rd sentence ARC, there is no limitation of the fine to the value of the assets transferred or to the fine appropriate for the legal predecessor.

! The provisions in secs. 81–86 ARC were comprehensively revised with the 10th amendment to the ARC in 2021 in order to implement the ECN+ Directive. The directive aims to strengthen the powers of national competition authorities and ensure more effective enforcement of EU competition law. Since it only provides for partial harmonisation, member states remain largely free to introduce stricter rules at the national level.

---

590 German Federal Cartel Office, Leitlinien für die Bußgeldbemessung in Kartellordnungswidrigkeitenverfahren, 2021, paras. 14 et seqq.

591 German Federal Cartel Office, Leitlinien zum Kronzeugenprogramm, 2021.

5.5.3 Private Enforcement

5.5.3.1 Invalidity of Contracts

Contracts that violate competition prohibitions are void pursuant to sec. 134 German Civil Code in conjunction with the relevant competition law provision. In the case of horizontal agreements, the nullity consequence of sec. 134 German Civil Code in conjunction with sec. 1 ARC also extends to implementation agreements concluded between cartelists or third parties that serve to enforce the restriction of competition.[592] Follow-up agreements, i.e., those concluded with non-cartelists, for example, for the purpose of supply or procurement, remain unaffected.

5.5.3.2 Claims for Injunctive Relief and Removal

In the event of a breach of prohibitions under national competition law or Articles 101, 102 TFEU, affected parties are entitled to a right to removal and, if there is a risk of repetition, a right to injunctive relief pursuant to **sec. 33(1) ARC**. These claims are **independent of fault**. The claimant does not have to prove negligence or intent with respect to the competition law violation.

▶ Example

In the case of abusive supply blocks, claims for delivery may arise as claims for removal.[593] If the unfair hindrance consists of a dominant undertaking withholding information from other market participants, a claim for information arises under sec. 33(1) ARC.[594] ◀

Pursuant to sec. 33(3) ARC, any competitor or market participant **affected** by the infringement may bring a claim. This is to be interpreted broadly: it is sufficient if a market participant is adversely affected in its competitive position, or if a disadvantage to its position and, as a result, potential damages are conceivable, even if they have not actually occurred.[595] Pursuant to sec. 33(4) ARC, industry associations and consumer organisations are also entitled to enforce claims for removal and injunctive relief.

Learning Goals

When it comes to claims against platform operators, courts are regularly faced with the issue of international jurisdiction, as platforms often do not have a registered office in Germany. In April 2025, the Higher Regional Court of Düsseldorf held that jurisdiction in matters relating to tort under Article 7(2) Brussels Ia Regulation applies even where a user contract exists between the parties.[596]

---

592 Glöckner (2021), sec. 2 mn. 269.

593 Franck (2024a), sec. 33 ARC mn. 30.

594 Regional Court of Hamburg 22 April 2013 – 408 HKO 95/12, WuW 2013, 772 – *Vermietung an Schilderprägebetrieb*.

595 Higher Regional Court of Duesseldorf 26 February 2014 – VI-U (Kart) 7/12, NZKart 2014, 154, 154 – *Presse-Grosso*.

596 Higher Regional Court of Duesseldorf 2 April 2025 – VI-U (Kart) 5/24, NZKart 2025, 262, 262 – Filmwerkstatt Düsseldorf II.

5.5.3.3 Claims for Damages

Basis for Claims

Sec. 33(1) ARC grants a claim for damages in addition to the negatory claims under sec. 33(1) ARC in the event of culpable violations of prohibitions under national competition law or Articles 101, 102 TFEU. This is a special tortious claim that takes precedence over claims under secs. 823 et seq. German Civil Code. Any person who has suffered damage is entitled to bring a claim. In contrast to sec. 33(3) ARC, the claimant does not need to be specifically affected.[597] If the injured party, such as a direct customer, is in a contractual relationship with the undertaking violating competition law, a contractual claim also arises under sec. 280(1) German Civil Code. However, other market participants who are not in a contractual relationship with a cartel member are also entitled to claims under sec. 33a(1) ARC. Examples include indirect customers, customers of non-cartel undertakings,[598] or end consumers.

Binding Effect

It can be very difficult for injured market participants and end customers to prove a competition law infringement. **Sec. 33b ARC** therefore provides that the decisions of the Commission and national competition authorities **are binding** in their favour. Courts are bound by the factual and legal findings of the authority. Consequently, the plaintiff no longer needs to prove the competition law infringement. Damages actions brought following official decisions are therefore common in practice and are referred to as **follow-on actions**, in contrast to stand-alone actions.

Proofing and Calculating Damage

Sec. **33a(2) ARC** provides a **rebuttable presumption** regarding the **existence of damage**. It applies to infringements of the cartel prohibition through horizontal restrictions of competition. The term 'cartel' is defined specifically for the purpose of this presumption in sec. 33a(2) 2nd–3rd sentencees ARC. According to sec. 33a(2) 2nd sentence ARC, a cartel includes agreements or concerted practices between two or more competitors aimed at coordinating their competitive conduct on the market or influencing relevant competitive parameters. Only **coordination between competitors** is covered, which primarily includes hardcore cartels. However, the presumption is not limited to these cases and does not require that an intended restriction of competition has actually been realized.[599]

The presumption of damage in sec. 33a(2) ARC is complemented by presumptions for the scenario of **passing-on** under **sec. 33c ARC**. Sec. 33c(1) 1st sentence ARC provides that damage caused by the purchase of goods at an inflated price is not excluded simply because the goods were resold. German case law has

597 Kersting (2025), sec. 33a ARC mn. 4.

598 They may suffer damage as a result of price umbrella effects, on further details, see. ECJ 5 June 2014 – C-557/12, ECLI:EU:C:2014:1317 – *Kone*.

599 Franck (2024a), sec. 33a ARC mn. 76.

considered the passing-on defence in the context of the equalisation of benefits (*Vorteilsausgleichung*).[600] According to this principle, the injured party must allow benefits that have an adequate causal connection to the damaging event to reduce the claim, if this corresponds to the purpose of the law on damages.[601] Sec. 33c(1) 2nd sentence ARC expressly clarifies this rule: damages are compensated even if the customer has passed on the price mark-up to its own customers. The damaging party bears the burden of proof for this defence. Recent case law has placed high demands on this burden and, in some proceedings, has denied the injuring party the defence of benefit equalisation.[602] Sec. 33c(1) 3rd sentence ARC further specifies that the passing-on defence applies only to damages resulting from price mark-ups and does not extend to loss of profit, as governed by sec. 252 German Civil Code.

The situation differs when an **indirect purchaser** brings an action for damages. In this case, the passing-on of the price mark-up by the direct purchaser is a circumstance that the indirect purchaser must demonstrate and prove as part of establishing the occurrence of damage. The presumption under **sec. 33c (2) ARC** operates in favor of the indirect purchaser. Accordingly, it is presumed that the direct purchaser has passed on the mark-up.

German competition law does not provide a presumption regarding the **amount of damages**. The court determines the amount in accordance with **sec. 287 German Code of Civil Procedure** (*Zivilprozessordnung, ZPO*). Under the difference hypothesis of sec. 249 German Civil Code, the court must first establish the price that would have prevailed on the affected market in the absence of the competition violation, in order to quantify the cartel-related price premium as damages. Various methods are used to approximate the hypothetical price level. Case law has primarily relied on the **comparative market method**, which identifies comparable markets in terms of geography, time, or product and uses the prevailing price levels on these markets as a reference for the hypothetical price.[603] Cost-based methods are also being trialled,[604] which calculate the price based on production costs plus a 'reasonable' profit margin. In practice, expert opinions are regularly obtained to assist in estimating damages.[605]

As there are considerable difficulties in proving the actual amount of damages, some have called for a legal presumption of a minimum percentage of damages or

---

600 German Federal Supreme Court 28 June 2011 – KZR 75/10, WRP 2012, 209, 211 et seqq. – *ORWI*.

601 German Federal Supreme Court 28 June 2011 – KZR 75/10, WRP 2012, 209, 211 et seqq. – *ORWI*.

602 German Federal Supreme Court 13 April 2021 – KZR 19/20, NZKart 2021, 566, 573 – *LKW-Kartell II*; German Federal Supreme Court 23 September 2020 – KZR 4/19, NZKart 2021, 44, 48 et seq. – *Schienenkartell V*.

603 Higher Regional Court of Berlin 1 October 2009 – 2 U 10/03 Kart, WuW 2010, 190, 196 – *Berliner Transportbeton*; Higher Regional Court of Celle 12 August 2021 – 13 U 120/16 (Kart), WuW 2021, 591, 594 et seqq. – *Spanplattenkartell*.

604 Commission, Practical guide quantifying harm in actions for damages based on breaches, 2013, pp. 36 et seq.

605 For further methods, see Laborde (2022), pp. 49, 50.

for the amount of damages to be directly stipulated in law.[606] Such rules exist in other national legal systems. In Hungary and Latvia, for example, a surcharge of 10 % is assumed in each case.[607] Under German law, it is possible to agree on contractual lump-sum damages. This is generally permissible, but must comply with the limitations of sec. 307 German Civil Code. In the *Schienenkartell IV* case, the Federal Court of Justice held that such lump-sum damages are permissible up to the amount of the contract sum in the context of procurement procedures, but that the tortfeasor may still prove that the actual damages incurred were significantly lower.[608]

Passive Legitimisation

Claims for damages can only be asserted in court against parties with legal capacity, i.e., primarily legal entities. Nevertheless, sec. 33a et seq. ARC define the term 'undertaking' in the sense of an economic entity, in line with the implementation of the Cartel Damages Directive. The ECJ has ruled that the Directive is based on the **functional concept of an undertaking** under EU competition law, as applied in the context of Articles 101, 102 TFEU and Regulation 1/2003.[609]

Undertakings belonging to an economic unit are liable for claims for damages under sec. 33a ARC as joint and several debtors pursuant to sec. 840(1), sec. 421 German Civil Code. Accordingly, it is not only the parent undertaking that may be liable for a breach by a subsidiary; subsidiaries can also be liable for breaches committed by their parent or sister undertakings.[610] However, liability is not automatic for all entities within the group.[611] The criteria established by case law regarding the economic relationship between the undertakings must be satisfied.

Checklist: Assessing a Claim under sec. 33a(1) ARC

1. Violation of competition law

breach of German competition law (secs. 1, 19, 20 ARC), Articles 101, 102 TFEU (or Articles 5, 6, 7 DMA)

2. Unlawfulness

Is the conduct prohibited and not justified by any defence (e.g. efficiency justifications)?

---

606 Krüger (2024), pp. 152, 152 et seqq.; Laborde (2022), pp. 49, 51.

607 Commission, Commission Staff Working Document on the implementation of Directive 2014/104/EU of the European Parliament and of the Council of 26 November 2014 on certain rules governing actions for damages under national law for infringements of the competition law provisions of the Member States and of the European Union, SWD (2020) 338 final, 2020, p. 9.

608 German Federal Supreme Court 10 February 2021 – KZR 63/18, NZKart 2021, 350, 355 – *Schienenkartell VI.*

609 ECJ 14 March 2019 – C-724/17, EU:C:2019:204, paras. 28–32 – *Skanska*; ECJ 6 October 2021 – C 882/19, ECLI:EU:C:2021:800, para. 40 – *Sumal.*

610 ECJ 6 October 2021 – C-882/19, ECLI:EU:C:2021:800, para. 40 – *Sumal.*

611 Franck (2024a), sec. 33a ARC mn. 30a.

3. Fault
Did the undertaking act negligently or intentionally?
4. Damage
(a) Existence of damage
(b) Quantification of damages (market comparables, cost-based methods, etc.)
(c) Equalisation of benefits – consider whether the claimant received any benefits that reduce the damages (sec. 33c ARC, passing-on defence).

5. Passive Legitimisation
Who are the liable party(ies)? Is the undertaking part of an economic unit?

5.6 Proceedings

5.6.1 Administrative Proceedings

Sec. 48 ARC determines which national competition authority is responsible for issuing cease-and-desist orders pursuant to sec. 32 ARC. The primary authorities include the German Federal Cartel Office and the competition authorities of the federal states (sec. 48(1) ARC). Pursuant to sec. 48(2) ARC, the German Federal Cartel Office is competent whenever the effects of the restrictive conduct extend beyond the territory of a single federal state.

Under sec. 54(1) ARC, the competent authority may initiate proceedings either **ex officio** or **upon application**. Applications are considered suggestions;[612] the authority retains full discretion over whether to open proceedings.[613] Pursuant to sec. 54(2) ARC, the undertakings against which the proceedings are directed must be involved. If proceedings are initiated based on an application, the applicant must also be involved. Additional parties may be summoned if their interests are significantly affected by the authority's decision (sec. 54(2) no. 3 ARC). It is sufficient that the official decision may potentially impact the economic or competitive circumstances of the summoned party.[614]

The competition authority has a **range of investigative powers** in administrative proceedings. It can seize objects that may serve as evidence, pursuant to sec. 58 ARC. Under sec. 59(1) ARC, it may require information and the submission of documents, and it is authorised to inspect and examine business records, cf. sec. 59a ARC. Pursuant to sec. 59b ARC, the authority may search business premises, homes, land, and other property if it suspects that relevant documents are located there. The parties involved have procedural rights, including the right to be heard. To safeguard this right, they must be given an opportunity to comment in accor-

612 Bach (2024), sec. 54 ARC mn. 2.
613 German Federal Supreme Court 6 March 2001 – KVZ 20/00, ZIP 2001, 807.
614 Higher Regional Court of Duesseldorf 2 July 2014 – VI-Kart 2/14 (V), NZKart 2014, 463 – *Radiusklausel*.

dance with sec. 56 ARC. Where the ARC does not provide specific rules, the general provisions of the German Federal Administrative Procedure Act apply.[615]

Cease-and-desist orders may be challenged by filing an **appeal (*Beschwerde*) under sec. 73 ARC** or an appeal on points of law (*Rechtsbeschwerde*) under sec. 77 ARC. Appelas do not have suspensive effect. If an order is not contested within the appeal period, it becomes final. The competent court for appeals is the Higher Regional Court responsible for the registered office of the competition authority (sec. 73(4) ARC). For orders issued by the German Federal Cartel Office in Bonn, this is the Higher Regional Court of Duesseldorf. The German Federal Supreme Court has jurisdiction over appeals on points of law.

The authorities can impose **interim measures** under **sec. 32a ARC**. For this, an infringement of competition law must be 'predominantly likely,' and the measure must be 'necessary to protect competition or to prevent imminent serious harm to another undertaking.' These requirements are less stringent than under Article 8 Regulation 1/2003, where the Commission may only adopt interim measures in 'urgent cases' involving a threat of 'serious and irreparable damage to competition.'[616] The legislator has rightly emphasised the need for swift intervention in digital markets.[617] The lower thresholds for action under sec. 32a ARC are compatible with EU law, as the ECN+ Directive[618] sets only minimum standards and allows member states to adopt more flexible rules. Nevertheless, it is doubtful whether interim measures under sec. 32a ARC will be effective in opening up digital markets. They are likely to remain exceptional instruments.[619]

5.6.2 Fine Proceedings

Before a fine can be imposed, a formal fine procedure must be conducted in accordance with the requirements of **administrative offence law**. This differs from European competition procedural law, where a single administrative procedure governs both cease-and-desist orders and fines.[620] The **German Federal Cartel Office** and the cartel office of the Federal States are primarily responsible for imposing fines, cf. sec. 82(1) no. 3 ARC, giving them a role similar to that of a public prosecutor.[621] Proceedings are generally initiated ex officio.

In addition to the investigative powers under **sec. 46(2) German Code of Administrative Offences**, which refers to the German Code of Criminal Procedure (*Strafprozessordnung; StPO*), the authorities may rely on secs. 59, 59b ARC pursu-

615 Emmerich (2024), sec. 32 ARC mn. 20.
616 For further details on Article 8 Regulation 1/2003, see ► 2.6.1.
617 Government justification for the 10th amendment to the ARC, BT-Drs. 19/23492, pp. 83 et seq.
618 Directive (EU) 2019/1 of the European Parliament and of the Council of 11 December 2018 on the strengthening of the competition authorities of the Member States with a view to ensuring more effective enforcement of the competition rules and the proper functioning of the internal market, OJ [2019] L 11/3.
619 Bach (2024), sec. 32a ARC mn. 2.
620 Klumpp (2020), pp. 9, 9.
621 Glöckner (2021), sec. 2 mn. 233.

ant to **sec. 82b ARC**. These provisions, drawn from administrative law, authorise the authority to request information regarding the offence (sec. 59 ARC) and to conduct searches (sec. 59b ARC). They implement Articles 6–9 of the ECN+ Directive.[622] At the same time, the rights of affected parties to refuse cooperation are restricted,[623] which raises potential concerns regarding the nemo tenetur principle.[624]

Pursuant to secs. 67 et seq. German Code of Administrative Offences in conjunction with sec. 83 ARC, an **objection** (*Einspruch*) to the Higher Regional Court of Duesseldorf is admissible. The time limit for filing an objection is two weeks from the service of the notice, cf. sec. 67 German Code of Administrative Offences. If an objection is lodged, the German Federal Cartel Office previously handed over the proceedings to the public prosecutor's office, retaining the right to make procedural requests, such as requests for evidence.[625] Since the 10th amendment to the ARC, however, the competition authority has the same procedural rights in court proceedings as the public prosecutor's office, pursuant to sec. 82a(1) 3rd sentence ARC. Appeals on points of law (*Rechtsbeschwerde)* against objection decisions can be further lodged with the German Federal Supreme Court, cf. secs. 79 et seq. German Code of Administrative Offences in conjunction with sec. 84 ARC.

5.6.3 Civil Proceedings

Civil actions under competition law must be brought before the regional court. The chambers for commercial matters have exclusive subject-matter jurisdiction, cf. secs. 87, 95 ARC and sec. 95(2) German Judicial System Act (*Gerichtsverfassungsgesetz; GVG*). Local jurisdiction is determined in accordance with secs. 12 et seq. German Code of Civil Procedure. In addition to the general place of jurisdiction under sec. 13, 17 German Code of Civil Procedure, the special rules for tortious acts pursuant to sec. 32 German Code of Civil Procedure also apply. Beyond the presumption rules (secs. 33a, 33c ARC) and the binding effect of competition authority decisions (sec. 33b ARC), plaintiffs benefit from facilitated **access to evidence** under **sec. 33g ARC**. The injured party may apply to the court for disclosure of evidence if it credibly demonstrates a claim for damages and identifies the relevant evidence as precisely as possible based on reasonably accessible facts. This constitutes an independent material claim. Restrictive conditions in sec. 33g(3) ARC are intended to prevent abusive or overly broad requests. Procedural aspects are further governed by sec. 89b ARC. Appeals (*Berufungen*) against decisions of the regional court are heard by the Higher Regional Court in accordance with secs. 93, 92(1) ARC. Appeals on points of law (*Revisionen*) to the German Federal Supreme Court are governed by sec. 94(1) no. 3 ARC.

622 Government justification for the 10th amendment to the ARC, BT-Drs. 19/23492, p. 137.
623 Critical Meyer-Lindemann (2020), pp. 16, 20 et seq.
624 Fritzsche and Bernhard (2021), pp. 599, 599 et seqq.; Giese et al. (2020), pp. 646, 647.
625 Biermann (2024), sec. 82a ARC mn. 5.

5.7 Review Questions

1. How can co-operative data sharing affect competition?

Co-operative data use can create competition law risks if competitors exchange sensitive information, potentially restricting secret competition (**5.2.2.2**). As with other forms of information sharing, the anticompetitive risk depends on the type of information disclosed. Participants in a data pool should primarily have access only to their own data and to final, aggregated information from other participants. Direct access to competitors' individual data should be avoided to prevent competition concerns.

2. Do platform bans violate the German ban on cartels?

Agreements with retailers that prohibit resale via online marketplaces are generally compliant with competition law if luxury goods are involved (► 5.2.3.3). Courts, however, differ in their assessment of whether a platform ban can serve as a legitimate qualitative criterion within a selective distribution system for branded goods. Some evidence suggests that platform bans may also be permissible for non-luxury products. The Commission's 2022 Vertical Guidelines further cite high-quality or high-tech products as examples of goods for which selective distribution that excludes certain platforms can be justified.

3. How are narrow price parity clauses assessed under sec. 1 ARC?

German courts and authorities have taken different positions on narrow price parity clauses (**5.2.3.3**). The Higher Regional Court of Duesseldorf initially held that such clauses are compatible with the cartel prohibition and may be exempted as necessary ancillary agreements or under the commercial agent privilege. In contrast, the German Federal Cartel Office and the Federal Court of Justice view them as restrictive of competition, since they limit retailers' pricing freedom and can effectively seal off the platform operator's market. However, narrow price parity clauses may benefit from an exemption under the VBER. Article 5(1)(d) VBER only covers broad price parity clauses.

4. Which criteria are particularly relevant for determining market dominance in multi-sided markets?

In addition to the general criteria in sec. 18(3) ARC, German competition law identifies special factors for multi-sided markets, cf. sec. 18(3a), (3b) ARC). These include direct and indirect network effects, parallel use of multiple services (single- vs. multi-homing), economies of scale combined with network effects, access to competition-relevant data, and innovation-driven competitive pressure. Sec. 18(3b)

ARC additionally covers intermediation power, meaning that when assessing the market position of an intermediary, the significance of its services for access to procurement and sales markets must also be considered (▶ 5.3.1.2; ▶ 5.3.1.2).

? 5. What characterizes an undertaking with paramount significance for competition across markets?

✓ An undertaking with paramount significance for competition across markets possesses the resources and strategic positioning to exert a significant influence on the business activities of third parties or to expand its own business activities into new markets and sectors. The prerequisite for this is that the undertaking has a consolidated position of power of some duration. The concept of paramount cross-market significance is an independent concept and not merely an extension of market dominance. Undertakings with paramount cross-market significance are addressed by sec. 19a ARC. While the provision does not define the concept, it provides a non-exhaustive catalogue of criteria for determining a paramount cross-market significance (▶ 5.3.2.2).

? 6. What characterises the system of sec. 19a ARC?

✓ Sec. 19a ARC is not directly applicable. An undertaking only becomes an addressee of this provision once the German Federal Cartel Office has formally determined that it is of paramount significance for competition across markets. This differs from the bans contained in sec. 19, 20 ARC, which address dominant undertakings and those with relative and superior market power. An additional order from the German Federal Cartel Office is required to prohibit an undertaking with paramount cross-market significance from engaging in specific conduct outlined in the catalogue of sec. 19a(2) ARC. The prohibition only takes effect once this order becomes final (**5.3.2.1**).

? 7. Why does sec. 19a (2) 1st sentence no. 3 ARC prohibit undertakings with paramount cross-market significance for competition from hindering competitors in a market in which they can rapidly expand their position?

✓ This rule is intended to make the 'rolling up of markets' more difficult. 'Rolling up of markets' refers to practices that allow the rapid expansion of market power without relying on fair competition. For example, undertakings with paramount cross-market significance are assumed to be able to expand their market power quickly if they enjoy significant advantages in accessing customers or data (▶ 5.3.2.3).

? 8. Which specific groups of cases relating to the digital economy does sec. 20(1), (1a) ARC address for establishing a position of relative market power?

Since the 10th amendment to the ARC, sec. 20 ARC includes two additional categories of dependency tailored to the digital context. These are dependency on intermediaries, cf. sec. 20(1) 2nd sentence ARC, and data-related dependency, cf. sec. 20(1a) 1st sentence ARC (▶ 5.3.3.2).

9. Under which provision can an undertaking with superior market power be obliged to provide access to data?

Pursuant to sec. 20(1a) 2nd sentence ARC, an undertaking with relative market power may be obliged to provide access to data if a refusal constitutes an exclusionary abuse. A refusal to grant access to such data, on which dependent undertakings rely, in return for an appropriate fee is considered abusive. The assessment focuses on whether the refusal of access is unfair. As part of the balancing of interests, it must be clarified whether the positive effects on competition outweigh the potential negative consequences arising from reduced incentives to invest in the acquisition of further data in the future (▶ 5.3.3.2).

10. Which conduct is captured by the provision in sec. 20(3a) ARC?

According to sec. 20(3a) ARC, an undertaking abuses its superior market power on a multi-sided market if it impedes competitors from independently realising network effects and thereby creates a serious risk that competition on the merits will be restricted to a not insignificant extent. This rule is based on the economic insight that digital markets tend to 'tip' due to their susceptibility to dominance, particularly through indirect network effects. Sec. 20 3(a) ARC is structured as an endangerment provision, enabling the competition authority to intervene at an early stage (▶ 5.3.3.3).

11. What is the special feature of the threshold under sec. 35(1a) ARC? Why was it introduced?

The threshold under sec. 35(1a) ARC is not only linked to turnover but also to the value of the consideration for the merger. Pursuant to sec. 35(1a) no. 3 ARC, the value of the consideration must exceed EUR 400 million. This rule was introduced with the 9th amendment to the ARC in 2017. It was triggered by the *Facebook/WhatsApp* merger, which was considered significant from a competition perspective but did not fall under Article 1 EUMR or sec. 35 ARC because *WhatsApp* generated insufficient turnover. The aim of the new threshold is to enable the German Federal Cartel Office to review killer acquisitions in digital markets (▶ 5.4.2.2).

12. How does the German Federal Cartel Office take innovation-driven competitive pressure into account when assessing a significant impediment to effective competition pursuant to sec. 36(1) ARC?

Innovation-driven competitive pressure is expressly included in sec. 18(3a) no. 5 ARC as a factor in assessing the creation or strengthening of a dominant position. According to the German Federal Cartel Office, it is not sufficient for a merger to merely concern digital markets in order to establish such pressure. Instead, there must be concrete evidence that dynamic innovation processes are likely to occur within the relevant forecast period (generally three to five years). Only then can innovation-driven competitive pressure be considered in the merger control assessment (▶ 5.4.3.2).

13. What special powers does the German Federal Cartel Office have after conducting a sector enquiry pursuant to sec. 32f ARC in the event of distortion of competition?

If the German Federal Cartel Office identifies a significant and persistent distortion of competition during a sector enquiry, it may impose both structural and behavioural remedies. These measures can be directed at undertakings whose conduct or market position significantly contributes to the distortion. In the case of undertakings with paramount cross-market significance for competition, the authority may even order ownership unbundling as an especially intrusive structural remedy pursuant to sec. 19a(4) ARC, cf. sec. 32f(4) ARC. The distinctive feature of this authorisation is that it applies irrespective of an infringement or fault. This marks a paradigm shift in German competition law (▶ 5.5.1.2).

14. How do presumptions and disclosure rights under the ARC strengthen the position of injured parties?

Where an action for damages is preceded by a cease-and-desist order issued by the Commission or the German Federal Cartel Office, plaintiffs benefit from the binding effect of sec. 33b ARC. They do not need to re-establish the breach of competition law, as the court is bound by the authority's findings of fact and law. In cases involving horizontal agreements, the presumption of harm under sec. 33a(2) ARC applies, though only with regard to the occurrence of damage, not its amount. Indirect purchasers further benefit from the presumption of passing-on in sec. 33c(2) ARC. Finally, injured parties can rely on claims for disclosure of evidence under sec. 33g ARC (▶ 5.5.3.3, ▶ 5.6.3).

15. Under what conditions may the German Federal Cartel Office impose interim measures?

The German Federal Cartel Office may impose interim measures pursuant to sec. 32a ARC. The requirements are less stringent than under European competition law (cf. Article 8 Regulation 1/2003). A competition infringement must be 'predominantly probable,' and the measure must be 'necessary to protect competition or to avert an imminent, serious impairment of another undertaking.' The legislator introduced this lower threshold to enable timely intervention, particularly in fast-moving digital markets (▶ 5.6.1).

References

Achleitner R (2022) Digital Markets Act beschlossen: Verhaltenspflichten und Rolle nationaler Wettbewerbsbehörden. NZKart 2022:359–366

Bach A (2024) ARC sec. 32a, 32b, 32c, 54. In: Immenga U, Mestmäcker E (founders) Kommentar zum Wettbewerbsrecht, 7th edn. C.H.Beck, Munich

Baranowski A, Glaßl R (2017) M&A im Internet: Transaktionen von Daten und Content. BB 2017:199–207

Bechtold R (2003) Zulassungsansprüche zu selektiven Vertriebssystemen unter besonderer Berücksichtigung der Kfz-Vertriebssysteme. NJW 2003:3729–3734

Berghaus F, Mekhalfia J (2021) Amazon als Preiskontrolleur – Zum Verhältnis von Marktmissbrauchskontrolle und Preisrecht. WuW 2021:82–86

Bien F, Becker B (2024) Das Anwerben von Mitarbeitern im Lichte der deutschen und europäischen Fusionskontrolle – Teil 1. WuW 2024:81–88

Biermann J (2024) ARC sec. 82a. In: Immenga U, Mestmäcker E (founders) Kommentar zum Wettbewerbsrecht, 7th edn C.H.Beck, Munich

Böhm F (1963) Die Bedrohung der Freiheit durch private ökonomische Macht in der heutigen Gesellschaft. Universitas – Zeitschrift für Wissenschaft. Kunst und Literatur 1963:37–48

Bourreau M, de Streel A (2020) Big Tech Acquisitions – Competition & Innovation Effects and EU Merger Control. Issue Paper, Brussels

Cetintas G (2020) Gefährlicher ('Tipping'-)Gefährdungstatbestand? – Eine Analyse von § 20 Abs. 3a des Referentenentwurfs für eine 10. GWB-Novelle. WuW:2020:446–453

Dethof S (2012) Die Beschränkung des Internetvertriebs der Händler nach Pierre Fabre. ZWeR 2012:503–521

Dreher M, Kulka M (2023) Wettbewerbs- und Kartellrecht - Eine systematische Darstellung des deutschen und europäischen Rechts, 12th edn. C.F.Müller, Heidelberg

Dreyer J, Lemberg N (2012) Möglichkeiten und Grenzen der Beschränkung des Internetvertriebs. BB 2012:2004–2010

Ecker B, Geerenstein D, Gronemeyer A, Janka S, Jansen G, Kiparski G, Lau N, Polley R, Scheibe A, Suchsland U, Wegner A (2021) Industrie 4.0 – Kartellrechtliche Betrachtungen, 2nd edn. Bundesministerium für Wirtschaft und Energie, Berlin

Ehricke U, Blask H (2003) Dynamischer Verweis auf Gruppenfreistellungsverordnungen im neuen GWB?, Dynamischer Verweis auf Gruppenfreistellungsverordnungen im neuen GWB? JZ 58(14):722–730

Ellger R (2024) ARC sec. 2, 3. In: Immenga U, Mestmäcker E (founders) Kommentar zum Wettbewerbsrecht, 7th edn. C.H.Beck, Munich

Emmerich V (2024) ARC sec. 32. In: Immenga U, Mestmäcker E (founders) Kommentar zum Wettbewerbsrecht, 7th edn. C.H.Beck, Munich

Emmerich V, Lange K (2024) Kartellrecht, 16th edn. C.H.Beck, Munich

Esser M, Höft J (2023) Die Einführung des SIEC-Tests durch die 8. GWB-Novelle – Folgen für die Praxis. NZKart 2013:447–457

Franck J (2024a) ARC sec. 33, 33a. In: Immenga U, Mestmäcker E (founders) Kommentar zum Wettbewerbsrecht, 7th edn. C.H.Beck, Munich

Franck J (2024b) Maßnahmen nach Sektoruntersuchung in der 11. GWB-Novelle. NJW 2024:246–252

Franck J, Peitz M (2021) Digital Platforms and the New 19a Tool in the German Competition Act. JECLAP 12(7):513–528

Fritzsche A, Bernhard T (2021) Der "Nemo-Tenetur"-Grundsatz nach der 10. GWB-Novelle – Vorschläge für eine verfassungskonforme Auslegung. NZKart 2021:599–606
Fuchs A (2024) ARC sec. 18, 19. In: Immenga U, Mestmäcker E (founders) Kommentar zum Wettbewerbsrecht, 7th edn. C.H.Beck, Munich
Furman J, Cyle D, Fletscher A, McAuley D, Marsden P (2019) Unlocking digital competition, Report of the Digital Competition Expert Panel. London. Available via: https://assets.publishing.service.gov.uk/media/5c88150ee5274a230219c35f/unlocking_digital_competition_furman_review_web.pdf. Accessed 10 July 2024
German Federal Cartel Office (2022) Fusionskontrolle im digitalen Zeitalter – Herausforderungen und Entwicklungsperspektiven. Bonn
German Federal Cartel Office (2020) Algorithmen und Wettbewerb. Bonn
German Federal Cartel Office (2016) Market Power of Platforms and Networks. Bonn
Giese P, Heinichen C, Janssen M, Klumpp U, Schelzke R, Steinle C (2020) Kartellbußgeldrecht in der 10. GWB-Novelle – Teil 2. NZKart 2020:646–652
Glöckner J (2021) Kartellrecht – Recht gegen Wettbewerbsbeschränkungen, 3rd edn. Kohlhammer, Stuttgart
Grave C, Nyberg J (2025) ARC sec. 3. In: Kersting C, Meyer-Lindemann H, Podszun R (eds) Kommentar zum Deutschen und Europäischen Kartellrecht, 5th edn. C.H.Beck, Munich
Grünwald A (2025) ARC sec. 19a. In: Jaeger W, Kokott J, Pohlmann P, Schroeder D, Seeliger D (eds) Frankfurter Kommentar zum Kartellrecht, 111th supp. Dr. Otto Schmidt, Cologne
Heyers J (2025) ARC sec. 2. In: Jaeger W, Kokott J, Pohlmann P, Schroeder D, Seeliger D (eds) Frankfurter Kommentar zum Kartellrecht, 111th supp. Dr. Otto Schmidt, Cologne
Kahlenberg H (2025) ARC sec. 36. In: Kersting C, Meyer-Lindemann H, Podszun R (eds) Kommentar zum Deutschen und Europäischen Kartellrecht, 5th edn. C.H.Beck, Munich
Kantzenbach E (1967) Die Funktionsfähigkeit des Wettbewerbs, 2nd edn. Vandenhoeck & Ruprecht, Göttingen
Käseberg T, Gappa S (2023) Article 1 DMA. In: Podszun R (ed) Commentary digital markets act. Nomos, Baden-Baden
Kersting C (2025) ARC sec. 33a, 37. In: Kersting C, Meyer-Lindemann H, Podszun R (eds) Kommentar zum Deutschen und Europäischen Kartellrecht, 5th edn. C.H.Beck, Munich
Kersting C, Dworschak S (2013) Leistungsschutzrecht für Presseverlage: Müsste Google wirklich zahlen? – eine kartellrechtliche Analyse. NZKart 2013:46–53
Klees A (2017) ARC sec. 130. In: Röhling A, Busche J (eds) Kölner Kommentar zum Kartellecht. Carl Heymanns, Cologne
Kling M, Thomas S (2016) Kartellrecht, 2nd edn. Franz Vahlen, Munich
Klumpe G (2025) ARC sec. 19. In: Kersting C, Meyer-Lindemann H, Podszun R (eds) Kommentar zum Deutschen und Europäischen Kartellrecht, 5th edn, C.H.Beck, Munich
Klumpp U (2020) Änderungen im Bußgeldrecht und -verfahren nach der 10. GWB-Novelle. NZKart 2020:9–14
Körber T (2025) Article 2 EUMR. In: Immenga U, Mestmäcker E (founders) Kommentar zum Wettbewerbsrecht, 7th edn. C.H.Beck, Munich
Körber T (2023a) Das GWB auf dem Weg zum more administrative approach? NZKart 2023:193–194
Körber T (2023b) Die 11. GWB-Novelle zwischen freiem und verwaltetem Wettbewerb. ZRP 2023:5–8
Körber T (2020) "Digitalisierung" der Missbrauchsaufsicht durch die 10. GWB-Novelle – Macht im Netz IV: Maßvolle Antwort oder übertriebene Regulierung der Digitalwirtschaft? MMR 2020:290–295
Körber T (2017) Konzeptionelle Erfassung digitaler Plattformen und adäquate Regulierungsstrategien. ZUM 2017:93–101
Körber T (2016) "Ist Wissen Marktmacht?" Überlegungen zum Verhältnis von Datenschutz, "Datenmacht" und Kartellrecht – Teil 1. NZKart 2016:303–310
Körber T (2012) Google im Fokus des Kartellrechts. WRP 58(7):761–772
Kohser K, Jahn S (2020) Die P2B-Verordnung – Neue Pflichten für Plattformbetreiber und Suchmaschinenanbieter. GRUR-Prax 2020:273–275
Krüger C (2024) Mit Voll(ab)gas zum kartelldeliktsrechtlichen Mindestschaden? NZKart 2024:152–156

5

Kühling J, Engelbracht T (2024) ARC sec. 32f. In: Immenga U, Mestmäcker E (founders) Kommentar zum Wettbewerbsrecht, 7th edn. C.H.Beck, Munich
Kühling J, Gauß N (2007) Expansionslust von Google als Herausforderung für das Kartellrecht. MMR 2007:751–757
Kühling J, Engelbracht T, Welsch J (2023) Verstoßunabhängige Maßnahmen zur Verbesserung des Wettbewerbs nach einer Sektoruntersuchung – der geplante § 32f GWB als Störung des Wettbewerbsrechts? (§ 32f GWB). WuW 2023:250–256
Laborde J (2022) Kartellschadensersatzklagen in Europa: Wie Gerichte kartellbedingte Preisaufschläge beurteilt haben – Teil 2. NZKart 2022:49–55
Legner S (2023) Die Marktabgrenzung im Kartellrecht. JURA 2023:175–181
Legner S (2012) Schadensberechnung bei Hardcore-Kartellen. KSzW 2012:218–224
Lettl T (2021) Kartellrecht, 5th edn C.H. Beck, Munich 2021
Lübbert H, Schöner M (2020) Sec. 24. In: Wiedemann G (ed) Handbuch des Kartellrechts, 4th edn. C.H.Beck, Munich, pp 1519–1548
Markert K (2024) ARC sec. 20. In: Immenga U, Mestmäcker E (founders) Kommentar zum Wettbewerbsrecht, 7th edn. C.H.Beck, Munich
Meyer-Lindemann H (2025) ARC sec. 35. In: Kersting C, Meyer-Lindemann H, Podszun R (eds) Kommentar zum Deutschen und Europäischen Kartellrecht, 5th edn, C.H.Beck, Munich
Meyer-Lindemann H (2020) Bußgeldsachen: Die stille Revolution im Windschatten der Digitalisierungsnovelle. WuW 2020:16–22
Möller S (2025) ARC sec. 35. In: Jaeger W, Kokott J, Pohlmann P, Schroeder D, Seeliger D (eds) Frankfurter Kommentar zum Kartellrecht, 111th supp. Dr. Otto Schmidt, Cologne
Möschel W (2014) Kartellrecht in Deutschland seit Stein-Hardenberg – Eine Reminiszenz. NZKart 2014:42–47
Müller-Feldhammer R (2019) Die Bieter- und Arbeitsgemeinschaft – kartellrechtlich ein Auslaufmodell? NZKart 2019:463–468
Nothdurft J (2021) ARC sec. 19a. In: Bunte H (ed) Kartellrecht – Commentary, 14th edn. Luchterhand, Munich
Otto J (2025) ARC sec. 32e. In: Kersting C, Meyer-Lindemann H, Podszun R (eds) Kommentar zum Deutschen und Europäischen Kartellrecht, 5th edn. C.H.Beck, Munich
Paal B (2025) ARC sec. 18, 19a, 20. In: Gersdorf H, Paal B (eds) Beck'scher Online-Kommentar Informations- und Medienrecht, 49th edn. C.H.Beck, Munich
Paal B (2019) Missbrauchstatbestand und Algorithmic Pricing – Dynamische und individualisierte Preise im virtuellen Wettbewerb. GRUR 2019:43–53
Paal B, Kieß F (2022) Ausweitung von Sektoruntersuchungen durch § 32f GWB-E: Gebotene Komplettierung oder Paradigmenwechsel? NZKart 2022:678–684
Paal B, Kumkar L (2021) Wettbewerbsschutz in der Digitalwirtschaft – Die wichtigsten Neuerungen der 10. GWB-Novelle im Überblick. NJW 2021:809–815
Paschke M (2025) ARC sec. 37. In: Jaeger W, Kokott J, Pohlmann P, Schroeder D, Seeliger D (eds) Frankfurter Kommentar zum Kartellrecht, 111th supp. Dr. Otto Schmidt, Cologne
Podszun R (2025) ARC sec. 18. In: Kersting C, Meyer-Lindemann H, Podszun R (eds) Kommentar zum Deutschen und Europäischen Kartellrecht, 5th edn. C.H.Beck, Munich
Podszun R (2024) ARC sec. 20. In: Immenga U, Mestmäcker E (founders) Kommentar zum Wettbewerbsrecht, 7th edn. C.H.Beck, Munich
Podszun R (2016) Die Ministererlaubnis – Einbruch der Politik ins Recht der Wirtschaft. NJW 2016:617–619
Podszun R, Schwalbe U (2017) Digitale Plattformen und GWB-Novelle: Überzeugende Regeln für die Internetökonomie? NZKart 2017:98–106
Polley R, Kaup R (2020) Paradigmenwechsel in der deutschen Missbrauchsaufsicht – Der Referentenentwurf zur 10. GWB-Novelle. NZKart 2020:113–119
Rehbinder E, von Kalben J (2024) ARC sec. 185. In: Immenga U, Mestmäcker E (founders) Kommentar zum Wettbewerbsrecht, 7th edn. C.H.Beck, Munich
Reiter J (2024) Internetökonomie als Endgegner des Kartellrechts? EuZW 2024:101–106
Riesenkampff A, Steinbarth S (2025) ARC sec. 37, 40. In: Kersting C, Meyer-Lindemann H, Podszun R (eds) Kommentar zum Deutschen und Europäischen Kartellrecht, 5th edn. C.H.Beck, Munich

Rittner F (2006) Vom Nutzen und Nachteil der Ökonomie für das Wettbewerbsrecht – Fünf Lehrstücke und 30 conclusiones. In: von Verschuer N, Gres J (eds) Liber amicorum für Alexander Riesenkampff zum 70. Geburtstag. C.H.Beck, Munich, pp 125–138

Rohner T (2023) Die 11. GWB-Novelle – Überblick und offene Fragen. WuW 2023:386–389

Schneider H (2021) ARC sec. 2. In: Bunte H (ed) Kartellrecht – Commentary, 14th edn. Luchterhand, Munich

Schweitzer H (2024) ARC sec. 19a. In: Immenga U, Mestmäcker E (founders) Kommentar zum Wettbewerbsrecht, 7th edn. C.H.Beck, Munich

Schweitzer H, Haucap J, Kerber W, Welker R (2018) Modernisierung der Missbrauchsaufsicht für marktmächtige Unternehmen. Available via: https://www.bmwk.de/Redaktion/DE/Publikationen/Wirtschaft/modernisierung-der-missbrauchsaufsicht-fuer-marktmaechtige-unternehmen.pdf?__blob=publicationFile&v=12. Accessed 18 June 2024

Stammwitz L (2025) ARC sec. 20. In: Kersting C, Meyer-Lindemann H, Podszun R (eds) Kommentar zum Deutschen und Europäischen Kartellrecht, 5th edn. C.H.Beck, Munich

Steinvorth T (2020) Sec. 19, 20. In: Wiedemann G (ed) Handbuch des Kartellrechts, 4th edn. C.H.Beck, Munich, pp 1011–1095, 1096–1197

Thomas S (2025) ARC sec. 35, 36, 37. In: Immenga U, Mestmäcker E (founders) Kommentar zum Wettbewerbsrecht, 7th edn. C.H.Beck, Munich

Wagner-von Papp F (2023) Habemus Regierungsentwurf 11. GWB-Novelle. WuW 2023:301–302

Volmar M (2020) Die Intermediationsmacht von Competitive Bottlenecks. NZKart 2020:170–176

Volmar M (2017) Marktabgrenzung bei mehrseitigen Online-Plattformen. ZWeR 2017:386–408

Westermann K (2025) Article 21 EUMR. In: Kersting C, Meyer-Lindemann H, Podszun R (eds) Kommentar zum Deutschen und Europäischen Kartellrecht, 5th edn. C.H.Beck, Munich

Westermann K (2022) ARC sec. 20. In: Montag F, Säcker F, Bien F, Meier-Beck P (eds) Münchener Kommentar zum Wettbewerbsrecht, 4th edn. C.H. Beck, Munich

Wiedemann G (2020) Sec. 3, 5, 23. In: Wiedemann G (ed) Handbuch des Kartellrechts, 4th edn. C.H.Beck, Munich, pp 70–92, 101–155, 1371–1518

Zimmer D (2024) ARC sec. 1. In: Immenga U, Mestmäcker E (founders) Kommentar zum Wettbewerbsrecht, 7th edn C.H.Beck, Munich

Supplementary Information

S. Legner, *Digital Competition Law*, Springer Textbooks in Law,
https://doi.org/10.1007/978-3-662-73213-7

Index

The manufacturer's authorised representative in the EU is Springer Nature Customer Service Centre GmbH, Europaplatz 3, 69115 Heidelberg, Germany. If you have any concerns regarding our products, please contact ProductSafety@springernature.com

Printed and bound by CPI Group (UK) Ltd, Croydon, CR0 4YY
05/10/2026
02228023-0008